THE CONDITION OF
THE WORKING CLASS IN ENGLAND

ENGELS

THE CONDITION
OF THE
WORKING CLASS
IN
ENGLAND

Translated and edited by
W. O. HENDERSON
and
W. H. CHALONER

STANFORD UNIVERSITY PRESS
STANFORD, CALIFORNIA

Stanford University Press
Stanford, California
© Basil Blackwell, 1958
First published by Basil Blackwell in 1958
Reissued by Stanford University Press in 1968
Cloth ISBN 0–8047–0633–6
Paper ISBN 0–8047–0634–4
Last figure below indicates year of this printing:
79

CONTENTS

EDITORS' NOTE vii

EDITORS' INTRODUCTION ix

ENGELS'S PREFACE TO THE FIRST GERMAN EDITION OF
1845 3

DEDICATION 'TO THE WORKING CLASSES OF GREAT-
BRITAIN' (1845) 7

CHAPTER

I HISTORICAL INTRODUCTION 9

II THE INDUSTRIAL PROLETARIAT 27

III THE GREAT TOWNS 30

IV COMPETITION 88

V IRISH IMMIGRATION 104

VI THE RESULTS OF INDUSTRIALISATION 108

VII THE PROLETARIAT 150

VIII THE PROLETARIAT (*continued*) 213

IX WORKING-CLASS MOVEMENTS 241

X THE MINERS 274

XI THE PROLETARIAT ON THE LAND 295

XII THE ATTITUDE OF THE BOURGEOISIE 311

CONCLUSION... 332

APPENDICES

I THE POSTSCRIPT OF 1846: AN ENGLISH STRIKE ... 337

II PREFACE TO THE AMERICAN EDITION OF 1887 352

III PREFACE TO THE ENGLISH EDITION OF 1892 360

IV LIST OF SOURCES QUOTED BY ENGELS 372

V EXAMPLES OF ENGELS'S METHODS OF QUOTING ... 375

INDEX 377

Maps and plans appear on pp. 57, 59, 66, 67, 72.

EDITORS' NOTE

This is a new translation of Engels's book on the condition of the working class in England in 1844. It is based upon the original German first edition of 1845, which was reprinted, with minor corrections, by the Marx-Engels-Lenin Institute in Karl Marx-Friedrich Engels, *Historisch-Kritische Gesamtausgabe: Werke, Schriften, Briefe*, Part I, Vol. 4 (1932), pp. 5–282.[1] The Institute edition includes notes by V. Adoratskij (pp. 519–25). We have added to our translation an account of a strike of building trade operatives in Manchester which Engels originally wrote for the periodical *Das Westfälische Dampfboot* (Bielefeld), 1846. The article was reprinted in the *Gesamtausgabe*, Part I, Vol. 4, pp. 393–405.

The main difference between this edition and all earlier German and English editions is that we have given the exact original text of all Engels's quotations, with one exception. A comparison with Mrs. Wischnewetzky's translation (first published in the U.S.A. in 1887 and in the United Kingdom in 1892) will show that many of Engels's 'quotations' were garbled abridgements of the original.

Certain interpolations have been made in the text [in square brackets] for the sake of clarity. Editors' footnotes are bracketed [in heavier type]. Engels's footnotes to the edition of 1845 and to the authorized English translation of 1887 have been left unbracketed.

The illustrations to the original German edition of 1845 have all been reproduced. The editors have added a contemporary map (1849) of the 'Little Ireland' district of Manchester.

We have to thank in particular Professor Arthur Redford, who first suggested that a new and critical translation of Engels's book was needed, Dr. Moses Tyson, the Librarian, University of Manchester, Mr. Sidney Horrocks, Reference Librarian, Manchester Public Libraries, Mr. F. G. B. Hutchings, City Librarian, Leeds, Dr. T. C. Barker, Mr. T. W. Freeman, Mr. Hugh Kearney, Mr. Donald Read, Professor Percy E. Schramm, Mr. D. C. Wollman and the officials of the Manchester Royal Infirmary. We owe a special debt of gratitude to the long-suffering Departmental Secretaries in the History School of Manchester University.

[1] This standard edition of the writings of Marx and Engels is in future cited as *Gesamtausgabe*.

EDITORS' INTRODUCTION

Marx and Engels

Few intellectual partnerships can ultimately have had such moment-ous consequence as that of Karl Marx and Friedrich Engels, the fathers of ' scientific' Socialism and Communism. Although Engels, the junior partner in the team, is not so well known as Marx, he was one of the leading Socialist writers in the second half of the nineteenth century. Engels's first visit to England, between November 1842 and August 1844, marked the climax of the formative period of his career during which he was preparing himself for his life's work as a Socialist agitator.

When Marx first met Engels in Cologne in the autumn of 1842— Engels was on his way to Manchester for the first time—there were no signs of the future close relationship between the two young men. Marx was apparently suspicious of Engels's motives in approaching him and this first meeting has been described as ' cool, even unfriendly'. But when Engels saw Marx again in Paris two years later—on Engels's return from England—the meeting was much more cordial. Marx appreciated the extent of Engels's intellectual development since their previous meeting and he was now ready to accept Engels as a collab-orator.

A Socialist Classic

As soon as he was home again in Barmen in the autumn of 1844 Engels wrote an account of the condition of the workers in England[1] and this was the major literary achievement of his early years.

Socialists and Communists have long regarded this work as a great socialist classic. They claim that, although many earlier writers had examined various aspects of social change brought about by the Industrial Revolution in England, Engels was the first to survey the problem as a whole. They argue that Engels did much more than merely describe what he had seen in the English manufacturing districts. He asked himself two questions: ' How did this state of affairs arise?' and ' How will it end?' It is said that by studying the history of the English workers Engels was able to show how the situation that he was describing was the inevitable outcome of a

[1] On November 19th, 1844, Engels wrote to Karl Marx that he was ' buried in English newspapers and books from which I am putting together my book on the condition of the working classes in England ', *Gesamtausgabe*, Part III, Vol. 1 (Berlin, 1929), pp. 4–8.

process of evolution. And since Engels had been able to show why social distress and injustice existed, he was able to forecast what was bound to happen in the future. Even before Karl Marx had formulated the doctrine of dialectical materialism, Engels used this method in studying the social condition of England in the 1840s.[1]

It is not surprising that Socialists and Communists should have taken so favourable a view of Engels's book since both Marx and Lenin held it in high esteem. Marx frequently referred to the book in glowing terms in his letters to Engels[2] and in the eighth and thirteenth chapters of the first volume of *Das Kapital*. In 1867 he declared that ' the fullness of Engels's insight into the nature of the capitalist method of production has been shown by the factory reports, the reports on mines, etc., that have appeared since the publication of his book '.[3]

In 1870, when Flerovsky's study of the workers in Russia appeared, Marx expressed the view that this was the most important work on such a subject ' since Engels's book on the condition of the proletariat in England '.[4]

Lenin was equally enthusiastic when he wrote:

> ' Many descriptions of the dreadful conditions under which the workers live had appeared before Engels came on the scene. And many people had urged that something should be done to improve the lot of the proletariat. But Engels was the *first* to show that the workers were something more than a social class in distress. He explained that the degraded economic condition of the proletariat was in itself the stimulus which would enable this class to make progress in the future. He saw that the situation in which the workers found themselves was in fact so deplorable that the proletariat would be forced to join in the struggle for freedom. Self-help is the motto of militant workers on the march to freedom. The workers' political movement will force the proletariat to grasp the fact that socialism—and socialism alone—is the goal at which they must aim to achieve their ends. On the other hand it is clear that socialism will never become a great political force until it becomes the goal for which the workers are striving in their political struggle.'

---

[1] In 1883, in an introduction to a new edition of the Communist Manifesto of 1848, Engels stated that for several years before 1845 he had been approaching the materialist conception of history. ' My book on *The Condition of the Working Class in England* shows how far I had travelled along that road by myself ' [i.e., independently of Marx].

[2] *Gesamtausgabe*, Part III, Vol. 1 (1929), pp. 5, 10, 14; Vol. 2 (1930), pp. 355 and 453; Vol. 3 (1930), pp. 135, 138, 154, 305 and 343–4; and Vol. 4 (1931), p. 36 and p. 275.

[3] Karl Marx, *Capital*, Vol. 1 (Everyman edn., 1930), pp. 240–1 (note).

[4] Karl Marx—Friedrich Engels, *Gesamtausgabe* . . . Part III, Vol. 4 (1931), p. 275.

'Those were the fundamental ideas expressed in Engels's book on the condition of the English workers. Those ideas are now a commonplace among workers who think for themselves. But in 1844 they were original ideas. They were clearly expressed in a book written with passionate fervour—a work which gives a deeply moving and a very convincing picture of the utter misery of the English workers. The book was a terrible indictment of capitalism and of the middle classes. It made a profound impression upon the minds of all who read it. Everywhere Engels's study came to be regarded as the best available contemporary account of the condition of the proletariat. And, indeed, neither before nor after 1845 has the depressed condition of the workers been so sharply and so accurately delineated.'[1]

The opinion of another Socialist—of a later generation—may be quoted. Franz Mehring, in his biography of Marx, declared that Engels's book was 'a fundamental Socialist work'. He considered that:

'the most admirable and at the same time the most noteworthy historical feature of the book is the thoroughness with which the twenty-four-year-old author understands the spirit of the capitalist mode of production and succeeds in explaining from it not only the rise but also the decline of the bourgeoisie, not only the misery of the proletariat but also its salvation.'[2]

The Socialist view that Engels's book is a masterly sociological study deserves closer examination. It may be doubted whether there is any substance in the claim that Engels showed unusual perspicacity when he traced the beginnings of social discontent back to its roots in the early days of the Industrial Revolution. If this book is really one of the first in which the doctrine of historical materialism is used in order to explain social phenomena, then the theory had a poor start in life. Engels was a brilliant political agitator but—at any rate at the age of twenty-four—he was no historian.

His historical introduction is based almost entirely upon a book called *The Manufacturing Population of England* (1833) and written by an obscure surgeon named Peter Gaskell.[3] Gaskell had contrasted the

---

[1] Quoted by V. Adoratskij in his introduction to Friedrich Engels, *Die Lage der arbeitenden Klasse in England* in *Gesamtausgabe*, Part I, Vol. 4 (1932), pp. ix–x.

[2] Franz Mehring, *Karl Marx: The Story of his Life* (trans. E. Fitzgerald, 1936, p. 105). Elsewhere Mehring refers to Engels's book as 'epoch-making' (see Franz Mehring, *Deutsche Geschichte vom Ausgang des Mittelalters* (Berlin, 1951), p. 182.

[5] Little is known of Peter Gaskell. His name appears in a *List of Persons who have obtained certificates of their fitness . . . to practise as apothecaries*, 1815–1840 (1840) as having secured the licence of the Society of Apothecaries on April 12th, 1827. Gaskell was also a member of the Royal College of Surgeons of England. He was admitted in February, 1828. At that time he was living in Camberwell, London.

horrors of working in the dark satanic mills of the factory towns with the alleged idyllic conditions of an earlier age. He had drawn a moving picture of the England of the mid-eighteenth century as a land of happy, prosperous yeomen and craftsmen who had not a care in the world. The view that the period before the Industrial Revolution was a sort of golden age is a myth. Many of the evils of the early factory age were no worse than those of an earlier period. Domestic spinners and weavers in the eighteenth century had been ' exploited ' by the clothiers as ruthlessly as the factory operatives were ' exploited ' by the manufacturers in the 1840's. Men, women and children worked long hours for low wages under the domestic system as under the factory system. The evidence collected by the Children's Employment Commission in 1842 shows that those who were employed in small workshops—such as the wretched apprentices to the nailmakers in Willenhall and the overworked sewing girls and shirtmakers in the East End of London—were treated far more cruelly than the little piecers in the cotton mills of Lancashire. It was because the factories brought the workers under one roof that it became possible to detect bad conditions which had formerly been hidden in isolated cottages and workshops. Engels accepted Gaskell's interpretation of social conditions in the eighteenth century and on these erroneous foundations he based his theories concerning the origins of the industrial proletariat.

This was by no means the only legend to which Engels helped to give currency. His account of the condition of the workers may have fostered the notion that the so-called ' Hungry Forties ' was a decade of exceptional social distress. In fact there is evidence which shows that the standard of living of the English workers in the 1840's was no worse than it had been in the 1820's and 1830's. Indeed it was probably better. Sir John Clapham, writing in 1926, observed that:

' the legend that everything was getting worse for the working man, down to some unspecified date between the drafting of the People's Charter and the Great Exhibition, dies hard. The fact that, after the price-fall of 1820–21, the purchasing power of wages in general— not, of course, of everyone's wages—was definitely greater than it

---

Later he lived in Bredbury, near Stockport, Cheshire. Gaskell published his first book on *The Manufacturing Population of England* in 1833. A revised and enlarged edition appeared in 1836 under a new title: *Artisans and Machinery*. Engels used the first edition of 1833. Gaskell died on July 19th, 1841, at the age of thirty-five, and was then living in Champion Grove, Camberwell, London. He was buried in the Nunhead Cemetery. See *The Times*, July 22nd, 1841, p. 7, col. 3 and the *Gentleman's Magazine*, September 1841, p. 329. Some information concerning Peter Gaskell has been kindly supplied by the Royal College of Physicians and the Royal College of Surgeons in England.

had been just before the Revolutionary and Napoleonic wars, fits
so ill with the tradition that it is very seldom mentioned, the work of
statisticians on wages and prices being constantly ignored by social
historians. . . .'[1]

Another myth to be found in Engels's book is the confident
assertion that social unrest in the factory districts—particularly in
Lancashire, the Black Country and the Potteries—in August 1842 was
deliberately brought to a head by the Machiavellian cunning of the
manufacturers who supported the Anti-Corn Law League. Engels
stated that the factory owners deliberately fomented strikes by reducing
wages so as to drive the workers onto the streets in the hope that
rioting would follow. In this way pressure could be brought to bear
upon Sir Robert Peel's government to repeal the Corn Laws. This
' explanation ' of the origin of the disorders appears to have originated
in the fertile brains of the Tory Croker[2] and the Chartist O'Connor
and it obtained wide circulation in both Chartist and Tory newspapers.
Although this view has been repeated since Engels's day[3] there is
little, if any, reliable evidence to support it. It is much more probable
that the Plug Plot riots in Lancashire and N.E. Cheshire were a spontaneous expression of discontent in the factory districts and were not
in any way fostered by the manufacturers.[4]

Engels can hardly be taken seriously as a historian. He cannot be
taken very seriously as a prophet either. This brash young man seems
to have imagined that as a result of a profound study of the early
history of the proletariat, coupled with a thorough examination of the
condition of the workers on the spot, he had lighted upon a great
historical truth. He thought that the historical trends that he had
discovered could be projected forward into the future. No astronomer
predicting the date of an eclipse could have asserted in a more positive
manner his conviction that the outbreak of social revolution in England
was imminent. He stated categorically that the next commercial crisis
must see a great rising of all the workers against their capitalist

[1] Sir John Clapham, *Economic History of Modern Britain: The Early Railway Age,*
1820–50 (1926), preface to the *first* edition, p. vii. See also Sir John Clapham's
paper on ' Corn Laws Repeal, Free Trade and History ' read to the Manchester
Statistical Society, October 10th, 1945, and W. H. Chaloner, *The Hungry Forties: a
Re-examination* (Historical Association pamphlet, 1957).
[2] See the anonymous article by J. W. Croker on 'Anti-Corn Law Agitation' in
the *Quarterly Review,* Vol. LXXI, no. 141, Dec. 1842.
[3] G. Kitson Clark, 'Hunger and Politics in 1842', *Journal of Modern History,* Vol.
XXV, No. 4, December 1953, pp. 355–74.
[4] A reply from the supporters of the Anti-Corn Law League to Chartists and
Tories who accused them of fomenting the strikes and disturbances in August 1842
will be found in Archibald Prentice, *History of the Anti-Corn Law League* (1853),
Vol. I, ch. 24, pp. 370–89).

oppressors. He foresaw an upheaval greater even than the French revolution of 1789.[1]

Reviewers of the first German edition of Engels's book had their doubts about the accuracy of this prophecy. The commercial crisis of 1847 and the revolutions on the Continent in 1848 heralded neither the Chartist triumph nor the social catastrophe that Engels had foretold. Engels was again living in Manchester between 1850 and 1870[2] and he could see for himself that neither the severe depression of 1857 nor the widespread unemployment and dire distress caused by the Cotton Famine of the early 1860's could rouse the Lancashire cotton operatives to revolt. Baernreither remarked in the 1880's that:

' the violent revolution which in 1844 Engels deemed inevitable never came to pass, and anyone who to-day, after a lapse of forty years, examines carefully the condition of the working classes in England, will be convinced that it never will.'[3]

The British working-class movement in fact developed on quite different lines from those which Engels so confidently predicted.

And Engels was also wrong in several other predictions. He was in error in supposing that the gulf between rich and poor in England would become ever wider and deeper.[4] He was wrong in supposing that child labour must always be an essential feature of modern industrialism.[5] He was mistaken in thinking that all the Chartist demands would soon be the law of the land.[6]

[1] As early as November 1842—immediately after arriving in London at the start of his visit to England and *before* he had ever seen the factory districts—Engels expressed the view that a social revolution in England was inevitable. See his two articles (both dated November 30th, 1842) which appeared in the *Rheinische Zeitung*, No. 343, December 9th, 1842, and No. 344, December 10th, 1842. The articles have been reprinted in *Gesamtausgabe*, Part I, Vol. 2 (1930), pp. 351-5.

[2] For this period of Engels's life, see W. O. Henderson and W. H. Chaloner, ' Friedrich Engels in Manchester ', *Memoirs . . . of the Manchester Literary and Philosophical Society*, Vol. 98 (1956-7).

[3] J. M. Baernreither, *English Associations of Working Men* (English translation, 1889), p. 5.

[4] G. von Schulze-Gaevernitz observed that according to Marx and Engels the development of industrialisation would mean ' a continuous degradation of the worker to the dead level of a hopeless proletariat, the accumulation of capital in the hands of the few, the disappearance of the middle class, and the rise of a party of social revolution. How do these predictions compare with the facts? The minute statistics of the Board of Trade prove that they have not been realised in England, and thereby cut the ground from under the feet of the revolutionary party '. See G. von Schulze-Gaevernitz, *Social Peace* (English translation, 1893), p. 282.

[5] G. von Schulze-Gaevernitz claimed in *Social Peace* (1893), p. 84, that official statistics refuted ' the contention of Engels and Marx that child labour inevitably supplants that of adults '.

[6] Engels was not always wrong in his predictions. In 1845 he foresaw that there would be a commercial crisis in 1846 or 1847 and he foresaw that the Corn Laws would soon be repealed.

A Social Survey of Britain

It is not only Socialists and Communists who have regarded Engels's account of the condition of the English workers as a book of major importance. Many scholars have accepted it as a reliable account of social England in the 1840's by a well informed contemporary. As early as 1848 the German economist and statistician Bruno Hildebrand declared that Engels was ' the most gifted and knowledgeable German writer on social problems '[1] and over a century later the compiler of a bibliography on urban sociology—prepared for the International Sociological Association in 1955—referred to Engels's book in glowing terms and accepted Engels's claim to have been the first to write about ' *all* the workers ' in England. In this bibliography it is claimed that Engels's account of the English factory towns:

' should still be studied as a model by those social scientists who talk so much nowadays about the need to introduce a " conceptual framework " and " hypotheses " into empirical research. . . . His description of Manchester . . . is a masterpiece of ecological analysis. And he was the only one of the Victorians who considered the social structure of cities systematically, who understood the significance of urbanism—for better and for worse—and also the reasons for anti-urbanism.'[2]

Both before and after the appearance of Engels's work numerous investigators had written detailed accounts of various aspects of the social problems that faced industrial England in the early railway age. In 1831 William Rathbone Greg criticised the factory system in his pamphlet, *An Enquiry into the State of the Manufacturing Population*. In 1832 Dr. J. P. Kay wrote a pamphlet on *The Physical and Moral Condition of the Working Classes employed in the Cotton Manufacture in Manchester* (first and second editions, 1832), while in the following year Peter Gaskell's account of *The Manufacturing Population of England* appeared. Dr. Andrew Ure discussed the condition of the workers in *The Philosophy of Manufactures* (1835) and in *The Cotton Manufacture of*

[1] Bruno Hildebrand in the periodical *Nationalökonomie der Gegenwart und Zukunft* (Frankfurt am Main), Vol. 1, 1848. But he added: ' Die Einzelheiten sind richtig, aber das Ganze ist falsch ' (p. 171). He criticised Engels for historical errors, sins of omission and incorrect deductions from the facts. See below, p. xix of Introduction.

[2] *Current Sociology*: ' Urban Sociology: (Research in Great Britain . . .) trend reports and bibliography ', U.N.E.S.C.O., Paris, Vol. 4, 1955, No. 4, p. 30. It may be added that Dr. Cunningham considered that ' Friedrich Engels's painstaking description of the housing of the Manchester poor is well worth perusal ' (W. Cunningham, *The Growth of English Industry and Commerce in Modern Times*, Part II (first edn., 1882), edition of 1925, p. 807). L. Brentano accepted as accurate Engels's account of social conditions in the 1840's: see L. Brentano, *Eine Geschichte der wirtschaftlichen Entwicklung Englands*, Vol. 3 (Part I), 1928, p. 140. See also David A. Wells, *Recent Economic Changes* (1891), p. 399 and footnote.

Great Britain (1836). The Todmorden cotton manufacturer John Fielden criticised factory evils in his pamphlet on *The Curse of the Factory System* (1836). J. C. Symons's account of *Arts and Artisans at Home and Abroad* was published in 1839; W. P. Alison's *Observations on the Management of the Poor in Scotland and its Effects on the Health of Great Towns* and his brother's (Sir Archibald Alison's) *The Principles of Population* both appeared in 1840. Two years later saw the publication of Edwin Chadwick's official report on *The Sanitary Condition of the Labouring Population of Great Britain* (1842). Thomas Carlyle's *Past and Present*—a book which Engels greatly admired—was first published in 1843, while James Leach's pamphlet on *Stubborn Facts from the Factories* appeared in 1844.

The report of Sadler's select committee on factory children had appeared in 1831–2 and this was soon followed by the two reports of the Factories Enquiry Commission of 1833, which were also concerned with child labour. A few years later another Commission reported on the condition of children working in mines and factories (1841–3). The Commissioners who investigated the condition of the handloom weavers reported in 1839. The first report of the Commissioners who enquired into the state of large towns appeared in 1844. The periodic reports of the Poor Law Board and of the factory inspectors as well as the transactions of the statistical societies of London and Manchester[1] also contain valuable information concerning the condition of the workers in the first half of the nineteenth century.

Here is a wealth of information about the workers in Britain in the 1840's.[2] How is it that Friedrich Engels's account has been so

---

[1] T. S. Ashton, *Economic and Social Investigations in Manchester*, 1833–1933: *a Centenary History of the Manchester Statistical Society* (1934)·

[2] The following books by foreigners may be mentioned: Eugène Buret, *De la misère des classes laborieuses en Angleterre et en France* (2 vols., 1840); C. E. Lester, *The Glory and Shame of England* (2 vols., New York, 1841); C. E. Lester, *The Condition and Fate of England* (2 vols., New York, 1843); Léon Faucher, *Etudes sur l'Angleterre* (2 vols., 1845); A. P. A. Ledru-Rollin, *De la décadence de l'Angleterre* (2 vols., 1850)— translated into English under the title *The Decline of England* (2 vols., 1850); and J. C. Cobden, *The White Slaves of England* (Buffalo, 1853). There are two interesting reports by German travellers—Friedrich von Raumer, *England im Jahre 1835* (first edition, 2 vols., Leipzig, 1836; second enlarged edition, 1842) and Gustav Mevissen, 'Englische Zustände' in the *Rheinische Zeitung*, September 13th, 18th and 20th, 1842, 264 et seq.). It may be added that the French scholar Charles Andler has criticised Engels for failing to acknowledge the extent to which he relied upon Buret's two volumes on the state of the English and French working classes. Andler considers that Engels's book is no more than 'une refonte et une mise au point' of Buret's volumes. Gustav Mayer remarks that Buret and Engels naturally used the same materials (e.g. the Factories Enquiry Commission reports) when writing their books, but he argues that Andler's criticism is much exaggerated. See G. Mayer, *Friedrich Engels: Eine Biographie* (The Hague, 2 vols., 1934), Vol. I, p. 195. See also Henri Sée, *The Economic Interpretation of History* (English translation, 1929), p. 126.

frequently read and quoted while all these—and many other—equally valuable contemporary sources of information have not been used by historians to anything like the same extent?

One reason is that Engels's book has been readily available since the 1890's while nearly all the other books, reports and pamphlets which have been mentioned have long been out of print and can be found only in the larger libraries. Moreover Engels attempted to survey the working classes as a whole—miners and farm workers as well as textile operatives—whereas other less ambitious writers had limited their enquiries in various ways. Thus Dr. J. P. Kay (Kay-Shuttleworth) was concerned only with the Manchester cotton operatives while W. P. Alison dealt only with Scottish workers.

Economic historians have tended to regard Engels's description of social conditions in the 1840's as a reliable account which they could safely recommend to their students. After all Engels was an eye-witness. He vividly describes what he himself saw. And he supplemented his personal observations by reading widely in the literature of the subject. His long quotations and his footnotes suggest that he had a thorough knowledge of the subject.

But was Engels a reliable witness? He lived in England for many years but his book on the condition of the workers was written after a visit of only twenty months or so. He could hardly have gained a comprehensive knowledge of a foreign country in so short a time. Manchester and Salford, which dominate his graphic description of the great towns, were places which he knew really well. He claimed that he was as familiar with Manchester as with his native Barmen: he knew Manchester ' more intimately than most of its residents '. He appears to have visited Oldham, Rochdale, Ashton-under-Lyne and other Lancashire towns and he crossed the Pennines to see Leeds, Bradford and Huddersfield. He was in London for a few weeks.[1] However well he knew industrial Lancashire there is no evidence that he was equally well acquainted with other factory and mining regions such as Clydeside, Tyneside, the Black Country, the Potteries and South Wales. It may be doubted whether he had any first hand knowledge of mining conditions or whether he ever spent much time in the country districts to see for himself how farm workers lived. His descriptions of textile—particularly cotton—mills are based upon personal inspection, but the information which he gives in his chapters on the miners and the agricultural labourers are derived from reports, pamphlets and the columns of the *Northern Star*.

[1] See Friedrich Engels's four ' Letters from London ' published in the *Schweizer-ische Republikaner*, May 16th and 23rd, and June 9th and 27th, 1843, and reprinted in *Gesamtausgabe*, Part I, Vol. 2 (1930), pp. 365-76.

A detailed examination of the material upon which Engels relied when compiling his book suggests that the range of sources which he used was more restricted than is sometimes supposed. He drew very heavily upon a relatively small number of books and pamphlets by Dr. J. P. Kay, Peter Gaskell, Dr. Andrew Ure, J. C. Symons, Sir Archibald Alison and James Leach. Two or three chapters are largely based upon evidence printed in the well-known Factories Enquiry Commission of 1833–4 and the Children's Employment Commission of 1841–3. The newspapers upon which Engels chiefly relied were the *Manchester Guardian,* the *Northern Star* and the *Weekly Dispatch.* Engels did not always consult the book or report in which a statement first appeared. He was content to reproduce at second hand a quotation that had appeared in a newspaper.

The way in which Engels handled his material falls well below generally-accepted standards of scholarship. It is an elementary axiom that quotations should be accurately reproduced. Engels repeatedly gave only a very garbled and abridged version of passages which he ' copied ', but he put them in inverted commas as if they were textual quotations. In a description of bad factory conditions or of insanitary dwellings Engels's ' quotations ' sometimes give the reader a gloomier impression than he would have gained if the original statement had been accurately reproduced. Engels showed little judgement in his assessment of the value of different sorts of evidence. He quoted statements taken on oath before a Royal Commission side by side with newspaper extracts without apparently realising that one carried much more weight than the other.

Although Engels was describing social conditions in the 1840's he sometimes relied upon ' evidence ' of a much earlier date. He referred to a factory in which the number of illegitimate babies born to female operatives doubled when night work was introduced. He omitted to mention that this was alleged to have occurred in 1801. When writing about the insanitary state of Edinburgh he referred his readers to an article by John Hennen in the *Edinburgh Medical and Surgical Journal.* He failed to mention that Hennen's paper had been written in 1818.[1]

---

[1] Engels was, of course, by no means the only reformer who used the device of stating what happened in earlier times and presenting his evidence in such a way as to suggest that the same abuses were still in operation. Professor W. H. Hutt in an article in *Economica* for March 1926—reprinted by F. A. Hayek in *Capitalism and the Historians* (1954), pp. 160–89—points out (p. 163) that Sadler did this when calling witnesses before the Select Committee on Factory Children's Labour in 1831–2 and that ' Fielden made use of the same device in *The Curse of the Factory System* (1836) '. It may be added that Francis Place had carefully coached working-class witnesses appearing before the committee which enquired into the working of the Combination Laws in 1824.

As an illustration of the way in which Engels was led astray by relying, from time to time, upon old books reference may be made to his statement that the workers who had murdered Mr. Thomas Ashton of Hyde had not been brought to justice. This was true when Peter Gaskell mentioned the affair in his book in 1833 but it was no longer true when Engels was writing in 1844-5. The murderers had been caught by that time, but Engels—apparently relying solely upon Gaskell—did not know this.

Again, there are numerous extracts from evidence presented to the Factories Enquiry Commission of 1833-4. The information contained in the first volume of this Commission's report described conditions which had existed before the passing of Althorp's Factory Act of 1833. Engels led his readers to believe that the grim picture of 1833 had not been materially altered by the 1840's. While Engels was right when he drew attention to the difficulties experienced by Factory Inspectors in enforcing the law he was wrong in assuming that virtually no improvements had occurred in the previous decade. Engels also quoted from Dr. Kay's well-known pamphlet on the Manchester cotton operatives which had appeared in 1832. The reader is left with the impression that Kay's strictures concerning housing and sanitation were all still valid in 1844. Engels does not appear to have appreciated the significance of the reforms in local government that had occurred in Manchester and other large industrial towns since the passing of the Municipal Corporations Act of 1835. Many of the factory towns were beginning to put their house in order at the very time when Engels was writing.

Engels's failure to handle satisfactorily the material at his disposal was exposed shortly after the appearance of the German edition of 1845. Bruno Hildebrand, a competent German economist, wrote a review of Engels's book in 1848. It is surprising that his detailed criticism of the way in which Engels assessed his evidence has been almost completely neglected. Hildebrand's discussion of Engels's work is too long to be briefly summarised. But the German economist, who had made a detailed study of English social conditions, ruthlessly exposed many of the faults of Engels's book. He showed, for example, that Engels was quite wrong in his interpretation of British criminal statistics and that his statement that English factory workers were worse off than the craftsmen of an earlier generation was not in accordance with statistical information available when he was writing.[1]

[1] Bruno Hildebrand in *Nationalökonomie der Gegenwart und Zukunft* (Frankfurt am Main), Vol. 1 (1848), pp. 155-61, 170-241.

A Political Tract

It has been seen that some at least of the merits which Marx and Lenin saw in Engels's ' classic ' exposition of the development of the working classes will not bear very close examination. It has been seen, too, that some economic historians have been at fault in accepting Engels's work as an unbiassed and authoritative account of social conditions in England in the 1840's.

The true significance of the book lies in the fact that it was a brilliant political tract. It is a furious indictment of the English middle classes in the early days of Victoria's reign. Engels denounced the factory owners as monsters of iniquity and the more widely the book became known among the working classes the stronger were the passions that it aroused.

At first the book does not seem to have had a very wide circulation. It was first published in 1845 and it was reprinted in 1848.[1] And then —despite many favourable references to it in *Das Kapital*—little more was heard of it. Not until the 1880's was there a revival of interest in *The Condition of the Working Class in England*. By that time there was a large Socialist party in Germany while in Britain and the United States the trade unions had become large and powerful bodies. In February 1885 Engels wrote:

> My friends in Germany say that the book is important to them just now because it describes a state of things which is almost exactly reproduced at the present moment in Germany.

He went on to say that ' a new German edition of my work is in actual preparation '. Two years later however Karl Kautsky was complaining that the book was still out of print and that many Socialists had never read it. In 1887 an ' authorised ' English translation by Mrs. Florence Wischnewetzky was published in the United States by the J. W. Lovell Company of New York. This translation was issued in England by Swan Sonnenschein & Co. in 1892.[2] In the same year a new German

---

[1] For reviews of the German editions of 1845 and 1848 see Victor Aimé Huber in *Janus: Jahrbücher deutscher Gesinnung, Bildung und That* (Berlin) (edited by V. A. Huber), 1845, Part II, pp. 387–389; Otto Lüning in *Deutsches Bürgerbuch*, 1846, Vol. 2, pp. 222–45; and Bruno Hildebrand in *Nationalökonomie der Gegenwart und Zukunft* (Frankfurt am Main), Vol. 1 (1848), pp. 155–62, 170–241. Both Huber and Hildebrand had recently visited the English factory districts. Huber agreed that many of the facts given by Engels were correct, but he opposed Engels's extreme political views.

[2] Mrs. Wischnewetzky's version of *The Condition of the Working Class in England* leaves much to be desired. The translation is little more than a word-for-word transcript of the original into another language. The reader can turn page after page before coming to a paragraph that bears some resemblance to the normal style of an English writer. The book as Engels wrote it is full of lively and vigorous

edition—published by J. H. W. Dietz of Stuttgart—at last appeared.

In a letter written while he was preparing the manuscript of *The Condition of the Working Class in England* and also in a Postscript—which was published separately as an article in 1846—Engels made his purpose crystal clear. His book was intended to reveal to the whole world the iniquities perpetrated by the English middle classes. He would expose the way in which they ground the faces of the poor. He would give chapter and verse to prove conclusively how these monsters in human form oppressed the wretched workers in a hundred ways. What did they care about dangerous and unhealthy factories, grossly insanitary slums, abuses of child labour and female labour, or the horrors of the Poor Law Bastilles if they got their profits as usual? Engels told Marx:

> I shall present the English with a fine bill of indictment. At the bar of world opinion I charge the English middle classes with mass murder, wholesale robbery and all the other crimes in the calendar. I am writing a preface in English which I shall have printed separately for distribution to the leaders of the English political parties, to men of letters and to Members of Parliament. These chaps will have good cause to remember me.[1]

Engels detested the factory system root and branch and his purpose was to amass evidence to condemn it. If a job demanded heavy physical labour then Engels declared that the employer was ruining the health of his hands. If only light repetitive work was required then Engels denounced the factory owner for reducing his workers to nervous wrecks by making them perform excessively tedious and boring tasks. If the manufacturer provided no amenities for his workers then Engels exhausted his extensive vocabulary of vituperation to

passages which have been translated in a very pedestrian fashion. Neither the spirit nor the style of Engels's book has been recaptured. Mrs. Wischnewetzky made no attempt to correct wrong dates or to put right elementary errors in addition in the statistical tables. Many of the passages from books and reports that Engels quoted at some length were not reproduced in the original English but were translated back into English from Engels's German version. A few passages have been arbitrarily omitted without informing the reader that this has been done. It is astonishing that generations of English scholars have been prepared to use so unsatisfactory a translation. For Mrs. Wischnewetzky's career (1859-1932) see page 392 of the German edition of Engels's book published by the Dietz Verlag of Berlin in 1952.

[1] Friedrich Engels to Karl Marx, November 19th, 1844, *Gesamtausgabe*, Part III, Vol. 1 (1929), Letter 2, pp. 4-8. Pierre Leroux once remarked that Karl Marx 'had a special faculty for seeing the evil side in human nature', W. Sombart, *Socialism and the Social Movement* (English translation, 1909), p. 51. The same might be said of Engels.

denounce him as a creature devoid of all common humanity. But if a millowner built cottages for his artisans Engels promptly accused him of being a greedy and tyrannous landlord. If a manufacturer built a school for the operatives' children Engels attacked him for trying to train a new generation of workers to be obedient slaves to the wicked capitalists. If a factory owner erected a reading room Engels complained because no copies of the *Northern Star* were displayed. As far as Engels was concerned no employer was ever in the right and the factory owner was always the villain of the piece.

Engels cast himself in the role of counsel for the prosecution against the capitalists. He did not pretend to be an impartial observer. He selected facts which strengthened his indictment of the middle classes and he suppressed or tried to explain away any evidence which did not support his thesis of the innate wickedness of the bourgeoisie. Sometimes he deliberately refrained from laying the full facts before his readers. Reference has already been made to a factory in which it was alleged that the female operatives had twice as many babies out of wedlock when night work was introduced. Engels failed to point out that the circumstances were quite exceptional. A mill had been burned down and—to avoid unemployment—a night shift was temporarily introduced at another mill. Engels criticised foremen because they treated factory children cruelly. He did not point out that in the cotton mills the little piecers were employed by the spinners and not by the foremen. It was the spinner rather than the foreman who beat the little piecers. Engels frequently drew attention to physical deformities brought about by excessive factory labour. It did not occur to him to quote Dr. Hawkins's remark that in Manchester in 1833 'deformities . . . appear to be far less frequent at present than formerly'.

Engels criticised the ruthless exploitation of girls in the shirt-making trade. They generally worked at home. Their hours were very long and their wages were very low. But the wretched condition of these unfortunate girls had received a good deal of newspaper publicity and their plight had evoked public sympathy. Engels might have mentioned a case—reported in his favourite newspaper—of a sewing girl who appeared before a court charged with pawning shirts entrusted to her. When the story of her poverty was made public a number of people sent money to the magistrate before whom she had appeared. The magistrate ordered that the girl's arrears of rent should be paid from the poor box and that money should be provided so that she could buy furniture for her room. He advised the girl to work for a shirt-manufacturer and to avoid any further dealings with middlemen.[1] This hardly looks as if the middle classes were utterly indifferent to the sufferings of the seamstresses.

Engels denounced a manufacturer for juggling with the factory clock so as to make his operatives work longer, but he did not tell his readers of the denial made on behalf of the factory owner to a representative of the Factories Enquiry Commission. Engels mentioned the case of eleven butchers charged before the Manchester Court Leet with selling bad meat. He failed to state that since this court met only twice a year the offences had been committed over a period of six months. When Engels discussed factory accidents he assumed that they were all due to the greed of capitalists who would not spend money on fencing dangerous machinery. Yet the newspaper reports of inquests on workers—reports to which Engels himself referred his readers—show that to some extent these fatalities were due to the operatives themselves who failed to take necessary precautions and disobeyed factory rules. Engels's account of coal-mining in Britain in the 1840s may give readers the impression that women and children worked underground in all the colliery districts. Actually at this time the employment of women underground was virtually confined to mines in the West Riding, Lancashire, Cheshire, Scotland and South Wales.[2] And when Engels was writing an Act was already on the Statute Book which forbade the employment of women and children underground. Engels asserted that this Act was virtually a dead letter since no inspectors had been appointed to enforce its provisions. In fact an inspector of mines had been appointed in 1843.

Engels's vivid imagination was sometimes used in lieu of facts. In the Postscript of 1846, in which he described a strike of building operatives in Manchester, Engels explained that he had not had an opportunity of seeing those copies of newspapers which would have

---

[1] *Northern Star*, No. 315, November 25th, 1843, page 7, col. 3. In 1843 an 'Association for the Relief and Protection of Young Persons employed in the Dressmaking and Millinery Departments in London' was established. See *The Illuminated Magazine*, Vol. 1, 1843, pp. 97–100 (article on ' Death and the Drawing Room or the Young Dressmakers ').

[2] Children's Employment Commission: *First Report: Mines* (1842), p. v and 24–37 and T. S. Ashton and J. Sykes, *The Coal Industry in the Eighteenth Century* (1929), pp. 21–4, 75 and 170–3. The Act of 1842 which forbade the employment of women and children underground has been described as ' perhaps the most high-handed interference with industry enacted by the State in the nineteenth century', B. L. Hutchins and A. Harrison, *A History of Factory Legislation* (1926), p. 82. The number of workers involved was quite small. In 1841 some 6,000 women and girls were employed underground and at the pithead in *all kinds* of mines in Great Britain. In the *coal mines* 1,185 females over the age of 20 and 1,165 females under that age were employed underground and at the pithead. See G. R. Porter, *The Progress of the Nation* (edn. of 1851), p. 79.

contained an account of the result of the strike. Nevertheless Engels confidently assured his readers that he knew what must have happened. A more honest and less self-opinionated writer would have refrained from saying anything if the necessary evidence was lacking.

Another weakness of Engels's description of the workers in the 1840s was that the author sometimes repeated the guarded assertions of cautious investigators as if they were proved facts. Sir Archibald Alison, for example, estimated in 1840 that there were between thirty thousand and forty thousand prostitutes in London. It is typical of Engels that he should have given the higher rather than the lower figure and that he should have tried to give his readers the impression that the existence of forty thousand prostitutes in London was an accepted fact. It was no more than a guess on Alison's part. No accurate statistics of prostitution are available.[1]

Engels refused to admit that recent reforms had improved the lot of the English workers. The abolition of truck (1830–1), the reduction of the hours worked by women and children in most textile factories (1833), the annual government grant to assist elementary education (from 1833), the reorganisation of municipal administration (1835), the exclusion of women and children from underground work in mines (1842) and Sir Robert Peel's reform of the tariff (1842) had all con- tributed towards alleviating the sufferings and raising the living standards of the workers. Some of the large cities were improving the condition of the working classes by exercising powers secured under local Acts of Parliament.

Time and time again Engels accused the middle classes—particu- larly the factory owners—of unworthy conduct and he habitually assumed that they were capable of acting only from the lowest motives. One charge which he repeatedly made was that an English factory was little better than a harem and that manufacturers had immoral relations with their female employees. Since his own mistress (Mary Burns) had been a cotton operative Engels was the last person to be entitled to make reckless accusations concerning the morals of the factory owners.[2]

Engels was fond of making sweeping statements concerning the reasons why the capitalists should have pursued a particular course of

---

[1] A higher estimate (80,000) appeared in the *Northern Star*, Dec. 2nd, 1843.

[2] Many years later—in 1872, when Engels was writing on the housing question (*Die Wohnungsfrage*, edited by Friedländer, 1930)—Engels accused Edward Akroyd of Halifax of immorality with his female employees. But no evidence was brought forward to substantiate the charge. See J. F. C. Harrison, *Social Reform in Victorian Leeds. The Work of James Hole* (1820–95) (Thoresby Society Monograph, No. 3, 1954), p. 66.

action. He was not deterred by the fact that it is far from easy to prove the motive which has inspired any action taken by an individual, let alone one taken by a whole social class. He was unable to appreciate the difficulty of disentangling the complex factors which might influence the middle classes in any particular set of circumstances. Engels confidently asserted that the abortive attempt to limit cheap railway travel to weekdays was due solely to a mean desire on the part of the middle classes to deprive the workers of the opportunity of travelling by train on the one day on which they were free. Yet opposition to Sunday ' parliamentary trains ' may well have come from a genuine desire to reduce Sunday work for railwaymen to a minimum and to maintain the Sabbath as a day of rest.[1]

A glance at Engels's early life and the circumstance in which his book on the English working classes was written may afford some clues as to the reasons for his bitter hatred of the capitalists.[2] Born in 1820—the son of a prosperous cotton manufacturer in Barmen in the Wupper valley (Rhineland)—Friedrich Engels grew up in a pious middle-class household where respect for Church and State was the order of the day. He received a grammar school education but left in October 1837 before taking his matriculation examination. He entered the family business. Part of his early training was in the office of Heinrich Leupold in Bremen (August 1838 to March 1841).[3] He then served for a year as a volunteer in the Prussian Guard Artillery

---

[1] See also an article on ' The Railway Bill—More Oppression for the Poor ' in *The Weekly Dispatch*, No. 2232, August 4th, 1844, p. 369, col. 4.

[2] The standard life of Friedrich Engels is Gustav Mayer, *Friedrich Engels: Ein Biographie* (The Hague, 2 vols., 1934). An abridged English translation in one volume entitled *F. Engels: A Biography* appeared in 1936. See also Karl Kautsky, *Friedrich Engels; sein Leben, sein Wirken, seine Schriften* (first appeared in the *Oesterreichische Arbeitskalender* of 1888 and then republished as a pamphlet by the Berlin newspaper *Vorwärts* in 1895 as a tribute to Engels at the time of his death); Zelda Kahan-Coates, *The Life and Work of Friedrich Engels* (Communist Party of Great Britain, 1920); Ernst Drahn, *Friedrich Engels* (Verlag Arbeiter Buchhandlung, Vienna, 1920) and an article in the *Handwörterbuch der Staatswissenschaften*, Vol. 3 (fourth edition of 1926); Max Adler, *Engels als Denker* (1935); D. Rjazanov, *Marx und Engels* (1927); and an article by H. Rössler and G. Franz in the *Biographisches Wörterbuch zur deutschen Geschichte* (1952). Engels's correspondence with Marx was published in four volumes in 1913. His correspondence with Eduard Bernstein was published in 1925. A collected edition (*Gesamtausgabe*) of the works of Marx and Engels was published by the Marx-Engels-Lenin Institute (Moscow). See also Moses Baritz, ' Frederick Engels in Manchester ' (letter to the *Manchester Guardian*, March 14th, 1933) and ' Engels: His twenty years in Manchester ' (article in the *Manchester Guardian*, October 10th, 1934); M. Jenkins, *Frederick Engels in Manchester* (Lancashire and Cheshire Communist Party, Manchester, 1951) and Edmund Wilson, *To the Finland Station* (1941), pp. 129-49.

[3] Heinrich Leupold was the head of a firm which was engaged in the export of Silesian cloths (mainly linens) to America. He was Consul for the Kingdom of Saxony in the Free Hanseatic City of Bremen.

in Berlin (1841–2) and he retained a lively interest in military affairs ever afterwards.

By 1842 Engels already held left-wing political views and he was contributing articles to the Cologne radical newspaper (the *Rheinische Zeitung*)[1] which was edited by Karl Marx. As Engels mentions in the introduction to his book on the English workers, many young German supporters of radical reform in the 1840's had been influenced by the materialist philosophy of Ludwig Feuerbach.[2] Engels, too, came under the sway of Feuerbach's doctrines at this time. But in his case the acceptance of extreme political views also represented a violent reaction against the whole way of life of the highly respectable middle-class household in which he had been reared. His own father was a cotton manufacturer and it was this very type of factory owner who was most savagely pilloried in Engels's book.

Two months after completing his military service Engels went to England to complete his business training by working in the offices of Ermen and Engels, a Manchester cotton firm of which his father was a partner.[3] It is understandable that he should have taken a gloomy view of the English scene when he arrived towards the end of 1842. There was unemployment in Manchester at that time. Indeed the whole of the industrial North was seething with unrest after the Plug Plot riots of August 1842.[4] And while Engels was in England in 1844 the coal miners of the North staged a great strike, while some of the southern counties were in the grip of a new outbreak of rick-burning reminiscent of the Swing riots of 1830. At this time agitators were denouncing the new Poor Law and its detested workhouses. They criticised the long hours worked in mines and factories; the

---

[1] The *Rheinische Zeitung* had been established in Cologne as a Liberal organ by Hansemann and Camphausen. Karl Marx, then only twenty-four years of age, was appointed editor in October 1842. The severity of the Prussian censorship led to his resignation in March 1843.

[2] For the views of Marx and Engels on Feuerbach, see their book entitled *Die Deutsche Ideologie*. One section was published as an article in 1847. The whole book was not published until 1932 when it was included in the *Gesamtausgabe . . .* , Part I, Vol. 5. In 1886 Engels wrote a series of articles on Feuerbach in *Die Neue Zeit*. The articles were reissued as a book in the same year. See Emile Burns (editor), *A Handbook of Marxism* (1937), pp. 214–23.

[3] The business had been established—probably in the early 1830's—by Peter Ermen. By 1838 he owned the Victoria Mills at Seedley near Pendleton. Engels's father (Friedrich Engels, senior) joined the firm as a partner in the late 1830's—probably in 1837. The Manchester offices of the firm in the early 1840's were at 5 Newmarket Buildings, Market Street. By 1845 new premises had been secured at South Gate, St. Mary's, off Deansgate.

[4] For Engels's first impression of Lancashire see his article ' Lage der arbeitenden Klasse in England ' in the *Rheinische Zeitung*, December 25th, 1842 (No. 359) reprinted in *Gesamtausgabe*, Part I, Vol. 2 (1930), pp. 361–2.

employment of young children; and the high price of bread. Advocates of the People's Charter, Corn Law repeal, and the Ten Hours Bill secured substantial popular support.[1]

Little wonder that Engels thought that he had come to a country that was on the whole very overworked, underpaid and underfed. He saw that there was a 'pool' of unemployment and he noted the presence of many beggars in the streets of the great cities. He visited slums and realised how wretchedly the workers were housed. His views were confirmed by information which he received from Chartist friends (such as Leach[2] and Harney[3]), from the secularist John Watts,[4] and from a group of German revolutionary leaders (Schlapper, Bauer and Moll) whom he met in London in 1843.[5]

Immediately after returning to Barmen in the autumn of 1844 Friedrich Engels began to write his book on the condition of the English workers. In November he told Marx that he was ' buried in English newspapers and books '. The young author worked under difficult conditions. He was engaged in Communist propaganda in Elberfeld and Barmen.[6] The Prussian police were beginning to show an unwelcome interest in his activities. He was involved in a love affair which seems to have ended somewhat abruptly. His relations with his father drifted from bad to worse. The elder Engels was deeply shocked when he realised that his eldest son had no intention either of entering the family business or of studying at a University, but was actually devoting his time to revolutionary agitation. Engels postponed a breach with his family long enough to complete his

[1] Lord Macaulay wrote on July 22nd, 1843: ' The aspect of foreign politics is gloomy. The finances are in disorder. Trade is in distress. Legislation stands still. The Tories are broken up into three or more factions which hate each other more than they hate the Whigs . . .' G. O. Trevelyan, *Life and Letters of Lord Macaulay* (pocket edn. two volumes, Vol. 2, p. 100).

[2] James Leach, a leading Manchester Chartist, was the author of an anonymous pamphlet entitled *Stubborn Facts from the Factories*, by a Manchester Operative, published by William Rashleigh, M.P. (1844). Engels referred to Leach as ' his good friend ' and as an ' honest, trustworthy and capable man '. For Leach see also below, p. 151.

[3] G. J. Harney (Leeds) edited the *Northern Star*. Engels made frequent use of this newspaper when writing his book on the English workers. For Harney's recollections of his first meeting with Engels see his article in the *Social Democrat*, Vol. 1 (1897), p. 7. For the *Northern Star*, see E. L. H. Glasgow, ' The establishment of the " Northern Star " newspaper ', *History*, Feb.–June, 1954, pp. 54–67.

[4] Dr. John Watts, secularist and Owenite socialist, lectured at this time at the Manchester Hall of Science. By 1851 Engels had lost confidence in Watts. See his letter to Marx in K. Marx-F. Engels, *Gesamtausgabe* . . . , Part III, Vol. 1 (1929), pp. 140–3. For Watts see the *D.N.B.*, Vol. 40, p. 71.

[5] *Gesamtausgabe*, introduction, p. xx, quoting a letter from Engels to Marx, May 6th, 1868.

[6] Two speeches made by Friedrich Engels at Elberfeld at this time are printed in *Gesamtausgabe*, Part I, Vol. 4 (1932).

manuscript, and by March 15th, 1845, the book was finished. Two days later Engels complained to Karl Marx that he was living 'a veritable dog's life' in Barmen. Soon afterwards he joined Karl Marx in Brussels.

All this helps to explain the fury with which Engels attacked the English middle classes in general and the factory owners in particular. At loggerheads with his family and watched by the police, he was a young man in a bad temper who vented his spleen in a passionate denunciation of the factory system as he had recently seen it in England. The unrestrained violence of his language and his complete failure to understand any point of view different from his own may—at any rate to some extent—be explained by the fact that in the winter of 1844-5 Engels was suffering from an overwhelming sense of frustration.

There were English critics of the fundamental errors of foreigners like Engels who attacked the British industrial society of the 1840s. A writer in the *Edinburgh Review*, for example, pertinently remarked in the spring of 1846[1] that

. . . whatever reproaches may be cast on the legislature of this country for the sufferings of the more indigent classes, it cannot be justly accused of having treated them with indifference or neglect. Its errors, if errors there have been, have not arisen from any reluctance to probe the wounds which are alleged to exist in this part of our social system. No other nation ever set to work with a more single-minded resolution, or a humanity more regardless of consequences, to discover and lay bare all its own defects and weaknesses. An incidental effect of these unsparing self-exposures, doubtless, has been the diffusion in foreign countries of utterly false and exaggerated notions respecting the state of the poorer classes amongst us. It is, we believe, generally thought on the Continent, even by persons well informed on other matters, that the English nation is divided into two portions—one consisting of enormously wealthy aristocrats and manufacturers, who are gorged with the spoils of their wretched serfs and operatives—the other, being the bulk of the community, who, by means of incessant toil, scarcely drive off want; numbers of whom are perpetually dying of starvation, and live in dwellings scarcely superior to the wigwams of savages. Such is the jealousy of England generally prevalent on the Continent, that every testimony against its prosperity which comes from an English source, is greedily seized upon by the editors of newspapers—reprinted by them with appropriate comments, and readily swallowed by the public; and thus not only the authentic facts disclosed in official reports, but the unscrupulous exaggerations of partisans, obtain implicit belief; and tend to foster an

[1] *Edinburgh Review*, January–April, 1846, p. 68.

impression that England is constantly on the verge of a social revolution—that her power reposes on an unsound basis—and that the whole system will crumble to pieces at the first severe shock from without.

Even if historians may no longer regard Engels's book as an authoritative work which gives a valuable picture of social England in the 1840s, Socialists will doubtless continue to accept his book as a pioneer standard work which shows what are the inevitable social consequences of rapid industrialisation. In fact the true significance of Engels's study lies in the light which it throws upon the intellectual development of a young revolutionary who was soon to become the chosen collaborator of Karl Marx.

W. O. HENDERSON.
W. H. CHALONER.

THE CONDITION OF
THE WORKING CLASS IN ENGLAND

ENGELS'S PREFACE

TO THE FIRST GERMAN EDITION OF 1845

This book was originally designed to form part of a more comprehensive work on English social history.[1] But I soon decided to publish it as an independent study of the working classes in England as this is in itself a topic of quite exceptional importance.

Since social distress in our day reaches its climax in the condition of the working classes it is obvious that the topics with which I am concerned in this book must form the basis of any effective approach to the examination of modern social movements. It is the condition of the workers which is directly responsible for the rise of working-class communism in France and Germany. It is also indirectly responsible for the French (Fourier) and English forms of socialism as well as that type of communism which has gained some middle class support in Germany. It is essential to have an adequate knowledge of the way of life of the proletariat if one is to form a sound judgment on the merits of socialist theories. Such knowledge is equally necessary if one is to sweep away the sentimental fantasies about the workers which lie behind so many arguments for and against socialist doctrines. It is only in the United Kingdom—and really only in England itself— that it is possible to study working class conditions in their ' classical ' form. Only in England is adequate material available for an exhaustive enquiry into the condition of the proletariat. Only in England do we have at our disposal a large number of official reports on various aspects of the lives of the workers.

I have had the opportunity, during a stay of twenty-one months in England, of seeing for myself how the proletariat lives. I have met many workers and I have had long talks with them. Through personal contact with the English workers I have learned something of their hopes and fears, their joys and sorrows. My own observations have been supplemented by studying authentic printed sources of information concerning the condition of the proletariat. This book is based upon what I have seen and heard for myself and also upon what I have

[1 Engels never completed writing a social history of England. He did, however, contribute several articles on this subject to the periodical *Vorwärts* (published in Paris) between August 31st and October 19th, 1844. These articles have been reprinted in *Gesamtausgabe*, Part I, Vol. 4 (Berlin, 1932), pp. 292–334. The first group of articles deals with England in the eighteenth century, the second with the English constitution].

read. I have no doubt that both the facts that I record and the comments that I make will be criticised in many quarters—particularly if my book falls into English hands. I realise too that here and there the critics will be able to point to some trifling mistakes in the book. But even an English author could hardly avoid making a few little slips in a study which covers so much ground and is based upon such far-reaching assumptions as this one. In England itself there is not a single volume which attempts—as mine does—to deal with *all* the various types of English workers. I have no hesitation in challenging the English middle classes to prove—with evidence as authentic as my own—that I am wrong in any single fact of major importance that is of real significance to the general conclusions that I have drawn.

My description of the present condition of the proletariat in so highly industrialised a country as the United Kingdom should be of particular interest to my German readers. The doctrines of German socialism and German communism have been derived from purely theoretical considerations to a much greater extent than similar doctrines elsewhere. Our German theorists have far too little knowledge of the world as it actually exists. That is why they have never been driven by 'the cold facts of hard reality' to demand reforms which would sweep away the social abuses of our time. Practically every single avowed champion of social reform in Germany has found his way to communism by studying Feuerbach's criticisms of Hegel's philosophy. So little is known of the way in which the proletariat really lives in Germany to-day that the well-meaning but blundering attempts of the middle classes to solve the great social problems of our time by founding societies 'to improve the condition of the workers' continually fail to achieve their object because their members hold preconceived views about the proletariat which are as ludicrous as they are absurd.

We Germans—more than any other people—ought to make ourselves acquainted with the true condition of the workers. In Germany the condition of the proletariat has not yet reached the same stage of development as in England but—since the two countries have basically the same social structure—a time will undoubtedly come when the position of the German workers will be the same as that of the English workers to-day. The only way of preventing this would be for the Germans to take heed while there is still time and drastically reform their entire social system.

On the other side of the North Sea the workers are suffering the most acute privations. They are poor. They are oppressed. The fundamental factors responsible for this deplorable state of affairs are also to be found in German society and they will one day bring about the same state of affairs as now exists in England.

There are two other matters that I should mention. First, I always use the word *Mittelklasse* in the English sense of ' middle class ' (or ' middle classes '—in the plural—which is the most common form). By the middle classes I mean the class which owns property. The French word *bourgeoisie* has the same meaning. When I use the term ' middle class ' I do not include the so-called aristocracy. It is the property-owning middle classes who wield effective power in national affairs. In France and England they do so openly, while in Germany they achieve the same result by controlling ' public opinion '. I always use the expressions ' workers ', ' working men ', ' working classes ', ' proletariat ' and ' non-property-owning class ' as synonymous terms.

Secondly, I want to explain why I always indicate the political affiliations of the authorities upon whom I rely in this book. In England it is nearly always the Liberals who condemn social distress in the agricultural districts while attempting to whitewash the deplorable conditions in the factory towns. But the Conservatives like to expose the social evils of the manufacturing districts though they turn a blind eye to the shocking conditions which exist in the rural parts of the country. Consequently when I am describing conditions in the factories I cite official Liberal reports so as to condemn the Liberals out of their own mouths and I rely upon the evidence of Tories or Chartists only if I know that they are telling the truth—either because I can corroborate what they say from personal observation or because of my confidence in their characters or in the manner in which they present their evidence.

F. ENGELS.

Barmen,
   March 15th, 1845.

TO THE WORKING CLASSES
OF
GREAT-BRITAIN[1]

Working Men!

To you I dedicate a work, in which I have tried to lay before my German Countrymen a faithful picture of your condition, of your sufferings and struggles, of your hopes and prospects. I have lived long enough amidst you to know something about your circumstances; I have devoted to their knowledge my most serious attention, I have studied the various official and non-official documents as far as I was able to get hold of them. I have not been satisfied with this, I wanted more than a mere *abstract* knowledge of my subject, I wanted to see you in your own homes, to observe you in your every-day life, to chat with you on your condition and grievances, to witness your struggles against the social and political power of your oppressors. I have done so: I forsook the company and the dinner-parties, the port-wine and champagne of the middle-classes, and devoted my leisure-hours almost exclusively to the intercourse with plain Working Men; I am both glad and proud of having done so. Glad, because thus I was induced to spend many a happy hour in obtaining a knowledge of the realities of life—many an hour, which else would have been wasted in fashionable talk and tiresome etiquette; proud, because thus I got an opportunity of doing justice to an oppressed and calumniated class of men who with all their faults and under all the disadvantages of their situation, yet command the respect of every one but an English money-monger; proud, too, because thus I was placed in a position to save the English people from the growing contempt which on the Continent has been the necessary consequence of the brutally selfish policy and general behaviour of your ruling middle-class.

Having, at the same time, ample opportunity to watch the middle-classes, your opponents, I soon came to the conclusion that you are right, perfectly right in expecting no supports whatever from them. Their interest is diametrically opposed to yours, though they always will try to maintain the contrary and to make you believe in their most hearty sympathy with your fates. Their doings give them the lie. I hope to have collected more than sufficient evidence of the fact, that

[1 This appeared in English as a preface to the original German edition in 1845.]

—be their words what they please—the middle-classes intend in reality nothing else but to enrich themselves by your labour while they can sell its produce, and to abandon you to starvation as soon as they cannot make a profit by this indirect trade in human flesh. What have they done to prove their professed good-will towards you? Have they ever paid any serious attention to your grievances? Have they done more than paying the expenses of half-a-dozen commissions of enquiry, whose voluminous reports are damned to everlasting slumber among heaps of waste paper on the shelves of the Home-office? Have they even done as much as to compile from those rotting blue-books a single readable book from which everybody might easily get some information on the condition of the great majority of ' free-born Britons'? Not they indeed, those are things they do not like to speak of—they have left it to a foreigner to inform the civilized world of the degrading situation you have to live in.

A Foreigner to *them*, not to *you*, I hope. Though my English may not be pure, yet, I hope, you will find it *plain* English. No working man in England—nor in France either, by-the-bye—ever treated me as a foreigner. With the greatest pleasure I observed you to be free from that blasting curse, national prejudice and national pride, which after all means nothing but *wholesale selfishness*. I observed you to sympathize with every one who earnestly applies his powers to human progress—may he be an Englishman or not—to admire everything great and good, whether nursed on your native soil or not. I found you to be more than mere *Englishmen*, members of a single, isolated nation, I found you to be MEN, members of the great and universal family of Mankind, who know their interest and that of all the human race to be the same. And as such, as members of this Family of ' One and Indivisible ' Mankind, as Human Beings in the most emphatical meaning of the word, as such as I, and many others on the Continent, hail your progress in every direction and wish you speedy success. Go on then, as you have done hitherto. Much remains to be undergone; be firm, be undaunted—your success is certain, and no step you will have to take in your onward march, will be lost to our common cause, the cause of Humanity!

FRIEDRICH ENGELS.

Barmen (Rhenan Prussia),
    March 15th, 1845.

CHAPTER I

HISTORICAL INTRODUCTION[1]

The history of the English working classes begins in the second half of the eighteenth century with the invention of the steam engine and of machines for spinning and weaving cotton. It is well known that these inventions gave the impetus to the genesis of an industrial revolution.[2] This revolution had a social as well as an economic aspect since it changed the entire structure of middle-class society. The true significance of this revolution in the history of the world is only now [1845] beginning to be understood. These momentous changes have occurred earlier and on a larger scale in England than elsewhere. The fact that these great changes sometimes took place without arousing much comment or publicity should not disguise their profound significance. In the circumstances it is only in England that the main social consequence of the Industrial Revolution—the emergence of an industrial proletariat—can be satisfactorily studied in all its varied aspects.

We do not propose to attempt to write the history of this Industrial Revolution or to attempt to assess its importance either for the present or for future generations. Such a task must be reserved for a more detailed study in the future. For our present purpose it will be sufficient to note the following points which have some bearing on the present [1845] conditions of the working classes in England.

Before the introduction of machinery in the textile industry the spinning and weaving of the raw materials took place in the home of the workers. Wives and daughters spun the yarn, which the men either wove themselves or sold to a weaver. Most of these weavers' families lived in the country near to a town and earned enough to live on. In those days the demand from the local market, which was virtually the only outlet for cloth, was steady and satisfactory. It was only later that the expansion of trade with the conquest of new markets abroad led to severe competition which had an adverse effect on the standard

[1 As Engels points out later (p. 78 below) much of this historical introduction is based upon P. Gaskell, *The Manufacturing Population of England* . . . (1833). The portion of Gaskell's work in question runs from pages 15 to 32. The translators have given a few extracts from Gaskell's book in footnotes to indicate the character of Engels's debt to this author].

[2 This is an early use of the term 'Industrial Revolution'. See G. N. Clark, *The Idea of the Industrial Revolution* (Glasgow, 1953).]

of living of the workers. Previously the home market had expanded steadily with the gradual increase in population, and consequently there was full employment. Competition between workers was impossible because they lived in rural isolation. This explains why it was possible for most weavers to save a little money and to rent smallholdings on which they could work in their spare time. In those days the weaver had as much free time as he wanted, because he could arrange his hours of work on the loom to suit his own convenience. It is true that he was a poor husbandman, who neglected his holding, so that the returns from his land were generally low. Nevertheless he was not a member of the proletariat and had, as the English say, a stake in the country. He owned property and was a step higher in the social scale than the modern [1845] English worker.[1]

In the circumstances the workers enjoyed a comfortable and peaceful existence. They were righteous, God-fearing and honest. Their standard of life was much better than that of the factory worker to-day [1845]. They were not forced to work excessive hours; they themselves fixed the length of their working day and still earned enough for their needs. They had time for healthy work in their gardens or smallholdings and such labour was in itself a recreation. They could also join their neighbours in various sports such as bowls and football and this too kept them in good physical condition. Most of them were strong, well-built people, whose physique was virtually equal to that of neighbouring agricultural workers. Children grew up in the open air of the countryside, and if they were old enough to help their parents work, this was only an occasional employment and there was no question of an eight- or twelve-hour day.

It is not difficult to form a judgment of the moral and intellectual character of this social class. The workers were cut off from urban life, because they never had occasion to visit the towns. Their yarn and cloth were sold to travelling agents who paid them on the spot for their work. Workers could live until old age quite close to towns without entering them, but eventually the machines robbed them of their livelihood and forced them to seek work there. Before this change took place the workers were, from a moral and intellectual point of

[1 Gaskell wrote: ' . . . he generally earned wages which were sufficient not only to live comfortably upon, but which enabled him to rent a few acres of land; thus joining in his own person two classes, that are now daily becoming more and more distinct. It cannot, indeed, be denied, that his farming was too often slovenly, and was conducted at times but as a subordinate occupation; and that the land yielded but a small proportion of what, under a better system of culture, it was capable of producing. It nevertheless answered an excellent purpose. . . . It gave him employment of a healthy nature, and raised him a step in the scale of society above the mere labourer ' (op. cit., pp. 16–7).]

view, on the same footing as countrymen, with whom they were linked by the fact that they themselves also cultivated small plots of land. They regarded the squire—the most important landlord in the district —as their natural superior. They went to him for advice from time to time. They asked him to settle their little disputes and they showed him that deference which naturally arose out of the patriarchal relationship between the squire and his dependents.[1] They were ' respectable ' people and good family men. In the absence of temptations to immorality they lived God-fearing decent lives. There were no low public houses or brothels in the neighbourhood. The innkeepers whose houses they did occasionally patronise were also respectable men, generally substantial tenant farmers, providing good beer and insisting on orderly behaviour and early closing. The workers' children were brought up at home, where they learned to fear God and obey their parents. This patriarchal relationship between parents and children continued until the young people left home to get married. Children grew up in idyllic simplicity and in happy intimacy with their playmates. It is true that sexual intercourse almost always took place before marriage, but this was only between engaged couples who fully intended to get married and in due course a wedding regularised the situation.[2] In short, the English industrial worker of those days lived very much in that state of seclusion and retirement which is still sometimes to be found here and there in Germany to-day [1845]. They were not much troubled with intellectual and spiritual problems and the even tenor of their lives was seldom disturbed. They could seldom read and it was still rare for them to be able to write. They went regularly to Church. They took no interest in politics, never formed secret societies, never concerned themselves about the problems of the day, but rejoiced in healthy outdoor sports and listened devoutly when the Bible was read to them. Their unquestioning humility enabled them to live peacefully side by side with the higher

[1 Gaskell wrote: ' The distinctions of rank, which are the safest guarantees for the performance of the relative duties of all classes, were at this time in full force; and the " Squire ", as the chief landed proprietor was generally termed, obtained and deserved his importance from his large possessions, low rents, and a simplicity and homeliness of bearing which, when joined to acknowledged family honours, made him loved and reverenced by his tenants and neighbours. He mingled freely with their sports—was the general and undisputed arbitrator in all questions of law and equity—was a considerate and generous landlord—a kind and indulgent master—and looking at him in all his bearings, a worthy and amiable man ' (op. cit., pp. 20-1).]

[2 Gaskell wrote: ' . . . sexual intercourse was almost universal prior to marriage in the agricultural districts. This intercourse . . . existed only between parties where a tacit understanding had all the weight of an obligation—and this was, that marriage should be the result. This, in nineteen cases out of twenty, took place sooner or later . . . ' (op. cit., p. 28).]

ranks of society. But this meant that they had no intellectual life and were interested solely in their petty private affairs, such as their looms and their gardens. They knew nothing of the great events that were taking place in the outside world. They vegetated happily, and but for the Industrial Revolution would never have left this way of life, which was indeed idyllic. Yet they remained in some respects little better than the beasts of the field. They were not human beings at all, but little more than human machines in the service of a small aristocratic class which had hitherto dominated the life of the country. The Industrial Revolution carried this development to its logical conclusion, turned the workers completely into mere machines and deprived them of the last remnants of independent activity. Yet it was this change which forced the workers to think for themselves and to demand a fuller life in human society. Political changes in France and economic changes in England aroused first the middle classes and later the working classes and brought them into the vortex of world affairs.[1]

The first invention which fundamentally changed the position of the English worker was that of the spinning jenny, which was constructed in 1764 by the weaver James Hargreaves of Stanhill, near Blackburn in North Lancashire.[2] This machine was the crude ancestor of the mule and could be operated by hand. Where the old spinning wheel had only one spindle, the jenny had sixteen or eighteen, which could be worked by a single artisan. It was therefore possible to produce much more yarn than formerly. At one time one weaver had always kept three spinners busy and there had been such a shortage of yarn that the weavers were often idle for lack of it. Now there was more yarn than the weavers could handle. The already lively demand for woven stuffs increased still further, because of lower prices which were due to the fall in the cost of production arising from the use of the jenny. There was a shortage of weavers and their earnings increased. Now that they could earn more by weaving they gradually stopped working on their smallholdings and devoted themselves entirely to industrial pursuits. At this stage, when trade was good and weavers were busy, four adults and two children (the latter being engaged in reeling) could earn £4 or more per week, working a ten-hour day. A single weaver could often earn as much as £2 per week.[3] Gradually the part-time weavers disappeared and were absorbed into

[1 This marks the end of Engels's borrowings from Gaskell for the time being.]
[2 Probably based upon Andrew Ure, *The Cotton Manufacture of Great Britain*, Vol. 1 (1836), p. 196. Both Ure and Engels wrongly wrote 'Stand-hill' instead of Stanhill.]
[3 Gaskell, op. cit., p. 34.]

the class of full-time industrial workers, who had no links with the soil either as owners or tenants of smallholdings. They were now purely members of the proletariat (working men). At the same time the old relationship between spinners and weavers came to an end. Hitherto, the spinning of the yarn and the weaving of the cloth had, as far as possible, been carried on under one roof. Now that both the jenny and the loom required considerable physical strength for their operation, men began to replace women as spinners. An entire family could live on a spinner's earnings and the old-fashioned spinning wheel was laid aside. On the other hand some families could not afford to buy a jenny and they had to live on the earnings of the head of the household from weaving. So began the division of labour between spinning and weaving which has since become more and more marked.

Although the jenny was an imperfect machine its appearance set in motion a train of events which led not only to the development of an industrial proletariat but also to that of an agrarian proletariat. Hitherto there had existed many independent owners of smallholdings called yeomen, who had led just as uneventful lives as their neighbours the farming weavers. They had cultivated their little plots of land just as their fathers had done before them and they resisted all innovations with the inevitable obstinacy of men who had inherited a way of life unchanged for generations. Among them there were also many small leaseholders. They were not, however, leaseholders in the modern sense of the term, but copyholders who cultivated their patches of land by virtue of hereditary or customary leases. In fact they were just as secure in the possession of their land as if they had been owners. When the weavers gave up their smallholdings and became industrial workers many plots of land came on to the market and they were acquired by a new class of substantial tenant-farmers who cultivated fifty, a hundred, two hundred or more ' Morgen '.[1] They were called tenants at will and their leases could be terminated at any time by giving twelve months' notice. These men were able by introducing better methods of farming to increase the output of the land. They could sell their products more cheaply than the small yeoman who thus found that he could no longer live on his smallholding and so was forced to sell it. These yeomen either bought a jenny or loom or else they became agricultural labourers on the big farms, so becoming members of the agricultural proletariat. The yeomen were too slow to adapt their inherited farming techniques to new conditions. They had cultivated their land inefficiently for generations and were now

[1 The Prussian ' Morgen ' was rather less than two-thirds of an acre.]

quite unable to compete against men of capital who farmed scientifically on a large scale.

Meanwhile industrial change continued. Here and there moneyed men began to assemble spinning jennies in factories and to drive them by water power. This enabled them to work with fewer spinners and to sell their yarn more cheaply than the individual spinner who worked his machine by hand. The spinning jenny was continually being improved, so that machines soon needed to be modified or even replaced entirely. The capitalist who used water-power might still make a profit for a time with relatively obsolete machinery, but this was not possible for the hand-spinner. In these developments may be seen the genesis of the factory system. The invention of the spinning throstle in 1767 by Richard Arkwright, a barber from Preston in North Lancashire, gave a great impetus to the erection of factories. This machine, usually called ' Kettenstuhl ' in Germany, shares with the steam engine the distinction of being the most important mechanical invention of the eighteenth century. The spinning throstle, constructed on entirely novel principles, was a power-driven machine from the beginning. In 1785[1] (*sic*) Samuel Crompton of Firwood[2] invented the mule which was a combination of the jenny and the throstle. At the same time Arkwright invented machines for carding and preparing the cotton wool for spinning. This group of inventions ensured the triumph of the factory system in the spinning of cotton. Gradually these machines were adapted by means of slight modifications to the spinning of wool and later—in the first decade of the nineteenth century—to the spinning of flax, so that in these textile industries too, handwork declined at the expense of machinery. Moreover, towards the end of the eighteenth century Dr. Cartwright, a country parson, invented the power-loom and by about 1804 he had improved this machine to such an extent that it competed successfully with the handloom weaver. The importance of all these machines was much increased by the invention in 1764 of James Watt's steam engine. After 1785 it was applied to the driving of spinning machinery.

These inventions have been improved from year to year and have brought about the victory of the machine over the hand worker in the main branches of British industry. The history of the hand-workers has been one of continued retreat in face of the advance of the machine. The results of this process were a rapid fall in the prices of all manu-

[1 At one time the date of Crompton's mule was generally given as 1775, but it is now known that the inventor completed his first mule in 1779. E. Baines, jun., *History of the Cotton Manufacture in Great Britain* (1835), p. 199.]
[2 Near Bolton, Lancs.]

factured articles, the expansion of commerce and industry, the conquest of virtually all unprotected foreign markets, the rapid expansion of capital and national wealth. On the other hand the process led also to a much swifter growth in the numbers of the proletariat. The industrial workers no longer owned any of the means of production, and they lost all security of employment. This led to the demoralisation of the workers and to political unrest. It led to a state of affairs which caused grave concern to wealthy property-owners. In the chapters which are to follow we shall describe in greater detail exactly how the industrial proletariat works and lives. We have already seen how the introduction of one new but primitive machine, such as the jenny, could have far-reaching effects on the economic and social condition of the workers. In the circumstances it is not surprising that the general transition from handwork to a system using intricate machinery in all stages of cloth manufacture should have had social consequences of a far-reaching character.

We may now follow the development of some of the main branches of British industry. The cotton industry is the most important branch of industry in Britain. Between 1771 and 1775, on the average, less than 5 million lb. of raw cotton were imported annually.[1] In 1841 these imports amounted to 528 million lb., while in 1844 they will amount to at least 600 million lb. In 1834 England exported 556 million yards of cotton piece goods, 76½ million lb. of cotton yarn and cotton hosiery to the value of £1,200,000 sterling.[2] In the same year the British cotton industry employed over 8 million mule spindles, some old-fashioned throstle-spindles, 110,000 power-looms and 260,000 hand looms.[3] According to McCulloch nearly one and a half million people were directly or indirectly employed in this branch of industry in the United Kingdom.[4] The factories themselves employed

[1 Baines, op. cit. (1835), p. 346.]
[2 See table in G. R. Porter *The Progress of the Nation*, Vol. 1 (1836), p. 208. That Engels was familiar with Porter's work is shown by the fact that in articles written for the German periodical *Vorwärts* in the autumn of 1844—while the book on the English working classes was in progress—Engels appears to have made extensive use of statistics taken from Porter's *Progress of the Nation*, which was issued in three volumes dated 1836, 1838 and 1843. A notebook has survived in which Engels summarised and commented upon the third volume of Porter's book. Adoratskij suggests that Engels made these notes in July and August 1845 in preparation for a new visit to England that he was planning with Marx. For Engels's notebook see *Gesamtausgabe*, Part I, Vol. 4 (1932), pp. 502-4.]
[3 Baines, op. cit., p. 383, and Porter, op. cit., Vol. 1, pp. 218-9.]
[4 J. R. McCulloch, *A Dictionary of Commerce* (ed. of 1840, Vol. 1, p. 444) estimated the number of persons dependent directly and indirectly upon the cotton industry as between 1.2 and 1.4 millions. For the 1847 edition of the same work he revised his estimate to between 1.0 and 1.2 million: op. cit. (ed. of 1847), Vol. 1, p. 438. See also Porter, op. cit., Vol. 1 (1836), p. 229.]

220,000 workers and used 33,000 h.p. of steam-driven machinery and 11,000 h.p. of machinery driven by water power. These statistics are now (1845) of course, out of date, and it may safely be assumed that since 1834 there has been a 50 per cent increase in the horse-power, the number of machines and the number of workers employed in the industry. The main centre of this industry is in Lancashire, where it started. The face of the country has been completely changed as a result of the Industrial Revolution. What was once an obscure, poorly-cultivated bog is now a thickly-populated industrial district. Lancashire's population has increased ten-fold in 80 years; and many large towns have grown up there. Liverpool and Manchester, for example, have together 700,000 inhabitants. Near at hand are Bolton (50,000 inhabitants), Rochdale (75,000), Oldham (50,000), Preston (60,000), Ashton and Stalybridge (40,000). These and many other factory towns have experienced a mushroom growth. Modern times can show few greater marvels than the recent history of South Lancashire. It is, however, astonishing how little the general public knows of these developments, brought about entirely by the expansion of the cotton industry. In addition, Glasgow and the adjacent counties of Lanarkshire and Renfrewshire form another subsidiary cotton district. Here, too, the main city in the area has increased in population tenfold, from 30,000 to 300,000 inhabitants, since the introduction of the cotton industry.[1] Two factors promoted the expansion of the hosiery industry in Nottingham and Derby. The first of these, as in cotton, was the fall in yarn prices, while the second was the improvement of the stocking-knitting frame, which enabled one machine to knit two stockings at the same time. The lace industry received an impetus in 1777 with the invention of a new machine. Shortly afterwards Lindley invented the point-net machine, while in 1809 Heathcote invented the bobbin-net machine which greatly simplified the manufacture of lace. A sharp reduction in the price of lace as a result of these inventions led to an expansion of the demand and now at least 200,000 persons are employed in this branch of manufacture.[2] The main lace centres are Nottingham and Leicester, but there are also factories in Wiltshire, Devonshire and elsewhere in the West of England. Various industries which depend on the manufacture of cotton such as bleaching, dyeing and calico printing have also expanded to a great extent. The time employed in bleaching was greatly reduced when the process was

[1 A. Alison, *The Principles of Population* (1840), Vol. 2, p. 87. Alison was quoting statistics, published by James Cleland, which showed that the population of Glasgow had increased from 31,000 in 1770 to 290,000 in 1839.]
[2 Porter, op. cit., Vol. 1 (1836), p. 247; Ure, op. cit. (1836), Vol. 2, pp. 342-4.]

modernised by the substitution of chlorine for the oxygen in the atmosphere. Dyeing and calico-printing benefited from the rapid extension of chemical knowledge. Calico-printing was further improved by a series of brilliant mechanical inventions. These three industrial processes would in any case have expanded with the growth of the cotton industry, but the inventions to which we have referred raised them to a hitherto unheard-of degree of prosperity.

Similar developments occurred in the woollen manufacture. Although this was at one time the most important British industry the output of wool textiles was much smaller in the last quarter of the eighteenth century than it is today [1845]. In 1782 the entire wool-clip of the previous three years was in store because there were not enough workers to handle it.[1] This situation was only alleviated by the appearance of new machinery which enabled the raw material to be spun. The new cotton spinning machines were successfully adapted to wool. There followed a rapid expansion in the woollen districts which recalled the progress made in the cotton industry. The output of woollen cloth in the West Riding of Yorkshire rose from 75,000 pieces in 1738 to 490,000 in 1817.[2] So rapidly did this industry develop that in 1834 the export of cloth was 450,000 pieces more than had been exported in 1825.[3] The amount of raw material worked up by the wool textile industry rose from 101 million lb. (7 millions of which were imported) in 1801 to 182 million lb. (of which 42 millions were imported) in 1835. The main centre of this industry is the West Riding of Yorkshire. At Bradford the long English wools are converted into worsted yarn, while in the other towns such as Leeds, Halifax and Huddersfield the short-stapled wools are used for the manufacture of [hand-spun] woollen yarn and cloth. In that part of Lancashire which adjoins Yorkshire, i.e. the Rochdale district, a good deal of flannel is manufactured as well as cotton goods. The finest cloths are manufactured in the West of England. The West Riding towns have expanded just as rapidly as those of Lancashire:

[1 The statement concerning the accumulation of wool in 1782 was quoted by Marx in *Capital* (Everyman edn.), Vol. 2, p. 667.]

[2 According to James Bischoff, *A Comprehensive History of the Woollen and Worsted Manufactures* (1842), Vol. 2, Appendix, Table IV), the number of pieces of woollen and worsted cloth milled in Yorkshire rose from 56,899 in 1738 to 483,729 in 1817.]

[3 See Bischoff, op. cit., Vol. 2, Appendix, Table VII. Engels's statement refers only to the expansion of the export trade in woollen and worsted stuffs, and does not include many other exports, such as flannels, blankets, etc. Engels's estimate refers to the expansion of the export trade between 1824 and 1833. The confusion may have arisen owing to the fact that the official figures are given for the year ending January 5th. Porter (op. cit., Vol. 1, (1836), p. 192) gives the figures for January 6th, 1824, to January 5th, 1825, under the year 1825.]

	Inhabitants	
	1801	1831
Bradford	29,000	77,000
Halifax	63,000	110,000
Huddersfield	15,000	34,000
Leeds	53,000	123,000
West Riding	564,000	980,000[1]

The population of the West Riding has certainly increased by between 20 and 25 per cent between 1831 and the present day [1845]. In the United Kingdom in 1835 there were 1,313 woollen spinning mills employing 71,300 workers.[2] This figure includes only a small part of the total number of workers engaged directly and indirectly in the manufacture of wool and excludes virtually all weavers.   The expansion of the linen industry occurred later owing to the technical difficulty of inventing a machine to deal with flax fibre. It is true that towards the end of the eighteenth century experiments in mechanical flax-spinning had been carried out in Scotland, but it was only in 1810 that a French inventor named Girard constructed a practicable flax-spinning machine. Even this invention had to be improved in England before it was generally adopted in Leeds, Dundee and Belfast, where it achieved a considerable measure of success. This led to a rapid expansion of the British linen industry. In 1814 Dundee imported 3,000 tons of flax, while in 1833[3] it imported 19,000 tons of flax and 3,400 tons of hemp.[4] The Irish linen sent to Great Britain rose from 32 million yards in 1800 to 53,000,000 yards in 1825, most of which was later exported overseas. The export of English and Scottish linen cloth rose from 24 million yards in 1820 to 51 million yards in 1833. The number of flax-spinning mills in 1835 amounted to 347, employing 33,000 workers. About half these mills were in southern Scotland; there were over 60 in the West Riding of Yorkshire (Leeds and district); there were 25 in Belfast, Northern Ireland, and the remainder were in Dorsetshire and Lancashire. Linen weaving was located mainly in Ireland, but also to some extent in southern Scotland and here and there in England.[5]

The progress of the silk industry was equally noteworthy. The raw material came in the form of skeins from Southern Europe and

[1 Porter, op. cit., Vol. 1 (1836), pp. 200–1.]
[2 Porter, op. cit., Vol. 1 (1836), pp. 196–7.]
[3 Porter, op. cit., Vol. 1 (1836), p. 267.]
[4] The English ton weighs 2240 lb. and 40 English lb. = 39 Prussian lb. [In the German edition of 1892 Engels gave the weight of the English ton as 'almost 1000 kilograms'.]
[5 Porter, op. cit., Vol. 1 (1836), pp. 265 and 272.]

Asia and the main function of the English industry was throwing the silk into fine threads. Until 1824 a heavy import duty on raw silk (4s. per lb.) greatly hampered the development of the silk industry, which could only compete with foreign silks in its protected home and colonial markets. As soon as the import duty on raw silk was reduced to 1d. per lb.[1] there was a rapid expansion in the number of silk factories. In a single year the number of doubling spindles rose from 780,000 to 1,180,000 and, although the commercial crisis of 1825 hampered the development of the industry temporarily, its output reached record heights in 1827.[2] British technical skill and inventive experience had brought silk-throwing machinery to a state of efficiency much greater than that of foreign competitors. In 1835 the United Kingdom had 263 [modernised] silk-throwing factories employing 30,000 workers, which were mainly situated in Cheshire (Macclesfield, Congleton, and district), Manchester and Somerset.[3] In addition there were numerous factories for manufacturing spun silk from silk waste from the cocoons. Even the silk-weaving sheds of Paris and Lyons used this English spun silk. The weaving of thrown silk and spun silk takes place in Scotland (Paisley, etc.), London (Spitalfields), Manchester and elsewhere.

The gigantic expansion which occurred in British industry after 1760 was by no means confined to textiles. Once the initial impetus to modern industrialisation had been given, one branch of manufacture after another was affected. There were many inventions which were quite unconnected with the progress in the textile industries which we have been discussing. These inventions would have been important in any event, but taken in conjunction with the innovations in the textile industries they became doubly important. Once the immense potentialities of industrial mechanisation had been appreciated, manufacturers and inventors made every effort to profit by this new knowledge and to extend the application of machinery as widely as possible. Many branches of industry and increasing numbers of workers were employed in constructing and erecting machines, in supplying the fuel consumed by the machines and in producing the raw materials for the new factories. The great coalfields of Britain first became important through the invention of the steam engine. The new engineering

[1 According to *Customs Tariffs of the United Kingdom from* 1800 *to* 1897 (c. 8706 of 1897) the import duty on raw silk was 5s. 6d. per lb. in 1823–24. This was reduced to 3d. per lb. on March 25th, 1824, and to 1d. per lb. as from July 5th, 1826.]

[2 Porter, op. cit., Vol. 1 (1836), p. 256.]

[3 Porter, op. cit., Vol. 1 (1836), pp. 260–1, 238 of these factories were at work and 25 idle in 1835.]

industry gave an impetus to the ironworks which supplied the raw material for the manufacture of machinery. The increased consumption of wool encouraged the rearing of sheep, while the increased imports of wool, flax and silk led to the expansion of the British mercantile marine. The most striking expansion occurred in the production of iron. Hitherto Britain's rich iron-ore deposits had been inadequately exploited because the iron-ore had to be smelted with charcoal. The shortage of home-grown timber, due to the depredations of the charcoal burners and the clearances undertaken by improving farmers, led to a serious shortage of charcoal and a consequent increase in its price. It was not until the eighteenth century that coke was used in smelting iron ore. At first only cast iron could be produced in this way, but in 1780 a new process was discovered by which wrought iron of satisfactory quality could be made by a coke-smelting process. The English call this method 'puddling' and it consists of extracting the carbon left in the iron after the first stages in the coke-smelting process. This led to a great expansion in the output of iron and the manufacture of iron goods. The size of the blast furnace increased five-fold; iron smelting was simplified by the introduction of the hot blast; and it was now possible to make from iron a large number of products which had formerly been made of wood and stone. The first iron bridge was erected in 1788 in Yorkshire by the well-known demo-crat Thomas Paine,[1] and this was followed by countless others. Today nearly all bridges, particularly railway bridges, are made of cast iron and one has actually been built over the Thames at London (South-wark). Iron pillars, foundations and supports for machinery are in universal use and the introduction of gas lighting and railways has opened up new markets for the English ironmasters. Even the manu-facture of nails and screws was eventually mechanised. In the 1740s[2] Huntsman of Sheffield invented a new labour-saving method of making cast steel which made possible the manufacture of many new cheap goods. The manufacture of metal goods in England now became important. Among the factors which made this development possible may be mentioned the higher quality of the raw material, improved tools, new machinery and a minute division of labour. Between 1801 and 1844 the population of Birmingham rose from 73,000 to 200,000, while that of Sheffield rose from 46,000 to 111,000. Sheffield's coal

[1 This statement is incorrect. Paine designed an iron bridge, the parts of which were cast near Rotherham in Yorkshire, but the bridge was never erected in York-shire. The first iron bridge in this country was built across the Severn at Coalbrook-dale between 1777 and 1779. See M. D. Conway, *Life of Thomas Paine* (1892), Vol. 1, pp. 239-67 and the article on Paine in *D.N.B.*]
[2 In the first German edition this date was wrongly given as 1790.]

consumption in 1836 amounted to 515,000 tons. Between 1805 and 1834 the export of iron goods rose from 4,300 to 16,200 tons, while in the same period the export of pig iron rose from 4,600 to 107,000 tons. The total output of pig iron was only about 17,000 tons in 1740 but had increased to 700,000 tons in 1834.[1] At the present time over 3 million tons of coal are used annually in the smelting of pig iron.[2] The progress made in the coal mining industry has been amazing. All the English and Scottish coalfields are being exploited. More than 5 million tons of coal are shipped yearly from the mines of Northumberland and Durham, which employ between 50 and 60,000 workers. According to the *Durham Chronicle*,[3] the number of collieries in operation in Northumberland and Durham has expanded as follows:

1753	... ...	14[4]
1800	... ...	40
1836	... ...	76
1843	... ...	130

All these mines are worked much more intensively than they used to be. There has been a similar expansion in the mining of tin, copper and lead. There has also been an expansion in the old-established glass industry. A new branch of industry is the making of pottery, which began to grow in importance about 1763 owing to the activities of Josiah Wedgwood. This great industrialist applied scientific principles and artistic designs to the production of earthenware. He founded the North Staffordshire Potteries, which is a district of eight square miles in area. This was once waste land, but is now covered with factories and houses and has a population of 60,000.

The whole of the economy was affected by this expansion. Fundamental changes occurred in agriculture. It has already been seen that new classes of landowners and cultivators appeared. Agriculture, however, was affected in other ways than this. The new large-scale tenant-farmers secured capital which they used to improve land by various means. They removed unnecessary fences, they drained and manured the soil, they used better farm implements and they introduced better rotation of crops. The progress of science helped the

[1 Porter, op. cit., Vol. 1 (1836), chap. IV.]
[2 The figure of 3 million tons of coal per annum appears in Porter, op. cit., Vol. 1 (1836), p. 345 and refers to the time at which this volume appeared. But on page 86 of his third volume, which was published in 1843, Porter gave a substantially higher figure (4,877,000). Engels, writing in the winter of 1844-45, should have used this higher estimate.]
[3 *Durham Chronicle, Sunderland Times, and Darlington and Stockton Gazette*, no. 1286, June 28th, 1844, p. 2, col. 8, article on ' The Coal Trade " Monopoly " '.]
[4 The *Durham Chronicle* states ' only about 14 '.]

farmer. Sir Humphry Davy successfully applied chemical knowledge to farming. Moreover, the progress of engineering also had beneficial effects on agriculture. So great was the demand for food, owing to the increased population, that between 1760 and 1834 no less than 6,840,540 acres of waste land were brought under cultivation.[1] In spite of this Britain now imports wheat, whereas formerly she had a surplus for export.

Important developments also took place in transport. Between, 1818 and 1829 a thousand miles of roads with the legal minimum width of 60 feet were constructed in England and Wales, and nearly all the old roads were remodelled on Macadam's principles. Since 1803 the Board of Public Works in Scotland has constructed 900 miles of highways and over 1000 bridges and this has brought the people of the Highlands into touch with civilisation for the first time. Formerly most of the Highlanders were poachers and smugglers, but now they have become smallholders and domestic industrial workers. Although schools have been established in order to foster Gaelic, the language and customs of the Celt are rapidly vanishing before the triumphant march of English civilisation. In an area which included parts of the counties of Cork, Limerick and Kerry in S.W. Ireland there was once a barren stretch of country without roads. Owing to its isolation this district had become the refuge of all sorts of criminals and was also the home of Celtic nationalism in Ireland. New roads were built through this wild district and opened it up to the influences of civilisation. Sixty years ago the English roads were just as bad as those of France and Germany. But today the country is covered with a network of excellent roads. Like practically everything else in England these roads were built by private enterprise and the State had little or nothing to do with them.

Before 1755 there were very few canals in England. In that year the Sankey Brook canal was constructed to St. Helens in Lancashire.[2] In 1759 James Brindley built the first important canal for the Duke of Bridgewater. This canal runs from Manchester and the adjacent coal-mining district to the Mersey estuary and crosses the River Irwell by an aqueduct at Barton. It was Brindley who gave the impetus to the construction of the modern English canal system. Today Britain has a network of canals and many rivers have been made navigable. England alone has 2,200 miles of canals and 1,800 miles of navigable

[1 Porter, op. cit., Vol. 1 (1836), p. 170.]
[2 The Sankey Navigation was, in fact, opened in 1757: T. C. Barker and J. R. Harris, *A Merseyside town in the Industrial Revolution: St. Helens 1750–1900* (1954), pp. 11–23.]

river. In Scotland the Caledonian canal intersects the country, while Ireland too, has several canals. These public works, like the roads and railways, have nearly all been undertaken by private persons and joint stock companies.

Railways are of more recent origin. The first of the more important railways was the Liverpool and Manchester, opened in 1830. Today [1845] all the big cities are linked by rail—London to Southampton, Brighton, Dover, Colchester, Cambridge, Exeter (via Bristol) and Birmingham; Birmingham to Gloucester, Liverpool and Lancaster (via Newton-le-Willows and Wigan and also Manchester and Bolton), and also to Leeds (via Manchester and Halifax and via Leicester, Derby and Sheffield); Leeds to Hull and Newcastle via York. Many smaller lines are being built or have been planned and it will soon be possible to travel by rail from London to Edinburgh in a day.

The application of steam power has not only revolutionized land transport, but it has also transformed travel by sea and river. The first steamship sailed on the River Hudson in North America in 1807, while in the United Kingdom a steamship sailed on the Clyde in 1811. Since that date over 600 steamships have been built in England[1] and in 1836 over 500 steamships were using British harbours.[2]

This in brief has been the development of British industry over the last sixty years, a development which has no parallel in the annals of mankind. Eighty, even sixty, years ago England was no different from any other country, with its little townships, only a few simple domestic manufactures and a relatively large but widely-scattered agricultural population. Today [1845] England is a unique country with a capital city of 2½ million inhabitants,[3] with huge factory towns; with industries which supply the needs of the whole world, making practically everything by means of the most complicated machines. England has an industrious, intelligent and dense population, two-thirds of which is engaged in industry. The population is composed of quite different classes than it used to be and these social groups make up a quite different sort of nation, with new customs and new needs. The Industrial Revolution has been as important for England as the political revolution for France and the philosophical revolution for Germany. The gulf between the England of 1760 and that of 1844

[1 This should read ' in the United Kingdom ': Porter, op. cit., Vol. 2, (1838), p. 45.]

[2 Porter, op. cit., Vol. 2 (1838), chapter II (Turnpike Roads), chapter III (Canals), chapter IV (Steam Navigation). Porter (op. cit., Vol. 2, p. 45) states that in 1836 there were 600 steamships employed in the ports of the United Kingdom and her colonies.]

[3 According to the census of 1841 London had a population of 1,949,277.]

is at least as great as that between France under the *ancien régime* and the France of the July Revolution. The most important result of this Industrial Revolution has been the creation of the English proletariat.

It has already been seen that the proletariat was called into existence by the introduction of machinery. The rapid expansion of industry led to the demand for more labour. This caused wages to rise and consequently hordes of workers migrated from the countryside to the towns. There was a very rapid increase in population and nearly the whole of this increase was due to the growth of the working class. Meanwhile, in Ireland, where law and order had only been fully established at the beginning of the eighteenth century, the population —formerly decimated by English barbarity—was expanding quickly. With the expansion of English industry many Irishmen migrated to England to seek work there. These are the reasons for the expansion of the great factory towns and commercial centres of the United Kingdom, in which at least three-quarters of the inhabitants are members of the working classes. Here the lower middle classes are represented only by small shopkeepers and by a mere handful of craftsmen. The new industries only became important with the change from tool to machine and from workshop to factory. This involved the transformation of the working middle classes into a toiling proletariat and at the same time transformed the wholesaler into the factory owner. This process involved the disappearance of the lower middle class and the emergence of a society in which workers and capitalists were sharply differentiated. But this process of social change was not confined to industry in the narrow sense of the term. It occurred also in craft work and even in commerce. Former masters and apprentices were replaced by large capitalists and workers. There was now no possibility that the workers would ever improve their position and rise out of their social group. Craftsmanship was now replaced by factory production. There was a strict division of labour. The result was that the small master could not compete with the big factories and so sank to the position of a mere worker. The disappearance of handicraft work and of the middle-class groups dependent upon it deprived the workers of the possibility of rising into this class of society. Hitherto there had always been a possibility that the craftsmen might establish himself as an independent master and might eventually employ apprentices himself. The disappearance of the old independent small masters and the large amount of capital required to start a factory made it impossible for the worker to rise out of his social class. The proletariat now became a definite class in the population whereas formerly it had only been a transitional stage towards entering into the middle classes. To-day [1845] he who is born a worker must remain a worker for the rest of his life. This is why it is only now possible for an organised working-class movement to spring up.

This is how the great masses of workers who now cover the whole of the United Kingdom have been brought together. The social problems of these workers are daily claiming more and more of the attention of the whole of the civilised world.

Since the Reform Act of 1832 the most important social issue in England has been the condition of the working classes, who form the vast majority of the English people. The problems are these: What is to become of these propertyless millions who own nothing and consume today what they earned yesterday? What fate is in store for the workers who by their inventions and labour have laid the foundations of England's greatness? What is to be the future of those who are now daily becoming more and more aware of their power and are pressing more and more strongly for their share of the social advantages of the new era? All the parliamentary debates of any consequence are in fact concerned with these questions. It is in vain that the English middle classes have hitherto tried to ignore the issue. It is useless for them to ignore these problems and to pretend that the interests of the middle classes are really identical with those of the nation as a whole. Such an attitude will not alter the facts of the situation. Every parliamentary session sees the working classes gain ground, while the influence of the middle classes declines. Although the middle classes at the moment are the main—indeed the only—power in Parliament, nevertheless the last session (1844) was in effect a continuous debate on working-class conditions. These debates covered the Poor Law Bill, the Factory Bill and the Master and Servant Bill. Thomas [Slingsby] Duncombe, the representative of the working classes in the House of Commons, was the leading figure of the Parliamentary session. On the other hand the Liberal middle-classes with their motion in favour of repealing the Corn Laws and the Radical middle classes with their motion against the payment of taxes, presented a truly miserable spectacle. Even the debates on Ireland were in reality discussions on the situation of the Irish proletariat and the means by which its condition could be improved. It is high time the English middle classes learned that they must be prepared to make concessions before it is too late, not only to the worker who begs, but to the worker who threatens to secure his demands by force. But the English middle classes prefer to ignore the distress of the workers and this is particularly true of the industrialists, who grow rich on the misery of the mass of wage earners. The middle classes, who consider themselves to be the most important social group, are ashamed to publish to the world the true facts concerning the workers. The property-owners and industrialists will not admit that the wage earners are suffering, because if they did they would have to accept moral responsibility for this misery. If one asks the intelligent English middle-class visitor to the Continent—and he is the only sort of Englishman who travels abroad—for his opinion concerning the condition of the working classes in England, one is met by an expression of mingled scorn and injured innocence. The fact that the whole English middle classes are totally ignorant about everything concerning the workers may be seen from the ludicrous blunders which their representatives commit both in and out of Parliamen whenever the situation of the workers is under discussion. The middle classes are living in frivolous unconcern, although the very ground beneath their feet is undermined and may give way at any moment. The imminence of this collapse may be foretold with the certainty of the laws of mathematics or mechanics. It is astonishing that there is not a single adequate account of the condition of the working classes, although for heaven knows how many years the middle classes have been enquiring into this problem and tinkering with it. No wonder that all the workers from Glasgow to London are deeply incensed against the wealthy, who systematically exploit the wage-earners and then callously leave them to their fate. The wrath of the workers must very soon—one can very nearly fix the date—lead to a revolution compared with which the French Revolution and the year 1794[1] will seem like child's play.

[1 Presumably this date should be 1793, the year of the Terror.]

CHAPTER II

THE INDUSTRIAL PROLETARIAT

We propose to discuss in detail the characteristics of the various sections of the English working classes. The arrangement of our material follows naturally from the history of the working classes that we have just sketched, and we will discuss each group in turn. The first members of the proletariat are the product of changes in manufacturing and they are the industrial workers engaged in working up raw materials. We shall consider this group first of all. Secondly we shall examine the workers engaged in the production of raw materials and fuel. This section of the proletariat increased in importance at a rather later stage. It includes coal miners and miners of metallic ores. The third group of workers are the farm labourers, who arose owing to the influence of the new industrial system on agriculture. The fourth group is the Irish proletariat. We shall find that, with the exception of the Irish, the closer the wage earners are associated with industry the more advanced they are. The industrial worker is more advanced than the miner, the miner is more advanced than the farm labourer, who is deplorably ignorant of the extent to which he is being exploited. The same distinction can be made between various groups within the industrial proletariat. We shall see that, from the earliest stages of modern industrialisation to the present day, the factory workers—the first propertyless wage earners of the new industrial age—have been the mainstay of the workers' movement. We shall see, too, how other workers have come to support this movement as their ancient crafts were engulfed by the progress of machine production. England's experience illustrates the political consequences that follow from the economic changes associated with the Industrial Revolution. There have been the closest links between industrialisation on the one hand and the growth of the workers' movement on the other.

At the present time virtually the whole of the industrial proletariat supports the workers' movement. This is not surprising because practically all the wage earners have been absorbed in large-scale industry and the different groups of workers face very similar problems. It will therefore be desirable to analyse the situation of the industrial workers as a whole before examining in greater detail the special characteristics of the workers in separate branches of industry.

We have seen how industry has been concentrated into fewer

hands. Industry needs large amounts of capital in order to erect colossal factories which work so efficiently and cheaply that they drive the lower middle class craftsmen out of business. The division of labour, the use of water power and steam power, and the introduction of modern machinery have been the three great forces which industry has used since the middle of the eighteenth century to upset the old economic and social order. Small-scale industry had fostered the growth of a middle class. Large-scale industry, on the other hand, has created a class of propertyless wage earners and has raised a small number of the middle classes to positions of great wealth and influence. This elevation of the chosen few has been spectacular, but their eventual downfall can be prophesied with certainty. No one can deny the obvious fact that the lower middle classes of the ' good old days '—once quite a large section of the population—have been destroyed by the Industrial Revolution. It is equally obvious that their place has been taken by the rich capitalists on the one hand and the poverty-stricken workers on the other.[1]

It was not only industry but population and capital which became centralised. There is nothing surprising in this because industry regards its workers not as human beings but simply as so much capital for the use of which the industrialist has to pay interest under the name of wages. Big industrial establishments need many hands massed together in one building. They have to live together and the labour force of even a relatively small factory would populate a village. Others are attracted to the vicinity of the factory to satisfy the needs of the operatives and these include such craftsmen as tailors, shoemakers, bakers, builders and joiners. The inhabitants of the new industrial village, particularly the younger generation, become skilled factory workers and become accustomed to the new way of life. There generally comes a time when the first factory cannot employ all the workers in the industrial village. This leads to a fall in wages, which in turn attracts new industrialists to the district. In this way a village grows into a little town and a little town expands into a city. The more the town grows the greater are the advantages which it has to offer to industrialists. It has railways, canals and roads and there is an ever-growing variety of skilled labour available. Competition between local builders and engineers reduces the cost of building

---

[1] See also my article on ' Outlines of a criticism of Political Economy ': *Deutsch-Französiche Jahrbücher*, 1844, pp. 86–115. The premiss from which the argument in this article starts is that of ' free competition '. But industry is free competition in action, and free competition is simply the principle on which industry is based. [The article appeared in 1844 and has been reprinted in the *Gesamtausgabe*, Part I, Vol. 2, pp. 379–404)]

new factories to a level below what has to be paid when a factory is built in a remote spot to which timber, machinery, building operatives and industrial workers have to be transported. The new town has its market and its exchange, which are crowded with buyers. It is in direct contact with the sources of raw materials and with markets in which manufactured goods can be sold. All this explains the remarkably rapid expansion of the great industrial towns.

On the other hand, the rural areas have the advantage that wages are normally lower there than in the urban centres. The countryside and the factory towns are continually competing against each other. Whenever the towns happen to have the advantage rural wages fall and it is again advantageous to set up new enterprises in the countryside. Such a development, however, does not lessen the tendency towards industrial centralisation and every new rural factory carries within it the seed of a future factory town. If it were possible for this furious expansion of industry to continue unchecked for another century every manufacturing district in England would become a single large factory town. Manchester and Liverpool, for example, would meet at Warrington or Newton-le-Willows. The trend towards centralisation may be seen in commerce as well as in industry and a few big ports such[1] as Liverpool, Bristol, Hull and London monopolise practically the whole overseas trade of Great Britain.

Industry and commerce attain their highest stage of development in the big towns, so that it is here that the effects of industrialisation on the wage earners can be most clearly seen. It is in these big towns that the concentration of property has reached its highest point. Here the manners and customs of the good old days have been most effectively destroyed. Here the very name of ' Merry England ' has long since been forgotten, because the inhabitants of the great manufacturing centres have never even heard from their grandparents what life was like in those days. In these towns there are only rich and poor, because the lower middle classes are fast disappearing. At one time this section of the middle classes was the most stable social group, but now it has become the least stable. It is represented in the big factory towns today partly by a few survivors from a bygone age and partly by a group of people who are anxious to get rich as quickly as possible. Of these shady speculators and dubious traders one becomes rich while ninety-nine go bankrupt. Indeed, for more than half of those who have failed, bankruptcy has become a habit.

The vast majority of the inhabitants of these towns are the workers. We propose to discuss their condition and to discover how they have been influenced by life and work in the great factory towns.

[1 In the German edition of 1892 the word ' grosse ' (big) was omitted.]

CHAPTER III

THE GREAT TOWNS

London is unique, because it is a city in which one can roam for hours without leaving the built-up area and without seeing the slightest sign of the approach of open country. This enormous agglomeration of population on a single spot has multiplied a hundred-fold the economic strength of the two and a half million inhabitants concentrated there. This great population has made London the commercial capital of the world and has created the gigantic docks in which are assembled the thousands of ships which always cover the River Thames. I know nothing more imposing than the view one obtains of the river when sailing from the sea up to London Bridge. Especially above Woolwich the houses and docks are packed tightly together on both banks of the river. The further one goes up the river the thicker becomes the concentration of ships lying at anchor, so that eventually only a narrow shipping lane is left free in mid-stream. Here hundreds of steamships dart rapidly to and fro. All this is so magnificent and impressive that one is lost in admiration. The traveller has good reason to marvel at England's greatness even before he steps on English soil.[1]

It is only later that the traveller appreciates the human suffering which has made all this possible. He can only realise the price that has been paid for all this magnificence after he has tramped the pavements of the main streets of London for some days and has tired himself out by jostling his way through the crowds and by dodging the endless stream of coaches and carts which fills the streets. It is only when he has visited the slums of this great city that it dawns upon him that the inhabitants of modern London have had to sacrifice so much that is best in human nature in order to create those wonders of civilisation with which their city teems. The vast majority of Londoners have had to let so many of their potential creative faculties lie dormant, stunted and unused in order that a small, closely-knit group of their fellow citizens could develop to the full the qualities with which nature has endowed them. The restless and noisy activity of the crowded streets is highly distasteful, and it is surely abhorrent to human nature itself. Hun-

---

[1] In a note to the German edition of 1892, Engels wrote: ' This was so nearly fifty years ago, in the days of the picturesque sailing vessels. In so far as such ships still ply to and from London they are now to be found only in the docks, while the river itself is covered with ugly, sooty steamers '.

dreds of thousands of men and women drawn from all classes and ranks of society pack the streets of London. Are they not all human beings with the same innate characteristics and potentialities? Are they not all equally interested in the pursuit of happiness? And do they not all aim at happiness by following similar methods? Yet they rush past each other as if they had nothing in common. They are tacitly agreed on one thing only—that everyone should keep to the right of the pavement so as not to collide with the stream of people moving in the opposite direction. No one even thinks of sparing a glance for his neighbour in the streets. The more that Londoners are packed into a tiny space, the more repulsive and disgraceful becomes the brutal indifference with which they ignore their neighbours and selfishly concentrate upon their private affairs. We know well enough that this isolation of the individual—this narrow-minded egotism—is everywhere the fundamental principle of modern society. But nowhere is this selfish egotism so blatantly evident as in the frantic bustle of the great city. The disintegration of society into individuals, each guided by his private principles and each pursuing his own aims has been pushed to its furthest limits in London. Here indeed human society has been split into its component atoms.

From this it follows that the social conflict—the war of all against all—is fought in the open. The type of society depicted by Stirner[1] actually exists in the great towns of England. Here men regard their fellows not as human beings, but as pawns in the struggle for existence. Everyone exploits his neighbour with the result that the stronger tramples the weaker under foot. The strongest of all, a tiny group of capitalists, monopolise everything, while the weakest, who are in the vast majority, succumb to the most abject poverty.

What is true of London, is true also of all the great towns, such as Manchester, Birmingham and Leeds. Everywhere one finds on the one hand the most barbarous indifference and selfish egotism and on the other the most distressing scenes of misery and poverty. Signs of social conflict are to be found everywhere. Everyone turns his house into a fortress to defend himself—under the protection of the law—from the depredations of his neighbours. Class warfare is so open and shameless that it has to be seen to be believed. The observer of such an appalling state of affairs must shudder at the consequences of such feverish activity and can only marvel that so crazy a social and economic structure should survive at all.

[1 ' Max Stirner ' was the pseudonym of Johann Kaspar Schmidt (1806–56), who published at Leipzig in 1845 a philosophical work entitled *Der Einzige und sein Eigenthum.*]

Capital is the all-important weapon in the class war. Power lies in the hands of those who own, directly or indirectly, foodstuffs and the means of production. The poor, having no capital, inevitably bear the consequences of defeat in the struggle. Nobody troubles about the poor as they struggle helplessly in the whirlpool of modern industrial life. The working man may be lucky enough to find employment, if by his labour he can enrich some member of the middle classes. But his wages are so low that they hardly keep body and soul together. If he cannot find work, he can steal, unless he is afraid of the police; or he can go hungry and then the police will see to it that he will die of hunger in such a way as not to disturb the equanimity of the middle classes. While I was in England at least twenty or thirty people died of hunger under the most scandalous circumstances, and yet when an inquest was held the jury seldom had the courage to bring in a verdict in accordance with the facts. However clear and unequivocal the evidence, the middle classes, from whom the juries were drawn, always found a loophole which enabled them to avoid a verdict of ' death from starvation '.[1] In such circumstances the middle classes dare not tell the truth, because if they did so, they would be condemning themselves out of their own mouths. The number of people who die from causes attributable to inadequate nourishment is far greater than the number of those who die of actual starvation. A continual lack of sufficient food leads to illnesses which prove fatal. An illness from which a well-fed person would speedily recover soon carries off those who are hopelessly undernourished. The English workers call this ' social murder ' and denounce a society which permits the perpetration of this crime. Is not their protest justified?

Of course, only a few actually die of hunger. But what guarantee has the worker that this will not be his fate to-morrow? Who will give him security of employment? If for any cause, reasonable or unreasonable, his employer dismisses him tomorrow, who will be responsible for maintaining the worker and his family until he finds fresh employment? Who will guarantee a man ' the right to work ' if he is willing to work? Who will ensure that success will follow the practice of honesty, hard work and thrift—those virtues so highly recommended to him by the middle classes in their wisdom? Nobody! The worker knows only too well that employment and food today do not mean employment and food tomorrow. He knows that any whim of his employer or any slackness in trade may throw him back into the

[1 For deaths from starvation in London at a later period (1868–1918) see R. F. Wearmouth, *Methodism and the Struggle of the Working Classes*, 1850–1900 (1954), pp. 25–30. This account is based upon information published in official returns.]

morass of unemployment from which he has extricated himself for the
time being. He knows that if he sinks into unemployment it will be
difficult, and indeed often impossible, to survive. He knows how
uncertain is the future for the industrial wage-earner.

We propose to examine more closely the conditions to which the
workers who own no property have been reduced by the class war.
We shall see what reward society gives to the worker for his labour
in the form of housing, clothing and food. We shall discover the
standard of living of that class which contributes most to the maintenance of the social system. Let us first consider housing conditions.

Every great town has one or more slum areas into which the
working classes are packed. Sometimes, of course, poverty is to be
found hidden away in alleys close to the stately homes of the wealthy.
Generally, however, the workers are segregated in separate districts
where they struggle through life as best they can out of sight of the
more fortunate classes of society. The slums of the English towns
have much in common—the worst houses in a town being found in
the worst districts. They are generally unplanned wildernesses of one-
or two-storied terrace houses built of brick. Wherever possible these
have cellars which are also used as dwellings. These little houses of
three or four rooms and a kitchen are called cottages, and throughout
England, except for some parts of London, are where the working
classes normally live. The streets themselves are usually unpaved and
full of holes. They are filthy and strewn with animal and vegetable
refuse. Since they have neither gutters nor drains the refuse accumulates in stagnant, stinking puddles. Ventilation in the slums is inadequate owing to the hopelessly unplanned nature of these areas. A
great many people live huddled together in a very small area, and so it
is easy to imagine the nature of the air in these workers' quarters.
However, in fine weather the streets are used for the drying of washing
and clothes lines are stretched across the streets from house to house
and wet garments are hung out on them.

We propose to describe some of these slums in detail. In London
there is the well-known ' rookery '[1] of St. Giles, which is to be demolished to make way for wide new thoroughfares.[2] St. Giles is situated
in the most densely-populated part of London and is surrounded by

[1 In English in the original.]
[2 Since writing this description I have seen an article in *The Illuminated Magazine*
for October 1844 which describes the working-class districts of London. This
account agrees almost word for word with my own. It is entitled ' The Dwellings
of the Poor, from the note-book of an M.D. ', [pp. 336–40. The author's initials,
' J.H.', only are given. A copy of this magazine is to be found in the British
Museum Library.]

splendid wide streets which are used by the fashionable world. It is close to Oxford Street, Trafalgar Square and the Strand. It is a confused conglomeration of tall houses of three or four stories. The narrow, dirty streets are just as crowded as the main thoroughfares, but in St. Giles one sees only members of the working classes. The narrowness of the roads is accentuated by the presence of street-markets in which baskets of rotting and virtually uneatable vegetables and fruit are exposed for sale. The smell from these and from the butchers' stalls is appalling. The houses are packed from cellar to attic and they are as dirty inside as outside. No human being would willingly inhabit such dens. Yet even worse conditions are to be found in the houses which lie off the main road down narrow alleys leading to the courts. These dwellings are approached by covered passages between the houses. The extent to which these filthy passages are falling into decay beggars all description. There is hardly an unbroken windowpane to be seen, the walls are crumbling, the door posts and window frames are loose and rotten. The doors, where they exist, are made of old boards nailed together. Indeed in this nest of thieves doors are superfluous, because there is nothing worth stealing. Piles of refuse and ashes lie all over the place and the slops thrown out into the street collect in pools which emit a foul stench. Here live the poorest of the poor. Here the worst-paid workers rub shoulders with thieves, rogues and prostitutes. Most of them have come from Ireland or are of Irish extraction. Those who have not yet been entirely engulfed in the morass of iniquity by which they are surrounded are daily losing the power to resist the demoralising influences of poverty, dirt and low environment.

St. Giles, however, is by no means the only London slum. In the vast mass of streets which make up the metropolis there are thousands of hidden alleys and passages where the houses are so bad that no one with an iota of self-respect would live in them unless forced to do so by dire poverty. Such dens of extreme poverty are often to be found close to the splendid mansions of the wealthy. Recently at a coroner's inquest an area near Portman Square—a very respectable part of London—was described as the abode of ' a large number of Irish demoralised by dirt and poverty '. In a street like Long Acre, which, although not fashionable, is still respectable, there are many cellar dwellings from which emerge into the light of day sickly children and half-starved, ragged women. In the immediate vicinity of the second most important theatre in London, that in Drury Lane, are to be found some of the worst streets in the metropolis. In Charles Street, King Street and Parker Street all the houses are crammed from cellar to roof with many poor families. In 1840, according to a report printed in the *Journal* of the Statistical Society of London,[1] there were in the parishes of St. John and St. Margaret, Westminster, 5,366 working-class families living in 5,294 'dwellings' (if they deserve this appellation!). Altogether there were 16,176[2] men, women and children thrown together without distinction of age or sex. Three quarters of the families lived in a single room. It is stated in the same *Journal*[3] that 1,465 working-class families totalling about 6,000 persons lived under similar conditions in [the Inner Ward of] the aristocratic parish of St. George, Hanover Square. In two-thirds of the families investigated the members were packed into a single room. How shamefully do the wealthier classes exploit, under the protection of the law, these miserable slum-dwellers, who are so poor that no thief would think of trying to rob them. The following [weekly] rents are charged for accommodation in the revolting dwellings near Drury Lane which we have just described: 3s. for cellars, 4s. for a room on the ground floor, 4s. 6d. on the first floor, 4s. on the second floor, 3s. for an attic. The starving inhabitants of Charles Street pay their landlord an annual tribute of £2,000, while the 5,366 families in Westminster mentioned above together pay an annual rent of £40,000.

The largest working-class district lies in Whitechapel and Bethnal Green to the east of the Tower of London. Here live the great majority of London's workers. The Rev. G. Alston, incumbent of St. Philip's, Bethnal Green, has given the following account of conditions in his parish:

'It contains 1,400 houses, inhabited by 2,795 families, comprising a population of 12,000. The space within which this large amount of population are living is less than 400 yards square, and it is no uncommon thing for a man and his wife, with four or five children, and sometimes the grandfather and grandmother, to be found living in a room from ten to twelve feet square, and which serves them for eating and working in. I believe that till the Bishop of London called the attention of the public to the state of Bethnal-green, about as little was known at the West-end of the town of this most destitute parish as the wilds of Australia or the islands of the South

---

[1 'Report of a committee of the Statistical Society of London on the state of the working classes in the parishes of St. Margaret and St. John': *Journal of the Statistical Society*, Vol. 3 (1840), pp. 14–24.]

[2 Engels states that the total number of persons covered by this report amounted to 26,830, but the table in the Report, pp. 17–18, shows that the total number of people enumerated was only 16,176. The figure given in the *Northern Star*, no. 338, May 4th, 1844, p. 6, col. 2, copied from the *Weekly Dispatch*, is 26,830.]

[3 C. R. Weld, 'On the conditions of the working classes in the Inner Ward of St. George's Parish, Hanover Square': ibid, Vol. 6 (1843), pp. 17–27.]

Seas. If we really desire to find out the most destitute and deserving, we must lift the latch of their doors, and find them at their scanty meal; we must see them when suffering from sickness and want of work; and if we do this from day to day in such a neighbourhood as Bethnal-green, we shall become acquainted with a mass of wretchedness and misery such as a nation like our own ought to be ashamed to permit. I was Curate of a parish near Huddersfield during the three years of the greatest manufacturing distress; but I never witnessed such a thorough prostration of the poor as I have seen since I have been in Bethnal-green. There is not one father of a family in ten throughout the entire district that possesses any clothes but his working dress, and that too commonly in the worst tattered condition; and with many this wretched clothing form their only covering at night, with nothing better than a bag of straw or shavings to lie upon.'[1]

This description enables us to appreciate the conditions inside these dwellings. We may add also some evidence given by public officials, who sometimes have occasion to enter the homes of the workers.

On November 16th, 1843, Mr. Carter, the coroner for Surrey, held an inquest on the body of a certain Ann Galway, who died at the age of 45.[2] We take the following account of her home from press reports. She lived in no. 3, White Lion Court, Bermondsey Street, London, with her husband and nineteen-year-old son. The family occupied a single small room in which there were neither beds, bedding nor other furniture. She lay dead by the side of her son on a heap of feathers which practically covered her naked body, for she had neither sheet nor blanket. The feathers had stuck so fast to her that the doctor was unable to examine the body until it had been washed. The doctor found that the body was emaciated and verminous. Part of the floor in the room had been torn up and the hole used by the family as a privy.

On Monday, January 15th, 1844, two boys appeared before the magistrate at Worship Street police court, London, charged with stealing a half-cooked cow-heel from a shop.[3] They immediately devoured their spoils as they were ravenous. The magistrate felt it necessary to enquire further into the circumstances and was given the following information by the police. The boys were brothers and

[1 *Northern Star*, no. 338, May 4th, 1844, p. 6, col. 2, copied from the *Weekly Dispatch*.]

[2 See the *Times*, Nov. 17th, 1843, p. 3, col. 5; and the *Northern Star*, no. 315, Nov. 25th, 1843, p. 7, col. 2. In the original edition Engels stated that the inquest took place on the 14th, whereas in fact it took place on the 16th.]

[3 See the *Times*, January 16th, 1844, p. 7, col. 2.]

their mother was a widow. Their father had served in the Army and had later been a policeman. After the death of her husband, the widow was left to struggle along as best she could with nine children. The family lived in dire poverty at no. 2 Pool's Place, Quaker Court, Spitalfields. When visited by a policeman she was found with six of her children. They were all huddled together and the only furniture consisted of two rush-bottomed chairs with seats gone, a little table with two legs broken, one broken cup and one small dish. Hardly a spark of fire came from the hearth and in one corner lay as many rags as would fill a woman's apron. It was on these rags that the whole family slept at night. As they had no blankets they slept in the miserable tatters worn during the daytime. The wretched woman told the policeman that she had had to sell her bed during the previous year in order to buy food. She had pawned her bedding with the grocer for food. Indeed everything had been sold to get bread. The magistrate made her a generous grant from the poor-box.

In February 1844 an application for assistance was made to the Marlborough Street magistrate on behalf of Theresa Bishop, a 60-year old widow, and her 26-year-old daughter who was ill.[1] She lived at no. 5, Brown Street, Grosvenor Square, in a little back room hardly bigger than a cupboard. The room contained no proper furniture. A *chest* was used both as table and chair, while a heap of rags in a corner served as a bed for both women. The mother earned a little money as a charwoman. Her landlord stated that she and her daughter had lived in this condition since May 1843. Gradually all their remaining possessions had been sold or pawned, but even so they had been unable to pay any rent. The magistrate allowed them 20s. out of the poor-box.

It is not, of course, suggested that all London workers are so poverty-stricken as these three families. There can be no doubt that for every worker who is rendered utterly destitute by society there are ten who are better off. On the other hand it can be confidently asserted that thousands of decent and industrious families—far more deserving of respect than all the rich people in London—live under truly deplorable conditions which are an affront to human dignity. It is equally incontestable that every working man without exception may well suffer a similar fate through no fault of his own and despite all his efforts to keep his head above water.

However wretched may be the dwellings of some of the workers—who do at least have a roof over their heads—the situation of the homeless is even more tragic. Every morning fifty thousand Londoners

[1 See the *Times*, Feb. 12th, 1844, p. 7, col. 6.]

wake up not knowing where they are going to sleep at night. The most fortunate are those who have a few pence in their pocket in the evening and can afford to go to one of the many lodging houses which exist in all the big cities. But these establishments only provide the most miserable accommodation. They are crammed full of beds from top to bottom—four, five and even six beds in a room—until there is no room for more. Each bed is filled to capacity and may contain as many as four, five or even six lodgers. The lodging house keeper allocates his accommodation to all his customers in rotation as they arrive. No attempt is made to segregate the sick and the healthy, the old and the young, the men and the women, the drunk and the sober. If these ill-assorted bed-fellows do not agree there are quarrels and fights which often lead to injuries. But if they do agree among themselves, it is even worse, for they are either planning burglaries or are engaged in practices of so bestial a nature that no words exist in a modern civilised tongue to describe them.[1] Those who cannot afford a bed in a lodging house sleep where they can, in passages, arcades or any corner where the police and the owners are unlikely to disturb their slumbers. A few find accommodation in the shelters provided by private charitable organizations. Others sleep on benches in the parks in full view of Queen Victoria's windows. An account of these conditions may be found in a leading article of the *Times* for October 12th, 1843:

'It appears from the report of the proceedings at Marlborough Street Police Office in our columns of yesterday, that there is an average number of 50 human beings, of all ages, who huddle together in the parks every night, having no other shelter than what is supplied by the trees and hollows of the embankment. Of these the majority are young girls, who have been seduced from the country by the soldiers, and turned loose on the world in all the destitution of friendless penury, and all the recklessness of early vice.

'This is truly horrible. Poor there must be everywhere. Indigence will find its way and set up its hideous state in the heart of a great and luxurious city. Amid the thousand narrow lanes and by-streets of a populous metropolis there must always, we fear, be much suffering—much that offends the eye—much that lurks unseen.

'But that within the precincts of wealth, gaiety, and fashion, nigh the regal grandeur of St. James's, close on the palatial splendour of Bayswater, on the confines of the old and new aristocratic quarters in a district where the cautious refinement of modern design has refrained from creating one single tenement for poverty; which seems, as it were, dedicated to the exclusive enjoyments of wealth—

[1 See Humphry House's remarks on Engels's reticence in *The Dickens World* (1941), pp. 217–9.]

that *there* want, and famine, and disease, and vice should stalk in all their kindred horrors, consuming body by body, soul by soul!

' It is, indeed, a monstrous state of things! Enjoyment the most absolute, that bodily ease, intellectual excitement, or the more innocent pleasures of sense can supply to man's craving, brought in close contact with the most unmitigated misery! Wealth, from its bright saloons, laughing—an insolently heedless laugh—at the unknown wounds of want! Pleasure, cruelly but unconsciously mocking the pain that moans below! All contrary things mocking one another—all contrary, save the vice which tempts and the vice which is tempted! . . .

' But let all men, whether of theory or of practice, remember this —that within the most courtly precincts of the richest city on GOD'S earth, there may be found, night after night, winter after winter, women—young in years—old in sin and suffering—outcasts from society—ROTTING FROM FAMINE, FILTH AND DISEASE. Let them remember this, and learn not to theorize but to act. God knows, there is much room for action now-a-days.'[1]

Reference has already been made to the shelters for the destitute. Two examples may be given to illustrate the hopeless overcrowding in these establishments. In a new Refuge for the Houseless in Upper Ogle Street [Marylebone], which has accommodation for 300, no less than 2740 persons were given shelter for one or more nights between January 27th, and March 7th, 1844.[2] Although it was a mild winter the number of people seeking accommodation in the shelter in Upper Ogle Street—and also in the hostels in Whitecross Street and Wapping —increased rapidly, and every night many applicants had to be refused admission. In another shelter, the Central Asylum in Playhouse Yard, the average number of persons accommodated in the first three months of 1843 amounted to 460. The total number of persons sheltered was 6,681, while the number of portions of bread distributed amounted to 96,141. Yet the committee responsible for the administration of this institution reported that only after the opening of the new Eastern Asylum had they been able to afford adequate provision for the applicants.[3]

These conditions can also be found in the other great cities of the

[1 *The Times*, October 12th, 1843, p. 4, col. 3.]
[2 For the Upper Ogle Street Refuge for the Houseless Poor, see *The Times* for 1844—Feb. 5th, p. 7, col. 3; Feb. 9th, p. 6, cols. 5–6; Feb. 12th, p. 6, col. 5. The significance of these refuges in the history of philanthropy is discussed by A. F. Young and E. T. Ashton in *British Social Work in the Nineteenth Century*, 1956, pp. 51, 84–5.]
[3 *The Times*, December 22nd, 1843, p. 3, col. 6, repeated in *Northern Star*, no. 320, Dec. 30th, 1843, p. 6, col. 2. See also *The Times*, November 24th, 1843, p. 5, col. 1; and *Northern Star*, no. 319, Dec. 23rd, p. 6, col. 4.]

United Kingdom. The traveller to Dublin finds the approach by water as imposing as when he visited London. Dublin Bay is the most impressive in the British Isles and the Irish even compare it to the Bay of Naples. The city itself is most attractive and its aristocratic quarter is laid out in a more tasteful manner than that of any other British town. By contrast the poorer districts of Dublin are among the ugliest and most revolting in the world. The national character of the Irish is partly responsible for this. The Irish are less bound by social convention than some of their neighbours and on occasion actually seem to be happy in dirty surroundings. Since thousands of Irish immigrants are to be found in every great town of England and Scotland and since every slum quarter gradually sinks into a state of squalor it cannot be claimed that the deplorable state of Dublin is unique. The same conditions can be found in any great city anywhere else in the world. The slums of Dublin are extensive. The filth, the dilapidation of the houses and the utterly neglected condition of the streets beggar description and are beyond belief. An official report of 1817 shows how the poor are herded together in the Dublin slums. The inspectors [appointed by the Governors of the Dublin House of Industry] stated that in Barrack Street[1] there were 52 houses in which 1,318 persons lived in 390 apartments while in Church Street and the adjoining courts there were 71 houses in which 1,997 persons were packed into 393 apartments. In the course of this report it was stated:

‘ Foul lanes, courts, and yards, are interposed between this and the adjoining streets. . . . There are many cellars which have no light but from the door. . . . In some of these cellars the inhabitants sleep on the floors which are all earthen; but in general, they have bedsteads. . . . Nicholson’s Court . . . . contains 151 persons in 28 small apartments, of whom 89 are unemployed; their state is very miserable, there being only two bedsteads and two blankets in the whole court.’[2]

The poverty in Dublin is so great that a single charitable organization known as the Mendicity Association makes provision for 2,500 persons daily, which is 1 per cent of the population. These people are provided with meals during the day, but do not receive accommodation during the night.[3]

[1] Wrongly given as ‘ Barrall Street ’ in the original German edition of 1845.]
    [2] Dr. W. P. Alison, *Observations on the Management of the Poor in Scotland* (1840), p. 5. [Alison quoted this extract from Drs. F. Barker and J. Cheyne, *An Account of the Rise, Progress and Decline of the Fever lately epidemical in Ireland* . . . , Vol. 2 (1821), pp. 160–1. This account refers to conditions prevailing about a quarter of a century before Engels was writing.]
    [3] Quoted by Dr. W. P. Alison, *Observations on the Management of the Poor in Scotland* (1840), p. 5. Engels added: ‘ The author is a pious Tory and brother of the

Dr. [W. P.] Alison gives a similar description of slum conditions in Edinburgh. This city, like Dublin, is beautifully situated and is known as the 'Athens of the North '. Yet here the brilliant aristocratic quarter in the New Town contrasts sharply with the stinking misery of the poor in the Old Town. Dr. Alison asserts that this huge slum is just as dirty and horrible as the worst districts of Dublin and that if the Mendicity Association were active in Edinburgh it would have to assist just as high a proportion of the population as in the Irish capital. Indeed Alison goes so far as to assert that the poor in Scotland, particularly in Edinburgh and Glasgow, are more wretched than the poor in any other district of the United Kingdom. He believes that the most wretched are native Scots and not Irish immigrants.[1] The Rev. Dr. [John] Lee, the minister of the Old Church in Edinburgh, stated on February 18th, 1836, in evidence before the Commissioners of Religious Instruction:

'I have seen much wretchedness in my time, but never such a concentration of misery as in this parish. Some of the Irish in it are very wretched, but by far the most wretched are Scotch. I have seen a mother and five daughters with another woman, in a house where there was neither chair nor table, stool, bed, or blanket, nor any kind of implement for cooking. She had the largest allowance given by the Charity Workhouse, 2s. 6d. a week . . . I frequently see the same room occupied by two married couples, neither having a bed . . . I have been in one day in seven houses where there was no bed, in some of them not even straw. I found people of eighty years of age lying on the boards. . . . Many sleep in the same clothes which they wear during the day. I may mention the case of two Scotch families living in a miserable kind of cellar, who had come from the country within a few months, in search of work. Since they came they had had two dead, and another apparently dying. In the place they inhabit it is impossible at noonday to distinguish the features of the human face without artificial light. There was a little bundle of dirty straw in one corner, for one family, and in another for the other. An ass stood in one corner, which was as well accommodated as these human creatures. It would almost make a heart of adamant bleed to see such an accumulation of misery in a country like this.'[2]

The existence of a similar state of affairs in Edinburgh is confirmed by a report published in the *Edinburgh Medical and Surgical Journal* [in

historian Archibald Alison '. [Engels's account of the Mendicity Association is a virtual quotation of the passage in Alison's work which apparently refers to the late 1830s.]

[1 This is not an assertion of Dr. W. P. Alison's, but a statement made by the Rev. Dr. Lee and quoted by Alison.]

[2 W. P. Alison, op. cit., pp. 11-12.]

1818] by John Hennen [Deputy Inspector of Military Hospitals in North Britain].[1] In the circumstances it is not surprising that a Parliamentary report[2] reveals the disgraceful squalor of the dwellings of the workers in Edinburgh. Hens roost on the bedposts, while dogs and even horses sleep in the same rooms as human beings. The inevitable consequences are that the rooms are not only disgustingly filthy, but smell abominably and harbour veritable armies of vermin.[3] The way in which Edinburgh has been built has been a major cause in bringing about this shocking state of affairs. The Old Town is built on two slopes of a hill along the crest of which runs the High Street. A large number of narrow crooked alleys branch off downhill from both sides of the High Street. They are called wynds, because of their many twists and turns, and form the working-class quarter of the city. The houses in Scottish towns are generally four, five or six stories high. In this respect Edinburgh is similar to Paris, but different from English towns, where as far as possible each family has its own house. In the Scottish towns a large number of different families live together in the same big house. In this way the evils of gross over-crowding are accentuated. An article on the health of the working

[1] Vol. 14 (1818), pp. 408–65 ('An account of the eruptive diseases which have lately appeared in the Military Hospitals of Edinburgh . . .'). On page 457 of this article Hennen describes overcrowding in the area round Edinburgh Castle a quarter of a century before Engels was writing. Mr. V. Adoratskij was unable to trace this article because his search in the files of the *Journal* was confined to the years 1836–45. There is no evidence that Engels used the article on sanitary con-ditions in Glasgow by Dr. R. Perry in the *Edinburgh Medical and Surgical Journal* for 1844 which Mr. Adoratskij suggested might have been the source of Engels's reference.]

[2] *Report . . . from the Poor Law Commissioners on an Inquiry into the Sanitary Condition of the Labouring Population of Great Britain, with Appendices*, July 1842—Parliamentary Papers, 1843, XII, p. 395. The *Report* was drawn up by Edwin Chadwick on the basis of reports from medical men. [For the Edinburgh slums, see Dr. Neil Arnott's description in Chapter I of the *Report*.]

[3] These last two sentences are a condensation of a report printed by Chadwick and refer to Tranent, eight miles east of Edinburgh, and not to the Scottish capital itself. The passage is as follows: ' Dr. Scott Alison in his report on Tranent, states: " In many houses in and around Tranent, fowls roost on the rafters and on the tops of the bedsteads. The effluvia in these houses are offensive, and must prove very unwholesome. It is scarcely necessary to say that these houses are very filthy. They swarm likewise with fleas. Dogs live in the interior of the lowest houses, and must, of course, be opposed to cleanliness. I have seen horses in two houses in Tranent inhabiting the same apartment with numerous families. One was in Dow's Bounds. Several of the family were ill of typhus fever, and I remember the horse stood at the back of the bed. In this case the stench was dreadful. In addition to the horse there were fowls, and I think the family was not under ten souls. The father died of typhus on this occasion. The families of most of the labouring people are crowded in consequence of the smallness of the apartment. Where there are many children, it is common for 10 or 12 people to inhabit one apartment, and for four children to lie in one bed, both in health and sickness. When a collier has few or no children, he sometimes takes single men and women as lodgers ".' (pp. 121–22, of the octavo edition of the *Report* cited in note 2 above).]

classes in large towns which has appeared in an English periodical states that:

'. . . the houses [of the Old Town of Edinburgh] are often so close together, that persons may step from the window of one house to that of the house opposite—so high, piled story after story with the view of saving room, that the light can scarcely penetrate to the court beneath. In this part of the town there are neither sewers nor any private conveniences whatever belonging to the dwellings; and hence the excrementitious and other refuse of at least 50,000 persons is, during the night, thrown into the gutters, causing (in spite of the scavengers' daily labours) an amount of solid filth and foetid exhalation disgusting to both sight and smell, as well as exceedingly prejudicial to health. Can it be wondered that, in such localities, health, morals, and common decency should be at once neglected? No; all who know the private condition of the inhabitants will bear testimony to the immense amount of their disease, misery, and demoralisation. Society in these quarters has sunk to a state indescribably vile and wretched. . . . The dwellings of the poorer classes are generally very filthy, apparently never subjected to any cleaning process whatever, consisting, in most cases, of a single room, ill-ventilated and yet cold, owing to broken, ill-fitting windows, sometimes damp and partially under ground, and always scantily furnished and altogether comfortless, heaps of straw often serving for beds, in which a whole family—male and female, young and old, are huddled together in revolting confusion. The supplies of water are obtained only from the public pumps, and the trouble of procuring it of course favours the accumulation of all kinds of abominations '.[1]

Conditions are no better in other great ports. With all its commerce, grandeur and wealth, Liverpool treats its workers with similar barbarity. Over a fifth of the population—more than 45,000 persons —live in the 7862 narrow, dark, damp, badly ventilated cellars which are to be found in this city.[2] In addition there are 2270 courts, which

[1 *The Artizan*, Oct. 1843, p. 230, col. 2 (quoted in *The Northern Star*, no. 313, Nov. 11th, 1843, p. 3, cols. 3 and 4). The original article (pp. 228–31) is No. 3 of a series and bears the title 'On the health of the working classes in large towns'. In the original German edition Engels gave an incorrect reference to *The Artizan* for October, 1842.]

[2 *Report of a Committee of the Manchester Statistical Society on the Condition of the Working Classes in an extensive manufacturing district in* 1834, 1835 *and* 1836 (1838), pp. 9–10. The figure of 7,862 inhabited cellars was supplied in September 1837 by M. I. Whitty, head constable of Liverpool, who had caused 'an accurate return' to be made. The statistics given in this report were often quoted by reformers and politicians at the time, e.g., R. A. Slaney, *State of the Poorer Classes in Great Towns* (1840), pp. 17–18 (this is an annotated version of a speech delivered in the House of Commons on Feb. 4th, 1840); and *Weekly Dispatch*, May 5th, 1844, p. 4: 'In Liverpool there is a population of 230,000, full one-fifth of whom inhabit dark, damp, confined, ill-ventilated, dirty cellars. Besides these 7,862 cellars, which are occupied by the working classes, there are 2,270 courts, in which several families reside '.]

are little yards, surrounded on all sides by buildings, and accessible only through a narrow passage, which is generally a covered one. They are built in such a way that they receive no ventilation at all. They are usually very dirty and are inhabited almost exclusively by the working classes. A more detailed description of such courts will be given in our account of housing conditions in Manchester. In Bristol, on one occasion 5,981 workers' families were visited and it was found that 2,800 of them (46.8 per cent) occupied only one room or a part of a room each.[1]

The same state of affairs is to be found in the factory towns. Nottingham has about 11,000 houses of which between 7,000 and 8,000 are back-to-back houses, which have no through ventilation. Generally there is only one privy to several dwellings. A recent investigation revealed that many rows of houses had been built over shallow drains covered only by the boards of the sitting-room floors.[2] Similar conditions exist in Leicester, Derby and Sheffield. Conditions in Birmingham are described as follows in the article in *The Artizan* already quoted:

'. . . in the older parts of the town there are many inferior streets and courts, which are dirty and neglected, filled with stagnant water and heaps of refuse. The courts of Birmingham are very numerous in every direction, exceeding 2,000, and comprising the residence of a large portion of the working-classes. They are for the most part narrow, filthy, ill-ventilated, and badly drained, containing from eight to twenty houses, each, the houses being usually three stories high, and often merely *single*, that is, built against some other tenement and the end of the courts being pretty constantly occupied by ashpits, etc., the filth of which would defy description. It is but just, however, to remark that the courts of more modern date are built in a more rational manner, and kept tolerably respectable; and the cottages, even in courts, are far less crowded than in Manchester and Liverpool, the result of which is, that the inhabitants, in epidemic seasons, have been much less visited by death than those of Wolverhampton, Dudley, and Bilston, at only a few miles distance. Cellar-residences, also, are unknown in Birmingham, though some few are, very improperly, used as workshops. The low lodg-

Engels may have relied on the *Weekly Dispatch's* version, as he gave 2,270 as the number of courts in Liverpool, whereas the Manchester Statistical Society's *Report* . . . states (p. 8, footnote) that there were 2,271 courts in the borough of Liverpool.]

[1 See C. B. Fripp, 'Report of an inquiry into the condition of the working classes of the city of Bristol': *Journal of the Statistical Society of London*, Vol. 2 (1839–40), pp. 368–75. Engels gave the number of families *visited* as 2,800, whereas the correct number is given in the text. See also Slaney, op. cit., p. 20.]

[2 W. Felkin, 'Statistics of the labouring classes and paupers in Nottingham': *Journal of the Statistical Society of London* (1839–40), Vol. 2, pp. 457–9. See also Slaney, op. cit., p. 17.]

ing-houses are pretty numerous (somewhat exceeding 400), chiefly in courts near the centre of the town; they are almost always loathsomely filthy and close, the resorts of beggars, trampers, thieves and prostitutes, who here, regardless alike of decency or comfort, eat, drink, smoke and sleep in an atmosphere unendurable by all except the degraded, besotted inmates.'[1]

In many respects conditions in Glasgow are similar to those in Edinburgh. Glasgow, too, has its wynds and apartment-houses. The article in *The Artizan* gives the following account of conditions in Glasgow:

' ... the population in 1840 was estimated at 282,000, of whom *about 78 per cent belong to the working classes*, 50,000 being Irish. Glasgow has its fine, airy, healthy quarters, that may vie with those of London and all wealthy cities; but it has others which, in abject wretchedness, exceed the lowest purlieus of St. Giles' or Whitechapel, the liberties of Dublin, or the wynds of Edinburgh. Such localities exist most abundantly in the heart of the city—south of the Trongate and west of the Saltmarket, as well as in the Calton, off the High-street, etc.— endless labyrinths of narrow lanes or wynds, into which almost at every step debouche courts or closes formed by old, ill-ventilated, towering houses crumbling to decay, destitute of water and crowded with inhabitants, comprising three or four families (perhaps twenty persons) on each flat, and sometimes each flat let out in lodgings that confine—we dare not say accommodate—from fifteen to twenty persons in a single room. These districts are occupied by the poorest, most depraved, and most worthless portion of the population, and they may be considered as the fruitful source of those pestilential fevers which thence spread their destructive ravages over the whole of Glasgow.'[2]

J. C. Symons,[3] one of the Assistant Commissioners on the official enquiry into the condition of the handloom weavers, gave the following report on this part of Glasgow:

'I have seen human degradation in some of its worst phases,

[1] *The Artizan*, Oct. 1843, p. 229, col. 2. It is interesting to note that Engels did not quote the opening sentences of this paragraph, which give a somewhat less gloomy estimate of the sanitary state of Birmingham: ' Birmingham, the great seat of the toy and trinket trade, and competing with Sheffield in the hardware manufacture, is furnished by its position on a slope falling towards the Rea, with a very good natural drainage, which is much promoted by the porous nature of the sand and gravel, of which the adjacent high grounds are mainly composed. The principal streets, therefore, are well drained by covered sewers; but still in the older parts . . . ' (ibid).]
[2] *The Artizan*, Oct. 1843, p. 230, col. 2; p. 231, col. 1.]
[3] J. C. Symons, *Arts and Artisans at Home and Abroad* (1839). The author, who, it appears, is himself a Scot, is a Liberal in politics and consequently a fanatical opponent of any independent workers' movement. Our quotations are from pp. 116 *et seq.* [For Symons's abilities as a Government Commissioner see D. Williams, *The Rebecca Riots* (1955), pp. 97-8.]

both in England and abroad, but I can advisedly say that I did not believe until I visited the wynds of Glasgow, that so large an amount of filth, crime, misery, and disease existed on one spot in any civilized country. . . . In the lower lodging-houses ten, twelve, and sometimes twenty persons of both sexes and all ages sleep promiscuously on the floor in different degrees of nakedness. These places are, generally as regards dirt, damp and decay, such as no person of common humanity to animals would stable his horse in.'[1]

And again, in another passage, Symons states:

' The wynds of Glasgow house a fluctuating population of between 15,000 and 30,000 persons. This district is composed of many narrow streets and square courts and in the middle of each court there is a dunghill. Although the outward appearance of these places was revolting, I was nevertheless quite unprepared for the filth and misery that were to be found inside. In some of these bedrooms we [i.e. Police Superintendent Captain Miller and Symons] visited at night we found a whole mass of humanity stretched out on the floor. There were often 15 to 20 men and women huddled together, some being clothed and others naked. Their bed was a heap of musty straw mixed with rags. There was hardly any furniture there and the only thing which gave these holes the appearance of a dwelling was fire burning on the hearth. Thieving and prostitution are the main sources of income of these people.[2] No

[1 Engels is quoting here not, as he states, from Symons's book, *Arts and Artisans* . . . , but from his report to the Royal Commission on Handloom Weavers (*Reports from Assistant Hand-Loom Weavers' Commissioners*) *Parliamentary Papers*, 1839, Vol. 42, no. 159, p. 51. See also R. A. Slaney, op. cit., pp. 23–6, and *Weekly Dispatch*, May 5th, 1844, which also reproduces passages from Symons's report of 1839.]

[2 Cf. Symons, *Arts and Artisans*, pp. 115–7: ' This district is bounded by the Clyde and the Trongate and extends in length from the Saltmarket to the Briggate. There are other similar districts skirting the High Street and in the Calton, comprising a fluctuating population of from 15,000 to 30,000 persons. The wynds near the Trongate are however, the densest and the dirtiest. . . . This quarter consists of a labyrinth of lanes, varying from 7 to 14 feet in width, out of which numberless entrances open into small square courts, appropriately designated ' closes ', with houses, many of them in a dilapidated state, of two stories high, and a common dunghill reeking with filth in the centre . . . revolting as was the outward appearance of these places, I confess I was little prepared for the filth and destitution within. In some of these lodging rooms we found a whole lair of human beings littered along the floor, sometimes 15 and 20 in number, some clothed and some naked, men, women and children all huddled promiscuously together. Their bed consisted of a layer of musty straw, intermixed with ambiguous looking rags, of which it was difficult to discover any other feature than their intense dirtiness. There was generally speaking, little or no furniture in these places; not even in the rooms let to families, beyond a few stools and one or two grimy platters and dilapidated pans. The sole article of comfort in these places was a good fire, and even of the very lowest and most destitute of these dens, where not an article of furniture was visible, I do not recollect one without a fire. Thieving and prostitution constitute the main sources of the revenue of this population . . . ' A similar description of the wynds of Glasgow occurs in Symons's report to the Royal Commission on Handloom Weavers, op. cit., pp. 51–2.]

one seems to have taken the trouble to clean out these Augean stables, this pandemonium, this nucleus of crime, filth and pestilence in the second city of the empire. A detailed investigation of the most wretched slums of other towns has never revealed anything half so bad as this concentration of moral iniquity, physical degradation and gross overcrowding. . . . In this part of Glasgow most of the houses have been condemned by the Court of Guild as dilapidated and uninhabitable—but it is just these dwellings which are filled to overflowing, because, by law, no rent can be charged on them.'[1]

Many large factory towns, rivalling those elsewhere, are to be found in the great, densely-populated industrial belt, comprising the West Riding of Yorkshire and South Lancashire, which stretches across the centre of the British Isles. The woollen district of the West Riding is a very pleasant part of the country. The green hills, a characteristic feature of this landscape, become steeper until they reach their greatest height at the sharp ridge of Blackstone Edge, which forms the watershed between the Irish Sea and the North Sea. Few parts of the country are pleasanter and more picturesque than the valleys of the Aire, in which Leeds is situated, and of the Calder, through which runs the railway from Manchester to Leeds. In these valleys lie many villages, towns and factories. It is indeed a pleasure to gaze upon the houses, built of rough grey stone, which look so clean and charming in comparison with the soot-blackened brick buildings of Lancashire. But a visit to the towns themselves leaves the stranger with a much less favourable impression. I can confirm from personal observation the description of Leeds given in *The Artizan*. The author of the article wrote:

'Leeds is situated on a slope running down towards the river Aire, which meanders about a mile and a half[2] through the town, and is liable to overflows during thaws or after heavy rains. The higher or western districts are clean for so large a town, but the lower parts contiguous to the river and its becks or rivulets are dirty, confined, and, in themselves, sufficient to shorten life, especially infant life; add to this the disgusting state of the lower parts of the town about Kirk-gate, March-lane, Cross-street, and Richmond-road, principally owing to a general want of paving and draining, irregularity

[1] Cf. Symons, *Arts and Artisans*, p. 120: '. . . my friends . . . were alike impressed with myself as to the fearful evil of such a nucleus of crime, filth and pestilence existing in the centre of the second city of the empire. No pains seemed to be taken to purge this Augean pandemonium. . . . Many of the houses are condemned by the Court of Guild as dilapidated, and remain there nevertheless. These are always the most inhabited, for where they are condemned, no rent can be enforced. . . .']

[2] Engels stated in a footnote that he was referring to English, and not German miles.]

of building, the abundance of courts and blind alleys, as well as the almost total absence of the commonest means for promoting cleanliness, and we have then quite sufficient data to account for the surplus mortality in these unhappy regions of filth and misery. . . . In consequence of the floods from the Aire,[1] the dwelling-houses and cellars are not unfrequently so inundated that the water has to be pumped out by hand-pumps, on to the surface of the streets; and at such times, even where there are sewers, the water rises through them into the cellars,[2] creating miasmatic exhalations, strongly charged with sulphuretted hydrogen, and leaving offensive refuse, exceedingly prejudicial to human health.   Indeed, during a season of inundation in the spring of 1839, so fatal were the effects of such an engorgement of the sewers, that the registrar of the North district made a report, that during that quarter there were, in that neighbourhood, *two* births to *three* deaths, whilst in all the other districts there were *three* to two deaths.   Other populous districts are wholly without sewers, or so inadequately provided as to derive no advantage therefrom.   In some rows of houses, the cellar-dwellings are seldom dry; in another district, several streets are described as being ' in that state in which a frequented road leading over a field to a brick-garth would be in wet weather.'   The inhabitants have from time to time vainly attempted to repair these streets with shovelsfull of ashes; and soil, refuse-water, etc., stand in every hole where a lodgment can be made, there to remain until absorbed by wind or sun . . . (see the Report of the Town Council in the *Statistical Journal*, Vol. 2, p. 404)[3]. . . . An ordinary cottage, in Leeds, extends over no more than about five square yards, and consists usually of a cellar, sitting room, and a sleeping chamber. This small size of the houses, indeed, . . . crammed almost to suffocation with human beings both day and night ' [is another factor which threatens both the health and the morals of the inhabitants.[4]]

[1] In the original text Engels interpolated here the following personal comment on the River Aire: ' It may be added that this river, like all others in the industrial, districts, enters the town crystal-clear and undefiled, and leaves it thick, black and stinking with every imaginable kind of refuse.'

[2] It should be emphasised that these cellars are not mere storerooms but human habitations.

[3] The passage from ' Other populous districts ' to ' wind or sun ' is largely a verbatim copy of a passage (p. 404) from the ' Report upon the Condition of the town of Leeds and of its inhabitants, By a Statistical Committee of the Town Council ', October 1839 (*Journal of the Statistical Society of London*, Vol. 2 (1839-40), pp. 397-424).]

[4] *The Artizan*, Oct. 1843, p. 229, col. 1. Engels's direct quotation from *The Artizan* ends at the phrase ' This small size of the houses, indeed, . . . crammed almost to suffocation with human beings both day and night ', and the phrase in square brackets which finishes the quotation in our text does not occur at this point in the article in *The Artizan*, but may have been taken from the second half of the first sentence of the complete passage, which is as follows: ' The confined size of the dwellings is another cause fraught with evils of a moral as well as physical nature. An ordinary cottage, in Leeds, extends over no more than about five yards square, and consists usually of a cellar, a sitting room, and a sleeping chamber.

And the extent of the overcrowding in these dwellings may be gauged from the report on the sanitary condition of the labouring population to which we have already referred.

'In the houses of the working classes [in Leeds], brothers and sisters, and lodgers of both sexes, are found occupying the same sleeping room with the parents, and consequences occur which humanity shudders to contemplate.'[1]

Bradford, which is only seven miles from Leeds, also lies on a little pitch-black, stinking river, and is also at the point where several valleys meet. On a fine Sunday the town presents a magnificent spectacle from the surrounding heights, but on weekdays it is covered with a grey cloud of smoke. The interior of Bradford is as dirty and uncomfortable as Leeds. The older parts of the town are built upon steep hillsides where the streets are narrow and irregular. Heaps of dirt and refuse disfigure the lanes, alleys and courts. The houses are dilapidated and dirty and are not fit for human habitation. In the immediate vicinity of the river I found a number of houses in which the ground floor, half buried in the hillside, was uninhabited. In general the workers' houses at the bottom of the valley are packed between high factory buildings and are among the worst-built and filthiest in the whole city. In the more recently built up area of Bradford, as of every other factory town, the cottages have been built in regular rows, but here, too, are to be found the usual evils which are to be found in all the houses built for the factory workers and which will be discussed in greater detail when we examine conditions in Manchester.

Similar conditions are to be found in the other towns of the West Riding, such as Huddersfield, Barnsley and Halifax. The charming situation and the modern style of building of Huddersfield have made it the most beautiful of all the factory towns in Yorkshire and Lancashire. Yet Huddersfield, too, has its slums. A committee appointed by a public meeting of the inhabitants to investigate conditions in the town reported as follows on August 5th, 1844:

'. . . it is notorious that there are whole streets in the town of Huddersfield, and many courts and alleys, which are neither flagged,

This small size of the houses, indeed, may perhaps be one of the causes of the tendency to consumption, which bears a high proportion here to other diseases, and prevails to a much greater extent than is generally imagined—for there can be no doubt, that the vitiated atmosphere of sleeping rooms so confined, crammed almost to suffocation with human beings during both day and night, predisposes the system to lung-diseases': *The Artizan*, Oct. 1843, p. 229, col. 1, quoting the *Statistical Journal*, Vol. 2 (1839–40). See also Slaney, op. cit., pp. 21–3.]

[1 *Report . . . from the Poor Law Commissioners, on an Inquiry into the Sanitary Condition of the Labouring Population of Great Britain* (1842), p. 126 (octavo edition). The quotation comes from Mr. Baker's report on the condition of the labouring classes in Leeds.]

paved, sewered, nor drained; where garbage and filth of every description are left on the surface to ferment and rot; where pools of stagnant water are almost constant; where the dwellings adjoining are thus necessarily caused to be of an inferior and even filthy description; thus where disease is engendered, and the health of the whole town perilled. . .'[1]

If we cross Blackstone Edge on foot or take the train we reach Manchester, the regional capital of South Lancashire, and enter the classic home of English industry. This is the masterpiece of the Industrial Revolution and at the same time the mainspring of all the workers' movements. Once more we are in a beautiful hilly countryside. The land slopes gently down towards the Irish Sea, intersected by the charming green valleys of the Ribble, the Irwell, the Mersey and their tributaries. A hundred years ago this region was to a great extent thinly populated marsh-land. Now it is covered with towns and villages and is the most densely-populated part of England. In Lancashire—particularly in Manchester—is to be found not only the origin but the heart of the industry of the United Kingdom. Manchester Exchange is the thermometer which records all the fluctuations of industrial and commercial activity. The evolution of the modern system of manufacture has reached its climax in Manchester. It was in the South Lancashire cotton industry that water and steam power first replaced hand machines. It was here that such machines as the power-loom and the self-acting mule replaced the old hand-loom and spinning wheel. It is here that the division of labour has been pushed to its furthest limits. These three factors are the essence of modern industry. In all three of them the cotton industry was the pioneer and remains ahead in all branches of industry. In the circumstances it is to be expected that it is in this region that the inevitable consequences of industrialisation in so far as they affect the working classes are most strikingly evident. Nowhere else can the life and conditions of the industrial proletariat be studied in all their aspects as in South Lancashire. Here can be seen most clearly the degradation into which the worker sinks owing to the introduction of steam power, machinery and the division of labour. Here, too, can be seen most the strenuous efforts of the proletariat to raise themselves from their degraded situation. I propose to examine conditions in Manchester in greater detail for two reasons. In the first place, Manchester is the classic type of modern

[1 *Northern Star*, No. 352, August 10th, 1844, p. 7, col. 5. The public meeting, summoned by the Commissioners of Huddersfield Waterworks for July 19th, had elected a Committee ' to enquire as to the desirability of embodying in any Act of Parliament that may be applied for, affecting the Town and Inhabitants of Huddersfield, in relation to the supply of Water and additional Waterworks, such other powers and provisions as may be deemed necessary and essential for the good government of the Town ' (ibid., p. 7, col. 4).]

industrial town. Secondly, I know Manchester as well as I know my native town and I know more about it than most of its inhabitants.

As far as the working-class districts are concerned the towns situated in the vicinity of Manchester closely resemble Manchester itself. In these smaller towns, however, the workers form an even larger proportion of the total population than in Manchester.[1] It should be explained that these towns are completely industrialised and all their commercial affairs are transacted in Manchester. They are dependent upon Manchester in every way and consequently are inhabited solely by workers, factory owners and petty shopkeepers. In Manchester on the other hand, there are a considerable number of persons engaged in commerce and there are many commission houses and high-class retail businesses. The towns in question include Bolton, Preston, Wigan, Bury, Rochdale, Middleton, Heywood, Oldham, Ashton, Stalybridge and Stockport. Although nearly all these towns have between 30,000 and 90,000 inhabitants, they are practically no more than huge working-class communities. The only parts of these towns not given over to housing the workers are the factory buildings, some main streets lined with shops, and a few semi-rural lanes where the factory owners have their villas and gardens. The towns themselves have been badly planned and badly built. They have dirty courts, lanes and back alleys. The pall of smoke which hangs over these towns has blackened the houses of red brick—the usual building material in this part of Lancashire—and has given them a particularly dingy appearance. Cellar dwellings are to be found everywhere. Wherever it is physically possible to do so, these subterranean holes are constructed and a very considerable proportion of the population lives in them.

Preston, Oldham and Bolton are three of the worst of these towns. I have on several occasions visited Bolton, which lies eleven miles north-west of Manchester, and as far as I can recollect it has only one main street which is a dirty thoroughfare. It is called Deansgate and serves as the town market. Even on a really fine day Bolton is a gloomy, unattractive hole, in spite of the fact that except for the factories it has only small houses of one or two stories. As in all these industrial towns, the older part of Bolton is particularly dilapidated and really unfit for human

[1 Compare James Bryce's remarks in the 1860s on the social structure of industrial Lancashire outside the great cities of Liverpool and Manchester:
‘ What is called the middle class is but small, there being few professional men, since neither a doctor's nor a lawyer's practice is lucrative in such places, and few rich shopkeepers, since all the better people do their shopping in Manchester or Liverpool, buying nothing but groceries and such like in the local store ’: School Inquiry Commission, Vol. 9 (*Parliamentary Papers*, c. 3966 of 1868), pp. 750–1.]

habitation. A black watercourse flows through the town and it would be difficult to decide whether this is a stream or a long chain of stinking puddles. Whatever it may be, it helps to pollute the atmosphere, which is far from pure in any case.

Although Stockport lies on the Cheshire side of the Mersey it forms part of the industrial region of Manchester. It lies on the Mersey in a narrow part of the valley, so that the main street runs steeply down one hill and then climbs steeply up the other. The railway from Manchester to Birmingham passes over the town and the whole ravine in which it lies by means of a lofty viaduct. Stockport is notoriously one of the darkest and smokiest holes in the whole industrial area, and particularly when seen from the viaduct, presents a truly revolting picture. But the cottages and cellar dwellings of the workers are even more unpleasant to look at. They stretch in long rows through all parts of the town from the bottom of the valley to the crests of the hills. I do not remember seeing elsewhere in the Manchester industrial district so many inhabited cellars in proportion to the total number of houses.

Ashton-under-Lyne lies a few miles north of Stockport. It is one of the newest factory towns in this district. Ashton lies on the slopes of a hill at the foot of which are situated a canal and the river Tame. In general the town, being recently built, has been comparatively well planned. Five or six long parallel roads run right along the slopes of the hill and are crossed at right angles by other roads running from the top of the hill to the valley. As the town has been planned in this way, the factories have necessarily been built away from the residential quarters. Other reasons for locating the factories on the valley bottom were the need for water from the river and for transport facilities along the canal. The factories are all built close together and thick clouds of smoke ascend from their chimneys. Owing to the way in which it has been built, Ashton has a much more agreeable appearance than most of the other manufacturing towns. The streets are broader and cleaner, while the new bright red cottages give every appearance of comfort. But the modern method of putting up houses for the working classes is not without its drawbacks. Hidden behind every street there is a back alley, which is approached by a narrow side passage. These back alleys are exceptionally dirty [on account of the restricted access]. Except for a few houses on the edge of the town, I did not see any cottages in Ashton which could have been more than fifty years old. Even so there are streets in which the cottages are becoming old and dilapidated. This can be seen in particular at the angles of the walls where the bricks are starting to work loose and fall out. Some walls are beginning to crack, so that inside the whitewash tends to flake off. There are some houses which look just as black and dirty as those in other industrial towns, but in Ashton this is the exception rather than the rule. A mile to the east of Ashton lies Stalybridge, which is also situated on the River Tame. After climbing to the top of the hill from Ashton the traveller sees both to the right and to the left fine, spacious gardens in which superb houses of the villa type have been built. These villas are in the imitation Tudor style,[1] which bears exactly the same relationship to the Gothic style as Catholicism does to Anglicanism.[2] A hundred paces further on and Stalybridge comes into view down in the valley. What a contrast does Stalybridge present to these stately homes and even to the humble cottages of Ashton! Stalybridge lies in a narrow, twisting ravine, which is even narrower than the valley in which Stockport is situated. On the slopes of both hills on either side of the valley there is a confused mass of cottages, houses and factories. On first entering the town the visitor sees congested rows of old, grimy and dilapidated cottages, which are quite typical of the rest of the town. There are only a few streets on the narrow floor of the valley. Most of the streets run in wild confusion up, down and across the hill-sides. Since so many of the houses are built on slopes it is inevitable that many of the rooms on the ground floors are semi-basements. It may well be imagined what a vast number of courts, back passages and blind alleys have been created as a result of this wholly unplanned method of building. It is from the hill-tops that one can get the most vivid impression of Stalybridge, for from such a vantage point a bird's eye view of this disgustingly filthy town can be obtained. It may well be imagined what a revolting impression Stalybridge makes on the visitor in spite of its beautiful setting.

Enough of these smaller towns! Each has its own local character-istics but on the whole the condition of the workers who live in them is exactly the same as in Manchester. Consequently I have done no more than indicate certain of the distinctive features of the lay-out of some of these towns. On the whole, however, the general description which I shall give of the condition of the workers' dwellings is equally applicable to those of the surrounding towns. We now turn our attention to Manchester.

Manchester lies at the foot of the southern slopes of a chain of hills which stretches from Oldham between the valleys of the Irwell and the Medlock to its last spur on Kersal Moor, which is both the race

[1 Engels called this style 'Elizabethan' and put the adjective in inverted commas.]
[2 In the German edition of 1892 Engels transposed 'Anglicanism' and Catholicism '.]

course and the *Mons Sacer*[1] of Manchester. Manchester proper lies on the left bank of the Irwell, between this river and two smaller streams, the Irk and the Medlock, which flow into the Irwell at this point. Salford lies on the right bank of the Irwell in a sharp bend of the river, while Pendleton lies further to the west. Higher Broughton and Lower Broughton are situated to the north of the River Irwell, while Cheetham Hill is situated to the north of the Irk. Hulme lies south of the River Medlock and Chorlton-on-Medlock lies further to the east. Beyond Chorlton-on-Medlock, in the east of Manchester, lies Ardwick. The whole of this built-up area is commonly called Manchester, and contains about 400,000 people. This is probably an underestimate rather than an exaggeration.[2] Owing to the curious lay-out of the town it is quite possible for someone to live for years in Manchester and to travel daily to and from his work without ever seeing a working-class quarter or coming into contact with an artisan. He who visits Manchester simply on business or for pleasure need never see the slums, mainly because the working-class districts and the middle-class districts are quite distinct. This division is due partly to deliberate policy and partly to instinctive and tacit agreement between the two social groups. In those areas where the two social groups happen to come into contact with each other the middle classes sanctimoniously ignore the existence of their less fortunate neighbours. In the centre of Manchester there is a fairly large commercial district, which is about half a mile long and half a mile broad. This district is almost entirely given over to offices and warehouses. Nearly the whole of this district has no permanent residents and is deserted at night, when only policemen patrol its dark, narrow thoroughfares with their bull's eye lanterns. This district is intersected by certain main streets which carry an enormous volume of traffic. The lower floors of the buildings are occupied by shops of dazzling splendour. A few of the upper stories on these premises are used as dwellings and the streets present a relatively busy appearance until late in the evening. Around this commercial quarter there is a belt of built up areas on the average

[1 The *Mons Sacer* was a hill near Rome to which, according to legend, the *plebs* seceded. Kersal Moor was the scene of numerous Radical and Chartist political meetings in the early nineteenth century.]

[2 The municipal borough of Manchester had been established in 1838. Its nucleus was the ancient *township* of Manchester to which had been added the townships of Hulme, Chorlton-upon-Medlock, Ardwick and Cheetham and also the district of Beswick. (The ancient *ecclesiastical parish* of Manchester, of course, covered a very much wider area, which included 30 townships). In 1844 the Manchester Borough Council stated that the population of the borough amounted to 235,139. See A. Redford and I. S. Russell, *History of Local Government in Manchester*, Vol. 2 (1940), p. 67 and map, facing p. 26. Engels's estimate of 400,000 presumably refers to a built-up area including not only the borough of Manchester but also the borough of Salford and other adjacent townships.]

one and a half miles in width, which is occupied entirely by working-class dwellings. This area of workers' houses includes all Manchester proper, except the centre, all Salford and Hulme, an important part of Pendleton and Chorlton, two-thirds of Ardwick and certain small areas of Cheetham Hill and Broughton. Beyond this belt of working-class houses or dwellings lie the districts inhabited by the middle classes and the upper classes. The former are to be found in regularly laid out streets near the working-class districts—in Chorlton and in the remoter parts of Cheetham Hill. The villas of the upper classes are surrounded by gardens and lie in the higher and remoter parts of Chorlton and Ardwick or on the breezy heights of Cheetham Hill, Broughton and Pendleton.[1] The upper classes enjoy healthy country air and live in luxurious and comfortable dwellings which are linked to the centre of Manchester by omnibuses which run every fifteen or thirty minutes. To such an extent has the convenience of the rich been considered in the planning of Manchester that these plutocrats can travel from their houses to their places of business in the centre of the town by the shortest routes, which run entirely through working-class districts, without even realising how close they are to the misery and filth which lie on both sides of the road. This is because the main streets which run from the Exchange in all directions out of the town are occupied almost uninterruptedly on both sides by shops, which are kept by members of the lower middle classes. In their own interests these shopkeepers should keep the outsides of their shops in a clean and respectable condition, and in fact they do so. These shops have naturally been greatly influenced by the character of the population in the area which lies behind them. Those shops which are situated in the vicinity of commercial or middle class residential districts are more elegant than those which serve as a facade for the workers' grimy cottages. Nevertheless, even the less pretentious shops adequately serve their purpose of hiding from the eyes of wealthy ladies and gentlemen with strong stomachs and weak nerves the misery and squalor which are part and parcel of their own riches and luxury. Deansgate, for example, changes in character as one goes due south from the Old Church. At first there are warehouses and factories. Next come shops of a somewhat inferior character. But on leaving the commercial quarter for the south, the traveller passes shops of an ever inferior character and the street becomes dirtier, while taverns and gin palaces become increasingly frequent. When he reaches the end of the street the appearance of the shops can leave no doubt in his

[1 L. M. Hayes wrote: ' In Manchester, about the year 1840 and onwards, the middle classes began to realise that town life was not very desirable, and families began migrating and settling in the various suburbs ': *Reminiscences of Manchester and some of its local surroundings from the year* 1840 (1905), p. 51.]

mind that no one but the workers would dream of patronising them. Market Street which runs in a south-easterly direction from the Exchange possesses the same characteristics. At first it is lined with really high-class shops, in the upper stories of which there are offices and warehouses. Market Street runs into Piccadilly, with its huge hotels and warehouses, but the further continuation of Piccadilly, London Road, which lies near the River Medlock, has a very different appearance. Here are to be found factories, public houses and shops which cater for the needs of the lower middle classes and the workers. By the time Ardwick Green is reached, the street has changed its character yet again and is flanked with residences occupied by the upper and middle classes. Beyond Ardwick Green lie the big gardens and the country villas of the wealthier factory owners and merchants. It is therefore possible for anyone who knows Manchester to judge the social character of any district merely by observing the appearance of the buildings fronting the road through which he is passing. On the other hand it is impossible to get a *true* picture from the main thoroughfare of the conditions of the working class districts which lie immediately behind the facade of the principal streets.

I am quite aware of the fact that this hypocritical town-planning device is more or less common to all big cities. I realise, too, that owing to the nature of their business, shopkeepers inevitably seek premises in main thoroughfares. I know that in such streets there are more good houses than bad ones, and that the value of land is higher on or near a main thoroughfare than in the back streets. But in my opinion Manchester is unique in the systematic way in which the working classes have been barred from the main streets. Nowhere else has such care been taken to avoid offending the tender susceptibilities of the eyes and the nerves of the middle classes. Yet Manchester is the very town in which building has taken place in a haphazard manner with little or no planning or interference from the authorities. When the middle classes zealously proclaim that all is well with the working classes, I cannot help feeling that the politically ' progressive ' industrialists, the Manchester ' bigwigs ',[1] are not quite so innocent of this shameful piece of town planning as they pretend.

It may be mentioned incidentally that nearly all the industrial establishments are situated on the banks of the three rivers or the various canals which intersect the town. I will now give a description of the working-class districts of Manchester. The first of them is the Old Town, which lies between the northern limit of the commercial quarter and the River Irk. Here even the better streets, such as Todd

[1 Engels, in the first German edition of 1845, wrote ' big Whigs ' in English. Either phrase would make sense in this context.]

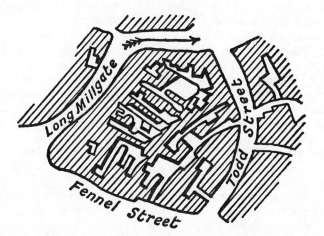

Street, Long Millgate, Withy Grove and Shudehill are narrow and tortuous. The houses are dirty, old and tumble-down. The side streets have been built in a disgraceful fashion. If one enters the district near the 'Old Church' and goes down Long Millgate, one sees immediately on the right hand side a row of antiquated houses where not a single front wall is standing upright. This is a remnant of the old Manchester of the days before the town became industrialised. The original inhabitants and their children have left for better houses in other districts, while the houses in Long Millgate, which no longer satisfied them, were left to a tribe of workers containing a strong Irish element. Here one is really and truly in a district which is quite obviously given over entirely to the working classes, because even the shopkeepers and the publicans of Long Millgate make no effort to give their establishments a semblance of cleanliness. The condition of this street may be deplorable, but it is by no means as bad as the alleys and courts which lie behind it, and which can be approached only by covered passages so narrow that two people cannot pass. Anyone who has never visited these courts and alleys can have no idea of the fantastic way in which the houses have been packed together in disorderly confusion in impudent defiance of all reasonable principles of town planning. And the fault lies not merely in the survival of old property from earlier periods in Manchester's history. Only in quite modern times has the policy of cramming as many houses as possible on to such space as was not utilised in earlier periods reached its climax. The result is that today not an inch of space remains between the houses and any further building is now physically impossible. To prove my point I reproduce a small section of a plan of Manchester. It is by no means the worst slum in Manchester and it does not cover one-tenth of the area of Manchester.

This sketch will be sufficient to illustrate the crazy layout of the whole district lying near the River Irk. There is a very sharp drop of some 15 to 30 feet down to the south bank of the Irk at this point. As many as three rows of houses have generally been squeezed on to this precipitous slope. The lowest row of houses stands directly on the bank of the river while the front walls of the highest row stand on the crest of the ridge in Long Millgate. Moreover, factory buildings are also to be found on the banks of the river. In short the layout of the upper part of Long Millgate at the top of the rise is just as disorderly and congested as the lower part of the street. To the right and left a number of covered passages from Long Millgate give access to several courts. On reaching them one meets with a degree of dirt and revolting filth, the like of which is not to be found elsewhere. The worst courts are those leading down to the Irk, which contain unquestionably the most dreadful dwellings I have ever seen. In one of these courts, just at the entrance where the covered passage ends there is a privy without a door. This privy is so dirty that the inhabitants of the court can only enter or leave the court if they are prepared to wade through puddles of stale urine and excrement. Anyone who wishes to confirm this description should go to the first court on the bank of the Irk above Ducie Bridge. Several tanneries are situated on the bank of the river and they fill the neighbourhood with the stench of animal putrefaction. The only way of getting to the courts below Ducie Bridge is by going down flights of narrow dirty steps and one can only reach the houses by treading over heaps of dirt and filth. The first court below Ducie Bridge is called Allen's Court. At the time of the cholera [1832] this court was in such a disgraceful state that the sanitary inspectors [of the local Board of Health] evacuated the inhabitants. The court was then swept and fumigated with chlorine. In his pamphlet Dr. Kay gives a horrifying description of conditions in this court at that time.[1] Since Kay wrote this pamphlet, this court appears to have been at any rate partly demolished and rebuilt. If one looks down the river from Ducie Bridge one does at least see several ruined walls and high piles of rubble, side by side with

[1] Dr. J. P. Kay, *The Moral and Physical Condition of the Working Classes employed in the Cotton Manufacture in Manchester* (2nd enlarged edn., 1832). Engels added the comment: 'This is an excellent book although the author confuses the factory workers with the working classes in general'. [The description of Allen's Court appears on pages 38 to 40 of the second edition of Kay's pamphlet. There was no reference to Allen's Court in the first edition. In the following year (1833) another Manchester physician, Henry Gaulter, published an equally revolting description of Allen's Court in *The Origin and Progress of the Malignant Cholera in Manchester* (1833), pp. 50–51. See also pages 44–49, 114 and plan facing page 206.]

PLAN OF MANCHESTER AND ITS SUBURBS

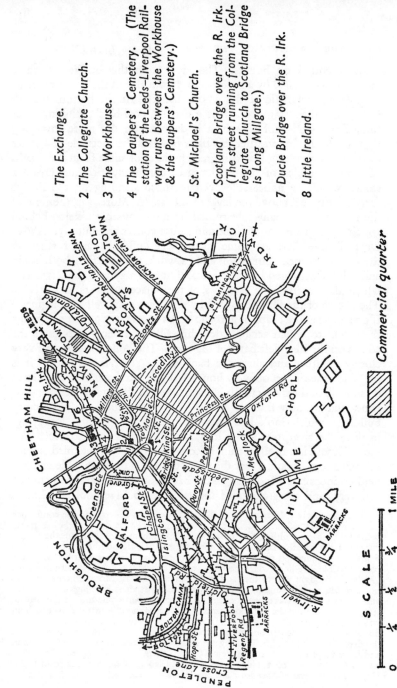

1   The Exchange.

2   The Collegiate Church.

3   The Workhouse.

4   The Paupers' Cemetery. (The station of the Leeds–Liverpool Railway runs between the Workhouse & the Paupers' Cemetery.)

5   St. Michael's Church.

6   Scotland Bridge over the R. Irk. (The street running from the Collegiate Church to Scotland Bridge is Long Millgate.)

7   Ducie Bridge over the R. Irk.

8   Little Ireland.

Commercial quarter

some recently-built houses. The view from this bridge, which is mercifully concealed by a high parapet from all but the tallest mortals, is quite characteristic of the whole district. At the bottom the Irk flows, or rather, stagnates. It is a narrow, coal-black, stinking river full of filth and rubbish which it deposits on the more low-lying right bank. In dry weather this bank presents the spectacle of a series of the most revolting blackish-green puddles of slime from the depths of which bubbles of miasmatic gases constantly rise and create a stench which is unbearable even to those standing on the bridge forty or fifty feet above the level of the water. Moreover, the flow of the river is continually interrupted by numerous high weirs, behind which large quantities of slime and refuse collect and putrefy. Above Ducie Bridge there are some tall tannery buildings, and further up there are dye-works, bone mills and gasworks. All the filth, both liquid and solid, discharged by these works finds its way into the River Irk, which also receives the contents of the adjacent sewers and privies. The nature of the filth deposited by this river may well be imagined.[1] If one looks at the heaps of garbage below Ducie Bridge one can gauge the extent to which accumulated dirt, filth and decay permeates the courts on the steep left bank of the river. The houses are packed very closely together and since the bank of the river is very steep it is possible to see a part of every house. All of them have been blackened by soot, all of them are crumbling with age and all have broken window panes and window frames. In the background there are old factory buildings which look like barracks. On the opposite, low-lying, bank of the river, one sees a long row of houses and factories. The second house is a roofless ruin, filled with refuse, and the third is built in such a low situation that the ground floor is uninhabitable and has neither doors nor windows. In the background one sees the paupers' cemetery, and the stations of the railways to Liverpool and Leeds.

[1 Engels's vivid descriptions of the Medlock (p. 71 below) and the confluence of the Rivers Irwell and Irk have obscured the fact that the Manchester rivers were not uniformly filthy. Sir John and Lady Clapham wrote: 'From the foulest corner of the greatest of them [i.e. the new towns], that corner in Manchester-Salford at the junction of the Irwell and the Irk where Engels, in 1844, saw ' the most horrible dwellings which he had ever yet beheld ', two and a half miles up a gentle hill brought you to the sand and heather of Kersal Moor, where there was horse-racing at Whitsuntide until 1846, and Chartist mass meetings later. (Next year the race-course was moved nearer in.) Not more than a mile and a half upstream from the foul corner, the little bourgeois of the forties thought that the river bathing was excellent; they knew ' a stretch of clean, nice, yellow sand, in which after our dip we could roll and dry ourselves in the hot summer sun '. There or thereabouts, the first Manchester and Salford regatta was rowed in September, 1842 ': Sir John and Lady Clapham, ' Life in the New Towns ' (*Early Victorian England*, 1830–1865, ed. G. M. Young, Vol. 1, (1934), p. 228. The Claphams' quotation is from L. M. Hayes, *Reminiscences of Manchester and some of its local surroundings from the year* 1840 (1905), pp. 61–2.]

Behind these buildings is situated the workhouse, Manchester's 'Poor Law Bastille'. The workhouse is built on a hill and from behind its high walls and battlements seems to threaten the whole adjacent working-class quarter like a fortress.

Above Ducie Bridge the left bank of the Irk becomes flatter and the right bank of the Irk becomes steeper and so the condition of the houses on both sides of the river becomes worse rather than better. Turning left from the main street which is still Long Millgate, the visitor can easily lose his way. He wanders aimlessly from one court to another. He turns one corner after another through innumerable narrow dirty alleyways and passages, and in only a few minutes he has lost all sense of direction and does not know which way to turn. The area is full of ruined or half-ruined buildings. Some of them are actually uninhabited and that means a great deal in this quarter of the town. In the houses one seldom sees a wooden or a stone floor, while the doors and windows are nearly always broken and badly fitting. And as for the dirt! Everywhere one sees heaps of refuse, garbage and filth. There are stagnant pools instead of gutters and the stench alone is so overpowering that no human being, even partially civilised, would find it bearable to live in such a district. The recently constructed extension of the Leeds railway which crosses the Irk at this point has swept away some of these courts and alleys, but it has thrown open to public gaze some of the others. So it comes about that there is to be found immediately under the railway bridge a court which is even filthier and more revolting than all the others. This is simply because it was formerly so hidden and secluded that it could only be reached with considerable difficulty, [but is now exposed to the human eye]. I thought I knew this district well, but even I would never have found it had not the railway viaduct made a breach in the slums at this point. One walks along a very rough path on the river bank, in between clothes-posts and washing lines to reach a chaotic group of little, one-storied, one-roomed cabins. Most of them have earth floors, and working, living and sleeping all take place in the one room. In such a hole, barely six feet long and five feet wide, I saw two beds—and what beds and bedding!—which filled the room, except for the fireplace and the doorstep. Several of these huts, as far as I could see, were completely empty, although the door was open and the inhabitants were leaning against the door posts. In front of the doors filth and garbage abounded. I could not see the pavement, but from time to time, I felt it was there because my feet scraped it. This whole collection of cattle sheds for human beings was surrounded on two sides by houses and a factory and on a third side by the river. [It was possible to get to this slum by only two routes]. One was the narrow path along the river bank, while the other was a narrow gateway which led to another human rabbit warren which was nearly as badly built and was nearly in such a bad condition as the one I have just described.

Enough of this! All along the Irk slums of this type abound. There is an unplanned and chaotic conglomeration of houses, most of which are more or less unhabitable. The dirtiness of the interiors of these premises is fully in keeping with the filth that surrounds them. How can people dwelling in such places keep clean! There are not even adequate facilities for satisfying the most natural daily needs. There are so few privies that they are either filled up every day or are too far away for those who need to use them. How can these people wash when all that is available is the dirty water of the Irk? Pumps and piped water are to be found only in the better-class districts of the town. Indeed no one can blame these helots of modern civilisation if their homes are no cleaner than the occasional pigsties which are a feature of these slums. There are actually some property owners who are not ashamed to let dwellings such as those which are to be found below Scotland Bridge. Here on the quayside a mere six feet from the water's edge is to be found a row of six or seven cellars, the bottoms of which are at least two feet beneath the low-water level of the Irk. [What can one say of the owner of] the corner house— situated on the opposite bank of the river above Scotland Bridge— who actually lets the upper floor although the premises downstairs are quite uninhabitable, and no attempt has been made to board up the gaps left by the disappearance of doors and windows? This sort of thing is by no means uncommon in this part of Manchester, where, owing to the lack of conveniences, such deserted ground floors are often used by the whole neighbourhood as privies.

We shall now leave the Irk in order to investigate the workers' houses on the other side of Long Millgate. This is a rather more recently built area which runs from St. Michael's Church to Withy Grove and Shudehill. Here at any rate there is more evidence of a planned building. In place of the chaotic layout [just described] we find that at least both the long through alleys and the cul-de-sacs are straight. The courts, built according to a plan, are usually square. On the other side of Long Millgate not a single house was erected in accordance with any sort of plan. Now we are in an area where although individual houses form part of a pattern the alleys and courts have been laid out in an irregular and unsystematic fashion without regard. The alleys may be straight but they change direction sharply, so that the unsuspecting stranger is continually finding himself in a blind alley or in a street which is leading him to the spot he left a few moments before. Only those who are reasonably acquainted with this maze can find their way through it. The ventilation of these streets and courts—if such a word could be used of this area—is just as inadequate as in the district along the Irk. Although this district is in some respects better than the slums in the valley of the Irk—at any rate the houses are rather newer and the streets do sometimes have gutters—nevertheless it must be pointed out that here there is nearly always a cellar dwelling underneath each house. In the valley of the Irk, on the other hand, it is rare to find cellar dwellings because of the greater age of the building and the more slovenly method of construction. Filth, heaps of refuse and ashes and dirty pools in the streets are common to both districts. However, in the area with which we are now concerned there are additional circumstances most deleterious to public cleanliness. There are large numbers of pigs, some of which are allowed to roam freely in the narrow streets, snuffling among the garbage heaps, while others are kept in little sties in the courts. In this area, as in most of the working-class districts of Manchester, pig breeders rent the courts and build the sties there. In nearly every court there are one or more little nooks in which pigs are kept. The inhabitants of the court throw all their garbage into these sties. This fattens the pigs, but also has the highly undesirable effect of impregnating the air—already stale because it is confined between four walls—with the disagreeable odour of decaying animal and vegetable matter. A wide and reasonably decent thoroughfare, Miller's Street, has been driven through this area and by this means the worst of the slums have been more or less hidden from the public gaze. If, however, anyone has sufficient curiosity to leave his road and go along one of the many alleys which lead to the courts, he will come across pigs and filth every twenty paces.[1]

This, then, is the Old Town of Manchester. On re-reading my description of the Old Town I must admit that, far from having exaggerated anything, I have not written vividly enough to impress the reader with the filth and dilapidation of a district which is quite unfit for human habitation. The shameful lay-out of the Old Town has made it impossible for the wretched inhabitants to enjoy cleanliness, fresh air, and good health. And such a district of at least twenty to thirty thousand inhabitants lies in the very centre of the second city in England, the most important factory town in the world. It is here that one can see how little space human beings need to move about in,

[1] It is impossible to translate Engels's play on words involved in the use of the word ' Schweinerei ' in this last sentence.]

how little air—and what air!—they need to breathe in order to exist, and how few of the decencies of civilisation are really necessary in order to survive. It is true that this is the *Old Town* and Manchester people stress this when their attention is drawn to the revolting character of this hell upon earth. But that is no defence. Everything in this district that arouses our disgust and just indignation is of relatively recent origin and belongs to the industrial age. The two or three hundred houses which survive from the earlier period of Manchester's history have long ago been deserted by their original inhabitants. It is only industry which has crammed them full of the hordes of workers who now live there. It is only the modern industrial age which has built over every scrap of ground between these old houses to provide accommodation for the masses who have migrated from the country districts and from Ireland. It is only the industrial age that has made it possible for the owners of these shacks, fit only for the accommodation of cattle, to let them at high rents for human habitations. It is only modern industry which permits these owners to take advantage of the poverty of the workers, to undermine the health of thousands to enrich themselves. Only industry has made it possible for workers who have barely emerged from a state of serfdom to be again treated as chattels and not as human beings. The workers have been caged in dwellings which are so wretched that no one else will live in them, and they actually pay good money for the privilege of seeing these dilapidated hovels fall to pieces about their ears. Industry alone has been responsible for all this and yet this same industry could not flourish except by degrading and exploiting the workers. It is true that this quarter of the town was originally built on a poor site, which offered few prospects for satisfactory development. But have either the landowners or the authorities done anything to improve matters when new buildings were erected? Far from adopting any such policy those responsible for recent developments have built houses in every conceivable nook and cranny. Even small passages which were not absolutely necessary have been built over and stopped up. The value of the land rose with the expansion of industry. The more the land rose in value the more furious became the search for new building sites. The health and comfort of the inhabitants were totally ignored, as a result of the determination of landlords to pocket the maximum profit. No hovel is so wretched but it will find a worker to rent it because he is too poor to pay for better accommodation. But the middle-classes salve their consciences by arguing that this state of affairs obtains only in the Old Town. Let us therefore see what the New Town has to offer.

The New Town, also known as Irish Town, on the other side of the Old Town, is situated on the clayey soil of the rising ground between the River Irk and St. George's Road. This district does not give one the impression that it is part of a big city. The New Town is composed of single rows of houses and groups of streets which might be small villages, lying on bare clayey soil which does not produce even a blade of grass. The houses—or rather the cottages—are in a disgraceful state because they are never repaired. They are filthy and beneath them are to be found damp, dirty cellar dwellings; the unpaved alleys lack any form of drainage. The district is infested with small herds of pigs; some of them are penned up in little courts and sties, while others wander freely on the neighbouring hillside. The lanes in this district are so filthy that it is only in very dry weather that one can reach it without sinking ankle-deep at every step. Near St. George's Road these isolated groups of houses are built closer together and one reaches a maze of lanes, blind alleys and back passages and courts. The nearer one gets to the centre of the town, the more closely packed are the houses and the more irregular is the lay-out of the streets. On the other hand, the streets here are often paved or at least have adequate pavements and gutters; but the filth, and the disgusting condition of the houses, particularly the cellars, remains unchanged.

It is pertinent at this stage to make some general observations on the normal lay-out of working-class quarters and the normal plan of constructing artisans' dwellings in Manchester. We have seen how, in the Old Town, there has been no systematic planning and that the siting of the houses has been purely fortuitous. Builders who erected new houses put them up without regard to the situation of older neighbouring property. The tiny gaps which exist between the houses are called ' courts ' for want of a more appropriate name. There is more evidence of planning in the rather newer parts of the Old Town, as well as in other working-class districts which date from the first stages of the Industrial Revolution. Here the spaces between the blocks of dwellings consist of regular—generally square—courts, from which there is access to the streets by a covered passage. [This may be seen from the accompanying diagram]. From the point of view of the health of the workers cooped up in these dwellings, this type of regular layout with wholly inadequate ventilation, is even worse than the unplanned streets of the Old Town. The air simply cannot escape and it is only up the chimneys of the houses—when fires happen to be burning—that any draught is provided to help the foul air from the courts to escape.[1] Moreover, the houses surrounding

[1] And yet, one of the wise English Liberals asserts in the *Report* of the Children's

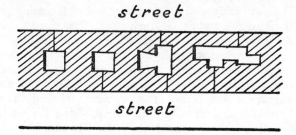

such courts are usually built back to back, with a common rear wall,[1] and this alone is sufficient to hinder any adequate circulation of the air, and since the police do not concern themselves with the state of these courts[2] everything thrown into the courts is allowed to lie there undisturbed, so that it is not surprising that dirt and heaps of ashes and filth are to be found there. I have had occasion to visit some of the courts lying in Miller's Street where the level of the ground was actually six inches lower than the level of the main street and yet no drains are available to carry away the water which accumulates in wet weather.

Subsequently another method of constructing workers' houses was introduced, but this has never become universal. Workers' cottages are now hardly ever built singly, but always in larger numbers —a dozen or even sixty at a time. A single contractor will build one or two whole streets at a time. The way in which these houses are built is illustrated by the accompanying diagram:

Employment Commission that courts such as these are masterpieces of town planning because they act in the same way as a number of little open spaces which facilitate ventilation and the circulation of the air. Of course the air would circulate if every court had two or four wide uncovered entrances opposite each other. In fact these courts never have even one. Nearly all have only narrow, covered entries. [This is a reference to a statement made by R. D. Grainger on the ' Manufactures of Birmingham ' in the *Appendix to the 2nd Report* of the Children's Employment Commission, Part I, p. F 23, para. 212. Grainger wrote:' The great number of courts [in Birmingham], amounting five years ago to 2030, must also promote the general health, being in fact so many small squares scattered over the town.']
    [[1] It will be seen that this fact is not illustrated in the diagram printed by Engels.]
    [[2] The Manchester Corporation's *police* force would not concern itself about these matters as it was not its function to do so. The courts were at this period regarded as private property. Professor Redford states: ' There were no powers in the local Acts for compelling the removal of middens from courts, passages and vacant lands . . . the only way in which redress could be obtained was by cumbrous and costly legal proceedings ': A. Redford and I. S. Russell, op. cit., Vol. 2, p. 148. In 1844, however, the Manchester Police Act was passed and this gave the local inspectors of nuisances rather wider powers.]

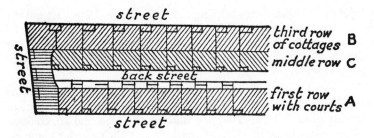

The cottages which face the street [at the bottom of the diagram] are of a somewhat superior character [Class A] and are fortunate enough to have a back door and a little backyard. The highest rents are charged for these cottages. Behind the back wall of these yards there is a narrow alley called a back street, which is enclosed at both ends. Access to this back street is either through a little entry or a covered passage. The cottages which have their front doors looking out on to the back street [Class C] pay the lowest rent and are indeed the most neglected. They have a party wall in common with the third row of cottages which face the street [at the top of the diagram]. This third row of cottages [Class B] pay a lower rent than the first class of cottages [A] but a higher rent than the middle row [C]. This method of construction ensures that the first row of cottages [A] is well ventilated. The ventilation of the cottages in the third row [B] 'is at any rate no worse than that to be found in the houses built on the older plan [which have a street frontage as distinct from a court frontage]. On the other hand the middle row of cottages [C] is just as badly ventilated as the older houses with front doors looking out on to courts. And the back streets of the newer houses are just as disgustingly filthy as the newer courts. The contractors prefer the newer lay-out, not only because it economises space, but because it gives them an opportunity of successfully exploiting the better paid workers who can pay higher rents for cottages which have front doors facing the street [A and B], [as distinct from the back alley]. This method of building workers' cottages in three rows is to be found throughout Manchester and indeed all over Lancashire and Yorkshire. Sometimes the old and the new method of construction are found side by side, but generally they are located in different parts of towns so that it is possible to distinguish without difficulty the older working-class districts from the newer.

There is also a third system of building working-class houses, which may be called the back-alley type of construction. This system predominates to an overwhelming degree in the working-class quarter [of Ancoats] to the east of St. George's Road, on both sides of the Oldham Road and Great Ancoats Street. It is also the commonest method of construction throughout the working-class districts of Manchester and its suburbs.

In the larger district we have just mentioned, which goes under the name of Ancoats, are to be found the majority, and the largest, of Manchester's factories. They are situated on canals and are colossal, six- or seven-storey buildings, towering, with their slender chimney-stacks, over the tiny cottages of the workers. The inhabitants of this district are for the most part factory workers, although hand-loom weavers are to be found in the worst streets. The streets lying closest to the centre of the town are the oldest and therefore the worst, though they are paved and have drains. I include in my description some streets parallel to Oldham Road and Great Ancoats Street [which lie outside Ancoats]. Further to the north-east there are several newly-built streets. Here the cottages have a clean and tidy appearance, for the doors and window frames have been newly painted and the rooms whitewashed. More fresh air gets into the streets themselves, while the empty spaces between the houses are larger and more frequent [than in the older districts]. But these remarks apply only to a relatively small number of the dwellings, because nearly every cottage has its inhabited cellar and many of the streets are unpaved and undrained. Above all, the present pleasing appearance of these cottages is only a pretence, because after ten years it will have vanished.[1] It is not only the lay-out of the streets, but the construction of the cottages themselves which is to be condemned. When newly built these cottages have a pleasant appearance and give the impression of being well-built. Their massive brick walls may well deceive the observer. Anyone looking at a newly-built row of workers' dwellings without examining either the back alleys or the construction of the houses might well be inclined to accept the assertions of the ' progressive '[2] manufacturers who claim that nowhere are the workers so well housed as in England. A closer inspection, however, soon reveals the fact that the walls of these cottages are as thin as it is possible to make them. The outer cellar walls which carry the weight of the ground floor and the roof, are only one brick thick. Generally the bricks are laid so that the long sides are together and the appearance of the wall from the outside may be represented as follows:

[1 Engels apparently assumes that no repainting would be carried out.]
[2 Engels used the phrase 'liberale Fabrikanten'.]

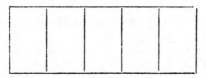

Yet I have seen several cottages of the same height—some actually still being built—where the thickness of the walls is equal to that of only half a brick. This is because the bricks are laid end to end, so that the outside wall has the following appearance:

This method of construction is adopted partly in order to save materials and partly because the builder is never the owner of the land on which the cottages are put up. The English practice is to lease building land for twenty, thirty, forty, fifty or ninety-nine years. When the lease falls in, possession of the land and the buildings on it reverts to the ground landlord, who does not have to pay any compensation for unexhausted improvements. The builder, therefore, constructs the cottages of a type unlikely to survive beyond the period of the lease. Since some leases are as short as twenty or thirty years it is easy to understand that builders are not likely to sink much capital into cottages built on such land. Moreover, the owners of the houses who are either bricklayers, joiners and carpenters or factory owners, are generally not prepared to spend very much money on repairing and maintaining their property. This is partly because they are not prepared to sacrifice any part of their profits, and partly owing to the system of short leases to which we have referred. When unemployment is rife during periods of bad trade whole rows of cottages often stand empty and in such circumstances they soon become virtually uninhabitable. It is generally estimated that on the average a worker's house is habitable for only forty years. This is indeed surprising when one looks at what appear to be the massive well-built walls of new cottages. Anyone would think they were intended to last for several centuries. False economy in the original construction, failure to maintain the property in good repair, frequent periods when they are unoccupied, are among the reasons which account for the fact that after forty years working-class property is generally in a ruinous condition. Moreover, it must be remembered that the house is particularly neglected during the last ten years or so of its life. The tenants during this period, who are generally Irish, actually use up all available woodwork for firing. The district of Ancoats has developed since the first expansion of manufactures and much of the property was built during the early years of the present [i.e. nineteenth] century. Nevertheless there are already many old and dilapidated houses in Ancoats, many of which will shortly be quite uninhabitable. What a mistake it has been to waste so much capital in this way! If only a little more money had been spent on these houses when they were first built and if only a small amount of repair work had been carried out regularly these houses might have been maintained in a clean, respectable and inhabitable condition for years. In fact the property is as I have described it, and I cannot think of any more scandalous and demoralising system of housing the workers than this. The worker is forced to live in such dilapidated dwellings because he cannot afford to rent better accommodation, or because no better cottages are available close to the factory in which he is working. It may even be that the cottage is owned by his employer and the worker is offered a job on condition that he rents the house. Of course working-class dwellings are not allowed to fall into decay quite so rapidly in a more central area where ground rents are high. In such parts of the town there is every prospect of finding a new tenant immediately an old one leaves the premises, and it is in the interests of the owners to maintain property in a habitable condition for a rather longer period. Even here, however, only the minimum amount of maintenance is carried out and some of these dwellings which have been repaired are among the worst in the country. Sometimes the threat of an epidemic arouses the normally very sluggish conscience of the health authorities and then there are signs of unwonted activity all over some working-class district. Complete rows of cellars and cottages may be closed and there are several such alleys near Oldham Road. The effects of such action soon wear off. The condemned dwellings rapidly find new tenants and the owners are placed in an advantageous position when searching for new tenants, for it is well-known that the health authorities will not trouble themselves again with this property for quite a time.

These eastern and north-eastern districts of Manchester are the only ones in which the middle classes have not built any houses for themselves. This is because for ten or eleven months in the year the winds blowing from the west and south-west always carry the smoke from the factories—and there is plenty of it—over this part of the town. The workers alone can breathe this polluted atmosphere.

A large working-class quarter is growing up south of Great Ancoats Street, on a hilly, bare stretch of land. Here a few irregularly built rows and square courts of houses have been erected between which lie broken muddy tracts where no grass grows. In wet weather it is almost impossible to cross these open spaces. The cottages are all old and dirty. They are often built at the bottom of the natural depressions in the soil and forcibly remind one of the workers' dwellings in the New Town. The area crossed by the railway to Birmingham has the most houses and is therefore the worst part of the district. Here the river Medlock flows with endless twists and turns through a valley which may be compared with that of the Irk. From its entry into Manchester to its confluence with the Irwell, this coal-black, stagnant, stinking river is lined on both sides by a broad belt of factories and workers' dwellings. The cottages are all in a sorry state. The banks of the Medlock like those of the Irk are generally steep and the buildings run down to the very edge of the river. The lay-out of the streets and houses is just as bad on the Manchester side of the river as it is on the opposite side where lie the districts of Ardwick, Chorlton and Hulme. This book would never be finished if I were to describe in detail every part of this district, but I might mention that the most disgusting spot of all is one which lies on the Manchester side of the river. It is situated to the south west of Oxford Road and is called Little Ireland. It lies in a fairly deep natural depression on a bend of the river and is completely surrounded by tall factories or high banks and embankments covered with buildings. Here lie two groups of about two hundred cottages, most of which are built on the back-to-back principle. Some four thousand people, mostly Irish, inhabit this slum. The cottages are very small, old and dirty, while the streets are uneven, partly unpaved, not properly drained and full of ruts. Heaps of refuse, offal and sickening filth are everywhere interspersed with pools of stagnant liquid. The atmosphere is polluted by the stench and is darkened by the thick smoke of a dozen factory chimneys. A horde of ragged women and children swarm about the streets and they are just as dirty as the pigs which wallow happily on the heaps of garbage and in the pools of filth. In short, this horrid little slum affords as hateful and repulsive a spectacle as the worst courts to be found on the banks of the Irk. The inhabitants live in dilapidated cottages, the windows of which are broken and patched with oilskin. The doors and the door posts are broken and rotten. The creatures who inhabit these dwellings and even their dark, wet cellars, and who live confined amidst all this filth and foul air—which cannot be dissipated because of the surrounding lofty buildings—must surely have sunk to the lowest level of humanity. That is the conclusion that must surely be drawn even by

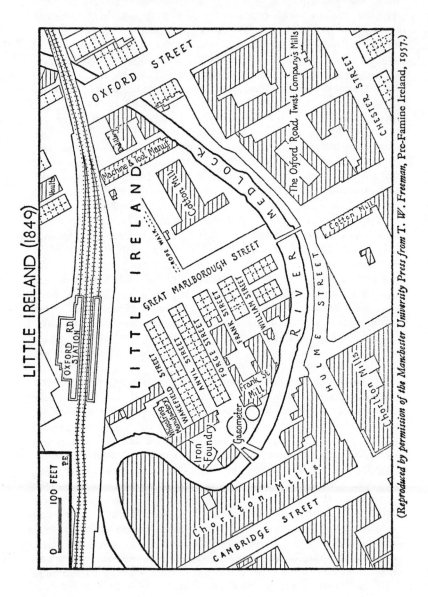

LITTLE IRELAND (1849)

100 FEET

(Reproduced by permission of the Manchester University Press from T. W. Freeman, Pre-Famine Ireland, 1957.)

any visitor who examines the slum from the outside, without entering any of the dwellings. But his feelings of horror would be intensified if he were to discover that on the average twenty people live in each of these little houses, which at the moment consist of two rooms, an attic and a cellar. One privy—and that usually inaccessible—is shared by about one hundred and twenty people. In spite of all the warnings of the doctors and in spite of the alarm caused to the health authorities by the condition of Little Ireland during the cholera epidemic, the condition of this slum is practically the same in this year of grace 1844 as it was in 1831. Dr. Kay describes how not only the cellars but even the ground floors of all the houses in this quarter were damp. He states that at one time a number of the cellars were filled with earth and that they were gradually emptied again and had now been re-occupied by the Irish. One particular cellar which lay below the level of the river was continually flooded with water which gushed in through a hole which had been stuffed full of clay. The handloom weaver who lived there had to clean out his cellar every morning and empty the water into the street.[1]

The district of Hulme lies further downstream on the left bank of the Medlock and this is really one big working-class quarter. Conditions in Hulme are practically identical with those already described in Ancoats. In those parts of Hulme in which the houses are built most tightly together the cottages are generally in a miserable and dilapidated state. In the less densely populated parts of the district the houses are of more modern construction and more open to the fresh air, but most of them are surrounded by filth. In general the cottages are damp and the type of lay-out, with back alleys and cellar dwellings, is similar to that of Ancoats.

On the opposite side of the Medlock, in Manchester itself is situated a second large working-class district which lies on either side of Deansgate and stretches as far as the commercial quarter of the city. Parts of this area are just as bad as the Old Town. This is true of the area between Quay Street, Bridge Street, Princess Street and Peter Street, which lies near the commercial centre of Manchester. Here the way in which buildings have been erected close to each other is even worse than in the narrowest courts of the Old Town. Here is a maze of long narrow lanes, linking the tiny courts and passages. The exits and entrances to the courts and passages are so irregularly

[1 Dr. J. P. Kay, op. cit., pp. 35–6. The story of the weaver who had to mop out his cellar every morning was not told by Kay himself but was quoted by Kay from a report made to the Manchester magistrates by a sub-committee of the local Board of Health on December 19th, 1831.]

placed that a visitor to this labyrinth is in danger of losing his way and finding himself in a blind alley or in a passage which leads in entirely the wrong direction. Only those who know every passage and every court can find their way about. Dr. Kay states that in these dilapidated and dirty houses along the narrow lanes there dwell the most demoralised classes in Manchester. There were the dens of thieves and prostitutes and as far as one can see Dr. Kay's description still holds true. When the sanitary authorities made an attempt to clean up this quarter in 1831 they found that it was just as dirty as Little Ireland and the districts round the Irk. They found that in Parliament Street there was only one privy for three hundred and eighty people and in Parliament Passage there was only one privy for thirty houses packed with human beings.[1] I can testify that things have not improved much since Kay wrote.

If we cross the Irwell to Salford we enter a town which is built on a tongue of land enclosed by a great bend of the river. The population numbers 80,000. Salford is really all one large working-class quarter through which runs a single broad main street. At one time Salford was more important than Manchester, being the principal town for the surrounding district, which is still called Salford Hundred. This explains why here, too, there is a fairly old and therefore now very unhealthy, dirty and dilapidated district which is situated opposite the ' Old Church ' of Manchester. This district is in just as bad a condition as the Old Town on the Manchester side of the Irwell. At some distance from the river there lies a more recently built-up area, but this, too, is over forty years old and therefore beginning to decay. The whole of Salford consists of courts and of lanes which are so narrow that they reminded me of the narrowest alleys I have ever seen, which are those in Genoa. From this point of view the lay-out out of Salford is in general even worse than that of Manchester. Moreover, Salford is dirtier than Manchester. In Manchester the authorities do at least once in a way—say every six or ten years—inspect the working-class districts and close the very worst dwellings. They try to clean out the filthiest corners of these Augean stables. Nothing of this sort ever seems to happen in Salford. I am sure that the narrow side streets and courts of Chapel Street, Greengate and Gravel Lane have never once been cleaned since they were built. Now the railway to Liverpool crosses the district and the construction of this line has led to the removal of some of the dirtiest parts of these slums. But what good does that do? The traveller crossing this viaduct can still look down on plenty of dirt and poverty. If he takes the trouble to go through

[1 Kay, op. cit., pp. 36–7.]

these alleyways and to peer through the open doors and windows into the houses and cellars he can satisfy himself time and time again that the Salford workers inhabit dwellings in which it is impossible to live in either cleanliness or comfort. Exactly the same conditions are to be found in the outlying districts of Salford—in Islington, along Regent Road, and behind the railway to Bolton. The working-class quarter situated between Oldfield and Cross Lane—it is divided by Hope Street—is one of the innumerable courts and lanes which are in a very bad condition. This district is just as dirty and overcrowded as the Old Town of Manchester. It was here that I found a man, who seemed to be about sixty years of age, living in a cow-shed. He had constructed a sort of chimney for his square-shaped hovel, which had no floor-boards, no plaster on the walls and no windows. He had installed a bedstead and here he lived although the rain came through the decaying roof. The man was too old for regular work, but he earned a living by removing manure and garbage with his handcart. Pools of filth lay close to his shed.

* * * *

Such are the various working-class districts of Manchester which I myself was able to see during my twenty months' stay in that town. I may sum up the impressions of my visits to these districts by stating that 350,000 workers in Manchester and the surrounding districts nearly all live in inferior, damp, dirty cottages; that the streets are generally in a disgraceful state of filth and disrepair, and that the lay-out of the dwellings reflects the greed of the builder for profits from the way in which ventilation is lacking. In a word, the workers' dwellings of Manchester are dirty, miserable and wholly lacking in comforts. In such houses only inhuman, degraded and unhealthy creatures would feel at home. And I am not the only one who takes this point of view. I have shown that Dr. Kay's recorded impressions of these districts tallied exactly with my own. I will add only a passage from a book by Nassau Senior, who is a Liberal and a fanatical opponent of all independent trade unions. His views are highly esteemed and recognised as authoritative by the great manufacturers. Nassau Senior writes:

But when I went through their [i.e. the Manchester operatives'] habitations in Irish Town, and Ancoats, and Little Ireland, my only wonder was that tolerable health could be maintained by the inmates of such houses. These towns, for such they are in extent and population, have been erected by small speculators with an utter disregard to everything except immediate profit. A carpenter and a bricklayer club to buy a patch of ground,[1] and cover it with what they call houses. In one place we saw a whole street following the course of a ditch, in order to have deeper cellars (cellars for people, not for lumber) without the expense of excavations. *Not a house in this street escaped cholera.*[2] And generally speaking throughout these suburbs the streets are unpaved, with a dunghill or a pond in the middle; the houses built back to back, without ventilation or drainage; and whole families occupy each a corner of a cellar or of a garret.[3]

I have already mentioned the unusual activity of the health authorities at the time of the cholera [in 1831–2]. When this epidemic threatened, the middle classes in Manchester were panic-stricken. They suddenly remembered the existence of the unhealthy dwellings of the poor; and they were greatly alarmed lest every one of these slums should become a centre from which this pestilence should spread death and destruction in all directions, and so reach the dwellings of the wealthier classes. A Board of Health was immediately appointed to inspect these slums and to make a detailed report to the municipal authorities.[4]

The investigations of this body covered all the police districts of Manchester with the exception of the 11th. Dr. Kay, who was a member of the Board, gives some extracts from the report.[5] Altogether 6,915 houses were inspected. These, of course, were all in Manchester proper [i.e. the township] and not in Salford or other adjacent districts. Of these 6,915 houses, 2,565 needed immediate whitewashing of the interior, 960 'were out of repair',[6] 939 were without adequate drainage, 1,435 were damp, 452 were badly ventilated while 2,221 lacked privies. Of the 687 streets inspected 248 were unpaved, 53 were only partially paved, 112 were badly ventilated and 352 contained 'heaps of refuse, stagnant pools, ordure, etc.'[7]

---

[1] That is to say, to lease for a number of years [inserted in the text by Engels].

[2] Engels's italics].

[3] Nassau W. Senior, *Letters on the Factory Act, as it affects the cotton manufacture, addressed to the Right Honourable the President of the Board of Trade* (1837), pp. 24–5.

[4] The Board of Health for the township of Manchester was set up in November 1831. It reported to the local magistrates and corresponded extensively with the Committees of the Manchester Police Commissioners.]

[5] See Kay, op. cit., p. 31.]

[6] Engels quotes these four words in English. The table prepared by the Manchester Board of Health showing the classification of houses inspected in the town is reproduced both by Kay (op. cit., p. 31) and Gaskell (op. cit., p. 134). In Kay's pamphlet column 3 of this table is headed 'No. of houses reported as requiring repair', but in Gaskell's book the phrase used is 'Houses out of repair'. This suggests that Engels had Gaskell's book in front of him when writing this passage.]

[7] Kay, op. cit., p. 30, quoted also by R. A. Slaney, *State of the Poorer Classes in Great Towns* (1840), p. 18.]

It was, of course, quite out of the question to clean an Augean stable of this sort before the onset of the cholera. All that could be done was to clean some of the filthiest streets and houses. Otherwise everything remained as before. It goes without saying that the places reverted in a few months to their previous filthy condition. Little Ireland was an example of this. This same Board of Health reported also on the condition of the interiors of these slum dwellings, and this investigation revealed conditions similar to those which we have already described in London, Edinburgh and elsewhere. Dr. Kay wrote:

'A whole [Irish] family is often accommodated on a single bed, and sometimes a heap of filthy straw and a covering of old sacking hide them in one undistinguished heap, debased alike by penury, want of economy and dissolute habits. Frequently the inspectors found two or more families crowded into one small house, containing only two apartments, one in which they slept, and another in which they eat; and often more than one family lived in a damp cellar, containing only one room, in whose pestilential atmsophere from twelve to sixteen persons were crowded. To these fertile sources of disease were sometimes added the keeping of pigs and other animals in the house, with other nuisances of the most revolting character.'[1]

It may be added that many families which have only one room take in boarders and lodgers, and it is not uncommon for both men and women lodgers to sleep in the same bed as their married hosts. The *Report . . . on . . . the Sanitary Condition of the Labouring Population* mentions half a dozen cases in Manchester in which a man sleeps not only with his wife but also with his adult sister-in-law.[2]

Common lodging houses, too, are very numerous in Manchester. Dr. Kay stated that in 1831 there were 267 of them in the township of Manchester,[3] and since that date their numbers have no doubt considerably increased. As each lodging house accommodates between twenty and thirty persons, the total number of people sleeping in them on any one night must be between five and seven thousand. The character of these houses and their clients is the same as in other towns. In every room five or seven beds are made up on the floor and human beings of both sexes are packed into them indiscriminately.

[1] Kay, op. cit., p. 32. Engels's translation of this passage into German contains a number of small errors and changes.]

[2] Evidence of James Riddall Wood (pp. 124-5): 'I have met with instances of a man, his wife, and his wife's sister, sleeping in the same bed together. I have known at least half-a-dozen cases in Manchester in which that has been regularly practised, the unmarried sister being an adult'.]

[3] Kay, op. cit., Table of 'pauper lodging houses', p. 33.]

There is no need for me to discuss the physical and moral state of these dens of vice. Every one of these houses is a breeding-ground of crime and also the scene of much conduct of an unnatural and revolting character.[1] Many of these offences might never have been committed at all had those who perpetrated them not visited lodging houses, which are hot-beds of unnatural vice.

Gaskell estimates that twenty thousand people live in cellars in Manchester proper.[2] This statement is confirmed by an estimate in the *Weekly Dispatch* 'from official sources' that 12 per cent of the workers live in cellars. The number of workers may be taken as 175,000 and 12 per cent of this number is 21,000.[3] As there are just as many cellars in the suburbs as in Manchester itself the total number of workers living in cellars in Greater Manchester must be between forty and fifty thousand. So much for the dwellings of the workers in the large towns.

The state of the workers' houses gives one a yardstick by which to measure the general standard of living of the workers. It would be natural to draw the conclusion that the inhabitants of the filthy slums that we have described must be clothed in rags and must be badly nourished. There is ample evidence to bear this out. The vast majority of the workers are clad in rags. The material from which the workers' clothes are made is by no means ideal for its purpose. Linen and wool have practically disappeared from the wardrobes of both men and women, and have replaced by cotton. Men's shirts are made of bleached or coloured cotton cloth. Women generally wear printed cottons; woollen petticoats are seldom seen on the washing-line.

[1 See note on p. 38 *supra*.]

[2] P. Gaskell, *The Manufacturing Population of England* . . . (1833). This book is mainly a description of the Lancashire workers. The author is a Liberal but he was writing at a time before it was regarded as a tenet of Liberalism to praise the 'good fortune' of the workers. Consequently Gaskell is an objective observer and does not ignore the evils of the modern factory system. He was, however, writing before the results of the enquiries of the Royal Commission on the Labour of Children in Factories [1833]. In the circumstances he makes use of some unreliable material and commits himself to assertions subsequently contradicted by the Royal Commission. Gaskell's book should, as far as its details are concerned, be used with some caution, not only for this reason, but also because the author, like Kay, confuses the factory hands with the working classes in general. With these reservations Gaskell's book can be recommended. I have used Gaskell's book extensively when writing the introduction to the present work. [On p. 138 of this work Gaskell stated that 'upwards of 20,000 individuals live in cellars in Manchester alone'.]

[3 *Weekly Dispatch* no. 2219, May 5th, 1844—article on 'Wild beasts *v.* rational beings'. In this article the total population of Manchester is given as 200,000. The same figure had been given in *Report of a Committee of the Manchester Statistical Society on the Condition of the Working Classes in an extensive manufacturing district in 1834, 1835 and 1836* (1838). See also Slaney, op. cit., p. 19.]

Men's trousers are generally made either of fustian or some other heavy cotton cloth. Overcoats and jackets are made from the same material. Fustian has become the traditional dress for working men, who are called 'fustian jackets'. Gentlemen, on the other hand, wear suits made from woollen cloth, and the term 'broadcloth' is used to designate the middle classes. When the Chartist leader, Feargus O'Connor, came to Manchester during the riots of 1842 he appeared before the workers in a fustian suit and received a great ovation. All workers in England wear hats and they are of the most varied shapes—round, cone-shaped, cylindrical, broad-brimmed, narrow-brimmed, or without a brim. Only the younger men in the factory towns wear caps. Anyone who does not possess a hat makes himself a low, four-cornered cap out of paper. Even if the workers' clothes are in good condition they are unsuitable for the climate. The air is damp and the temperature is liable to change suddenly. This, more than anything else, causes people to catch colds. Members of the middle classes nearly all wear flannel vests next to the skin, cummerbunds round the stomach and flannel scarves and shirts. The working classes, on the other hand, have to do without this extra protection, and indeed very seldom wear woollen clothing of any kind. Their heavy cotton clothes, though thicker, stiffer and heavier than woollen cloth, do not keep out the cold and wet to anything like the same extent as woollens. Cotton garments, owing both to their thickness and to the very nature of the material, absorb dampness more than woollen cloth. In fact cotton cloth has not got the same compact texture as felted woollen cloth. If once in a way a worker has enough money to buy a woollen coat, he has to go to a 'cheap shop', where he buys a garment manufactured from 'devil's-dust cloth', and therefore 'made to sell well, but not to wear well'. In a fortnight it tears or grows threadbare. Alternatively, the worker may go to an old-clothes dealer and buy a shabby second-hand garment which has seen better days and is only likely to give a few weeks' further service. In addition it must be remembered that most workers have very few clothes, and from time to time they find it necessary to pawn the better garments. A very large number of workers, particularly the Irish, wear extremely ragged clothing, which is either incapable of being patched any more or has been so often patched in the past that the original colour can no longer be detected. But both English and Anglo-Irish workers do go on patching their clothes and have achieved a remarkable proficiency in this art. It is remarkable how they can patch fustian clothes with pieces of woollen cloth and sacking, or woollen clothing with fustian. But the recent arrivals from Ireland hardly ever patch their clothes except in the last resort—to stop them from falling apart. Usually an Irishman's ragged shirt can be seen protruding through the tears and holes in his jacket and trousers. Thomas Carlyle describes their clothing as ' a suit of tatters, the getting off and on of which is said to be a difficult operation, transacted only in festivals and the hightides of the calendar.'[1]

The growing habit of going about barefoot in England has been introduced by Irish immigrants. In all factory towns we can now see, particularly women and children, going about barefooted and this custom is gradually being adopted by the poorer class of English.

The situation with regard to food resembles that which has been discussed concerning clothing. The workers only get what is not good enough for the well-to-do. The very best food is to be had in all the big towns of England, but it is expensive, and the worker, who has only got a few coppers to spend, cannot afford it. The English worker is not paid until Saturday evening. In some factories wages are paid on Fridays, but this desirable reform is far from general. Most workers can only get to market on Saturdays at four, five or even 7 o'clock in the evening, and by that time the best food has been purchased in the morning by the middle classes. When the market opens, there is an ample supply of good food, but by the time the worker arrives the best has gone. But even if it were still there, he probably could not afford to buy it. The potatoes purchased by the workers are generally bad, the vegetables shrivelled, the cheese stale and of poor quality, the bacon rancid. The meat is lean, old, tough and partially tainted. It is the produce either of animals which have died a natural death or of sick animals which have been slaughtered. Food is generally sold by petty hawkers who buy up bad food and are able to sell it cheaply because of its poor quality. The poorest of the workers have to employ yet another stratagem in order to be able to buy foodstuffs even of the poorest quality. Since all shops have to close at midnight on Saturdays and no trading is allowed on Sundays, the shopkeepers sell very cheaply between ten o'clock and midnight those foodstuffs which would otherwise go bad if kept until the Monday morning. But nine-tenths of the foodstuffs still on sale at 10 p.m. will in fact have gone bad by Sunday morning. And yet it is such food that the poorest workers have for their Sunday dinners. The meat the workers buy is very often unpalatable, but simply because money has been spent on it, it has to be eaten.[2] If I remember rightly it was on January 6th, 1844 (sic) that eleven butchers were punished by the Manchester Court Leet for selling tainted meat. Between them they exposed for sale a

---

[1] *Chartism* (1839), p. 28.   [2 Compare Gaskell, op. cit., pp. 111–113.]

whole cow, a pig, several sheep and from fifty to sixty pounds of meat. All this bad meat was confiscated. One of the offenders had fifty-four dressed Christmas geese for sale which had not been sold in Liverpool and were therefore offered for sale in a putrefying condition in the Manchester market. These, too, were confiscated. The *Manchester Guardian* gave a detailed account of the affair, with the names of the offenders and the amounts of the fines.[1] In the six weeks between July 1st, and August 14th [1844] the same newspaper reported three similar cases. On July 3rd it reported that at Heywood the carcase of a pig, weighing 200 lb., was cut up and exposed for sale although tainted. This pork was confiscated.[2] On July 31st the *Manchester Guardian* reported that two Wigan butchers, one of whom had already been convicted previously for a similar offence, were fined £2 and £4 respectively for exposing for sale meat unfit for human consumption.[3] On August 10th, the same paper reported that a hawker at Bolton had been fined 20s. for offering 26 unwholesome hams for sale. The hams were confiscated and publicly burnt.[4] To estimate the average number of such cases that occur annually it would be necessary to take into account more than three instances in six weeks. The *Manchester Guardian*, which appears twice a week, often reports at least one case of this kind in the neighbouring factory districts in every number. Many cases are obviously never reported because the markets are so extensive —they are to be found in all the main streets—and from the lack of an adequate inspectorate to check the evil. How else can we explain the impudence with which shopkeepers expose for sale an entire carcase [that is unfit for human consumption]. Moreover the fines imposed by the courts are scandalously low and it must be remembered that the condition of the meat is very bad indeed before the inspectors are prepared to order its confiscation. In these circumstances it is obviously impossible to believe that the workers are, in general, able to buy wholesome and nourishing meat.

The working classes are cheated in other ways by the greed of the

[1 Engels's memory was at fault. The cases against the 11 butchers, summoned before the Manchester Court Leet, were reported in the *Manchester Guardian* of May 10, 1843, page 6, col. 1 (not January 6th, 1844). Since the Court Leet met only twice a year the offences had been committed over a period of 6 months—from Nov. 12th, 1842, to April 22nd, 1843. See also *The Court Leet Records of the Manor of Manchester* . . . Vol. 12 (1832–46) (1890), session of May, 1843, pp. 191–223. The dressed geese were exposed for sale on Dec. 10th, 1842, and the number involved was 54 not 64, as stated in the original German edition.]

[2 *Manchester Guardian*, July 3rd, 1844, p. 7, col. 1.]

[3 *Manchester Guardian*, July 31st, 1844, p. 7, col. 5. Both butchers had previous convictions.]

[4 *Manchester Guardian*, August 10th, 1844, p. 7, col. 2. Two men were engaged in selling the hams.]

middle classes. Producers and shopkeepers adulterate all food stuffs in a disgraceful manner, with a scandalous disregard for the health of the ultimate consumer. My previous examples have been taken from the *Manchester Guardian*, but I will now take my evidence from the pages of the *Liverpool Mercury*, another middle-class newspaper. I enjoy making my opponents provide me with evidence. The *Liverpool Mercury* writes:

. . . salt butter is moulded into the form of pounds of fresh butter, and *cased* over with fresh. . . . In other instances, salt butter is moulded into the shape of fresh, and not cased at all; but a pound of fresh is conspicuously placed to be tasted; but *that* pound is not sold; and in other instances salt butter, washed, is moulded and sold as fresh. . . . Pounded rice and other cheap materials are mixed in sugar, and sold at full monopoly price. A chemical substance—the refuse of the soap manufactories—is also mixed with other substances and sold as sugar . . . chicory [is mixed] in good coffee . . . Chicory, or some similarly cheap substance, is skilfully moulded into the form of the coffee berry, and is mixed with the bulk very liberally . . . Cocoa . . . is extensively adulterated with fine brown earth, wrought up with mutton fat, so as to amalgamate with portions of the real article.. . . The leaves [of tea] are mingled with sloe leaves and other abominations, to swindle the public. Used leaves are also re-dried, and re-coloured on hot copper plates, and sold as tea. . . . Pepper is adulterated with dust from husks etc.; port wine is altogether *manufactured* (from spirits, dyes, etc.)[1] by certain parties, it being notorious that more [port] wine, so called, is drunk in this country than is made in Portugal. . . . Nasty things of all sorts, if cheap, are mixed with the weed [tobacco] in all its manufactured forms. . . .'[2]

[1] The words in brackets '(from spirits, dyes, etc.)' were interpolated by Engels.]
[2 *Liverpool Mercury*, Feb. 9th, 1844, p. 46, col. 1. Engels's extracts are a severely abridged version of the article and his translation of it into German was a fairly free one. In the original article the order in which the various adulterated substances are discussed is slightly different. On the subject of adulteration Engels naturally did not quote the following extract from the *Liverpool Mercury* of January 26th, 1844 (p. 32, col. 3), which showed that both the authorities and the press were alive to the need for suppressing such practices:

'. . . The Excise authorities, it appears, are actively engaged in detecting instances of adulteration throughout the country. The *Morning Chronicle* says:

"As the whole of these nefarious practices are reported to the Board of Excise in London, and samples of the adulterated articles transmitted for examination, some idea may be formed of their number when it is known that a practical chemist, who is kept by the Board, and who is furnished with a complete laboratory at the office in Broad-street, has been constantly engaged for the last two months on analyzing the various seizures of spurious and adulterated pepper alone, which amounts in the gross to several tons " . . .'

The article then went on to give further examples of adulteration and listed successful Excise prosecutions in various parts of the country during the previous week.]

It may be added that one of the most respectable of the tobacco merchants in Manchester publicly declared last summer that owing to the universal practice of adulterating tobacco, it was impossible for any tobacconist to carry on business successfully without resorting to it. No cigar selling for threepence or less, he declared, could possibly be made solely from tobacco leaf.[1] Among other methods of deceit in the sale of food, the shameful practice of mixing gypsum or chalk with flour may be mentioned.[2] Of course I could give many more examples of swindles of this description.

Deceit occurs in the sale of all articles offered for sale to the workers —flannel and stockings are stretched to make them appear to be larger than they really are and they shrink the first time they are washed. Narrow cloth is sold as if it were $1\frac{1}{2}$ or 3 inches broader than it really is.[3] Crockery is so thinly glazed that the glazing might just as well not exist, for the article cracks at once.[4] Hundreds of other petty deceits might be mentioned, *tout comme chez nous*. It is the worker who suffers most from deceptions of this kind. Those who can afford to pay more are not affected, because they pay the higher prices charged by the big shops which have a reputation to maintain, and could themselves be the first to suffer if they stocked such rubbishy goods. In addition, rich people are spoilt by good food and their nice palates would soon detect adulteration and taint more easily. The poor worker has got to make a few coppers go a long way and must buy a large quantity of goods with very little money. Consequently, he is in no position to be particular and to demand goods of high quality. In any case he has never had the opportunity of acquiring a sense of taste which would enable him to detect adulterated and often positively poisonous foodstuffs. He has to patronise the petty shopkeeper, and sometimes even has to buy on credit. These petty shopkeepers are unable to sell as cheaply as the better-class retailers because they begin with very little capital and their overheads are proportionately greater if they sell goods of high quality. They know that their customers can pay only very low prices and they know that there is

[1 The Excise authorities were particularly active in 1843-44 in prosecuting tobacconists for selling adulterated tobacco (*Manchester Guardian*, Feb. 14th, 1844, p. 7, cols. 3-4; April 27th, 1844, p. 5, cols. 1-3, p. 6, cols. 5-6; *Liverpool Mercury*, Sept. 6th, 1844, p. 295, col. 5, Sept. 22nd, 1844, p. 310, col. 5). One of the Liverpool tobacconists, Thomas Nelson, stated at the trial: 'I was obliged to do it in self-defence, for I could not make a living along with others if I did not': *Liverpool Mercury*, April 26th, 1844, p. 143, col. 1.]

[2 *Liverpool Mercury*, July 12th, 1844, p. 232, col. 2; July 19th, 1844, p. 240, col. 5, August 2nd, 1844, p. 255, col. 1. William Pattinson of Cuddington Mill, Weaverham, was fined for having gypsum in his possession.]

[3 *Liverpool Mercury*, Feb. 9th, 1844, p. 46, col. 1.]

[4 *Liverpool Mercury*, loc. cit.]

fierce competition between small shopkeepers. And so, knowingly or unknowingly, they stock adulterated and inferior goods. If a high-class retailer is detected in the sale of such articles, the ruin of his reputation brings about the collapse of his business and the loss of the large capital invested in it. The petty trader's customers are confined to those living in one street. What does it matter to him if his mal-practices are detected? If his reputation in Ancoats has gone, he simply goes to Chorlton or Hulme, where no one knows him and he can continue his career of duplicity. It may be added that legal penalties affect only a few kinds of adulteration and deception and are mainly those involving frauds on the excise revenue. The English workers are cheated not only with regard to the quality, but also in respect of the quantity of the goods they buy. The petty shopkeeper generally uses false weights and measures. Every day there are reports in the provincial press of an incredible number of prosecutions for this offence. How common this sort of deceit is in the factory districts may be illustrated by a few examples taken from the pages of the *Manchester Guardian*. They cover only a short period and not all issues of the paper are available at the moment:

June 15th,[1] 1844: Rochdale Sessions—Four shopkeepers fined from 5s. to 10s. for using deficient weights. Stockport Sessions—Two shopkeepers fined a shilling; one of them had seven deficient weights and defective scales.[2] Both had been previously warned for committing the same offence.
June 19th, 1844: Rochdale Sessions—A shopkeeper fined 5s. and two farmers fined 10s.[3]
June 22nd, 1844: Manchester magistrates' Court: nineteen shop-keepers fined between 2s. 6d. and 40s.[4]
June 26th, 1844: Ashton Petty Sessions—Fourteen dealers and farmers fined from 2s. 6d. to 20s. Hyde Petty Sessions—nine farmers and dealers sentenced to pay 5s. and costs.[5]
July 6th,[6] 1844: Manchester—Sixteen shopkeepers fined up to 10s. and costs.
July 13th, 1844: Manchester—nine shopkeepers fined from 2s. 6d. to 20s.

[1 Not June 16th as in the original German edition.]
[2 One shopkeeper was fined 1s. and 11s. 6d. costs, while the other was fined 20s., including costs; the exact amount of the fine was not given.]
[3 The shopkeeper was fined 10s. and costs and the two farmers 5s. and costs each.]
[4 In each case defendants had to pay 8s. 6d. costs in addition to the fine.]
[5 In the case in Hyde the penalties imposed ranged from a 5s. fine and costs to the payment of costs only.]
[6 Not 9th July as in the original German edition.]

July 24th, 1844: Rochdale Sessions—four shopkeepers fined from 10s. to 20s.[1]

July 27th, 1844: Bolton—twelve beersellers and innkeepers sentenced to pay costs.

August 3rd, 1844: Bolton—three shopkeepers fined 2s. 6d. and 5s.

August 10th, 1844: Bolton—a shopkeeper fined 5s.

The workers suffer more than the wealthier classes from short weight for the same reasons as they suffer more from the bad quality of the goods offered for sale.

The normal diet of the individual worker naturally varies according to his wages. The better-paid workers—particularly when the whole family works in the factories—enjoy good food as long as they are in employment. They have meat every day and bacon and cheese for the evening meal. The lower-paid workers have meat only two or three times a week, and sometimes only on Sundays. The less meat they can afford, the more potatoes and bread they eat. Sometimes the meat consumed is cut down to a little chopped bacon mixed with the potatoes. The poorer workers can afford no meat at all and they eat cheese, bread, porridge and potatoes. The poorest of all are the Irish, for whom potatoes are the staple diet. In addition, most workers drink weak tea to which perhaps sugar, milk, or spirits are added. In England and even in Ireland tea is regarded as being just as essential as coffee is in Germany and only those who suffer from the direst poverty give up their tea.

In this discussion on diet, it has been assumed that the worker is in employment. If he is out of work it is a matter of chance whether he eats at all or starves. The unemployed worker has to rely on charity, begging or theft. And if he gets nothing he just has to starve, as we have already observed.[2] It is obvious that both the quality and the quantity of the diet is governed by the amount of the wages the worker receives. A poorly-paid worker, even if he has only a small family to support, goes short of food even when he is in employment. The number of poorly-paid workers is very large. This is particularly true of London, where there are many such, because in this great city there is a surplus of unskilled labour and competition for low-paid jobs is consequently fierce. A similar problem arises in a less acute form in other large urban centres. In cases of dire necessity the poorest

[1 Three of the defendants were fined 10s. and costs; the fourth defendant had to pay costs only.]

[2 In making this sweeping allegation Engels ignores the existence both of the Poor Law and of numerous private organisations which endeavoured to relieve poverty.]

workers will resort to any expedient to stay the pangs of hunger and will actually eat potato peelings, vegetable waste and even rotten vegetables[1]—in fact they will consume anything that contains even an atom of nourishment. If wages have been spent before the end of the week, then in the period remaining before pay-day the family only gets the barest minimum of food to save them from actual starvation. Such a way of living naturally fosters many illnesses. It is the bread-winner of the family, who is probably engaged in heavy manual labour, and therefore in the greatest need of food, who is the first to fall ill! When this happens the family faces a real crisis and then we can see all too clearly with what callous brutality society treats those who most need assistance.

Let us summarise the facts revealed by our enquiries. The vast majority of the inhabitants of the great towns are workers. Given favourable circumstances, there is only one middle-class inhabitant to two, three and sometimes even four, workers. The workers do not possess any property and nearly all live from hand to mouth on their wages. Society having degenerated into a collection of selfish individuals, no one bothers about the workers and their families. The workers are not given the means whereby they can make satisfactory and permanent provision for their families. Even the most highly-skilled worker is therefore continually threatened with the loss of his liveli-

---

[1] *Weekly Dispatch*, April or May 1844, according to Dr. Southwood Smith's report on the condition of the London poor. [The *Weekly Dispatch* of May 5th, 1844, contains the following passage in the article entitled ' Wild beasts *v.* rational beings ' already quoted: ' Dr. Southwood Smith, in an admirable report which appeared in *The Weekly Dispatch* a few months since, gave a frightful descrip-tion of the dwellings, and a general state of the poor in Whitechapel, Bethnal-green, Southwark, Lambeth, and Westminster, where, in consequence of their pent-up dwellings and their wretched food, which often consists of potato peelings, raw turnips, and decayed vegetables, fever rages in a most fatal and frightful manner'. This was a reference to Dr. Southwood Smith's report on the work of the London Fever Hospital during 1843, summarised in the *Northern Star* of February 24th, 1844, p. 7, col. 3 (see below, p. 112). Dr. Thomas Southwood Smith was a recognised authority on sanitary conditions in the east end of London in the 1830s and 1840s. He was a powerful advocate of sanitary legislation to reduce the incidence of disease in the slums. He reported to the Poor Law Commissioners on the insanitary state of Bethnal Green and Whitechapel in 1838 (see *Parliamentary Papers*, 1837–38, Vol. 28, *Fourth Annual Report* of the Poor Law Commissioners, Appendix A, No. 1, Supplements 2 and 3, pp. 83–96) and on the prevalence of fever in twenty metro-politan Unions or parishes in 1839: *Parliamentary Papers*, 1839, Vol. 20, *Fifth Annual Report* of the Poor Law Commissioners, Appendix C, No. 2. He also gave evidence before the Select Committee on the Health of Towns in 1840 (*Report from the Select Committee on the Health of Towns, Parliamentary Papers*, 1840, Vol. 11). See also evidence of Dr. T. Southwood Smith, questions 1–130, on June 15th, 1843, before the Commissioners for inquiring into the state of large towns and populous districts: *Parliamentary Papers*, 1844, Vol. 20, *First Report*, evidence, pp. 68–86, and R. A. Lewis, *Edwin Chadwick and the Public Health Movement*, 1832–1854 (1954), pp. 394–5.]

hood and that means death by starvation. And many do indeed die in this way. The working-class quarters of the towns are always badly laid out. Their houses are jerry-built and are kept in a bad state of repair. They are badly ventilated, damp and unhealthy. The workers are herded into the smallest possible space and in most cases all the members of (at the least) one family sleep together in a single room. The furnishings and household equipment are poor, and there are some workers' families where even the barest essentials are lacking. The clothing of the workers is also normally inadequate and many workers go about clad in rags. The workers' diet is generally poor and often almost inedible. From time to time many workers' families actually go short of food and in exceptional cases they actually die of hunger. The working classes of the great cities exhibit a variety of standards of living. In favourable circumstances some of them enjoy, at least temporarily, a modest prosperity. Sometimes high wages can be earned, particularly for the hardest kinds of physical labour, and this provides reasonable living accommodation and a respite from the consumption of poor quality food. This standard of living, [poor as it may seem to the middle classes,] is prized by the worker, who has almost certainly known the real meaning of want. In bad times, however, the unlucky worker may sink into the deepest poverty, actually culminating in homelessness and death from starvation. On the average the condition of the worker approximates much more closely to the worst we have described than to the best. The various standards of living cannot be equated with any fixed groups of workers. It is never possible to single out any particular group of workers as permanently enjoying a satisfactory standard of living. While it is true that particular groups of workers have an advantage over their fellows and are relatively well off, nevertheless the condition of all workers is liable to fluctuate so violently that every single worker is faced with the possibility of passing through the stages that lead from relative comfort to extreme poverty and even death from starvation. Practically every English worker can recall considerable vicissitudes in his own personal fortunes. The causes of such changes must now be examined in greater detail.

Chapter IV

COMPETITION

We have shown in our introduction how, at the very beginning of the Industrial Revolution, it was competition that called the working classes into existence. The increased demand for cloth raised the wages of the weavers and so led the peasants who had worked at the loom in their spare time to give up their work on the land in order to earn more by weaving. We have seen how the growth of large farms forced the peasants off their holdings, turned them into wage-earners and then in some cases drove them into the towns. We saw, too, how the lower middle-classes were also to a great extent ruined and depressed to the condition of wage-earners. We have seen capital becoming concentrated into the hands of a small group of people, while the population has been concentrated in the great towns. Those are the various ways and means by which competition both created the working classes and increased their numbers. It is in modern industry that competition first becomes a factor of major importance and has been given free rein to develop unchecked to its furthest limits. We propose to examine the influence of competition on the working-classes of to-day. The effects of competition between the workers themselves and the consequences of such competition may be considered first.

Competition is the most extreme expression of that war of all against all which dominates modern middle-class society. This struggle for existence—which in extreme cases is a life and death struggle—is waged not only between different classes of society but also between individuals within these social groups. Everybody competes in some way against everyone else and consequently each individual tries to push aside anyone whose existence is a barrier to his own advancement. The workers compete among themselves, and so do the middle classes. The powerloom weaver competes with the handloom weaver. Among the handloom weavers themselves there is continual rivalry. Those who are unemployed or poorly paid try to undercut and so destroy the livelihood of those who have work and are earning better wages. This competition of workers among themselves is the worst aspect of the present situation as far as the proletariat is concerned. This is the sharpest weapon which the middle classes wield against the working classes. This explains the rise of trade unions, which represent an attempt to eliminate such fratricidal conflict between the workers themselves. It explains, too, the fury of the middle classes against trade unions, and their ill-concealed delight at any setback which the unions suffer.

The worker is helpless; left to himself he cannot survive a single day. The middle classes have secured a monopoly of all the necessities of life. What the worker needs he can secure only from the middle classes, whose monopoly is protected by the authority of the State. In law and in fact the worker is the slave of the middle classes, who hold the power of life and death over him. The middle classes offer food and shelter to the worker, but only in return for an ' equivalent,' i.e. for his labour. They even disguise the true state of affairs by making it appear that the worker is acting of his own free will, as a truly free agent and as a responsible adult, when he makes his bargain with the middle classes. A fine freedom indeed, when the worker has no choice but to accept the terms offered by the middle classes or go hungry and naked like the wild beasts. A fine ' equivalent ', when it is the bourgeoisie alone which decides the terms of the bargain. And if a worker is such a fool as to prefer to go hungry rather than accept the ' fair ' terms of the middle classes who are his ' natural superiors '[1] —well, then it is easy enough to find another worker. The working classes are numerous enough in all conscience and not all of them are so stupid as to prefer death to life.

This illustrates the effect of competition among the workers themselves. If only all the workers would firmly announce their intention of starving rather than working for the middle classes, then the employers would soon have to surrender their monopoly. Such unity among the workers does not exist and is indeed unlikely to occur. As a result the middle classes are in clover. One thing alone sets a limit to competition between the workers: no worker is prepared to work for a wage which is insufficient to keep body and soul together. If he has got to starve he would rather go hungry in idleness than in work. Even this is only a relative limitation [to the competition of the workers among themselves]. One worker needs more than another, because the former is accustomed to a higher standard of living than the latter. The Englishman, who is not yet wholly uncivilised, needs more than the Irishman, who goes about in rags, eats potatoes and lives in pigsties. This does not prevent the Irishman competing with the Englishman and gradually dragging down his wages and standard of living to his own level. Certain jobs can only be performed by workers who have reached a certain degree of civilisation and prac-

[1] A favourite expression of English industrialists.

tically all industrial employment falls into this category. Consequently wages for these jobs must, in the interests of the middle classes themselves, be high enough to maintain the living standards of the worker at a level appropriate to the job. The newly-arrived immigrant from Ireland would make a poor factory worker. His level of culture is so low that he camps in the first stables that he comes across and if he got a decent cottage he would be evicted every week because he squanders his wages in drink and cannot pay the rent. It is also in the interests of the middle classes that factory wages should be high enough to enable the workers to bring up their children, who will in due course be fit for regular industrial employment. On the other hand, the worker's wages must be low enough to force him to send his children to the factory rather than encourage them to improve their lot by training for something better than mere factory labour. From this point of view, too, the limits set to competition among the workers themselves—the minimum wage necessary for existence—is relative. When an entire family is working the wages of the individual can be cut down [so long as the income of the whole family is adequate to maintain life]. The middle classes have craftily succeeded in depressing men's wages, while at the same time they draw profit from the work of women and children in factories made possible by the new machinery. Of course it is not possible for every member of every worker's family to find employment in the factory. And it would go hard with a family which included only one or two members who were employed in the factory, if the rates of wages paid to them were calculated on the assumption that several more members of the family were wage earners. In practice actual wage-rates must therefore be a little higher than those which could be paid if all workers' families included a large number of wage-earners. Consequently a household which includes a number of wage-earners is fairly well off, while a household where there are only one or two wage-earners can barely make ends meet. But an unemployed worker prefers to give up the little luxuries to which he has been accustomed rather than to have no wages coming in at all. He would rather sleep in a pigsty than in the open air; he would rather wear rags than go naked; he would rather live on potatoes than go hungry. He would rather be satisfied with half wages—in the hope that conditions will improve—than drop down dead in the street from lack of food, as not a few workers have done. This pittance, therefore, this something a little more than nothing is ' minimum wages '.[1] And if there are more workers than the middle

[1 It will be seen from this definition that Engels uses the term ' minimum wage ' in a different sense from modern usage.]

classes are pleased to employ—if the full play of competition between workers still leaves a pool of unemployed—then there is nothing for it but that the surplus workers should starve, because the middle classes probably will not be prepared to find jobs for men unless the goods they produce can be sold at a profit. This explains the phenomenon of the 'minimum wage'.

On the other hand the 'maximum wage' is fixed by the competition among members of the middle classes. It has already been seen that competition also exists within this social group. Members of the middle classes can increase their capital only by engaging in commerce or industry. In either case the services of workers are essential. Even if members of the middle classes invest their capital they still need the services of workpeople in an indirect way, because it is only by using the money in commerce or industry that the borrower is in a position to pay any interest. Although, in a general sense, the middle classes are dependent upon the workers, this does not mean that the middle classes depend upon the workers for their daily needs. After all, at a pinch, the middle classes can live upon their accumulated capital. The middle classes use the workers not to live but to enrich themselves in the same way as they use an article of commerce or a beast of burden. The workers fashion the goods which the middle classes sell at a profit. If the demand for these goods increases to such an extent that there is full employment or even a surplus of jobs for workers who are normally competing for them, competition between the workers themselves ceases and competition among the middle classes begins. The capitalist who is looking for workers knows very well that rising prices, due to an increasing demand for goods, raise profits and so he is prepared to pay somewhat higher wages rather than to lose his profits altogether. He throws out a sprat to catch a mackerel and if he succeeds in landing the mackerel he gladly lets the worker have the sprat. If two or more capitalists are chasing one worker then wages rise. This increase, however, is limited by the increase in the demand [for goods]. The capitalist may well be prepared to sacrifice a little of the increased profits [due to the increased demand for goods] but he takes good care not to give up any part of his 'normal' profits and if that danger should arise he is careful not to pay more than 'average' wages.

These considerations enable us to determine the 'average' rate of wages. Conditions may be regarded as 'normal' when there is no intensification of the usual competition either among the workers or among the capitalists. This state of affairs exists when exactly the right number of workers are available for employment to produce precisely the correct quantity of goods to satisfy current demands. In such a state of equilibrium wages will be a little more than the ' minimum '. The extent to which the level of the ' average ' wage is above that of the ' minimum ' wage depends upon the standard of living and the level of culture of the workers. If the workers are accustomed to eat meat several times a week then the capitalists have to face the fact that they must pay wages sufficiently high to make such a diet possible. The capitalist is not in a position to pay less than this, because [in a state of equilibrium] the workers are not competing among themselves and therefore cannot be compelled to reduce their standard of living. On the other hand the capitalist will not pay a higher level of wages, because [in a state of equilibrium] the capitalists are not competing amongst themselves and have no incentive to try to attract labour by offering higher wages or other special inducements.

We have already explained that the average standard of living and average level of culture vary from one group of workers to another and are determined by complicated factors called into existence by modern industry in England. They are therefore difficult to measure. Most industrial activities demand the steady application of a certain degree of skill, and this—combined with the need for maintaining a reasonable standard of living for the worker—makes it necessary for the employer to pay wages which will induce the worker to acquire the necessary skill and the habit of regular work. This is why the wages of industrial workers are normally higher than those engaged in unskilled or irregular labour [e.g. porters, dockers and coal heavers]. Industrial wages are considerably higher than those paid to farm labourers. Another factor favouring higher wages in industry as compared with agriculture is the high cost of living in the towns. In plain English, the worker is both legally and in fact the slave of the middle-class capitalists. He is a slave because he is sold in the same way as goods are sold. The price of the worker rises and falls like the prices of goods. If the demand for workers increases, then the cost of employing a worker goes up. If the demand for labour falls, then the cost of the worker falls. Should the demand for labour fall so low that some of the workers cannot be sold and have to remain ' warehoused ', they are simply abandoned to idleness and since they cannot live for ever without wages, they die of hunger. In the jargon of the economists, the unemployed worker would not ' reproduce ' the money which would have to be spent in maintaining him in idleness. Such money would simply be thrown away, and no one does that with his capital. To this extent Malthus's theory of population is quite correct. The only difference between the old-fashioned slavery and the new is that while the former was openly acknowledged the latter is disguised. The worker *appears* to be free, because he is not bought and sold outright. He is sold piecemeal by the day, the week, or the year. Moreover he is not sold by one owner to another, but he is forced to sell himself in this fashion. He is not the slave of a single individual, but of the whole capitalist class. As far as the worker is concerned, however, there can be no doubt as to his servile status. It is true that the apparent liberty which the worker enjoys does give him some *real* freedom. Even this genuine freedom has the disadvantage that no one is responsible for providing him with food and shelter. His real masters, the middle-class capitalists, can discard him at any moment and leave him to starve, if they have no further use for his services and no further interest in his survival. These arrangements are much more favourable to the middle classes than was the old system of slavery. They can now get rid of their workers whenever it pleases them without losing any of their capital. Adam Smith has consoled the middle-class capitalists by pointing out that they secure their labour at a much cheaper rate than they would do if they were slave owners.[1]

From this it follows that Adam Smith is also quite right when he lays down the principle ' that the demand for men, like that for any other commodity, necessarily regulates the production of men; quickens it when it goes on too slowly, and stops it when it advances too fast '.[2] *Like that of any other commodity*—if too little labour is available, then its cost, that is to say, wages, rise, and the condition of the worker improves. In such circumstances, more workers marry and the population increases. This goes on until the working-class population has increased sufficiently to meet the demand for labour. On the other hand, if too much labour is available, its cost [i.e. wages] falls, and shortage of food, distress and starvation lead to epidemics carrying off the ' surplus population '. Malthus, who elaborated Adam Smith's observations on the subject of wages, was also correct, according to his lights, when he asserted that there was always a superfluous

[1] Adam Smith, *An Inquiry into the Nature and Causes of the Wealth of Nations* (ed. J. R. MCulloch, 1st edn., vol. 1, 1828, p. 134): ' The wear and tear of a slave, it has been said, is at the expense of his master; but that of a free servant is at his own expense. The wear and tear of the latter, however, is, in reality, as much at the expense of his master as that of the former. The wages paid to journeymen and servants of every kind must be such as may enable them, one with another, to continue the race of journeymen and servants, according as the increasing, diminishing, or stationary demand of the society may happen to require. But though the wear and tear of a free servant be equally at the expense of his master, it generally costs him much less than that of a slave. The fund destined for replacing or repairing, if I may say so, the wear and tear of the slave, is commonly managed by a negligent master or careless overseer.' [2] Adam Smith, op. cit., p. 133.

population in existence. Malthus argued that there were always too many people in the world. He was wrong when he expressed the view that more people existed than could be fed from available resources. The real reason for the existence of the superfluous population is the competition of the workers among themselves. This forces the individual worker to do as much work in a day as is humanly possible. If a factory owner who employs ten workers for nine hours a day finds that nine of them are willing to work for ten hours a day, then he can turn one of his workers on to the street and get the job done by the other nine. At a time when the demand for labour is not very great, the employer can force nine of his workers, on pain of dismissal, to work for an extra hour, i.e. ten hours instead of nine, for the same wages, then he can dismiss the tenth worker, and save the money formerly spent on his wages.[1]

The same process, on a much larger scale, takes place in the country as a whole. A number of workers lose their means of subsistence for various reasons, such as the competition of the workers among themselves, which forces each worker to labour to his maximum capacity; the division of labour; the introduction of machinery; the subjugation of the forces of nature. These unemployed workers are deprived of their purchasing power in the markets. They are no longer consumers. The goods which they formerly demanded are no longer needed and therefore it is no longer necessary to manufacture them. Consequently the workers engaged in making these goods are thrown out of work and themselves cease to be consumers. And so a vicious spiral is engendered, which would continue indefinitely were it not for the intervention of a new factor in the situation. This is because the increased industrial productivity, brought about by the methods already described, eventually leads to a fall in the prices of manufactured goods and consequently to increased consumption. The result is that a large number of the unemployed workers, after a long period of distress, eventually find employment in new kinds of jobs. It must be remembered, too, that in the past sixty years English manufacturers have been conquering new overseas markets, which has led to a rapid and continuous expansion in demand. This in turn has led to an increase in the demand for labour which has fostered a proportionate growth in population. Far from declining, the popula-

[1 The difference between the two cases does not seem to be very clear. It may be that in the first instance Engels assumes that the dismissal of the tenth worker is caused by competition between the workers themselves, i.e. the initiative for the dismissal of the tenth worker comes in effect from the other nine. In the second instance the initiative is taken by the employer at a time when the demand for labour is low.]

tion of the United Kingdom has been expanding rapidly and this increase continues. The ' official ' parties—Tories, Whigs and Radicals —all deplore the continued existence of a large ' surplus population ' and there can be no doubt that competition between the workers themselves has been greater than the competition between employers for the services of workers. Yet the tempo of industrial expansion has been increasing and, on the whole, there has been, in England, an ever-increasing demand for labour.

Here is an apparent contradiction which requires elucidation. The explanation is to be sought in the very nature of modern industry and competition and the commercial crises to which they give rise. In the modern world both industrial production and the division of the means of subsistence are wholly unplanned; no attempt is made to satisfy undoubted needs. On the contrary profits alone determine what shall be produced and who shall consume it. Everyone works on his own with an eye to his own profits. It is hardly surprising that such a system should be continually breaking down. England, for example, supplies a number of countries with a very wide variety of manufactured goods. The individual manufacturer may well know how many articles of a particular kind are consumed annually in particular countries, but he does not know how many goods are being stored abroad. Still less does he know how many goods his competitors are exporting. All he can do is to make estimates of a dubious character about such matters from the evidence of continually fluctuating prices. He exports his goods in the hope that they will be absorbed by the market. He sends everything blindly overseas and leaves the rest to chance.[1] On the slightest indication that some particular market is a favourable one, everyone exports as much as possible and consequently such a market is soon overstocked. There follows a fall both in sales and cash returns and before long English industry has no more employment to offer the workers. In the early phase of the Industrial Revolution these crises were confined to particular branches of trade and particular markets. In time, however, the small individual crises coalesced and they have now developed into a recurrent cycle of major depressions. This development has been due to the unifying force of competition. The unemployed workers of one branch of industry are thrown on to such other branches of manufacture as are easiest for them to learn. Similarly goods which are superfluous in one overseas market are thrown on to other markets. A crisis now comes once every five years, after a short

[1 For the auction system in the export trade in textiles see N. S. Buck, *The Development of the Organisation of Anglo-American Trade* (1925), pp. 135-148].

period of boom for the manufacturers and prosperity for the workers. In times of depression, home and foreign markets are glutted with English manufactured goods and their disposal inevitably takes time. Practically all branches of industry are adversely affected. There are failures among the smaller factory owners and those merchants who cannot carry on without the remittances due to them. At the height of the crisis the larger manufacturers transact no business. They either close their factories or put their workers on 'short time', i.e. about half a day. Wages fall owing to competition between the unemployed as well as the reduction of working hours and the lack of profitable orders. The workers suffer great distress. The small savings of the individual worker are soon spent and charitable organizations are overwhelmed with appeals for help. The poor rates are doubled or even trebled and, even so, are inadequate to alleviate the distress. The number of those who are starving increases and general panic is created by the sudden realisation of the existence of a great mass of 'superfluous population'. This state of affairs continues for some time. The 'superfluous' workers may or may not survive. The charitable organizations and the poor law authorities provide enough relief to enable a number of the miserable unemployed to keep body and soul together. Other workers manage to survive by finding work in such branches of manufacture as are less affected by competition, or they follow an occupation which is not connected with industry. It is astonishing on what a low standard of life survival for the worker is still possible. Gradually the state of trade improves. The goods which have been warehoused are consumed. Manufacturers and merchants, depressed by the vicissitudes of trade, hesitate to resume production quickly and to fill the gaps in stocks caused by the revival in consumption. Eventually, however, rising prices, combined with more favourable reports of trade prospects, encourage manu-facturers to increase production. Most of the markets are distant ones; while these new exports are on the high seas, the demand for goods is increasing continuously and consequently prices are also rising. When the first exports reach their destination they are eagerly snapped up. These first sales stimulate trade still further. Exporters are now tempted by still higher prices to send more goods overseas. Traders now speculate in anticipation of still higher prices and divert to overseas markets supplies which are badly needed at home. Specu-lation increases prices still further as new traders enter the [foreign] markets and buy up [English] goods as quickly as they arrive. When news of this boom reaches England the wheels of industry turn quickly once more. New factories are built and every means used to profit from the favourable turn of events. Here again speculation takes a hand, with the same results as those already noted in foreign markets. Prices rise, goods are diverted from home to overseas markets, and these two factors together encourage manufacturers to the greatest possible efforts. Now come the speculators who are mere men of straw. These are traders who live on credit and work with fictitious capital. They would be ruined if they did not sell at once the goods passing through their hands. These men fling themselves into the universal and frenzied race for profits. The hectic scramble for orders and for a quick turnover, in which these speculators indulge, increases the prevailing confusion and drives up both prices and output to fantastic heights. It is a crazy struggle, in which even the most sober and experienced businessmen take a hand. The ironworks, the spinning mills and the weaving sheds become hives of activity. One would think that all humanity needed to be supplied and that some thousands of millions of new consumers had been discovered on the moon. [Suddenly the situation changes.] Speculators abroad, who have no capital behind them, need cash quickly and have to sell goods which they are holding at a sacrifice. One such sale soon leads to others. The whole price-structure is undermined. Panic-stricken speculators frantically offer their goods at cut prices, and the market becomes disorganized; credit is shattered. One firm after another stops payment. Bankruptcy follows upon bankruptcy. Then merchants realise that they have in their warehouses or on the high seas three times as many goods as are ever likely to be sold. When news of this state of affairs reaches England—where in the meantime production has gone on unceasingly—the whole business world is engulfed by a wave of panic. English firms are dragged to ruin by the failures abroad. Output now declines and this leads to more failures. In England, as abroad, all available goods are thrown onto the market at once, and this increases the panic still further. That is how a commercial crisis begins. From then onwards trade develops in the way that has already been described, and in due course depression gives way to boom. And so it goes on. English industry passes through a continuous series of cycles of boom and slump. It has been seen that each cycle lasts for about five or six years.[1]

Consequently English industry must always have a reserve of unemployed workers, except during the short period when the boom is at its height. The existence of such a reserve is essential in order

[1 For a modern view of the trade cycle for the period when Engels was writing, see R. C. O. Matthews, *A Study in Trade-Cycle History: Economic Fluctuations in Great Britain*, 1833–1842 (1954).]

that labour may be available to produce the great quantities of goods which are needed during the few months when the business boom reaches its climax. The size of this reserve varies with the state of trade. When trade is good and more hands are wanted the number of workers in the pool of unemployed declines. For a time, at the height of the boom, the labour force is supplemented by drawing upon workers from the agricultural districts, from Ireland and from those branches of industry not affected by the boom. These workers are a minority of the additional hands engaged, but they, too, belong to the pool of unemployed. These groups of workers differ from the main body inasmuch as it is only at times of exceptionally good trade that they realise that they are in fact part of the reserve army of labour[1] [upon which the capitalists can call in time of need]. Employers who lose workers in this way during the height of a boom deal with the situation by imposing longer hours of work upon their employees and by using the labour of women and young people. When the boom is over many of the workers temporarily engaged in busy trades find that their former jobs have been filled and that their services are no longer required. During a slump the reserve of unemployed swells to formidable dimensions. Even when trade is moderately active—in between the extremes of boom and depression—there are still many workers who are unemployed. This pool of unemployed is the ' surplus population ' of England. When they are out of work these people eke out a miserable existence by begging and stealing, by sweeping the streets, by collecting horse-dung, by pushing barrows or driving donkey-carts, by hawking and peddling and by turning their hands to anything that will bring in a copper or two. In all the big towns one can see many people of this type, who—as the English say —' keep body and soul together ' by doing odd jobs. It is remarkable what tasks the ' surplus population ' will perform. The London crossing sweepers[2] are famous all over the world. It is not only in the capital but also in other big cities that the services of the unemployed have been used in this way by the municipalities and poor law authorities. Now, however, machines have been invented to do this work and they rattle through the streets every day and deprive the unemployed of an opportunity of getting work.[3] On all the main

[[1] This doctrine of the 'reserve army of labour' appears to have been first enunciated in *The Northern Star* of June 23, 1838: Sir John Clapham, *Economic History of Modern Britain*, Vol. I (1926), p. 557.]
[[2] Engels added in English the words ' cross sweeps '.]
[[3] For Whitworth's patent road-sweeping machine in the 1840s see A. Redford and I. S. Russell, *History of Local Government in Manchester*, Vol. 1 (1939), pp. 368-9 and Vol. 2, pp. 141, 162-6.]

roads leading into big towns there is a great deal of wheeled traffic, and a large number of people are to seen with little carts in which they collect freshly-dropped horse-dung for sale. At the risk of their lives these people dart on to the street between fast moving carriages and omnibuses. Frequently they have to pay a few shillings a week for the privilege of collecting the dung. In many places, however, the practice of collecting it is prohibited because the local authorities sell the street refuse and their customers will not accept it as manure unless it contains the right proportion of horse dung. One of the 'surplus population' who possesses a handcart considers himself fortunate in that he can earn a trifle by fetching and carrying. Still more fortunate is he who can raise enough money to become the proud possessor of a donkey as well as a cart. The donkey has to forage for himself. The most he is likely to get from his master is a little vegetable refuse. Even so the donkey can bring in a little money. Most of the 'surplus population' are engaged in petty trading. Particularly on Saturday evenings, when practically the whole working class population is to be found on the streets, it is possible to get an impression of the large numbers of people who get a living from petty trading. Countless men, women and children are offering for sale shoe laces, braces, string, oranges, cakes and all sorts of other articles. On other days, too, one can at any moment see these pedlars either standing in the streets or on the move offering their oranges, cakes, ginger-beer or nettle-beer.[1] Among other articles sold by these pedlars are such things as matches, sealing-wax, and patent fire-lighters. Then there are the odd-job men[2] who go from street to street looking for occasional work. A few may be lucky enough to get a day's work, but many are less fortunate. The Rev. W. Champneys, one of the incumbents of East London, writes:

> At the gates of each of the [London] docks, hundreds of poor men may be seen before day-break waiting for the opening of the gates in the hope of obtaining a day's work; and when the youngest and most able-bodied, and those best known, have been engaged, hundreds still may be seen returning to their destitute families with that 'sickness of heart' which arises from 'hope deferred'.[3]

---

[1] These are two fizzy, cooling drinks. The first is made from water, sugar and some ginger; the second from sugar, water and nettles. They are popular drinks among the workers, especially with those who practise temperance.

[[2] Engels used the word 'jobbers' in English.]

[[3] *Northern Star*, no. 338, May 4th, 1844, p. 6, col. 2 (quoting the *Weekly Dispatch*). See also Champneys's letter to the *Northern Star*, no. 317, Dec. 9th, 1843, p. 6, col. 1. William Weldon Champneys (1807–75) was Rector of St. Mary's, Whitechapel for twenty-three years (1837–60). He set up one of the first 'ragged schools'

If these people can find no work and are not prepared to rebel against society, what else can they do but beg? No wonder that there exists a great army of beggars, mostly able-bodied men, with whom the police are in perpetual conflict. The way in which these men beg is somewhat peculiar. They perambulate the streets with their families, appealing to the benevolence of the charitable by singing doleful ballads or by reciting an account of their misfortunes. It is very noticeable that such beggars are to be found only in working-class districts and that they subsist almost exclusively on the charity of the working classes. Sometimes the whole family will stand immobile, and, without saying a word, will allow the mere sight of their helplessness to plead for them. They, too, rely solely on the sympathy of the workers, who know from personal experience what it is like to go hungry and who themselves may at any moment share the same fate. Those who make this silent but very moving appeal are to be found practically only in such streets as are frequented by the workers themselves and at such times as it is likely that many workers will pass by. This is particularly true of Saturday evenings. Indeed it is at that time that the ' secrets ' of life in the working-class districts are revealed in the main streets of a town. Consequently, at such times members of the middle classes do not frequent the districts sullied by the presence of the workers. Those members of the ' surplus population ', who—goaded by their distress—summon up enough courage to revolt openly against society become thieves and murderers. They wage open warfare against the middle classes, who have for so long waged secret warfare against them.

According to the reports of the Poor Law Commissioners the average size of the ' surplus population ' in England and Wales is 1½ million.[1] The average number of unemployed in Scotland cannot be estimated because of the absence of a poor law.[2] We shall discuss below the question of unemployment in Ireland. The one and a half million English unemployed include only those who apply to the poor

in London and founded a workers' provident society and a shoeblack brigade. Engels spelt the name ' Champney ' and the error was repeated in Mrs. Wischnewetzky's translation. For Champneys see the *Dictionary of National Biography*, and obituary notices in *The Guardian*, February 10th, 1875, p. 168 and February 17th, 1875, p. 209.]

[1 The number of paupers relieved in England and Wales during the quarter ending Lady-day 1842 was 1,429,356: *Journal of the Statistical Society of London*, Vol. 6 (1843), p. 256. See also T. Carlyle, *Past and Present* (1843), p. 2, fn. 1 (Everyman edn., 1912.)]

[2 This is incorrect. For a list of sources on the Scottish poor law in the nineteenth century see, for example W.O. Henderson, ' The Cotton Famine in Scotland and the relief of distress ': *Scottish Historical Review*, Vol. 30, no. 110, p. 157, *n*. 5.]

law authorities for assistance. Many of those who are out of work are most reluctant to apply for relief and they are therefore not included in the poor law statistics. On the other hand, a fairly high proportion of the one and a half million come from the country districts and with these we are not at the moment concerned. When there is a slump this average figure is, of course, greatly increased, and at the climax of a trade depression a very large number of people are out of work. We propose to examine the situation that occurred at the time of the crisis of 1842. This is not only the most recent, but also the most serious, of England's commercial crises. Each depression is more serious than the one which preceded it. The next crisis is due to occur in 1847 at the latest[1] and, as far as one can judge, it will last longer and will be of a more serious character. During the crisis of 1842, poor rates rose to record heights in all the towns. In Stockport, for example, these rates amounted to 8s. in the £, so that the poor rate alone amounted to an addition of 40 per cent to the rents paid by householders. A number of streets in Stockport were uninhabited and the population declined by at least 20,000. On the doors of empty houses were to be found the words: ' Stockport to let '.[2] In Bolton in an average year the rateable value for poor law purposes was £86,000. In 1842, however, it fell to £36,000, and at the same time the number of paupers increased to 14,000, which was more than 20 per cent of the entire population. In Leeds in 1842 the poor law authorities had £10,000 in reserve. Both this sum and a further £7,000 were spent before the crisis reached its height. This state of affairs was universal. A report was made in January 1843 by a committee of the Anti-Corn Law League which described conditions in the previous year based upon detailed information supplied by manufacturers.[3] This report states that the poor rate was generally twice as high in 1842 as it had been in 1839. The number of persons applying for poor relief was three times—sometimes even five times—greater in 1842 than in 1839. It was stated further that many of the paupers belonged to a class of people who did not usually apply for poor relief

[1 In the first English edition (published in New York in 1887) Engels added in a footnote: 'And it came in 1847 '.]

[2 In English in the original German edition. For the exceptionally severe effects of the economic crisis of 1836–42 in Stockport, see *The Report of the Statistical Committee appointed by the Anti-Corn Law Conference, held in London on March 8th, 9th, 10th, 11th and 12th, 1842* (London, n.d. ? 1842), pp. 32–3, and *A copy of the Evidence taken and Report made, by the Assistant Poor Law Commissioners sent to enquire into the state of the population of Stockport: Parliamentary Papers,* 1842, vol. 35, no. 158, passim.]

[3 This report of the Committee of Manufactures of the Anti-Corn Law League is summarised in the *Manchester Guardian,* Feb. 4th, 1843, p. 5, col. 6.]

According to the report, the amount of food consumed by the working classes fell in 1842 to one-third of what they had eaten in 1834–6. The consumption of meat in particular declined sharply. In some places the decline amounted to only 20 per cent, but in others it was as much as 60 per cent. The report also stated that even skilled craftsmen, such as blacksmiths and bricklayers, who are normally busy even in times of trade depression, suffered from reductions in earnings and lack of work on this occasion. As late as January 1843 the earnings of these craftsmen were still falling. All this information is derived from a report drawn up by factory owners themselves. The hungry workers, whose employers had closed their factories and turned them adrift, were to be found everywhere begging, either singly or in groups. Crowds of them invaded the main thoroughfares and pestered those who passed by. They did not appeal for help in any servile fashion, but adopted a threatening attitude. Their large numbers, their gestures and their demands for money were calculated to put fear into the hearts of passers-by. This occurred in all the industrial districts from Leicester to Leeds and from Manchester to Birmingham. Here and there sporadic disturbances occurred, as in the Potteries of North Staffordshire. The greatest excitement prevailed among the workers and this culminated in severe rioting throughout the factory districts in August. When I arrived in Manchester at the end of 1842 many unemployed were still standing at street corners and many factories were still idle. Between then and the middle of 1843 the situation improved. The factory wheels began to turn again and those who had been lounging at street corners through no fault of their own gradually disappeared.

I need hardly attempt to describe the various degrees of want and misery suffered by the unemployed during such a crisis. Poor rates are quite insufficient to deal with the situation. The charity of the wealthy is a mere drop in the ocean, the effect of which lasts only a moment. When so many are in want begging is of little avail. In times of crisis the petty shopkeepers give the unemployed credit for as long as they can, recouping themselves eventually by charging a high rate of interest on the debts. Moreover, the workers help each other in times of trouble. It is only by these means that large numbers of the surplus population manage to survive a crisis. Were it not for credit from shopkeepers and the self-help of the poor, thousands of the unemployed would die of hunger in times of trade depression. The period of really acute distress is usually short, lasting for a year— at the most two or two and a half years—and so most of the unemployed manage to survive, but only after severe privations. We propose to examine later certain indirect consequences which follow upon each crisis. Thousands of workers fall victims to illnesses caused by malnutrition. In the meantime, however, we shall turn our attention to another factor which contributes to the degradation of the English worker. This factor [—the immigration of the Irish—] continually operates to depress the standard of life of the working classes to even lower levels.

Chapter V

IRISH IMMIGRATION

We have already had occasion to refer several times to the Irish who have settled in England; and we now propose to discuss in greater detail the causes and effects of this Irish immigration.

The rapid expansion of British industry could not have taken place if there had not been available a reserve of labour among the poverty-stricken people of Ireland. The Irish had nothing to lose at home and much to gain in England. From the time that the Irish realised that across St. George's Channel strong able-bodied men could find permanent employment at good wages, hordes of them have flocked to Great Britain every year. It has been estimated that so far over a million have emigrated to Britain, and fifty thousand more are coming in year by year. Nearly all of them settle in the big cities of the industrial areas, where they form the lowest stratum of the community. There are 120,000 Irish poor in London, 40,000 in Manchester, 34,000 in Liverpool, 24,000 in Bristol, 40,000 in Glasgow and 29,000 in Edinburgh.[1] These folk have grown up in a virtually uncivilized condition. From childhood they have been accustomed to a life of austerity. They are uncouth, improvident, and addicted to drink. They introduce their brutal behaviour into a section of English society by no means noted for civilized habits or moral principles. Let Thomas Carlyle speak on this subject:

The wild Milesian features, looking false ingenuity, restlessness, unreason, misery and mockery, salute you on all highways and byways. The English coachman, as he whirls past, lashes the Milesian with his whip, curses him with his tongue; the Milesian is holding out his hat to beg. He is the sorest evil this country has to strive with. In his rags and laughing savagery, he is there to undertake all work that can be done by mere strength of hand and back; for wages that will purchase him potatoes. He needs only salt for condiment; he lodges to his mind in any pighutch or dog-hutch, roosts in outhouses; and wears a suit of tatters, the getting off and on of which is said to be a difficult operation, transacted only in festivals and the hightides of the calendar. The Saxon man if he

---

[1] Archibald Alison, *The Principles of Population* . . . , 2 vols. 1840. This Alison is the historian of the French Revolution and, like his brother, Dr. W. P. Alison, is a religious Tory. [See A. Alison, op. cit., Vol 1, p. 529 footnote, where the figure for Manchester is 38,000 and not 40,000.]

cannot work on these terms, finds no work . . . the uncivilised
Irishman, not by his strength but by the opposite of strength, drives
out the Saxon native, takes possession in his room. There abides he,
in his squalor and unreason, in his falsity and drunken violence, as
the ready-made nucleus of degradation and disorder. Whosoever
struggles, swimming with difficulty, may now find an example how
the human being can exist not swimming but sunk.

That the condition of the lower multitude of English labourers
approximates more and more to that of the Irish competing with
them in all markets; that whatsoever labour, to which mere strength
with little skill will suffice, is to be done, will be done not at the
English price, but at an approximation to the Irish price: at a price
superior as yet to the Irish, that is, superior to scarcity of third-rate
potatoes for thirty weeks yearly; superior, yet hourly, with the arrival
of every new steamboat, sinking nearer to an equality with that.[1]

Carlyle's description is a perfectly true one, if we overlook his exaggerated and prejudiced defamation of the Irish national character.
These Irish workers pay only fourpence passage-money to get to
England and they are often packed like cattle on the deck of the steamboat. They are to be found everywhere. The worst accommodation is
good enough for them; they take no trouble with regard to their
clothes which hang in tatters; they go barefoot. They live solely on
potatoes and any money left over from the purchase of potatoes goes
on drink. Such folk do not need high wages. The slums of all the big
towns swarm with Irish. One may depend upon seeing mainly Celtic
faces, if ever one penetrates into a district which is particularly noted
for its filth and decay. These faces are quite different from those of
the Anglo-Saxon population and are easily recognisable. The Irish,
of course, can also be identified by their accent, for the true Irishman
seldom loses the sing-song, lilting brogue of his native country. I
have even heard the native Irish language spoken in the most densely-
populated parts of Manchester. The majority of cellar-dwellers are
nearly always Irish in origin. In short, as Dr. Kay has pointed out,
the Irish have discovered ' what is the minimum of the means of life,
upon which existence may be prolonged . . . and this secret has been
taught the labourers of this country by the Irish '.[2] The Irish have
also brought with them filth and intemperance. Dirty habits, which
have become second nature to the Irish, do no great harm in the
countryside where the population is scattered. On the other hand, the
dangerous situation which develops when such habits are practised

---

[1] T. Carlyle, *Chartism* (1839), pp. 28–9, 31–2.

[[2] Dr. J. P. Kay, *The Moral and Physical Condition of the Working Classes employed
in the Cotton Manufacture in Manchester* (1832), 2nd edn., p. 21.]

among the crowded population of big cities, must arouse feelings of apprehension and disgust. Among the nasty habits which the Irish have brought with them is that of emptying all their filth and refuse out of the front door, and this causes filthy puddles and heaps of garbage to accumulate and so a whole district is rapidly polluted. The Irish have brought with them the habit of building pigsties immediately adjacent to their houses. If that is not possible, the Irishman allows the pig to share his own sleeping quarters. This new, abnormal method of rearing livestock in the large towns is entirely of Irish origin. The Irishman loves his pig as much as the Arab loves his horse. The only difference is that the Irishman sells his pig when it is fat enough for slaughter. The Irishman eats and sleeps with his pig, the children play with the pig, ride on its back and roll about in the filth with it. Thousands of examples of this may be seen in all the big cities of England. Only those who have actually seen this state of affairs can form an adequate idea how impossible it is to find any home comforts in such incredibly filthy conditions. The Irish are not used to furniture: a heap of straw and a few rags too tattered to wear in the daytime suffice for bedding. The Irish need only a bare plank, a broken chair and an old chest for a table. All that the Irishwoman needs in her kitchen are a teapot, a few saucepans and coarse dishes. The kitchen also serves as a living room and bedroom. If an Irishman is short of fuel, everything within reach is thrown on the fire—chairs, door posts, skirting boards, shelves and floor boards, if they are still there. Why should an Irishman want anything more than the minimum accommodation? At home, in Ireland, he lived in a mud cabin where a single room sufficed for all purposes. In England, too, his family needs no more than one room. And, owing to the immigration of the Irish, this custom of living in one room has spread widely among the English as well. The poor devil must get some pleasure out of life and so he goes and drinks spirits. Society has debarred him from other pleasures. Two things make life supportable to the Irishman—his whiskey and his lively, happy-go-lucky disposition. He drinks himself into a state of brutish intoxication. Everything combines to drive the Irishman to drink—his light-hearted temperament, akin to that of the Mediterranean peoples, his coarseness, which drags him down virtually to the level of a savage, his contempt for all normal human pleasures, which he is incapable of appreciating because of his degraded condition, combined with his dirty habits and his abject poverty. The temptation is so great, that he cannot resist it; whenever he has any money in his pocket he tosses it down his throat in the form of whiskey. What else is to be expected? Society treats him in such a way that it is virtually impossible for him to avoid becoming a drunkard. Society neglects the Irish and allows them to sink into a state bordering upon savagery. How can society complain when the Irishman does, in fact, become a habitual drunkard?

It is with such people that the English workers have to compete. They are competitors whose standard of living is the lowest conceivable in a civilised country and consequently they are able to work for lower wages than anyone else. In the circumstances Carlyle is right when he observes that in all occupations where English and Irish workers compete it is inevitable that the wages earned by the English should be continually forced down to even lower levels. There are many such occupations. All occupations which demand little or no skill are open to the Irish. Of course, the dissolute, volatile, and drunken Irish are unfitted for tasks which demand either a regular apprenticeship or that degree of skill which can only be secured by a long period of unremitting application to one's job. In order to become a mechanic—the English term ' mechanic ' includes all those accustomed to handling machinery—or a skilled factory worker, the Irishman would first have to assimilate English civilisation and customs. In other words he would have to become an Englishman. The Irishman, however, is just as capable as the Englishman of undertaking simple tasks involving brute strength rather than skill and precision. So workers in occupations of this kind have to face a flood of Irish competitors, for example, handloom weavers, builders' labourers, porters and odd-job men. Thousands of Irish gain their livelihood in doing jobs of this kind, and it is in these occupations that the infiltration of the Irish on a large scale has led to a lowering of wages, a decline in the standard of life of the workers. And even if the immigrant Irish in other occupations were forced to become more civilised they would still retain a sufficient number of bad habits to have a degrading effect upon their English fellow-workers. An Irish environment would undoubtedly be detrimental to English standards of conduct. A fifth or a quarter of the workers in every big town are either immigrant Irish or the English-born children of immigrant Irish, who have grown up in Irish filth. It is not therefore surprising that the life of the entire working class has been deeply influenced by the strong Irish element in its environment. The habits and the intellectual and moral attitudes—indeed the whole character—of the working class, have been strongly influenced by the Irish immigrants. So it is not surprising that a social class already degraded by industrialisation and its immediate consequences should be still further degraded by having to live alongside and compete with the uncivilised Irish.

CHAPTER VI

RESULTS OF INDUSTRIALISATION[1]

We have already described in some detail the conditions under which the English urban factory workers live. Now we propose to elaborate this topic somewhat and to draw some further conclusions from the condition of the working classes to-day. Let us see then what has happened to the workers who exist in the conditions we have described. Let us see what sort of people they are, and how industrialisation has affected their bodily, intellectual and moral conditions.

If one individual inflicts a bodily injury upon another which leads to the death of the person attacked we call it manslaughter; on the other hand, if the attacker knows beforehand that the blow will be fatal we call it murder. Murder has also been committed if society[2] places hundreds of workers in such a position that they inevitably come to premature and unnatural ends. Their death is as violent as if they had been stabbed or shot. Murder has been committed if thousands of workers have been deprived of the necessities of life or if they have been forced into a situation in which it is impossible for them to survive. Murder has been committed if the workers have been forced by the strong arm of the law to go on living under such conditions until death inevitably releases them. Murder has been committed if society knows perfectly well that thousands of workers cannot avoid being sacrificed so long as these conditions are allowed to continue. Murder of this sort is just as culpable as the murder committed by an

[1 Engels's rather bald title for this chapter consisted of the single word 'Resultate '.]

[2] Here and elsewhere I speak of society as a responsible entity which has its rights and duties. But by ' society ' I do not mean the whole population, but only that social class which at this moment actually wields political and social authority. It is this class which is responsible for the position of those members of society who are excluded from exercising any political or social authority. In England, as in other civilised countries, this position as the ruling class is held by the middle classes. As this book is being written for German readers there is no need for me to approve the proposition that society as a whole, and in particular the middle classes —which wield social power—have the duty of at least protecting the lives of all individual citizens and must take measures to prevent anybody from starving. If I were writing for the English middle classes I would have to explain this in greater detail [*Note by Engels to first edition.*] *Engels added to the English translation of* 1887: And so it is now in Germany. Our German capitalists are fully up to the English level in this respect at least, in the year of grace, 1886. *Engels added a further note to the German edition of* 1892: How things have changed in the last fifty years. To-day there are members of the English middle classes who recognise that society has duties to the individual citizen—but as for the German middle classes?!?

individual. But if society murders a worker it is a treacherous stab in the back against which the worker cannot defend himself. At first sight it does not appear to be murder at all, because responsibility for the death of the victim cannot be pinned on any individual assailant. Everyone is responsible and yet no one is responsible, because it appears as if the victim has died from natural causes. If a worker dies no one places the responsibility for his death on society, though some would realise that society has failed to take steps to prevent the victim from dying. But it is murder all the same. I shall now have to prove that, every day and every hour, English society commits what the English workers' press rightly denounces as social murder. I shall now have to prove that English society has created for the workers an environment in which they cannot remain healthy or enjoy a normal expectation of life. I shall have to prove that English society gradually undermines the health of the workers and so brings them to an early grave. Moreover I shall also have to prove that English society *is fully aware* how dangerous is this environment to the health and life of the workers, and yet takes no action to reform the situation. I shall have proved my point if I can produce evidence concerning the deaths of workers from such unimpeachable sources as official documents, Parliamentary papers and Government reports. Evidence of this kind proves conclusively that society is aware of the fact that its policy results not in manslaughter but in murder.

It is self-evident that a social class which lives under the conditions that we have described and is so poorly supplied with the most indispensable necessities of existence can enjoy neither good health nor a normal expectation of life. Let us, however, review once more the various factors which have a detrimental effect upon the state of health of the English workers. The concentration of the population in great cities has, in itself, an extremely deleterious influence. The air of London is neither so pure nor so rich in oxygen as that of the countryside; two and a half million pairs of lungs and two hundred and fifty thousand coal fires concentrated in an area of three to four geographical square miles[1] use up an immense amount of oxygen, which can only be replaced with difficulty since the layout of English towns impedes ventilation. The carbon dioxide gas produced by people breathing and fires burning fails to rise from the streets because of its specific gravity and is not dispersed by the winds which blow over the rooftops. The inhabitants of the towns do not take in sufficient oxygen when they breathe and this leads to mental torpor and low physical vitality. Consequently the dwellers in great towns suffer

[1] The German geographical mile is 7.42 kilometres or 4.64 English miles.

from chronic ailments to a greater extent than country people who breathe a purer atmosphere.

On the other hand the town dweller is less exposed to acute attacks of inflammatory disorders. If life in the great towns is unhealthy, how much worse must it be for those who live in the unwholesome atmosphere of the working-class quarters where, as we have already seen, everything combines to pollute the air. In the country no harm may come from having a dung heap near a house, because it is more exposed to the fresh air. In the middle of a big town, on the other hand, it is quite a different matter to have dung heaps in alleys and courts in built up areas where there is no ventilation. Decaying animal and vegetable refuse produces gases which are injurious to health and if these gases are not blown away they pollute the atmosphere. The filth and the stagnant pools in the working class quarters of the great cities have the most deleterious effects upon the health of the inhabitants because they engender just those gases which give rise to disease. The same effect follows from the miasma exuded by foul streams. But that is not the whole story by any means. The way in which the vast mass of the poor are treated by modern society is truly scandalous. They are herded into great cities where they breathe a fouler air than in the countryside which they have left. They are housed in the worst ventilated districts of the towns; they are deprived of all means of keeping clean. They are deprived of water because this is only brought to their houses if someone is prepared to defray the cost of laying the pipes. River water is so dirty as to be useless for cleansing purposes. The poor are forced to throw into the streets all their sweepings, garbage, dirty water, and frequently even disgusting filth and excrement. The poor are deprived of all proper means of refuse disposal and so they are forced to pollute the very districts they inhabit. And this is by no means all. There is no end to the sufferings which are heaped on the heads of the poor. It is notorious that general overcrowding is a characteristic feature of the great towns, but in the working-class quarters people are packed together in an exceptionally small area. Not satisfied with permitting the pollution of the air in the streets, society crams as many as a dozen workers into a single room, so that at night the air becomes so foul that they are nearly suffocated. The workers have to live in damp dwellings. When they live in cellars the water seeps through the floor and when they live in attics the rain comes through the roof. The workers' houses are so badly built that the foul air cannot escape from them. The workers have to wear poor and ragged garments and they have to eat food which is bad, indigestible and adulterated. Their mental

state is threatened by being subjected alternately to extremes of hope
and fear. They are goaded like wild beasts and never have a chance of
enjoying a quiet life. They are deprived of all pleasures except sexual
indulgence and intoxicating liquors. Every day they have to work
until they are physically and mentally exhausted. This forces them to
excessive indulgence in the only two pleasures remaining to them. If
the workers manage to survive this sort of treatment it is only to fall
victims to starvation when a slump occurs and they are deprived of
the little that they once had.

How is it possible that the poorer classes can remain healthy and
have a reasonable expectation of life under such conditions? What
can one expect but that they should suffer from continual outbreaks of
epidemics and an excessively low expectation of life? The physical
condition of the workers shows a progressive deterioration. Let us
examine the facts concerning the health of the workers.

There is ample proof that the dwellings of the workers who live
in the slums, combined with other adverse factors, give rise to many
illnesses. The article in the *Artizan*[1] which we have already quoted is
perfectly right in stating that lung diseases must inevitably follow in
such living conditions and are in fact particularly rife among the
workers.[2] The flushed appearance of many of the passers-by in the
streets of London indicates to what an extent the polluted atmosphere
of the capital, particularly in the workers' quarters, fosters the prevalence of consumption. If one goes into the streets of London, when
people are on their way to work, it is astonishing to note how many of
them appear to be suffering to a greater or lesser degree from consumption. Even in Manchester one does not see these pale, emaciated,
narrow-chested and hollow-eyed ghosts who are to be met with in
such large numbers every minute in London. From their appearance
one would judge them to be weak, flabby, and lacking in all energy.
But, of course, large numbers of people also die every year of consumption in the factory towns of the North. In addition to consumption
the workers suffer from other lung infections, to say nothing of scarlet
fever. Above all typhus is the illness which is most deadly as far as
the workers are concerned. The official report on the health of the
working classes[3] states that this widespread scourge is due to bad living

[1 Engels prints this as *Artisan*.]

[2 *The Artizan*, October 1843, p. 229, col. 1. This passage is a summary of a
paragraph on p. 406 of the report on Leeds in the *Journal of the Statistical Society of
London*, Vol. 2 (1839–40)].

[3 Engels is presumably referring either to Dr. T. Southwood Smith's two
reports to the Poor Law Commissioners on sanitary conditions in Bethnal Green
and Whitechapel in 1838 and on the prevalence of fever in twenty metropolitan
areas in 1839, or to Edwin Chadwick's *Report on the Sanitary Condition of the Labouring
Population of Great Britain* (1842).]

conditions, in particular to bad ventilation, damp and dirt. This report was written by some of the leading doctors in England on the basis of information supplied by other medical men. These experts state that any badly ventilated court or undrained cul-de-sac—particularly if grossly overcrowded and if organic refuse is allowed to decay there—may well engender fever and does in fact nearly always do so. This fever is nearly always of the same type and practically always develops into definite cases of typhus. The disease is to be found in the working-class quarters not only of all the great cities, but even in isolated groups of slum dwellings in smaller places, where its effects are naturally felt most severely, but, of course, there are occasional cases of typhus in better class quarters. In London it has been endemic for some time; and the violent epidemic of 1837 gave rise to the report to which reference has already been made. Dr. Southwood Smith, in the annual report on the London Fever Hospital for 1843 stated that 1,462 patients were admitted in that year, which represented an increase of 418 over any previous year. Typhus raged in the damp, dirty slums of East, North and South London. Many of the patients [in the London Fever Hospital] were migrants from the provinces who had endured dire privations both on the way to London and on their arrival in the capital. Unable to find work, they suffered from lack of food and had to sleep in the streets with insufficient clothing to cover them. It was in these circumstances that they caught fever. They were in such a weak condition when taken to hospital that unusually large quantities of stimulent such as wine, brandy and ammonia had to be administered to them. Deaths among those admitted amounted to 16.5 per cent.[1] This malignant fever is also to

[1] This passage appears to be a summary of the following paragraph in the *Northern Star*, no. 328, February 24th, 1844, p. 7, col. 3:

RECORD OF DESTITUTION

FRIGHTFUL SPREAD OF FEVER FROM DESTITUTION

Dr. Southwood Smith has just given his annual report upon the state of the London Fever Hospital during the past year, from which it appears that the admissions during the period were 1,462, being an excess of 418 above that of any preceding year. Fever raged most violently in the Central, Northern, and Southern Districts, which was attributable to the undrained, close, and filthy condition of these localities. A large proportion of the inmates were agricultural labourers or provincial mechanics, who had come to London in search of employment, and who were seized with the malady either on the road or soon after their arrival, evincing the close connexion between fever and destitution. These poor creatures ascribed their illness—some of them to sleeping by the sides of hedges, and others to a want of clothing, many being without stockings, shirts, shoes, or any apparel capable of defending them from the inclemency of the weather; while the larger number attributed it to want of food, being driven by hunger to *eat raw vegetables, turnips, and rotten apples.* Their disease was attended with such extreme prostration as generally to require the administration of an

be found in Manchester. It has never been wholly stamped out in such bad slums as those of the Old Town, Ancoats and Little Ireland, though it must be admitted that here, as in other English provincial towns, typhus has not spread so much as one would expect. In Scotland and Ireland, on the other hand, typhus rages with a violence which is difficult to credit. In Edinburgh and Glasgow there were violent epidemics of typhus in 1817, after the famine, and both in 1826 and 1827, after the commercial crises. On each of these occasions the epidemic lasted for about three years before there was any appreciable decline in its incidence. In Edinburgh there were 6,000 cases of typhus in 1827 and 10,000 in 1837. Each new epidemic was characterised by an increase in the number of cases, the violence of the disease, and the mortality rate.[1] But the violence of the typhus in earlier times seems to have been mere child's play compared with what happened after the commercial crisis of 1842. One-sixth of all the poor in Scotland were laid low by fever. The disease was spread with extreme rapidity by beggars tramping the country. In two months there were more cases of fever than in the whole of the previous twelve years. In Glasgow in 1843 there were 32,000 cases of fever and this represented 12 per cent of the population. Nearly one-third (32 per cent) of those stricken by the disease died. In Manchester and Liverpool, on the other hand, the mortality from typhus is usually only 8 per cent of those affected. The disease reaches its crisis on the seventh and fifteenth days. The patient usually assumes a yellow hue on the fifteenth day and Dr. Alison suggests that this shows that the disease is not purely physical in origin but is due to excitement and anxiety.[2] In Ireland, too, fever is endemic. In 21 months of 1817–18, 39,000 cases were admitted to the Dublin hospitals.[3] Sheriff A. Alison, in the second volume of his *Principles of Population*,[4] says there were actually 60,000 admissions in a subsequent year. In Cork the fever hospital admitted [a number of patients exceeding] one-seventh of the population of the town in the two years 1817–18; at Limerick at the same period a quarter of the

unusually large proportion of wine, brandy, and ammonia, and other stimulants. The gross mortality was 16½ per cent. An unprecedented number of nurses and other servants of the hospital were attacked with fever, namely twenty-nine, of whom six died.]

[1] Dr. W. P. Alison, *Management of the Poor in Scotland* (1840) [pp. 12–3 (Edinburgh and Glasgow).]

[2] Dr. W. P. Alison's paper to the British Association for the Advancement of Science read at York in October 1844. [See *Journal of the Statistical Society of London*, Vol. 7 (1844), pp. 316–8: 'Notes on the Report of the Royal Commissioners on the operation of the Poor Laws in Scotland '.]

[3] Dr. W. P. Alison, *Management of the Poor in Scotland* (1840), p. 16.

[4] Sir Archibald Alison, *Principles of Population* (1840), Vol. 2, p. 80.]

population was laid low by the disease, while nineteen-twentieths of the inhabitants of the slums of Waterford were attacked by the disease.[1]

In view of all the circumstances it is indeed surprising that so infectious a disease as this fever is not more widespread. Consider how the workers live; how tightly packed are the dwellings of the poor; how every corner is crammed with human beings; how sick and healthy sleep together in one room and even in one bed. Consider how little medical care is available for those who fall ill; how many of them are ignorant of the commonest rules of diet to be observed by fever patients. In view of these facts the mortality from fever is by no means excessive. Dr. Alison, who has much experience of this disease, ascribed it to the low standard of living and general wretched conditions of the poor. The report to which reference has already been made stresses the same points.[2] Dr. Alison asserts that privation and insufficient food, clothing and shelter make the poor incapable of resisting the ravages of the disease. This is the reason why fever epidemics spread with such rapidity. Dr. Alison explains that in Scotland and Ireland a period of depression—a commercial crisis or harvest failure—always leads to the appearance of a typhus epidemic, and that its full fury is felt almost exclusively by the working classes. Dr. Alison draws attention to a striking feature of the epidemics: the majority of the typhus victims are the fathers of families and are therefore those who can least be spared by their families. The Irish doctors quoted by Alison also draw attention to this aspect of the epidemics.[3]

Other diseases are due less to the poor dwellings than to the poor food of the workers. The food commonly consumed by the working classes is difficult for adults to digest and is quite unsuitable for the diet of young children. The workers have neither the time nor the money to procure proper food for their children. In addition reference should be made to the widespread custom of giving children brandy, even opium. Poor diets, combined with the generally unsatisfactory environment in which the children of the poor grow up, are the cause of various stomach disorders which affect the children for the rest of their lives. Nearly all workers suffer from weak stomachs, but nevertheless they are forced to continue on the very diet which originally caused the complaint. They are ignorant of the cause of their illness;

[1 Dr. W. P. Alison, *Observations on the Management of the Poor in Scotland* (1840), pp. 16–17, quoting Drs. F. Barker and J. Cheyne, *An Account of the Rise, Progress and Decline of the Fever lately epidemical in Ireland* . . . , Vol. 2 (1821), pp. 16, 26, 40.]

[2 Presumably Dr. Southwood Smith's report on the work of the London Fever Hospital for 1843, quoted in the *Northern Star*, no. 328, Feb. 24th, 1844, p. 7, col. 3—'Frightful Spread of Fever from Destitution'.]

[3 Dr. W. P. Alison, *Management of the Poor in Scotland* (1840), pp. 16–7, 18–32.]

even if they knew what was wrong with them, how could they procure more suitable food unless they adopted a different way of life and enjoyed a better education? These digestive troubles lead to new illnesses even in childhood. Scrofula is an almost universal complaint among the working classes. Scrofulous parents have scrofulous children, especially if the original cause of the illness continues to operate in full force upon the inherited tendency of the children. Rickets[1] is another consequence of insufficient nourishment in the early years of growth and is consequently very common among the children of the workers. The hardening of the bones is delayed and the development of bodily structure is stunted; so that in addition to the usual effects of rickets it is quite common to find that the victims of the disease suffer from deformities of the spine and legs. It is obvious that these diseases are aggravated by the fact that the workers suffer so much from fluctuations in trade. At times of industrial crisis their wages are reduced and they must go short of food. Practically every worker at some time in his life has had to go short of food and this naturally aggravates conditions caused by long periods of living on an unsuitable (though not inadequate) diet. Children who do not get enough to eat at the very time when they most require adequate nourishment, inevitably fall victims to digestive troubles, scrofula and rickets. Very many suffer in this way during periods of bad trade and even at times of comparative prosperity. Common observation shows how the sufferings of childhood are indelibly stamped on the adults. The vast mass of the workers' children are neglected; this leaves traces which are never wholly removed and leads to the weakening of a whole generation of workers. Moreover the workers wear unsuitable clothing which does not give them adequate protection from catching cold. They are forced to work as long as they possibly can when they fall ill, because they know that if they are unable to work their families will suffer. When the poor are ill they very seldom have any medical attention. All these unfavourable circumstances inevitably have a deleterious effect on the health of the English working classes. I do not propose to discuss, at this stage, the occupational diseases to which workers in particular branches of industry are liable.

There are still other factors which have an adverse effect on the health of the workers. Of these, drink is the most important. The worker is under every possible temptation to take to drink. Spirits are virtually his sole form of pleasure and they are very readily avail-

---

[1] Engels adds: ' Die englische Krankheit (" The English disease "): knotty protuberances on the joints '.

able. The worker comes home tired and exhausted from his labours. He finds that his comfortless and unattractive dwelling is both damp and dirty. He urgently needs some stimulant; he must have something to recompense him for his labours during the day and enable him to face the prospect of the next day's dreary toil. He is out of sorts; his nerves are on edge and he feels thoroughly depressed. This state of mind arises originally from his poor state of health, particularly his indigestion. It is greatly aggravated by the circumstances in which he finds himself—the uncertainty of his job, his lack of resources to fall back on, his state of insecurity, his complete inability to do anything to make his position more secure, make him think that life is unbearable. His physique is poor and his health has been undermind by bad air and poor food. So the worker urgently feels the need of some stimulant. Moreover, his need for company can be satisfied only in the public house, for there is nowhere else where he can meet his friends.

In these circumstances the worker is obviously subject to the strongest temptation to drink to excess, and it is hardly surprising that he often succumbs. Given these conditions, it is in fact inevitable that a large number of workers should have neither the moral nor the physical stamina to resist the temptation. Quite apart from the influences, which are mainly of a physical nature, driving the worker to drink, it should be remembered that many other factors of a different nature contribute to this result. These include the desire to follow the crowd; the neglected education of the workers; the impossibility of shielding young people from the temptation to drink; the frequent example of hard-drinking parents who actually give spirits to their children; and the certainty that drink will, at any rate for a few hours, enable the worker to forget the hard and miserable life that he leads. These and a hundred other influences are so powerful that no one could really blame the workers for their excessive addiction to spirits. In view of the general environment of the industrial workers, drunkenness ceases to be a vice for which the drunkard must accept responsibility. It becomes a phenomenon which must be accepted as the inevitable consequence of bringing certain influences to bear upon workers, who in this matter cannot be expected to have sufficient willpower to enable them to act otherwise. The responsibility lies with those who turned the factory hand into a soulless factor of production and have thus deprived him of his humanity. If it is inevitable that many workers should be driven to drink, it is equally inevitable that they should suffer physically and morally from over-indulgence. All the diseases to which the workers are liable because of the way in which they live and work are aggravated by drink. The ravages of lung diseases, of abdominal complaints and of typhus are immensely increased by gross intemperance.

Another reason for the poor state of health of the working classes is to be found in the impossibility of securing skilled medical attention in the event of illness. It is true that there are a number of charitable institutions which try to meet this need. The Manchester Infirmary, for example, deals with 22,000 patients a year; some of these are treated in the hospital; others are out-patients who are given medicine and advice—but what does that amount to in a city in which, according to Gaskell, three-quarters of the inhabitants need medical attention every year?[1] English doctors charge high fees which the workers are unable to pay. The workers either do without medical advice, or they are forced to patronise charlatans and make use of quack remedies which, in the long run, do more harm than good. A very large number of quack doctors ply their trade in all the towns of England. By means of advertisements, posters and other publicity stunts they recruit their clients from the poorer classes. In addition large numbers of patent medicines are sold as cures for all sorts of actual and imaginary complaints. Morrison's Pills, Parr's Life Pills, Dr. Mainwaring's Pills and thousands of other pills, medicines and ointments which are all capable of curing all the illnesses under the sun. While these medicaments seldom contain substances which are actually harmful, they often have injurious effects if taken frequently or in too large quantities. Since the ignorant workers are told in all the advertisements that no one can ever consume too much of these medicines, it is not surprising that they continually consume quantities far in excess of their needs. It is by no means unusual for the manu-facturers of Parr's Life Pills to sell between 20,000 and 25,000 boxes of these wonderful nostrums in a week. They are taken to relieve

---

[1] P. Gaskell, *The Manufacturing Population of England* (1833), chapter 8. [Gaskell gave the number of patients admitted to the Manchester Royal Infirmary in 1831 as 21,196—see p. 230. The figures for patients treated in the Manchester Royal Infirmary (for the twelve months ending June 24th, in each case) are as follows:

1827–8	...	...	...	...	...	16,680
1828–9	...	...	...	...	...	18,002
1829–30	...	...	...	...	...	16,237
1830–1	...	...	...	...	...	19,628
1831–2	...	...	...	...	...	21,349
1832–3	...	...	...	...	...	21,232

(compiled from the official annual reports of the Manchester Royal Infirmary).]

an astonishing variety of different complaints—constipation as well as diarrhoea, fever as well as lassitude. Just as peasants in Germany go to be bled or cupped at certain seasons of the year, so the English workers now gulp down their patent medicines, injuring themselves while filling the pockets of the proprietors. One of the most harmful of these patent medicines is a preparation of opiates, particularly laudanum, which is sold under the name of Godfrey's Cordial.[1] Women who work at home and have to look after their own and other people's children dose them with this medicine, not only to keep them quiet, but because of a widely prevalent notion that it strengthens the child. Many women give the children this medicine while they are new-born infants, and go on dosing them without realising the harmful consequences of this method of 'strengthening the heart' until the children die. When the child's system develops a greater resistance to the effects of opium, the dose is gradually increased. When Godfrey's Cordial is no longer effective it is replaced by pure laudanum and doses of from fifteen to twenty drops at a time are given. In evidence before a Parliamentary enquiry[2] the Nottingham coroner stated that one druggist had admitted using 13 cwt of treacle in a year in the manufacture of Godfrey's Cordial.[3] The effects on the children dosed in this way can easily be imagined. They become pale, stunted and weak, generally dying before they are two years old. The use of this medicine is widespread in all the great cities and industrial towns of the country.[4]

All these adverse factors combine to undermine the health of the workers. Very few strong, well-built, healthy people are to be found among them—at any rate in the industrial towns, where they generally work indoors. And it is with the factory workers that we are concerned here. They are for the most part, weak, thin and pale. The bone structure is prominent but gives no evidence of strength.

[1 Godfrey's Cordial consisted of a mixture of tincture of opium (laudanum) and treacle.]

[2 *Report of Commission of Inquiry into the Employment of Children and Young Persons in Mines and Manufactories.* . . . This report is usually referred to as the 'Children's Employment Commission's Report'. It is one of the best official reports of its kind and contains an immense quantity of evidence which is both valuable and horrifying. The first report was issued in 1842 and the second in 1843. [See *Appendix to 2nd Report* (Trades and Manufactures) Part 1, Reports and Evidence from Sub-commissioners (1842) F 10-11, f 60-2.]

[3 In the 1887 American edition the translator amended this sentence to read: 'used thirteen hundredweight of *laudanum* in one year in the preparation of Godfrey's Cordial', and this mistake was approved by Engels.]

[4 For the widespread use of Godfrey's Cordial in Wolverhampton see Children's Employment Commission, *Appendix to 2nd Report* (1842), Part 2, Q 30.]

All their muscles are flabby, except for those which may have been abnormally developed because of the nature of their work. Nearly all suffer from digestive troubles, and consequently they suffer from more or less permanent mental depression and general irritability, so that their outlook on life is a gloomy one. Their weakened bodies are in no condition to withstand illness and whenever infection is abroad they fall victims to it. Consequently they age prematurely, and die young. This is proved by the available statistics of death rates.

The Report of Mr. G. Graham, the Registrar General, states that the annual death rate for England and Wales is a little under $2\frac{1}{4}$ per cent, i.e., one in every 45 persons[1] die every year. This was the average for the registration year 1839–40. The following year (1840–1) the death rate declined somewhat and only amounted to one in 46. In the big cities, however, the situation is quite different. Official statistics printed in the *Manchester Guardian* of July 31st, 1844,[2] which is now lying before me, include the following data concerning the death rates in some of the great towns. In Manchester, including Salford and Chorlton, the death rate was 1 in 32.72, and excluding Salford and Chorlton, 1 in 30.75. In Liverpool, including the suburb of West Derby, the death rate is 1 in 31.9, and excluding West Derby, 29.9. On the other hand, in all those parts of Cheshire, Lancashire and Yorkshire included in this return—and these include many rural and semi-rural districts—the average death rate in a population of 2,172,506 persons is 1 in 39.8. How unfavourably situated the urban worker is from this point of view may be seen from the mortality of Prescot in Lancashire. This is a colliery town and since coalmining is a relatively unhealthy occupation the health of the town falls somewhat below the standard of that in an agricultural community. But the workers in Prescot live in the countryside and the death rate is 1 in 47.54, which is better by nearly $2\frac{1}{2}$ than the national average of 1 in 45. The figures which have been quoted from the *Manchester Guardian* of July 31st, 1844, all refer to the year 1843. The death rate in Scottish towns is higher still—in Edinburgh in 1838–39 it was 1 in 29 and in 1831 it was actually 1 in 22 in the Old Town. Dr. [Robert] Cowan in his paper 'Vital Statistics of Glasgow [illustrating the sanitary condition

---

[1] *5th Annual Report* of the Registrar-General of Births, Deaths and Marriages [(1843), p. iii.]

[2] *Manchester Guardian*, July 31st, 1844, p. 6, cols. 4–5: article on 'Quarterly Table of Mortality' in 115 registrars' districts for the quarter ending June 30th, 1844. Engels's figures for the death rates appear to have been calculated from a table in this article giving the population of certain towns in 1841 and the deaths registered therein in 1843.]

of the population] '[1] states that since 1830 the average death rate in that city has been 1 in 30, and in certain years between 1 in 22 and 1 in 24. There is overwhelming evidence that this drastic reduction in the average span of life falls mainly on the working classes. Indeed the death rate among the workers is obviously somewhat higher than the average for the whole country, since the members of the upper and middle classes live longer than the workers. Among the most recent evidence available is that collected by Mr. P. H. Holland [surgeon], of Manchester. He undertook an official survey of the Manchester suburb of Chorlton-on-Medlock.[2] He classified both the houses and streets into three categories and found the following differences in the death rates:

Class of Streets	Class of Houses	Rate of Mortality
1st	1st	1 in 51
	2nd	1 in 45
	3rd	1 in 36
2nd	1st	1 in 55
	2nd	1 in 38
	3rd	1 in 35
3rd	1st	not given
	2nd	1 in 35
	3rd	1 in 25[3]

From the evidence supplied by Mr. Holland in several other tables it is clear that the death rate in *streets* of the second class is 18 per cent higher than in those of the first class. The death rate in *streets* of the third class is 68 per cent higher than in those of the first class. The death rate in *houses* of the second class is 22 per cent higher than in those of the first class and the death rate in houses of the third

[1 *Journal of the Statistical Society of London*, Vol. 3, 1840, p. 265. Cowan's table of the mortality in Glasgow was:

		1 in
1831	... ...	33.845
1832	... ...	21.672
1833	... ...	35.776
1834	... ...	36.312
1835	... ...	32.647
1836	... ...	28.906
1837	... ...	24.634
1838	... ...	37.939
1839	... ...	36.146]

[2 *Report of the Commission of Enquiry into the State of large Towns and Populous Districts*, 1st Report, 1844, Appendix [pp. 202–17.]

[3 Engels may have taken these figures from the article on 'Sanitary Condition of Large Towns' in the *Manchester Guardian* of July 31st, 1844, p. 6, cols. 3–4.]

class is 78 per cent higher than in those of the first class. Mr. Holland
also showed that in slum streets which had been improved the death
rate had declined by 25 per cent. He concludes his report with a
comment which is unusually frank for a member of the English middle
classes:

> When we find the rate of mortality four times as high in some
> streets as in others, and twice as high in whole classes of streets as in
> other classes, and further find that it is all but *invariably* high in those
> streets, which are in bad condition, and almost as invariably low
> in those whose condition is good, we cannot resist the conclusion
> that multitudes of our fellow-creatures, *hundreds of our immediate
> neighbours*, are annually destroyed for want of the most evident
> precautions.[1]

The *Report on the Sanitary Condition of the Labouring Population*
contains corroborative evidence of this. In 1840 in Liverpool the
average age at death of the ' gentry and professional persons ' was 35
years, of ' tradesmen and their families ' 22 years and ' labourers,
mechanics and servants ' was actually only 15 years.[2] The same parliamentary report contains many statistics of a similar nature.[3]

The main reason for the high death rate is the heavy mortality
among infants and small children. A child's constitution is normally
so weak that it is least able to withstand the harmful effects of a low
standard of living. If both parents go out to work for their living, or if
either parent is dead, the child is so neglected that its health inevitably
suffers. In the circumstances it is not surprising to learn from the
report that we have just cited that in Manchester, for example, nearly
54 per cent[4] of the workers' children die before attaining their fifth
birthday. On the other hand only 20 per cent of the children of the
middle classes die before they are five. In the rural districts rather less
than 32 per cent of all children die before they are five.[5]

[1 *Manchester Guardian*, July 31st, 1844, p. 6, col. 4.]
[2 E. Chadwick, *Report on the Sanitary Condition of the Labouring Population* (1842),
p. 159, octavo edition.]
[3 See ' Tabular views of the ages at which deaths have occurred in different
classes of society ', *ibid.*, pp. 162–3.]
[4 Engels wrote ' over 57 per cent '.]
[5 This information appears to have been extracted partly from the Second
Report of the Factories Enquiry Commission (1833), D3, p. 5—medical reports by
Dr. Bisset Hawkins, who in turn relied on information supplied by Mr. J. Roberton,
described as ' the chief statistical authority of Manchester '. Engels's statement
that ' only 20 per cent of the children of the middle classes die before they are five ',
was taken from Edwin Chadwick's *Report on the Sanitary Condition of the Labouring
Population of Great Britain* (1842), p. 162. Chadwick arrived at his figure by taking an
average of the mortality of children under 5 born to ' Gentry and Professional
Persons ' in nine localities (Manchester, Leeds, Liverpool, Bath, Bethnal Green and
the poor law unions of the Strand, Kendal, Wiltshire and Rutland).]

The article in the *Artizan*[1] to which we have already frequently referred gives more detailed information concerning infantile mortality in England. The article lists the proportion of deaths due to various diseases in both urban and rural districts. These tables prove that epidemics in Manchester and Liverpool generally kill three times as many children as in rural districts[2]; that diseases of the nervous system are five times more fatal in the towns than in the country; that diseases of the digestive organs kill more than twice as many children in the towns than in the rural districts, while diseases of the respiratory organs are two and a half times as deadly in the towns as in the country. Fatal cases of smallpox, measles, whooping cough and scarlet fever carry off four times as many infants in the cities as in the rural districts. Similarly deaths from water on the brain are three times and convulsions ten times more deadly in urban than in rural districts.

Another acknowledged authority may be quoted on this subject. This is Dr. Wade, who has written a *History of the Middle and Working Classes* (London, 1835, 3rd edition). In this work Dr. Wade abstracts the following table from the Report of Sadler's Committee:

COMPARATIVE DURATION OF LIFE IN EVERY 10,000 PERSONS IN MANUFACTURING AND AGRICULTURAL DISTRICTS[3]

	Under 5 Years	5–19	20–39	40–59	60–69	70–79	80–89	90–99	100 and upwd.
Rutland, healthy county:	2,865	891	1,275	1,299	1,189	1,428	938	112	3
Essex, marshy:	3,159	1,110	1,526	1,413	953	1,019	630	77†	3
Carlisle, 1779–1787, before manufactories:	4,408	911*	1,006	1,201	940	826	533	153	22
Carlisle, now partly manufacturing and spinning:	4,738	930	1,261	1,134	677	727	452	80	1
Preston, factories, cotton spinning:	4,947	1,136	1,379	1,114	553	532	298	38	3
Leeds, factories, woollen, flax, silk:	5,286	927	1,228	1,198	593	512	225	29	2

[† Engels wrongly gave 177 instead of 77.]
[* Engels wrongly gave 921 instead of 911.]

[1] October 1843, pp. 228 *et seq.*]
[2] See ' Comparative Table of Mortality from various classes of disease in England and Wales . . .': *Artizan*, Oct. 1843, p. 228.]
[3] Engels based this table on that printed on p. 560 of Dr. John Wade's *History*

The very high mortality among infants and small children is caused not only by various diseases, which are the inevitable consequence of the neglect and oppression of the poorer classes, but also by other factors which must be taken into account. In many families the wife leaves home to go to work as well as the husband, and this results in the utter neglect of the children, who are either locked in the house or handed over to somebody else's care. No wonder that hundreds of such children lose their lives owing to all kinds of mishaps. Nowhere are so many children drowned or burnt to death as in the great cities of England. Deaths from burns or from being scalded by boiling water are very common. In Manchester and in London at least one case of this kind occurs ever week in the winter months. It is rare, however, for these cases to be reported in the press. I have by me, however, a copy of the *Weekly Dispatch* for December 15th, 1844, which reports six such incidents [in London] alone during the week ending December 7th.[1] These unfortunate children, who come to such a shocking end, are simply the victims of our extremely defective social arrangements, which are perpetuated in the interests of the property-owning classes. It may well be that this frightful and painful death is a blessing in disguise for the children, since it spares them from a long life of toil and wretchedness, rich in suffering and poor in enjoyment. This is actually the position in England to-day. The middle classes read these things every day in the newspapers, and do nothing at all about it. But they have no grounds for complaint if I accuse them of social murder and support my charge by producing the official and unofficial witnesses I have already cited, of whose evidence they cannot possible be ignorant. The middle classes should either put an end to this scandalous state of affairs, or they should hand over to the working classes the power to make regulations for the common good. The bourgeoisie have no desire to surrender their powers and—so long as they are blinded by their middle-class prejudices—they are powerless to set matters right. After hundreds of thousands have fallen victim to neglect the middle classes have at last embarked upon a few precautionary reforms of trifling significance. The Metropolitan Buildings Act [1844] has been passed which restricts

of the Middle and Working Classes, 1st edn., 1833. Wade, in turn, abstracted it from pp. 608–612 of the Report from the Select Committee on the Bill to regulate the labour of children in the mills and factories of the United Kingdom: *Parliamentary Papers*, Session 1831–2, Vol. 15, no. 706.]

[1 *Weekly Dispatch*, no. 2251, p. 598, col. 3—'Mortality in the Metropolis'. The news item states: 'Among the violent deaths are six cases. The unfortunate victims, with one exception being very young children, were burnt to death from their clothes taking fire'.]

to some extent the more blatant cramming of working-class dwellings on to a limited space. The middle classes pride themselves upon measures which barely touch the fringe of the problem, which in no way approach the root of the matter, and even fail to satisfy the minimum requirements of any self-respecting health authority. Such measures in no way absolve the middle classes from the accusations I have made. The only choice before the English bourgeoisie is this —either to plead guilty to the irrefutable charge of [social] murder and to keep power in spite of such an admission, or to abdicate its authority in favour of the working classes. So far the bourgeoisie has chosen the first alternative.

We turn now to consider the cultural and educational state of the workers, as distinct from their physical condition. Since the middle classes allow the workers only a bare minimum standard of living, it is not surprising that they receive only as much education as will serve the interests of their masters, which in fact amounts to very little. In relation to the size of the population the educational facilities in England are negligible. There are a very limited number of day schools available to working-class children; they are of a poor standard and attract only a very few scholars. The teachers are retired workers or other unsuitable persons who, unable to earn a living in any other way, have turned to teaching as a last resort. The vast majority of these 'teachers' are themselves virtually uneducated and lack the moral qualities essential in a teacher. Moreover, they are under no sort of public control. In education, as in everything else, free competition is the rule, and as usual the wealthy derive all the advantages from this arrangement. The poor, on the other hand, have to put up with all its disadvantages, because for them the competition is not really free at all, as they have not the necessary knowledge to make for themselves any judgement [about the quality of the schooling offered]. There is no compulsory education in England. In the factories, as we shall see, compulsory education exists only in name. During the parliamentary session of 1843 the Government proposed to enforce compulsory education for factory children. The factory owners resisted this proposal vigorously, although it was supported by the workers themselves. Large numbers of children work throughout the week in factories or at home and consequently have no time to attend school. There are evening institutes which are intended to serve the needs of such children and young workers, who are fully employed during the day-time. These institutes have very few scholars and those who do attend derive no profit from the instruction given. It is really too much to expect a young person who has been at work for twelve hours to go to school between 9 p.m. and 10 p.m. Most of those who do attend fall asleep, as is proved by hundreds of statements by witnesses before the Children's Employment Commissioners.[1] It is true that there are also Sunday schools in existence, but they are quite inadequately staffed and are of value only to pupils who have already learnt something in a day school. The interval between one Sunday and another is too long for an ignorant child to remember on the second attendance what he has learnt on the first a week before. On the basis of thousands of proofs contained in the statements of witnesses examined on behalf of the Children's Employment Commission, the Report[2] of this Commission emphatically declares that the existing provision of day schools and Sunday schools is wholly inadequate for the present needs of the country.

This Report gives a picture of the abysmal ignorance of the English working classes which one might expect to find in such countries as Spain and Italy.[3] What else is to be expected? The middle classes have little to hope and much to fear from the education of the workers. In an enormous budget of £55,000,000 a mere £40,000 is devoted to public education. If it were not for the fanaticism of the religious sects—which does at least as much harm as good—the amount of education available would be even less. The Anglicans have established their National schools and the various dissenting bodies have founded theirs, too, simply and solely in order to bring up children of their members in their particular faiths; and, if possible, now and again to filch the soul of some poor little child from a rival religious body. The result is that polemical discussions—the most sterile aspect of religion—dominate the school curriculum. The minds of the children are crammed with dogmas and theological principles which they do not understand. Consequently a narrow sectarianism and a fanatical bigotry are awakened in the children at as early an age as possible, to the serious neglect of any reasonable instruction in religion and morals. The working classes have often enough demanded from Parliament the introduction of a purely secular system of public education, which would make religious instruction solely the responsibility of the ministers of the various churches. They have not been able to obtain anything approaching a sympathetic hearing from any Government. This need cause no

[1 Children's Employment Commission: *Second Report of the Commissioners*: *Trades and Manufactures* (1843) pp. 141–194, paras. 752–1020, 'Moral Condition of Children and Young Persons employed in Collieries and Mines, and Trades and Manufactures'.]

[2 The Children's Employment Commission in fact made two reports.]

[3 But see R. K. Webb, *The British Working Class Reader*, 1790–1848 (1955).]

surprise. The [Prime] Minister is the obedient lackey of the middle class, which is divided into countless religious bodies. Every church is prepared to grant the workers the dangerous privilege of education only on condition that this education is vitiated by the poisonous dogmas of that particular church. The churches are still to this day quarrelling and so, for the time being, the working classes must remain steeped in ignorance.

The factory owners boast that the vast majority of the children in their employment have been taught to read, but the standard of reading is very inferior, as may be gathered from the reports of the Children's Employment Commission. Anyone who knows his alphabet claims to be able to read and with that the manufacturers are content. This ignorance is easily understandable when we remember the pitfalls of English spelling, which make the ability to read a real achievement, and one which can be acquired only after a long period of instruction. Very few English people can write and spell at all well, and this is true even of the ' educated ' classes. The Sunday schools maintained by the Anglicans, the Quakers and, I believe, several other religious bodies, do not give any instruction in writing at all because ' this is too secular an occupation for Sunday '.[1] A few examples may be given to illustrate the level of education of the English workers at the present day. They are taken from the Report of the Children's Employment Commission, which unfortunately does not include information concerning the true factory areas:[2]

[Sub-]Commissioner R. D. Grainger wrote of Birmingham:[3]

' With respect to the children and young persons who came under my observation . . . in the aggregate they are entirely destitute of anything which can be called . . . an useful education. It is especially to be deplored that notwithstanding the instruction in the existing schools is, with a few exceptions, exclusively limited to

[1 A somewhat similar phrase was used by Edwin Ford, a Wolverhampton Wesleyan Sunday school teacher, in his evidence to Sub-Commissioner R. H. Horne. Writing was not taught because it ' was not thought quite proper for Sunday '. But he went on to say: ' there are two nights in the week when writing is taught in this school ' (Children's Employment Commission, *Appendix to 2nd Report*, Part II, statement no. 98, p. q21. See also p. Q17). Of Sheffield J. C. Symons reported: ' In some of the Methodist New Connexion, and other dissenting Sunday schools, writing is still taught, though a strong feeling against this or any secular instruction on the Sabbath is growing up '. (Children's Employment Commission, *Appendix to 2nd Report*, Part I, p. E26, para. 203).]

[2 Engels is here drawing attention to the fact that very little evidence in the *Reports* came from the textile industries of S.E. Lancashire, N.E. Cheshire and the West Riding of Yorkshire (except for the finishing branches, e.g., calico-printing). But these industries had already been covered by the early factory enquiries.]

[3 Grainger's report—a portion of which Engels summarised—covered not only Birmingham, but Nottingham, Derby, Leicester and London.]

religious knowledge, a most awful ignorance was generally evinced upon this, the most important of all subjects.'[1]

In Wolverhampton [Sub-]Commissioner R. H. Horne found among others the following examples: A girl of eleven years who had attended both day and Sunday school, but had ' Never learnt of another world, nor of heaven, nor of another life. . .'[2] Another young person, 17 years of age, ' did not know how many two and two made, nor how many farthings there were in two-pence, even when the money was placed in his hand '.[3] ' . . . You will find boys who have never heard of such a place as London, nor of Willenhall (which is only three miles distant, and in constant communication with Wolverhampton) '.[4] ' . . . Some [of the children] have never heard the name of Her Majesty, nor such names as Wellington, Nelson, Buonaparte, etc. But it is to be especially remarked, that among all those who had never even heard such names as St. Paul, Moses, Solomon, etc., there was a general knowledge of the character and course of life of Dick Turpin, the highwayman, and more particularly, of Jack Shepherd, the robber and prison-breaker '.[5] A youth of 16 did not know ' how many twice two make ', nor ' how much money six farthings make, nor four farthings '.[6] A youth of seventeen asserted that ' 10 farthings make 10 halfpence ';[7] a third, sixteen[8] years old, answered several very simple questions with the brief statement ' He be'nt no judge o' nothin' '.[9]

These children, who are crammed with religious doctrines for four or five years at a stretch, know as little at the end as at the beginning. One child had ' attended a Sunday school regularly for five years. . . Does not know who Jesus Christ was, but has heard the name of it. Never heard of the twelve apostles. Never heard of Samson, nor of Moses, nor Aaron, etc.'[10] Another had ' attended a Sunday school regularly nearly six years. Knows who Jesus Christ

---

[1] ' On the Education and Comparative Condition of the Young Persons employed in the occupations included in this Report '. Children's Employment Commission, *Appendix to 2nd Report*, Part I, p. F35, para. 339.

[2] Children's Employment Commission, *Appendix to 2nd Report*, Part II (1843), p. q13, statement no. 55 (by Mary Field, ' going of 11 ').

[3] Ibid, p. Q52, para. 564 (Report of R. H. Horne on the town of Willenhall, Staffs. [This was William Southern, whose statement (no.161) appears on page q36.]

[4] Ibid, page Q19, para. 216.

[5] Ibid, page Q52, para. 564.

[6] Ibid, page q45 (Joseph Gibbs, statement no. 210).

[7] Ibid, pages q46–q47 (Moses Giles, statement no. 226).

[8] Engels gave the age of this witness as 17.]

[9] Ibid, page q47 (John Hutton, statement no. 233). [This statement was incorrectly reported by Engels as ' he was ne judge o' nothin '.]

[10] Ibid, page q36 (anonymous boy, ' aged 17 nearly ', statement no. 160).

was, he died on the cross to shed his blood, to save our Saviour.
Never heard of St. Peter or St. Paul '.[1] A third ' attended the Sunday
schools of different kinds about seven years; can read, only in the thin
books, easy words of one syllable; has heard of the Apostles; does not
know if St. Peter was one, nor if St. John was one, unless it was St.
John Wesley '.[2] To the question who Christ was, Horne received,
among others, the following answers: ' Yes, Adam ', ' He was an
Apostle ', ' He was the Saviour's Lord's Son ', and (from ' a young
person 16 years of age '): ' Jesus Christ was a king of London a long
time ago '.[3] In Sheffield [Sub-]Commissioner J. C. Symons made the
Sunday school children read to him.[4] The children could not tell
what they had been reading about, or what sort of people apostles
were. After he had put this question, ' to nearly every one of the 16
in succession without a correct answer, a little sharp-looking fellow
cried out with great glee, " Please, Sir, they were the lepers " '.[5] A
similar state of affairs is reported from the Potteries and from Lancashire.

This shows what the middle classes have done for the education
and improvement of the working classes. Fortunately the circumstances in which the workers live are such as to give them a practical
training which is not only a substitute for mere book-learning, but also
renders harmless the confused religious instruction which is associated
with the knowledge gained at school. The workers are actually in the
vanguard of the national movement in England.[6] Necessity is the
mother of invention, and what is even more important, is also the
mother of thought and action. Although the average English worker
can hardly read, let alone write, he nevertheless has a shrewd notion
of where his own interest and that of his country lie. He knows, too,
where the selfish interest of the bourgeoisie lies, and what he may
expect from the middle classes. He may not be able to write, but he
can at least speak and he can speak in public. He may not be very
good at arithmetic but he knows enough about the facts and figures of
political economy to see through and to defeat the attempts of the
middle classes to foist Corn Law repeal on him. He may still be
somewhat uncertain concerning spiritual affairs—in spite of all the

---

[1] Ibid, page q36 (William Southern, statement no. 161).

[2] Ibid, page q34 (Walter Brindley, statement no. 152). Engels explained that
John Wesley was ' the founder of Methodism '.

[3] Ibid, page Q52 (R. H. Horne's report on Willenhall).

[4 The incident to which Engels refers took place during a visit paid by Symons
to the Red Hill Methodist Sunday school. It is not a comment on *all* the Sunday
schools in Sheffield.]

[5] Children's Employment Commission, *Appendix to 2nd Report*, Part I, p. E27,
para. 207.   [6 This is presumably a reference to Chartism.]

preachings of the parsons—but he is no fool when it comes to dealing with secular, political, and social problems. We propose to discuss this matter further at a later stage, but for the time being we proceed to discuss the moral characteristics of the workers.

In England no distinction is made between moral instruction and religious education. Consequently the worker can hardly be expected to obtain any clear idea of the way in which everyday conduct should be guided by moral principles. The uneducated worker is wholly ignorant of the simple principles which should regulate the behaviour of human beings towards one another in society—principles which have been utterly debased by the unbridled play of free competition in the modern world. This ignorance is due to two facts. First, these principles are enunciated in the form of arbitrary rulings of which the worker receives no explanation. Secondly, they are embodied in the form of unintelligible religious commandments. The evidence of the best authorities, and in particular of the Children's Employment Commission, makes it clear that the schools contribute virtually nothing to the moral improvement of the workers. The English middle classes are so recklessly stupid and smug, that in their blind egotism they do not even take the trouble to instruct the workers in their own bourgeois moral code, in spite of the fact that this ramshackle code has been patched up in their own selfish interests! Even self-interest does not stir the sleepy sluggish middle classes to action. The time will come when they will bitterly rue their present inactivity. But the middle classes cannot complain if the workers know nothing of bourgeois morality and do not follow its tenets.

From a moral point of view, as in the physical and intellectual spheres, the workers are neglected and spurned by the possessing classes. The middle classes control the worker not by inculcating moral principles but simply by means of the shackles imposed on them by the legal system. The workers are treated like dumb beasts who can only be taught by means of the whip. If the workers threaten the interests of their superiors even to the slightest extent, the middle classes do not reason with them but use the brutal discipline of legal repression. In the circumstances it is not surprising that workers who are treated like beasts either behave like beasts or are able to maintain their self-respect as human beings only by continually harbouring hatred of the powerful oppressors. The workers retain their humanity only so long as they cherish a burning fury against the property-owning classes. They become animals as soon as they submit patiently to their yoke, and try to drag out a bearable existence under it without attempting to break free.

That is all the middle classes have done for the education of the workers. When we recall all the other circumstances of the workers' lives we can hardly blame the workers for their hatred of the oppressors. Neither at school nor in later life does the worker receive even that form of moral discipline which is acceptable to the middle classes. Immorality is fostered in every possible way by the conditions of working class life. The worker is poor; life has nothing to offer him; he is deprived of virtually all pleasures. Consequently he does not fear the penalties of the law. Why should he restrain his wicked impulses? Why should he leave the rich man in undisturbed possession of his property? Why should he not take at least a part of this property for himself? What reason has the worker for *not* stealing? It is all very well to chatter happily about the ' sacredness of private property ', but obviously property automatically loses its sacred qualities for those who have none. Mammon is the God of this world. The middle classes deprive the worker of his money and so turn him into a practising atheist. No wonder that the worker remains firm in his atheism and no longer respects either the sacredness or the power of this God of the middle classes. The poorer the worker becomes, the more he lacks the necessities of life, the more he suffers from hunger and distress, the less respect he has for the social order and its institutions. Most of the middle classes are well aware of this fact. Symons remarks that ' poverty has the same effect on the mind that drunkenness has on the body '.[1] And Sheriff Alison explains precisely to the property-owning classes the inevitable consequence of the social oppression from which the worker suffers.[2] Distress due to poverty gives the worker only the choice of starving slowly, killing himself quickly or taking what he needs where he finds it—in plain English—stealing. And it is not surprising that the majority prefer to steal rather than to starve to death or commit suicide. Of course, even among the workers there are some who have a moral sense which is strong enough to prevent them from stealing, even when they suffer beyond the bounds of human endurance. These are the workers who either starve or die by their own hands. At one time suicide was the envied privilege of the upper classes. But in England it has also become the fashion among the workers and now a number of these poor people kill themselves to avoid the miseries of an existence from which no other way of escape seems possible.

[1] J. C. Symons, *Arts and Artisans at Home and Abroad* . . . (1839), p. 147. [Engels inserts the adjective ' debasing ' before the word ' effect ', and does not put the quotation in inverted commas.]

[2] Sir Archibald Alison, *Principles of Population* (1840), Vol. 2, 196–199.

Insecurity is even more demoralising than poverty. English wage-earners live from hand to mouth, and this is the distinguishing mark of their proletarian status. The lower ranks of the German peasantry are largely filled with men who are also poor, and often suffer want, but they are less subject to that sort of distress which is due solely to chance. They do at least enjoy some measure of security. But the proletarian is in quite a different position. He possesses nothing but his two hands and he consumes to-day what he earned yesterday. His future is at the mercy of chance. He has not the slightest guarantee that his skill will in future enable him to earn even the bare necessities of life. Every commercial crisis, every whim of his master, can throw him out of work. He is placed in the most revolting and inhuman position imaginable. A slave is at least assured of his daily bread by the self-interest of his master, while the serf at any rate has a piece of land on the produce of which he can live. Slaves and serfs are both guaranteed a basic minimum existence. The proletarian on the other hand is thrown wholly upon his own resources, and yet at the same time is placed in such a position that he cannot be sure that he can always use those resources to gain a livelihood for himself and his family. Everything that the factory worker can do to try and improve his position vanishes like a drop in the bucket in face of the flood of chance occurrences to which he is exposed and over which he has not the slightest control. He is the passive sufferer from every possible combination of mishaps, and can regard himself as fortunate if he keeps his head above water even for a short time. And it is self-evident that the character of the worker and his way of life should be moulded by this state of affairs. He may fight for survival in this whirlpool; he may try to maintain his dignity as a human being. This he can do only by fighting the middle classes,[1] who exploit him so ruthlessly and then condemn him to a fate which drives him to live in a way unworthy of a human being. On the other hand, the worker may give up the struggle to improve his position, as being of no avail, and seek only to snatch what profit he can from any circumstances favourable to himself which may present themselves. It is useless for him to try and save, because he can never put aside any more money than will keep him going for a few weeks, and if he falls out of work he is usually unemployed for far more than a few weeks. He has no opportunity of acquiring any property, and if he could do so, he would cease to be a worker and someone else would take his place in the working classes. So what else can the worker do when he is

---

[1] We shall see later how the struggle of the English working classes against the middle classes has been legalised by the right to form free associations.

earning good wages, except spend the money on high living? The English middle classes are shocked to the marrow by the reckless expenditure of workers in periods of high wages. In fact such conduct is not only natural but sensible. Situated as the workers are, it is obvious that they will enjoy life while they have the opportunity, instead of accumulating savings which will eventually be eaten away by moths and rust, in the shape of the bourgeoisie. Such a way of life is the most demoralising of all. What Thomas Carlyle says of the cotton spinners applies to all the English industrial workers:

> . . . their trade now in plethoric prosperity, anon extenuated into inanition and ' short-time ', is of the nature of gambling; they live by it like gamblers, now in luxurious superfluity, now in starvation. Black mutinous discontent devours them; simply the miserablest feeling that can inhabit the heart of man. English Commerce with its world-wide convulsive fluctuations, with its immeasurable Proteus Steam-demon, makes all paths uncertain for them, all life a bewilderment: sobriety, steadfastness, peaceable continuance, the first blessings of man, are not theirs . . . this world for them no home, but a dingy prison-house, of reckless unthrift, rebellion, rancour, indignation against themselves and against all men. Is it a green flowery world, with azure everlasting sky stretched over it, the work and government of a God; or a murky-simmering Tophet, of copperas-fumes, cotton-fuz, gin-riot, wrath and toil, created by a Demon, governed by a Demon?[1]

And Carlyle continues:

> Injustice, infidelity of truth and fact and Nature's order, being properly the one evil under the sun, and the feeling of injustice the one intolerable pain under the sun, our grand question as to the condition of these working men would be: Is it just? And first of all, What belief have they themselves formed about the justice of it? The words they promulgate are notable by way of answer; their actions are still more notable. . . . Revolt, sullen revengeful humour of revolt against the upper classes, decreasing respect for what their temporal superiors command, decreasing faith for what their spiritual superiors teach, is more and more the universal spirit of the lower classes. Such spirit may be blamed, may be vindicated; but all men must recognise it as extant there, all may know that it is mournful, that unless altered it will be fatal.[2]

Carlyle is right in his facts, but he is wrong in criticising the savage resentment of the workers against the upper classes. This resentment

---

[1] *Chartism* (1839), pp. 34-5.
[2] Ibid, pp. 40-1.

and anger surely prove that the workers realise how inhumanly they are being treated. It shows that they are determined not only to resist attempts to depress their standards to the level of those of mere animals, but to free themselves without delay from the slavery imposed upon them by the middle classes. The extent to which the workers are degraded may be seen from the conduct of those who submit passively to this state of affairs. Some of them submit to their fate and exist as best they can as respectable law-abiding citizens. They take no interest in public affairs and actually help the middle classes to tighten the chains which bind the lower orders of society. They have not moved with the times and still behave as though they were living in the long-vanished age that preceded the Industrial Revolution. Other workers [who make no attempt to resist bourgeois oppression] are content to take their chance in the new industrial world. Since they have lost not merely economic security but also moral stability, they lead a hand-to-mouth existence, drink too much gin and run after the girls. Whether they submit passively to their fate or take to drink, they are equally no more than animals. The behaviour of this [debauched] section of the working classes is the main cause of that ' rapid increase in vice ' which so disgusts the sentimental middle classes, although they are themselves actually responsible for the conditions which inevitably give rise to it.

Another reason why the workers are demoralised is the fact that they are condemned to a lifetime of unremitting toil. Man knows no greater happiness than that which is derived from productive work voluntarily undertaken. On the other hand, man knows no more degrading or unbearable misery than forced labour. No worse fate can befall a man than to have to work every day from morning to night against his will at a job that he abhors. The more the worker feels himself a man, the more must he detest work of this kind—the more acutely is he aware of the fact that such aimless labour gives rise to no inner spiritual satisfaction. Does he work from any natural impulse, or because he enjoys the tasks that he performs? Of course not. He works for money. He works for something which has nothing to do with the tasks that he has performed. He works because he must. If only because his hours of labour are so long and so dismally monotonous, the worker must surely detest his job after the first few weeks, assuming that he possesses a spark of humanity. The division of labour has intensified the brutalizing effects of forced labour. In most branches of industry the task of the worker is limited to insignificant and purely repetitive tasks which continue minute by minute for every day of the year.[1] How much human feeling or ability can a man of thirty expect to retain if since childhood he has spent twelve hours or more daily making pin heads or filing cogwheels, and in addition has dragged out the normal existence of a member of the English proletariat? The introduction of steam-power and machinery has had the same results. The physical labour of the worker has been lightened, he is spared some of his former exertion, but the task itself is trifling and extremely monotonous. Although a job of this kind gives the worker no scope for exercising his intelligence, [it is not purely repetitive] since the operator must pay some attention to the machine to ensure that nothing is going wrong, and so he is prevented from thinking about anything else. It is obvious that a man must be degraded to the level of a beast if he is condemned to work of this kind—work which occupies the whole of his time, which barely gives him the opportunity to eat or to sleep, which affords him no freedom to enjoy the beauties of Nature and the open air, and certainly deprives him of any opportunity for intellectual activities. Once more there are only two courses open to the worker. He may submit to his fate and become a ' good worker ', ' faithfully ' serving the interests of the middle classes—and if he does so he is absolutely certain to become a mere animal—or he can resist and fight for his rights as far as is humanly possible and that necessarily involves the most strenuous opposition to the middle classes.

If all these causes result in an appalling degree of demoralisation among the working classes there is another factor in the situation which intensifies this demoralisation to an extreme degree. This is the concentration of the population. The English bourgeois writers are everlastingly condemning the evil effects of life in the great towns. These perverted Jeremiahs weep crocodile tears not over the destruction of cities, but over their expansion. Sheriff Alison blames almost everything on the dense growth of urban populations, while Dr. Vaughan in his book on *The Age of Great Cities* goes even further in his over-emphasis on this aspect of the problem.[2] This is quite

---

[1] Shall I once again quote evidence from a middle-class authority? I select only one, available to all, which appears in Adam Smith's *Wealth of Nations* (ed. J. R. McCulloch) 4 vols., 1828, Vol. 3, Book V, Chap. I, pp. 296–7. [The reference given by Engels to ' chapter VIII ' is incorrect.]

[2 Robert Vaughan, *The Age of Great Cities: or, Modern Civilization viewed in its relation to Intelligence, Morals, and Religion*, second edition (1843), pp. 221–98. For Robert Vaughan see the *D.N.B.* Vaughan, a Congregationalist pastor, was one of the few writers of the nineteenth century who looked with favour on the growth of towns. In Vaughan's view ' the new industrial economy, and with it the " great cities ", brought the promise of social, political and cultural progress: they were the agents of rationality and liberation. Cities, he thought, both represented and

understandable, because, if they were to lay adequate stress upon the other reasons for the physical and moral degradation of the workers, they would come too near to revealing the extent to which this state of affairs is connected with the vital interests of the possessing classes. If they were to confess that the main causes of degradation are poverty, insecurity of employment, long hours of work and forced labour, everyone would realise—and they would have to admit it themselves —what action must be taken to solve the problem. The necessary reforms would have to include endowing the poor with property, fixing a minimum standard of living and the passing of laws to curtail excessive hours of labour. The middle classes, however, are not prepared to agree to the introduction of such reforming measures. The big cities have sprung up spontaneously and people have flocked in to them of their own free will. In the circumstances the possessing classes are wholly unable to appreciate that these great cities were in fact created solely by industry and by the middle classes which profited by the new factories. It is easy for the possessing classes to delude themselves into a belief that the demoralisation of the workers has been due to these quite unavoidable causes. The middle classes also comfort themselves with the reflection that, after all, the social evils of the great cities existed in embryo in the smaller towns characteristic of a former age. Alison is at least humane enough to recognise this; he is not a fully fledged Liberal industrialist, but only a partially developed Tory bourgeois, and consequently can occasionally see things to which the highly developed member of the middle class is completely and utterly blind. Let him speak for himself:

The great difficulty in the management of the poor occurs in great cities. It is there that vice has spread great temptation, and pleasure her seductions, and folly her allurements: that guilt is encouraged by the hope of impunity, and idleness fostered by the frequency of example. It is to these great marts of human corruption, that the base and the profligate resort from the simplicity of country life: it is there that they find victims whereon to practise their iniquity, and gains to reward the dangers that attend them. Virtue is there depressed from the obscurity in which it is involved: guilt is matured from the difficulty of its detection: licentiousness is rewarded by the immediate enjoyments which it promises. If any person will walk through St. Giles's, the

promoted social interdependence and change. While Vaughan was fully aware of the sick and sordid state of the industrial towns, he tried to weigh up the positive versus the negative potentialities of urbanism ' (*Current Sociology*, ' Urban Sociology: trend reports and bibliography', U.N.E.S.C.O., Paris, Vol. 4, 1955, no. 4, p. 30). It is clear that Engels's comment does not give a fair impression of Vaughan's point of view.]

crowded alleys of Dublin, or the poorer quarters of Glasgow at
night, he will meet with ample proof of these observations: he will
no longer wonder at the disorderly habits and profligate enjoyments
of the lower orders: his astonishment will be, not that there is so
much, but that there is so little crime in the world.

The great cause of human corruption in these crowded situations,
is the contagious nature of bad example, and the extreme difficulty
of avoiding the seductions of vice, when they are brought into close
and daily proximity with the younger part of the people. Whatever
we may think of the strength of virtue, experience proves that the
higher orders are indebted for their exemption from atrocious
crime or disorderly habits, chiefly to their fortunate removal from
the scene of temptation: and that where they are exposed to the
seductions which assail their inferiors, they are noways behind them
in yielding to their influence. Solomon never showed his wisdom
more than in recommending to the young to fly from the allurements
of the strange woman; knowing well, that to remain and to resist
were more than could be expected of human nature. It is the
peculiar misfortune of the poor in great cities, that *they cannot fly*
from these irresistible temptations: but that, turn where they will,
they are met by the alluring forms of vice, or the seductions of
guilty enjoyment. . . . It is the experienced impossibility of *concealing
the attractions of vice* from the younger part of the poor in great cities,
which exposes them to so many causes of demoralization from
which their superiors are exempted; and renders the contagion of
guilt so infinitely more rapid than the influence of good example.

After a lengthy description of the moral condition of the workers our
author continues:

All this proceeds, not from any unwonted or extraordinary
depravity in the character of these victims of licentiousness, but
from the almost irresistible nature of the temptations to which the
poor are exposed. Doubtless all in every rank are by nature prone
to corruption; but this inherent tendency to evil does not attach to
one class of society more than another. The rich who censure their
conduct would in all probability yield as rapidly as they have done
to the influence of similar causes. There is a certain degree of misery,
a certain proximity to sin, which virtue is rarely able to withstand,
and which the young in particular are generally unable to resist.
The progress of vice in such circumstances is almost as certain, and
often nearly as rapid as that of physical contagion.

And later in the book:

When the higher orders, for their own profit, have drawn the
labouring classes in great numbers into a small space, the contagion
of guilt becomes rapid and unavoidable. The lower orders, situated
as they are in so far as regards moral or religious instructions, are

frequently hardly more to be blamed for yielding to the temptations which surround them, than for falling victims to the typhus fever.[1]

Enough of this! Although Alison has one foot in the middle-class camp and has a narrow-minded approach to the question, his writings do reveal to us the disastrous consequences of the growth of the great towns on the moral condition of the workers. Another writer, Dr. Andrew Ure,[2] who is completely bourgeois in outlook, and a man after the heart of the Anti-Corn Law League, makes revealing admissions concerning another aspect of the problem. He explains to us how life in the great towns facilitates working-class organization and gives power to the masses. If the urban workers are not given any education—and by education Ure means the inculcation of obedience to the middle classes—there is a real danger that they will view economic problems solely in the light of their own selfish interests, and so fall victims to the wiles of unscrupulous demagogues. Dr. Ure fears that the urban workers may actually adopt an envious and hostile attitude towards the frugal, enterprising industrialists, who are actually the workers' *greatest benefactors*. Only a sound education for the proletariat can stave off the national bankruptcy and other calamities which would inevitably follow from a workers' revolution. The fears expressed by this middle-class writer are fully justified. If the concentration of population in urban centres furthers the expansion of middle-class power, at the same time it leads to an even more rapid development among the working classes. The workers begin to feel themselves members of a homogenous social group. They realise that, although they are weak as individuals, they are strong if united. Urban life tends to divide the proletariat from the middle classes. It helps to weld the proletariat into a compact group with its own ways of life and thought and its own outlook on society. The worker begins to realise that he is being oppressed and the proletariat develops into a class which has both social and political significance. In this way the great cities are the birthplace of the working-class movement. It is there that the workers first began to reflect upon the conditions under which they live and began the struggle to alter them. The cities first saw the rise of the workers and the middle classes into opposing social

---

[1] Sir Archibald Alison, *Principles of Population*, Vol. 2, pp. 76–7, 82–3, 135. [In his quotation from Alison's book Engels omits some sentences without indicating that this has been done. Such of the omissions as are necessary to follow the argument have been restored.]

[2] *Philosophy of Manufactures* (London, 1835), p. 406 et seq. We shall have occasion to refer elsewhere to this precious work. [Ure's reference to 'secret cabal and co-operative union' among factory workers occurs in one paragraph on p. 407 of his book.]

groups. It was in the towns that the trade-union movement, Chartism and socialism all had their origin. The sickness of society, which was chronic in the countryside, became acute in the towns, with the result that its true nature and the proper means of effecting a cure were both revealed. But for the growth of the big towns and their stimulating influence on the discussion of the questions of the day, the workers would not have made the progress which in fact they have done. The workers have destroyed the last vestiges of the old system of benevolent paternalism in the relationship between masters and men. Here again the development of large factories contributed to bring this about because it led to a substantial increase in the number of workers dependent upon a single capitalist. The middle classes bitterly lament the passing of the old relationship between the employer and his hands and they have every reason to do so, because this former state of affairs gave the middle classes comparative security against rebellious discontent among their employees. In those days the middle-class employer could lord it over his men and exploit them to his heart's content. He could actually expect obedience, gratitude, and devotion into the bargain from these stupid folk, if he were graciously pleased to make a friendly gesture or bestow a trifling favour—which cost him nothing—over and above the wages which he had agreed to pay. Such concessions appeared to be made entirely out of the goodness of his heart; in fact, of course, they did not represent one-tenth of what the capitalist really owed his men. It may be granted that as an individual capitalist, placed in a situation not of his own creation, he did not wholly neglect his obligations [towards the workers]. On the other hand, as a representative of the ruling class—a class which is accountable to the whole community because it holds power, and assumes responsibility for the common welfare—he accepted no social obligations, but on the contrary actually plundered the nation as a whole for his own private advantage. In the days when there was a patriarchal relationship between master and man, a situation which hypocritically disguised the fact that the proletariat was enslaved, the individual worker was inevitably morally and spiritually inert. He remained wholly ignorant concerning the nature of his own interests and was no more than a cipher. Only when the worker became estranged from his employer did the situation change. Then it became clear to the worker that he was linked to his master only by selfish interest and the cash nexus. Then the bond of personal devotion, which was incapable of bearing the slightest strain, snapped completely. Then at last the worker ceased to be a slave of the capitalist in thought, sentiment and action.

The growth of large-scale industry and of great cities has contributed to a considerable extent to bring about these changes. Another factor which has had a great influence on the attitude of the English workers is the wave of Irish immigration to which we have already referred in this connection. It has been observed that the arrival of the Irish has degraded the English workers, lowering both their standard of living and the level of their behaviour. On the other hand the Irish immigrants have helped to widen the gulf that separates the capitalists from the workers, thus inevitably hastening the approaching cataclysm. The social disorder from which England is suffering is running the same course as a disease which attacks human beings. It develops according to definite laws. It has its crises and it is the last and most violent of these which decides the fate of the patient. But this final crisis [which may kill a human sufferer] cannot kill an entire nation. The English people must emerge reborn and rejuvenated from this ordeal. Consequently we must welcome any circumstances which bring the disease to its climax. The Irish immigration is hastening this process because the passionate, excitable sides of the Irish character have had their effects on the English workers. In many ways the English are to the Irish as the Germans are to the French. In the long run this union of the livelier, more mercurial and more fiery temperament of the Irish with the stolid, patient and sensible character of the English can only be mutually beneficial. The harsh egotism of the English middle classes would have kept its hold much more firmly on the English proletariat, if it had not been for this Irish element.

It is in the nature of the Irish to be generous to a fault and to be swayed almost wholly by sentiment. Through inter-marriage and by daily contact in the workaday world these Irish attributes have softened the cold and rational aspects of the English character.

In the circumstances it is not surprising that the working classes have become a race apart from the English bourgeoisie. The middle classes have more in common with every other nation in the world than with the proletariat which lives on their own doorsteps. The workers differ from the middle classes in speech, in thoughts and ideas, in customs, morals, politics and religion. They are two quite different nations, as unlike as if they were differentiated by race. We on the Continent have only met one of these two nations—the English bourgeoisie. Yet it is the other section of the population, the proletariat, which will be of far greater importance for England's future.[1]

---

[1] *Engels's note to the German edition of* 1892: It is well known that at about the same time Disraeli in his novel *Sybil, or the Two Nations,* realised that large-scale industry had split the English people into two different nations.

We shall have occasion in due course to discuss the political principles of the English workers and the influence exerted on public affairs by working men through their associations. For the time being we propose to confine ourselves to the way in which the circumstances which we have just been discussing have affected the private lives of the working classes. I have already pointed out that a beggar directs his appeals to the workers alone, and that the working classes do far more than the bourgeoisie to support the poor. This statement can be substantiated every day and it is confirmed by the Rev. Richard Parkinson, canon of Manchester:

The poor give more to each other than the rich give to the poor. I am confirmed in this assertion by the testimony of one of our oldest, most learned, and most observant physicians [Dr. Bardsley], whose humanity is as conspicuous as his learning and talent, and who has often publicly declared that the experience of nearly fifty years has convinced him that the aggregate sum given in each year by the poor to each other exceeds that contributed by the rich in the same period.[1]

There are many other shining examples of the kindliness of the workers. They themselves have experienced bitter suffering and consequently are sympathetic towards those in dire need. A worker regards all his fellow-beings as men, [whatever their condition], whereas the middle classes look down on the workers as something less than human. And so the workers are more sociable and more friendly [towards those who are less fortunate than themselves]. Although the workers cannot really afford to give charity on the same scale as the middle classes, they are nevertheless more charitable in every way. The workers look at money from a different angle than the middle classes. To a worker money has no more worth than the value of the things that it will buy. On the other hand, the middle classes believe that money has a specific inherent God-like quality and it is this attitude which makes the bourgeois a nasty, vulgar ' money grubber '. Consequently the workers, in whom money does not inspire this kind of awe, are much less grasping than the middle classes. The bourgeoisie will stop at nothing to acquire wealth, and regard the filling of their money bags as the main purpose of existence. The workers are therefore much less prejudiced than the middle classes.

[1] Richard Parkinson, B.D., Canon of Manchester, *On the Present Condition of the Labouring Poor in Manchester . . .*, 3rd edn., London and Manchester, 1841, pp. 9–10 [Engels's version of this quotation is a shortened one. For a brief biography of Parkinson, see John Evans's ' Canon Parkinson : a biographical sketch ': *Papers of the Manchester Literary Club*, iv, 1877–8 (1878), pp. 79–94].

They are not blinded to the facts of everyday life by selfishness, as are the middle classes. The workers are shielded by their defective education from the prejudices of religion, and do not worry about things of which they are ignorant. They are quite free from that religious fanaticism which holds the bourgeoisie in its grip. If any of the workers do possess some veneer of religion it is only a nominal attachment to some religious body, and does not indicate any spiritual conviction. In practice the workers live only for this world and try to make themselves as comfortable as possible here below. All bourgeois writers are agreed that the workers have no religion and do not go to church. Exceptions to this are the Irish, a few of the older workers and those wage-earners who have one foot in the middle-class camp—overlookers, foremen and so on. Among the mass of the working-class population, however, one nearly always finds an utter indifference to religion. At most one finds traces of Deism, but this is so primitive a belief that it is little more than a figure of speech, or else a vague fear of being called an infidel[1] or atheist. Although the clergy of all denominations have only recently lost their influence over the workers, they are now greatly disliked by working men. The mere cry: ' He's a parson '[2] is often enough to force a clergyman off the platform at a public meeting. Compared with the bourgeoisie, the workers—lacking religious convictions and education, and labouring under other disadvantages [already discussed] —are relatively free from prejudice and from the restrictions imposed by inherited principles and hidebound opinions.

The members of the bourgeoisie are imprisoned by the class prejudices and principles which have been ruthlessly drummed into them from childhood. Nothing can be done about people of this sort. In practice the middle classes support the established order of things, however progressive they may sometimes appear to be. Their interests are completely bound up with the present economic and social structure and they will never be able to adapt themselves to changing conditions. The middle classes are losing their position as leaders of a phase in historical development. The just claim of the workers to replace them will one day be realised.

These aspects of working-class life, coupled with the public activities of the workers to which we shall later refer, together reveal the favourable side of the character of the English workers. The unfavourable traits can be quickly summarised, and arise naturally out of the circumstances already discussed. Drunkenness, fornication,

[1 Engels uses the word ' infidel ' in English.]
[2 Engels uses the phrase ' He is a parson ' in English.]

brutality and thieving are the main crimes of which the middle classes accuse the workers. It is not surprising that the workers should drink heavily. Sheriff Alison asserts[1] that 30,000 workers are drunk in Glasgow every Saturday night. And this is certainly no under-estimate. He states that in 1830 there was in Glasgow one public house to every twelve dwelling houses. By 1840 there was one public house to every ten dwelling houses. He goes on to state that the quan-tity of spirits on which excise was paid in Scotland rose from 2,300,000 gallons in 1823 to 6,620,000 gallons in 1839. Comparable figures for England are: 1,976,000 gallons in 1823 and 7,875,000 gallons in 1837.[2] In 1830 the Beer Act was passed, which made it easier to open beer-houses, the so-called ' [Tom and] Jerry shops '. The owner of such a shop was licensed to sell beer for consumption on the premises.[3] This Act encouraged drunkenness by increasing the opportunities for beer-drinking.[4] Practically every street has several beer-houses and in the countryside, where one finds two or three houses together, one of them will certainly be a jerry-shop. There are also ' hush-shops ' which are unlicensed beer-shops, and therefore illegal. In addition there are an equal number of drinking places which harbour illicit stills and produce large quantities of spirits. They are to be found in the centre of the great cities, down side streets seldom visited by the police. Gaskell estimates that in Manchester alone there are over a hundred of these illicit stills with an annual output of 156,000 gallons.[5] Manchester also has over a thousand ' inns, beer-houses and gin-vaults '[6] and in proportion to the number of houses there are at least

[1] Sir Archibald Alison, *The Principles of Population*, Vol 2, 1840, p. 80. [Alison's actual words are: ' . . . at Glasgow nearly 30,000 persons are every Saturday night in a state of brutal intoxication '.]

[2 The increase in the quantity of spirits on which excise was paid in Scotland between 1823 and 1837 was by no means wholly due to an increased consumption on the part of the workers. Nearly double the quantity of spirits was submitted for excise in 1824 (4,350,301 gallons) as compared with 1823 (2,303,286 gallons). This was due to a reduction in the excise duty in 1823 from 6s. to 4¾d. a gallon. This resulted in the produce of many illicit stills being brought forward for submission to duty, as it was no longer as profitable to evade the law. In other words, the quantity of spirits which paid excise before 1823 was not an accurate measure of consumption. In comparing consumption between 1823 and 1837 the increase of population in Scotland should also be borne in mind: J. R. McCulloch, *A Dictionary of Commerce* (2 vols., edn. of 1847) ii, 1168–9. In England there was no change of excise in 1823, but in 1826 the excise duty was reduced from 11s. 4¼d. to 7s. per gallon and this was raised to 7s. 6d. in 1830: ibid, 1170.]

[3 Engels wrote the words ' to be drunk on the premises ' in English. A beer-shop sold beer only, but a public house sold spirits as well as beer.]

[4 P. Gaskell, *The Manufacturing Population of England* (1833), pp. 349–51.]

[5 P. Gaskell, *The Manufacturing Population of England* (1833), pp. 125–6.].

[6 Gaskell, op. cit., p. 117, stated ' In Manchester alone there are very near if not quite one thousand inns, beer-houses, and gin-vaults. . .']

as many beer shops in Manchester as in Glasgow. The same is true of all the other great cities. Quite apart from all the usual consequences of drunkenness, it must be remembered that in these various drinking places men, women and children, and even mothers with babies in their arms, meet with thieves, prostitutes and swindlers, who are the most degraded victims of the bourgeois régime. When one recalls that some mothers actually give spirits to children in arms, it must surely be admitted that it is highly demoralising to visit these drinking places. It is particularly on Saturday evenings that intoxication can be seen in all its bestiality, for it is then that the workers have just received their wages and go out for enjoyment at rather earlier hours than on other days of the week. On Saturday evenings the whole working class streams from the slums into the main streets of the towns. On such an evening in Manchester I have seldom gone home without seeing many drunkards staggering in the road or lying helpless in the gutter. On Sunday the same sort of things happen, but with less noisy disturbances. And when the revellers have no money left they go to the nearest pawnshop with whatever they have. Every great city has many pawnshops—Manchester, for example, has over sixty, while in Salford there are ten or twelve in Chapel Street alone. On every Saturday evening [after receiving their wages] the workers redeem vast quantities of furniture, Sunday clothes (if they have any) and crockery, but these articles are nearly always pawned again by the following Wednesday. Eventually, owing to some chance, it proves impossible to redeem the pledges, and so one article after another falls into the hands of the moneylender. Sometimes goods are pawned again and again until they are worn out and the pawnbroker will not advance another farthing on them.[1] When we consider the vast extent of drunkenness among the English workers, Lord Ashley's assertion that the workers spend £25,000,000 sterling a year on spirituous liquor can be readily accepted.[2] It is easy to see the consequences of widespread drunkenness—the deterioration in personal circumstances, the catastrophic decline in health and morals, the breaking up of homes. The temperance societies have, it is true, done

[1 Gaskell, op. cit., pp. 123–4.]
[2] House of Commons debate of February 28th, 1843. [This refers to a debate on the condition and education of the poor on February 28th, 1843. What Ashley was reported as saying is as follows:
' In the year 1834 a committee was appointed on the motion of Mr. Buckingham, to investigate the causes and effects of drunkenness. That committee produced a report . . . from that report we learn that the sum annually expended by the working-people in the consumption of ardent spirits is estimated at twenty-five millions! and ' I have no doubt ', says a witness of great experience, ' That it is, in fact, to a much larger extent ': *Hansard's Parliamentary Debates*, 3rd series, Vol. 67 (1843), col. 62.]

a great deal, but what are a few thousand teetotallers[1] among millions of workers? When Father Mathew,[2] the Irish apostle of temperance, visits an English town, from thirty to sixty thousand workers will often take the pledge,[3] but within four weeks most of them have lapsed. If you add up the number of people in Manchester who have taken the pledge in the last three or four years they amount to more than the whole population of the town. And yet there has been no noticeable decline in the amount of drunkenness in Manchester.

Apart from over-indulgence in intoxicating liquors, the sexual immorality of many English workers is one of their greatest failings. This, too, inevitably follows from the circumstances in which this class of society is placed. The workers have been left to themselves without the moral training necessary for the proper control of their sexual desires. While burdening the workers with numerous hardships the middle classes have left them only the two pleasures of drink and sexual intercourse. The result is that the workers, in order to get something out of life, are passionately devoted to these two pleasures and indulge in them to excess and in the grossest fashion. If people are relegated to the position of animals, they are left with the alternatives of revolting or sinking into bestiality. Moreover the middle classes are themselves in no small degree responsible for the extent to which prostitution exists—how many of the 40,000 prostitutes who fill the streets of London every evening[4] are dependent for their livelihood on the virtuous bourgeoisie? How many of them were first seduced by a member of the middle classes, so that they now have to sell their persons to passers-by in order to live? Truly, the middle classes are least entitled to accuse the workers of sexual licence. Indeed, all the failings of the workers may be traced to the same sort of origin— an unbridled thirst for pleasure, to lack of foresight, inability to adjust themselves to the disciplines of the social order, and above all, the inability to sacrifice immediate pleasure for a future advantage. But who can blame them for this? A class which can only buy a very few —and those the most sensual—pleasures in return for the hardest labour, can hardly be criticised for blindly indulging in those pleasures to wild excess. The workers form a class whose education has been grossly neglected and whose welfare is threatened by all sorts of

[1 Engels printed the word ' teetotallers ' in English.]
[2 For Father Theobald Mathew, see the *Dictionary of National Biography*.]
[3 The word ' pledge ' is in English in the original.]
4 Sir Archibald Alison, *The Principles of Population* (1840), Vol. 2, 147. [What Alison actually wrote was: ' When we reflect that thirty or forty thousand young women have embarked in a mode of life in London, which entails degradation in themselves, and dissolute habits in others. . .']

mishaps. They know nothing of security. Why on earth should they
be provident in any way? Why should they lead ' respectable ' lives
and think of some future happiness instead of indulging in some
immediate pleasure which happens to come their way? For *them*, of
all people, future happiness is something of a hypothetical nature,
because of the perpetually shifting and uncertain conditions under
which they are forced to exist. The proletariat has to suffer all the
drawbacks of the present social order without enjoying any of its
advantages. The workers regard this social order as highly inimical
to their interests. Why then should they respect it? That indeed
would be asking too much. But the working classes cannot escape the
social order while it survives and if an individual worker has the
temerity to rebel against it he suffers grievous penalties. Family life
for the worker is almost impossible under the existing social system.
All he has is a dirty and comfortless hovel which is barely adequate as
sleeping quarters. It is badly furnished and unheated. Often the roof
leaks and there is no comfort to be found in the stifling atmosphere
of an overcrowded room. The various members of the family only see
each other in the mornings and evenings, because the husband is away
at his work all day long. Perhaps his wife and the older children also
go out to work and they may be in different factories. In these
circumstances how can family life exist? It has already been seen that
the constant lure of the public house is another factor inimical to the
stability of family life. All the same, the worker cannot escape from
his home and must live with his family. Consequently there are endless
domestic troubles and family quarrels, which are highly demoralising
both for the children and the parents. Among the English workers it
is all too common to find that household duties are totally neglected
and that children are left entirely to their own devices. These faults
are due entirely to existing social conditions. And how can the
children grow up into decent, sober adults if they have been left to
run wild when young and if they have grown up in surroundings of a
demoralising character? The parents, of course, have themselves
helped to create the thoroughly unsatisfactory environment in which
the children have been reared. The self-satisfied middle classes are
really asking too much if they expect children brought up under these
conditions to become respectable members of society later on.

The clearest indication of the unbounded contempt of the workers
for the existing social order is the wholesale manner in which they
break its laws. If the demoralisation of the worker passes beyond a
certain point then it is just as natural that he will turn into a criminal—
as inevitably as water turns into steam at boiling point. Owing to the

brutal and demoralising way in which he is treated by the bourgeoisie, the worker loses all will of his own and, like water, he is forced to follow blindly the laws of nature. There comes a point when the worker loses all power [to withstand temptation]. Consequently the incidence of crime has increased with the growth of the working-class population and there is more crime in Britain than in any other country in the world. The annual statistics of crime issued by the Home Office show that there has been an extraordinarily rapid growth of crime. The number of those committed for trial on criminal charges in England and Wales alone has increased sevenfold in thirty-seven years:

1805 ...	...	4,605	1830... ...	18,107
1810 ...	...	5,146	1835... ...	20,731
1815 ...	...	7,818	1840... ...	27,187
1820 ...	...	13,710	1841... ...	27,760
1825 ...	...	14,437	1842... ...	31,309[1]

In Lancashire alone in 1842 the number of persons committed for trial came to 4,497, which amounted to over 14 per cent of the total committals. In Middlesex, including London, 4,094 persons were com-

---

[1 See G. R. Porter, *The Progress of the Nation*, new edn., 1851, p. 635. In the original German edition of 1845 Engels wrongly gave the figures for 1815 as 7,898. It may be added that the number of *convictions* in these years was substantially less. e.g.

1805	...	...	2,783	1830	12,805
1810	...	...	3,158	1835	14,729
1815	...	...	4,883	1840	19,927
1820	...	...	9,318	1841	20,280
1825	...	...	9,964	1842	22,733

(Porter, op. cit., p. 635).

Engels failed to take two factors into account when discussing British criminal statistics—the increase of population and the improvement in the machinery for the detection and punishment of evil-doers, particularly after 1829. As Mrs. Jenifer Hart has pointed out in her article, 'Reform of the borough police, 1836–56' (*English Historical Review*, July 1955, p. 412):

There exist figures showing the number of persons charged with the more serious offences, and the numbers convicted, year by year. These would be sufficient for our purpose if we could assume that a variation in the charge and/or conviction rates represented a corresponding variation in the amount of crime. But this is not an assumption we are warranted in making, for charges and convictions were no doubt affected by other factors, such as changes in the efficiency of the police and in the criminal law (of which there were many during this period) and in the ease of prosecuting. . . .

Between 1835 and 1844 more than 120 municipal corporations established police forces, on the model of the Metropolitan Police of 1829, particularly after the passing of the Municipal Corporations Act of 1835 (see table, op. cit., p. 416). For Bruno Hildebrand's criticism of Engels's misinterpretation of British criminal statistics see *Nationalökonomie der Gegenwart und Zukunft* (Frankfurt am Main), Vol 1 (1848), pp. 211–7.]

mitted for trial, which represented over 13 per cent of the total. These statistics show that two regions which include great towns with a large working class population accounted for over a quarter of the total crime in the country, although the inhabitants of Lancashire and Middlesex by no means represent anything like a quarter of the total population of the country. Other evidence from the criminal statistics proves that the working classes are responsible for nearly all the crime in the country. In 1842, for example, 32.35 per cent of the criminals were totally illiterate, 58.32 per cent had an imperfect knowledge of reading and writing, while only 6.77 per cent could read and write properly, and only 0.22 per cent had received any form of higher education. No information was available concerning the education of 2.34 per cent of lawbreakers. Crime has increased even more rapidly in Scotland [than in England and Wales.] Here only 89 persons were charged with criminal offences in 1819; by 1837, however, the number of persons committed for such offences had increased to 3,126[1] and in 1842 to 4,189. In Lanarkshire, where Sheriff Alison himself was responsible for making the official return, the population doubled in thirty years, but the number of persons committed for trial doubled every five and a half years. Crime therefore increased six times more rapidly than population. In Britain as in all civilised countries, by far the greatest number of offences are crimes against property. Such offences are obviously due to poverty of one sort or another, because no one needs to steal what he already possesses. In the Netherlands there is one offence against property for every 7,140 of the population, and in France there is one such offence to every 1,804 persons. In England, however, at the time when Gaskell was writing [1833] the ratio was 1:799. With regard to the ratio between offences against the person and total population the figures for the three countries are as follows: the Netherlands 1:28,904, France 1:17,573 and England 1:23,395.[2]

In England, taking into consideration all forms of crime, the ratio between population and offences is 1:1,043 in agricultural districts and 1:840 in [certain] manufacturing districts.[3] In the whole of

[1] Engels gave this figure as 3,176. The correct figure is given in Porter, op. cit., p. 658.]
[2] Gaskell took this information from the table on page 16 of W. R. Greg's anonymous pamphlet of 1831 entitled *An Enquiry into the State of the Manufacturing Population, and the causes and cures of the evils therein existing.* Greg gave full references to the sources of the table.]
[3] P. Gaskell, *The Manufacturing Population of England* (1833), chap. 10, pp. 285-287. [See also J. Fletcher, 'Progress of Crime in the United Kingdom . . .' *Journal of the Statistical Society of London,* Vol. VI, 1843.]

England, however, the ratio is now 1:660,[1] although it is hardly ten years since Gaskell's book appeared. These facts are surely more than sufficient to make everybody—even a member of the middle classes—aware of the seriousness of the consequences of such a state of affairs. What will be the consequences if demoralisation and crime increase in the same degree in the next twenty years? And should English industry be less prosperous in the next twenty years then the rate of increase in crime will be greater still. Already we see society in the process of dissolution. No one can pick up a newspaper without finding conclusive evidence of the way in which all social ties are being strained to breaking point. I will pick up at random just one newspaper from a file lying before me—it is the *Manchester Guardian* for October 30th, 1844, which contains three days' news. The paper no longer bothers to give a comprehensive account of events in Manchester, but confines itself to reporting isolated items of particular interest: in this copy there is an account of a strike for higher wages in a mill and the workers have been forced to go back to work by a J.P.; in Salford some boys have committed robberies, while a bankrupt tradesman has tried to swindle his creditors. Fuller reports are given of events in neighbouring towns. In Ashton there have been two cases of theft, one of burglary and one suicide; in Bury, there has been a case of theft; in Bolton, there have been two cases of theft and one infringement of excise regulations; in Leigh one theft. In Oldham, there have been a strike for higher wages, a theft, and a brawl between Irish women, as well as an assault by trade-unionist hatters on a blackleg, and a mother beaten by her son. In Rochdale there have been several brawls, an attack on a constable, and a case of sacrilege. From Stockport it is reported that some of the workers were dissatisfied with their wages. There was a theft, a swindle, a brawl and a case of wifebeating. In Warrington there was a case of theft and a street fight. In Wigan there was a case of theft and a case of sacrilege.[2] The reports of the London papers are still worse. They are full of accounts of swindles, thefts, robberies with violence and serious family quarrels. I pick up a copy of *The Times* for September 12th, 1844, at random, which reports the events of only a single day. In this number there are reports of a robbery, a [fatal] attack on a policeman, a bastardy order against the father of an illegitimate child, the abandonment of a child by its parents, and the poisoning of a man by his wife.[3]

---

[1] The total population (about 15 millions) divided by the number of convicted offenders (22,733). [22,733 is the figure of convictions for offences in England and Wales in 1842 (Porter, op. cit., p. 635).]

[[2] See *Manchester Guardian*, Oct. 30th, 1844, pp. 4–7.]

[[3] See *The Times*, Sept. 12th, and 13th, 1844.]

Similar events are chronicled in all English newspapers. There can be no doubt that in England the social war is already being waged. Everyone looks after his own interests and fights only for himself against all comers. Whether in doing so he injures those who are his declared enemies is simply a matter of selfish calculation as to whether such action would be to his advantage or not. It no longer occurs to anybody to come to a friendly understanding with his neighbours. All differences of opinion are settled by threats, by invoking the courts, or even by taking the law into one's own hands. In short, everyone sees in his neighbour a rival to be elbowed aside, or at best a victim to be exploited for his own ends. The criminal statistics prove that this social war is being waged more vigorously, more passionately and with greater bitterness every year. Social strife is gradually developing into combat between two great opposing camps—the middle classes and the proletariat. No one need be surprised at the existence either of the social war of all against all or of the struggle between the workers and the bourgeoisie. These conflicts are no more than the logical consequence of the fundamental principle upon which free competition is based. It is, however, somewhat surprising that the bourgeoisie should remain so complacent and placid in the face of the thunderclouds which are gathering overhead and grow daily more threatening. How can the middle classes read about these things in the newspapers every day without showing some anxiety as to the consequences? Do they not see that the individual crimes of which they read will one day culminate in universal revolution? It would, of course, be too much to expect from the middle classes any sign of indignation at the state of affairs which gives rise to this threat of social upheaval. For, after all, this is the bourgeoisie, and as such is naturally blind to the facts of the situation and to the consequences which will follow from this state of affairs. It is indeed astonishing that ingrained prejudices and preconceived ideas should afflict a social class to such an extent that this blindness might well be called a form of madness. Meanwhile national affairs take their course, whether the middle classes realise what is happening or not, and one fine day the property-holding class will be overwhelmed by events far beyond their comprehension and quite outside their expectations.

CHAPTER VII

THE PROLETARIAT

[(a) Factory Workers in the main textile industries]

We now propose to discuss in greater detail the condition of the industrial proletariat in some of the more important branches of manufacture. In doing so we follow the principle discussed at the beginning of chapter two, that is to say we shall begin by considering those workers who are covered by the Factory Act.[1] This Act regulates the hours of work in factories in which wool, silk, cotton and flax are spun and woven by machines driven by water- or steam-power. The Act therefore covers the most important branches of English industry. The factory hands employed in these industries belong to that group of workers whose mode of life was first changed by the Industrial Revolution. They form the most numerous, the most intelligent, most energetic and also the most unruly section of the English working classes. Of all the English workers they are those most hated by the middle classes. These workers, particularly the cotton operatives, are in the van of the working-class movement just as their masters, especially those in Lancashire, form the spearhead of middle-class agitations.

In our historical introduction we showed how the textile workers were the first to be uprooted from their customary way of life by the introduction of new machinery. It is not surprising, therefore, that in later years, too, it was the workers in these very industries who were again most radically and most permanently affected by technological progress. Histories of the modern development of the cotton industry, such as those of Ure,[2] Baines[3] and others, tell on every page of technical innovations. Most of these have been adapted to work up textile fabrics other than cotton. Machinery has replaced hand labour in practically all processes [of textile manufacture], and water-power or steam-power now drive virtually all the machines. This process continues and every year there are fresh improvements to be chronicled.

In a well-ordered society such improvements would indeed be welcome, but social war rages unchecked and the benefits derived

[1 On page 27, however, Engels defines the first group of industrial workers as those ' engaged in working up raw materials '.]

[2 Dr. Andrew Ure, *The Cotton Manufacture of Great Britain*, 2 vols. (1836).

[3 Edward Baines, jun., *History of the Cotton Manufacture in Great Britain* . . . , (1835).

from these improvements are ruthlessly monopolised by a few persons, while the vast majority [of the workers] lose their very means of subsistence. Every improvement in machinery leads to unemployment, and the greater the technical improvement the greater the unemployment. Every improvement in machinery affects a number of workers in the same way as a commercial crisis and leads to want, distress and crime. A few examples may be given. The jenny, the first of these inventions[1] could be operated by a single worker and produced in a given time at least six times as much yarn as the spinning wheel. Consequently every new jenny put five hand spinners out of work. The throstle, which produced much more yarn than the jenny and was also operated by one worker only, once more led to fresh unemployment. The mule, which once more employed fewer workers in relation to the amount of yarn produced, had the same effect. Every improvement of the mule—that is to say, every increase in the number of spindles to each mule—goes on reducing the number of operatives required. This expansion of the number of spindles on each mule is so significant that very large numbers of operatives have been thrown out of work in this way. At one time a spinner[2] assisted by a few children (piecers) could keep 600 spindles going. He can now supervise between 1,400 and 2,000 spindles on two mules. The result is that two adult spinners and some of their piecers have been thrown out of work. Subsequently self-acting mules have been introduced into a large number of spinning establishments. This has resulted in the disappearance of the [skilled] spinner whose functions are now performed by machinery. I have before me a book based on the experience of James Leach[3] who is one of the acknowledged leaders of the Manchester Chartists.[4] Leach has worked in various branches

[1 Engels wrote ' see above ' in the text. He is referring to page 12.]
[2 Engels uses the English word ' spinners '.]
[3 Anon. [James Leach], *Stubborn Facts from the Factories by a Manchester Operative*. (Published and dedicated to the working classes by William Rashleigh [jun.], M.P., London 1844, pp. 28, 32, 34). [According to Adoratskij, Engels is the only writer who identifies Leach as the Manchester operative concerned. The pamphlet attacks the Anti-Corn Law League and Rashleigh exhorted the workers as follows: ' Read the following pages. They are written by one of your own order '.]
[4 James Leach, a factory worker who later became a printer, appears to have entered the Chartist movement early in 1840. He rose rapidly and took a leading part in establishing the National Charter Association in Manchester (1840). In 1842 he was vice-chairman of the Chartist National Convention in London. Six years later he was again a Manchester delegate to the National Convention and was arrested on a charge of conspiracy in 1848. He was then said to be 42 years of age. Leach was a Protectionist, and a strong opponent of the Anti-Corn Law League, the meetings of which he tried to disrupt in 1839, as described by Engels (*infra*, p. 342). Leach also attacked the introduction of labour-saving machinery in industry. (We are indebted to Mr. Donald Read of Leeds University for information about Leach).]

of industry both in factories and coalmines and is known to me personally as an upright, trustworthy and capable fellow.[1] Owing to his position in the Chartist movement he had access to very detailed information about various factories collected by the workers themselves. According to Leach's tables it appears that in 35 factories [about which information was secured] there were 1,083[2] fewer mule spinners in 1841 as compared with 1829, although the number of spindles in these 35[3] factories had increased by no less than 99,429.[4] Leach mentions five factories in which no coarse spinners were employed because in these establishments only self-actors are used.[5] Whereas the number of spindles had increased by 10 per cent the number of mule spinners declined by more than 60 per cent. He adds that in the past three years so many improvements have been made in various ways, particularly by installing two rows of spindles instead of one (i.e. double-decking)[6] that in some of the factories to which he refers half of the remaining spinners have been dismissed since 1841. In one factory alone there are now only 20 [fine] spinners where not long ago 80 were employed. The remainder have either been dismissed or forced to accept children's work at children's wages.[7] Other evidence provided by Leach discloses a similar state of affairs in Stockport. Here only 140 spinners were employed in 1843[8] as compared with 800 in 1835–6,[9] in spite of the fact that Stockport's [cotton] industry has expanded considerably in the past eight or nine years. Similar improvements have now been made in carding engines which have resulted in throwing half the workers out of employment. In one factory improved drawing frames were installed with the result that four girls out of eight lost their jobs. Moreover those still at work found that their [weekly] wages were reduced from 8s. to 7s.[10] The

[1 Engels referred to Leach as his ' good friend ' in an article in the *Westphälisches Dampfboot*, 1846, p. 21. See above p. 342].

[2 Engels originally wrote 1,060 instead of 1,083. See tables in Leach, op. cit., pp. 28–29.]

[3 I.e. 20 of the largest mills spinning coarse counts and 15 spinning fine counts.]

[4 Here Engels wrote 99,239 instead of 99,429. This was caused by an error in the table (Leach, op. cit., pp. 28–29).]

[5 According to Leach, these were the factories belonging to Clark, Beever, Dodson, Norris, and Birley (op. cit., p. 28).]

[6 ' Double-decking ' is in English in the original.]

[7 Leach, op. cit., p. 30.]

[8 In the original German edition of 1845 Engels wrote ' 1843 ', and this is the date mentioned by Leach. In the American edition of 1887 it was given as 1840 and this was repeated in the first edition brought out in England in 1892.]

[9 The source of this information is described by Leach as a ' report got up intending to show the condition of the working people in the town of Stockport, in 1843 ': op. cit., p. 32. See also *supra*, p. 101, and the *Northern Star*, no. 294, July 1st, 1843, p. 1, col. 5 (news item on the state of Stockport).]

[10 Leach, op. cit., p. 34.]

same thing has happened in the weaving section of the industry. The power loom has taken over one branch of hand weaving after another. Here again many workers have been thrown out of employment by the power-loom, since this machine has a much greater output than the hand-loom, and one worker can operate two power-looms. A similar state of affairs exists in all [textile] factories—in flax spinning, wool spinning and silk twisting. The power-loom has even been introduced into certain sections of woollen and linen weaving. In Rochdale alone there are more power-looms than hand-looms in flannel weaving and in other sections of woollen weaving.

When criticisms are made about the hardships resulting from the introduction of improved machinery, the stock answer of the middle classes is that technical innovations, by reducing production costs, enable manufactured goods to be sold more cheaply. These low prices bring about such an increase in demand that the unemployed workers soon find jobs in newly erected factories. The middle classes are no doubt right from one point of view. In certain favourable circumstances—when the economy as a whole is expanding—it is true that every fall in the price of such manufactured goods as are made from *cheap* raw materials will result in an increase in consumption and in the erection of new factories. But there is not an atom of truth in the rest of the argument. The middle classes coolly ignore the fact that it takes years before the fall in the prices of manufactured goods leads to the opening of new factories. Moreover, the middle classes fail to mention the fact that every technical innovation shifts more and more of the physical labour from the worker to the machine. Consequently tasks once performed by grown men are now no longer necessary. The much less strenuous duty of supervising the operations of the machine can be performed by women and even by children at one third or half of the wages earned by the men. The middle classes do not tell us that owing to improvements in machinery entire branches of industrial activity disappear or are so radically changed that the worker is forced to acquire a fresh skill. The bourgeoisie carefully suppresses the fact—which it actually emphasises when someone proposes to ban the work of small children in factories—that the training of an efficient factory hand involves starting work as a child before the age of ten.[1] The middle classes fail to mention that the speed of technical innovation has increased to such an extent that the

[1] See various statements before the Factories Enquiry Commission. [i.e. the Royal Commission appointed to collect information in the manufacturing districts as to the employment of children in factories, 1833–34: *Parliamentary Papers*, 1833, vols. 20, 21, 1834, vols. 19, 20.]

workers are unable to keep up with it. If it really should happen that an operative were to succeed in mastering a new trade, the introduction of an improved machine would soon throw him out of work again. Thus he would lose the last shreds of his feeling of security in the industrial world. The middle classes, however, secure the advantage of technical innovation. This is particularly true of the years immediately following the introduction of new machinery. At a time when many old machines are still in use and the new technique has not been universally introduced, [those who have the new machine] reap vast profits. It would indeed be asking too much to expect the middle classes to appreciate the fact that improved machinery has its draw-backs as well as its advantages.

The workers persistently claim that improved machinery leads to wage reductions, but this, too, is denied by the middle classes. The bourgeoisie assert that although piece rates fall when productivity increases [with the use of new machines], weekly earnings have tended to rise rather than to fall, so that on the whole the position of the factory hand is better, not worse. It is difficult to discover the truth. The argument of the workers is nearly always based upon piece rates alone. It is, however, certain that in various branches of industry weekly wages have also fallen when new machinery has been introduced. The so-called fine spinners (who turn out fine mule yarn) are in a somewhat exceptional position and do draw high wages, which amount to thirty or forty shillings a week. This is due to two causes. First, the fine spinners have a strong trade union, which helps to keep up their wages, and secondly, fine spinning is a highly-skilled occupation which takes a long time to learn. The coarse spinners, on the other hand, are in a less fortunate position. They have had to struggle against the self-acting mule, which makes coarse yarn, but not fine yarn. The coarse spinners' trade union has been weakened by the introduction of these machines. Consequently the coarse spinners are able to secure only very low wages in comparison with the fine spinners. One mule-spinner told me that he did not earn more than 14s. a week and this agrees with the information given by Leach in his pamphlet. He states that in some factories fine[1] spinners earn less than 16s. 6d. a week and that one [coarse] spinner who was earning 30s. a week three years ago now earns barely 12s. 6d., which represents his average wage during the past twelve months.[2] It may well be true

[1 Engels wrote ' coarse ' instead of ' fine ' (Leach, op. cit., p. 30.)]
[2 Leach (op. cit., p. 31) quotes the following statement made to him by a spinner: ' Three years ago I could earn 30s. per week easier than I can now earn 12s. 6d., which is about the average I have received during the last twelve months '.]

that the wages of women and children have not fallen so much, but that is only because their wages never were very high. I know several women—widows with children to support—who have to work hard to earn from 8s. to 9s. a week, and everyone who is aware of the cost of living in England will agree with me that they cannot bring up a family properly on such wages. All workers are *unanimously* agreed that wages in general are lowered by improved machinery. On every occasion when there is a gathering of working men in the factory districts, the assertions of middle-class manufacturers that machinery has improved the lot of the workers are denounced as blatant lies. And what would follow even if it were true that only piece rates have fallen, while the total weekly wages have remained stable? It would mean that the workers have had to stand by quietly while their masters the manufacturers have swelled their bank balances and have gained the whole advantage from improved machines without passing on even a fraction of these gains to the operatives. When they fight the workers, the middle classes forget the most elementary principles of their economics. Normally they swear by Malthus, but now fear of the workers makes them cry: 'How would the many millions of England's increased population find work without machinery?'[1] What a stupid point of view! The middle classes know perfectly well that these 'millions of workers' would never have been called into existence and reared without the new machines and the industrial expansion which followed their invention. Machinery has benefited the workers simply by making them realise the imperative necessity of social reform. The workers now realise that machinery must no longer be used to their detriment but to their advantage. Why don't

---

[1] This is the question posed by J. C. Symons in *Arts and Artisans at Home and Abroad* (1839). [The rhetorical question in the text is not a quotation, but summarises Symons's point of view, as expressed on pages 154–5, where he wrote:

Although the progress of machinery is among the reasons why hand-loom weaving cannot rise in the scale of wages, I by no means admit that, had power-looms never been invented, the weaving trade could have been one iota less depressed than it is. There seems to be always an omission of half the case on the part of the rapidly expiring economists who infer that machinery depresses the wages of manual labour. They seem wholly to forget the millions of our doubled population to whom the capital produced by machinery has, since its introduction, afforded other employment. It were well if the gentlemen who are so assiduous in their calculations of the amount of work taken from hand-loom weaving by the power-loom, would also set about a calculation of the number of hands which, in all the varied trades of the country, power-looms have kept away from the hand-loom; and which, were it not for the employment afforded them by the capital machinery has created, would have deluged hand-loom weaving with an excess of hands and a depression of wages far greater than they labour under. In fact, machinery has been the sole salvation of the working classes from inevitable starvation.]

the middle classes in their wisdom for once in a way ask the street sweepers of Manchester and elsewhere what they used to do for a living?[1] Or for that matter let them ask the beggars or those who sell salt, matches, oranges and shoelaces in the streets.[2] Many of them could reply that they were factory workers who were now unemployed because of the introduction of machinery.[3] In the existing state of society improvements in machinery can only be detrimental to the interests of the workers, and are often extremely so. Every new machine brings with it unemployment, want and suffering. In a country like England which nearly always has a ' surplus population ', loss of his job is generally the worst fate that can befall a worker. It must be emphasised that this haunting fear of unemployment due to technical improvements has an unnerving and dispiriting effect on the morals of the workers, who are in any case in a very insecure economic position. In his despair the worker either revolts against the middle classes or drowns his sorrows in drink and debauchery. The history of the English working classes tells of hundreds of riots against machinery and we have already discussed elsewhere the demoralisation of the workers. This demoralisation is indeed another symptom of the workers' desperate reaction against the existing order of society.

The most oppressed workers are those who have to compete against a new machine which is in process of replacing hand labour. When the same goods are made both by machinery and by hand labour the price at which both types of goods sell is fixed by the cost of machine production. Consequently the handicraft worker is forced to accept very low wages. The same situation arises when a worker using an old, out-of-date machine competes with the worker who uses an improved machine. As things are, it is inevitable that the worker should suffer from the change to better machinery. The manufacturer does not want to scrap an out-of-date machine and does not wish to lose by continuing to work it. An obsolete and inanimate machine cannot be made to work better, but a living worker can be made to work for a lower wage. It is as usual the worker who has to bear all

[1] Engels adds in the text ' Street sweepers have disappeared owing to the invention and use of a mechanical street cleaner '. [Engels's information appears to have come from Leach: op. cit., p. 30. For the use and eventual abandonment of Whitworth's patent automatic street sweeper in Manchester between 1842 and 1848, see A. Redford and I. S. Russell, *The History of Local Government in Manchester*, Vol. 1 (1939), pp. 368–9, Vol. 2 (1940), pp. 141, 162–166. It was finally decided that hand-sweeping was both more economical and more efficient.]

[² See, for example, James Leach's description (op. cit., p. 30) of the displaced operatives as ' this unfortunate and degraded class '.]

[³ Ashley's speech in the House of Commons, March 15th, 1844: *Hansard's Parliamentary Debates*, 3rd series, Vol. 73, col. 1085-6 This information was supplied privately to Ashley in June 1841.]

the hardships involved in industrial change. Of all the workers who
compete against machinery the most oppressed are the handloom
weavers in the cotton industry. These workers receive the lowest
wages and even when in full employment cannot earn more than 10s.
a week. One branch of hand weaving after another is challenged by
the power-loom. Moreover handloom weaving is the refuge of workers
who have lost their livelihood in other sections [of the cotton industry].
The result is that there is always a surplus of handloom weavers, and
they consider themselves fortunate if on the average they can earn
between 6s. and 7s. a week for fourteen to eighteen hours a day spent
behind the loom. Most types of cloth have to be produced in a damp
atmosphere so that the weft does not break continually. This factor,
combined with the poverty of the workers, who cannot afford to
pay much rent, accounts for the poor state of the weavers' workshops
which, for the most part, have neither wooden nor stone floors. I
have visited many of these weavers' workshops, which are usually in
cellars, situated down obscure, foul courts and alleys. Frequently
half a dozen of these handloom weavers—some of them married
people—live together in a cottage[1] which has one or two workrooms
and one large common bedroom. They live almost entirely upon
potatoes, supplemented perhaps with a little porridge. They seldom
drink milk and they hardly ever eat meat. A large number of them are
Irish or of Irish descent. These poor wretches are the first to be
thrown out of work when there is a commercial crisis and last to be
taken on again when trade improves. The middle classes actually
point to the sufferings of these hand-loom weavers in order to justify the
factory system which provides a higher standard of living for the
operatives. ' Look,' cries the bourgeois triumphantly, ' compare the
lot of these poor starving hand-loom weavers with that of the thriving
factory operatives, and *then* pass judgment on the factory system '.[2]
In fact, of course, it is this very factory system and the machinery
associated with it, which has reduced the handloom weavers to such a
degraded situation, and the middle classes are as well aware of this as
I am. But this touches the financial interests of the middle classes and
when they are at stake a few lies and a bit of hypocrisy are neither here
nor there.

[1] [The word ' cottage ' is in English in the original].
[2] See for example, Dr. Andrew Ure's *Philosophy of Manufactures* (1835). [Engels
does not put this sentence in inverted commas as it is not an actual quotation. It is
almost certainly based upon a paragraph on pages 7–8 of Ure's book. The passage
on pages 353–4 of Ure's book which Adoratskij suggests as the basis of Engels's
remarks compares the urban and rural proletariats rather than the factory operatives
and the handloom weavers].

Let us examine a little more closely the process whereby machine-continually supersedes hand-labour. When spinning or weaving machinery is installed practically all that is left to be done by hand is the piecing together of broken threads, and the machine does the rest. This task calls for nimble fingers rather than muscular strength. The labour of grown men is not merely unnecessary but actually unsuitable, because the bones and muscles of their hands are more developed than those of women and children. The greater the degree to which physical labour is displaced by the introduction of machines worked by water- or steam-power, the fewer grown men need be employed. In any case women and children will work for lower wages than men, and, as has already been observed, they are more skilful at piecing than grown men. Consequently it is women and children who are employed to do this work. In the spinning mills women and girls alone work the throstle spindles. Frames of mule spindles are supervised by a [male] spinner helped by several piecers who tie up the broken threads. The piecers are nearly always women and children, but occasionally one finds young men aged between 18 and 20 and even an old spinner[1] who would otherwise be unemployed. When self-actors are introduced it is possible to dispense with the services of the male spinner.

Power looms are generally worked by young women aged between 15 and 20 or a little more; there are also some young men employed at this work, but they are seldom kept on beyond the age of about 21. In the preparatory processes the machinery is normally attended by women although a few men are employed to sharpen and clean out the carding machines. Moreover, the factories also employ a number of children as doffers to fix and take down the bobbins[2] as well as a few grown men as overlookers, an engineer and some men to tend the steam engine. Men are also employed as carpenters, porters, etc. The bulk of the work is performed by women and children. This, however, is denied by the manufacturers, who last year issued elaborate tables with the object of demonstrating that men were not being displaced by machinery. These statistics show that rather more than

---

[1] Leonard Horner, H.M. Inspector of Factories, reported in October 1843 as follows:

There is at present a very anomalous state of things in regard to wages in some departments of cotton mills in Lancashire; for there are hundreds of young men, between 20 and 30 years of age, in the full vigour of life, employed as piecers and otherwise, who are receiving not more than eight or nine shillings a week; while under the same roof, children of 13 years of age are getting five shillings, and young women between 16 and 20 are getting from ten to twelve shillings a week.

Leonard Horner's report for the quarter ending September 30th, 1843, in *Reports of the Inspectors of Factories . . . for the half year ending 31st Dec.*, 1843 (1844), p. 4.

[2 The technical phrase for this operation is ' tubing and doffing ' the bobbins.]

half (52 per cent) of all factory workers are females and about 48 per cent are males.[1] Over half these workers are over 18 years of age. So far, so good. But the manufacturers are careful not to tell us what proportion of the *adult*[2] labour force is male and what female. And that is the real point at issue. Obviously the factory owners have included in their returns the engineers, the carpenters and all the grown men who are employed in any capacity at all in an industrial establishment. But millowners lack the courage to tell the whole truth. These statistics are riddled with inaccuracies and distortions of all kinds. They include many calculations of averages, which may befog the layman but do not deceive the expert. The statistics conceal the most vital information and all that these prove is the selfish blindness and dishonesty of the factory owners. On March 15th, 1844, Lord Ashley spoke in the House of Commons in the debate in committee on the Ten Hours Bill. Lord Ashley[3] gave some statistics concerning the age and sex of factory workers. These data, however, cover only a section of British industry. Ashley's statistics have not been refuted by the factory owners. Of the 419,590[4] factory workers [in the major branches of the textile industry] in the United Kingdom in 1839 nearly half (192,887) were under 18 years of age. Of the 242,296 females 112,192 were under 18 years of age. Consequently there remain 80,695 male workers under 18 years of age and 96,599[5] adult male workers. This shows that less than one quarter, i.e. 23 per cent, of the total labour force in the factories was composed of adult males over the age of 18. The proportion of female workers in the textile industry was as follows:

[1 Engels derived this information from a *Statement of Facts . . . submitted by the Deputation of Master Manufacturers and Millowners in the County of Lancaster*. See *Manchester Guardian*, May 1st, 1844, p. 5, cols. 4–5 and *Liverpool Mercury*, April 26th, 1844, p. 139. Information was given concerning 412 firms in the Lancashire industrial district. The number of persons employed in these factories was 116,281. Deductions drawn from this information did not, of course, necessarily apply to the whole country. The return included information concerning the distribution of the labour force by sexes in the 412 establishments:

Number of male workers over 21	28,459
under 21	26,724
	55,183—48%
Number of female workers over 21	26,710
under 21	34,388
	61,098—52%.]

[2 Translators' italics.]
3 *Hansard's Parliamentary Debates*, 3rd series, 1844, vol. 73, cols. 1073–1101.
[4 In the original German edition Engels gave this figure incorrectly as 415,960.]
[5 In the original German edition Engels gave this figure incorrectly as 96,569.]

Cotton factories 56½ per cent; woollen [and worsted] factories 69½ per cent; silk factories 70½ per cent; flax spinning factories 70½ per cent. These figures show clearly to what extent the adult males have been displaced in the factories. It is only necessary to visit the nearest well-run textile factory in order to satisfy oneself on this point. All this has led to a complete reversal of normal social relationships. The working classes have had no choice but to submit to this change, which has the most evil effects. When women work in factories, the most important result is the dissolution of family ties. If a woman works for twelve or thirteen hours a day in a factory and her husband is employed either in the same establishment or in some other works, what is the fate of the children? They lack parental care and control. They are looked after by foster-parents, who charge 1s. or 1s. 6d. a week for this service. It is not difficult to imagine that they are left to run wild. This can be seen by the increase in the number of accidents to little children which occur in the factory districts. The main cause of such accidents is the lack of proper supervision. According to a report by Dr. Bisset Hawkins,[1] the Manchester coroner's statistics show that, in 9 months, out of 215[2] deaths 69 were due to burns, 56 to drowning, 23 to falls and 67[3] to other accidents.[4] In Liverpool, which is not a factory area, there were only 146 similar accidental deaths in twelve months. It should be noted that in both towns accidents in coal mines are excluded, and since the Manchester coroner has no jurisdiction in Salford the two populations which are being compared are approximately the same.

The *Manchester Guardian* is continually reporting cases of children who die from burns. It is, moreover, self-evident that the total death

---

[1] *Second Report* of Factories Enquiry Commission, Parliamentary Papers, 1833, Vol. 21, report of Dr. Bisset Hawkins, D.3, p. 3. [These accidental deaths were those for all age-groups of the population and not merely those of children.]
[2 Engels gave this figure incorrectly as 225.]
[3 Engels gave this figure incorrectly as 77.]
[4] In 1843 there were 189 admissions to Manchester Royal Infirmary of persons who had been accidentally burned. How many of these proved fatal is not recorded. [Engels is wrong in giving the year as 1843. He arrived at the figure 189 by adding together the following casualties admitted to the accident out-patients department during the year 1842:

				Caused by Machinery	Other Causes	Total
Burns	...	...	...	28	60	88
Scalds	...	...	...	21	80	101
						189

('A Table of the Injuries of the Accident Out-patients: *Admitted during the year 1842*', printed in *Report of the State of the Manchester Royal Infirmary . . . from June 25th, 1842, to June 25th, 1843*).]

rate for small children is increased by the fact that their mothers go out to work. There is ample evidence to prove this statement. It is often only two or three days after confinement that a woman returns to the factory, and of course, she cannot take the baby with her. When there is a break in the factory routine she has to rush home to feed the infant and get her own meal. It is obvious that this is no proper way to rear a child. According to Lord Ashley the following statements were made [to him] by certain women working in factories:

M. H. aged twenty, leaves a young child in care of another, a little older, for hours together; leaves home soon after five, and returns at eight; during the day the milk runs from her breasts, until her clothes have been as wet as a sop. . . . H. W. has three children; leaves home at five on Monday; does not return until Saturday at seven; has then so much to do for her children that she cannot go to bed before three o' clock on Sunday morning. Oftentimes completely drenched by the rain, and has to work all day in that condition. [She states:] My breasts have given me the most shocking pain, and I have been dripping over with milk.[1]

The use of narcotic medicines to keep children quiet can only be encouraged by this infamous system, and it is a very widespread practice in the factory districts. Dr. Johns, Superintendent Registrar [of Births, Deaths and Marriages] in the Manchester district[2], states that this practice is the main cause of the frequency of death from convulsions [among infants]. It is inevitable that if a married woman works in a factory family life is inevitably destroyed and in the present state of society, which is based upon family life, its dissolution has the most demoralising consequences both for parents and children. A married woman cannot really be regarded as a mother if she is unable to spare the time to look after her child; if she hardly sees the infant at all, and if she cannot satisfy her baby's elementary need for loving care. Such a mother is inevitably indifferent to the welfare of the child, which she treats without love and without proper care as if it were a stranger. Children who grow up under such conditions have no idea of what a proper family life should be. When they grow up and have families of their own they feel out of place because their own early experience has been that of a lonely life. Such parents foster the universal decadence of family life among the workers. Similar evil consequences for the family follow from child labour. When

[1 *Hansard*, 3rd series, 1844, Vol. 73, col. 1094.]
[2 W. Johns, ' Report upon the working of the Registration and Marriage Acts during the two years 1837–38 and 1838–39 in the registration district of Manchester ', in *Journal of the Statistical Society of London*, Vol. 3, 1840, pp. 191–205; *Hansard*, 3rd series, 1844, Vol. 73, col. 1094.]

children earn more than the cost of their keep they begin to make a contribution to the family budget and to keep the rest as pocket money. This often occurs when they are no more than fourteen or fifteen.[1] In brief, the children become emancipated and regard their parents' house merely as lodgings, and quite often, if they feel like it, they leave home and take lodgings elsewhere.

Very often the fact that a married woman is working does not lead to the complete disruption of the home but to a reversal of the normal division of labour within the family. The wife is the bread-winner while her husband stays at home to look after the children and to do the cleaning and cooking. This happens very frequently indeed. In Manchester alone there are many hundreds of men who are condemned to perform household duties. One may well imagine the righteous indignation of the workers at being virtually turned into eunuchs. Family relationships are reversed, although other social conditions remain unchanged. I have before me a letter written to Oastler by an English working man named Robert Pounder. In order that the middle classes can look him up I will give his address which is Barron's Buildings, Woodhouse Moorside, in Leeds. The naïvety can only be partially reproduced in a German translation. The spelling and the Yorkshire dialect cannot be reproduced in German.[2] Pounder relates how a working class acquaintance of his, being on tramp in search of work, passed through St. Helens in Lancashire, and met an old friend: [Pounder wrote to Oastler]:

> . . . Well Sir he found him out—and when he got to is Cot what was it think you, Why a Low Damp Seller the Discriptun he gave of the funitoure was has follows, 2 old Chares, a round 3 legd table, a Box, no Bed Stocks, but a quantety of old Strow in one Corner with some Durty Bed Linen thrown opon it, and too peseses of wood was placed by the Fire Place, and when my poor friend Entered the Doar—poar Jack (for that is is name) was sat by th Fire Jarm on one of the Cloggs of wood and what wor he Dowing think you? Why he was sat mending is wife Stocking Eeels, with the Darning Neadle, but as soon has he sow is old

---

[1] Factories Enquiry Commission, *First Report*, Parliamentary Papers, Vol. 20, 1833; Power's Report (C. 2) section on Leeds, p. 47, and Tufnell's Report (D. 2) section on Manchester, p. 17 [Joseph Bell Clarke (reply to E. C. Tufnell): ' I believe that every child that is employed in the mills receives his own wages, and when they receive as much money as will more than pay for their living, they contract with their parents for board and lodging and put the rest in their pockets.']

[2] In order to enable his German readers to realise that the letter was written in dialect, Engels turned it into the sort of German that an uneducated worker would use and introduced deliberate mis-spellings. The translators have reproduced the relevant portions of the original letter of August 5th, 1844, from Oastler's periodical, *The Fleet Papers*, Vol. 4, no. 35, August 31st, 1844, pp. 486–88.]

Matey at the Door post, he endevered to hide them—but Joe
(for that is my poar friend's name) was to sharp for him and he
sead ' Jack what Ever is thow Dowing? whear is the wife? what,
that is not thy job, Im shour? ' poar Jack was ashamed, and sead
' No I know that this is not my job, but t' poar wife is at the Mill,
she has to go at ½ past 5 oClock and work untill 8, and she is so
poley that she is not able to do Eneything when she comes home
so I do all that I can for her, for I have no wark nore have Ed Eney
for more then 3 years, and I think that I never shall heave Eney,
Eney more.' And then Sir, he weept the big Tear,—' No, Joe,
there is plenty of Wark for Wemen and Barns in this quarter but
very Little for men—thou may as well go try to finde a hondred
pounds, as go to find wark aboats heare—but I hed not ment
neather thee nor eney one Els to have seen me mending t'wifes
stockings, for its a poar job, but she is almost nockt of her feet—
I ham sadely afrad that she will be thrown up altogather, and then,
if she is, I do not now what is to become of us, for she as been
t'man now for a Long time, and me t'woman—it is hard wark
Joe ';—and then poor Jack crayed bittly and sead ' It did not
use to be so '—' No ', sead Joe, ' it did not Lad—and if thou has
being out of wark so Long as that how Ever has ta Gotten on all
t'time? ' Well, Joe, I wall tell thee, as well as I can, I have gotten
on in a very misserable way all the time—thow knows that when I
Gat Wead—I had plenty of wark and something for warking, and
thou nows that I was not Idle '—' No Jack thou wasn't '—' and we
gat on very well—we gat a good firnished House " (' Ye Did Lad—
has Ever Eney poar man need put a foot into ')—' thire was no nead
for—Mary to go to wark then—I could wark for us boath '—(' yes
that thou could ') ' but now t'world is turned up side down, Mary
has to turn out to wark and I have to stop at home to mind Barns—
and to Wash and Clean—Bake and mend, for, poar Lass—when she
comes home at night, she is down up—thou nows Joe this is ard
wark for one that wants to Dow Different '.—Joe sead, ' I Lad it
is ard Wark '—then poor Jack weept agane and sead that he wisht
that he had never being Wead and that he never had being Born—
but he did not think when Marred Mary that things would have
comed to this, ' I have meney a cry about it ', sead poor Jack.

Well Sir—when Joe heard poar Jacks tale, he towld me that he
Could not help—Curseing both the factarys and the factary masters
and the Government also for premetting it with all the Curseses
that a mind Edecated in a factary is Capperble of.[1]

[1 Owing to Engels's misleading abridgement of the beginning of this letter
it has previously been assumed that this incident took place in a house in St. Helens,
but the relevant passage in the original letter, now reprinted for the first time,
leaves the location vague:
    ' a shot time since a friend of mine that was out of work and who ust to

Can one imagine a more senseless and foolish state of affairs than that described in this letter? It deprives the husband of his manhood and the wife of all womanly qualities. Yet it cannot thereby turn a man into a woman or a woman into a man. It is a state of affairs shameful and degrading to the human attributes of the sexes.[1] It is the culminating point of our highly-praised civilization. It is the final result of all the efforts of hundreds of generations to improve the lot of humanity both now and in the future. If all that can be achieved by our work and effort is this sort of mockery, then we must truly despair of humanity and its aspirations. If not, then we must admit that human society has followed the wrong road in its search for happiness. We shall have to accept the fact that so complete a reversal of the role of the two sexes can be due only to some radical error in the original relationship between men and women. If the rule of the wife over her husband—a natural consequence of the factory system—is unnatural, then the former rule of the husband over the wife must also have been unnatural. To-day, the wife—as in former times the husband— justifies her sway because she is the major or even the sole bread-winner of the family. In either case one partner is able to boast that he or she makes the greatest contribution to the upkeep of the family.

work with me, at a former pearead, but who had being out of Wark for a Long time wor Compeld to go, on what we Labouring men Call, the tramp and having got to a place Calld Sant Hellins (I think it is in Lonckshire) and meeting with no sucsess, he thought that he would bend is way towards Monchester, and just as he was Leaving the place, he herd of one of his old mateys Leaving Close on the way—so he resolved that he would make him out if poseble—for he wishd to see him, thinking that he might perhaps help him to a job, and if not, he might give him a mouthfull of something to Eat, and a nights Lodgings, has he said he was very heard-up' (*The Fleet Papers*, Vol. IV, no. 35, August 31, 1844, p. 487).

It would, of course, be a mistake to assume that the state of affairs reported by Pounder was in any way typical of St. Helens in the early 1840s, which was a town of heavy industry rather than a textile centre. T. C. Barker and J. R. Harris comment as follows: '. . . it seems probable that the celebrated story recounted by Engels, of the poor, helpless wretch, found in a miserable, damp cellar at St. Helens mending the stockings of his wife who was out working, was a product of this period' of depression in 1841–3: *A Merseyside Town in the Industrial Revolution: St. Helens, 1750–1900* (1954), p. 321.]

[1 Engels's 'Victorian' belief that women's place was in the home was shared by Peter Gaskell. See P. Gaskell, *The Manufacturing Population of England* (1833), pp. 166–7:

Nothing would tend more to elevate the moral condition of the manufacturing population, than the restoration of woman to her proper social rank: nothing would exercise greater influence upon the form and growth of her offspring, than her devotion to those womanly occupations which would render her a denizen of home. No great step can be made till she is snatched from unremitting toil, and made what Nature meant she should be—the centre of a system of social delights. Domestic avocations are those which are her peculiar lot. The poor man who suffers his wife to work, separated from him and from home, is a bad calculator.']

Such a state of affairs shows clearly that there is no rational or sensible principle at the root of our ideas concerning family income and property. If the family as it exists in our present-day society comes to an end then its disappearance will prove that the real bond holding the family together was not affection but merely self-interest engendered by the false concept of family property.[1] A similar disturbance in family relationships takes place when children do not pay lodging money as such, but are the sole breadwinners in a family when the parents are unemployed. Dr. Hawkins testifies in the Factories Enquiry Commission's Report that this situation frequently occurs and is certainly a common state of affairs in Manchester.[2] In this case it is not the wife, but the children who rule the household, and Lord Ashley gives an example of this in his speech to the House of Commons on March 15th, 1844.[3] Lord Ashley states that a father rebuked his two daughters for frequenting a public house, and they turned on him, saying that they no longer recognised his authority: ' Damn you, we have you to keep '.[4] They said that they were entitled to spend at least a part of their earnings as they pleased. The girls left home and abandoned their father and mother to their fate.

The unmarried girls who work in the mills are no better off than their married sisters. Obviously a girl who has been an operative since the age of nine has never had a chance to acquire a skill in household duties. Consequently all the factory girls are wholly ignorant

---

[1] The great number of married women working in factories is shown by the following statistics issued by the factory owners themselves. In 412 factories in Lancashire 10,721 married women were employed. Only 5,314 of their husbands were also at work in factories; 3,927 of the husbands were engaged in other trades, while 821 were out of work and no information was available concerning 659 others. This shows that on the average in every factory two or even three husbands were being supported by their wives. [These statistics are to be found in the *Statement of Facts . . . submitted by the Deputation of the Master Manufacturers and Millowners in the County of Lancaster.* (See *Manchester Guardian*, May 1st, 1844, p. 5, cols. 4–5).]

[2] *2nd Report* of Factories Enquiry Commission, 1833, *Parl. Papers*, Vol. 21. Dr. Hawkins wrote in his medical report on the Lancashire district (D3, p. 4): ' The degree in which parents are supported by their youthful offspring at Manchester is a peculiar feature of the place, and an unpleasing one; the ordinary state of things in this respect is nearly reversed.']

[3] *Hansard's Parliamentary Debates*, 3rd series, Vol. 73, cols. 1096–7.

[4] The words ' Damn you, we have you to keep ' are in English in the original German edition. It is clear from Lord Ashley's speech that Engels is here confusing two illustrations of the point made by the speaker. Lord Ashley said:
Children and young persons take the same advantage of parents that women do of their husbands, frequently using harsh language, and, if corrected, will turn round and say, ' —— you, we have you to keep '. One poor woman stated that her husband had chided two of their daughters for going to a public-house; he made it worse, for they would not come home again, stating, ' they had their father to keep, and they would not be dictated to by him ': *Hansard*, 3rd series, Vol. 73, cols. 1096–7.]

of housewifery and are quite unfitted to become wives and mothers. They do not know how to sew, knit, cook or wash. They are ignorant of the most elementary accomplishments of the housewife, and as for looking after babies, they have the vaguest notion of how to set about it. The Report of the Factories Enquiry Commission gives dozens of examples of this state of affairs and Dr. Hawkins, the medical commissioner who reported on Lancashire, stated:

But let us suppose one of these young females about to assume the character of wife, mother, nurse, housekeeper,—which she too often undertakes prematurely and improvidently. She has had no time, no means, no opportunities of learning the common duties of domestic life; and even if she had acquired the knowledge she has still no time to practise them. In addition to the twelve hours' labour [there] is an additional absence from home in the going and returning. There is the young mother absent from her child above twelve hours daily. Who has the charge of the infant in her absence? Usually some little girl or aged woman, who is hired for a trifle and whose services are equivalent to the reward. Too often the dwelling of the factory family is no home; it sometimes is a cellar, which includes no cooking, no washing, no making, no mending, no decencies of life, no invitations to the fireside. I cannot help on these and on other grounds, especially for the better preservation of infant life, expressing my hope that a period may arrive when married women shall be rarely employed in a factory.[1]

Further examples may be found in evidence collected by Cowell and Tufnell.[2]

But we have not yet discussed the worst results of women's work in factories. The moral evils are worse than those aspects of the problem already discussed. In the factories members of both sexes of all ages work together in a single room. It is inevitable that they should come into close contact with each other. The crowding together of a large number of men and women who lack the advantages or moral or intellectual instruction is not exactly calculated to promote the favourable development of the female virtues. Even if a factory owner desires to maintain moral standards in his establishment he can only intervene after something really scandalous has happened. With the best will in the world he cannot discover, let alone prevent, those subtle types of corruption which are particularly apt to undermine the morals of weak characters and of young people. These

---

[1] Factories Enquiry Commission, 1833, *2nd Report*, Parl. Papers, vol. 21, Dr. Hawkins's report, D3, p. 5. [Engels gave only an abridged and garbled version of this quotation.]

[2] Factories Enquiry Commission, *1st Report*, Cowell, D.1, pp. 35–39, 50, 57, 72, 77, 82; Tufnell, D.2, pp. 9, 15, 45, 54. See also Power, D.2, p. 8.

influences are among the most harmful to the workers. The Factory
Commissioners of 1833 frequently denounced the language used in
factories as ' indecent ', ' low ', and ' dirty ' and so forth. Cowell,
for example, draws attention to this on several occasions.[1] Things
are no better in the factories of the smaller towns. The concentration
of population affects the workers in the same way whether they work
in a big town or a little factory. If the factory is a small one, the
contacts between the workers are even more intimate than in the
larger establishments; the inevitable consequences follow. According
to the Factories Enquiry Commission, a witness from Leicester stated
that he would rather see his daughter beg than go into the factories,
which were ' complete hell-holes ', and that most of the prostitutes in
Leicester had the factories to thank for their present degradation.[2]
[A Manchester witness] ' had no hesitation in stating that three quarters
of girls between 14 and 20 who worked in factories were unchaste '.[3]
Mr. Cowell, another Commissioner, was of the definite opinion that
the moral standards of the factory worker were somewhat lower than
the average standard of the working classes.[4] And Dr. Hawkins
stated:

> An estimate of sexual morality is scarcely possible to be reduced
> into figures; but if I may trust my own observations, and the
> general opinion of those with whom I have conversed, and the
> spirit of our evidence, then a most discouraging view of the influence
> of the factory life upon the morality of female youth obtrudes itself.
> . . .[5]

It will, of course, be appreciated that the girls who work in a
factory, even more than girls working in other occupations, find that
they have to grant to their employers the *ius primae noctis*. In this
respect, too, the factory owner wields complete power over the
persons and charms of the girls working for him. Nine times out of

[1] Factories Enquiry Commission, *First Report*, 1833, D. 1, pp. 35–37—evidence
taken by J. W. Cowell.
    [2] Op. cit., 1833, C. 2, p. 8—evidence taken by A. Power.
    [[3] Engels placed this passage in inverted commas, and attributed it to evidence
taken by J. W. Cowell (Factories Enquiry Commission, *First Report*, 1833, D. 1,
p. 57), but the evidence to which he refers is as follows:
    [Cowell:] Then as to morality in intercourse between the sexes, what should
you say was the number out of a thousand factory girls, between the ages of
fourteen and twenty, who are unchaste? [S. Cundy, witness:] If I were to give
an answer to the extent of my conscience, it must be to a great extent, but I
would not like to give a hard answer; I should not feel any restraint upon my
conscience in saying three-fourths.]
    [4] Op. cit., 1833, D. 1, p. 82 (evidence taken by J. W. Cowell).
    [5] Factory Enquiry Commission, *Second Report*, 1833, D. 3, p. 4 (medical report by
Dr. Francis Bisset Hawkins.)

ten, nay, in ninety-nine cases out of a hundred, the threat of dismissal is sufficient to break down the resistance of girls who at the best of times have no strong inducement to chastity. If the factory owner is sufficiently debased—and the Report of the Factories Enquiry Commission[1] recounts several such cases—his factory is also his harem. As far as the girls are concerned the situation is not altered by the fact that not all manufacturers take advantage of their opportunities in this matter. In the early days of the factory system most of the manufacturers were uneducated upstarts, and quite uninhibited by social hypocrisies from denying themselves the exercise of their vested rights.

Before we are in a position correctly to assess the consequences of factory work on the physical condition of women, it will be necessary to examine child labour and the nature of the work itself. Child labour was a feature of the factory system from the very beginning. This was because in the early days machines were small [and could therefore be tended exclusively by children]. Now bigger machines are used. In early days the children were recruited from workhouses and large numbers of them were hired out as apprentices to the manufacturers for a term of years. They were housed and clothed communally and were, of course, the complete slaves of their masters, by whom they were treated with the greatest indifference and barbarism. As early as 1796 Dr. Thomas Percival and Sir Robert Peel (himself a master cotton spinner and father of the present Prime Minister) expressed public disapproval of this disgraceful system in so energetic a manner that Parliament passed the Health and Morals of Apprentices Act[2] in 1802, which suppressed the worst abuses of the system. The competition of free labour gradually reduced the operation of this apprenticeship system. In time more and more factories were built in the towns; machines increased in size and workrooms were better ventilated and more healthy. More jobs became available for adults and young persons and consequently there was a certain decline in the proportion of the factory labour force consisting of children. There was also a rise in the minimum age at which children were generally put to work in the mills. Few children under the age of eight or nine were employed. As we shall see, the authority of the law was eventually invoked on several occasions to give children some protection against exploitation by the rapacious middle classes.

[1 There is a certain amount of evidence in the Factories Enquiry Commission's Reports for the existence of immorality among the young operatives, but little to support Engels's statement about the immoral conduct of the factory owners.]
[2 Engels used the words 'Apprentices Bill' in English in the original.]

The high mortality among the children of workers, particularly factory workers, is sufficient proof of the unhealthy conditions under which their early years are spent. These unfavourable factors naturally affect also those children who manage to survive, but not unscathed. The very least that they suffer is ill health, arrested development, and general constitutional weakness. The nine-year-old child of a factory worker may well have endured various vicissitudes, including want, privation, damp, cold and inadequate clothing and accommodation. Such a child is not likely to have the same capacity for labour as one brought up in a healthier surroundings. When nine years old, the child is sent to the factory where he or she works a $6\frac{1}{2}$ hour day. Formerly this was 8 hours, and at an earlier period between 12 and 14 —even 16—hours were worked. Between the ages of 13 and 18 young persons work a 12 hour day. Children and young people in the mills are still subject to the factors already mentioned which lead to ill-health, but now the work itself is an additional unfavourable influence. It may be admitted that a nine-year-old child, even a worker's child, can work for $6\frac{1}{2}$ hours a day without his or her health being visibly impaired thereby. At the same time no one can claim that work in the excessive heat and steamy damp of the factory contribute to good health. In any case it is obviously wrong that children still of an age when all their time should be devoted to bodily and mental development should be sacrificed to the greed of the unfeeling middle classes. It is wrong to take children from school and the fresh air, in order to exploit them for the benefit of the manufacturers. The middle classes reply that if children were not employed in factories, their environment would be detrimental to their healthy development in the future. True enough—but the fact of the matter is this. First of all, the middle classes create a situation which is highly unfavourable to the workers' children. Then they coolly exploit that unsatisfactory situation to their own advantage. They defend themselves by drawing attention to a state of affairs for which they themselves are just as much to blame as they are to blame for the very existence of the factory system. They actually try to excuse to-day's evil by drawing attention to yesterday's evil, for both of which they are responsible. The Factory Act has to some extent tied the hands of the middle classes. If no such Act existed it would be easy to imagine how the workers would be treated by these ' benevolent ' and ' humane ' members of the middle classes. To hear them talk, one would think that these kind-hearted industrialists establish factories solely for the benefit of the workers. Let us see how the manufacturers behaved before the Factory Inspector had his eye on them. Let us convict them out of their own mouths by examining their evidence before the Factories Enquiry Commission of 1833.

The report of the Central Board of the Commission states that manufacturers usually employed children in factories from the age of eight or nine; but occasionally younger children were to be found at work, a few of them as young as five. The hours of work varied from fourteen to sixteen a day, exclusive of mealtimes. The factory owners allowed their workers to beat and otherwise maltreat the children. The owners themselves sometimes struck children. The Report tells of one Scottish manufacturer who went on horseback after an absconding 16-year-old worker and whipped him all the way back to the factory.[1] In big cities, where there was more resistance on the part of the workers to ill-treatment, such occurrences were rarer. Even these long hours of work did not satisfy the greed of the capitalists. They were determined by all means at their disposal to extract the maximum profit from the capital they had invested in their buildings and machinery. The machines should stand idle as little as possible. Consequently the factory owners introduced the shameful system of night work. Some owners employed two shifts, each capable of manning all the machinery in the factory. One shift worked for twelve hours during the day and the second for twelve hours during the night. It is easy to see what bad effects this arrangement would have upon the night shift. These workers were permanently deprived of their sleep at night, and this can never be replaced by sleeping during the day. The physical condition of children, young people and even adults was bound to suffer. The inevitable consequences were the appearance of nervous disorders, and a general lassitude and bodily weakness. In addition the workers' health was undermined by succumbing to the temptations of excessive drinking and irregular sexual habits. One factory owner stated[2] that during the two years when his establishment was on night work the number of illegitimate children born was doubled. The morale of the factory became so deplorably low that night work had to be discontinued. Even more barbarous was the conduct of those factory owners who forced many operatives to work continuously for thirty to forty hours at a stretch.

[1] Factories Enquiry Commission, *First Report*, 1833, A.1, p. 35 (evidence taken by James Stuart) [John Ross, the worker in question, was 22 years of age when he gave evidence and merely said that the incident occurred ' some years ago '].

[2] Op. cit., D. 2, p. 91—evidence taken by E. C. Tufnell. [This evidence was given by Aaron Lees, who stated that this increase in illegitimacy occurred at a Stalybridge mill as long ago as 1801. The information came from his father, a partner in the mill. The night work had been introduced as a temporary measure because a mill had been burnt down, and the owners operated double shifts in another mill to keep their workers employed.]

This was repeated several times a week because there were not enough hands on the regular night shift. Those who worked these very long hours were only allowed to snatch a few hours' sleep. That section of the Commission's report relating to this barbarous practice and its consequences reveals more revolting conditions than anything I have come across elsewhere. The disgusting occurrences mentioned in the Report are indeed unique in their depravity. And yet it is this very report that the middle classes like to quote as supporting their case. There is ample evidence in the Commission's report of the evil consequences which quickly follow from the malpractices described. A number of cripples gave evidence before the Commission, and it was obvious that their physical condition was due to their long hours of work. Deformity of this type generally affects the spine and legs. [In Dr. Loudon's Report, information is given by two Leeds surgeons —Francis Sharp, M.R.C.S., and William Hey]. The former writes:

During my practice at the hospital, where I have seen about 35,000 patients, I have observed the peculiar twisting of the ends of the lower part of the thigh bone. This affection I had never seen before I came to Leeds, and I have remarked that it principally affected children from 8 to 14 years of age. At first I considered it might be rickets, but from the numbers which presented themselves, particularly at an age beyond the time when rickets attack children, and finding that they were of recent date, and had commenced since they began work at the factory I soon began to change my opinion. I now may have seen of such cases (but as to the numbers I cannot positively say) nearly 100, and I can most decidedly state they were the result of too much labour. So far as I know they all belong to factories, and acquired this knockkneed appearance from the very long hours the children are worked in the mills. The greatest number have attributed their disease to this cause themselves. Many of those cases have been shown to medical men, and, with few exceptions, they coincided with my opinion as to the cause.

My attention has also been called to other ailments as resulting from factory labour; and I have seen ulcers of the legs in about 100 young persons both male and female, who were employed in factories, with and without varicose state of the veins, which are not to be observed in other classes of society at the same period of life, and which by themselves and by me have been attributed to long standing at the labour of the factories. I have also seen of the falling in of the arch of the foot above 200 cases altogether, of the cause of which I have no doubt it was owing to the long standing at their labour.

Of distortions of the spine, which were evidently owing to the same cause, perhaps the number of cases might not be less than 300.[1]

Mr. [William] Hey,[2] who had eighteen years' experience in the Infirmary at Leeds, states:

> During my hospital practice diseases of the spine amongst people employed in factories presented themselves very frequently. . . . Some were the result of pure labour; others were the result of labour on a constitution perhaps congenitally weak, or rendered feeble by bad food and other causes. . . . The deformities of the limbs appear to be more frequent than the spinal diseases. What I have particularly remarked has been the falling-in of the arch of the foot, the bending in of the knees, relaxation of the ligaments of the ankles was very frequent, and the bending of the large bones. The heads of the large bones have especially been increased and twisted to a considerable extent; and these cases I have found to have come from those mills and factories where long hours have been said to be common.[3]

Similar evidence is given by two Bradford surgeons, Beaumont and Sharp. The Reports of Commissioners Drinkwater, Power and Loudon contain many references to the physical deformities of the workers. On the other hand, E. C. Tufnell and Sir David Barry (a medical man) are less interested in this aspect of the question and give fewer examples.[4] The Commissioners for Lancashire—Cowell, Tufnell and Dr. Hawkins—virtually ignored the effect of the factory system on the physique and health of the factory workers, although Lancashire can undoubtedly compete with Yorkshire in respect of the number of workers who have been crippled in their factories. I have seldom walked through Manchester without seeing three or four cripples whose deformities of the spine and legs were exactly the same as those described by Mr. Sharp of Leeds. I have had ample oppor-

---

[1] Factories Enquiry Commission, *Second Report*, 1833, C 3, pp. 12–13—medical report by Dr. C. Loudon, quoting statement made by Mr. Francis Sharp of Leeds. [Engels's version of this extract is both garbled and abridged].

[2] In the first German edition Engels wrote ' Dr. Kay ', which is an error for ' Mr. Hey '. For William Hey II (1771–1844), for twenty years surgeon to the Leeds Infirmary, see the *Dictionary of National Biography*, and the Rev. R. W. Taylor, *The Biographia Leodensis* (1865), p. 403.]

[3] Op. cit., 1833, C. 3, p. 16—medical report by Dr. C. Loudon, quoting William Hey of Leeds. [Engels abbreviates this extract.]

[4] Factories Enquiry Commission, *First Report*, 1833, C. 1, pp. 69 (two brothers) 72, 80, 146, 148, 150 (two cases), 155 and many others—evidence taken by J. E. Drinkwater; in Leeds: C. 2, pp. 29, 31, 40, 43, and 53 onwards; in Bradford: C. 2, pp. 63, 66, 67 (two cases), 68 (three cases), 69 (two cases—evidence taken by A. Power); D. 2, pp. 5, 16—evidence taken by E. C. Tufnell. *Second Report*, 1833, C. 3, pp. 4, 7 (four cases) 8 (several cases)—medical reports of Dr. C. Loudon, A. 3, pp. 6, 8, 13, 21, 22, 44, 55 (three cases)—medical reports of Sir David Barry.

tunities of observing these cripples closely. I know one cripple personally whose deformities are exactly the same as those described above by Mr. Hey, the surgeon.[1] This operative got into this condition through working in Mr. Douglas's mill in Pendleton. This factory has a very bad reputation among the workers because of the long hours of night work which are customary there. It is easy to identify such cripples at a glance, because their deformities are all exactly the same. They are knock-kneed and deformed and the spinal column is bent either forwards or sideways. But it is the philanthropic silk manufacturers of Macclesfield who seem to have done most to ruin the physique of those who work for them, because they employed very young children aged from only 5 to 6 years in their mills. Commissioner Tufnell includes, in a supplementary report, a statement made by Mr. Wright, steward in a factory in Macclesfield. According to Mr. Wright, his two sisters had been deformed as a result of factory work. He also affirmed that he had once counted the number of cripples living in various streets in Macclesfield, which included some of the cleanest and prettiest in the town. He discovered that there were 10 cripples in Townley Street, 5 in George Street, 4 in Charlotte Street, 15 in Watercots, 3 in Bank Top, 7 in Lord Street, 12 in Mill Lane, 2 in Great George Street, 2 in the workhouse, 1 on Park Green, and 2 in Pickford Street. The relatives of all these cripples unanimously declared that these deformities were due to excessive work in the factories. Mr. Tufnell also refers to a boy who was so crippled that he could not walk upstairs and to girls whose backs and hips were deformed.[2]

Among the other deformities caused by overwork flat-footedness deserves particular mention. Both Sir David Barry[3] and the doctors and surgeons of Leeds[4] give numerous examples of this complaint in the Report of the enquiry of 1833. Some young workers, for various reasons, were able to work long hours without actually becoming cripples. They might enjoy better food and there might be other circumstances which would enable these workers to ward off the effects of barbarous exploitation. Nevertheless they still suffer from pains in the back, hips and legs. They suffer from swollen joints,

---

[1 In the first German edition and in the Marx-Engels-Lenin Institute edition (ed. Adoratskij) this is wrongly given as ' Dr. Kay '].

[2] Factories Enquiry Commission, *Second Report*, D. 2, pp. 26–7—evidence taken by E. C. Tufnell from John Wright, of the silk factory of Brinsley and Shatwell, Macclesfield.

[3] Factories Enquiry Commission, *Second Report*, A. 3, p. 21 (two cases)—medical reports by Sir David Barry.

[4] Factories Enquiry Commission, *Second Report*, C. 3, pp. 13, 16 etc. (medical reports by Dr. Loudon).

varicose veins and large, deep-seated abscesses in the thighs and shins. These are almost universal complaints among the workers. Hundreds of such cases are reported by Stuart, Mackintosh and Sir David Barry. Indeed, these doctors were hardly able to find a worker who was free from one or other of these afflictions. Other reports from many other doctors confirm the widespread nature of these complaints among the workers. Further confirmation is provided by the reports relating to Scotland. These reports can leave no doubt in the reader's mind concerning the seriousness of the situation. It is clear that if young workers aged between 18 and 22 work for thirteen hours a day that these evil consequences must inevitably result. This applies to the flax spinning mills of Dundee and Dunfermline, and the cotton mills of Glasgow and Lanark.

All these evils can be easily explained by the very nature of factory work. Admittedly, as the manufacturers claim, this is very ' light ' work,[1] but just because it is light it is more enervating than any other type of labour. Factory workers have little to do, but they have to be on their feet the whole time and they have no opportunity for resting. Anyone who sits down on a window ledge or basket is fined. The physical disabilities to which we have referred are obviously caused by continual standing. Spine, hips and legs have to bear an unnaturally heavy strain. The nature of the work, however, does not necessarily demand continual standing. In Nottingham seats have been introduced, at any rate into the doubling rooms, with the result that the women were found to be free from the physical disabilities which we have been discussing, and had no objection to working long hours. [If seats were generally introduced] in factories where the operatives work only to earn profits for the middle classes and have little incentive to work hard, they would probably sit down more frequently than would be agreeable and advantageous to the manufacturers. In order to prevent damage to a little of the raw material, the middle classes force the workers to sacrifice their health and strength.[2] Standing for long periods—combined with the unwholesome atmosphere of the factories—brings with it other evils. The whole vitality of the worker is sapped, and this undermines his general physical condition as well as causing specific ailments. The atmosphere in the factories is generally both damp and warm—usually warmer than

[1 See E. Baines, *History of the Cotton Manufacture* (1835), p. 156. Baines stated that in cotton mills ' the labour is light, and requires very little muscular exertion '.]

[2] Seats have also been introduced into the spinning room of a Leeds mill (Factories Enquiry Commission, *First Report*, C. 1, p. 85—seats allowed in Harris's mill—evidence taken by J. E. Drinkwater). [Engels's original note referred the reader to p. 80.]

is necessary. Even if the ventilation of the factory is *very* good, the air is still foul, stuffy, and deficient in oxygen. It is polluted with dust and the smell of stale machine oil, with which the floor is generally impregnated. Owing to the heat the workers are scantily clad and so are liable to chills because of changes in the temperature of the work-rooms. Owing to the heat the workers feel discomfort when exposed to draughts and they become languid. All their physical movements and actions are slowed down. The temperature of the body, which ought to be maintained at a normal level, falls to such an extent that the worker actually prefers to breathe continually the warm air of a room of which all the windows are kept closed. In addition we have to consider the effect of the sudden change in temperature to which the worker is subject when he leaves the humid atmosphere of the factory for the cold, damp or frosty air outside. The worker is too poor either to buy adequate clothing to protect him against the rain or to change out of his wet clothes when he gets home. All these circumstances make the workers continually liable to catch cold. All the time that he is working the operative hardly uses a single muscle with any degree of vigour, except for those in his legs. He does nothing to counteract the lassitude that inevitably creeps over him. He makes no movements which would revive his flagging sinews and flabby muscles. From childhood the workers have no opportunity for exercise in the open air. In these circumstances it will cause no surprise to learn from the doctors whose opinions are given in the Factories Enquiry Commission's report that the operatives have virtually no power of resistance to the attacks of disease. The doctors refer to a general lowering of vitality and a persistent lassitude which affects both body and mind. First let us hear what Sir David Barry has to say:

But although both the young and the adult millworkers may command more abundant food and better clothing than their unemployed neighbours, there are causes to whose operation they are exposed, which, in a sanitary point of view, counterbalance the advantage alluded to:

1. The first and most influential of all is the indispensible, un-deviating necessity of forcing both their mental and bodily exertions to keep exact pace with the motions of machinery propelled by an unvarying, unceasing power.
2. The continuance of an erect posture for periods unnaturally prolonged and too quickly repeated.
3. The privation of sleep.[1]

[1 In the middle of the quotation from Barry Engels inserts at this point in brackets the words '(due to long hours of work, pains in the legs and general physical exhaustion)'.]

To these causes and deviations from the ordinary appearance of particular times of life inseparable from all factories, are often added low, crowded, dusty, or damp rooms; impure air, heated atmospheres, constant perspiration. Hence it is that male children particularly, after they have worked some time in mills lose—with very few exceptions indeed—the rosy chubbiness of boyhood, and become paler and thinner than boys not so employed generally are. Even the draw-boy[1]. . ., who stands with his bare feet, on the earthen floor of his master's shop as long as the shuttle is moving, preserves his appearance much better than the mill-boys, because the former goes to play while the weaver dresses his web (three or four times a day), whilst he smokes his pipe, and has always two or three holidays between the finishing of one web and the fitting up the tackle of another. But the mill-worker never has a moment's respite except at meals, and never gets into the open air except when he is going to look for them; yet his work is by no means so heavy as that of the draw-boy.

All the adult male spinners are pale and thin; they are subject to capricious appetite and dyspepsia; but being prohibited from smoking they generally chew tobacco largely, and often commence that pernicious practice at an early age. As all the spinners have been piecers, and brought up in the mills from their very childhood, it is fair to conclude that their mode of life is not favourable to the development of the manly forms, seeing that few, or none of them are tall athletic men.

Females are much less deteriorated in their appearance by mill work than males. . . .[2]

It is quite natural that mill girls should appear to be healthier than the men; but we shall see that they, too, have their illnesses.
Power wrote in a similar strain:

I can have no hesitation, however, in stating my belief, from what I saw myself, that a large mass of deformity has been produced at Bradford by the factory system; . . .
The effect of long and continuous work upon the frame and limbs is not indicated by actual deformity alone; a more common indication of it is found in a stunted growth, relaxed muscles, and slender conformation.[3]

[1 At this point Sir David Barry draws attention to a definition of draw-boys in a previous document: ' Children who draw over pullies, certain parts of the warp at each traverse of the shuttle in pattern-work weaving ': *Second Report*, A. 3, p. 43.]
    2 Factories Enquiry Commission, *Second Report*—A. 3, p. 72, general report by Sir David Barry. [Engels's version of this extract is severely abridged.]
    3 Factories Enquiry Commission, *First Report*, 1833, C. 2, p. 74—A. Power's report from Yorkshire.

Mr. Francis Sharp, a surgeon[1] to whose evidence reference has already been made, told Dr. Loudon that he had moved to Leeds from Scarborough:

The general appearance of the children in Leeds immediately struck me as much more pallid, and also the firmness of the fibre as much inferior as what I had seen in Scarborough and the adjacent country. Observed also many of those who applied for hospital aid to be more diminutive for their age, comparatively and absolutely than the bulk of those people I had seen in the North Riding...

Innumerable cases of scrofula, affections of the lungs, mesenteric diseases, and dyspepsia, have also occurred, which I have no doubt, as a professional man, were owing to the same cause. Asthmatic cases, and other affections of the lungs, particularly of those who are employed in the dusty parts of the mill, not infrequently occur; but I have no tables to show the relation of them. . . . The nervous energy of the body I consider to be weakened by the very long hours, and a foundation laid for many diseases. . . . Were it not for the individuals who join the mills from the country, the factory people would soon be deteriorated.[2]

Mr. Beaumont, a Bradford surgeon, also testifies:

. . . I also consider the system of working in the factories in and around here induces for the most part a peculiar laxity of the whole system, rendering the children highly susceptible of either prevailing epidemics or casual medical disorders. . . . I certainly consider the want of wholesome regulations in the most of the factories, whether as to ventilation or cleanliness, to be productive in a great measure of that peculiar tendency or susceptibility of morbid affections of which my own practice affords ample experience.[3]

Similarly Mr. William Sharp, jun.,[4] has this to say about Mr. Wood's factory at Bradford:

The object of my evidence is to represent:—

1. That I have had an opportunity of observing the effect of the factory system in (sic) the health of children under the most advantageous circumstances[5]; 2. That this effect is decidedly, and, to a

[1] At this point Engels explains for the benefit of German readers, the distinction made in England between a physician and a surgeon. He thought that, in general, people often preferred to consult surgeons rather than physicians.
[2] Factories Enquiry Commission, *Second Report*, C. 3, pp. 12–3—medical report by Dr. C. Loudon—evidence of F. Sharp.
[3] Factories Enquiry Commission, *Second Report*, 1833, C. 3, p. 22—medical report by Dr. C. Loudon—evidence of Thomas Beaumont.
[[4] Engels wrote 'Dr. Kay'. Evidence was given to the Factories Enquiry Commission by William Hey, surgeon, but the particular piece of evidence given here was by William Sharp, jun., surgeon.]
[[5] At this point Engels adds, in brackets, the information that Sharp had been the medical officer in Wood's factory, which was the best-regulated establishment in Bradford from the point of view of the employment of children.]

great extent, injurious, even under those favourable circumstances of having every attention paid to the health and comfort of the children which the system will allow; 3. That during the year 1832[1] out of about 500 children employed in one mill thus circumstanced, upwards of 300 had medical assistance from me; 4. That the most injurious effect is not in the prevalency of *deformed* bodies, but *debilitated* and *diseased* constitutions; 5. That though the effect on the general health be the most serious and lamentable, yet the bones and joints, particularly of the lower extremities, frequently suffer very *materially*; 6. And that as I have stated above, since the time of labour has been reduced to about ten hours, the health of the children has been much improved.[2]

Dr. Loudon, the Commissioner who quotes these witnesses, himself writes:

In conclusion, I think it has been clearly proved that children have been worked a most unreasonable and cruel length of time daily, and that even adults have been expected to do a certain quantity of labour which scarcely any human being is able to endure. The result of this has been, that many have met with a premature death; many have been affected constitutionally for life; and the idea of posterity being injured from the shattered frames of the survivors is, physiologically speaking, but too well founded.[3]

Finally I quote from Dr. Hawkins on the subject of Manchester:

I believe that most travellers are struck by the lowness of stature, the leanness, and the paleness which present themselves so commonly to the eye at Manchester, and above all among the factory classes. I have never been in any town in Great Britain nor in Europe in which degeneracy of form and colour from the national standard has been so obvious. The married women fall remarkably short of the usual characteristics of the English wife; in fact, in addition to the labour of twelve hours daily, they have other cares which engross almost the undivided attention of married women in many other classes of life.[4]

[Previously Dr. Hawkins had stated:]

I cannot help remarking, that the boys and girls whom I examined from the Manchester factories very generally exhibited a depressed look, and a pallid complexion; none of the alacrity, activity, and hilarity of early life shone on their countenances and gestures. This is more perceptible on the side of the boys than of the girls. A large

[1 Engels gave the date wrongly as 1842, not 1832.]

[2] Factories Enquiry Commission, *Second Report*, 1833, C. 3, p. 23. [Sharp was a nephew of William Sharp, sen.]

[3] Op. cit., 1833, C. 3, p. 24 (Concluding remarks of Dr. Charles Loudon).

[4] Factories Enquiry Commission, *Second Report*, D. 3, p. 3.

number of both, in reply to my questions, declared that they had no wish to play about on the Saturday afternoon and on the Sunday, but that they preferred remaining quiet.[1]

I will add here another passage from Hawkins, which is only partly relevant to this discussion, but may conveniently be given here:

> . . . Intemperance, debauchery and improvidence are the chief blemishes on the character of the factory workpeople, and those evils may easily be traced to habits formed under the present system, and springing from it almost inevitably . . . but on all sides it is admitted that indigestion, hypochondriasis and languor affect this class of the population very widely. After twelve hours of monotonous labour and confinement, it is but too natural to seek for stimulants of one kind or another; but when we superadd the morbid states above alluded to, the transition to spirits is rapid and perpetual.[2]

Confirmation of all these statements by doctors and Commissioners is contained in the main body of the Report itself which gives hundreds of additional examples [of ill health due to factory labour]. Numerous cases are cited of young workers whose health has suffered owing to the nature of their work. Mr. Cowell, for example, gives the weights of 46 boys who attended a particular Sunday school. All were aged 17.[3] Twenty-six of these boys worked in factories and their average weight was 104.5 lb. On the other hand the twenty boys who came from working-class families but did not work in factories weighed on the average 117.7 lb. One of the most important Manchester manufacturers, and the leader of the factory owners against the workers[4]—I think it was Robert Hyde Greg—admitted that if this state of affairs were allowed to continue the Lancashire factory operatives would soon be a race of pigmies.[5] A recruiting

---

[1] Ibid., D. 3, p. 2.

[2] Ibid., D. 3, p. 4.

[3] Factories Enquiry Commission, *First Report*, 1833, D. 1, p. 89—evidence taken by J. W. Cowell. [The sample was taken from boys attending two Sunday schools and not one.]

[4 The phrase ' of the factory owners ' was omitted by Engels in the English translation published in the U.S.A. in 1887.]

[5 Speaking in the House of Commons on March 15th, 1844, Lord Ashley stated: ' I have, moreover, the authority of one of the most ardent antagonists, himself a mighty mill-owner, that, if the present system of labour be persevered in, the " county of Lancaster will speedily become a province of pigmies " ': *Hansard*, 3rd series, Vol. 73 (1844), col. 1100. The three Greg brothers, Robert Hyde (1795–1875), Samuel (1804–76) and William Rathbone (1809–81) all wrote pamphlets on the condition of the factory population in the 1830s and early 1840s. W. R. Greg, for example, published an anonymous tract in 1831 entitled *An Enquiry into the State of the Manufacturing Population, and the causes and cures of the evils therein existing*. It was used extensively by Peter Gaskell in writing *The Manufacturing Population of*

officer[1] stated that factory workers rarely came up to the standards required for admission to the army. They looked thin and delicate and often failed to pass their medical examination. In Manchester he could rarely find men who were 5 ft. 8 ins. high; most of them were about 5 ft. 6 ins. or 5 ft. 7 ins. in height, whereas in agricultural districts most of the recruits were 5 ft. 8 ins.[2]

As a result of all this working men grow old before their time. Most of them are no longer fit for work at 40. A few manage to keep going until they are 45, but hardly any are able to work to the age of 50. This is due not only to general physical debility but also to the failing eyesight which affects mule spinners. They have to watch closely a bank of fine parallel moving threads, and this must place a great strain on the eyes. Of 1,600 workers employed in several factories in Harpur [?Harpurhey, near Manchester] and Lanark, only ten were over the ages of 45, while out of 22,094 operatives in various factories in Stockport and Manchester only 143 were over the age of 45. Of these 143, sixteen were kept on as a special favour and were employed on light work normally done by children. On one occasion the owner of a factory turned down applications for employment from 131 spinners because they were 'too old'; yet only seven of them were over the age of 45. Of 50 Bolton spinners who were laid off and lost their livelihood because of old age, only two were over 50 and the average age of the remainder was under 40. Mr. Ashworth, a leading manufacturer, admitted in a letter to Lord Ashley that when spinners were about forty years old they were no longer capable of producing a sufficient quantity of yarn [in a given time] and were therefore 'sometimes' discharged. He refers to operatives in their forties as

England (1833)—see pp. 63, 70-1, 72, 85, 137, 196—and was quoted with approval by John Fielden: The Curse of the Factory System (1836), pp. 35-6. Robert Hyde Greg, however, dismissed his young brother's pamphlet as being ' little more than a college thesis, written before he had any experience, and scarcely any acquaintance with factories, or factory population ': The Factory Question, considered in its Relation to its Effects on the Health and Morals of those employed in Factories: and ' The Ten Hours Bill ' . . . (1837) pp. 69-70. The phrase ' a race of pigmies ' was not used by W. R. Greg in his pamphlet of 1831, but on pages 16-17 he dealt with ' the injurious influence which the weakened and vitiated constitution of the women [employed in cotton factories] has upon their children '. Gaskell, writing on the same subject, went somewhat further and stated, ' . . . it may be asserted—that a diminutive and ill-shaped race, possessing little muscular strength, and fitted as labourers only to act in subservience to a more powerful agent, will be the product of the present mode of manufacture ': The Manufacturing Population of England (1833), p. 170.]

[1] Factories Enquiry Commission, First Report, D. 2, pp. 60-61 (Statement of Colour Sergeant John Wilmot).

[2 The final sentence of this paragraph is omitted. For the benefit of the German readers Engels explains the difference between the English foot and the Prussian Fuss.]

' old men '[1] Mr. Mackintosh, one of the Factory Commissioners, states in the Report of 1833:[2]

Although prepared by seeing childhood occupied in such a manner, it is very difficult to believe the ages of the men advanced in years as given by themselves, so complete is their premature old age.

Mr. James Smellie, a Glasgow surgeon, whose main practice was among the factory operatives, asserts that they [i.e. cotton spinners] are old at forty.[3] Further confirmation is to be found in the evidence of Messrs. Tufnell and Hawkins.[4] In Manchester the premature ageing of the working-class population is so universal that practically all operatives in their forties look between ten and fifteen years older than this.[5] On the other hand both men and women of the well-to-do classes are well-preserved in middle age unless they drink to excess.

Factory work also has characteristic effects on the physique of the women operatives. Long hours of work lead to much more serious deformities in women than in men. The pelvis becomes deformed, partly because the malformation of the hip bones already apparent in youth becomes more pronounced in adult years. Another contributory cause is the malformation of the base of the spinal column. Dr. Loudon states in the concluding remarks to his medical reports:[6]

Although no cases presented themselves of deformed pelvis, varicose veins, ulcers in the young people under 25 years of age, and some others of the diseases which have been described, yet their ailments are such as every medical man must expect to be the probable consequences of young people working, in some instances,

---

[1] All this information is derived from Lord Ashley's speech of March 15th, 1844, in the House of Commons. [*Hansard*, 3rd series 1844, Vol. 73, cols. 1082–4.]

[2] Factories Enquiry Commission, *First Report*, A. 2, p. 96—Report of Robert Mackintosh.

[3] Factories Enquiry Commission, *First Report*, A. 1, p. 101—evidence taken by James Stuart.

[4] For evidence taken by Tufnell see *First Report*, D. 2, pp. 3, 6, 15 [and not, as Engels stated, page 9.] For evidence taken by Hawkins see Second Report, D. 3, pp. 4, 11 [and not page 14 as stated by Engels.]

[[5] But see the *Statement of Facts* . . . *submitted by the Deputation of the Master Manufacturers and Millowners in the County of Lancaster* (*Manchester Guardian*, May 1st, 1844, p. 5, cols. 4–5). This return referred to 412 mills in the Lancashire industrial area, and stated that:

The percentage of persons above 40 engaged in mills is only 7¾ per cent; this does not arise so much from superannuation, as from the number of mill-hands who are enabled by their savings, to enter into superior occupations. Of these 197 have been traced in the town and vicinity of Ashton-under-Lyne. . . . Of these 197 we found that 14 have become master spinners and manufacturers, 61 shopkeepers, 42 publicans and beer retailers, 11 grocers and tea dealers, and the rest have found other respectable means of obtaining a livelihood. . .]

[6] Factories Enquiry Commission, *Second Report*, C. 3, p. 24.

nearly forty consecutive hours twice a week, and, besides, labouring from twelve to fourteen hours on those days of the week when night-work was not expected; and they are recorded by men of the highest professional and moral character.[1]

Many midwives and others who assist at childbirth state that female factory operatives experience more difficult labour in childbirth than other women, and that miscarriages are more frequent among them than is normal. This is stated in evidence collected by Dr. Hawkins on behalf of the Factories Enquiry Commission.[2] Moreover, during pregnancy the women operatives—who suffer from the general ill health common to factory workers of both sexes—continue to work right up to the hour of their confinement. If a pregnant operative left work too early she would be afraid of dismissal and of finding her place taken by another when she wished to return to work. In addition, absence from work means loss of wages. It is quite common for women to be working in the evening and for the child to be delivered the following morning, and it is by no means uncommon for babies to be born in the factory itself among the machinery. Gentlemen of the bourgeoisie may well show no concern at this state of affairs. Their wives, however, might be prepared to admit that it is not only a disgrace, but an infamous barbarism, virtually to force a pregnant woman to work from twelve to thirteen—formerly even longer—hours at a job which entails both standing and frequent stooping. But this is not all. If a woman can afford to stay away from the factory for a fortnight after the birth of her child, she considers that she is lucky and has had a long rest. Some women are back at work in the factory in a week—or even after three or four days—and they actually do a full day's work. I am told that the owner of a factory once asked one of his overlookers: ' Is so-and-so not back yet? ' ' No ', [replied the overlooker]. ' How long is it since she had her baby? ' 'A week'. ' Surely she ought to have been back long ago. That girl over there only stays at home for three days when she has a baby '. Of course, the behaviour of the second girl is easy to understand. It is fear of dismissal and fear of hunger which drive her into the factory in spite of her weakness and her pain. It is not in the interest of the factory owner that his workers should be at home on sick-leave. They are not supposed to fall ill or to stay away during childbirth. If such goings on were allowed, the factory owner would be forced to stop his machinery or he would actually have to rack his precious brains

[1 Engels gives only a very abbreviated version of Dr. Loudon's somewhat guarded statement.]

[2 *Second Report*, D. 3, pp. 11, 13. [Evidence of Mary Woodhouse, midwife, pp. 11–12, and Elizabeth Taylor, midwife, pp. 13–14.]

to devise some temporary arrangement while his workers were ill.
But factory owners are not prepared to suffer any inconvenience whatever and dismiss their workers outright if they are so presumptuous
as to fall ill. One of the witnesses [examined by Mr. J. W. Cowell],
obviously very ill, was asked ' Why don't you ask for leave to stay
away? ' [The witness, a girl 16½ years old, replied] ' Well, sir, the
master is queer at letting us off; if we are off a quarter [i.e. a quarter of
a day] we stand a chance of being turned away.'[1]

And Sir David Barry in one of his medical reports cites the case
of Thomas McDurt, a cotton operative, aged 34. Barry reported
as follows concerning this workman:

> Rheumatic pains; twenty-six years at mill-work; white tongue
> and slight fever just now, and cannot venture to be off work more
> than four days, for fear of losing his work; has had hernia and is
> now better.[2]

The same thing is happening in practically all factories. The fact
that young girls are at work during the period of adolescence has
many unfortunate effects, in addition to those already mentioned.
Some girls particularly those who are better nourished [than the aver-
age], develop more quickly than they should do because of the heat of
the factory rooms. There are some cases of girls aged between twelve
and fourteen who are already physically mature. We have already
referred to Mr. John Roberton, who is stated in the Factories Enquiry
Commission's Report to be an eminent gynaecologist in Manchester.
This doctor states in the *North of England Medical and Surgical Journal*
that he knew of an eleven-year-old girl who was not only completely
mature physically, but was actually pregnant.[3] He stated that it was
not at all unusual in Manchester for girls of fifteen years of age to
bear children. In such cases the heat of the factory has the same effect
as a tropical climate. In both cases nature revenges herself on precocious physical development by premature old age and debility.
On the other hand, there are also cases of retarded physical develop-

---

[1] Factories Enquiry Commission, *First Report*, D. 1, p. 77—evidence collected
by J. W. Cowell. [Engels wrote ' half day ' instead of a ' quarter '].

[2] *Second Report*, A. 3, p. 44—Sir David Barry's medical report. [Engels gave
only a garbled version of this evidence].

[3] John Roberton, 'An inquiry respecting the period of puberty in women ',
North of England Medical and Surgical Journal, Vol. 1 (August 1830–May 1831), pp.
69–85, 179–191. Although Roberton gives a number of examples of menstruation
in the eleventh year (pp. 72–73), he gives no example of pregnancy at that age.
Engels was obviously relying here on the account of Roberton's paper given by
Peter Gaskell (*The Manufacturing Population* (1833), pp. 77–8 and in particular
footnote 2, p. 78), who made the same mistake. Gaskell did, however, state:
' Two similar cases have occurred to the author, and very many others to his
professional friends '.]

ment among young women. Cowell[1] gives examples of cases in which the breasts mature late or not at all. Menstruation often does not begin until the seventeenth or eighteenth year, and occasionally is even postponed to the twentieth year. Often it does not occur at all.[2] Medical evidence is unanimous that girls in factories suffer from irregular menstruation, coupled with great pain and various disorders, such as anaemia, which is particularly common.

It is too much to expect healthy children to be born to such young women, especially if they are obliged to work during pregnancy. The medical evidence in the Factories Enquiry Commission's Report, particularly with regard to Manchester, is virtually unanimous in describing these children as unhealthy. Only Sir David Barry asserts that these children are healthy, but he admits that in Scotland, where he collected evidence, hardly any married women worked in the factories. Most of the Scottish factories, except those in Glasgow, are situated in country districts, and this makes the children healthier. The children of the working classes in the immediate vicinity of Manchester nearly all have a healthy and robust appearance, whereas those who live in the town itself are pale and scrofulous. But soon after the country children enter the factories at the age of nine they lose their healthy colour and before long it is impossible to distinguish them from the town children.

There are in addition certain branches of factory labour which have particularly injurious effects on the workers. In the cotton and flax spinning mills there are many rooms in which the air is filled with fluff and dust. This leads to chest and bronchial complaints, particularly among the workers in the carding and combing rooms. Some people are able to breathe the atmosphere of these rooms without any ill effects, but other workers suffer from the complaints we have mentioned. The operative, of course, has no choice in the matter. He must work in the room in which there is employment for him, whatever the state of his chest. The usual consequences of inhaling factory dust are the spitting of blood, heavy, noisy breathing, pains in the chest, coughing and sleeplessness—in short, all the symptoms of asthma, which, in the worst cases, culminates in consumption.[3] The wet

---

[1] E.g. Factories Enquiry Commission, *First Report*, D. 1, p. 35. (J. W. Cowell).

[2] Factories Enquiry Commission, *Second Report*, A. 3, p. 5 (opinion of Dr. Douglas mentioned by Sir David Barry in one of his medical reports); C. 3, p. 14 (evidence of Francis Sharp, sen., in one of Dr. Loudon's medical reports); D. 3, p. 11 (evidence of Mary Woodhouse, midwife, in Dr. Hawkins's medical reports).

[3] Factories Enquiry Commission, *First Report*, A. 1, pp. 13, 70, 101, 125 (report and evidence collected by Stuart); A. 2, p. 94 (Mackintosh's reports); C. 2, pp. 15, 17, 37 (Power's Reports on Nottingham and Leeds); and D. 1, p. 33 (Cowell's Report on Manchester); *Second Report*, A. 3, pp. 12 (five cases in one factory), 17, 44, 52, 60, 72 (Barry's evidence); C. 3, p. 13 (Loudon's Report).

spinning of linen yarn, which is performed by young girls and children, is a particularly unhealthy occupation. The water spurts from the spindles on to the operatives, so that the front of their clothing is always wet and they are soaked to the skin. They are continually standing in water. In the doubling rooms of cotton mills the same state of affairs prevails, though to a lesser degree, and these operatives, too, are continually suffering from colds and chest ailments. Practically all textile operatives, particularly wet spinners and doublers, speak with hoarse voices. Messrs. Stuart and Mackintosh and Sir David Barry condemn the unhealthiness of this type of work in the strongest terms and denounce the callous disregard shown by most employers for the welfare of girls engaged in it. Flax spinners also suffer from a peculiar distortion of the shoulder. The right shoulder blade becomes deformed and thrust forward as a result of the character of the work. Both flax spinning and the throstle-spinning of cotton frequently produce injuries to the knee-cap, which the spinners use to stop the spindles while broken threads are being tied. In the two branches of work to which we have referred, the machinery is so constructed as to impose frequent stooping on the operatives, and this, too, has deleterious effects upon their health. I cannot recall having seen a single healthy and well-built girl in the throstle room of the mill in Manchester in which I worked. The girls were all small and stunted and suffered from a marked stoop. The general appearance of their figures was far from pleasing.

In addition to all their illnesses and deformities, the physical condition of the workers suffers in another way. Accidents occur to operatives who work in rooms crammed full of machinery.[1] Many of them lead to injuries of a more or less serious character and render the victim partly or wholly incapable of earning a living. The most common injury is the loss of a joint of the finger. It is less common for a machine to crush an entire finger, a hand or part of a hand or even an arm. Even a minor injury can lead to major consequences and death from lockjaw is by no means infrequent. In Manchester one sees not only numerous cripples, but also plenty of workers who have lost the whole or part of an arm, leg or foot. The most dangerous

[1 A different point of view about accidents in factories at this time was expressed in the *Statement of Facts . . . submitted by the Deputation of the Master Manufacturers and Millowners in the County of Lancaster*: *Manchester Guardian*, May 1st, 1844, p. 5, cols. 4-5. They asserted:
From the return of accidents (by coroners, etc.) sent with this return, it appears that, out of upwards of 850 accidents, occasioning loss of life, only 29 (or 3⅜ per cent) have been occasioned by factory machinery while 79 have been caused by carts, etc. and 85 in coalpits.]

part of a machine is the belt which conveys power from the shaft to the individual machines. When these belts have buckles they are particularly dangerous; but few belts of this type remain in use. When an operative is caught in the belt he is quickly thrown up to the ceiling and down to the floor with such force that practically every bone in his body is broken and he is killed instantly. The following serious accidents (minor injuries are not reported) were recorded in the *Manchester Guardian* between June 12th and August 3rd, 1844:

12th June, 1844: A boy died in Manchester from lockjaw after his hand had been crushed by the wheels of a machine.[1]

15th June, 1844: A youth from Saddleworth died of dreadful injuries after being caught in a machine.[2]

29th June, 1844: A young man of Greenacres Moor, near Manchester, working in a machine shop, had two ribs broken and suffered from many cuts as a result of falling under a grindstone.[3]

24th July, 1844: An Oldham girl died after being swung round fifty times in machinery belting, every bone in her body being broken.[4]

27th July, 1844: In Manchester a girl fell into a blower (the first machine used in preparing raw cotton) and died [of lockjaw] as a result of serious injuries.[5]

3rd August, 1844: A Dukinfield bobbin turner was caught in a belt and had all his ribs broken.[6]

The Manchester Infirmary, in the year 1842[7] alone, treated 962 cases of injuries from machinery. All other accidents dealt with in the same period at the Infirmary totalled 2,426.[8] This shows that

[1 *Manchester Guardian*, 12th June, 1844, p. 4, col. 6. There is no mention of lockjaw in the report of the accidental death of John Whitehead, aged 12. At the inquest it was stated that the boy was employed in another part of the works and had no right to be touching the machine in which his hand was trapped].

[2 *Manchester Guardian*, 15th June, 1844, p. 6, col. 5.]

[3 *Manchester Guardian*, 29th June, 1844, p. 6, col. 3.]

[4 *Manchester Guardian*, 24th July, 1844, p. 7, col. 2. The person involved was not a girl, but a married woman aged about 30. The report states: ' No portion of her body was mutilated, but she was dreadfully shaken, and died in about twenty minutes. The deceased is said to have repeatedly ventured upon cleaning machinery at improper times, and her death is generally attributed to her own rashness.']

[5 *Manchester Guardian*, 27th July, 1844, p. 5, col. 1. Engels does not mention that the girl was trying to clean the machine while it was still in motion, whereas she should have waited until it was stopped for the tea-break. At the inquest the jury imposed a deodand (fine) of £10 upon the machinery, which, in their opinion, should have been fenced.]

[6 *Manchester Guardian*, 3rd August, 1844, p. 6, col. 4.]

[7 Engels wrote 1843 instead of the correct date 1842.]

[8 *Report of the State of the Manchester Royal Infirmary. . . from June 25th, 1842, to June 24th, 1843* (1843)—'A table of the injuries of accident out-patients admitted during the year 1842 '. It is assumed from the nature of the injuries that many of these out-patients immediately became in-patients.]

two out of every five accidents were caused by machinery. These figures include neither accidents which occurred in Salford nor injuries treated by private doctors. When such accidents occur, whether the victim is totally incapacitated or not, the factory owner usually does no more than pay the doctor's fee. If he is very generous he may pay the operative his wages while he is out of work. If the operative is too badly injured to return to work the factory owner shows no interest in his fate.

The Factories Enquiry Commission's Report recommends that the responsibility for all accidents should be laid on the shoulders of the factory owners. Child workers are obviously too young to look after themselves properly, and adults may be assumed to take precautions, if only in their own interest. But since this is a report drawn up by the middle classes it is not surprising that the writers should contradict themselves by qualifying their remarks about the owners' responsibility by hypocritical observations on the so-called ' culpable temerity '[1] of the workers. The truth of the matter is that if children *cannot* look after themselves, their employment must be prohibited. If adults are careless, one explanation might be that their mental age is that of a child who cannot fully appreciate the extent of the danger [from machinery in motion.] If that is true, where does the fault lie, save with the middle classes, who keep the workers in a state which precludes them from developing their intelligence to the full? Another possibility is that the lay-out of the machinery may be defective. If that is so, the machinery should be adequately fenced. This, too, is the responsibility of the middle classes. Again, it may be that the worker has reasons for taking undue risks when operating machinery. He may, for example, have to work quickly in order to earn enough money, and have no time to take care. Once more the middle classes are to blame. Many accidents occur when workers are cleaning machines in motion. The reason for this is that the bourgeois factory owner makes the operative clean the stationary machinery during meal breaks. The worker naturally does not relish the prospect of giving up any of his free time to the middle classes. If the factory owners would only give the operatives time during working hours to clean stationary machinery, not a single one would dream of trying to clean a machine in motion. In short, it is the factory owner who is always at fault, whatever may be the cause of these accidents. It would be reasonable to ask that the factory owner should grant a pension for life to any worker permanently incapacitated as the result

[1 ' Culpable temerity ' is in English in the original: see Factories Enquiry Commission, *First Report*, 1833, p. 72 (last paragraph).]

of an accident. The family of a worker involved in a fatal accident should also receive a pension for life. In the early days of industrialisation accidents were relatively much more common than they are to-day. At one time the machines were smaller, more liable to break down and crowded more closely together. Moreover, fencing was virtually unknown. We have, however, shown that although some improvements have been made the toll of accidents is still large enough to give cause for alarm. No one can be complacent about a situation which injures and cripples so many workers for the benefit of a single class. It is tragic that so many industrious workers are injured in the factories and so are condemned to a lifetime of poverty and hunger. Their middle-class employers must bear the sole responsibility for this disgraceful state of affairs.

A fine list of diseases and injuries due solely to the revolting greed of the middle classes! Simply in order to fill the pockets of the bourgeoisie, women are rendered unfit to bear children, children are crippled, while grown men are stunted and maimed. The health of whole generations of workers is undermined, and they are racked with diseases and infirmities. Let us recall a few of the more barbarous cases [brought to light by the Factories Enquiry Commission's Reports.] Stuart reports that children were dragged naked out of bed by overseers and driven with blows and kicks to the factories, their clothes over their arms.[1] Blows had at first aroused them from their slumbers, but before long they were asleep again over their work. A case is reported of a wretched child being roused by a shout from the foreman, when the machinery had stopped working. Still half asleep, the child, with eyes still closed, automatically went through the motions of working the silent machine. We read of children who were too tired [when the day's work was over] to go home, but hid themselves under the wool in the drying room, only to be driven from the factory by blows from a strap. We read of hundreds of children who come home from the factory every evening so tired that they cannot eat their supper from lack of sleep and lack of appetite. Their parents found them on their knees at their bedside, where they had fallen asleep while saying their prayers. These, and hundreds of other revolting and infamous occurrences, are to be found scattered through the pages of the Factories Enquiry Commission's Reports. The evidence was all given on oath and was confirmed by several witnesses. It comes from men whose reliability is accepted without question by the

---

[1] Factories Enquiry Commission, *First Report*, 1833, A. 1, p. 39 (evidence of Robert Arnot taken by James Stuart). [Some of Arnot's evidence clearly refers to events a few years before he gave evidence in 1833.]

Commissioners themselves. Remember that this is a ' Liberal ' report;
it is a middle-class report. It was embarked upon in order to contradict
an earlier report by the Tories. It was intended to clear the name of the
factory owners and vindicate the purity of their motives. Remember
that the Commissioners themselves were on the side of the middle
classes and reported these things most unwillingly. Does not all this
make one's blood boil? Should one not detest the middle classes, who
so hypocritically boast of their humanity and sacrifice, while really
they are concerned solely with filling their pockets? But let us hear
what the middle classes have to say through their mouthpiece, Dr.
Ure, the chosen lackey of the bourgeoisie. In his *Philosophy of Manufactures*[1] Ure criticises those who tell the workers that there is no
relationship between the wages they receive and the efforts they make
in earning them. Such a doctrine injures good relationships between
masters and men. Ure strongly advises the workers to bring themselves
to the favourable notice of their employers by industry and application
to duty. They should rejoice in the fact that they are in a position to
make themselves useful to their masters. If the workers follow this
advice they may become overlookers, managers and even partners
and so (Oh! Wisdom, thou speakest as the dove!) will 'have increased
at the same time the demand for their companions' labour in the
market '!'[2] ' Had it not been for the violent collisions and interruptions
resulting from erroneous views among the operatives, the factory
system would have been developed still more rapidly and beneficially
for all concerned than it has been . . . '[3] There follows a long jeremiad
against the rebellious spirit shown by the workers during a strike of
the fine spinners who are among the highest paid workers. He makes
the following naive comment:

> In fact, it was their high wages which enabled them to maintain
> a stipendiary committee in affluence, and to pamper themselves into
> nervous ailments by a diet too rich and exciting for their indoor
> occupations.[4]

Listen to the description of children at play given by this middle-
class writer:

> I have visited many factories, both in Manchester and in the

---

[1] Dr. Andrew Ure, *Philosophy of Manufactures* (1835), pp. 279–80.
    [2 Op. cit., p. 280.]
    [3] Ure, op. cit., p. 280 [Engels gives an abbreviated version of this statement as
if it were a quotation from the original and puts it in italics].
    [4] Ure, op. cit., p. 298. [Ure is referring to a strike which took place in 1818, or
nearly twenty years before the publication of his book. For the Lancashire and
Cheshire cotton operatives' strike of 1818, see A. Aspinall, *The Early English Trade
Unions* (1949), pp. 246–310].

surrounding districts, during a period of several months, entering the spinning rooms, unexpectedly, and often alone, at different times of the day, and I never saw a single instance of corporal chastisement inflicted on a child, nor indeed did I ever see children in ill-humour. They seemed to be always cheerful and alert, taking pleasure in the light play of their muscles,—enjoying the mobility natural to their age. The scene of industry, so far from exciting sad emotions in my mind, was always exhilarating. It was delightful to observe the nimbleness with which they pieced the broken ends, as the mule-carriage began to recede from the fixed roller beam, and to see them at leisure, after a few seconds' exercise of their tiny fingers, to amuse themselves in any attitude they chose, till the stretch and winding-on were once more completed. The work of these lively elves seemed to resemble a sport, in which habit gave them a pleasing dexterity. Conscious of their skill, they were delighted to show it off to any stranger. As to exhaustion by the day's work, they evinced no trace of it on emerging from the mill in the evening; for they immediately began to skip about any neighbouring play-ground, and to commence their little amusements with the same alacrity as boys issuing from a school.[1]

Obviously! It is self-evident that it would be essential for workers to exercise all their muscles in order to ease limbs which had become stiff through lack of exercise, but Dr. Ure should have waited to see whether this momentary vigour lasted for more than a minute or two. Incidentally Ure could only see this at mid-day after the children had been working for five or six hours. He could not see it in the evening.

When he discusses the health of the workers Dr. Ure has the boundless effrontery to pretend that the Report of the Factories Enquiry Commission of 1833—extracts from which we have already given—contains evidence to show that the factory operatives enjoy excellent health. He actually tries to show by quoting isolated extracts wrenched out of their context that none of the operatives suffer from scrofula. He points out quite correctly that the factory workers are free from all acute diseases, but he omits to mention that this is counter-balanced by liability to all kinds of chronic infection.[2] I must emphasise that the Factories Enquiry Commission's Report consists of three thick folio volumes and the well-fed English middle classes would never think of ploughing right through them. Only an examination of the contents would enable one to measure the impudence with which our friend Ure deceives the English public with the grossest of falsehoods.

[1] Ure, op. cit., p. 301. [Engels gives an abridged version of this passage between inverted commas as if it were an exact version].

[2] A. Ure, *Philosophy of Manufactures* (1835), Book 3, chapter II on 'Health of factory inmates', pp. 374–403.

Consider his views on the Factory Act of 1833,[1] which was passed by the Liberal middle classes and—as we shall see later—places only the most necessary restrictions upon the factory owners. Ure argues that the provision concerning the compulsory education of factory children was an absurd and despotic restriction upon the factory owners. He claims that when this Act came into full force all children under the age of twelve would run the risk of losing their livelihood. And with what result? The children, deprived of their light and useful employment, would now receive no education at all: '... they are thrown out of the warm spinning rooms upon the cold world to exist by beggary or plunder ... a life woefully contrasted with their former improving state at the factory and its Sunday-school '.[2] Ure declares that under the guise of philanthropy this Act aggravates the sufferings of the poor, and will powerfully restrict, if it does not entirely stop, the useful labours of conscientious manufacturers.[3]

Attention was drawn at an early date to the ruinous consequences of the factory system. We have already drawn attention to the passing of the Health and Morals of Apprentices Act of 1802. In about 1817 Robert Owen, the future father of English Socialism, who was at that time a manufacturer at New Lanark in Scotland, began to draw the attention of the authorities by petitions and memorials to the necessity of protecting by law the health of industrial workers, particularly factory children. The late Sir Robert Peel and other philanthropists supported him, and their agitation led to the passing of the three Factory Acts of 1819, 1825 and 1831. The first two of these Acts were inoperative and the third was only enforced here and there. The Factory Act of 1831, based upon a motion brought forward by Sir John Cam Hobhouse, included the following provisions. Night work was prohibited for cotton operatives under the age of 21. This prohibition covered the period from 7.30 p.m. to 5.30 the following morning. In all factories young people under the age of 18 were to work for no more than twelve hours a day, except on Saturdays, when their work was not to exceed nine hours. This Act, too, was largely a dead letter, since workers would not dare to give evidence against their masters for fear of being dismissed. In the great towns, however, where there was industrial unrest, the owners of the larger factories agreed among themselves to abide by the law; but there were many factory owners in the big towns who followed the example of their

[1 Engels gives this date, in error, as 1834.]
[2] Ure, op. cit., p. 406.
[3] Ure, op. cit., pp. 405 et seq. [Book 3, chapter iii—' State of Knowledge and Religion in Factories '.]

colleagues in the country districts, and disregarded Hobhouse's Act. Meanwhile an agitation in favour of a Ten Hours Bill had begun among the workers. The object of the movement was to secure the passing of a law which would forbid all young people under 18 to work in factories. The trade unions supported this agitation, which received widespread support in all the factory districts. The project was taken up by Michael Sadler, the leader of the humanitarian wing of the Tory Party, and he raised the question in Parliament. Sadler secured the appointment of a Select Committee of the House of Commons to enquire into the factory system and its findings were presented in 1832.[1] This is a very partisan document, which was drawn up entirely by enemies of the factory system for purely political purposes. Sadler was led astray by his passionate sympathies [for the oppressed] into making assertions of a most misleading and erroneous kind. He asked witnesses questions in such a way as to elicit answers which, although correct, nevertheless were stated in such a form as to give a wholly false impression. The manufacturers were enraged at a Report which held them up to public condemnation as monsters of iniquity. They thereupon asked for a new official enquiry knowing full well that *now* such an investigation would only be to their advantage. This was because the Whigs by this time were firmly in the saddle. They were a genuine middle-class party and were on good terms with the factory owners. The Whigs were opposed to placing any restrictions upon industry. The manufacturers secured a new enquiry without any difficulty. This time the Royal Commission was packed with representatives of the Liberal bourgeoisie. It is the Report of this Commission that I have frequently quoted in this chapter. This enquiry comes somewhat closer to the truth than Sadler's Committee, but errs in the opposite direction. On every page there is sympathy for the factory owners and distrust for Sadler's Report. Distaste for independent working class agitation and the supporters of the Ten Hours Bill is a marked feature of the Report. Nowhere does the Commission recognise the worker's right to be treated as a human being. The Commission actually criticises the workers, who admitted that they were thinking of their own as well as their children's interests when they agitated for the Ten Hours Bill. The Commission condemns

---

[1] Report from the Select Committee on the Bill to regulate the labour of children in the mills and factories of the United Kingdom, 8th August 1832, *Parliamentary Papers*, 1831–32, Vol. 15.
[In fact no report of any substance was made and only the minutes of evidence were laid before the Commons. For an analysis of the Report of Sadler's Committee, see W. H. Hutt, ' The factory system of the early nineteenth century ': *Capitalism and the Historians* (ed. F. A. Hayek, 1954), pp. 160–88.]

organized workers as demagogues, rogues, mischief-makers, etc.—in short it is a truly middle-class report. Yet even the authors of this Report cannot whitewash the manufacturers completely. The evidence of the factory owners themselves provides so many examples of scandalous conditions in the factories that there can be no doubt where the heavy burden of responsibility lies. In the circumstances there is every justification both for the Ten Hours agitation and for the hatred of the workers against the manufacturers to which the report refers. There is also ample justification for the criticisms of the factory owners contained in the Report. There is this difference between the two Reports. In Sadler's enquiry the manufacturers were [in effect] charged with open and undisguised brutality. On the other hand, the Royal Commission shows how the exercise of this brutality is generally hidden beneath a veneer of civilisation and benevolence. Dr. Bisset Hawkins, the medical Commissioner for Lancashire, actually gives unequivocal support to the Ten Hours Bill in the very first paragraph of his report.[1] Commissioner Robert Mackintosh admits that his report does not contain the full truth since it is very difficult to get the workers to testify against their masters.[2] He states that manufacturers often made special preparations to receive him by sweeping out their factories and by reducing the speed of their machinery.[3] Moreover, agitation among the workers had already forced the factory owners to show them greater consideration. The Lancashire manufacturers in particular, were fond of resorting to the device of introducing the foreman of the workroom as a ' worker '.[4] The foreman would then testify as to the humane conduct of his employers, the healthy nature of the work and the indifference—even the opposition—of the workers to the Ten Hours Bill. These foremen, however, are no longer genuine workers. They have betrayed and deserted their class. They have been tempted by increased pay to enter the service of the middle classes and to fight against the worker in the interest of the capitalists. The interests of

---

[1] Factories Enquiry Commission, 2nd Report (1833), D. 3, p. 1.

[2] Ibid., 1st Report (1833), A. 2, p. 94.

[3] Mackintosh made no such statement in his report (op. cit., A. 2, pp. 94-8), but he commented as follows on the evidence taken by him at Dunfermline (A.2, p. 6): ' One of the overlookers ... informed me that preparations were made at this as well as at the other mills for our arrival, by cleaning, etc.' For the slowing down of machinery see A. 2, p. 26.]

[4] E.g. Factories Enquiry Commission, 1st Report, D. 2, pp. 71-72 (evidence taken by E. C. Tufnell from five Rochdale overlookers who stated that they did not know one Rochdale operative who was in favour of the Ten Hours Bill); D. 2, pp. 108-9 (evidence taken by E. C. Tufnell from James Belshaw, manager of a cotton mill in Manchester).]

the foremen are the same as those of the middle classes. The workers probably hate these renegades more than they hate their employers. But when all is said and done, the report of the Royal Commission is a wholly inadequate exposure of the most shameful recklessness with which the bourgeois mill owners maltreat their workers, and the utter infamy and inhumanity of the modern system of industrial exploitation. It makes one's blood boil to read in this report the catalogue of illnesses and deformities brought about by gross over-work—and then on another page to see how the manufacturers use the cold, calculated precepts of political economy to show that these very statistics demonstrate that they and all England would inevitably be ruined if they were stopped from maiming their annual quota of helpless children. Dr. Ure's opinions, which we have just quoted, would be even more revolting if they were not so preposterous.

The Factory Act of 1833[1] which was passed as a result of this Report, forbade the employment of children under the age of 9 (except in silk mills). Children aged between 9 and 13 were not to work for more than 48 hours a week or 9 hours a day. Young persons aged from 14 to 18 were not to work more than 69 hours a week, or 12 hours on any one day. The minimum break for meals was fixed at 1½ hours a day. Night work for all persons under the age of 18 was once again forbidden. At the same time it was made compulsory for factory children under the age of fourteen to have two hours schooling a day. Manufacturers were liable to penalties if they employed children without an age certificate from the factory surgeon;[2] and a school attendance certificate from the teacher. The employer was entitled to deduct a penny a week as school money from the wages of the children in order to pay the teacher's salary. In addition, factory doctors and inspectors were appointed who had the right of entry to the factory at any time. They had the power to take evidence from factory workers on oath and they had the duty of enforcing the law by laying information with a view to prosecution before a Justice of the Peace. Those are the provisions of the law which Dr. Ure denounces in such unmeasured terms!

As a result of the passing of this Act—particularly owing to the appointment of inspectors—the average hours of work were reduced to between twelve and thirteen. As children [under 9 years of age] could now no longer be employed, the employers had to replace

---

[1 Engels gave the date of this measure inaccurately as 1834.]
[2 The Act of 1833 stipulated that the operative should obtain an age certificate not from a factory surgeon but from ' some surgeon or physician in the neighbourhood of his residence ': M. W. Thomas, *The Early Factory Legislation* (1948), p.129.]

them as best they could. The most blatant evils of the factory system
virtually disappeared. Only workers of very poor physique now
suffered from deformities. The evil effects of factory labour now
became less conspicuous. Nevertheless the Report of the Factories
Enquiry Commission contains ample evidence of the prevalence of
minor evils. These include swellings of the ankles, weakness and pain
in the legs, hips and spine, varicose veins, ulcerated limbs, general
lassitude, bowel complaints and nausea. Lack of appetite alternates
with ravenous hunger. The workers suffer also from digestive complaints, melancholia and, finally, chest complaints due to the dust and
foul atmosphere in the factories. All these complaints occurred
among operatives who worked the shorter hours (12 to 13) laid down
in Hobhouse's Act of 1831. These evils were not eradicated by the
passing of the Factory Act of 1833[1] and continue to undermine the
health of the workers to the present day. By this Act the brutal greed
of the middle classes has been hypocritically camouflaged by a mask of
decency. The law checks the worst excesses of the manufacturers,
who now apparently have a plausible excuse for flaunting their sham
humanitarianism. And that is all the difference it really makes. If a
new Factory Commission were to be appointed to-day it would find
that conditions in the factories had not materially changed. The
attempt to introduce compulsory education for factory children has
failed, since the Government did not provide good schools. The
manufacturers employed retired factory workers as teachers, to whom
the children were sent for two hours a day. The letter of the law was
observed, but the children learnt nothing. Although the work of the
Factory Inspectors is confined strictly to ensuring the observance of
the Factory Act, nevertheless their reports contain ample evidence
to prove that the evils to which we have referred are still an inevitable
feature of the factory system. Messrs. Horner and Saunders, two of
the Inspectors, state in their reports for October and December 1843[2]
that in those processes in which child labour is no longer available
the manufacturers engage adults who would otherwise not find
factory employment. Such workers have to toil from 14 to 16 hours a
day or even more.[3] Work formerly done by children is now also

[1 Engels gives the date of the first effective Factory Act, incorrectly, as 1834.]
[2 In the original German edition of 1845 Engels gave the date as 1844 instead
of 1843.]
[3 This statement is made by R. J. Saunders in his report of October 20th, 1843,
in *Reports of the Inspectors of Factories for the half-year ending 31st December*, 1843 (1844).
He wrote: ' I am equally well satisfied that persons are employed as adults, for very
long hours physically unfit for the work they are called upon to do, and often
unwillingly on their part. In this remark I refer principally to females, who have

performed by young people who are just old enough to escape the
protection of the law. Other manufacturers defy the law by reducing
the meal hours and by making the children work longer than the Act
allows. They take the risk of being prosecuted since any fine that
may be inflicted is a trifling penalty when compared with the profits
they gain by breaking the law. Since trade is booming at present the
manufacturers are under strong temptation to defy the law in this way.

The passing of the Factory Act of 1833 did not stop the workers
from continuing their agitation in favour of the Ten Hours Bill. By
1839 the agitation was in full swing again. Sadler was now dead, but
his place [as leader of the factory reformers] in the House of Commons
was taken by Lord Ashley and in the country by Richard Oastler.
Both were Tories. Oastler had been continuously engaged in propaganda in the factory districts since Sadler's day and was a great
favourite with the working classes. They called him their ' good, old
King ' and ' the King of the factory children '. In all the industrial
districts there is not a child who does not know and honour the name
of Oastler. When he visits a town the children join the adults in forming processions to welcome him. Oastler was also a very energetic
opponent of the new Poor Law of 1834. This brought him into
conflict with his Whig employer, Mr. Thornhill.[1] Oastler was the
steward of Mr. Thornhill's estate. He owed Mr. Thornhill some money
and was thrown into a debtors' prison. On several occasions the Whigs
offered to pay his debts and to confer other favours on him if only he
would withdraw his opposition to the new Poor Law. Oastler refused
and continued to languish in prison. He continued, however, to
agitate against the factory system and the new Poor Law and his
Fleet Papers were issued from prison.[2]

Attention was again focussed on factory legislation when the
Tory government took office in 1841. Sir James Graham, the Home
Secretary, introduced a bill in 1843 to reduce the hours to be worked
by children to 6½ a day, and to facilitate the enforcement of compulsory
education for factory children by building better schools. The bill
was lost because of Nonconformist opposition; it had been proposed
to place the new schools under the general supervision of the Church of

just completed the age of 18. I have seen many such employed for 13, 14, or 15
hours a day . . . ' (p. 8).

See also L. Horner's remarks, ibid., report of October 21st, 1843, pp. 3–4, and
the reports by the same two inspectors for the last quarter of 1843 (ibid., pp. 12–17,
22–27).]

[1 Engels gave the name of Oastler's employer wrongly as ' Thornley '.]

[2 For *The Fleet Papers* see Cecil Driver, *Tory Radical: the Life of Richard Oastler*
(1946), pp. 416–8, 461. They were issued from 1841 until September 7th, 1844.]

England, although the children of Dissenters would not have been compelled to attend Anglican religious instruction. Moreover, it was intended to make the Bible the basic reading book and so religious instruction would have been the foundation of the curriculum in these schools. Consequently the Nonconformists felt that their interests were threatened. They were supported by the manufacturers and by all the Liberals. The workers themselves were divided on the religious question and this prevented them from giving wholehearted support to the measure. However, the workers in many of the great manufacturing towns, such as Salford and Stockport, gave solid support to the bill. Elsewhere, as in Manchester, support for the bill was so strong that its opponents only criticised a few of its provisions. Nevertheless the critics of the bill were able to secure some two million signatures to their petitions. Sir James Graham bowed to the opposition and withdrew the whole measure. In 1844 he introduced a new bill which omitted the previous school clauses and simply proposed to limit to 6½ hours per day the labour in factories of children aged between eight and thirteen. This was to be achieved by allowing the children to work only in the morning or in the afternoon. The labour of young persons between the ages of thirteen and eighteen and also of all women was limited to twelve hours a day. The bill also aimed at preventing the frequent breaches of the existing law. No sooner had the bill been published than the Ten Hours agitation was revived more vigorously than ever. Oastler's debts were paid by his friends and by a subscription raised among the workers. He came out of prison and threw himself energetically into the Ten Hours movement. Meanwhile the number of M.P.s supporting the Ten Hours Bill had increased. From all over the country masses of petitions in support of the Ten Hours Bill poured in. This secured still further converts to the movement in the House of Commons. On March 19th, 1844, Lord Ashley's proposal that the word ' night ' in the Factory Bill should be defined as meaning the hours between 6 p.m. and 6 a.m. was accepted by 179 votes to 170.[1] By specifically pro-hibiting night work this decision automatically brought the number of hours to be worked a day down to twelve, including mealtimes. This, in fact, was a ten-hour working day, as two hours were allowed for meals. But the Government would not agree to this. Sir James Graham threatened to resign from the Cabinet. On the next occasion

[1 The motion that the working day should extend from 6 a.m. to 8 p.m. was rejected by 179 votes to 170. Ashley's amendment to this clause (limitation of the working day to the period between 6 a.m. and 6 p.m.) was carried by 161 to 153 votes. It was this vote which Graham described as ' a virtual adoption of a Ten Hours Bill '. See M. W. Thomas, *The Early Factory Legislation* (1948), p. 204.]

when the bill was debated [in Committee] both the twelve-hour working day and the ten-hour working day were rejected by small majori-
ties.[1] Graham and Peel now declared that they would introduce a
new bill and threatened to resign if it were not passed. For all practical
purposes the new bill was identical with the old bill in its original
form before the House had accepted Ashley's amendment. The
House of Commons, which had rejected the main clauses of the old
bill in March, now swallowed the whole of the new bill. This *volte
face* occurred because the majority of the supporters of the Ten Hours
Bill were Tories who were prepared to sacrifice the bill rather than
see the Government go out of office. Whatever may have been the
motives of the M.P.s, there can be no doubt that the House of Commons
by changing its mind in this way has earned the contempt of all
the workers. The Commons have shown how right the Chartists are
in demanding parliamentary reform. Three M.P.s, who before had
voted against the Government, now changed their minds and voted
for it. In this way the Government was saved. In all the divisions
on these bills practically the whole of the Opposition voted in favour
of factory reform, while the majority of the Government supporters
voted against the Cabinet.[2] Graham's proposals for a $6\frac{1}{2}$-hour working
day for young persons and a twelve-hour working day for adult
operatives are now the law of the land. It is therefore now practically
impossible for the twelve-hour limit to be exceeded. Even the making
up of lost time when there has been a breakdown in the machinery or
a failure of water power owing to frost or drought, is now restricted.
Other permissible methods of extending the twelve-hour day are also
of quite minor significance.[3] There can be little doubt that the Ten
Hours Bill will be passed very soon. The manufacturers are, of course,
all opposed to it—it is doubtful if ten of them could be found to
support it. They have used every method, honourable and dis-

---

[1] [See M. W. Thomas, op. cit., pp. 204-5. This debate was on March 22nd,
1844. The twelve-hour day was rejected by 186 to 183, while the ten-hour day was
rejected by 188 to 181].

[2] It is well known that the House of Commons had made itself look ridiculous
on a serious occasion in the same session. This was on the sugar question, when the
Commons reversed its previous decision, which was unfavourable to the Ministry,
at the crack of the 'Government whip'.

[3 *Hansard's Parliamentary Debates*, 1843, Vols. 67, cols. 422-424, 70, cols. 94-
101, 1299-1300, 72, cols. 277-286; *Northern Star*, no. 278, March 11th, 1843, p. 4,
cols. 1-3—'Factory Labour'; no. 281, April 1st, 1843, p. 4, cols. 5-6, p. 5, cols. 1-3
('The Government Factory Bill: from our second edition of last week'); no. 283,
April 15th, 1843, p. 4, cols. 2-5—'National Education and the Government
Factory Bill'; no. 284, April 22nd, 1843, p. 4, cols. 2-3—'The Government Factory
Bill'; no. 337, April 27th, 1844, p. 6, cols. 1-4 (meetings in favour of the Ten
Hours Bill.)]

honourable, to prevent the bill from passing, and all they have got for their pains is to draw upon themselves the ever-growing hatred of the workers. The bill will pass because in the end the workers can get anything they really set their hearts upon. The events of last spring have made it quite clear that the workers are behind the Ten Hours Bill. The manufacturers use various arguments of an economic nature against the Ten Hours Bill. They say that it will increase the cost of production, with the result that English industry will not be able to withstand foreign competition in overseas markets. The manufacturers allege that this will inevitably lead to a fall in wages. There is something in these arguments, but they merely prove that the industrial greatness of England rests simply upon the barbarous treatment of the workers, the destruction of their health and the social, physical and moral neglect of future generations. Taken by itself the Ten Hours Bill might conceivably ruin England, but, of course, such a reform could necessarily be brought about only in conjunction with other measures which will open an entirely new era in the affairs of the country. It is for this reason that the Ten Hours Bill must be regarded as a valuable reform.

We propose now to examine another aspect of the factory system which gives rise to certain different evils. Efforts may be made by Acts of Parliament to check the complaints arising from these evils, but the fundamental cause of the trouble is less amenable to legislative action. We have already discussed in general terms the nature of work in factories and we are now in a position to draw some further conclusions from our observations. To tend machinery—for example, to be continually tying broken threads—is an activity demanding the full attention of the worker. It is, however, at the same time a type of work which does not allow his mind to be occupied with anything else. We have also seen that this type of factory work gives the operative no opportunity of physical exercise or muscular activity. This is really no work at all, but just excessive boredom. It is impossible to imagine a more tedious or wearisome existence. The factory worker is condemned to allow his physical and mental powers to become atrophied. From the age of eight he enters an occupation which bores him all day long. And there is no respite from this boredom. The machine works ceaselessly. Its wheels, belts and spindles hum and rattle ceaselessly in his ears, and if he thinks of taking even a moment's rest, the overlooker is always there to punish him with a fine. It is nothing less than torture of the severest kind to which the workers are subjected by being condemned to a life-sentence in the factory, in the service of a machine which never stops. It is not only the body of the worker which is stunted, but also his mind. It would indeed be difficult to find a better way of making a man slow-witted than to turn him into a factory worker. If in spite of all this the factory operatives have not only managed to save their reason but have actually developed their minds and sharpened their wits to a greater extent than any other class of worker, it is because they have been inspired by violent hatred against their fate and against the bourgeoisie. This and this alone fills the thoughts of the operatives when they are tending their machines. And if they are workers who are not inspired to a fury of indignation against their oppressors, then they sink into drunkenness and all other forms of demoralising vice. Dr. Bisset Hawkins,[1] one of the officials appointed by the Factories Enquiry Commission, stated that the demoralisation of the operatives was due to physical exhaustion and to the illnesses commonly to be found in factories. If demoralisation is caused by the factors mentioned by Hawkins, it is obvious that the condition of the workers is made much worse by the fact that they also suffer from mental lassitude and its attendant effects. No one need be surprised at the extent to which drunkenness and sexual licence prevail in the factory towns.[2] Moreover, the slavery which the middle classes have imposed on the workers can be seen most clearly in the factory system. There, in law and in fact, the operative loses all his rights. He must arrive at the factory by half-past five in the morning. He is fined if he arrives a few minutes late. If he is ten minutes late he is locked out until after breakfast and loses a quarter of a day's pay, although he has only actually missed 2½ hours work out of twelve. He is forced to eat, drink and sleep to a fixed routine. He is allowed only the minimum

---

[1] Factories Enquiry Commission, 2nd Report (1833), D 3, p. 4.
[2] Read what Dr. J. P. Kay, another qualified observer, has to say on this subject:
    When this example [i.e. of the Irish] is considered in connexion with the unremitted labour of the whole population engaged in the various branches of the cotton manufacture, our wonder will be less excited by their fatal demoralization. Prolonged and exhausting labour, continued from day to day, and from year to year, is not calculated to develop the intellectual or moral faculties of man. The dull routine of a ceaseless drudgery, in which the same mechanical process is incessantly repeated, resembles the torment of Sisyphus—the toil, like the rock, recoils perpetually on the wearied operative. The mind gathers neither stores nor strength from the constant extension and retraction of the same muscles. The intellect slumbers in supine inertness; but the grosser parts of our nature attain a rank development. To condemn man to such severity of toil is, in some measure, to cultivate in him the habits of an animal. He becomes reckless. He disregards the distinguishing appetites and habits of his species. He neglects the comforts and delicacies of life. He lives in squalid wretchedness, on meagre food, and expends his superfluous gains in debauchery. *The Moral and Physical Condition of the Working Classes Employed in the Cotton Manufacture in Manchester* (1832), first edition, pp. 7-8.

time to satisfy the most urgent demands of nature. The manufacturer does not worry if the worker lives half an hour's walk or even a full hour's walk away from the factory. The tyrannical bell calls the wretched worker from his bed and summons him to breakfast and to lunch.

And what happens to the worker once the doors of the factory close upon him? There the despotic will of the manufacturer reigns supreme. He issues his arbitrary edicts and modifies them as he sees fit. However absurd his rules may be, the worker can get no redress from the Courts. The magistrate says to him: 'After all, you are your own master. You need not have entered into such a contract if you didn't wish to do so. You have freely accepted the terms of your employment and now you must abide by them '. And so the worker has to put up with the sarcasm of the middle-class magistrate quite apart from the fact that he suffers from the iniquity of the law, which has been enacted by the bourgeoisie. The courts have frequently handed down such decisions. In October 1844 there was a strike of the operatives in Messrs. Kennedy's mill in Manchester. Kennedy prosecuted them [for breach of contract] on the grounds that there was a notice displayed in the factory that no more than two workers in each room could give in their notice at the same time. The court decided in Kennedy's favour and the workers received the explanation given above.[1] The following factory rules are quite common:

1st. The door of the lodge will be closed ten minutes after the engine starts every morning, and no weaver will afterwards be admitted till breakfast-time. Any weaver who may be absent during that time shall forfeit three-pence per loom.

2nd. Weavers absent at any other time when the engine is working, will be charged three-pence per hour each loom for such absence; and weavers leaving the room when the engine is working without the consent of the overlooker, shall forfeit three-pence.

3rd. Weavers not being provided with nippers or shears, shall forfeit one penny for every day they are so unprovided.

9th. All shuttles, temples, brushes, oil-cans, wheels, windows, &c., if broken, shall be paid for by the weaver.

10th. One week's notice will be required previous to any weaver leaving the mill, or the work in hand will be forfeited. The master may discharge any hand without notice, for bad work or misconduct.

[1 *Manchester Guardian*, October 30th, 1844, p. 4, col. 6—' Turnout at Messrs. Kennedy's factory '. See above p. 148, for an earlier reference by Engels to this strike. The rule at Messrs. Kennedy's factory at this time was that no more than two operatives in each room should give notice *in any one week*.]

11th. If any hand in the mill be seen *talking* to another, *whistling*, or *singing*, [he or she] will be fined *sixpence*.[1]

I have before me another set of factory rules, which state that a worker who is three minutes late loses a quarter of an hour's pay, while anyone who is 20 minutes late loses a quarter of a day's pay. An operative who does not arrive at the factory until after breakfast is fined 1s. on Mondays and 6d. on other days. These regulations were in force at the Phoenix Mill, Jersey Street, Manchester. It will be argued that such rules are necessary to ensure the smooth co-ordination of the various processes carried on in a big, well-run factory. It will be said that stern discipline of this kind is just as necessary in the factory as in the army. That may be true enough, but how can one defend a state of society which can only survive by the exercise of such shameful tyranny? [The advocates of factory discipline may argue that] the end justifies the means. [On the other hand, the opponents of such tyranny] are entitled to argue that if they can show that the means employed by the manufacturers to preserve discipline are bad, they are thereby proving the inherent wickedness of the whole factory system. Anyone who has served in the army knows what it is like to be subject to military discipline even for a short time. These workers, however, are condemned to such iron discipline both moral and physical, from the age of nine until they die. Their slavery is more abject than that of the negroes in America because they are more strictly supervised. Moreover, the worker is expected to behave, to think and to feel like a human being. Obviously their human qualities can find expression only in burning hatred against their oppressors, and against the social order which treats them as if they were mere machines. It is even more shameful to have to report —on the strength of the *unanimous* opinion of the workers—that there are several manufacturers who show the most heartless severity in collecting every farthing of the fines levied on their operatives. In this way they inflate their own profits by a few coppers filched from the penniless operatives. James Leach, too, asserts that the factory clock is often moved forward a quarter of an hour [between the end of work in the evening and the resumption of work] on the following morning, so that the operatives find the gates closed when they arrive. Meanwhile a clerk is busily going through the factory rooms and entering in the fine-book the names of the numerous absentees. Leach states that on one occasion he counted 95 workers who had been

[1] James Leach, *Stubborn Facts from the Factories*, p. 13; also quoted in a review of Leach's pamphlet in the *Northern Star*, no. 353, Aug. 17th, 1844, p. 3, col. 3. Neither Leach nor the *Northern Star* printed all these rules.]

locked out of a factory [at half-past five in the morning]. The clock of this factory was a quarter of an hour slow when compared with the public clocks of the town in the evening, but was a quarter of an hour fast on the [following] morning.[1] The Report of the Factories Enquiry Commission contains similar cases. In one factory the clock was moved back during working hours so that the operatives had to work longer than they should have done. Of course they earned no extra wages for this.[2] In another factory, a full quarter of an hour's work was put in by the operatives [because the factory clock had been tampered with]. From a third factory it was reported that two clocks were in use: one was a normal time-piece, while the other recorded the revolutions of the main shaft. If the machinery was running slowly the hours of work were regulated by the clock attached to the machinery. Work continued until the number of revolutions of the shaft were equivalent to a normal twelve hours [even although more than twelve hours had passed since the factory opened]. On the other hand, if the machinery was running quickly and the normal number of revolutions of the shaft were completed in less than twelve hours then work went on until twelve hours work had been completed [measured by the ordinary clock].[3] The witness added that he knew some girls who had good jobs and worked overtime, but who became prostitutes rather than endure tyranny of this kind.[4] To return for a moment to the question of fines, it may be mentioned that Leach states that he has repeatedly seen women far advanced in pregnancy being fined 6d. for sitting down for only a minute or two while at their work. Fines for bad work are levied in a most arbitrary fashion. When the goods reach the warehouse they are examined, and the warehouse supervisor makes a list of the fines without giving the workers any opportunity of appeal. The operative only discovers that he has been fined when the foreman pays him his wages. By that

---

[1] James Leach, *Stubborn Facts* . . . pp. 14–15.

[2] Factories Enquiry Commission, *1st Report* (1833) C. 1, p. 79 (evidence taken by Drinkwater from William Hebden, who had previously given evidence before Sadler's Committee). [This is an alleged case of moving a clock *forward* in order to shorten the workers' dinner hour, a practice actively resented by the workers. On the other hand Thomas Saul, employed in the same mill (Messrs. Titley, Tatham and Walker of Leeds) stated: 'I never heard of such a thing as the clock being put forwards or backwards at meal-times'. He admitted that the clock was slightly erratic owing to a 'looseness somewhere in the tubes', but claimed that, taking one-half hour with the next, the irregularities cancelled themselves out (C. 1, pp. 124–5).]

[3] Factories Enquiry Commission, *1st Report* (1833) C. 1, p. 86. [Evidence given to Drinkwater by John Hannam of Leeds concerning the unfair use of a 'speed-clock'.]

[4] Factories Enquiry Commission, *1st Report* (1833), C. 1, p. 87—evidence given to Drinkwater by John Hannam.]

time the goods in question have been put into stock or even sold. Leach has in his possession an actual list of fines which is ten feet long and gives details of fines amounting to £35 17s. 10d. Leach states that in the factory in which this list was compiled a newly-appointed warehouse supervisor was dismissed, because he did not levy enough fines, with the result that the manufacturer was losing £5 a week [on what he formerly gained from this source].[1] Let me repeat that I know Leach to be a thoroughly reliable person, incapable of telling a lie.

In other ways, too, the operative is no more than the slave of his employer. If a wealthy manufacturer is attracted by the wife or daughter of one of the workers, he has only got to drop a hint, and she is forced to gratify his base desires. If a manufacturer is getting up a petition in support of some middle-class interest, he has only to send it to his factory in order to get a long list of signatures. If he is interested in a local parliamentary contest, he simply marches all his workers who have votes down to the poll, where they have to vote for the middle-class candidate whether they want to or not. If he wants to pack a public meeting he lets his employees out of the factory half an hour earlier than usual and lets them fill the front seats reserved for them near the platform, where he can keep an eye on them.

There are two other circumstances which greatly strengthen the master's hold over his men. These are the truck system and the tied cottage system. Under the truck system workers are paid in goods instead of in cash and at one time this method of payment was universal in England. The manufacturers would open a shop, ' for the convenience of the workers, and in order to protect them from the high prices charged by the petty shopkeepers '. These shops were small general stores, selling a variety of goods. The goods offered for sale in these ' tommy shops ' were generally 20 per cent to 30 per cent dearer than elsewhere. To stop the workers from patronising the cheaper shops the workers were forced to deal at their employer's shop. Instead of getting his wages in cash the workers received vouchers exchangeable only at the ' tommy shop '. Owing to the

[1 J. Leach, *Stubborn Facts . . .* , p. 15:
  'At this mill, a short time ago, one of the cut-lookers was discharged, and another placed in his situation. When he had been there a fortnight, the master asked him, " How it was that he had so little on his *bate-book*; ' the man replied,' " I think there's a great deal, I 'bate the weavers so much that I can't for shame look them in the face when I meet them in the street." The master answered, " *You be d—d*; you are five pounds a week worse *to me* than the man that had this situation before you, and I'll kick you out of the place ". The man was discharged to make room for another who knew his duty better.' (Also quoted in *Northern Star*, no. 353, Aug. 17th, 1844, p. 3, col. 3.)]

universal discontent aroused by this infamous system the Truck Act was passed in 1831. This Act declared that—at any rate for the vast majority of workers—payment in kind was henceforward made an offence punishable at law. Like so many other English laws this enactment has only been enforced here and there. It is true that it is now generally enforced in the towns, but in country districts the truck system survives both openly and in disguised forms. The truck system still flourishes in the town of Leicester. I have before me copies of the *Manchester Guardian* and *Northern Star*, dating from the period between November 1843 and June 1844, which record about a dozen cases of employers being successfully prosecuted for infringements of the Truck Acts. Of course, the truck system cannot be operated so blatantly now as was at one time possible. The workers now generally get their wages in cash, but the employer still has means at his disposal to force his workers to buy their goods in his truck shop and nowhere else. Since the manufacturer is obeying the letter of the law by giving his workers their wages in cash, he is now safe from prosecution. The *Northern Star* of April 27th, 1844, prints a letter from a worker of Holmfirth in Yorkshire, referring to the conduct of a manufacturer named Bowers. [I quote the letter in full:]

It is almost strainge to see that the accursed truck sistim should exist to the enormoust extent that it dose in Holmfirth, and no one to be found to have the moral courage to attempt to put a stop to it. Thaire are a greate many honest handloome weavers that is suffering by that accurssed sistim. This is one specimen. Out of the many of that precious freetraid crew, thaire is one manufacturer that lives not a hundred miles from Upper-Bridge-End, that as the curse of the whole neighbourhood upon im, for is baseness towards is weavers. When they finnish a warp, which comes to £1 14s, or £1 16s, he gives them £1, and the rest in goods, wearing apparel, at 40 or 50 per cent dearer then at the regular shopkeeppers, and many a time the goods are rotton. But as the Free-Trade *Mercury* says by the factory labour, ' they are not bound to take it; its quite optional '. O, yes; but thay must eather take it or starve. If thay whant any more than the £1 0s. 0d for rent, or any thing no matter what, thay must wait of a warp a week or a fortnight; but if thay take the £1 0s 0d and the goods, thaire is always a warp for them. This is free traidism. Lord Brohom says ' we should lay something by in our young days, that we may be independent in our old age of parochial relief '. Must we lay by these rotton goods? If this did not come from a lord, thay would think is brains wear as rotton as the goods wee got for our labour. When the unstampt newspapers wear in circulation theair wear no lack of informers in Holmfirth. Thaire wear the Blyths, the Estwoods, &c.; but wear are thay now?

O, but this is quite diffrent. Our truckster is one of the free trading pious crew. He goes to the church twise every Sunday, and repeats after the parson very fervently: ' we have left undone those things wich we hought to have done; we have done those things wich we hought not to have done; and thaire is no help in us; but spare us, good Lord '. Yes, spare us wile morning, and we will pay our weavers wages in rotton goods again.[1]

The system of tied cottages appears on the face of it to be less objectionable than the truck system. The origin of the tied cottage is not open to criticism to the same extent. Nevertheless the tied cottage enslaves the worker as much as the ' tommy shop '. When a new factory is built in the country there is often no suitable accommodation for the workers in the vicinity. The manufacturer has to build cottages himself and he gladly does so, since he can obtain a high rate of interest on his capital outlay. Any landlord normally expects to receive a return of 6 per cent on capital invested in working-class dwellings; and it is therefore safe to suppose that the manufacturer who owns houses tenanted by his workers secures a 12 per cent return on his capital. The reason for this is that so long as this factory is not actually shut down the manufacturer will always have tenants in his cottages who pay the rent punctually. The manufacturer is thus free from the two main difficulties which confront other property owners—none of his cottages are ever empty and he runs no risk of losing any rent due to him. The rent of a cottage which is not tied to a factory is so calculated as to cover the landlord against these contingencies. The factory owner charges the same level of rent without having to take the risks to which we have referred, so makes a gilt-edged investment at from 12 to 14 per cent—and all at the expense of his operatives. It is obviously unjust that, when the manufacturer turns landlord, he should make profits up to twice as great as those of his competitors and at the same time try to stifle competition. It is a still greater injustice that the manufacturer should filch these extra profits from the pockets of the poorest class in the community who have to count every penny that they earn. But there is nothing unusual in this, since the whole of the manufacturer's wealth is amassed at the expense of the workers. The injustices of the tied cottage system become infamous when the mamufacturer—and this happens often enough—forces his operatives on pain of dismissal to occupy one of his houses, to pay a higher rent than is normal or even to rent houses that they do not occupy. The London Liberal

[1 *Northern Star*, no. 337, April 27th, 1844, p. 4, cols. 5–6—article on ' Truck-ism '.]

newspaper, *The Sun*, quoting from the *Halifax Guardian*, states that hundreds of workers in Ashton-under-Lyne, Oldham and Rochdale, etc. are forced to pay rent for cottages whether they occupy them or not.[1] The tied cottage system is universal in the case of factories situated in the country. Villages and even small towns have been built in this way, and usually the manufacturer has not got to face any competition in the provision of housing. Since he enjoys a virtual monopoly he is in the position of being able to charge what he pleases. And what power does the tied cottage place in the manufacturer's hands if he is involved in a dispute with his workers! If the men strike he gives them a week's notice to quit their cottages. At the end of the week the worker is not only without food, but no longer has a roof over his head. He becomes a homeless wanderer liable to be sentenced to a month on the treadmill by the merciless operation of the Vagrancy Laws.

I have now described the factory system as fully as space permits. I have been as impartial as it is possible to be in the light of the heroic triumphs of the middle classes over the defenceless workers. It is impossible to be indifferent when contemplating these triumphs. In such circumstances indifference would indeed be a crime. Let us compare the situation of the free-born Englishman in 1845 with that of the Saxon serf under the whip of the Norman baron in 1145. The serf was *adscriptus glebae*, that is, he was bound to the soil. The free factory worker is tied in the same way by the cottage system. The mediaeval lord of the manor exacted the *jus primae noctis* from his serfs. The modern factory goes much further and demands the right on any night. The serf was unable to acquire any property of his own. His lord could seize anything which he had acquired. The free factory worker also owns no property. He is not in a position to acquire property owing to the pressure of competition. The factory owner goes further than the Norman baron. By means of the truck system, he actually controls so personal a part of the life of the worker as his daily housekeeping. In mediaeval times the relations between lord and serf were regulated by traditions and by laws which were observed because they conformed with the customs of the time. To-day, on the other hand, although the relations between master and man are on a legal basis, the law is in fact not carried out because it does not conform

---

[1] *Sun*, end of November 1844. [This statement appeared originally in the *Halifax Guardian* (no. 571, Nov. 4th, 1843, p. 5, col. 6) in an article entitled ' The Truck System Extraordinary '. It was copied by the *Sun* and then re-quoted by the *Northern Star* (no. 315, Nov. 25th, 1843, p. 4, cols. 4–6, p. 5, col. 1). Engels's reference is therefore a year out, and he appears to have read the account given in the *Northern Star*.]

either to the interests or the traditions of the masters. In mediaeval times the lord of the manor could not eject the serf from his holding. Serf and land were indissolubly linked. The lord could not sell the serf because in practice he could not sell his land, since ne held his land not on freehold tenure, but as a fief from the Crown. To-day the middle classes force the worker to sell himself. The mediaeval serf was tied to the land on which he was born, while the modern worker is tied to the money that he must have to acquire the necessaries of life. Both are the slaves of material objects. The serf's livelihood was guaranteed by the existence of feudalism, in which everyone had his allotted place in society. The modern free worker has no similar guarantee because he is only certain of a place in society when the middle classes require his services. On the other hand, when the bourgeoisie has no use for the worker they simply ignore him and pretend that he does not exist. The serf risked his life in the service of his master in time of war, while the modern factory worker risks his life for his master in times of peace. The feudal lord was a barbarian who treated his serfs as beasts of burden. The modern civilised factory owner treats his workers as if they were machines. In short there is little to choose between the position of the mediaeval serf and the free worker of the present day. If anything, the situation of the factory operative is less enviable than that of the mediaeval serf. Slavery has been the lot of both the serf and the factory worker. While in mediaeval times serfdom was an honourable status, undisguised and openly admitted, the slavery of the working classes to-day is hypocritically and cunningly disguised from themselves and the public. It is a far worse type of slavery than mediaeval serfdom. The Tory humanitarians were justified in referring to the factory operatives as ' white slaves '. But in one respect the new slavery is better than the old. The society which accepts this hypocritically camouflaged form of servitude does at least pay lip-service to the ideal of liberty. It pays outward homage to a public opinion which worships the principles of freedom. To this extent progress has been made, and the new slavery is not as bad as the old, since at any rate the *principle* of liberty has been accepted. The oppressed workers will surely see to it that this principle is really carried into effect.

In conclusion I will quote a few verses of a poem giving the workers' own point of view concerning the factory system. The author is Edward P. Mead of Birmingham, but he gives expression to the views which are now held by a majority of the workers.[1]

[1 *Northern Star*, no. 274, February 11th, 1843, p. 3, col. 1. Engels omitted the last two verses of this poem.]

THE STEAM KING

There is a King, and a ruthless King;
Not a King of the poet's dream;
But a tyrant fell, white slaves know well,
And that ruthless King is Steam.

   He hath an arm, an iron arm,
   And tho' he hath but one,
   In that mighty arm there is a charm,
   That millions hath undone.

Like the ancient Moloch grim, his sire
In Himmon's vale that stood,
His bowels are of living fire,
And children are his food.

   His priesthood are a hungry band,
   Blood-thirsty, proud, and bold;
   'Tis they direct his giant hand,
   In turning blood to gold.

For filthy gain in their servile chain
All nature's rights they bind;
They mock at lovely woman's pain,
   And to manly tears are blind.

   The sighs and groans of Labour's sons
   Are music in their ear,
   And the skeleton shades, of lads and maids,
   In the Steam King's hell appear.

Those hells upon earth, since the Steam King's birth,
Have scatter'd around despair;
For the human mind for Heav'n design'd
With the body, is murdered there.

   Then down with the King, the Moloch King,
   Ye working millions all;
   O chain his hand, or our native land
   Is destin'd by him to fall.

And his Satraps abhor'd, each proud Mill Lord,
Now gorg'd with gold and blood,
Must be put down by the nation's frown,
As well as their monster God.

[The cheap bread crew will murder you
By bludgeon, ball or brand;
Then your Charter gain and the power will be vain
Of the Steam King's bloody band.

Then down with the King, the Moloch King
And the satraps of his might:
Let right prevail, then Freedom hail
When might shall stoop to right.]

*   *   *   *   *   *

APPENDIX TO CHAPTER VII

[*In the first German edition of* 1845 *this appendix appeared as a long footnote to the poem which concludes this chapter.*]

I have neither the time nor the space to embark upon a lengthy discussion of the attempts made during the last twelve years by the manufacturers to justify their conduct in the light of the charges made against them. It is simply impossible to discuss these matters with the factory owners who are completely deaf to any argument once their own private interests are at stake. I have already in this chapter dealt with a number of their arguments and I will add only a few words more.

Let us suppose that a visitor comes to Manchester and wants to know something of the state of affairs in England. He naturally takes the precaution of bringing with him suitable letters of introduction to 'respectable' people in the town. The visitor indicates that he is interested in securing information concerning the condition of the factory population. He is referred to the leading progressive manufacturers, such as Robert Hyde Greg, Edmund Ashworth or Thomas Ashton.[1] The stranger makes known the purpose of his visit. The factory owner knows at once what he has to do. He takes the visitor to his mill in the country—Mr. Greg to Quarry Bank in Cheshire, Mr. Ashworth to Turton near Bolton, Mr. Ashton to Hyde. The manufacturer shows his visitor through an imposing, well-appointed building, which is perhaps fitted with ventilators. He draws his guest's attention to the lofty, airy workrooms, the fine machinery and now and again he is able to point out an operative who is the very

[1 This is presumably a reference to Dr. Andrew Ure and W. Cooke Taylor, who visited these mills in the 1830s and in the early 1840s respectively. See A. Ure, *The Philosophy of Manufactures* (1835), passim and W.C. Taylor, *Notes on a Tour in the Manufacturing Districts of Lancashire* (1842), passim.]

picture of health. He gives the visitor an excellent breakfast, and then suggests a conducted tour of the worker's dwellings. The mill-owner shows his guest a row of newly-erected cottages which, from the outside, present a clean and attractive appearance. The mill-owner personally shows his guest the interior of one or two of the cottages. He is naturally careful to select only houses occupied by overlookers and skilled mechanics, so as to be sure that the family is one completely devoted to the manufacturer's interests. A visit to one of the other cottages showed that only the wife and children were working in the factory and that the husband was darning socks at home. The visitor is not in a position to ask [the workers] indiscreet questions since the mill-owner is present. The workers all appear to be well paid and to be in comfortable circumstances. They are in relatively good health because of the fresh country air that they breathe. The investigator begins to wonder whether his previous notions concerning distress and famine among the factory workers were not exaggerated. He does not realise, however, that the tied cottage system enslaves the operatives and that the employer's ' tommy shop ' may well be just round the corner. The visitor does not know the extent to which the workers detest their master. In the presence of the mill-owner the workers have naturally no opportunity of giving vent to hatred for their employer. No doubt the mill-owner has provided a school and a church and a reading room. But he uses the school to inculcate strict obedience in the children's minds. He allows the reading room to stock only such books as support the middle-class point of view. The mill-owner dismisses workers who read Chartist and Socialist newspapers and books. All this is hidden from the eye of the visitor. He sees only a happy patriarchal relationship between master and man, and gets to know only the overlooker's mode of life [and not that of the ordinary worker]. He sees the realisation of what the middle classes promise the workers if only they will slavishly accept a way of life dictated by the interests of the bourgeoisie. The ' country mill ' has always been the hobby of the manufacturer. Here he avoids the drawbacks—particularly the bad sanitation—of the factory system [in the towns], because to some extent the fresh air of the open country itself promotes good health. Here, too, the *patriarchal* slavery of operatives survives far longer than in the towns. Dr. Ure sings a song of praise on this theme. But the fatherly affection of the mill-owner for his workers quickly evaporates if they should presume to think for themselves and become Chartists. Moreover, if the visitor to Manchester should ask to be shown the working-class quarters of the town itself —if he should show some interest in the practical effects of the growth of large-scale manufacture in an urban district—he would have to wait a long time before a rich middle-class millowner would help to satisfy his guest's curiosity! The millowners are quite ignorant of the conditions under which their workers live [in the towns] and are completely out of touch with working-class hopes and aspirations. The millowners must shut their eyes to these things, for fear of learning something which might prick their consciences or might even force them to act in a way detrimental to their financial interests. But it is quite immaterial what policy the millowner adopts, for the workers will achieve reform by their own exertions.

CHAPTER VIII

THE PROLETARIAT (*continued*)

[(*b*) *Other industrial workers*]

In the previous section we considered at some length the factory system [as it has affected the textile workers], because this system is something entirely novel which has grown up in the new industrial age. We can deal with the workers in the remaining [and less highly mechanized] branches of manufacture more briefly, since much of what we have already written concerning the industrial proletariat and the factory system applies also, either wholly or in part, to these other workers whose conditions of employment we now propose to examine. We intend to confine our attention to the question of how far the factory system has penetrated those branches of manufacture in which these workers are engaged. We shall discuss also certain features peculiar to the occupations of these various groups of workers.

We have already dealt with the four industries covered by the Factory Acts. These are textile industries engaged in working up various kinds of yarn and cloth. Let us now examine the condition of the workers in those branches of industry whose raw materials are the yarns and cloths produced by the textile manufacturers. We shall now consider the framework knitters in the counties of Nottingham, Derby and Leicester who make stockings. According to the Report of the Children's Employment Commission [of 1841–3] these operatives are paid such low wages that they have to work very long hours. Framework knitting is a sedentary occupation and places a great strain on the eyes. Consequently the framework knitters are usually of poor physique and are particularly liable to eye trouble. Their work cannot be done in the evening except under a strong light, which is obtained by placing the flame of the lamp behind a glass globe [filled with water.] By this method a brighter light is obtained, but the worker runs a great risk of eyestrain. Nearly all these framework knitters need to wear spectacles by the time they are forty. The health and physique of their children, who are engaged in winding the thread on spools and hemming, also suffer seriously. They begin work when they are 6, 7 or 8 years old and work from 10 to 12 hours in small, stuffy rooms. Many faint at their work. They are too weak to perform the most ordinary domestic duties and they are so shortsighted that they have to wear spectacles even at a tender age. The

Commissioners stated that many of these workers had all the symptoms of scrofula and that manufacturers in other trades generally refuse to employ such girls because they are not strong enough.[1] Mr. R. D. Grainger denounced the condition of the children employed in this industry as ' altogether disgraceful in a Christian country ' and he suggested that they should be protected by law from this sort of exploitation.[2]

The Factories Enquiry Commission's Report states that the framework stocking knitters were the worst-paid of all the operatives in Leicester.[2] They normally earned 6s. a week, but could make 7s. if they worked very hard. Their hours of work varied from 16 to 18 per day. At one time they used to earn between 20s. and 21s. a week, until they were ruined by the introduction of wider frames. Most of the knitters still used the older, simpler frames and were waging a losing battle against the progress of the improved machines. Here is another example of the way in which every technical advance represents a loss to the worker. Mr. Power, the Commissioner, states that, in spite of this state of affairs, the framework stocking knitters are proud that they are free and that they do not have to obey the summons of the factory bell, which would regulate their hours for working, sleeping and eating. The information collected by the Factories Enquiry Commission refers to the year 1833. The condition of this group of workers, as far as wages are concerned, is no better to-day—competition from the stockingers of Saxony, who themselves live on the verge of starvation, sees to that. The English have to meet this competition in all foreign markets and, as far as the coarser qualities are concerned, actually in the home market. How the patriotic German stocking knitter must rejoice that by going hungry himself he reduces the English stockinger to beggary. Will he not be proud and happy to continue to starve for the greater glory of German industry? Does not Germany's honour demand that his plate should go on being only half-full? Is not competition and the struggle between nations for industrial supremacy a truly wonderful thing? In December 1843 the *Morning Chronicle*, a Liberal newspaper, the acknowledged organ of the bourgeoisie, printed two letters[3] from a stockinger in Hinckley concerning the condition of his fellow-workers. In the course of

---

[1] *Appendix to 2nd Report* of the Children's Employment Commission: Trades and Manufactures, Part I (1842), F. 15. sects. 132-137.

[2] *Appendix to 2nd Report* of the Children's Employment Commission: Trades and Manufactures, Part I (1842), F. 16, sect. 141.

[3] *Morning Chronicle*, Dec. 1st, 1843, p. 5, col. 5 (' Distress at Hinckley '); Dec. 9th, 1843, p. 3, col. 4 (' Letters to the Editor '). The first letter was reprinted in the *Northern Star*, no. 317, Dec. 9th, 1843, p. 6, cols. 1 and 2.]

these letters he referred to the deplorable condition of 50 families, comprising 321 people. These families were dependent on 109 knitting frames. The average weekly earnings on each frame were 5s. 2d. The average weekly earnings of each family were 11s. 4d. From this it was necessary to deduct 5s. 10d. for house-rent, frame-rent, coal, candles, soap and needles. This left a mere 1½d. a head per day for food and absolutely nothing for clothing. The writer stated:

'Eye hath not seen, ear hath not heard, the heart cannot conceive', the half of the suffering endured by this poverty-stricken people.

Some families were entirely without beds; in other families some members only had them. The children were in rags and running about barefoot. The men declared with tears in their eyes: 'We never tasted meat this many a day '—'We have almost forgotten its taste.' Some of these knitters actually worked on Sundays, although the noise of the frames could be heard by all the neighbours and there is nothing that public opinion condemns so much in England as Sabbath-breaking. One of them defended his action by saying: 'Look at my children, and my home, and ask no more: I will tell you, however, why I work on this day. It is because my poverty compels me; I *cannot* and *will* not hear my children cry for bread without taking the only means honestly to get it. Last Monday morning I rose at two o'clock and worked till near midnight. I rose at six o'clock each succeeding morning and worked until between eleven and twelve each night, and now you see what I have for dinner. I cannot do it longer. I shall go to an untimely grave if I do; I will therefore end my labours at ten o'clock each night and make up the time lost by labouring on the Sunday '.[1]

Neither in Leicestershire, Derbyshire nor Nottinghamshire have wages risen since 1833. What is worse, the truck system, as has already been mentioned, is rife in Leicestershire, so that it is not surprising the framework knitters of this district have taken a very active part in all working-class movements.[2] Their agitation has been all the more effective because most of these operatives are men. The districts in which the framework knitters live are also the main centres for the lace manufacture. There are 2,760 lace machines at work in the three counties of Leicester, Derby and Nottingham, whereas in all other

[1 All the extracts are from the second letter printed in the *Morning Chronicle*, Dec. 9th, 1843, p. 3, col. 4. The stocking frame is referred to throughout as a 'loom'.]

[2 See A. Temple Patterson, *Radical Leicester: a history of Leicester*, 1780–1850 (1954).]

parts of England there are only 787.[1] The manufacture of lace is an industry in which the division of labour has been carried to an extreme limit. There are therefore many distinct processes in lace making. First of all the yarn must be put on the spools by the winders, who are girls aged 14 or over. Next the threaders, who are boys aged from 8 upwards, fix the wound spools on the machines and insert the threads correctly into small holes. On the average each machine has 1,800 of these apertures.[2] Now the weaver gets to work on his frame and produces lace in a form which resembles a broad piece of cloth. Very small children, who are called lace runners, are engaged in a process which is called ' lace running ' or ' lace drawing '. By this process the threads are again separated. Finally comes the finishing process, after which the lace is ready for sale. Both winders and threaders have no fixed working hours. Their services are needed whenever the spools of a machine are empty. Since the machines run by night as well as by day, the winders and threaders are liable to be called at any time into the factory or the lacemakers' workshop.[3] Erratic hours of labour, frequent night work, and irregular habits are the cause of many physical and moral evils. All witnesses agree that these workers are both precocious and disorderly in their sexual behaviour. The work is very hard on the eyes. Although the threaders do not appear to suffer from any permanent disability of vision nevertheless their eyes are inflamed and, while engaged in threading, they suffer from inflammation and watery eyes and their sight is temporarily impaired.[4] The winders, on the other hand, suffer permanent ill-effects from their work. Quite apart from the fact that they frequently suffer from inflammation of the cornea, they are also subject to amaurosis and cataract. The framework knitters themselves are engaged upon work which becomes continually more exacting, because the machines are constantly being widened. At present practically all the frames in use are those which have to be worked by three men, each of whom works a four-hour shift before being relieved by a colleague. The frame is kept running continuously for 24 hours, and during this time each knitter works two four-hour shifts. This explains why the winders and threaders often have to work at night, so that the machines do not have to stand idle for long. It takes three children two hours to

[1 *Appendix to 2nd Report* of the Children's Employment Commission, Trades and Manufactures, Part I (1842) F. 1 (R. D. Grainger's report on the manufacture of lace). Engels gives the figure of 786 instead of 787 for the total number of machines ' in the West of England and the Isle of Wight '.]

[2 Ibid., F. 7, para. 57.]

[3 Ibid., F. 6, para. 51.]

[4 Ibid., f54–56, no. 173: ' Memorandum . . . on the diseases of the eyes . . . in . . . the Nottingham trade ' by Dr. J. C. Williams].

thread each machine with its 1,800 eyes. Moreover some machines are now operated by other machines, and this throws some of the hand knitters out of work. The Report of the Children's Employment Commission refers to 'lace manufactories' in which children are employed. It would appear, therefore, either that the work of the framework knitters has been transferred from workshop to factory or that steam-power is now generally used in this branch of industry. Further development would represent yet another extension of the factory system.

The runners are engaged in the most unhealthy occupation of all. Most of them are children of seven but some of them are actually only four or five years old. Indeed Mr. Grainger actually found a child aged two engaged in this work.[1] Their work consists in keeping track of a solitary thread which is picked out from a complicated pattern by means of a needle. This work is very damaging to the eyesight, particularly when, as is usual, fourteen to sixteen hours is the usual length of the spell of duty. These children are lucky if they escape with extremely short sight. If they are unlucky, and many of them are, they go blind from amaurosis, for which there is no cure. In addition the children are adversely affected by sitting continually in a crouched position. This leads to general debility, pigeon chests, digestive troubles and scrofula. Nearly all the girls suffer from disturbances of the functions of the uterus.[2] The runners also suffer from spinal defects, and it is considered that ' a " lace runner " can be known by her walk '.[3]

Workers engaged in embroidering lace also suffer from similar physical defects and from the effects of eyestrain. Medical men are unanimously of the opinion that the health of children engaged in embroidering lace suffers severely. These children are pale, weak, delicate, stunted and much less able than normal children to resist disease. The most common complaints from which these children suffer are: general debility, frequent fainting fits, pains in the head, sides, back and hips, palpitations, nausea, vomiting, lack of appetite, spinal curvature, scrofula and tuberculosis. The health of women workers in this branch of the lace manufacture is severely and continually undermined. Grainger in his Report produced a wealth of evidence regarding the prevalence of such complaints as anaemia, difficulties in childbirth and miscarriages among the female operatives.[4] Grainger, a sub-commissioner of the Children's Employment Com-

[¹ Ibid., f.42, nos. 156-9 (Mrs. Houghton's family) and F. 10, para. 76.]
² Ibid., F. 11, para. 87.
³ Ibid., f. 5, no. 25 (evidence of Anne Corbett collected by R. D. Grainger.)
⁴ Ibid., f. 57-59, nos. 174-77 (reports by Nottingham doctors).

mission, also stated that the children engaged in lace embroidery were often clothed only in rags and suffered from inadequate nourishment. Their diet consisted mainly of bread and tea, and they often went without meat for months at a time. The moral conditions of these children was described by Grainger as follows:

> In the town of Nottingham all parties, clergy, police, manufacturers, workpeople, and parents agree that the present mode of employing children and young persons as threaders and winders is a most fertile source of immorality. There can, in fact, be but few states more immediately leading to vice and profligacy. Children of both sexes are called out of their parents' houses at all hours of the night, and as it is quite uncertain how long they may be required, whether for two hours or the whole night, a ready and unanswerable excuse for staying out is furnished. The threaders, who are usually boys, and the winders, who are generally girls, are required at the same time and thus have every facility for forming improper connexions. The natural results of such a noxious system are but too apparent, and must have contributed, in no slight degree to the immorality which, according to the opinion universally expressed, prevails to a most awful extent in Nottingham.
>
> In addition to the immediate evils to the children themselves, the domestic peace and comfort of the families of which they are members are sacrificed to this most unnatural state of things.[1]

Another branch of the lace industry, the manufacture of bobbin-lace,[2] is carried out in the counties of Northampton, Oxford, Bedford and Buckingham, which are agricultural districts. Large numbers of children and young people are employed. Their diet is poor and they seldom eat meat. The work is very unhealthy. The children work in small, badly-ventilated and damp rooms, where they sit bent almost double over their lace-pillows. To support the body in this exhausing position, the girls wear stays with a wooden support. Since most of the girls are quite young and their bones are still very soft, their breast-bones and ribs become completely deformed and they generally become pigeon-chested. After suffering from acute digestive disorders most of these girls die of tuberculosis, which they contract because of the sedentary nature of their occupation and the bad atmosphere in which they work. They are almost wholly uneducated, and receive virtually no moral training. They also love fine clothes. These factors combine to lower their moral standards to such an extent that prostitution is almost universal among them.[3]

---

[1] Ibid., F 9, para. 72.   [2] Or pillow-lace.

[3] *Appendix to 2nd Report* of Children's Employment Commission Part I, 1842, A. 12–13 [(report by Major J. A. Burns on lace-making in Northants, Oxfordshire, Bedfordshire and Buckinghamshire, A. 50–56, and evidence which he collected).]

That is the price which society pays in order that the fine ladies of the middle classes can enjoy the luxury of wearing lace! Is not the the price a small one? It amounts to only a few thousand blind workers, a few consumptive daughters of the proletariat, a chronically debilitated generation of the vulgar herd who will hand on their diseases to their equally vulgar children and grandchildren. Is this really anything to worry about? Of course not! Our English middle classes will lay aside the reports of the Government Commission without turning a hair, and will continue to allow their wives and daughters to deck themselves out with lace as before. Is not the serene complacency of the English bourgeoisie something to marvel at?

A large number of workers are employed in the calico-printing works of Lancashire, Derbyshire and the West of Scotland. In no other branch of English industry has the introduction of machinery had such striking results, yet nowhere else are the workers so oppressed. The introduction of engraved cylinders turned by steam and the discovery of how to print between four and six colours simultaneously with these cylinders has superseded hand-block printing. This development has had just as drastic results as the mechanization of spinning and weaving. Moreover, the new calico-printing machines have cut down the labour force required to an even greater extent than the spinning and weaving improvements. One man, assisted by a child, now performs with a machine the work formerly done by 200 hand printers. A single machine prints 28 yards of cloth a minute. The result is that the calico printers are in a deplorable state indeed. A petition from them to the House of Commons stated that in the year 1842 11 million pieces of calico were printed in the counties of Lancashire, Derby and Cheshire. Of this number only 100,000 were printed by hand alone, while 900,000 were printed partly by machinery and partly by hand. On the other hand, machinery, printing up to six colours, was responsible for the printing of no less than 10 million pieces of calico. Since most of the machines are new and are continually being improved the number of hand printers is far too great in relation to the work available. Obviously many of them are unemployed. The petition to which we have referred stated that a quarter of the hand printers were out of work. Those who had managed to secure employment generally worked on only one, two or at the most three days a week, and were very badly paid.[1] James Leach asserts that at a printworks at Deeply Vale, near Bury in Lancashire, the hand block printers earned on the average no more

[1 James Leach, *Stubborn Facts from the Factories* (1844), pp. 45–47.]

than 5s. a week.[1] On the other hand the machine printers were fairly well paid. It may be seen therefore that the calico printworks have been completely mechanized. But they are not subject to the provisions of the Factory Act.[2] These works are engaged in the manufacture of goods the demand for which is strongly influenced by the vagaries of fashion. The work is therefore of an irregular nature. If the printworks have not many orders, they work only half-time. On the other hand, if a printworks turns out a design which catches the public fancy, sales expand. Then they are busy until ten or twelve o'clock at night. Indeed there are occasions on which calico printers work throughout the night. There was a calico printworks not far from my lodgings near Manchester, where work sometimes went on far into the night. When I got home the building was still lit up and I have often been told that the children working in this establishment sometimes had to work such long hours that they snatched a few minutes of rest and slept on the stone steps of the factory and in corners of the outbuildings. I could not prove this to a court of law. If I were in a position to do so I would name the firm. The Report of the Children's Employment Commission deals with the children employed in calico printworks in a very superficial manner. It merely states that in England, at any rate, the children are fairly well clothed and nourished. In fact the way in which the children are clothed and fed depends on the wages earned by the parents at any particular time. The Report also states that the children's education is totally neglected and that their moral standards leave much to be desired.[3] It is only necessary to bear in mind that these children are in the grip of the factory system. We need therefore only recall that our previous remarks about factory children in other occupations apply equally well to these children, and pass on.

There is little to say concerning operatives employed in other branches of the textile industry. The work of the bleachers is very unhealthy because they are continuously inhaling chlorine, which is dangerous to the lungs. The dyers follow a healthier occupation. They are often very fit because their work exercises all their limbs. Little is known about the wages earned by bleachers and dyers. This suggests that they do not earn less than the average wage earner, because if they did complaints would be heard.[4] Owing to the increased demand for velvet a fair number of workers are engaged in fustian

[1 Leach, op. cit., p. 47.]
[2 In fact they were brought under regulation in 1845 by 8 and 9 Vict., cap. 29.]
[3 Ibid., B. 16–19 (report of J. L. Kennedy on the employment of young children in print grounds . . . in Lancashire . . .).]
[4 Ibid., B. 43 (bleaching), B. 45–6, para. 316 (dyeing).]

cutting—probably between 3,000 and 4,000. These operatives have suffered seriously in an indirect way from the growth of the factory system. At one time fustian was woven by hand, the cloth was uneven when it came off the loom, and skill was needed in trimming it. To-day fustian is woven on a power-loom. The cloth is therefore quite regular and no great skill is required in the cutting process. Various types of worker who lost their employment through the introduction of machinery tried to take up fustian cutting. This competition led to a reduction in wages. Then the manufacturers discovered that women and children could cut fustian and so wages fell still further.[1] Consequently hundreds of men lost their employment. Moreover the manufacturers discovered that fustian cutting could be done more cheaply in a factory than in a domestic workshop for which the factory owner was indirectly paying rent. To-day the attics of many cottages which were once fitted out as cutting rooms have fallen empty or are used as dwellings, while the fustian cutter has lost his freedom to decide his own hours of work and has been brought under the discipline of the factory clock. I have been told by a fustian cutter aged about 45 that he could remember the time when he could earn 8d. a yard for cutting cloth for which he would now only be paid 1d. a yard. It is true that he can cut the more regular fustian produced by the power-loom more rapidly than he could cut the hand-woven fustian. He cannot, however, cut twice as much of the new cloth in an hour. Consequently he can earn less than a quarter of his former wages in a week. Leach gives a table which compares piece rates paid in 1827 and 1843 for the cutting of different kinds of cloth. From this table it will be seen that the following prices were paid per yard to the cutters:

1827	1843
4d	1½d
2¼d	¾d
2¾d	¾d
1d	⅜d

According to Leach the average weekly earnings of cutters for doing this work were as follows:

[1 A distinction should be made between fustian cutting and fustian dressing. In the early 1840s fustian cutting was 'done invariably by adults', while 'in the preparing of fustians and velveteens' a great number of children were employed (Children's Employment Commission, *Appendix to 2nd Report*, Part I, B. 45, paras. 311-2—report by J. C. Kennedy). There is no suggestion in Kennedy's report that women and children were employed in *cutting* at this time.]

1827 £ s d	1843 £ s d
1 6 6	10 0[1]
1 2 6	7 0
1 0 0	6 8
1 6 6	10 0

There were hundreds of workers who could not make ends meet on the low wages paid in 1843.[2]

We have already discussed the condition of the handloom weavers in the cotton industry. The weaving of other textiles is carried out for the most part by handloom weavers and many of them, like the fustian cutters, are suffering from an influx of workers displaced by machinery. Moreover, these handloom weavers, like the factory operatives, suffer from a direct system of fines for bad work. This may be illustrated from the case of the silkweavers. Mr. [John] Brocklehurst, one of the largest silk manufacturers in the whole of England, gave a Parliamentary Committee the following information from his business records concerning the piece rates paid in 1821 and 1831 for the same classes of work.

1821 s. d.	1831 s. d.
30 0	9 0
14 0	7 6
3 6	2 3
9	4
1 1	6
10 0	6 3

On this occasion decline in piece-rates cannot be ascribed to improvements in machinery. The rates paid by Mr. Brocklehurst may well be regarded as typical for the whole of England. The table from which we have already quoted shows that in Mr. Brocklehurst's silk mill the average net weekly earnings of a weaver [i.e. ' clear of all deductions '] declined from 16s. 6d. in 1821 to 6s. in 1831.[3] Since the latter year

[1 Engels gave this figure wrongly as 10s. 6d. in the first German edition.]
[2] James Leach, *Stubborn Facts from the Factories* (1844), p. 35.
[3 For Brocklehurst's evidence on July 16th, 1832, see the *Report of the Select Committee* [of the House of Commons] *on the Silk Trade* in *Parliamentary Papers*, 1831–2, Vol. 19, no. 678, pp. 775–804. The table is printed on page 791.]

wages have fallen still further. One fabric (single sarsnets) which in 1831 was paid for at the rate of 4d. per yard now brings in only 2½d. a yard. Indeed, many country weavers can get this work only if they will do it for 1½d. or 2d. a yard, and even these prices are subject to arbitrary deductions. Every weaver who collects warp to work up at home receives a ticket on which is recorded the exact date and hour at which the materials have been received. [This ticket also lays down the conditions under which the work is given out. It] states that a weaver who cannot work because he is ill must report the fact to the warehouse within three days. If he omits to do this, sickness will not be accepted as an excuse for failure to complete the work on time. The ticket states that if work is handed in late, it is not a valid excuse for the weaver to allege that he has had to wait for yarn to use as weft. It is laid down that certain defects in the work— for example if a certain length of fabric has more than the stipulated number of weft threads, *at least* half the wages will be deducted. The fine for late work is 1d. per yard.[1] In order to illustrate how severe are the penalties which can be inflicted in this way the case may be mentioned of a ' putter-out ' [i.e. manufacturer's agent] who goes twice a week to Leigh in Lancashire to collect finished fabrics and collects on behalf of his master at least £15 in fines on each occasion. This information comes from the agent himself—and he has the reputation of being one of the fairest in the business.[2] At one time disputes on these matters were referred to the J.P.s for decision but complaints to them generally led to the dismissal of the worker concerned. To-day this practice has come to an end and the manu-facturer is free to act as arbitrarily as he pleases. He is prosecutor, wit-ness, judge, and law-maker rolled into one and carries out the sentence into the bargain. If a worker should appeal to a J.P. he is told that having accepted the employer's card he has made a contract with the manufacturer by which he is now bound. In this respect the domestic silk weaver is no better placed than the factory operative. Moreover [every time that fines are imposed] the manufacturer makes the silk weaver sign a declaration agreeing to the deductions that have been made.[3] Leach states that if a weaver should resist all the manufacturers in the town are at once informed that he is ' an enemy *to all ticket-made law and social order* ' and has the impudence to dispute ' the wisdom of those whom he, *ignorant fellow*, ought to know are his superiors in society '.[4]

[1 Leach, op. cit., pp. 37–38]   [2 Leach, op. cit., p. 38.]
[3 Leach, op. cit., p. 38–40.]
4 James Leach, *Stubborn Facts* . . . pp. 39–40.

Of course, these weavers are completely free. No manufacturer forces them to accept either his warp or his tickets, but he says to them—and Leach translates what he says into plain English: ' If you don't like to be frizelled (*sic*) in my frying-pan you can take a walk into the fire '.[1] It may be added that the silk weavers of Spitalfields in London have for many years suffered periods of distress from time to time. How dissatisfied they are with their lot may be seen from the fact that they are among the most active supporters of working-class movements in London. It was among these depressed workers in the East End of London that an epidemic of fever broke out and this led to the appointment of a Royal Commission to enquire into the sanitary state of the labouring population. But the most recent report of the London Fever Hospital shows that fever is still raging in this district.

Metal goods are, next to textiles, the most important products of British industry. The main centres for the production of metal goods are Birmingham, where the finer types of article are made, Sheffield, where all kinds of cutlery are made, and Staffordshire, particularly Wolverhampton, where locks, nails and many other iron goods are produced. We propose to begin our description of the workers in these industries by considering the state of affairs in Birmingham. In that city, as in most other places where metal goods are produced, the industry retains something of its traditional domestic character. The small masters still survive. Some practise their craft with the assistance of apprentices in their domestic workshops But those who require steam power rent a workshop which is situated in a large factory. In each room in the factory there is a shaft driven by steam, and this turns the machinery required by the craftsmen. Léon Faucher gives the name of ' industrial democracy ' to this type of industrial organisation, which obviously differs from the large factories characteristic of Lancashire and Yorkshire.[2] Faucher shows that this system was far from beneficial to either the masters or the apprentices. This

---

[1] Leach, op. cit., p. 41.

[[2] Engels adds in the text in brackets after Faucher's name the following sentences: 'Author of a series of articles in the *Revue des Deux Mondes* concerning working-class conditions in England, which shows at any rate some evidence of serious study on his part. Anyhow it is a better account than any hitherto given either by an English or a German author '. Léon Faucher's writings on England appeared as a series of articles in the *Revue des Deux Mondes* in 1843 and 1844, and were subsequently incorporated in the *Études sur l'Angleterre* (2 vols., Paris, 1845). The reference to ' industrial democracy ' in Birmingham occurs in Volume 2, p. 147. Faucher wrote: ' C'est la démocratie industrielle à l'état domestique et en quelque sorte patriarcal. Birmingham va nous présenter un phénomène non moins extraordinaire, la démocratie industrielle dans une vaste cité et jusque dans les ateliers que la vapeur fait mouvoir '.]

observation is perfectly correct, because in the first place the small masters cut down their own profits by competition among themselves and, secondly, they secure only a modest share of profits which [in Lancashire or Yorkshire] would find their way into the pockets of a single factory owner. Consequently these small masters do not enjoy a high standard of living. When capital does become concentrated in this industry it bears heavily upon the small masters. For one who succeeds ten are ruined, while a hundred others suffer from the competition of a single wealthy manufacturer who can undercut them. It is self-evident that if a small craftsman starts a business in the face of competition from a big capitalist he has the greatest difficulty in overcoming competition of this kind. We shall see that the apprentices are treated just as badly by the small masters as they would be by big manufacturers. The only difference is that they themselves will one day become masters and will in this way attain a certain degree of independence—that is to say, they are not exploited by the middle classes in so direct a manner as if they were factory hands. These master craftsmen are not genuine members of the proletariat, because to some extent they exploit their apprentices; they sell a finished product and they are not themselves wage-earners. On the other hand, they are not genuine members of the middle class since what they sell is in the main the product of their own labour. These Birmingham craftsmen are in an exceptional and intermediate position, since they are partly workmen and partly employers. This accounts for the fact that Birmingham craftsmen have never thrown themselves heart and soul into the English working-class movement. In politics the city has been Radical rather than Chartist.

In addition to these small masters there are also a number of large capitalist firms, which have introduced the factory system in its entirety. In these works the division of labour has been carried to its logical conclusion, the manufacture of needles being a particularly good example of this. Steam power has been introduced. These two factors[1] have made possible the employment of women and children on a large scale. The Report of the Children's Employment Commission shows that conditions in these Birmingham factories are just as unsatisfactory as in industrial establishments elsewhere. [Here again we read of] pregnant women working until the hour of their confinement, lack of skill as housewives, the neglect of household duties, the neglect of the children, indifference to—even hostility towards —family life, and general social demoralisation. Here again are cases of men losing employment, of progressive improvement of machinery,

[1 I.e., the division of labour and steam power.]

of the loss of parental control over children at an early age, and of women and children supporting their menfolk. It is reported that the children [of Birmingham] are clothed in rags and often go short of food—it is said that half of them never get a square meal to eat.[1] Many of them have to survive throughout the day on a pennyworth of bread. For others their lunch is the first meal of the day. Examples are actually given of children who went without food from 8 in the morning until 7 in the evening. The children's clothing was reported to be often inadequate to cover them decently. Many of them go barefoot even in winter. Consequently all these children are weak and stunted for their age, and seldom grow up into robust adults. When we consider the poor diet of these children and young people and their long and hard hours of work in stuffy workrooms it is not surprising to learn that few adults in Birmingham are fit for military service. A surgeon [who had examined all the recruits enlisted in Birmingham for ten years] stated:

> The mechanics are shorter, more puny, and altogether inferior in their physical powers. Many of the men presented for examination, are distorted in the spine and chest. . . .[2]

According to the statement of a recruiting sergeant, the people in Birmingham are smaller than elsewhere, the normal height being 5 ft. 4 in. to 5 ft. 5 in.[3] [Another witness stated that], out of 613 would-be recruits, only 238 were approved for service.[4] We have already given several examples from the Children's Employment Commission's Report concerning the state of morals and education of Birmingham and the Black Country.[5] In addition we also gather from this report that in Birmingham over half the children between the ages of 5 and 15 do not go to school. The school population of the city changes very rapidly, with the result that it is impossible for the children to get any permanent benefit from their education.[6] All school children leave to go to work at a very early age. The Report makes it clear that the standard of the teaching staff leaves much to be desired. A mistress in a dame school was asked if she gave the children any

---

[1] *Appendix to 2nd Report* of the Children's Employment Commission, Part I (1842), F. 17–24—R. D. Grainger's report on Birmingham and evidence f. 119 et seq.]

[2] *Appendix to 2nd Report* of Children's Employment Commission, Part I (1842) f. 175, no. 492—evidence of E. T. Cox, surgeon, taken by R. D. Grainger on Dec. 31st, 1840.]

[3] Ibid., f. 176, no. 495—evidence of Sgt. H. Buchan, taken by R. D. Grainger.]

[4] Ibid., f. 175, no. 493—evidence of Lieut. D. Herbert, taken by R. D. Grainger. Engels attributed Herbert's statements to Buchan.]

[5] See above, p. 235.

[6] Ibid., f. 197, no. 516—evidence of Mrs. E. Chell, taken by R. D. Grainger.]

moral instruction. She replied ' No, I can't afford it for 3d. a week '.[1]
Several teachers did not even grasp the meaning of this enquiry;
others declared that giving moral instruction was not part of their
duties. Another woman teacher said that she did not teach morals as
such, but that she strove to instil sound principles into the children
(and she made a blunder in English in saying so).[2] Mr. Grainger
reported that in the schools the level of discipline was low and there
was continual noise and disorder.[3] The moral state of the children
was most deplorable. Half of all the criminals in the [Birmingham]
district were under 15 years of age. In a single year 90 children [in
Birmingham] aged 10 committed offences of which 44 were of a
serious nature.[4] Mr. Grainger stated that sexual misconduct [in
Birmingham and Nottingham] was almost universal and started at a
very early age.[5]

In the Black Country,[6] the centre of the South Staffordshire iron
industry, conditions are even worse. Neither steam power, nor
machinery, nor—with certain exceptions—the division of labour,
characterises the manufacture of the relatively coarser types of iron
products which are produced in this region. The main industrial
centres in the Black Country are Wolverhampton, Willenhall, Bilston,
Sedgeley, Wednesfield, Darlaston, Dudley, Walsall and Wednesbury.
[Owing to the backwardness of the local manufacture of iron goods]
there are fewer big establishments [than in Birmingham] but there are
more little smithies in which small master craftsmen work either on
their own or with the help of one or more youths who are apprenticed
until the age of 21. These small masters are in much the same position
as their counterparts in Birmingham, but their apprentices are gener-

---

[¹ This evidence comes from the *Report on the State of Education in Birmingham*
compiled in 1838 by a Mr. Wood for the Birmingham Statistical Society for the
Improvement of Education. Grainger reprinted extracts from this report in the
Appendix to 2nd Report of the Children's Employment Commission (1842), Part I,
f. 185-191, no. 503. Grainger remarks that some of the Anglican clergy had
criticised the report, but he considered that it gave a ' tolerably accurate view ' of
the state of education in Birmingham. The answer given by Engels was printed on
the top of page f. 188 of the document.]
[² Ibid., f. 188. The teacher had said that ' she strove to *imbibe* good principles
into them '.]
[³ Ibid., F. 35, para. 337. Grainger made a special report on education in the
districts he had inspected (F. 34-42).]
[⁴ Ibid., F. 39, para. 371.]
[⁵ Ibid., F. 39, para. 372.]
[⁶ For the Black Country see *Appendix to 2nd Report* of the Children's Employment Commission, Part II (1842)—report by R. H. Horne, Q.1-Q. 93 and evidence
q. 1-q. 84. For more modern descriptions of this district see W. H. B. Court, *The
Rise of the Midland Industries*, 1600-1838 (1938) and G. C. Allen, *The Industrial
Development of Birmingham and the Black Country*, 1860-1927 (1929).]

ally in a much worse position. The meat that they are given to eat consists almost solely of the flesh of animals which have died a natural death, aborted calves, and pigs suffocated in railway vans. Tainted meat and rotten fish are also included in the apprentices' diet. It is not only small master craftsmen who treat their young workers in this way, but also the owners of larger works employing between 30 and 40 apprentices. This state of affairs appears to be universal in Wolverhampton. Naturally such a diet has adverse effects on health and the apprentices often suffer from stomach troubles and other complaints. Young apprentices rarely get enough to eat and seldom possess any garments other than their working clothes. That is why these youngsters do not attend Sunday school. The workers' dwellings are often so dilapidated and dirty that the inhabitants suffer from a chronic state of ill health, so that although the work is reasonably healthy bad housing conditions are responsible for many physical disabilities among young people. The youngsters are small, stunted, weak and often severely deformed. In the Willenhall workshops, continuous filing at the lathe has been responsible for innumerable bent backs and crooked legs. One leg only is affected, and the result is that [when the worker stands up] his legs have the shape of a letter K. The deformed leg is popularly called the 'hind leg'.[1] Moreover it is said that at least a third of the Willenhall workers suffer from rupture. In Wolverhampton and in Willenhall there are frequent cases of retarded puberty. Up to the age of nineteen not only boys but even girls—for they too toil in the smithies—suffer from this condition. Sedgeley and the surrounding district are devoted almost exclusively to the making of nails. Here people work and live in miserable hovels little better than stables. The dirt here has to be seen to be believed. Boys and girls are set to work when they are only ten or twelve years old and are not regarded as fully skilled until they can turn out one thousand nails a day. They get paid at the rate of 5¾d. for every 1,200 nails.[2] Each nail has to be struck twelve times, and since the hammer weighs 1¼ lbs. the worker has to lift 18,000 lbs. in order to earn this miserable pittance. The heavy character of the work and the inadequacy of the diet make it inevitable that the young should be physically weak and stunted. Statements made by the members of the Children's Employment Commission confirm this supposition. We have already given

[1 *Appendix to 2nd Report* of the Children's Employment Commission, Part II (1842), q. 28, no. 128 (evidence of John Putnam taken by R. H. Horne).]

[2 Certain figures relating to the payments for nailmaking are given in Horne's report on Sedgeley: *Appendix to 2nd Report* of the Children's Employment Commission, Part II (1842), q. 76, para. 753 (based on evidence of William Hilton, no. 281, q. 59); but they do not tally exactly with the figures given by Engels.]

elsewhere some facts concerning the state of education in the Black Country. In this industrial district the standard of education is incredibly low. Half the children do not even go to Sunday school and those who do go are very irregular in their attendance. Standards of literary education among children and young persons in the Black Country are very low as compared with other industrial districts. Few can read and still fewer can write. This is perfectly understandable since the children start work between the ages of 7 and 10, and it is just at this time that children are best able to profit from schooling. The Sunday school teachers in this district are generally smiths or miners who themselves are often unable to read and can hardly sign their own names. The moral state of the workers is what might be expected from their lack of education. Mr. Horne, an official of the Children's Employment Commission, stated that in Willenhall the workers lack all moral sense, and he gives ample evidence to support this assertion.[1] In general he found that children had no affection for their parents and recognised no obligations towards them. These children were so brutish and so stupid that they did not realise what they were saying. It was by no means unusual for them to assert that they were well treated and perfectly happy, although in fact they worked for twelve to fourteen hours, were dressed in rags, were not given enough to eat and were beaten so hard that they felt the effects for several days afterwards. They simply had no experience of any other way of life than to slave away from morn till night until they were given permission to stop. They had never before been asked whether they were tired and did not know the meaning of the question.

Wages are higher in Sheffield than in the Black Country and consequently the workers enjoy a better standard of life. But here, too, there are certain types of work which have an exceptionally deleterious effect on the health of the workers. Certain tasks involve the continual pressure of a tool against the breast and this often causes tuberculosis. Certain other occupations such as file cutting lead to stunted physical development and digestive disturbances. Workers engaged in shaping bones for knife handles suffer from headaches and biliousness. Many girls do this work and they suffer from anaemia. The most unhealthy type of work is the grinding of knife blades and forks which, especially where a dry stone is used, always leads to the death of the operative at an early age. The unhealthy nature of this work is caused partly by the fact that the grinder works in a bent position. His breast and stomach suffer from the pressure put upon them. But the main

[1 Ibid., Q. 49-53, paras. 541-569. It is clear from Horne's report that conditions in Willenhall were quite exceptional, even for the Black Country.]

danger of this trade comes from breathing in particles of sharp metallic dust thrown up into the air during the grinding process. The average expectation of life of a dry grinder is barely 35 years, while that of the wet grinder is rarely more than 45. Dr. Knight, of Sheffield, reports as follows:

> Grinding is a most pernicious trade; so much so, that they who frequent the beer-houses, and are the greatest drinkers among the grinders, are sometimes the longest lived, owing to their more frequent absence from their work.[1]

[He had previously written in an article in a medical journal:]

> ... The grinders are divided into two classes, the dry and the wet grinders—and there is a third class, who grind both wet and dry—altogether they amount to about two thousand five hundred, of this number about one hundred and fifty, viz. eighty men and seventy boys, are fork grinders—these grind dry, and die from twenty-eight to thirty-two years of age. The razor grinders grind both wet, and dry, and they die from forty to forty-five years of age. The table-knife grinders work on wet stones, and they live to betwixt forty and fifty years of age.[2]

The same medical man gives the following description of the course of the disease known as grinders' asthma:

> Those who are are to be brought up grinders, usually begin to work when they are about fourteen years old: there are, however, many exceptions to this custom, as the children of grinders are frequently employed in the lighter branches of the trade as early as eight or nine years of age.... Grinders, who have good constitutions seldom experience much inconvenience from their trade until they arrive at about twenty years of age: about that time the symptoms of their peculiar complaint begin to steal upon them, their breathing becomes more than usually embarrassed on slight exertions, particularly on going upstairs or ascending a hill; their shoulders are elevated in order to relieve their constant and increasing dysproea; they stoop forward, and appear to breathe the most comfortably in that posture in which they are accustomed to sit at their work, viz: with their elbows resting on their knees. Their complexions assume a muddy, dirty appearance; their countenance indicates anxiety ; they complain of a sense of tightness across the chest; their voice is rough, and hoarse; their cough loud, and as if the air were drawn through wooden tubes: they

[1 *Appendix to 2nd Report* of Children's Employment Commission, Part I (1842), E. 12, no. 23—evidence of Dr. Arnold Knight, taken by J. C. Symons, and E. 5, para. 29.]

[2 Dr. Arnold Knight, 'On the grinders' asthma': *North of England Medical and Surgical Journal*, Aug. 1830–May 1831, Vol. 1, p. 86.]

occasionally expectorate considerable quantities of dust, sometimes mixed up with mucus, at other times in globular or cylindrical masses enveloped in a thin film of mucus. . . . Haemoptysis,[1] inability to lie down, night sweats, colignative diarrhoea, extreme emaciation, together with all the usual symptoms of pulmonary consumption at length carry them off; but not until they have lingered through months, and even years of suffering, incapable of working so as to support either themselves or their families. . . . It is desirable that the public mind should be repeatedly impressed with this important truth, that all the attempts which have hitherto been made, to prevent or to cure the grinders' asthma have utterly failed.[2]

Since the days when Knight wrote ten years ago the number of grinders has increased and so have the ravages of the disease which attacks them. Attempts have been made to protect the grinders by covering the grinding wheels and by drawing off the dust by suction. Some measure of success has attended these efforts but the grinders themselves are not in favour of these precautions and have sometimes actually destroyed the safety apparatus. Their attitude is explained by the fact that they fear that if their trade becomes safer, it will attract more workers and so lead to a fall in wages. They believe in ' a short life and a merry one '. Dr. Knight stated that he had often warned grinders in whom he had detected the first symptoms of asthma that they would die if they went back to the grindstone. His advice was never taken. Once a man had become a grinder he appeared to be bewitched as if he had sold himself to the devil. The level of education in Sheffield is very poor. A clergyman who had devoted much time to the collection of educational statistics gave his opinion that out of 16,500 working-class children who were in a position to attend school hardly 6,500 could read.[3] This was because the children left school at an early age—some at the age of seven—and none stayed longer than the age of twelve. The clergyman stated that the quality of the schoolmasters left much to be desired. One of them was a convicted thief who could find no other employment when he came out of prison. Immorality among the young people of Sheffield appears to be worse than anywhere else. It is indeed difficult to decide which town

[1 The spitting of blood.]
[2 Dr. Arnold Knight, ' On the grinders' asthma ': *North of England Medical and Surgical Journal*, Vol. 1, August 1830–May 1831, pp. 170–171, 178. Engels appears to have copied the extracts from this article given in *Appendix to 2nd Report* of the Children's Employment Commission, Part I (1842), E 5–6.]

[3 *Appendix to 2nd Report* of the Children's Employment Commission, Part I (1842), E. 20, para. 147—report by J. C. Symons on Sheffield. The statement was made by Symons himself and not the clergyman. There is a table on page E19 compiled in 1838 by the Rev. Thomas Sutton, vicar of Sheffield, but this contains no estimate of the number of children who could read.]

should be awarded the prize for the grossest immorality. Whenever I have read one of the official reports about a particular place, I feel strongly inclined to make the award to that town. In Sheffield on Sundays young people hang about the streets all day gambling by tossing coins or by organizing dog fights. They frequent gin shops assiduously, where they sit with their girl-friends until late in the evening, when it is time for the couples to take their solitary walks. In one low beer shop visited by the Commissioner [J. C. Symons] forty to fifty young people of both sexes were sitting. Nearly all of them were under 17 years of age and every youth had his girl-friend with him. [In several of the beershops visited afterwards] the young people were playing cards, while in others they were dancing. But in all of them drinking was going on. Known prostitutes were among the company. In the circumstances it is not surprising to hear from many witnesses that in Sheffield it is very common for irregular sexual intercourse to take place at an early age and that girls as young as 14 or 15 years have already become prostitutes. Crimes of savage violence are of common occurrence. Only a year before the Commissioner paid his visit a gang composed almost entirely of young men was seized in the act of trying to set the town on fire. They were fully equipped with pikes and inflammable material.[1] We shall see later that the working-class movement in Sheffield is also characterised by the most brutal violence.[2]

In addition to these main centres of the metal-working industries there are also pin-making workshops in Warrington, Lancashire, several nail forges in the vicinity of Wigan in Lancashire and in the East of Scotland. Those who work in the Warrington pin-making workshops, particularly the children, are sunk in extreme poverty, immorality and ignorance. The reports concerning the workers in the nail forges of Wigan and the East of Scotland show that conditions there are very similar to those already described as existing in Staffordshire.[3] One other branch of the metal industries should be mentioned; this is the manufacture of machinery. Machinery is produced mainly in the manufacturing districts, particularly in Lancashire. In this remarkable industry machines are made with the help of machine

[1 *Appendix to 2nd Report* of the Children's Employment Commission, Part I (1842) E. 14–16, paras. 105–127—report by J. C. Symons on the employment of children and young persons in the trades of Sheffield.]
[2 Ibid., E. 3, para. 13.]
[3 Ibid. (J. L. Kennedy's report on print grounds and miscellaneous trades in Lancashire) B. 40, para. 276—Atherton, Leigh, Billinge and Upholland nail-forges; B. 38–40, paras. 270–75—Wigan pinmaking workshops; *Appendix to 2nd Report* of the Children's Employment Commission, Part II (1842) K.3–6, paras. 17–37—report of R. H. Franks on the nailworks of Stirlingshire in East Scotland.]

tools. At one time the worker displaced by machinery sought refuge in engineering workshops where the machines which had taken away his livelihood were constructed. Now he finds that even the making of machinery is done by machine tools. Machines for planing and boring, machines for cutting nuts, screws and wheels, and mechanical lathes have thrown out of work many skilled artisans who formerly secured regular and well-paid employment. Anyone who is interested can find plenty of these unemployed craftsmen in Manchester.[1]

We turn now to the Potteries, which is an industrial district lying to the north of the Black Country. The main manufacturing centre in the Potteries is the borough of Stoke. Other centres are the localities of Hanley, Burslem, Lane End, Lane Delph, Etruria, Cobridge, Longport, Tunstall and Goldenhill. Together these places contain 70,000 inhabitants.[2] We have extracted the following inform-ation about the Potteries from the Report of the Children's Employ-ment Commission. In some establishments in the pottery industry the children are engaged only in light work in warm, well-ventilated workshops.[3] On the other hand, in other branches of the industry their work is hard and exhausting. Their diet is poor and their clothing inadequate. Many children complain:

I . . . don't go to a Sunday-school; never went to a day-school; don't know the reason why, except that mother's so poor and havn't (*sic*) got no clothes. I am very happy in my work, but don't get enough to eat and drink; I get mostly dry tatoes and salt . . . never get meat, never get bread. . . .'[4]

' We are very badly off at home; don't get meat every day; got nothing at all today for dinner; they don't at home get a dinner every day; what I get chiefly is tatoes and salt, and sometimes bread. . . .'[5]

' This is all the clothes I got; I have no change at home for Sunday.'[6]

[1 Ibid., B. 41–42, paras. 281–285 (machine making in the Manchester district); James Leach, *Stubborn Facts from the Factories* (1844), pp. 42–45.]

[2 Engels gave the figure of 60,000 but the figure given by Samuel Scriven in the *Appendix to 2nd Report* of the Children's Employment Commission, Part I (1842), C. 1, para. 1 is 70,000.]

[3 Ibid., C. 3, para. 8 where Scriven states that the new factories erected by Minton and Boyle, Alcock and John Ridgway ' contain large, well-ventilated, light, airy, commodious rooms . . .']

[4 Ibid., C. 4, no. 14 (evidence collected by S. Scriven from William Hall, aged 13). Engels gave a garbled version of this evidence and omitted the statement that the boy was happy in his work.]

[5 Ibid., C. 5, no. 20 (evidence collected by S. Scriven from William Rowley, aged 17.)]

[6 Ibid., C. 2, no. 7 (evidence collected by S. Scriven from George Burton, aged 9). The witness went on to say ' Overseer is kind to me, so is master '.]

The mould runners are among the young workers whose labour is most injurious to their health. They carry into the drying room the finished earthenware objects in the moulds in which they have been placed. When the chinaware has been sufficiently dried they have to carry the empty mould back again. All day long they carry to and fro weights which are too heavy for children of such tender years. The high temperature in which they have to do this makes their labours exceedingly exhausting. Almost without exception these children are thin, pale, weak, small and stunted. Nearly all of them suffer from stomach troubles, nausea, and lack of appetite and many of them die of phthisis. The 'jiggers' are almost equally unhealthy. These boys are known as 'jiggers' because they turn a wheel which is called a 'jigger'.[1] The most scandalous way in which the health of the workers is undermined is when they have to handle pottery which has been dipped in a fluid [glaze] which contains large quantities of lead and also much arsenic. Some workers actually have to put their hands into the liquid. Both men and boys do this work. Their hands and clothes are consequently always wet. Their skin becomes soft and the continuous friction results in sores. Their fingers bleed and their hands are in such a state that there is great danger that they will absorb poison into the system. These workers suffer from violent pains, serious stomach and intestinal complaints, severe constipation, colic, and, in some cases, tuberculosis. As far as children are concerned, the commonest [occupational] disease is epilepsy. The men usually suffer the partial loss of the use of the muscles of the hands, painter's colic, and total paralysis of the limbs.[2] One witness [before the Children's Employment Commission] stated that two boys who worked with him actually died from fits as a result of the nature of their employment.[3] Another witness who had worked for two years as a boy in the dipping room stated that at first he suffered from severe pains in the bowels. This was followed by a bad fit which caused him to be confined to bed for two months. From that time the attacks became steadily more frequent and when the evidence was taken he sometimes had from ten to twenty fits a day. His right side is paralysed and the doctors tell him that he will never recover the full use of his limbs.[4] One firm employed four men in two dipping houses and they all suffered from fits and severe pains. Eleven boys were also employed, some of whom

[1 Ibid., C. 5–6, paras. 17–19—work of mould runners and jiggers.]
[2 Ibid., C. 4–5, para. 15 (Scriven's report.)]
[3 Ibid., C. 27, no. 99—evidence taken by S. Scriven from Ralph Bowyer, aged 38.]
[4 Ibid., C. 21, no. 76—evidence taken by S. Scriven from Thomas Hassall, aged 19.]

were already suffering from fits.[1] In fact the ravages of epilepsy are very common among those who are employed in the dipping houses, and all this suffering enables the middle classes to increase their profits. In the rooms in which earthenware is scoured the air is full of fine pulverized flint dust. It is just as dangerous to health to work in this atmosphere as it is for the Sheffield grinders to inhale steel dust. The workers suffer from shortage of breath and cannot lie down in comfort. They suffer from sore throats, severe coughing and they lose their voices, so that one can hardly hear what they say. In the end, they all die of tuberculosis. Schools in the Potteries are said to be relatively numerous [as compared with other industrial districts]. But the children have to go to work in the factories at so early an age and they have to work such long hours—12 hours a day or even longer—that they are not in a position to take advantage of such educational opportunities as exist. Mr. Scriven, of the Children's Employment Commission, found that three quarters of the persons[2] whom he examined could neither read nor write and, indeed, that the whole of the Potteries was sunk in the deepest ignorance. Children who had been attending Sunday school for years were unable to distinguish one letter of the alphabet from another. Indeed the whole district is on a very low educational, religious and moral level.[3]

In the manufacture of glass, too, there are jobs which do not appear to harm male workers very much, but are injurious to the health of children. The work is heavy, the hours of labour are long. There is much night-work and the workshops are very hot (100 deg. to 130 deg. Fahrenheit). These factors—particularly the last—weaken the physique of the children and lead to stunted growth. They suffer especially from eye-troubles, bowel complaints, bronchitis and rheumatism. Many of the children are pale. Their eyes are inflamed and they often go blind for weeks at a time. They suffer also from violent nausea, vomiting, coughs, colds and rheumatism. When removing glass-ware from the furnaces the children often work in such heat that the boards on which they are standing burst into flames. Glass blowers have only a short expectation of life and they usually die of general debility and diseases of the lung.[4]

[1 Ibid., C. 10, no. 40—evidence taken by S. Scriven from Charles Barker, aged 33. Engels referred to only one dipping house.]
[2 Engels wrote 'children'.]
[3 Ibid., C. 8-12, paras. 28-49. Most of Engels's references are to paras. 29-34.]
[4 *Appendix to 2nd Report* of the Children's Employment Commission, Part II (1842), I. 56-58, paras. 213-221, and i. 76, no. 160 (Report by T. Tancred on glass-works in the West of Scotland); K. 7, para. 45-48 (Report of R. H. Franks on glass manufacture in the East of Scotland); L. 1-3, paras. 1-19 (Report by J. R. Leifchild on the glassworks of Northumberland and Durham.)]

In general the Report of the Children's Employment Commission makes it clear that in all branches of industry the factory system is slowly but surely making headway. This is particularly clear when one examines the increase in the employment of women and children. I have not thought it necessary to give a detailed description for each industry of the progress of machinery and of the supersession of the adult male worker. Anyone who has even a slight acquaintance with modern industry will be able to look up this information for himself. I have no space in this chapter to make a detailed examination of this aspect of the present method of industrial production, since I have already discussed this in general terms in a previous chapter [on the results of industrialisation on the workers]. Machines are being introduced everywhere and they are destroying the last vestiges of the independence of the worker. Everywhere the work of women and children is leading to a dissolution of family life. Sometimes, when the husband is unemployed, while his family are at work, the normal structure of the family is reversed. Everywhere the inevitability of the increased use of machinery places more power in the hands of the capitalist, who controls both the business and the workers in it. There is no halt to the continued concentration of property; every day society becomes more sharply divided. On the one hand there are the great capitalists and on the other hand the workers who possess no property. The industrial expansion of England moves forward with giant strides towards an inevitable crisis.

I have already pointed out that the power of capital, coupled with the division of labour, has led to the same results in the workshops of the craftsmen as in the great factories. The little man has been pushed aside and in his place stand the great capitalist and the property-less wage earner. Little needs to be said about the craftsmen because their position is much the same as that of the industrial proletariat. The nature of their work and its effects upon their health have changed little since the early days of the Industrial Revolution. Nearly all the independent skilled craftsmen have now become active supporters of the working class. Many factors have contributed to this development. The close contact between the independent artisans and the factory workers has become closer. Great capitalists have been able to exercise considerable pressure on the independent craftsmen and thus have loosened the old personal links between these craftsmen and their apprentices. The influence of life in the great towns and the decline in earnings have also contributed to bring the craftsmen and the factory workers closer together. We shall have something further to say on this topic. Meanwhile we turn our attention to a group of workers in London whose conditions of work merit investigation because of the extraordinary barbarity with which they are exploited by the greedy middle classes. I refer to milliners and seamstresses.

It is characteristic [of industrial England to-day] that it is precisely the workers engaged in the manufacture of those articles intended for the personal adornment of middle-class ladies whose health is most seriously threatened by the nature of their employment. We have already come across one example of this when we were describing conditions among the lacemakers. An examination of the conditions under which women work in the dressmaking and millinery establishments of London provides further proof of the assertion which we have already made. These establishments employ many young girls —there are said to be 15,000 in all—who have their meals and sleep on the premises.[1] Since most of them are country girls they are held in a state of complete servitude by their employers. During the London season, which lasts for about four months every year, even the well-conducted establishments work fifteen hours a day. If they are exceptionally busy, even eighteen hours a day may be worked. In most of the dressmaking workshops there are no fixed hours of labour at all during the London season and the girls never get more than six hours' sleep out of the twenty-four. Often they get only three or four hours' sleep and occasionally they get only two hours' sleep. They work between 19 and 22 hours at a stretch and frequently they have to work all through the night. The only limit to their labour is the physical impossibility of holding a needle any longer. On one occasion one of these helpless creatures worked for 9 consecutive days at a stretch, without ever undressing. She snatched only a few minutes' rest on a mattress and was given food which had already been cut up into small pieces so that she could swallow it in the shortest possible time [and get back to her sewing].[2] These unfortunate girls have been driven by their modern slave-drivers—the threat of dismissal takes the place of the whip—to work such long and unbroken periods of work as a strong man could not be expected to perform. Yet young girls aged between fourteen and twenty are driven to carry out these tasks. Moreover it must be remembered that both the workrooms and bedrooms of these girls are very stuffy. The girls have to bend continually

[1 *Appendix to 2nd Report* of Children's Employment Commission, Part I (1842) F. 26–42 (R. D. Grainger's reports on trades in London, chiefly dressmaking and shirtmaking), f. 204–38 (evidence collected by R. D. Grainger).]

[2 Ibid., F. 30, para. 283, f. 233–34, no. 623—evidence of F. Tyrrell, ophthalmic surgeon. In the last paragraph of his statement Tyrrell referred to a girl aged 17 who had become blind through overwork. She had worked continuously for nine days and nights. Engels writes as if several girls had worked for nine consecutive days and nights, but the witness mentions one case only.]

over their work and their food is both poor and difficult to digest. All this, and in particular, the long hours of work and the lack of fresh air have tragic results as far as the health of these girls is concerned. They do not work long before they begin to suffer from headaches, listlessness, exhaustion, general debility, loss of appetite and pains in the shoulders, back and hips. These complaints are followed in due course by more permanent ill-effects, such as curvature of the spine, round shoulders, and loss of weight. Continual inflammation and running of the eyes is a painful complaint which soon leads to short-sightedness. In addition they suffer from coughs, pigeon chests and shortage of breath, and those specifically female complaints associated with a girl's sexual development. Very often the eye complaints to which we have referred end in complete and incurable blindness. If [a dressmaker or] a milliner does retain sufficient eyesight to continue with her work, her brief and tragic career generally ends in tuberculosis. Even those who leave this work before it is too late find that their health has been permanently impaired. Their constitutions have been undermined for good, and they always suffer from chronic weakness and ill-health. This is particularly evident if they marry. Their children are sickly and puny. All the doctors examined by the Children's Employment Commission were unanimously of the opinion that it would be impossible to imagine any type of work which would be more likely than this one to destroy health and lead to premature death.

The needlewomen, particularly those who work in London, are exploited just as cruelly as the dressmakers.[1] In this case, however, the employer exploits the workers in an indirect fashion [because the needlewomen work in their own homes]. Girls employed in stay-making are engaged in hard and tiring work, which inflicts a great strain on their eyes. And what do they get paid for this? I do not know. But what I do know is, that the agent who gives out the work to them, to the individual needlewoman, gets 1½d. a piece. This agent, of course, has to give security [to the manufacturer] for the material which he distributes among the needlewomen. The agent will take at least a halfpenny a piece as his commission, and this leaves only a penny for the poor girl [who has done the work]. The girls who sew up cravats have to accept a 16-hour working day for which they receive only 4s. 6d. a week.[2] The condition of the shirt-makers is worst of

[1 Needlewomen generally worked in their own homes, while dressmakers were employed in workshops.]
[2 *Weekly Dispatch*, March 17th, 1844, p. 123, col. 4, article on 'Horrifying Conditions of the Stay-Makers and Stock-makers'. See also a later article on 'Horrifying Conditions and Starvation Wages of Stay-Makers' in *The Weekly Dispatch*, no. 2235, Aug. 25th, 1844, p. 399, col. 4.]

all.[1] They earn only 1½d. for sewing an ordinary shirt. At one time they received between 2d. and 3d., but because St. Pancras workhouse, which is administered by a Radical bourgeois Board of Guardians, began to do the work for 1½d., the unfortunate independent needle-women had to accept the same rate. Sixpence each is paid for fine or fancy shirts, which can be done in a long working day of eighteen hours. According to ample evidence both from the workers themselves and their employers these needlewomen can earn only 2s. 6d. to 3s. a week. To make as much as this they have to work very hard and they have to work far into the night.[2] The most infamous aspect of this barbarous system is that these wretched needlewomen must put down as a deposit part of the value of the materials entrusted to them. It is obvious that they can do this only by pawning a portion of the goods entrusted to them, and the employer knows very well that this is what happens. When the material in pawn is redeemed it can only be done at a loss, which falls on the needlewomen. If they cannot redeem the material, they have to appear before a Justice of the Peace. An instance of this happening in November 1843 was reported in the press.[3] Another poor girl, who got herself into this plight, drowned herself in a canal in August 1844.[4] These poverty-stricken needlewomen usually live in little attics, where as many herd together as space will permit. In winter they crowd together for warmth, as they have no other source of heat. There they sit bent over their work and sew from four or five in the morning until midnight. Their health is ruined in a few years and they sink into an early grave, without having been able to earn the barest necessities of life.[5] In the streets below the gleam-

[1 *Appendix to 2nd Report* of Children's Employment Commission Part I (1842) F. 33-4 (report by R. D. Grainger on shirtmaking in London). See letter from 'Censorius' on this evidence in *The Weekly Dispatch*, Nov. 19th, 1843.]

[2 Ibid., f. 265-66, no. 738 (letter from Messrs. Silver and Co.) f. 268, no. 747 (shirtmaking in St. Pancras workhouse). Owing to the considerable variations in the quality and type of shirts mentioned in the evidence, it is difficult to make generalizations as to the average earnings of the shirt-makers and their assistants. There is little doubt that in general earnings were miserably low and that they had been considerably depressed by competition from 'slopwork' in the workhouses of East and Central London.]

[3 *Weekly Dispatch*, no. 2193, Nov. 5th, 1843, p. 535, col. 3—Elizabeth Harding, shirt-maker, charged with pawning a shirt entrusted to her; *Northern Star*, no. 315, Nov. 25th, 1843, p. 7, col. 3—Mary White, shirt-maker, brought before a magistrate, on a charge of pawning shirts entrusted to her.]

[4 *Northern Star*, no. 355, Aug. 31st, 1844, p. 6, cols. 2-5—inquest on Eliza Kendall, shirt-maker, aged 19, who committed suicide by jumping into the Grand Surrey Canal. She and her sister had 'borrowed a trifle from the rent money, and, being unable to make it up, she pawned some of the shirts intrusted to them to make . . . ' (reported earlier in the *Weekly Dispatch*, no. 2235, August 25th, 1844, p. 399, col. 4.]

5 Thomas Hood, the most talented of the present generation of English humor-

ing carriages of the wealthy middle classes rattle past, and close at hand some wretched dandy is gambling away at faro in a single evening as much money as a needlewoman could hope to earn in a year.

Such is the condition of the English industrial proletariat. Everywhere we find permanent or temporary suffering, sickness and demoralisation all springing either from the nature of the work or from the circumstances under which they are forced to live. Everywhere the workers are being destroyed. Slowly but surely they are ceasing to be human beings, either physically or morally. Can this state of affairs go on? It cannot and will not last, because the workers, who form the vast majority of the community, are determined that it shall not endure. Let us see what they themselves have to say about these conditions.

ists, like all humorists, has strong sympathies with suffering humanity, but his character lacks all dynamic energy. Early in the year 1844, when all the press was full of accounts of the distress among the needlewomen, he wrote a fine poem called ' The Song of the Shirt ', which wrung many compassionate but ineffectual tears from the daughters of the bourgeoisie. I have not sufficient space to reproduce the poem here. It appeared originally in *Punch* and was subsequently reprinted in other papers. Since the condition of the sewing girls was discussed in all the newspapers at that time, it is unnecessary to me to give more detailed references to the subject. [' The Song of the Shirt ' first appeared in the Christmas number of *Punch* in 1843 (Vol. 5, July–Dec., 1843, p. 260) and not in 1844. For an exposure of conditions on the men's side of the tailoring trade see Charles Kingsley, *Cheap Clothes and Nasty* (1850), reprinted in A. C. Ward (ed.) *A Miscellany of Tracts and Pamphlets* (Oxford, 1927). See also A. Whitley, ' Thomas Hood and *The Times* ' (*Times Literary Supplement*, May 17, 1957, p. 309).]

CHAPTER IX

WORKING-CLASS MOVEMENTS

Even if I had not given so many examples as I have done to
illustrate the condition of the working classes in England, it would
still be self-evident that the proletariat can hardly feel happy at the
present situation. It will surely be granted that the state of affairs I
have described is not one in which either an individual or a social class
can think, feel and live in a civilised manner. The workers must strive
to escape from this position, which degrades them to the level of
animals. They must try to achieve for themselves a better and more
human status. They can do this only by attacking the interests of the
middle classes who live by exploiting the workers. But the bourgeoisie
defends its interests in the most vigorous fashion. It has at its disposal
not only the power of property, but also the resources of the authority
of the State. Every attempt the worker makes to free himself from
his present bondage meets with the open hostility of the bourgeoisie.

Moreover, the worker is made perpetually aware of the fact that
the middle classes treat him as if he were an inanimate object and a
piece of property rather than a human being, and for this reason alone
he is the declared enemy of the bourgeoisie. I have already given a
hundred examples, and I could have given another hundred, to illustrate the fact that under present circumstances the worker can only
retain his self-respect by rising in anger against the middle classes.
There can be no doubt that the worker is well able to protest with all
the fury at his command against the tyranny of the capitalist, if only
because of the way in which he has been brought up—or rather his
lack of proper upbringing. In addition the fact that there is now a
large hot-blooded Irish element in the English proletariat also stimu-
lates the workers' animosity against their oppressors. The English
worker to-day is no longer an Englishman [of the old school]. He no
longer resembles his capitalist neighbour in being a mere machine for
making money. His capacity for feeling has developed. He has thrown
off his native Nordic reserve. He has cast aside his inhibitions.
Given free rein, his passions have therefore been able to develop so
that they now readily stimulate him to action. Among the middle
classes the emphasis laid on the cultivation of the reasoning faculty has
greatly increased the tendency towards selfishness and, indeed, has
promoted greed to the position of a guiding principle in the conduct of

affairs. For the bourgeoisie, love of money has become the ruling passion of life. All this is lacking in the worker, who is therefore able to give full play to passions as strong and unbridled as those of the foreigner. All feelings of patriotism have been crushed in the heart of the worker.

We have seen the only way in which the worker can retain his self-respect is by fighting against the way of life imposed upon him. It is natural, therefore, that it is when he is taking action against his oppressors that the English worker is seen at his best. It is then that he appears to the fullest advantage—manly, noble and attractive. We shall see that all the vigour and activity of the worker is concentrated upon this struggle. We shall see that even his efforts to cultivate his mind have a direct connection with his fight against the bourgeoisie. It is true that we shall have to report isolated cases of violence and even brutality. It must be remembered, however, that in England the social war has been openly declared. There are occasions on which it is the interest of the middle classes to wage this war with the weapons of hypocrisy, and to try and cover up their deeds under the disguise of peace and even of philanthropy. When this happens the worker can reply only by tearing off this mask of hypocrisy, so as to reveal the true state of affairs. Acts of violence committed by the working classes against the bourgeoisie and their henchmen are merely frank and undisguised retaliation for the thefts and treacheries perpetrated by the middle classes against the workers.

Since its beginning in the early days of the Industrial Revolution the revolt of the workers against the middle classes has passed through several phases. I do not propose to examine here the historical significance of these phases in the history of the English people. This must be reserved for a later study. For the time being I propose to confine myself to a brief survey of the principal facts concerning the hostility of the workers to the middle classes in order to show what effect this has had upon the development of the English proletariat.

Criminal activities were the first, the crudest and the least successful manifestation of this hostility. The worker lived in poverty and want, and saw that other people were better off than he was. The worker was not sufficiently intelligent to appreciate why he, of all people, should be the one to suffer—for after all he contributed more to society than the idle rich, and sheer necessity drove him to steal in spite of his traditional respect for private property. We have already pointed out how crime has increased as industry has expanded. It has been shown that there has been a constant relationship between the number of arrests and the annual consumption of bales of cotton.

The workers, however, soon realised that crime did not forward their cause. The criminals, by their thefts, could protest against the existing social order only as individuals. All the mighty forces of society were hurled against the individual law-breaker and crushed him with their overwhelming power. In addition theft was the blindest and most stupid form of protest and consequently this never became the universal expression of the workers' reaction to industrialisation, although many workers doubtless sympathised privately with those who broke the law. The first organised resistance of the workers, as a class, to the bourgeoisie, was the violence associated with the movements against the introduction of machinery. This occurred in the earliest stage of the Industrial Revolution. Even the earlier inventors of new machines, such as Arkwright, were attacked in this way and their machines destroyed. Subsequently there were many instances of machine breaking. These generally followed the same course as the printers' riots in Bohemia in 1844, when both workshops and machines were destroyed.

This type of protest was also far from universal. It was limited to certain localities and was confined to resistance to one aspect of industrial change. If the immediate object of the machine breakers was attained, then the defenceless law breakers had to face the full fury of the established order. The criminals were severely punished and the introduction of the new machinery went on unchecked. It was clearly necessary for the workers to find a new method of expressing their discontent.

This was facilitated by a law passed by the old unreformed oligarchical Tory Parliament. This Act repealed the Combination Laws, and it was a law which would certainly not have been carried through the House of Commons after the Reform Act of 1832, because this reform of the franchise gave legal recognition to the conflict between the bourgeoisie and the proletariat and raised the status of the bourgeoisie to that of the ruling class. The repeal of the Combination Laws in 1824 annulled all the legislation which had formerly forbidden workers to unite for the protection of their interests. In this way the workers secured the right of free association, which had hitherto been confined to members of the bourgeoisie and aristocracy.[1] There have, of course, always been secret societies among the workers, but there are no substantial achievements to their credit. Symons reports the existence of such

[1 Engels's account of the repeal of the Combination Laws is not in accordance with the facts. See Mrs. M. D. George's two articles in *Economic History* (supplement to the *Economic Journal*), Vol. 1, no. 2 (May 1927), pp. 214–28, and *Economic History Review*, Vol. 6, no. 2, April 1936, pp. 172–8].

societies in Scotland, and mentions that as early as 1812 a secret combination of weavers in Glasgow called a general strike.[1] A similar strike took place in 1822. On this occasion two workers who refused to join the union, and were regarded by their fellow-workers as traitors to their class, were blinded by sulphuric acid.[2] In 1818 a union of coal miners was strong enough to bring about a general stoppage of work throughout Scotland.[3] These unions bound their members by an oath of fidelity and secrecy, and kept accurate membership lists, possessed funds and rendered regular financial accounts. Local branches were established, but the secrecy in which affairs of these unions had to be conducted crippled their development. As soon as the workers were granted the right of free association in 1824 trade unions sprang up all over England and they became powerful. Unions were set up by workers in all branches of industry, their declared object being to protect the individual artisan against the tyranny and indifference of the middle classes. They aimed at fixing wages by collective bargaining with their employers. They wished to regulate wages according to the profits of the employers. They desired to raise wages whenever a favourable opportunity presented itself. Their policy was to maintain uniform rates of wages in different occupations throughout the country. Consequently the trade unions negotiated with the capitalists to secure the establishment of wage-scales which would be universally applied, and they threatened to strike against any individual employer who refused to pay wages at this level. Trade unionists tried to restrict the number of apprentices in each trade. By setting limits on the expansion of the labour force in this way they hoped to maintain competition between employers for the available skilled workers, and so to keep wages high. Unionists also strenuously opposed attempts to reduce wages by such underhand methods as the introduction of new machinery and tools. Finally unemployed workers received financial assistance from their unions. This was done either by a direct grant from the union funds or by supplying the unemployed worker with a card, which certified that he was a union member,

[1 All that Symons says is: ' In 1812, a serious strike took place at Glasgow among the weavers, and they were tried under the then combination laws ': J. C. Symons, *Arts and Artisans at Home and Abroad* (1839), p. 143].

[2] See Symons, op. cit., pp. 139-43. [Symons quotes from material supplied to him by the Sheriff's Clerk of Glasgow. From this account it appears that three men were attacked in this way on different occasions—Wilkie, Armstrong and M'Callum. It seems that only M'Callum was actually blinded.]

[3 One of the documents submitted to Symons by the Glasgow Sheriff's Clerk stated: ' In January 1818, I was called (says the Procurator-Fiscal) to aid in protecting Mr. Dixon of the Calder Iron Works, against an alarming combination of the colliers throughout Scotland . . . ' (See Symons, op. cit., p. 137).]

and therefore entitled to receive subsistence and information about vacant jobs, from other branches when he was seeking work in other parts of the country. These arrangements are called ' the tramping system ' and those who use them to find work are called ' tramps '.[1] In order to carry out their policy the trade unions appoint two salaried officials known as the president and the secretary. It is necessary to pay these officials, because no employers can be expected to give them work. The affairs of the trade union are controlled by a committee which is responsible for collecting the weekly subscriptions of the members and for seeing that the funds are used for carrying out the objects of the association. Should some real advantage appear to be gained from doing so, the skilled workers in one district try, if possible, to combine with similar unions in other districts to form a federation which holds regular meetings of delegates. There have been isolated attempts to hold national conferences representing unionists in particular trades. On several occasions, the first being in 1830, efforts have been made to establish a universal trade union for the whole country, delegates from all types of trade unions being summoned. Attempts to form nation-wide associations, however, have generally proved abortive, and even when initially successful, have never lasted for very long. Only if circumstances brought about a quite exceptional wave of enthusiasm would a union of this kind be both possible and successful.[2]

The following steps are taken by trade unions to gain their ends: if one or more masters refuse to pay the wages demanded by the union, a deputation waits upon the employer. Alternatively a petition is handed in, and this procedure shows clearly that the workers appreciate the absolute power wielded by the manufacturer in his little kingdom. If nothing is achieved by these methods, the union orders its members to down tools and all the workers go home. This is called a ' turn-out ' or strike. If all the employers are involved then the strike is a general one. If only some of the manufacturers refuse to pay the wages suggested by the union, then only a partial strike is called. Provided that proper notice of the strike has been given—and this is not always done—this course of action is legal. No further pressure on the employers is possible within the existing law. These legal methods of resistance are, however, too weak to be effective, so long as there are workers who are either not members of the union or who

---

[1 For this system, see E. J. Hobsbawm, ' The Tramping Artisan ' (*Economic History Review*, 2nd series, Vol. 3, no. 3, 1951, pp. 299–320.)]

[2 See G. D. H. Cole, *Attempts at General Union: a study in British Trade Union History*, 1818–1834 (1953).]

can be bribed by the bourgeoisie to desert their union. When there
is only a partial stoppage it is easy for the employer to secure workers
from amongst these blacklegs, who are called 'knobsticks', and so
break the resistance of the workers who are loyal to the union. Usually
these blacklegs are threatened by the loyal union members. They are
molested and beaten up. Everything is done to intimidate them. As
soon as one of the blacklegs who has been assaulted brings a charge
the power of the trade union is nearly always broken on the very first
occasion on which one of its members is guilty of a breach of the peace.
The law-abiding bourgeoisie controls the administration of justice
and in this way ensures the defeat of the union.

The history of trade unionism is the story of many defeats of the
workers and of only a few isolated victories. It is obvious that all
these efforts on the part of trade unionists cannot change the economic
law by which wages are fixed according to supply and demand in the
labour market. Consequently the trade unions are helpless in the face
of the major factors influencing the economy. Thus, if there is a trade
depression, the unions themselves have to acquiesce in a reduction of
wages or go out of existence. Similarly if there is a striking increase in
the demand for labour the trade unions are not in a position to secure
for their members higher wages than those which they would in any
case obtain as a result of free competition between the capitalists for
skilled men. On the other hand, the trade unions are in a position to
exercise considerable influence over minor and less important factors
in the economy. If the manufacturers did not have to face mass organised opposition from the workers they would always increase their own
profits by continually reducing wages. Competition between the
manufacturers themselves would force the individual capitalist to
depress the wages of his workers to the minimum. Unless exceptional
circumstances prevail, it is true to say that the united opposition of
the workers can limit the evil consequences of unrestrained competition between manufacturers. It is one thing for a manufacturer
to reduce wages when all other manufacturers are doing the same
thing because the general state of the economy makes this necessary.
It is another matter for one employer to attempt to cut wages on his
own account at a time when there is no economic justification for
doing so. The manufacturer who does this knows that he will have to
meet a strike, which will injure him because his capital will lie idle
and his machinery will go rusty. He knows that he cannot be sure of
imposing a reduction in wages, while he can be certain that, if successful,
his example will be followed by his rivals. This will lead to a fall in
the price of the goods he is making and will soon deprive him of any

advantage gained by the original reduction in wages. Again the trade unions are often able to bring about a more rapid increase in wages after a trade crisis than would occur if the workers were entirely unorganised. It is not in the interest of the individual manufacturer to raise wages until he is forced to do so by the competition of rival manufacturers. In fact, the workers themselves demand more wages as soon as business improves and they are often able to force the manufacturer to pay higher wages by threatening a strike. If the manufacturer is short of workers he is not able to resist such a demand. But as we have pointed out, the trade unions are unable to make any headway against the more important factors influencing the state of the labour market. In such circumstances hunger gradually forces the operatives to go back to work on whatever terms the employer dictates. Even if only a few of the strikers return to work, the power of the union is broken, since the labour of the blacklegs and the fact that there are still supplies of goods in the market enable the middle classes to overcome the worst consequences of the disturbance caused to business by the stoppage. Union funds are soon exhausted if large sums have to be disbursed in strike-pay. Small shopkeepers are prepared to sell goods on credit, at a high rate of interest, but only for a short time. Consequently necessity forces the worker back under the yoke of the middle classes. The workers have discovered that most strikes are unsuccessful. In their own interests the manufacturers do not wish to cut wages unless a reduction is unavoidable. Indeed it is the organised opposition of the workers that has forced the employers to adopt this policy. If a reduction in wages has to take place because the state of business makes this imperative the workers' standard of life naturally falls. It may well be asked why the workers go on strike when it is clear that the stoppage cannot prevent a reduction in wages which cannot be avoided owing to slack trade. The answer is, simply, that the workers must protest both against a reduction in wages and also against the circumstances which make that reduction necessary. They must assert that since they are human beings they do not propose to submit to the pressure of inexorable economic forces. On the contrary they demand that economic forces should be adapted to suit *their* convenience. If trade unionists failed to register their protest by striking, their silence would be regarded as an admission that they acquiesced in the pre-eminence of economic forces over human welfare. Such acquiescence would be a recognition of the right of the middle classes to exploit the workers when business was flourishing and to let the workers go hungry when business was slack. The workers must protest against this state of affairs so long as they have not lost all human feeling. Their protest takes the form of strikes because Englishmen are practical people, who believe in the efficacy of deeds rather than words. They are not German theorists, who cheerfully go to sleep as soon as their protest has been officially received and left to slumber in a pigeon-hole for ever. The practical manner in which Englishmen protest has helped to set certain limits to the greed of the middle classes. It has kept alive the opposition of the workers to the overweening political and social power of the capitalist class. But the workers are also learning from practical experience that trade unions and strikes are not of themselves sufficient to break the might of the middle classes. The real importance, however, of trade unions and strikes is that they constitute the first attempt of the workers to put an end to competition amongst themselves. They are based on a recognition of the fact that the power of the middle classes over the workers is due entirely to the existence of competition between workers themselves—that is to say, their lack of solidarity and their intestine rivalries. Trade unions have proved to be so dangerous to the existing social order simply because they have—if only to a limited degree—firmly opposed that competition of workers among themselves, which is the very corner-stone of modern society. The workers could not have chosen a more vulnerable chink in the armour of the middle classes and of the present social structure than by organising trade unions and strikes. The sovereign power of property must come to an end if competition among workers is impaired and if all the operatives are determined not to allow themselves to be exploited by the middle classes. Wages have come to depend upon the law of supply and demand and upon the state of the labour market at any particular moment, simply because the workers have hitherto allowed themselves to be treated as chattels which can be bought and sold. The whole modern system of political economy, with its law of wages, will collapse as soon as the workers make up their minds that they are not going to allow themselves to be passively bought and sold any longer. Its doom is sealed as soon as they act like human beings who can think as well as toil, and show their determination to secure a just share of the fruits of their labour. It is true that the law of wages would eventually come into force again if the workers went no further than to secure the removal of competition amongst themselves. But such a limitation of their aims would bring the present trade union movement to an end, and would actually cause a revival of competition among the workers. Such a policy is out of the question. Necessity will force the trade unions to bring to an end not merely *one* aspect of competition, but all competition. And this result will be achieved. Every day it becomes clearer to workers how they are affected by competition. They appreciate even more clearly than the middle classes that it is competition among the capitalists that leads to those commercial crises which cause such dire suffering among the workers. Trade unionists realise that commercial crises must be abolished, and they will soon discover *how* to do it.

It is obvious that the activities of the trade unions contribute substantially towards inflaming the bitterness and hatred of the workers against the capitalist class. This explains why, in times of exceptional unrest, individual trade unionists, acting with or without the knowledge of their leaders, are guilty of deeds which can be explained only by the existence of hatred nourished in the depths of despair, and by ungovernable passions which cannot be restrained. I have already illustrated this when I mentioned cases of vitriol throwing, and I will now select a few more examples. In 1831, at a time of serious labour unrest, young Mr. [Thomas] Ashton, [the son of] 'a manufacturer of Hyde, near Manchester, was shot dead one evening while walking across some fields. No trace of the murderer was ever discovered.[1] There is no doubt that this deed was committed by the workers and inspired by vengeance. There have been many cases of arson and of attempts to wreck workshops by using explosives. On Friday, September 29th, 1843, an explosion caused serious damage to Mr. Padgin's saw-making factory in Howard Street, Sheffield. The device used was a piece of piping filled with powder and sealed at both ends.[2] On the next day, September 30th, a similar attempt at sabotage occurred at Mr. Ibbetson's factory for making cutlery and files at Shales Moor, near Sheffield. Mr. Ibbetson had made himself obnoxious to the workers because he had played a leading part in various middle-class movements. Moreover he paid low wages, he refused to employ trade unionists and used the machinery of the Poor Law for his own ends. At the time of the trade depression of 1842, he forced his workers to accept a reduction in wages by reporting to the Guardians the names of those men who rejected his terms. They

[1 See *Annual Register*, 1831, Chronicle, pp. 7–8. Engels's statement that the murderers were never apprehended is incorrect. Three years after the crime had been committed, two brothers, Joseph and William Mosley, and William Garside, were tried at Chester Assizes for the murder. William Mosley turned King's evidence (there were rewards at stake amounting to £2,000) and the other two were convicted and eventually hanged in London (*Annual Register*, 1834, Chronicle, pp. 290–6). Engels's blunder may be due to reliance on the account of the affair given by P. Gaskell in *The Manufacturing Population of England* (1833), pp. 299–300, at a time when the murderers had not been caught.]
[2 *Northern Star*, no. 308, Oct. 7th, 1843, p. 3, col. 2.]

were therefore declared ineligible for relief because they had refused to accept work when it was offered to them. Much damage was done to Mr. Ibbetson's works by this explosion. The only regret expressed by workers who came to see the damage was ' that the whole concern was not blown over the church '.[1] On Friday, October 6th, 1843, there was an attempt at arson at Ainsworth and Crompton's mill at Bolton. No damage was done. This was the third or fourth attempt to burn down this factory within a very short space of time.[2] At a meeting held on Wednesday, January 10th, 1844, the police surveyor showed the Sheffield Borough Council a bomb made of cast iron. It had been discovered in Mr. Kitchen's works in Earl Street, Sheffield. It contained four pounds of powder and was equipped with a fuse. It was clear that the fuse had been lit, but the flame had gone out before reaching the powder.[3] On Sunday, January 21st, 1844, an explosion occurred in a saw-mill owned by Messrs. Bentley and White of Bury in Lancashire. This was caused by a quantity of gunpowder, thrown into the workshop with disastrous results.[4] The Soho [Grinding] Wheel works in Sheffield were set on fire on Thursday, February 1st, 1844 and completely gutted.[5] These six cases have all occurred within four months, and are due solely to the hatred of the workers for their employers. I need hardly stress the fact that this is evidence of a deplorable state of industrial relations. These incidents prove that the social war has broken out in England and rages unchecked even during a period of commercial prosperity such as existed in the latter part of 1843. And yet the English middle classes are blind to what is happening. The most striking case, however, is that of the Glasgow thugs,[6] which came before the local assizes from January 3rd to 11th,

[1] *Northern Star*, no. 308, Oct. 7th, 1843, p. 3, col. 1. Engels appears to have based his account of Ibbetson on the *Northern Star's* remarks:
    ' The cause of the attempt seems to be a mystery, although rumour attributes it to the odium that attaches to Mr. Ibbetson as an employer. He is a leading man among the Methodists, and the great gun of the ' free-booters ' [i.e. Free Traders]: his works is a refuge for all *outlaws*, or men who will not join the Union; and who are working considerably under the general prices of the town. It is said too that he took advantage of the late depression and went to the Board of Guardians, and caused men who were receiving parish relief to be compelled to work for his prices or perish for want. . . .']
[2] *Manchester Guardian*, Oct. 11th, 1843, p. 6, col. 5.]
[3] *Northern Star*, no. 323, Jan. 20th, 1844, p. 5, col. 2, quoting *The Times*, Jan. 13th, 1844.]
[4] *Manchester Guardian*, Wednesday, Jan. 24th, 1844, p. 7, col. 2. Engels gave the date wrongly as January 20th.]
[5] *Sheffield and Rotherham Independent*, Saturday, February 3rd, 1844.]
[6] These workers were called thugs after the well-known tribe in India whose sole occupation is the murder of all strangers who fall into their hands.

1838.[1] It is clear from these proceedings that a trade union of cotton spinners had existed in Glasgow since [at least] 1816,[2] and that they were exceptionally well-organized and powerful. Members were bound by oath to accept the decision of the majority. All strikes were controlled by a secret committee, the composition of which was unknown to most members of the union. This committee had unrestricted control over the finances of the union. The Committee put a price on the heads of all blacklegs[3] and obnoxious factory owners, and deliberately organized arson in factories. One factory to be set on fire had women blacklegs on the premises who had taken the place of men at the spinning machines. A certain Mrs. MacPherson, the mother of one of these girls, was murdered and those responsible were shipped off to America at the expense of the union.[4] As early as 1820 a blackleg named M'Quarry had been shot at and injured. The perpetrator of this deed had been awarded £15 by the union.[5] Subsequently a man named Graham had been shot at and the person who shot him received £20. He was, however, caught and sentenced to transportation for life.[6] Finally, in May 1837, there were disturbances in Glasgow owing to strikes at the Oakbank and Mile-end [cotton] factories during which a dozen blacklegs were roughly handled. In July of the same year there was fresh unrest and a blackleg named [John] Smith was so badly mishandled[7] that he died. The members of the secret committee were now arrested, and were brought to trial. The president and principal members of the committee were found guilty of forming an illegal association, intimidating and injuring blacklegs and burning down the factory[8] of James and Francis Wood. They were sentenced to seven years' transportation.[9] What do our good Germans say to all this?[10]

[1 Accounts of the trial may be found in Archibald Swinton (ed.) *Report of the Trial of Thomas Hunter, Peter Hacket, Richard M'Neil, James Gibb and William M'Lean, operative cotton-spinners in Glasgow* . . . (Edinburgh, 1838) and *Annual Register* for 1838 (Chronicle), pp. 6–12.]

[2 *Annual Register* for 1838, p. 7 (evidence of James Moat) and p. 8 (evidence of James Murdoch).]

[3 Engels uses the word ' knobstick' which was current when he wrote in 1845.]

[4 *Annual Register* for 1838, p. 9 (evidence of James Murdoch.) From the account of James Murdoch's evidence given in the *Annual Register* it is not clear exactly when Mrs. MacPherson was murdered but it was certainly not in 1837.]

[5 *Annual Register* for 1838, p. 9 (evidence of James Murdoch].

[6 *Annual Register* for 1838, p. 9 (evidence of James Murdoch)].

[7 Although Engels uses the word ' mishandled ', Smith was in fact shot in the back: *Annual Register* for 1838, pp. 10–11].

[8 The indictment says ' house ' not ' factory ': *Annual Register* for 1838, p. 6.]

[9 A verdict of ' not proven ' was returned on eight of the twelve counts in the indictment: *Annual Register* for 1838, pp. 6, 12].

10 ' What kind of "wild-justice" must it be in the hearts of these men that prompts

The capitalists, and particularly the factory owners, who come into direct contact with the working classes, are strongly opposed to trade unions. They are continually trying to persuade the workers that such associations are useless. Insofar as the capitalists appeal to the science of economics in support of their case, they are using arguments which might be regarded as valid. But simply because their case rests on economic grounds it is only a half-truth, and can have no application whatsoever to the workers' actual conditions. The very fact that the middle classes press these arguments with such zeal is proof enough that the advice they are giving to the workers is by no means unbiased. On the one hand it is obvious that a strike will harm the middle classes. On the other hand it is equally clear that anything the factory owners put in their pockets must necessarily be filched from those of the workers. The workers are well aware of the fact that trade unions are able, to some extent, to curb the insatiable propensity of the employers to indulge in competitive wage-cutting. Even if the workers did not fully appreciate this they would nevertheless contrive to strike simply in the hope of injuring their natural enemies, the factory owners. In a war any injury to one side is of advantage to the other, and since a state of war does in fact exist between the workers and the employers, it is natural that the working classes should adopt the same policy as is adopted by the Great Powers when hostilities break out between them. Of all members of the middle classes our old friend, Dr. Ure, is the most rabid opponent of all trade union activity. He positively foams at the mouth in his fury at the ' secret tribunals ' of the cotton spinners, who are the most powerful section of organised labour. [Ure wrote:]

They boasted of possessing a dark tribunal, by the mandates of which they could paralyze every mill whose master did not comply with their wishes, and so bring ruin on the man who had given them profitable employment for many a year.[1]

He speaks of a time ' when the inventive head and the sustaining heart of trade were held in bondage by the unruly lower members . . .'[2] What a pity that the good doctor cannot palm his fairy stories

them, with cold deliberation, in conclave assembled, to doom their brother work-man, as the deserter of his order and his order's cause, to die as a traitor and deserter; and have him executed, since not by any public judge and hangman, then by a private one;—like your old Chivalry *Femgericht* (*sic*), and Secret-Tribunal, suddenly in this strange guise become new; suddenly rising once more on the astonished eye, dressed now not in mail-shirts, but in fustian jackets, meeting not in Westphalian forests but in the paved Gallowgate of Glasgow! Not loyal loving obedience to those placed over them, but a far other temper, must animate these men! It is frightful enough. Such temper must be widespread, virulent among the many, when even in its worst acme, it can take such a form in a few.'—T. Carlyle, *Chartism* (1839), p. 40.   [¹ Dr. Andrew Ure, *The Philosophy of Manufactures* (1835), p. 282.]
    [² Ibid., p. 282.]

off on to the English workers as easily as Menenius Agrippa pulled the wool over the eyes of the plebs in the days of ancient Rome! Finally Dr. Ure tells the following story: on one occasion the mule spinners producing coarse yarn ' abused their powers beyond endurance '. They received high wages, but this did not awaken any sense of gratitude towards their employers. Nor did it induce them to improve their minds in any way. When Dr. Ure refers to ' improvement of mind ' he really means that the workers should occupy themselves with innocuous studies which might actually benefit their employers. In many cases increased wages led to sinful pride. The money was actually used to support strikes by refractory workmen. One group of millowners[1] after another have suffered from this arbitrary abuse of power. On one occasion when these unhappy industrial disputes affected Hyde, Dukinfield and neighbouring districts, the millowners, fearing lest French, Belgian and American competitors would drive them out of the market, asked the firm of Sharp, Roberts and Company whether Mr. [Richard] Roberts[2] could not invent an automatic mule ' in order to emancipate the trade from galling slavery and impending ruin '.[3] '. . . he produced in the course of a few months, a machine apparently instinct with the thought, feeling, and tact of the experienced workman . . . Thus, the *Iron Man*, as the operatives fitly call it, sprang out of the hands of our modern Prometheus at the bidding of Minerva—a creation destined to restore order among the industrious classes, and to confirm to Great Britain the empire of art. The news of this Herculean prodigy spread dismay through the Union, and even long before it left its cradle, so to speak, it strangled the Hydra of misrule '.[4] Dr. Ure goes on to state that the invention of the four-colour and five-colour printing machines in the textile industry was brought about by unrest among the [journeymen] calico-printers.[5] Ure gives several other examples to illustrate his point, including the installation of a new sizing machine for dressing warp when the yarn dressers showed signs of insubordination.[6] And this is the same author who only a little earlier in the same book had devoted several pages to explaining how beneficial machinery was to the workers! Dr. Ure, of course, is by no means the only critic of trade unions. In

[[1]Engels wrote ' Fabrikanten ' (i.e. factory owners) but Dr. Ure had written ' millowners ' (op. cit., p. 366).]

[[2] Engels gives the name Sharp instead of the correct one, Roberts (Ure, op. cit., p. 366). For Richard Roberts, see H. W. Dickinson ' Richard Roberts, his life and inventions ' (*Trans. Newcomen Society*, Vol. 25, 1945-7, pp. 123-27).]

[[3] Ure, op. cit., p. 367.]

[[4] Ure, op. cit., p. 367.]   [[5] Ure, op. cit., p. 369.]

[[6] Ure, op. cit., p. 370.]

evidence before the Factories Enquiry Commission, several manufacturers, including the well-known industrialist, Mr. [Henry] Ashworth, lost no opportunity of venting their wrath on combinations of
workers.[1] These clever representatives of the middle classes—like
certain [reactionary] governments—denounce all movements that
they do not understand as inspired by the machinations of wicked
agitators, evilly-disposed persons, demagogues, tub-thumpers and
irresponsible youths. They claim that the paid agents of the trade unions
foment this unrest, because it is a bread and butter question as far as
they are concerned. In fact, of course, it is the middle classes themselves
who make it necessary for the trade unions to support these agents,
because the bourgeoisie refuses to allow them to earn a livelihood in
industry.

The incredible frequency of strikes affords the best proof of the
extent to which the social war now rages in England. Not a week
passes—indeed hardly a day passes—without a strike occurring somewhere. There are numerous causes for these stoppages—reductions
in wages, refusals to raise wages, the employment of non-union
labour, the continued existence of abuses or bad conditions of work,
the introduction of new machinery and a hundred other causes.
Nevertheless, these strikes are often nothing more than skirmishes in
the social war, though sometimes they develop into more serious
clashes. They may be only minor engagements but they prove conclusively that the decisive battle between the proletariat and the bourgeoisie is approaching. These stoppages of work are a training ground
for the industrial proletariat and a preparation for the great campaign
which draws inevitably nearer. Strikes are the manifestoes by which
particular groups of trade unionists pledge their adherence to the cause
of the working classes. The *Northern Star* is the only newspaper
which contains reports of all aspects of the workers' movement.
Anyone who examines all the issues which have appeared in a year
will realise that both urban and rural industrial workers are united in
trade unions and are accustomed from time to time to demonstrate
openly against the tyranny of the middle classes. Trade unionism is an
ideal preparation for social war. It is in these organisations that the
characteristic courage of the Englishman finds its best expression.
Continental observers argue that Englishmen—particularly English
workers—lack the courage to succeed as revolutionaries because
English workmen seem to accept middle-class rule without complaint:
it is said that, unlike the French, they are not always prepared to man

[[1] *First Report* of the Central Board of the Factories Enquiry Commission (1833),
p. 50 and evidence, E4–7. See last paragraph of evidence.]

the barricades at a moment's notice.[1] This opinion is entirely erroneous. The English workers are as courageous as those of any other
country. They are just as discontented as the French, but their methods
of fighting are different. The French workers have politics in their
blood, and so they fight social evils with political weapons. The
English workers hold aloof from politics, which they look upon as a
game played solely in the interests of middle-class groups. Therefore,
instead of fighting against the government, the English workers
strike directly at their middle-class enemies and, for the time being, this
struggle can be waged only by peaceful means and not by violence. In
France commercial depression and the resulting social distress led in
1834 to the armed rising of the Lyons workers in favour of the
Republic. In England, somewhat similar conditions in 1842 led to a
general strike in Manchester in support of the People's Charter and
higher wages. Courage is needed not only by armed rebels but also
by strikers. Indeed, it is obvious that a striker needs greater courage
and a keener and steadier determination than the man at the barricades.
It is no mere trifle for a worker with first-hand experience of poverty to
face hunger and distress with wife and child for months on end and
still remain steadfast in the cause. Death or the galleys face the French
worker who takes part in an armed rising. But what is such a fate
compared with that of the English striker who daily sees his family in
the grip of slow starvation, and who knows that in the long run he
cannot escape the vengeance of the middle classes, who are determined
to crush him under the capitalist yoke? We propose later to give an
example of the obstinate, unconquerable spirit of the English workers,
which only surrenders to superior strength when all further resistance

[1 Compare the opening paragraphs of chapter III (' Manchester Insurrection ')
of Thomas Carlyle's *Past and Present* (1843) pp. 14–15 (Everyman edition, 1912):
   ' Blusterowski, Colacorde, and other Editorial prophets of the Continental-
Democratic Movement, have in their leading-articles shown themselves disposed
to vilipend the late Manchester Insurrection, as evincing in the rioters an extreme
backwardness to battle; nay as betokening, in the English People itself, perhaps a
want of the proper animal courage indispensable in these ages. A million hungry
operative men started up, in utmost paroxysm of desperate protest against their
lot; and, ask Colacorde and company, How many shots were fired? Very few in
comparison! Certain hundreds of drilled soldiers sufficed to suppress this
million-headed hydra, and tread it down, without the smallest appeasement or
hope of such, into its subterranean settlements again, there to reconsider itself.
Compared with our revolts in Lyons, in Warsaw and elsewhere, to say nothing
of incomparable Paris City past or present, what a lamblike Insurrection!
   The present Editor is not here, with his readers, to vindicate the character of
Insurrections; nor does it matter to us whether Blusterowski and the rest may
think the English a courageous people or not courageous. In passing, however,
let us mention that, to our view, this was not an unsuccessful Insurrection; that
as Insurrections go, we have not heard lately of any that succeeded so well.']

is obviously hopeless. The character of the English worker indeed deserves our respect when we see how in such circumstances he bears his sufferings with patient fortitude and determination. The striker's steadfastness is tested a hundred times a day and still he stands firm. Men who are prepared to suffer so much to break the will of a single obstinate factory owner will one day be able to smash the power of the whole bourgeoisie.

[It might be argued that the failure of the Plug Plot riots in Lancashire in 1842 showed that English workers lacked the courage of their convictions]. But it is easy to account for the failure of this strike movement. The conflict was badly timed, for the workers allowed themselves to be provoked by the middle classes into taking premature action. The men were far from clear in their own minds as to why they were on strike. Above all, the workers were not united.

But, apart from failures of this kind, ample evidence exists of the courage of the English workers—particularly when they have clearly defined social objectives in view. The Welsh rising of 1839 is a case in point.[1] I propose to discuss at greater length a strike which culminated in violence in Manchester when I was there in May 1843. Messrs. Pauling and Henfrey decided to increase the size of the bricks made at their works.[2] They naturally proposed to charge more for the new bricks than for the smaller ones but they failed to raise the wages of the men who made them. A wage-claim was rejected by the employers, the men went on strike and the men's trade union supported them by blacklisting the firm. Messrs. Pauling and Henfrey succeeded, though not without great difficulty, in securing blackleg labour from Manchester and district. The strikers threatened with violence those who persisted in working for the firm and then Messrs. Pauling and Henfrey engaged twelve men, all ex-soldiers or former policemen, and armed them with flintlocks for the defence of the brick yard. Having failed to intimidate the blacklegs, the strikers proceeded to sterner measures. At ten o'clock one night a disciplined force of strikers— the front rank armed with blunderbusses—marched on the brickworks, which were only four hundred yards away from an infantry barracks.[3] The strikers pressed on. As soon as they saw the guards, they fired on them, trampled on the wet bricks spread out to dry, scattered the stacks of finished bricks and destroyed everything in their path. Then

[1] For the Newport rising, see David Williams, *John Frost: a study in Chartism* (1939).]

[2] For subsequent labour disputes at this establishment see Engels's postscript of 1846 below, p. 338].

[3] [The brickworks were] at the junction of Cross Lane and Regent Road—see plan of Manchester, facing p. 58.

they broke into the house of the manager, beat up his wife, and destroyed the furniture. Meanwhile the guards were able to fire on the strikers from a safe vantage point which they had taken up behind a hedge. The rioters were now standing around a kiln in which bricks were being fired; they were clearly silhouetted against the fire. Consequently every bullet fired by the guards found its mark, while the return fire of the strikers was wholly ineffective. The firing went on for over half-an-hour until supplies of ammunition ran out. By this time, however, the object of the attack—the demolition of what could be destroyed in the brickyard—had been accomplished. When the military appeared the brickmakers retreated to Eccles, which is three miles from Manchester. Shortly before reaching Eccles, a roll-call was held and each man had to answer to his number. The men thereupon dispersed, but it is not surprising that they immediately fell into the hands of the police who were closing in upon them from all sides. The number of wounded must have been very considerable, but only some of them were arrested. One of them had been hit three times, in the thigh, the calf and the shoulder, and yet had managed to walk for over four miles. Surely it cannot be denied that these strikers showed all the courage needed by revolutionaries and did not flinch from a hail of bullets.[1] The circumstances of the demonstrations of 1842 were quite different. Then unarmed crowds, who had no clear common objective in view, were easily held in check by a handful of dragoons and police in enclosed market places. The forces of law and order had only to block a few roads leading to the markets. These demonstrators were not lacking in courage, for they would have behaved in the same way even had the minions of the bourgeoisie not put in an appearance. When the workers have a clear objective, they show no lack of courage. An example of this was at Birley's mill which eventually had to be protected by the mounting of artillery.[2]

Incidentally it may be worth while saying a word or two here concerning the sanctity of law in England. The middle classes certainly are all in favour of the sanctity of the law. That is not surprising. They have made the law; they approve of it; they are protected by it and they gain advantages from it. The bourgeoisie appreciate that, even although some particular enactment may injure their interests, the whole body of laws protects their interests. The

[1 For the attack on the brickworks, see *Northern Star*, no. 289, May 27th, 1843, p. 5, col. 5: 'Atrocious and Alarming Outrage '.]
[2 For the riot at Birley's mill, see *Northern Star*, no. 248, August 13th, 1842, p. 5, col. 1.]

middle classes know full well how firmly their position in the social order is buttressed by this principle of the sanctity of law—a principle established by an act of will on the part of one section of society and passively accepted by the other section. The middle classes hold fast to the sanctity of law because they believe that the law has been made, like their God, in their own image. That is why the policeman's truncheon, which is really their own weapon, is such a reassuring symbol of authority. But the worker naturally regards the law in quite a different way. He knows from long and bitter experience that the law is a rod which the bourgeoisie has in readiness for him. The worker has no confidence in the law and, if at all possible, he avoids it. It is ridiculous to assert that the English workers are afraid of the police. In Manchester policemen are beaten up every week by the workers, and last year the workers even attempted to storm a police station which was protected by iron doors and shutters. I have already pointed out that the victory of the police in the disturbances caused by the strikes of 1842 was due solely to vacillations of the workers.

Since the workers do not respect the law, but merely submit to it when they are not strong enough to change it, it is natural that they should put forward proposals for new laws. It is natural that they should aim at replacing the law of the middle classes by the law of the working classes. This proposed law of the proletariat is the People's Charter, which is purely political in outward form and calls for a fully democratic House of Commons. Chartism is the expression of a common policy which unites the workers solidly against the middle classes. When workers make common cause in trade unions or when they combine to go on strike to fight the middle classes their opposition is of only a local or piecemeal character. When there were signs that the economic struggle against the bourgeoisie was being fought on a wide front, this could hardly be ascribed to the deliberate intentions of the workers. It was a purely political movement—Chartism—which was mainly responsible for uniting the workers against their oppressors. The whole working class is behind the great Chartist assault on the middle classes—above all against the political and legal fortress which the bourgeoisie has erected to guard its interests. The origins of Chartism are to be found in the 1780s, when a democratic party developed simultaneously with the growth of the proletariat. The French Revolution fostered this democratic movement, particularly in London. After the end of the Napoleonic Wars in 1815 the movement—now known as the 'Radical' party—was strongest in Birmingham and Manchester. The Radicals allied themselves with the Liberal middle classes to break the power of the oligarchy which dominated the unreformed House of Commons and to secure the passing of the Reform Bill. Since then the organization of the Radicals has steadily improved and they have moved to the left to become a working-class party opposed to the middle classes.

In 1838 the London Working Men's Association, under the leadership of William Lovett, drew up the People's Charter.[1] It had six points: (i) Every male adult over the age of 21, being of sound understanding and not convicted of any criminal offence, was to be entitled to a vote. (ii) Parliament was to be elected annually. (iii) Members of Parliament to be paid, so that membership of the House of Commons should be open to the poorest. (iv) Voting for members of Parliament to be by ballot, to prevent bribery and intimidation of the voters by the middle classes. (v) Equal electoral districts, so that each member of Parliament should represent the same number of voters. (vi) Abolition of the—admittedly ineffective—property qualification for candidates for election, who are supposed to possess landed property to the [annual] value of £300.[2] This provision would have qualified every voter to be a candidate.

These six points are all concerned with the constitution of the House of Commons. They may look innocent enough, but if they were granted they would undermine the whole English Constitution, including the position of the Queen and the House of Lords. The so-called monarchical and aristocratic elements of the Constitution can survive only because it is in the interests of the middle classes to maintain the facade of a sham monarchy and aristocracy, neither of which enjoys more than the outward semblance of authority. But as soon as public opinion is solidly behind the House of Commons—as soon as the Commons represent the will of the whole people and not merely of the middle classes—that body will become all-powerful and Queen and Lords will lose even the last trappings of outward authority. The English worker has no respect whatever either for the Queen or the nobility. The middle classes place Queen and peerage on a pinnacle and accord them every honour, but in fact leave them with little effective power. An English Chartist is a republican, though he seldom, if ever, uses the term. He prefers to describe himself as a democrat, although he gives his sympathy to republican parties all over the world. Indeed, he is more than a republican, because the democracy that he supports is not only political [but social and economic as well].

[1 The People's Charter was first published on May 8th, 1838, not in 1835 as stated by Engels.]

[2 According to the Act of 1710 the property qualification of candidates for borough seats was the possession of land bringing in an income of £300 a year and, in the case of county seats, £600 a year.]

Nevertheless it may be observed that, although from its beginnings in 1835[1] Chartism was a working-class movement, it was not sharply differentiated from the Radical movement supported by the lower middle classes. Working-class Radicalism went hand in hand with bourgeois Radicalism. The two groups mingled in their annual National Conventions and both accepted the points of the Charter as their objective. At one time they appeared to form a united party. At that time the lower middle classes were bitterly disappointed over the results of the Reform Bill and they were badly hit by the commercial depression of 1837–9. Consequently they were in a highly bellicose and blustering mood and threw themselves heart and soul into the Chartist movement. Here in Germany no one appreciates the full-blooded vigour of this agitation. The Chartists incited the people to take up arms and rise in revolt. The days of the French Revolution were recalled when the making of pikes became a popular hobby. In 1838 a certain Methodist minister called Stephens, advocated violence at a mass meeting of workers in Manchester:

There is no need for you to fear the power of Government. Do not be afraid of the soldiers, bayonets, and cannon, with which your oppressors threaten you. You have something which is mightier than them all. You possess a weapon against which bayonets and cannon are powerless, and a ten-year-old child can wield this weapon. All you need to do is to take a bundle of straw dipped in pitch and a few matches, and we shall see what Government and its hundreds of thousands of soldiers will be able to do when this weapon is boldly used.[2]

At the same time the characteristic social aspect of the working-class side of the Chartist movement was clearly demonstrated. Thus this same Stephens told a demonstration of 200,000 people at Kersal Moor, the *Mons Sacer* of Manchester[3]:

This question of Universal Suffrage was a knife and fork question after all; this question was a bread and cheese question, notwith-

[1 The origin of Chartism is usually dated in the following year, 1836, which saw the foundation of the London Working Men's Association].

[2] We have seen how the workers are taking this advice to heart. [This footnote was omitted in Mrs. F. K. Wischnewetzky's translation of 1887. This speech of Stephens's has been retranslated from the German. For the Rev. Joseph Rayner Stephens see the *Dictionary of National Biography*. Examples of speeches in which he incited the workers to violence may be found in G. J. Holyoake, *Life of Joseph Rayner Stephens, preacher and political orator* (1881), chap. VII, pp. 112–131 and *Wigan Gazette*, Nov. 16th, 1838. For the technique of torchlight processions at this time see R. G. Gammage, *The History of the Chartist Movement* . . . , Part I (1854), pp. 103–8.]

[3 Two references to Kersal Moor as the 'Mons Sacer' of Manchester had already been made in Croker's article on the Anti-Corn Law agitation in the *Quarterly Review* of December, 1842, Vol. 71, no. clxi, pp. 268, 275.]

standing all that had been said against it, and if any man asked him what he meant by Universal Suffrage, he would answer that every working man in the land had a right to have a good coat to his back, a comfortable abode in which to shelter himself and his family, a good dinner upon his table and no more work than was necessary for keeping him in health, and as much wages for that work as would keep him in plenty, and afford him the enjoyment of all the blessings of life which a reasonable man could desire (*Tremendous cheers*).[1]

Two other popular agitations, which were very closely associated with Chartism, were those against the new Poor Law and in favour of the Ten Hours Bill. The Tory, Oastler, was very active at public demonstrations at this time. The national petition in favour of the People's Charter was adopted at Birmingham, but there were also hundreds of other petitions demanding various social reforms for the benefit of the workers. The agitations were as active in 1839 as they had been in the previous year. Towards the end of 1839, however, the enthusiasm of the workers appeared to be waning. Thereupon Bussey, Taylor and Frost[2] planned simultaneous risings in the North of England, in Yorkshire and in Wales. Frost's plans were betrayed, his rising broke out prematurely, and it was easily suppressed. The Northern plotters heard the news of Frost's failure in time to cancel their plans. Two months later, in January 1840, several so-called ' spy-outbreaks ' took place in Sheffield, Bradford and elsewhere in Yorkshire,[3] and after that the unrest gradually subsided.

Meanwhile the attention of the middle classes was diverted to a more practical and more advantageous plan.[4] This was the repeal of

[1 *Northern Star*, no. 46, Sept. 29th, 1838, p. 6—meeting at Kersal Moor, on Monday, Sept. 24th. Engels gives only a very abbreviated version of this well-known passage in the speech. For the significance of the meeting at which this speech was made, see M. Hovell, *The Chartist Movement* (1918), pp. 118–119.]

[2 For Peter Bussey, Dr. John Taylor and the events of 1839 see Mark Hovell, *The Chartist Movement* (1918), chap. XI: ' Sedition, Privy Conspiracy and Rebellion (1839–1840)'; for John Frost, see *supra* p. 256, *n*. 1]

[3 For these minor outbreaks see Hovell, op. cit., pp. 186–7. By using the English words ' spy-outbreaks ' Engels appears to imply that they were fomented by *agents provocateurs*.]

[4 Engels's account of the origins and course of the Plug Plot riots of 1842 is undoubtedly based upon that given in an article on the Anti-Corn Law agitation in the *Quarterly Review* of December 1842 (Vol. 71, no. cxli, pp. 244–314). It was written by a rabid Tory, J. W. Croker, and made a vicious and unscrupulous attack upon the League. For Croker's authorship of this article, see *The Correspondence and Diaries of the late Rt. Hon. John Wilson Croker* . . . (ed. L. J. Jennings), Vol. 2 (1884), pp. 388–93 and M. F. Brightfield, *John Wilson Croker* (1940), pp. 433, 453, 458. Engels was not, as Halévy stated, ' an eye witness ' of the riots (E. Halévy, *The Age of Peel and Cobden: a History of the English People, 1841–1852* (1947), p. 22, fn. 1). Croker was supplied with material for the article by the Home Secretary, Sir James Graham, and the Prime Minister, Sir Robert Peel, himself read the proofs.]

the Corn Laws. The Anti-Corn Law Association was founded in Manchester and this resulted in a loosening of the bonds which linked the Radical elements in the bourgeoisie with the proletariat. The workers soon realised that they would gain little from the repeal of the Corn Laws, which would, however, be very beneficial to the middle classes. In the circumstances the working classes were not prepared to support the agitation for Corn Law repeal. In 1842, when there was much economic distress and social unrest, the agitation in favour of Corn Law repeal revived and was as vigorous as it had been in 1839. On this occasion it was the wealthy members of the middle classes engaged in industry who supported the movement, because they had been particularly hard hit by the commercial crisis.[1] The Anti-Corn Law League—a federation of societies which had developed from the original association founded by the Manchester manu-facturers[2]—now adopted a decidedly Radical and bellicose attitude. The journals and agitators of the League became frankly revolutionary in tone. This change in the attitude of the leaders of the League may be attributed to the fact that [Peel's] Conservative Government had been in power since 1841.[3] The League incited the workers to revolt in much the same way as the Chartists had done a few years before. Meanwhile the workers themselves were by no means inactive, for after all they had suffered most from the depression of 1842. This is shown by the fact that in 1842 the Chartists drew up a national petition which secured three and a half million signatures. Although the working-class and bourgeois wings of the Radical party had become somewhat estranged, circumstances nevertheless brought them together again in 1842. On February 14th[4] of that year a meeting of Liberals and Chartists was held in Manchester and agreement was reached on the terms of a petition which demanded not only the repeal of the Corn Laws but also the adoption of the Charter. On the following day both parties endorsed this decision and approved the petition. In the spring and summer of 1842 there was much unrest and distress. The middle classes were determined to push through Corn Law repeal while conditions remained favourable—business depression, social misery and widespread unrest. Since the Tories were now in office, the middle classes on this occasion actually deviated

[1 *Quarterly Review*, Dec. 1842, p. 270.]
[2 The Anti-Corn Law League had been founded as far back as 1839.]
[3 *Quarterly Review*, Dec. 1842, pp. 254–58.]
[4 Engels wrote February 15th, but see *Northern Star*, No. 223, February 19th, 1842, p. 3, col. 2, on 'The Chartists and the League'. The writer of the *Quarterly Review* article also gave February 15th as the date of this meeting (Dec. 1842, p. 270).]

for a time from their normal respect for the sanctity of the law. They wanted to gain their ends by revolutionary means and they wanted the support of the working classes for their policy. The workers were to pull the chestnuts out of the fire and burn their fingers for the benefit of the middle classes. Already in many quarters there was a revival of the plan already put forward by the Chartists in 1839. This project was called a 'Sacred Month' and there was to be a general strike during that period. But in 1842 it was not the workers who wanted to go on strike. It was the manufacturers who wanted to close their factories and lock out their workers, in the hope that unemployed men would leave the towns and swarm into the countryside over the estates of the landed aristocracy.[1] In this way the factory owners hoped to force the Government and the Tory Parliament to repeal the Corn Laws. If this plan had been put into operation it would, of course, have culminated in a workers' rising. But the middle classes kept themselves safely in the background and could await the success of their schemes. If the worst came to the worst, the middle classes would not themselves be compromised. In July [1842] business began to improve. It was now or never [for the middle-class plot]. Although *trade was actually getting better*[2] three Stalybridge firms proposed to reduce their employees' wages. I would not care to say whether they did this on their own initiative, or whether they had an understanding with other manufacturers, particularly the members of the Anti-Corn Law League. Two of the Stalybridge firms soon gave up the idea of cutting wages, but William Bayley and Brothers stood fast by their decision. When their workers complained to them they replied that if they were not satisfied with the firm's offer, 'You had, perhaps, better go and play for a few days'.[3] The remark was no more than a piece of sarcasm, but the men took their employers at their word. The men left the factory cheering loudly and marched through Stalybridge, calling upon workers in other mills to join them. In a few hours every mill in the town stood idle and the workers had marched off in procession to Mottram Moor for a meeting. This was on August 5th. Five thousand of the men marched from Stalybridge to Ashton and Hyde on August 8th. This led to the closure of all the factories and collieries in the immediate neighbourhood.[4] At their meetings the men did not demand the repeal of the Corn Laws, as the middle classes

[1 *Quarterly Review*, Dec. 1842, pp. 258, 271.]
2 See the trade reports from Manchester and Leeds from the end of July to the beginning of August [1842]. [The *Quarterly Review*, Dec. 1842 (pp. 185–6) published reports from the *Manchester Guardian* and *Leeds Mercury* of July and August 1842 to the effect that trade was reviving in the Northern textile districts.]
[3 *Quarterly Review*, Dec. 1842, pp. 291–2.]   [4 Ibid., Dec. 1842, p. 293.]

had hoped. They demanded ' a fair day's wages for a fair day's work '.[1] On August 9th they marched to Manchester. Here, the municipal authorities, who were all Liberals, allowed the demonstrators to enter the town, and on their arrival all the factories closed down. The first occasion upon which the demonstrators were resisted was on August 11th, when they had reached Stockport, and this was because they attacked the workhouse, the favourite child of the English middle classes.[2] On the same day there was a general strike in Bolton, coupled with much unrest, but here again the authorities refrained from checking these demonstrations[3]; soon the rising had spread to all the industrial districts, and everybody was on strike with the exception of those who were getting the harvest in or engaged in handling foodstuffs. The angry strikers showed very great self-control. They had been manoeuvred into this situation against their better judgment. With one exception—[Hugh Hornby] Birley, the Manchester Tory—the employers had offered no resistance to the strike, and this was absolutely contrary to their normal practice.[4] When the whole business started the workers had no definite objective in mind,[5] but they were at least united on one point. They were all determined not to be shot down to oblige their Anti-Corn Law League employers.[6] Some of them hoped to gain the People's Charter, others thought that it was premature to hope for the Charter and would have been satisfied with a return to the wage-rates of 1840.[7] This was why the rising collapsed completely: had it been a deliberate and carefully thought-out workers' insurrection from the beginning it would probably have succeeded. In fact, masses of workers were turned loose on the streets by their employees whether they liked it or not. They had no definite objective in view, and so could achieve nothing. Meanwhile the middle classes had not moved a finger to implement the alliance of February 14th, 1842.[8] The bourgeoisie soon realised that it was not possible to use the workers as catspaws; the middle classes realised that they themselves had endangered their own position by departing from their normal rôle as guardians of law and order. So they promptly became once more staunch upholders of the prin-

---

[1 Ibid., Dec. 1842, p. 293. The Rev. J. R. Stephens had used this phrase in a speech at Norwich as early as November 1838: *Northern Star*, Nov. 10th, 1838.]
[2 *Quarterly Review*, Dec. 1842, pp. 301-3.]
[3 Ibid., Dec. 1842, p. 300.]
[4 *Quarterly Review*, Dec. 1842, p. 295. For a recent account of this incident see G. Kitson Clark, ' Hunger and Politics in 1842 ': *Journal of Modern History*, Vol. 25, no. 4, Dec. 1953, pp. 362-3.]
[5 *Quarterly Review*, Dec. 1842, pp. 293-4.]
[6 Ibid., Dec. 1842, pp. 297-8.]
[7 Ibid., Dec. 1842, p. 294.]   [8 See above, p. 262 and footnote 4.]

ciple of the sanctity of the law. They now allied themselves with the Government against the workers, whom they had first stirred up and then let loose upon the streets. They themselves, together with their trusty henchmen, were sworn in as special constables. Even the German merchants of Manchester wasted their time by parading through the town as special constables, smoking cigars and carrying staves. In Preston the special constables fired on the crowd. Suddenly the aimless insurgents found themselves opposed not only by Government troops but also by all the resources that the capitalists could summon to their aid. The workers, who in any case had no common objective in view, gradually dispersed, and the insurrection petered out without serious consequences. Afterwards the middle classes disgraced themselves by committing one shameful act after another; they tried to whitewash their own conduct by pretending to be horrified by this most recent example of popular violence. Such an attitude was hardly consistent with their own inflammatory language of the previous spring. Now the middle classes blamed the rising on Chartist ' agitators ', although actually they themselves were far more to blame for the outbreak than the Chartists. Once more the middle classes came forward as champions of the sanctity of the law. The brazen effrontery of this attitude was surely unique. We have seen that the Chartists had played a very minor part in the outbreak, for they did no more than to make the most of the opportunities afforded by the situation. The middle classes themselves would have been only too glad to do the same thing. But it was the Chartists who were brought to trial and punished, while the middle classes came to no harm and actually took advantage of the stoppage of work to dispose of their stocks at a good profit.[1]

The failure of this rising led to a complete split between the working classes and the bourgeoisie. Hitherto the Chartists had made little attempt to hide the fact that they were prepared to try all means, not excluding revolutionary methods, to gain their ends. The middle classes had by now realised the danger to their own position of any violent upheaval, and so were opposed to the use of ' physical force '. They were prepared to secure their ends only by the use of moral force—as if this were anything else but a threat eventually to resort to physical force in one form or another. [At this time two fundamental issues divided the Chartists from the middle classes]. One concerned the respective merits of physical force and moral force. But this difference of opinion was subsequently resolved when the Chartists asserted that they also were firmly opposed to the use of physical force

[1 *Quarterly Review*, Dec. 1842, pp. 304-5.]

—and the Chartists are quite as worthy of credence as the Liberal middle classes. The second—and more important—point at issue between the Chartists and the middle classes was the question of the repeal of the Corn Laws, and here the shining integrity of the Chartist movement was fully in evidence. The Radical middle classes had a direct interest in Corn Law repeal, but the working classes had not. So the Chartists split into two groups. Although on paper their political programmes might appear to be identical, these rival sections of the movement in fact pursued different and irreconcilable objectives.

When a National Convention was held at Birmingham in [December 1842 and] January 1843, Sturge, the representative of the Radical middle classes, suggested that the word ' Charter ' be dropped from the rules of the Association. The reason he advanced for making this proposal was that owing to the popular rising in the previous year the word ' Charter ' had now acquired a sinister and revolutionary significance. We might add that the name ' Charter ' had, in fact, had such a significance for some years without Mr. Sturge having found it necessary to say anything about it. The workers refused to drop the name ' Chartist ' and Sturge was outvoted. The worthy Quaker thereupon suddenly rediscovered his long-lost loyalty and led a minority of the Radical middle classes from the hall to found a Complete Suffrage Union.[1] The middle classes, who had so recently been tainted with Jacobinism, were now so anxious to forget their former policy that they actually dropped the use of the familiar phrase ' Universal Suffrage ' in favour of the ridiculous term ' Complete Suffrage '. The workers hooted with derision and quietly went their own way.

From this moment Chartism became a purely working-class movement, and was free from all the trammels of bourgeois influence. The periodicals which supported Sturge's [Complete Suffrage] Union—the *Weekly Dispatch*, the *Weekly Chronicle*, the *Examiner* etc.—gradually lapsed into that somnolence which is typical of all the other Liberal newspapers. They had less and less to say about Radicalism; they espoused Free Trade, attacked the Ten Hours Bill and all other reforms which would have benefited the working classes. The Radical bourgeoisie made common cause with the Liberals in attacking the Chartists. The main plank in their platform was now Corn Law repeal, which for Englishmen is the issue of free competition. And so the Radical section of the middle class fell under the domination of the Liberals, and now plays a very miserable rôle indeed on the political scene.

[1 See Mark Hovell, op. cit., pp. 264–5.]

On the other hand, the Chartist workers resumed the fight of the lower classes against the middle class in all its aspects. They detested free competition which had brought so much misery to the proletariat, and the Chartists were therefore the declared enemies of the bourgeoisie, who stood for this abominable principle. Should no limit whatever be set to the freedom of competition, the position of the workers would be worse than ever. The reforms hitherto demanded by the workers had included the Ten Hours Bill, protection of workers against capitalists, a fair wage, security of employment, and the repeal of the new Poor Law. All these proposals are in direct opposition to free competition and free trade, and they are all just as much a part of Chartism as the ' Six Points '. It is therefore not surprising that the workers have no use for free competition, Free Trade or Corn Law repeal. They are completely indifferent to the fate of the Corn Laws, but detest wholeheartedly the supporters of Repeal. The middle classes, to a man, are quite incapable of appreciating the workers' attitude to these questions. The Corn Law issue is fundamental. It divides the proletariat from the bourgeoisie and the Chartists from the Radicals. The middle class world cannot grasp the significance of this, because the middle classes are incapable of understanding the working classes.

Herein lies the difference between Chartist democracy and all former brands of bourgeois political democracy. *Chartism is essentially a social movement.*[1] The middle-class Radicals had regarded the ' Six Points ' of the Charter as the be-all and end-all of the movement, but the working classes consider that the ' Six Points ' and any further constitutional reforms to which they might give rise, are only a means to an end. Nowadays the rallying cry of the Chartists is: ' Political power brings social happiness '. The ' knife and fork question ' to which the Reverend [J. R.] Stephens referred in 1838 was in those days accepted by only a section of the Chartists as the aim of their movement. By 1845 it had become the slogan of the entire movement. Not one of the Chartists to-day is content to agitate solely for the political objectives of the ' Six Points '. It is true that the form of Socialism professed by the Chartists is not a very highly developed one. It is true that the main Chartist remedy for distress is the introduction of smallholdings[2]—an anachronism since small-

[1 At this point Mrs. F. K. Wischnewetzky added the words ' a class movement ', for which there is no authority in the original German edition of 1845. But Engels approved the English translation of 1887.]

[2 Engels uses the words ' allotment system ' in English in the first German edition of 1845. It is now generally called the system of smallholdings. For O'Connor's land scheme, to which this is a reference, see Mark Hovell, op. cit., pp. 267–84.]

holdings disappeared with the rise of modern industry.[1] It is true that most of the Chartists' practical proposals, such as the demand for 'the protection of the worker',[2] might at first sight appear to be an attempt to return to the conditions of an age which has passed away. Nevertheless, these proposals of the Chartists are not so impractical as they might appear on the surface. They do at least clarify the issue which faces the English working classes. The proletariat must either give up the fight against the power of competition and fall back into its former servitude or the workers must themselves utterly destroy the competition system. Again, it will be appreciated that at the moment Chartism is in a state of flux. Chartism has shaken off those supporters who regarded it as a purely political movement. The result is that to-day the significant feature of Chartism lies in its social aims. And it is this aspect of Chartism which must inevitably develop in the future. It cannot be long before Chartism moves towards Socialism. This is particularly likely to happen during the next commercial crisis in England. In view of the present prosperity of manufacturers and commerce the latest date at which this crisis may be expected is the year 1847.[3] Indeed it will probably strike the economy next year [1846]. The magnitude and fury of this crisis will be far greater than that of any former business depression. When it comes the workers will suffer so severely that they are certain to demand radical social remedies rather than purely political measures and it is a foregone conclusion that the workers will then get their Charter.[4] But at the moment the workers are by no means clear in their own minds as to what they can achieve once the Charter has been accepted, and it will be absolutely necessary for them to devote a great deal of thought to this matter, so that they will know to what use to put political power when they achieve it. Meanwhile the Socialist agitation is making progress. In this connection we are concerned with English Socialism only in so far as it influences the workers. The English Socialists demand the gradual introduction of ' home colonies of united interests '[5] of between 2,000 and 3,000 people. These

[1] At this point Engels refers readers to his introduction, *supra*, p. 9.

[2] The meaning of this vague phrase is not clear. It might refer to the protection of craftsmen such as the handloom weavers who were waging a losing battle against machines.]

[3] In the German edition of 1892 Engels added the triumphant footnote: 'Arrived punctually '.]

[4] Engels made no comment on the non-fulfilment of this prophecy in later editions of his book.]

[5] See, for example, the use of this phrase in the original rules of the Rochdale Pioneers Society of 1844, printed by Bland, Brown and Tawney, *English Economic History: Select Documents* (1914), p. 643.]

communities will be engaged in both industry and agriculture. The members enjoy equal rights and [their children are to receive] the same education. Other objects of the Socialists include easier divorce, and the introduction of an enlightened system of government, with complete freedom of opinion. Punishments are to be abolished and are to be replaced by more intelligent treatment of criminals. These are the practical proposals of the Socialists. We are not concerned for the moment with the theoretical principles of English Socialism. Robert Owen was the founder of Socialism.[1] He was a millowner himself and, although his theories developed from an appreciation of the antagonism between the middle classes and the workers, nevertheless his practical proposals unduly favoured the bourgeoisie and were often less than just to the proletariat. The Socialists are mild-mannered and entirely law-abiding. They accept existing conditions, however bad they may be, and refuse to countenance any other method of reform save that of the peaceful persuasion of public opinion. In fact, however, the public will never be convinced by the Socialist arguments, which are at present presented in far too abstract a form. At the same time the English Socialists are constantly bewailing the demoralisation of the lower orders. But they fail to recognise that this dissolution of the social order is in fact a sign of progress. They cannot see that the demoralisation of private interests and the hypocrisy of the capitalist classes are far worse than any failings that the workers may possess. They do not appreciate the significance of historical development. They want to realise the Communist ideal immediately and do not grasp the fact that the transition to this state of society can be achieved only by the pursuit of a definite policy culminating in the dissolution of the existing social order. It is true that they do understand why the working classes are the sworn enemies of the middle classes. Yet although this enmity is the only means by which the workers can further their aims, the modern English Socialists preach the much less effective doctrine of philanthropy and universal love. The Socialists understand only the psychological development of man and are concerned with the improvement of humanity in the abstract. This abstract approach to the problem takes no account of the extent to which modern man has been moulded by the past. In fact the whole world and, indeed, all individuals in it are the product of historical circumstances. The English Socialists are consequently too intellectual and too metaphysical, with the result that their practical achievements have been negligible. They have secured some support

[1 For Robert Owen see F. Podmore, *The Life of Robert Owen* (2 vols., 1906) and Margaret Cole, *Robert Owen of New Lanark* (1954).]

from the working classes, but only a small minority of the proletariat is imbued with the Socialist creed. But it must be admitted that this tiny minority includes those workers with the best education and the firmest characters. In its present form Socialism in England will never be a rallying cry for the workers. The Socialists will have to come down to earth, if only for a short time, and support the Charter as a practical objective. On the other hand, genuine working-class Socialists, who have played their part in a Chartist movement purged of its middle-class elements, will before long play an important role in the political development of the English people. There are already many such working-class Socialists, some of whom entered the movement through Chartism.[1] English Socialism rests on a firmer foundation than French Socialism. On the other hand French Socialism has made greater progress than English Socialism. English Socialists will have to learn something from the example of their French comrades, so that they can ultimately make further progress themselves. Meanwhile it is not to be expected that the French Socialists will be standing still.

It may be added that the lack of religious belief among the proletariat is most clearly seen in the Socialist doctrines. This is all the more significant when we consider that although English workers reject religion in practice without much conscious thought, they nevertheless recoil from an open admission of their lack of faith. Once more it may be expected that hard necessity will force the workers to give up their religious beliefs. They will come more and more to realise that these beliefs serve only to weaken the proletariat and to keep them obedient and faithful to the capitalist vampires.

We have seen that the Chartists and the Socialists are the two main groups into which the working-class movement is divided. The Chartists are genuine members of the working class, true representatives of the proletariat; but their policy is far less mature than that of the Socialists. The Socialists, on the other hand, are more far-sighted, and have put forward practical proposals to relieve working-class distress. Unfortunately, when their movement started the Socialists were not in a position to join forces with the proletariat because of their middle-class origin. The next step will be to unite Socialism and Chartism, and give an English dress to the principles of French Communism. This process has indeed already begun. Only when it is finally accomplished will the working classes really rule England. While this is happening it may be expected that the growth

[1] Engels added a footnote to German edition of 1892: ' Socialists, of course, in the general sense of the term and not in the Owenite sense.'

and evolution of the Chartist movement will be favoured by political and social changes [that can be confidently anticipated].

We have examined three aspects of the working-class movement —trade unionism, Chartism and Socialism. These three movements differ in character to a great extent, though there is a not inconsiderable overlap in their membership. They have, of course, frequently differed on points of policy. All three have from their own resources established schools and reading rooms to provide educational facilities for their members. Nearly all the Socialist and Chartist groups maintain such educational centres. Many local trade union branches and working men's clubs provide similar facilities. Here the children receive a genuine proletarian education, free from middle-class influences, while the reading rooms contain very few books or newspapers except those devoted to the interests of the working classes. The middle classes naturally regard these institutions with great alarm and they have succeeded in withdrawing some of them from the influence of the workers and turning them into new centres called Mechanics Institutes. These new institutes are organs of the middle classes and their purpose is to encourage the study of those branches of ' useful knowledge ' which it is to the advantage of the bourgeoisie that the workers should possess.[1] The Mechanics Institutes provide classes in those fields of scientific study which are thought likely to wean the workers from their opposition to the middle classes. The middle classes hope also that by fostering such studies they will stimulate the inventive powers of the workers to the eventual profit of the bourgeoisie. At the moment the workers are not interested in the natural sciences. Since they live in great cities and work for very long hours they have little opportunity of obtaining any first-hand knowledge of nature at all. Mechanics Institutes also offer classes in that brand of political economy which takes free competition as its God. The teachers of this subject preach the doctrine that it does not lie within the power of the workers to change the existing economic order. The proletariat is told that they must resign themselves to starving without making a fuss. In the Mechanics Institutes the teaching is uninspired and flabby. The students are taught to be subservient to the existing political and social order. All that the worker hears in these schools is one long sermon on respectful and passive obedience in the station in life to which he has been called.

Of course the vast majority of the workers will have nothing to do with these institutes and patronise working-class reading rooms where they can join groups which can discuss matters which really affect

[1 For an instance of this, in 1843–45, see W. H. Chaloner, *The Social and Economic Development of Crewe*, 1780–1923, 1950, pp. 234–5.]

their own interests. The smug middle classes thereupon intone ' Dixi
et salvavi '[1] and contemptuously turn their backs upon workers who
actually ' prefer the impassioned harangues of wicked demagogues to
the advantages of a sound education.' There can be no doubt that the
workers are interested in acquiring a sound education, provided that
it is not tainted by the ' wisdom ' spread by prejudiced middle-class
teachers. This is proved by the popularity of lectures on economics
and on scientific and aesthetic topics which are frequently held at
working-class institutes, particularly those run by Socialists. I have
sometimes come across workers, with their fustian jackets falling
apart, who are better informed on geology, astronomy and other
matters, than many an educated member of the middle classes in
Germany. No better evidence of the extent to which the English
workers have succeeded in educating themselves can be brought forward
than the fact that the most important modern works in philosophy,
poetry and politics are in practice read only by the proletariat. The
middle classes, enslaved by the influences generated by their environment, are blinded by prejudice. They are horror-stricken at the very
idea of reading anything of a really progressive nature. The working
classes, on the other hand, have no such stupid inhibitions and devour
such works with pleasure and profit. In this connection the Socialists
have a wonderful record of achievement, for they have promoted the
education of the workers by translating the works of such great
French materialist philosophers as Helvetius, Holbach and Diderot.
These books, as well as many standard English books have been widely
circulated among the workers in cheap editions.[2] [D. F.] Strauss's
Life of Jesus[3] and [P.–J.] Proudhon's book on *Property*[4] are also read in

[1 The full phrase is: *Dixi et salvavi animam meam* = I have spoken and saved my
soul.]

[2 The file of Robert Owen's periodical *The New Moral World* contains advertisements for popular editions of Shelley's *Queen Mab* and translations of Rousseau's
Social Contract and of Holbach's *System of Nature.*]

[3 In an article entitled ' Die Lage Englands '—a review of Thomas Carlyle's
Past and Present which originally appeared in the *Deutsch-Französische Jahrbücher* (ed.
by Karl Marx and Arnold Ruge, Paris, 1844, Parts I and II, pp. 86–114 and pp.
181–182), reprinted in *Gesamtausgabe . . . ,* Part I, Vol. 2 (1930), pp. 405–431—Engels
stated that when Strauss's book on Jesus appeared no ' respectable ' person in
England would translate it and no ' respectable ' bookseller would sell it. But a
' Socialist lecturer ' made a translation which was issued in parts which were sold
at a penny each. And so ' it was the workers of Manchester, Birmingham and
London who were Strauss's only readers in England ': *Gesamtausgabe,* Part I,
Vol. 2: F. Engels, *Werke und Schriften bis Anfang 1844 nebst Briefen und Dokumenten*
(Marx-Engels-Lenin Institute, 1930), pp. 407–8. The ' Socialist lecturer ' was
Henry Hetherington (1792–1849) who apparently used Littré's French translation
of 1839. The first authorized translation of Strauss's book—by Mary Ann Evans
(' George Eliot ')—appeared in 1846, in three volumes.]

[4 Proudhon's well-known work *Qu'est-ce la Propriété?* (1840) was not translated
into English until 1876.]

England only by the workers. Again it is the workers who are most familiar with the poetry of Shelley and Byron. Shelley's prophetic genius has caught their imagination, while Byron attracts their sympathy by his sensuous fire and by the virulence of his satire against the existing social order. The middle classes, on the other hand, have on their shelves only ruthlessly expurgated 'family' editions of these writers. These editions have been prepared to suit the hypocritical moral standards of the bourgeoisie.

Bentham and Godwin—particularly the latter—are the two great practical philosophers of recent times, and both are virtually studied only by the workers. It is true that Bentham has a school of followers among the middle-class Radicals, but only enlightened working-class students and Socialists have been able to evolve a progressive doctrine from his writings. Such are the foundations upon which the English working classes are building up their own literature. It is to be found mainly in periodicals and pamphlets, and it is far superior in content to the whole body of middle-class literature. We shall discuss this matter again later.

Finally, it may be observed that it is the factory workers, particularly in the Lancashire cotton districts, who form the solid core of the working-class movement. Manchester is the headquarters of the most powerful trade unions, the focal point of Chartism, and the stronghold of the Socialist movement. As one branch of handicraft industry after another is transformed by the factory system, so more and more workers flock into the various working-class movements. The wider the gulf which separates workers from capitalists, the more openly class-conscious does the proletariat become. The small independent master craftsmen of Birmingham, although they suffer, in company with the workers, from recurrent trade depressions, are poised uneasily between the Chartism of the proletariat and the Radicalism of the petty shopkeepers. In general, however, all the industrial workers support one or other of the three main working-class movements, and so are ranged against the capitalists and the bourgeoisie. They are all proud to call themselves 'working men',[1] which is the usual opening form of address in the speeches at Chartist meetings. The workers are conscious of the fact that they form a separate class, and have their own interests, policies, and points of view, which are opposed to those of the capitalist property owners. Above all they are conscious of the fact that on their shoulders rests the real power of the nation and the hope of its future progress.

[¹ In English in the original.]

CHAPTER X

THE MINERS

A very large labour force is naturally required to produce the raw materials and the fuel required by the vast operations of British industry. The only raw materials which Britain herself produces are metallic ores and coal. Wool can be left on one side, as it is an agricultural product. Rich deposits of copper, tin, zinc and lead ore are found in Cornwall. Iron ore is to be found in large quantities in Staffordshire, North Wales and elsewhere. Supplies of coal which are more than ample for the country's needs are found nearly everywhere in Northern and Western England, in central Scotland, and in a few places in Ireland.[1]

Mining in Cornwall is partly underground and partly open-cast. Here 19,000 men and 11,000 women and children are employed. In the mines themselves the labour force is composed practically entirely of men and boys over the age of 12. According to the report of the Children's Employment Commission (1841–3) the condition of these workers appears to be reasonably satisfactory.[2] Indeed, Englishmen are fond of referring with pride to the strong and daring Cornish

[1] According to the Census of 1841 the number of persons employed in or around mines in Great Britain (excluding Ireland) was as follows:

Description	Men over 20 years of age	Men under 20 years of age	Women over 20 years of age	Women under 20 years of age	Total
1. Coal Mines ...	83,408	32,475	1,185	1,165	118,233
2. Copper Mines ...	9,866	3,428	913	1,200	15,407
3. Lead Mines ...	9,427	1,932	20	20	11,419
4. Iron ore Mines ...	7,773	2,679	424	73	10,949
5. Tin Mines ...	4,602	1,349	68	82	6,101
6. Miscellaneous ...	24,162	6,591	472	491	31,716
Total ...	139,238	48,454	3,102	3,031	193,825

Since coal mines and iron works are often under joint management some of the coal miners listed in the above table [under description 1] should also be included as workers in the iron industry. A substantial part of the 'unspecified' [category 6] miners were also employed in ironworks. [G. R. Porter, *The Progress of the Nation* (edn. 1851), p. 79.]

[2 Children's Employment Commission, *1st Report*: *Mines* (1842), section III, 'Tin, Copper, Lead and Zinc Mines . . .', pp. 203–55.]

miners who are not afraid to seek out new veins of ore even under the sea bed. But the Children's Employment Commission's report does not in fact support this boast, and gives a different picture of the physical condition of these workers. Dr. Charles Barham's[1] excellent report shows that those employed in the [Cornish] mines suffer from serious diseases of the lungs, heart and digestive organs. These illnesses are caused by inhaling air deficient in oxygen and impregnated with particles of dust and smoke from the gunpowder used in blasting operations. Dr. Barham draws attention to the evil consequences which follow from the performance of feats which overtax the physical strength of the workers. This is due in particular to the fact that miners have to climb up and down long ladders in the mine shafts.[2] In some mines it takes even strong young men over an hour a day, both before and after their work, to ascend or descend the ladders. Consequently those male underground workers who enter the mines at an early age are much inferior in physique to the female labourers who work at the surface. Many of the men die young, of galloping consumption, and those who survive to middle age succumb to slow consumption. Many miners become unfit to continue at work between the ages of 35 and 45.[3] It is quite common for them to contract a fatal illness through coming suddenly into the cold air at the top of the shaft after working in the stuffy atmosphere below and perspiring heavily owing to the exertion of climbing the ladders. Under these conditions a severe bronchial cold will prove fatal to a miner whose respiratory organs have already been weakened by the nature of his work.[4] The tasks at the top of the mineshafts—the breaking up and sorting of the ore—are performed by women and children and are said to be very healthy because the work is carried on in the open air.

The important lead mines of Alston Moor[5] are to be found in the North of England on the boundary between the counties of Northumberland and Durham. Dr. Mitchell, who reported on this district for the Children's Employment Commission, gives a description of conditions very similar to those in Cornwall.[6] Here, too, there are complaints of lack of oxygen, excessive dust, the fumes of gunpowder,

[[1] Children's Employment Commission, *Appendix to 1st Report*: Mines, pp. 731–820; evidence, pp. 821–54.]

[[2] Ibid., p. 780, para. 164.]   [[3] Ibid., p. 795, para. 226.]

[[4] Ibid., p. 796, para. 229.]

[[5] For these mines, see Dr. A. Raistrick, *Two Centuries of Industrial Welfare: the London (Quaker) Lead Company*, 1692–1905 (1938). Dr. Raistrick does not appear to have used the evidence collected by the Children's Employment Commission, and his book is based mainly on the manuscript records of the Company.]

[[6] Children's Employment Commission, *Appendix to 1st Report*: Mines, Part II (1843), pp. 721–86.]

choke-damp and sulphureous gases in the mine galleries. The result is that, as in Cornwall, these miners have a stunted physique and nearly all of them suffer from diseases of the chest from the age of 30 onwards. If, as nearly always happens, they go on working, their illness develops into acute consumption. This naturally reduces the average expectation of life of these miners. The fact that the Alston miners sometimes live longer than the Cornish miners may be explained by the fact that they do not go underground until the age of 19. In Cornwall, on the other hand, as already noted, they go underground from the age of 12. Yet even in the district of Alston Moor, according to medical reports, the majority of the miners die between the ages of 40 and 50. Of 79 miners whose deaths were registered in the district [between July 1st, 1837, and June 30th, 1841] 37 died of consumption and 6 of asthma. The average age at death was 45.[1] The average expectation of life in neighbouring towns and villages (Allendale, Stanhope, and Middleton) is 49, 49 and 47 years respectively, while deaths from chest complaints were 48 per cent, 54 per cent and 56 per cent respectively of all deaths.[2] It must be remembered that all these figures apply to miners who only began work underground at the age of 19.[3] Let us compare these figures with the so-called 'Swedish Tables'—detailed mortality tables covering the whole Swedish population[4]—which have hitherto been regarded in England as giving the closest approximation to the mortality rates for English workers. According to these tables men reaching the age of 19 can, on the

[1 Children's Employment Commission, *Appendix to 1st Report*: *Mines*, Part II, (1843), p. 751. Dr. Mitchell observed that 4 of these 79 persons, although women, were under the age of 19 and were probably not working in the mines regularly. See also footnote, below.]

[2 The information may be tabulated as follows:

July 1st, 1837, to June 30th, 1841

	Total deaths of miners over 19 years of age	Average age at death	Deaths from consumption and asthma	Percentage of deaths from asthma and consumption
Allendale (Northumberland) ...	79	48	38	48%
Stanhope (Weardale) ...	129	49	70	54%
Middleton (Teesdale) ...	57	47	32	56%

(Ibid., pp. 751-2.)]

[3 This sentence was omitted by Mrs. F. K. Wischnewetzky from the English translation of 1887.]

[4 For the Swedish tables, see Joshua Milne, *A Treatise on the Valuation of Annuities and Assurances on Lives and Survivorships* ..., 2 vols. (1815) and James Bonar, *Malthus and his Work* (1885), p. 72.]

average, expect to live to the age of 57½. Consequently, owing to the nature of their work the [lead] miners are robbed on the average of ten years of their lives. It must be emphasised that the Swedish tables are considered to be an accurate forecast of the expectation of life [not of the English population as a whole] but *only of the English working classes*. We have seen that the expectation of life of the English workers in general is poor, because of the unsatisfactory conditions under which they exist. The expectation of life of these [lead] miners is low even by the poor standards normally attained by English workers.

In the Alston Moor lead-mining district one comes across the same sort of lodging houses and other sleeping quarters which we have already met in the great industrial towns, and they are just as filthy, nauseating and overcrowded as those already described. Mitchell states that he was in one of these bedrooms which was 18 feet long by 15 feet wide. The room accommodated 56 persons (42 men and 14 boys) in 14 beds.[1] These were arranged in bunks as on board a ship, so that half the occupants of the room slept above the other half. There was no ventilation to get rid of the foul air, so although at the time of Mitchell's visit no one had slept there for three nights the stench was still so overpowering that the visitor had to leave immediately. What must this room have been like on a hot summer's night if it was filled to capacity, with 56 sleeping lodgers? And this is the abode of ' free-born Britons ', not between decks on an American slaver!

We turn now to the coal and ironstone mines which are the most important branches of mining in England. The Children's Employment Commission's report [of 1841–3][2] discusses these mines together,[3] and the description is as detailed as one would expect from the importance of the subject. Nearly the whole of the first part of this report is devoted to the condition of the workers employed in these mines. Since we have already given a detailed account of how the workers live in the factory districts, I propose to deal with the miners in

[1 Children's Employment Commission, *Appendix to 1st Report: Mines*, Part II (1843), pp. 740-2—report by Dr. James Mitchell on lead mines in Northumberland, Durham and Cumberland. The figure of 42 men and 14 boys was the *maximum* number which the 14 beds could be made to accommodate in exceptional circumstances. Normally between 30 and 40 persons slept in the room.]

[2 Children's Employment Commission, *1st Report: Mines* (1842) — section I, ' Coal Mines ', pp. 6–194; section II, ' Ironstone Mines and the Manufacture of Iron ', pp. 195–203.]

[3 The *Report* itself deals separately with the mining of coal, ironstone and the non-ferrous ores, but the reports of individual sub-commissioners on particular mining districts deal with all types of mines together.]

somewhat briefer fashion—at least as far as the wealth of material in this report will allow.

Children of 4, 5 and 7 years work in coal and ironstone mines, where very similar methods of extraction are used. But most of the children are over 8 years of age.[1] They carry the loosened coal or ironstone from the face either to the underground tramway or to the bottom of the shaft. Their services are also used to open and shut the ventilation doors which divide the various parts of a mine, so as to allow the passage of men, carts and tubs. The smallest children are usually given the task of minding the doors. They have to sit alone for 12 hours every day in a narrow, dark passage which is generally damp. They are not even given enough to do to save them from the idle boredom which gradually turns them into stupid animals. The transport of coal and ironstone, on the other hand, is very heavy work, because these minerals are moved about in fairly large tubs which have no wheels. The tubs have to be hauled over the bumpy ground of the underground passages, often through wet clay or even water. Sometimes the tubs have to be hauled up steep inclines and are brought through passages which are so narrow that the workers have to crawl on their hands and knees. The older boys and girls have to perform this heavy work. Sometimes one of the older youths has to handle the tub by himself, but sometimes the work is given to two younger children one of whom pushes and the other pulls. The actual hewing of the coal or ironstone is done by grown men or by physically well-developed youths of 16 or more. This also is very exhausting work. The normal working day in the mines is between 11 and 12 hours, but may often be longer. In Scotland miners work up to 14 hours a day. Double shifts are frequently worked, and this means that all miners are frequently at work for 24, or even 26, hours without coming to the surface. There are rarely any set times for meals, so that the hungry miners take their meals when they can.

The standard of living of the miners in general appears to be reasonably good. Their wages are high in comparison with neighbouring farm workers, who, however, are often virtually starving. On the other hand, in the Irish coalfields, and in parts of the Scottish coalfields there is serious distress. We shall have occasion to refer to the standard of life of the miners again, and we should once more remind the reader that the comparison we have made with the agricultural labourers is with the poorest class in all England. Meanwhile we propose to consider the evils inherent in coal mining as at present carried on in England. The reader will himself then be able to judge

[1 This sentence was omitted in Mrs. F. K. Wischnewetzky's translation of 1887.]

whether any wage, however high, could really compensate the miner for the sufferings of such a life.

All the children and young people employed in hauling coal and ironstone complain of being very tired. Not even in a factory where the most intensive methods of securing output are employed do we find the workers driven to the same limits of physical endurance as they are in the mines. Every page of the report to which we have referred gives chapter and verse for this assertion. It is a very common occurrence for children to come home from the mine so exhausted that they throw themselves on to the stone floor in front of the fire. They cannot keep awake even to eat a morsel of food. Their parents have to wash them and put them to bed while they are still asleep. Sometimes the children actually fall asleep on the way home and are eventually discovered by their parents late at night. It appears to be the almost universal practice of these children to stay in bed most of Sunday in an attempt to recover from the exertions of the previous week's work. Only a few go to church or Sunday school. The teachers at these schools complain that their pupils are very tired and listless. The women and older girls are also habitually exhausted owing to the brutal way in which they are overworked. This utter weariness, actually painful to bear, naturally affects the physique of these women adversely.[1] The most obvious consequence of their unnatural physical exertions is that all the strength in their bodies is concentrated into muscular development. In particular, the muscles of the arms, legs, back, shoulders and chest are over developed because they take the strain of pushing and pulling [the heavy coal tubs]. The rest of their bodies, on the other hand, are crippled owing to lack of nourishment. Nearly all miners are physically stunted, except those in Warwickshire and Leicestershire who work under particularly favourable conditions. Next it may be mentioned that both among boys and girls puberty is delayed—among boys often until as late as the eighteenth year. J. C. Symons actually came across a 19-year-old

[1 Engels's account of the effects of early employment in coal mines upon the physical condition of the miners appears to be based largely upon the section of the *First Report* (1842) of the Children's Employment Commission, entitled ' Peculiar Effects upon the Physical Condition of Early Employment in Coal Mines ', pp. 173–194. The extent to which Engels is indebted to the *Report* may be seen from the headings of the sub-sections of the *Report* which are as follows:
1. Immediate Effects of Overworking.
2. Extraordinary Muscular Development.
3. Stunted Growth.
4. Crippled Gait.
5. Irritation of the Head, Back, etc.
6. Diseases.
7. Premature Old Age and Death.]

youth who, except for his teeth, had the physique of a boy aged between 11 and 12. This prolongation of the period of childhood is a proof of retarded development and naturally has its consequences in later years. Miners are either bandy-legged or knock-kneed and suffer from splayed feet, spinal deformities and other physical defects. This is due to the fact that their constitutions have been weakened and they are nearly always forced to work in a cramped position. Many people, including even doctors, say that in Yorkshire, Lancashire, Northumberland and Durham it is possible to pick a miner out from among a hundred other people because of his physical defects. The women, in particular, appear to be half crippled. They seldom, if ever, have backs which are as straight as those of other women. Distortion of the pelvis leads these women to have difficult and sometimes fatal confinements. All this is to be attributed to the nature of their work. In addition to these physical deformities, which are peculiar to coalmining, there are the illnesses which they share with all types of miners. It is easy to see the connection between these illnesses and the nature of the occupation they follow. They suffer particularly from stomach troubles. They lose their appetites and are subject to internal pains, nausea and vomiting. In addition they are liable to become very thirsty and very often the only water available is the filthy, tepid water in the mine. They suffer from severe indigestion and this aggravates the other stomach troubles mentioned. Further complaints among miners are various diseases of the heart—particularly enlargement and inflammation of the heart and pericardium, contraction of the auriculo-ventricular communications, and contortion of the commencement of the aorta.[1] There is much evidence to show that all these diseases are common among miners, and it can easily be seen that they are almost certainly caused by undue physical exertion. The same is true of ruptures, which are also due to excessive muscular strain.

Many miners suffer also from painful and dangerous lung diseases, particularly asthma. This is due partly to the causes we have already discussed, and partly to the foul dusty atmosphere impregnated with carbonic acid gas and carburretted hydrogen gas. These gases could easily be dispersed. In some districts most miners suffer these diseases by the time they are 40, and then they are soon unfit for further work. Sometimes the effects of these diseases are seen as early as the age of 30. Those employed in wet workings are naturally the first to suffer from chest complaints. In some districts of Scotland young miners

[1 Engels is here following very closely the evidence given by Dr. S. Scott Alison (East Lothian), quoted in the *First Report* of the Children's Employment Commission (1842), p. 189.]

aged only between 20 and 30 are particularly susceptible to inflammation of the lungs and other feverish complaints. A disease which is largely confined to miners is ' black spittle '. It arises because the lungs become impregnated with fine coal dust and this leads to general debility, headaches, constriction of the chest and the expectoration of thick black mucus.[1] In some coalmining districts this complaint occurs only in a mild form, but in certain areas, particularly in Scotland, it is so virulent as to appear to be quite incurable. In Scotland the symptoms of black spittle—in addition to those already mentioned— are constant shortness and quickness of breath, a rapid pulse (over 100 beats in a minute), and a hacking cough. When general emaciation and weakness set in, the patient is soon unfit for work. The illness is always fatal. Dr. Makellar of Pencaitland, East Lothian, states that this illness does not occur in those mines which are adequately ventilated. Many examples could be given of miners who moved from well-ventilated to badly-ventilated mines and caught the disease.[2] It is solely due to the colliery owners' greed for profit that this illness exists at all. If the coalowners would pay to have ventilation shafts installed the problem would not exist. Except in Warwickshire and Leicestershire rheumatism is an occupational disease of miners. It is naturally most severe in the wetter coal mines.

Owing to these illnesses the coalminers in all districts, *without exception*, become prematurely aged and unfit for work after they are 40 years old. The average age of retirement, of course, varies from district to district. It is very rare for a miner to be still at work after he is 50 or even 45. It is generally agreed that a miner is practically an old man at the age of 40. That is true of the coalhewers. The loaders who lift heavy lumps of coal into the tubs, become old when they are 28 or 30, so that there is a saying in the coal districts: ' Loaders are . . . old men before they are young ones '.[3] It goes without saying that, since miners age prematurely, they die young. It is very rare indeed to come across a miner who is 60 years of age.[4] Even in South Staffordshire where the coal mines are relatively healthy, comparatively few workers reach the age of 51.[5] Since the workers become old so soon it is natural that there should be much unemployment among parents in the mining as well as in the factory districts. The parents are often supported by children who are still very young.

Dr. Southwood Smith, one of the Commissioners, briefly sum-

[1 *First Report* (1842) of Children's Employment Commission, p. 190.]
[2 Op. cit., p. 190-1.]
[3 Op. cit., p. 192 (Evidence of J. M. Fellows, reporting statement by Phoebe Gilbert.]   [4 Op. cit., p. 193, statement by William Wardle.]
[5 Op. cit., p. 193.]

marises the effects of their occupation on the miners as follows. He points out that the period of childhood is unduly prolonged while the period of adult life is curtailed. Consequently, when a man should be in the prime of life and in full possession of his powers, his life is prematurely cut short by an early death.[1] And for all this the middle class is solely responsible.

So far we have been describing conditions in the average English mine. But there are many mines in which conditions are much worse. These are in the mines with thin seams of coal. It would be too expensive to remove not only the coal but also some of the sand and clay that sticks to it. The coalowner insists that only the coal itself must be cut. Consequently in mines with thin seams the underground passages, instead of being four foot, five foot and more in height, are so low that it is impossible for the worker to stand up straight in them. The miner has to lie on his side, use his elbow as a lever and hack away at the coal with his pick. This causes inflammation in the elbow. If the miner has to kneel to do his work then his knees are liable to become inflamed. In such mines the women and children, who haul the coal, have to crawl on the hands and knees fastened to the tub by a harness and chain which is generally passed between their legs. Another worker pushes the tub with his head and hands. This pressure on the head causes inflammation, painful swellings and abscesses. Moreover the passages are often wet so that these workers have to crawl through several inches of water. The water may be filthy or salty and this causes inflammation of the skin. It is easy to see how the illnesses to which the miner is subject by the nature of his occupation are aggravated by such disgusting slave labour as we have described.

Even now we have not exhausted the dangers that the unfortunate miners have to face. In no industry in the United Kingdom are there so many fatal accidents as in mining. The coalmines are the scene of many terrible disasters for which the financial greed of the middle classes is entirely responsible. The carburetted hydrogen gas which frequently occurs in coalmines forms an explosive mixture when it comes into contact with the air. A naked light causes it to explode and to kill everybody in the vicinity. Such explosions are almost a daily occurrence in some mine or other. There was one at Haswell Colliery in County Durham on September 28th, 1844, when ninety-six people

[1 Op. cit., pp. 194-6, footnote by Dr. T. Southwood Smith, who ended his comment as follows: work in the mines ' protracts the period of childhood, shortens the period of manhood, and anticipates the period of old age, decrepitude, and death.']

were killed.[1] Another noxious gas—carbonic acid gas—is also to be found in coalmines. It accumulates in the deeper parts of the mines where it frequently rises above the height of the average man. It is fatal to enter a part of a mine where this has gas accumulated. Doors have been erected between different parts of the mines so as to prevent the fires and noxious gases from spreading. Unfortunately these doors are controlled by little children who often fall asleep or neglect their duties so that this method of protecting the miners fails to achieve its object. The evil effects of both gases could be neutralised if only the ventilation of the mines were improved by constructing air shafts from the surface to the underground workings. The middle classes, however, will not pay money out for this purpose. They tell the miners to use Davy lamps. But these lamps are often quite useless because they give too poor a light. The miner uses a candle instead. So when an explosion occurs the middle classes say that the miner has been careless and has only himself to blame. In fact it is the middle classes who are to blame because if they would provide good ventilation there would be hardly any explosions in the mines.

Moreover, there are continual falls of coal and sometimes the roofs of the workings collapse completely. When this happens the miners are either buried or their limbs are crushed. It is in the interest of the middle classes that every seam should be worked as completely as possible and that is why there are so many accidents of this type. In addition it may be mentioned that the ropes by which the workers descend the mine are frequently so worn that they break and the wretched miners are dashed to pieces at the bottom of the shaft.

According to the *Mining Journal* all these accidents—I have no time to give more details—are responsible for 1,400 deaths every year.[2] The *Manchester Guardian* reports two or three fatal accidents every week in the Lancashire mines alone. In nearly all the coalmining districts the coroner's juries are dependent upon the coalowners, and, even when that is not the case, immemorial custom sees to it that a verdict of 'accidental death' is automatically returned. Yet the Report of the Children's Employment Commission does not beat about the

[1 95, according to W. P. Roberts (*Northern Star*, no. 361, Oct. 12th, 1844, p. 5, col. 6.]
[2 *The Mining Journal* . . . , Vol. 13, no. 420, Sept. 9th, 1843, p. 291. The *Journal's* figure of 1,400 fatalities a year in mines was only an estimate. It was based on the fact that the *Journal* had recorded the deaths of 93 miners between May 6th and September 9th. There is further discussion of the question in the *Mining Journal* on November 11th, and December 2nd, 1843. See also the Children's Employment Commission, 1*st Report*, 1842, pp. 135–53. In this report it is stated, on information supplied by the Registrar General, that in 1838 there were only 349 deaths in mines or pit-banks (in 55 registration districts containing mines).]

bush in placing the responsibility for the great majority of the accidents fairly and squarely on the shoulders of the mineowners.

According to the report of the Children's Employment Commission the education and morals of the mining population of Alston Moor are actually described as excellent. In Cornwall they are said to be fairly satisfactory. On the other hand in the remaining mining districts they are, on the whole, very poor. The miners live in remote, neglected parts of the country and so long as their hard work gets done not a soul—except the police—bothers about them in the slightest. It is for this reason—and because the children start work at so tender an age—that the education of the miners is completely neglected. They cannot go to the day-schools. It is a waste of time to provide evening institutes and Sunday schools since the teachers are worthless. Few miners are able to read and still fewer can write. The Commissioners stated that the one thing that the miners do appreciate is that they are grossly underpaid for their hard and dangerous work on which they are engaged.

The miners rarely if ever go to church. All the clergy complain of the shocking ignorance of the miners on religious matters. Their abysmal lack of knowledge concerning both religious and secular affairs could be illustrated by even more striking examples than those already given to show the ignorance of the factory workers. Only when they swear do the miners show any acquaintance with religion. Their standards of morality are undermined by the very nature of their work. To such an extent are they overworked that it is inevitable that they should take to drink. In the dark loneliness of the mines men, women and children work in great heat and the majority of them take off most (if not all) of their clothes. You can imagine the consequences for yourself. There are more illegitimate children in the mining districts than elsewhere, and this is in itself sufficient evidence of what these half savage creatures are doing when they get below ground. But it suggests that sexual irregularities have not degenerated into large-scale prostitution in the mining districts as they have in the big cities.

When the Children's Employment Report was laid before Parliament Lord Ashley promptly brought forward a bill which prohibited female labour in the mines[1] and greatly reduced the extent of child labour. The Bill was passed, but it has remained a dead letter in many coalmining regions because no mining inspectors were appointed to enforce its provisions.[2] If a coalmine is situated in a rural area

[1 I.e. underground.]
[2 *Northern Star*, No. 321, January 6th, 1844, p. 4, columns 5–6: article entitled

evasion of the law is in any case a relatively simple matter. So it need cause no surprise to discover that last year (1843) an official memorial laid before the Home Secretary by the Miners' Association stated that over sixty women were employed on the Duke of Hamilton's collieries in Scotland.[1] Nor need it cause surprise to learn that the *Manchester Guardian* reported that a girl had been killed in a colliery accident—if I remember rightly—at Wigan.[2] No one bothered that these cases revealed flagrant breaches of the law. Here and there female labour in the mines may have come to an end, but in general there has been no change in the state of affairs that we have described.

Those are by no means all the grievances of the miners. The middle classes are not content to ruin the health of the miners, to endanger their lives at every hour of the day, to deprive them of all chances of learning anything. They exploit the miners still further in an utterly shameless manner. In this industry the truck system is the rule and not the exception. It is conducted in the most obvious and disgraceful fashion. The tied cottage system, too, is universal in the coalmining districts. Indeed, it is generally a necessity, but it is used to exploit the workers more effectively. In addition all sorts of other deceits are practised upon the miners. Coal is sold by weight but the miners' wages are generally calculated by the tub. If a miner's tub is not absolutely full he gets no pay for the whole tub, yet if the tub is overful the miner does not get an extra farthing. If the tub contains more than a fixed quantity of slack—and this depends much more upon the nature of the seam than upon the skill of the miner—

' The Coal Kings, and the Non-Employment of Women Law '. Engels does not mention the fact that H. Seymour Tremenheere had been appointed an Inspector of Mines and Collieries on November 28th, 1843. From 1844 onwards he made annual reports on the enforcement and working of the Act of 1842. The Act came into force on March 1st, 1843, and it is clear from Tremenheere's first Report that, particularly in Scotland, there had been difficulties in enforcing the law, but they were by no means as great as Engels led his readers to suppose. The difficulties appear to have been removed without serious trouble: *Report of the Commissioner appointed under the provisions of the Act 5 and 6 Vict., c. 99 to inquire into the operation of that Act . . . ,* (1844), *Parly. Papers,* c. 592 of 1844.]

[1 *Northern Star,* no. 306, Sept. 23rd, 1843; no. 308, Oct. 7th, 1843, p. 4, col. 5; no. 312, Nov. 4th, 1843, p. 4, cols. 5–6 and no. 321, Jan. 6th, 1844, p. 4, col. 5. According to the *Northern Star* the memorial sent to Sir James Graham, the Home Secretary, was drawn up by W. Daniells, and came from the colliers of Falkirk (no. 311, Oct. 28th, 1843, p. 4, col. 3).]

[2 *Report of the Commissioner appointed under the provisions of the Act 5 and 6 Vict. c. 99 to inquire into the operation of that Act . . .* 1845 (c. 670 of 1845), pp. 5–6. Tremenheere stated that in 1844–45 about 200 women were still illegally employed in the Wigan colliery district. He refers to the death of a woman in one of the pits of the Standish Colliery, which led to strong local protests against the continued contravention of the law. It is presumably this case to which Engels referred, although a nine-year-old *boy,* Thomas Taylor, was killed in a Wigan pit disaster in November 1844; *Manchester Guardian,* Nov. 23rd, 1844, p. 3, col. 5.]

the miner is not only paid nothing for that tub, but he is fined as well. The system of fines is so highly developed in the coalmines that it is actually possible for a poor devil to work for a whole week and then when he goes to the foreman for his wages—and the foreman makes up the pay-packets on his own without consulting the men— he learns not only that no wages are due to him but that he owes the company something in fines. The foreman has absolute power as far as the calculation of wages is concerned. He makes a record of the amount of coal produced by each miner. The miner cannot appeal against the foreman's decision and must accept the wages as they have been worked out by the foreman. In some collieries where coal is paid for by weight false weighing machines are used and there is no official check on the accuracy of the weights. At one coalmine it was actually laid down that a miner must give the foremen *three weeks' notice* if he wished to make a complaint concerning the weighing of coal.

In many coalfields, particularly in the northern counties, it is customary for miners to sign a yearly contract. They promise not to work at any other mine during that period. But the mineowner gives no promise to find work for the miners for the whole of the year. So a miner may be out of work for months at a time and yet if he gets a job in another mine he gets six weeks' hard labour at the treadmill for breach of contract. Some contracts promise the miner a guaranteed wage of up to 26s. for every fortnight but the owners fail to pay up. In certain districts the owners give the miners trifling advances of wages (to be repaid later in instalments) in order to get a hold over the men. In the North of England it is everywhere customary for wages to be paid one week in arrears so as to tie the miners down. To complete the enslavement of the miners it is normal for the magistrates in the coalmining districts to be coalowners, or their relatives or friends. The justices of the peace have almost unlimited powers in poor uncivilised districts where few newspapers circulate—and the local press is entirely under the thumb of the ruling classes—and where political activities are almost unknown. One can hardly credit the extent to which these unfortunate miners are dominated and tyrannised by the magistrates who, after all, are judging their own cases.[1]

For a long time matters went on in this way. The mine workers knew no better than to allow themselves to be exploited to the last drop of their blood. Gradually however a spirit of resistance to the shameless oppression of the ' Coal Kings ' began to evince itself,

[1 For the miners' grievances in the 1840s, see *Hansard's Parliamentary Debates,* 1844, Vol. 75, col. 261—speech by T. S. Duncombe.]

particularly in collieries in the manufacturing districts where they came into contact with factory workers who were more intelligent than themselves. They began to establish trade unions and every now and again they went on strike. In the more enlightened districts they even threw in their lot body and soul with the Chartists. But the great coalfield in the North of England—isolated from the manufacturing districts—remained backward in this respect. At last, however, in 1843—after much effort and many false starts—a general spirit of revolt was generated even in this coalfield. This was due partly to the efforts of the Chartists and partly to the labours of the more intelligent miners. So determined was the spirit of the miners of Northumberland and Durham that they took the lead in establishing a trade union which united all the miners in the country. They appointed the Chartist solicitor, W. P. Roberts[1] of Bristol[2] to be their 'Attorney General'. He had already distinguished himself at various Chartist trials as a representative for the defence. The Miners' Union spread and soon covered most of the coalfields. Agents were appointed everywhere, demonstrations were held, and new members were enrolled. When the Union held its first conference at Manchester in January 1844 it had a membership of over 60,000 miners.[3] Six months later, when a second conference was held in Glasgow, the membership had already grown to over a hundred thousand. All matters concerning the miners were discussed at these conferences and decisions were taken concerning the more important strikes. Many journals were established to advocate the cause of the miners, one of the most important being *The Miners' Advocate*, a fortnightly periodical which was published at Newcastle-on-Tyne.

On March 31st, 1844, all the miners' contracts of service in the Northumberland and Durham coalfield expired. Roberts, on behalf of the miners, drew up a proposed new contract. The miners demanded

(1) Payment by weight [of coal cut] and not by measure.

(2) Amount of coal cut to be determined by ordinary beam and scales; scales and weights to be checked by inspectors.

(3) Miners' contracts to run for six months.

(4) Abolition of the system of fines: miners to be paid according to the actual amount of coal produced.

(5) Owners to agree to find at least four days' work a week for

[1 For W. P. Roberts see the *Dictionary of National Biography*. There is a memoir of him in *The Northern Star*, Feb. 24th, 1844, p. 4, cols. 1–2.]

[2 But according to Sidney and Beatrice Webb, *The History of Trade Unionism* (edition of 1920), Roberts ' became a solicitor in Manchester ' (p. 182, note 2).]

[3 For this conference see the *Northern Star*, no. 321, January 6th, 1844, p. 8, cols. 2–3: article on ' The Great National Conference at Manchester '.]

miners whom they regularly employed. In default of four days' work in the week the miners should receive pay for four days' work [i.e. a guaranteed wage on the basis of four days' work].[1]

The proposed contract was submitted to the ' Coal Kings ' and the miners appointed a deputation to negotiate with the owners. But the owners replied that as far as they were concerned the Union did not exist. They would deal with individual miners but they would not recognise the Union. The owners put forward a new contract of their own which ignored all the proposals made by the miners. The Union naturally rejected the contract suggested by the owers. And so war was declared.

On March 31st, 1844, forty thousand miners laid down their picks and all the collieries in Northumberland and Durham came to a standstill. So large were the funds at the disposal of the Union that every miner's family was assured of strike pay at the rate of half a crown a week for several months. While the workers were putting the patience of their masters to the test Roberts organised the strike and the agitation with unexampled vigour. He travelled the length and breadth of England, collected subscriptions for the strikers, advocated non-violence and respect for the law, and at the same time waged a campaign against the despotic magistrates and ' truck-masters '. Such a thing had never been seen in England before. He had begun his agitation early in 1844. Whenever a miner was sentenced by a magistrate, Roberts secured a writ of *habeas corpus* from the Court of Queen's Bench, brought his clients before the Court in London and always secured their freedom. In the Queen's Bench on January 13th, 1844, Mr. Justice Williams set free three miners who had been sentenced by the Bilston (South Staffordshire) magistrates. Their ' crime ' was that they had refused to work in a part of the mine where the roof was in danger of falling in—and which had in fact collapsed by the time they got back to it! In a previous case Mr. Justice Patteson had freed six workers, so by this time the name of Roberts was beginning to alarm the magistrates in the coalmining districts. In Preston six of Roberts's clients were in prison. Early in February he went there to look into their case only to discover that the miners had already been let out of goal *before* completing their sentences. In Manchester seven of Roberts's clients were in prison. He applied to Mr. Justice Wightman for a writ of *habeas corpus* and secured the unconditional release of all seven miners. In Prescot (South Lancashire) seven miners had been found guilty of alleged breach of the peace and were awaiting

[1 *Northern Star*, no. 336, April 20th, 1844, p. 3, cols. 3–4—a review of the first two numbers (March and April) of *The Miners' Monthly Magazine*, ed. W. P. Roberts.]

sentence. When Roberts arrived he was able to secure their immediate discharge. All this happened in the first half of February, 1844.[1]

In April 1844 Roberts was able by the same means to free one miner from Derby House of Correction, four from Wakefield Gaol (Yorkshire) and four from Leicester Gaol. And so things went on for a time, until the 'Dogberries'—as these justices of the peace are called after the well-known character in Shakespeare's *Much Ado About Nothing*—began to have a measure of respect for the 'Miners' Attorney General'.[2]

The same thing happened with regard to the truck system. One by one the dishonourable mineowners were hauled up by Roberts before the courts. And the magistrates were reluctantly forced to find case after case proved against them. The 'Miners' Attorney General' acted with incredible speed—he seemed to be everywhere at once— and he struck terror into the hearts of the coalowners. For example on one occasion when he reached Belper (near Derby) he found that Messrs. Haslam had anticipated his arrival by issuing the following notice:[3]

PENTRICH COLLIERY

Messrs. Haslam think it right (*to prevent mistake*), to give notice that all men employed at their colliery will receive their wages wholly in money, and be at liberty to spend it where they like.

If they buy at Messrs. Haslam's shop they will be supplied (as heretofore) at wholesale prices; but they are not expected to buy there, and will have the same work and wages whether they go to that shop or any other.

[April 9th, 1844.[3]]

These triumphs aroused the most lively feelings of satisfaction among all the English workers and attracted many new members to the Miners' Union. Meanwhile the strike in the Northumberland and Durham coalfield continued. Newcastle, the main English port for the export of coal, actually received coals from Scottish ports— although in England the saying 'to carry coals to Newcastle' has the same meaning as the French saying 'to carry owls to Athens' (i.e. to do something quite superfluous). At first—so long as the strike

[1] For these cases see the *Northern Star*, no. 322, Jan. 13th, 1844, p. 8, col. 1; no. 323, Jan. 20th, 1844, p. 4, cols. 3–4 ('Liberation of the Staffordshire Colliers'); no. 326, Feb. 10th, 1844, p. 4, col. 5 and no. 328, Feb. 24th, 1844, p. 4, cols. 5–6.]
[2] *Northern Star*, no. 338, May 14th, 1844, p. 5, cols. 1–2—'More Liberations of Miners': 'Lord Denman . . . will bring the Dogberries to their senses at last'.]
[3] *Northern Star*, No. 336, April 20th, 1844, p. 4, cols. 3–5: article entitled 'Mr. Roberts—Belper—Messrs. Haslam. "To prevent any Mistake"'.]

fund lasted—everything went well, but during the summer the miners found it difficult to carry on the struggle. There was great distress among the miners. They had no money. As so many miners were on strike the subscriptions from workers in other industries were inadequate. The strikers had to get credit from small shopkeepers at usurious rates. They had the whole English press—except for a few workers' journals—against them. The middle classes (even the tiny minority which had a sufficient sense of justice to support the cause of the miners) read all the lies about the strike which appeared in the venal liberal and conservative newspapers. A deputation of twelve miners went to London to secure financial help from the workers for the strikers in the North. But the sum collected in this way did not go very far among so large a number of strikers. Nevertheless the strikers stayed out. And to their credit let it be said that they remained quiet and peaceful in the face of every provocation that the coal-owners and their faithful lackeys could devise. No act of vengeance occurred: no blackleg was molested: no theft was committed. The strike had lasted for four months and the mineowners had no prospect of getting the upper hand. But one weapon remained in their hands. They remembered the system of tied cottages. It occurred to them that, after all, the houses in which the recalcitrant miners lived were *their* [i.e. the coalowners'] property. In July 1844 the strikers received notices to quit their cottages and within a week all forty thousand of them had been put into the street. This was done in an incredibly savage way. The sick, the infirm, the aged, the infants and even pregnant women were ruthlessly kicked out of their beds and thrown into the street. One agent of the landlord enjoyed himself by pulling a woman (far gone in pregnancy) by the hair out of bed with his own hands and dragging her out of the house. The justices of the peace, who were in charge of the evictions, would only have had to raise a hand for the large contingents of police and soldiers who were present to attack the strikers at the first sign of resistance. The home-less miners—remembering Roberts's warnings—offered no resistance. They carried their furniture to the moors or to fields (from which the grain had been harvested) and patiently continued the struggle. Some, who could find nowhere else to camp, settled down in ditches at the roadside. Those who camped on other people's property found themselves in court charged with doing damage ' to the value of one halfpenny '. They were told to pay twenty shillings costs, but of course did not have so much money, and were sentenced to terms of imprisonment with hard labour at the treadmill. And so the strikers and their families survived for another eight weeks or more in the

open during the wet summer of last year [1844]. They had no shelter
for themselves or their children except for the cotton sheets from their
beds. The only money they received came from their own union.
And now the credit formerly given by the small shopkeepers was
drying up. Thereupon Lord Londonderry,[1] who owns large coalmines
in [County] Durham, threatened the shopkeepers of ' his town ' of
Seaham with his august disapproval if they continued to give credit to
' his ' recalcitrant miners. Indeed this ' noble ' lord was the prize
clown of the whole affair. He was in the habit from time to time of
issuing ridiculous, pompous, badly-written ' ukases ' to his workers—
only to make himself the laughing-stock of the whole country.[2] When
all else had failed the northern coalowners, at great expense, fetched
miners from Ireland and from the remote corners of Wales, where
no one had ever heard of trade unions. The arrival of these new miners
increased the labour force in the district and re-established competition
among the workers themselves. At last the strike collapsed. The coalowners forced the men to leave their union, to dismiss Roberts and to
accept the terms which they dictated. And so, early in September 1844,
the great struggle of the mineworkers against their employers, which
had lasted for five months, came to an end. The oppressed miners
were greatly admired for the courage, the persistence, the intelligence
and the discretion with which they had conducted the strike. We have
seen that in 1842[3] the Children's Employment Commission's Report
described the miners as coarse and uncouth. Yet two years later
they gave evidence of possessing a truly remarkable intelligence,
strength of character and firmness of purpose. And remember that
there were forty thousand of them. How severe must have been the
oppression that brought these forty thousand miners to rise as one
man. What an inspired army of fighters they were—inspired by a
single will—to carry on the conflict in cold blood but without violence
until a point was reached when further resistence was absolutely
impossible. And what a struggle it was—not a fight against visible
enemies who could be struck down but a fight against passions which
were debauched almost to madness by the brutality of wealth.
If the strikers had allowed themselves to give way to violence they
would have been shot down in a trice—for they had no arms—and the
capitalists would have been victorious in a few days. The strikers were

[1 *Northern Star*, No. 350, July 27th, 1844, p. 4, cols. 4–6: articles entitled ' The
Mad Marquis again ' and ' The Labour Struggle '.]
[2 For a reappraisal of the part played by Londonderry in the strike, see A. J.
Taylor, ' The Third Marquis of Londonderry and the North Eastern Coal Trade ':
Durham University Journal, Dec. 1955, pp. 21–27.]
[3 Engels wrote ' 1840 '.]

law-abiding not because they feared the police but because they believed that non-violence would be a better policy than violence. That surely is the best proof of the intelligence and the self-control of the workers.

The workers had again been defeated by the might of capitalism in spite of their unexampled resistance to their oppressors. But the struggle was not in vain. Above all, the nineteen-week strike of the miners of Durham and Northumberland has shaken them free for ever from their former mental and spiritual torpor. They have ceased to slumber. They are awake to their own interests. They have entered the stream of modern civilisation and they form a part of the working-class movement. The strike has for the first time brought the complete barbarity of the mineowners to the light of day. It has established for all time the working-class opposition to the capitalists of Durham and Northumberland—and it has turned at least three quarters of the miners there into Chartists. And the acquisition of thirty thousand such fine and energetic supporters is indeed a great gain for the Chartist movement. Again, this long-drawn-out strike, which was fought without resorting to violence—coupled with the agitation that accompanied it—have forced the general public to take some notice of the condition of the coalminers. When there was a debate in the House of Commons on the export duty upon coal Thomas [Slingsby] Duncombe—the one Member of Parliament who energetically espouses the Chartist cause—raised the question of the condition of the workers in the coalmines and laid a petition from the miners on the table of the House. His speech forced even the middle-class newspapers to give space—if only in their reports on the proceedings of Parliament—for a truthful account of the state of affairs in the coalfields.[1]

Immediately after the great strike [of 1844] came the explosion at Haswell. Roberts went straight to London, succeeded in obtaining an interview with Sir Robert Peel, [the Prime Minister], and—on behalf of the coalminers—demanded that an exhaustive enquiry should be made into the causes of the disaster. It was owing to his efforts that Professor Lyell and Professor Faraday—the most eminent geologist and the most eminent chemist in England—were sent to Haswell to pursue their enquiries on the spot. Soon afterwards several other explosions occurred [in coalmines]. Again Roberts laid the facts before the Prime Minister and this time Peel promised that, if possible, he would submit legislative proposals to increase safety measures in the coalmines during the next—i.e. the present (1845)—session of

[1 *Hansard's Parliamentary Debates*, 1844, Vol. 75, col. 154 (petition presented) and cols. 259–62: speech of T. S. Duncombe, June 4th, 1844.]

parliament.[1] All this would not have happened if the coalminers had not—by their behaviour during the strike—shown themselves to be freedom-loving and respectable people. And it would not have happened if the miners had not had Roberts to plead their cause.

Hardly had it been made known that the coalminers of the North had been forced to give up their trade union and to dismiss Roberts than some ten thousand Lancashire miners established a trade union and appointed Roberts as their 'Attorney General' at a salary of £1,200 a year. In the autumn of the previous year they had collected £700 a month. Rather more than £200 was spent each month on salaries, legal expenses and so forth, leaving most of the rest of the money to be paid out to miners who were out of work. Some had been laid off while others were on strike owing to disputes with their employers. Thus the workers are more and more coming to realise that if they unite they are powerful and—if the worst comes to the worst—they can pit their strength against the middle classes. That the English workers, and above all the miners, have realised this is due to the great stand made by the coalminers of Durham and Northumberland in the strike of 1844. It cannot be long now before the gap between the factory workers and the miners—the former being more intelligent and energetic than the latter —will be closed. In the future the miner will stand shoulder to shoulder with the factory workers on a basis of complete equality. Thus one stone after another of the fortress of the middle classes is being knocked away. How long will it be before the whole edifice of State and Society—and the foundations upon which it rests—crumble and collapse?

But they refuse to see the writing on the wall. The middle classes have only been more embittered by the opposition of the coalminers. Instead of accepting the fact that the great strike of 1844 represented a step forward of the whole working-class movement—instead of coming to its senses—the capitalist class merely took the opportunity to show its implacable hostility to a group of workers who had been so foolish as to oppose a method of settling contracts hitherto regarded as traditional. They saw in the just claims of the miners only shameful discontent, stupid opposition ' against the established divine and human organisation of society '. They saw in the strike—if things went in their own favour—a golden opportunity to crush with all the weapons at their disposal the ' wicked demagogues who thrive upon

[1 *Northern Star*, no. 360, Oct. 5th, 1844, p. 1, cols. 4–5, p. 5, cols. 2–6; no. 361 Oct. 12th, 1844, p. 5, cols. 2–3 and 6 (' The Haswell Murder ') and no. 363, October 26th, 1844, p. 4, col. 6 (' Mr. Roberts and the Lancashire Miners ') and p. 5, cols. 4–6 (' The Lancashire Coal Miners ').]

agitation and are too idle to turn their hands to honest work '. They tried—of course with no success—to persuade the miners that people like Roberts and the full-time agents of the union (who obviously had to be paid for their labours) were swindlers who were trying to entice the last farthing out of the workers' pockets. If the capitalist class is as mad as all that, and if they are so blinded by temporary success that they cannot understand the most obvious signs of the times—then we must indeed give up all hope of seeing a peaceful solution to the social question in England. The only possible outcome of this state of affairs is a great revolution and it is absolutely certain that such a rising will take place.

Chapter XI

THE PROLETARIAT ON THE LAND

In our introduction we pointed out that the smallholders and peasants on the land were ruined at the same time as the craftsmen and the lesser members of the bourgeoisie. This came about when the link between craftwork and work in the fields was snapped. The fields from which the peasants had fled were thrown together into big leasehold farms. The peasants were driven away by competition from the large units of agrarian production. The peasant was no longer a small freeholder or even a leaseholder. He was forced to give up his land and take service with a substantial tenant farmer of the owner of a great landed estate. He was now simply a wage-earner. Although his situation was much worse than it had formerly been it was nevertheless not intolerable. For a time the expansion of industry kept pace with the growth of the population. But a time came when the pace of industrial expansion faltered and then it was no longer possible for the urban factories to find employment for all the surplus workers who were leaving the countryside. From that time onward the distress which had hitherto been confined to the factory districts —and then only from time to time—spread to the agricultural regions. This development took place practically simultaneously with the ending of the long wars against France which had lasted for a quarter of a century. During the war British agriculture had been artificially fostered by exceptional circumstances—the reduced output of the countries in which fighting was taking place, the prohibition of imports and the necessity of sending supplies to the British army in Spain. At the same time, owing to the war [a number of] agricultural workers were taken from the land. But [when the war was over] the restrictions on imports, the need to export and the shortage of workers suddenly came to an end. And the result was 'agricultural distress'. The tenant farmers could get only poor prices for their corn and so were forced to pay low wages to their men. Consequently the corn law of 1815 was passed to prohibit the importation of corn so long as the price was less than eighty shillings a quarter. This law was naturally a failure and it has had to be changed on several occasions. But this has not alleviated the agricultural distress. The only consequence of the corn laws was this: if there had been no such import restrictions, and if foreign corn had been freely admitted, then the sickness afflicting English farming would soon have become acute and would have come to a head as an agricultural crisis. In fact the corn laws have turned 'agricultural distress' into a chronic illness which continually presses severely upon the unfortunate farm workers.

Soon after the appearance of the agricultural proletariat the old patriarchal relationships began to break down in the countryside—as they were already breaking down in the urban factories. These patriarchal relationships still survive [1845] in nearly the whole of the German countryside. So long as these relationships survived in England distress in the agricultural districts was not so frequent and not so severe as it has since become. In those days the farm workers shared the fortunes of the tenant farmers and lost their jobs only when conditions were exceptionally bad. To-day all this has changed. Now the farm workers are nearly all day-labourers and are employed only when they are wanted. Consequently they are often without any work for weeks on end—particularly in the winter. In the old days the agricultural labourers and their families lived on the farm The farmer made every effort to find work for the children of his labourers when they grew up. Day-labourers were then the exception rather than the rule. In fact the total number of men employed on a farm was generally greater than was strictly necessary. This was one reason why it was in the interest of the farmer to bring this state of affairs to an end. It was in his interest to drive the workers from the farm and to turn them into day-labourers. This happened practically everywhere in the late 1820s. What was the result? To borrow an expression from physics, we may say that the surplus population—hitherto 'latent'—was now 'free'. And so wages have fallen and the poor rates have increased enormously. From that time onwards the agricultural districts have been the seat of *permanent* pauperism, while the factory districts have been the seat of *fluctuating* pauperism. The reform of the poor laws was the first step taken by the authorities to try and stay the progressive pauperisation of the English countryside. Moreover the size of farms is continually increasing. Machines for threshing and other purposes are being introduced, and more and more women and children are being employed in the country. Indeed the labour of women and children is now so common in the agricultural districts that the whole problem has recently been the subject of an official enquiry.[1] All these factors have aggravated unemployment on the land. So here again we see the characteristics which we have already discussed when dealing with the industrial economy—large units of production, the disappearance of the old patriarchal relationship

[1 See the *Reports of Special Assistant Poor Law Commissioners on the Employment of Women and Children in Agriculture* (1843)—*Parliamentary Papers*, c. 510 of 1843.]

between masters and men—which is particularly significant in agriculture—the introduction of machinery and steam-power, and the increased employment of women and children. Thus what was once the most stable working-class group has now been drawn into the revolutionary movement. The very fact that the relationship between masters and men had so long been a stable one on the land has made it all the more difficult for the modern farm labourer to shoulder the burden that he has to bear. In the countryside [even more than in the factory districts] we see the complete dissolution of old-established social relationships. The ' surplus population ' suddenly came to light and was not—as in the factory districts—absorbed by increased industrial production. As long as new customers could be found it was always possible to set up new factories. But there was no new land. After 1815 a good deal of capital had been invested in attempts to cultivate waste land but this had proved to be a risky speculation. The result was that the competition of the farm labourers among themselves reached a climax and wages were driven down to a very low level indeed. As long as the old Poor Law survived it was possible to supplement the low wages of the farm labourers from the rates. This, however, inevitably led to further wage reductions since the farmers naturally wanted as much as possible of the cost of maintaining their workers to be borne by the Poor Law. The burden of the poor rates would, in any case, have increased with the rise in population. The policy of supplementing agricultural wages, of course, greatly aggravated the position. It was this situation which made it necessary to introduce the new Poor Law which we shall discuss later.

The situation, however, was not improved by the new Poor Law. Agricultural wages did not increase; the surplus population did not disappear; and the savage cruelty of the new Poor Law aroused great hostility. There was for a few years a reduction in the poor rates, but before long they returned to the old high level. The only achievement of the new Poor Law was this: formerly there had been between three and four million semi-paupers. Now a million of them became complete paupers and the remainder—although they got no help from the poor law authorities—were in fact still semi-paupers. Every year saw an increase in agricultural distress. The farm workers now live in a state of extreme poverty. Entire families have to survive on 8s. a week—or even on 7s. or 6s. And there are times when they are out of work and can earn nothing at all.

Here is a description of the farm workers written as early as 1830 (*sic*) by a Liberal Member of Parliament:[1]

[1 Edward Gibbon Wakefield was never a Member of Parliament.]

What is that defective being, with calfless legs and stooping shoulders, weak in body and mind, inert, pusillanimous, and stupid, whose premature wrinkles and furtive glance tell of misery and degradation? That is an English peasant or pauper; for the words are synonymous. His sire was a pauper, and his mother's milk wanted nourishment. From infancy his food has been bad as well as insufficient; and he now feels the pains of unsatisfied hunger nearly whenever he is awake. But half-clothed, and never supplied with more warmth than suffices to cook his scanty meals, cold and wet come to him, and stay by him with the weather. He is married, of course; for to this he would have been driven by the poor laws, even if he had been, as he never was, sufficiently comfortable and prudent to dread the burden of a family. But, though instinct and the overseer have given him a wife, he has not tasted the highest joys of husband and father. His partner, and little ones being, like himself, often hungry, seldom warm, sometimes sick without aid, and always sorrowful without hope, are greedy, selfish and vexing; so to use his own expression, he ' hates the sight of them ', and resorts to his hovel, only because a hedge affords less shelter from the wind and rain. Compelled by parish law to support his family, which means to join them in consuming an allowance from the parish, he frequently conspires with his wife to get that allowance increased, or prevent its being diminished. This brings begging, trickery, and quarrelling; and ends in settled craft. Though he have the inclination, he wants the courage to become, like more energetic men of his class, a poacher or smuggler on a large scale; but he pilfers occasionally, and teaches his children to lie and steal. His subdued and slavish manner towards his great neighbours shows that they treat him with suspicion and harshness. Consequently, he at once dreads and hates them; but he will never harm them by violent means. Too degraded to be desperate, he is thoroughly depraved. His miserable career will be short; rheumatism and asthma are conducting him to the workhouse, where he will breathe his last without one pleasant recollection, and so make room for another wretch who may live and die in the same way.[1]

The author adds that in addition to these farm labourers there is another class of English peasants to be considered. The men in this second class are of a more energetic type. They are physically, morally and intellectually superior to the first class. They live as miserably as the first group, but were not bred and born in extreme destitution. It is said that they usually make good husbands and affectionate

---

[1] Edward Gibbon Wakefield, *Swing Unmasked; or, the Causes of Rural Incendiarism* (dated London, Dec. 17th, 1831), pp. 9–10. [Engels gives a shortened version of the extract. Wakefield's pamphlet is rare. George Grote's copy is in the University of London Library].

parents, but they engage in smuggling and poaching and are often involved in murderous conflicts with gamekeepers and customs officials. They have served many terms of imprisonment and have consequently become embittered against the forces of law and order. In this respect they resemble the first group of farm labourers because of the hatred they bear towards the privileged classes of the country-side. The writer of the pamphlet concludes: ' By courtesy, the entire body is called " the bold peasantry of England " '.[1]

This description remains even to-day [1845] an accurate account of the condition of the vast majority of the English farm labourers. In July 1844 *The Times* sent one of its correspondents into the agricultural districts to report on the condition of the farm workers.[2] His account tallies in every way with that given by Wakefield in 1831. According to the correspondent of *The Times* there were some districts where the farm labourers were earning no more than six shillings a week. This is no higher than the wages of German agricultural workers, but the cost of the necessities of life is twice as high in England as it is in Germany. The way in which the English farm labourers live is easy to imagine. Their food is meagre and poor in quality. Their clothes are in rags and their dwellings are small and poorly furnished. They inhabit wretched little cottages which have no home comforts. The young people live in lodging houses where no proper provision is made for the privacy of men and women, so that sexual irregularities are not uncommon. If they are out of work even for a few days in a month the farm workers are in a desperate situation. They cannot form trade unions in order to secure better wages because they are too scattered. If one of their number refuses to work for the very low wages that are offered then there are dozens of unemployed farm labourers—or paupers from the workhouse—who would be happy to work for any wage, however miserable it might be. Anyone who refuses to accept work on the land finds himself treated by the poor law authorities as a wretched, idle fellow for whom there is no relief outside the detested workhouse. This is because local government in the countryside is dominated by the farmers. And it is only from the farmers—or from their neighbours and sympathisers—that the unemployed farm worker can hope to get a job. Reports of this state of affairs are by no means confined to any particular agricultural district in England. On the contrary the misery of the farm workers

[1 Op. cit., pp. 10–13. Engels attributed the phrase ' the bold peasantry of England ' to Shakespeare. In fact it appears in Goldsmith's *Deserted Village* (line 51: 'A bold peasantry, their country's pride ')].

[2 See *The Times*, June 7th, 1844, page 6, col. 1–2; June 10th, 1844, page 7, col. 1–2; June 21st, 1844, page 5, col. 1 and page 6, col. 1.]

is universal—north, east, south and west. The condition of the farm labourer in Norfolk and Suffolk is exactly the same as in Devonshire, Hampshire and Sussex. Wages are as low in Dorsetshire and Oxfordshire as they are in Kent, Surrey, Buckinghamshire and Cambridgeshire.

The game laws are more severe in England than in any other country and are a barbarous instrument of oppression. It is astonishing how frequently the farm workers break these laws. By custom and tradition the English farm worker has always regarded poaching as a noble and natural way of showing his courage and daring. Now his natural inclination to poach is aggravated when he compares his own wretched poverty with the disdainful way in which the great lords rear thousands of hares, grouse and partridge so as to indulge their private pleasures. The farm worker snares and even shoots game. He does no harm to the lord who has far more game than he knows what to do with. But a hare or a bird in the pot over the fire represents a meal for the agricultural worker's family. If a poacher is caught he is imprisoned. If he repeats the offence he will be transported for at least seven years. It is the severity of the punishment that accounts for the frequency of bloody encounters with gamekeepers. Every year several of these affrays have fatal consequences. The gamekeeper not only has a dangerous job but he is despised and detested. Last year two gamekeepers shot themselves rather than carry on with their work. That is the price that has to be paid to enable the landed aristocracy to enjoy the noble pleasures of the chase. But this does not worry the ' lords of the soil '.[1] They are wholly indifferent to the fate of a few members of the ' surplus population '. Indeed the philanthropic English capitalists argue that if half the surplus population disappeared it would be a good thing because the other half would be better off!

Various factors make it difficult to change things in the countryside—the structure of rural society, the isolation in which the countryman lives, the nature of his work and of his mental processes. But even in the country poverty and distress produce their inevitable results. The first phase of resistance to gross social injustice is crime on the part of the individual. The workers in the factories and mines soon passed through this phase, but the farm labourers are still resisting oppression by individual acts of violence. Their favourite weapon in the social war is incendiarism. In the winter of 1830–31—just after the July revolution in France—incendiarism became universal in the

[1 The words ' lords of the soil ' are in English in the first German edition of 1845].

rural districts of England. There had already been trouble in Sussex early in October [1830] owing to changes in poor law administration, low wages, the introduction of machinery, and the strengthening of the force of revenue officers stationed on the coast. The increased activity of customs officials had checked smuggling, with the result that—according to one farmer—the coastal districts were ruined. Before long there was unrest throughout Sussex and the adjacent districts. In the winter [of 1830-1] the farmers found that their hay stacks and corn ricks in the fields were being set on fire. Even barns and cow-sheds were fired under their very noses. Several such fires were started every night and the wrath of the landlords and farmers knew no bounds. The fire-raisers were seldom, if ever, caught and people began to attribute the fires to a mythical person called Swing. There was much discussion concerning Swing's identity and the causes of the madness that possessed the farm workers. Very few people seemed to realise that it was dire poverty and ruthless oppression that led to incendiarism. From that time onwards incendiarism has been a regular annual occurrence. The outbreaks are always most serious in the winter, when there is most unemployment among farm workers. Incendiarism was particularly prevalent in the winter of 1843-4. I have before me a file of the *Northern Star* for that period. Every number of the paper includes particulars of several cases of incendiarism and in each case the source of the report is given. My file is incomplete but the missing numbers no doubt contain reports of several other acts of incendiarism. In any case the *Northern Star* cannot be expected to report all such cases.

The following information is taken from the issues of the *Northern Star* which are listed:

November 25th, 1843: two cases of incendiarism and references to to several others [reported in earlier issues].

December 16th, 1843: In the previous fortnight there had been widespread excitement and unrest in Bedfordshire owing to the frequency with which acts of incendiarism were committed. Several fires occurred every night. Recently two large farm houses were destroyed. In Cambridgeshire two farms were burnt down. In Hertfordshire a farmhouse was set on fire. Fifteen other fires were reported from various agricultural districts.

December 30th, 1843. The following cases of incendiarism were reported—one in Norfolk, two in Suffolk, two in Essex, three in Hertfordshire, one in Cheshire, one in Lancashire, and twelve in Derby, Lincoln and the southern counties.

January 6th, 1844. Ten cases of incendiarism reported.

January 13th, 1844. Seven cases of incendiarism reported.

January 20th, 1844. Four fires reported from the agricultural districts.[1]

From then onwards the *Northern Star* reported three or four cases of incendiarism every week. At one time these fires stopped in the spring but in 1844 they continued until July and August. English and German periodicals which have recently come to hand show that the coming of the severe winter of 1844-5 caused an increase in the number of cases of incendiarism.

What do my readers think of this state of affairs in the peaceful, idyllic English countryside? Is this social war or is it not? Is this to be regarded as a normal state of affairs which can go on for ever? But the landlords and farmers in the agricultural districts have nothing to learn from the factory owners in the towns—or indeed from the middle classes in general—when it comes to being stupid and obdurate and blind to anything that doesn't put hard cash into their pockets. The manufacturers tell their workers that all their troubles will be over when the Corn Laws are repealed. The landlords and the majority of the farmers promise the farm labourers a heaven on earth if only the Corn Laws are preserved. But neither group of capitalists has succeeded in persuading the workers to support their own favourite panacea. Both factory workers and farm labourers are quite indifferent as to whether the Corn Laws are repealed or not. Yet the issue is an important one for both classes of worker. If the Corn Laws are repealed the principle of free competition—the hallmark of the existing economic relationship between social groups—will be completely unchecked. In such circumstances any new advance within the existing social and economic framework would be impossible and the only way to secure further progress would be by means of a radical social revolution.[2] The Corn Law question is also of importance to the farm workers for another reason. If the laws are repealed the tenant farmers will cease to be dependent, from an economic point of view, upon their landlords. How this will come about I cannot discuss at this point. But the result will be that the Tory farmer will become a Liberal farmer. The one valuable achievement of the Anti-Corn Law League has been to pave the way for this important

---

[1 *Northern Star*, no. 315, November 25th, 1843, p. 4, col. 1 and p. 6, col.4; no. 318, December 16th, 1843, p. 6, cols. 3-6; no. 320, December 30th, 1843, p. 6, col. 1-2; no. 321, January 6th, 1844, p. 6, col. 1; no. 322, January 13th, 1844, p. 5, col. 6; and no. 323, January 20th, 1844, p. 6, col. 6.]

[2] Engels's note to the English translation of 1887: 'This has been literally fulfilled. After a period of unexampled extension of trade, Free Trade has landed England in a crisis which began in 1878 and is still increasing in energy in 1886'.

change. Once the farmers become ' Liberal ' in politics—that is to say once they throw in their lot with the middle classes—it is inevitable that the farm workers will become Chartists and Socialists and throw in their lot with the proletariat. The second development follows logically from the first.

Already a new movement has begun among the agricultural labourers. This may be seen by what happened at a meeting held in October 1844 by the Liberal landlord, Lord Radnor, at Highworth, where his property is situated. His object in calling the meeting was to pass resolutions in favour of Corn Law repeal. But the farm labourers were apathetic as far as Corn Law repeal was concerned. They showed that they were interested in other matters. They told Lord Radnor a few home truths to his face and demanded small-holdings and low rents.[1] In this way the working-class movement is spreading to remote and stable agricultural districts which from the point of view of new ideas have long been dead. But in the countryside dire distress and misery will very soon lead to the development of a working-class movement which will be as active as it now is in the factory districts.[2]

Although the farm labourers have more contacts with religion than the factory workers, nevertheless they have, to a great extent, broken with the Church. Nearly all the labourers in the country districts belong to the Church of England. A correspondent of the *Morning Chronicle*[3] [July 1843] writing under the pen-name ' One who has whistled at the Plough ' described conditions in various agricultural districts which he had visited. He placed on record a conversation on the question of the Church which he had had with a farm labourer to whom he spoke after a service:

> . . . I inquired if the clergyman who had preached was the one who usually ministered there? The answer of one of the men . . . was ' Yes, blast him! he be our own parson sure enough—he be

[1 See *Northern Star*, no. 363, Oct. 26th, 1844, p. 6, cols. 2–6 for this meeting.]
[2] Engels added the following footnote to the English translation of 1887: ' The agricultural labourers have now a Trade's Union; their most energetic representative, Joseph Arch, was elected M.P. in 1885.'
[3 See *Morning Chronicle*, July 6th, 1843, p. 3, cols. 2–4: article entitled: ' The Farm Labourer. What is to be done?—More Churches or more Employment? (being a second notice of the Reports on the Employment of Women and Children in Agriculture, lately presented to Parliament by Command of Her Majesty) '. For Alexander Somerville, the writer of the article, see his autobiography, which was first published anonymously in 1848. A new edition appeared in 1951: Alexander Somerville, *The Autobiography of a Working Man* (ed. John Carswell). Somerville's articles on agricultural topics were reprinted in an abridged form under the title, *The Whistler at the Plough* (Manchester, 3 vols., 1852–3).]

always a begging[1]; he be always, sin' ever I knowed him'. 'And sin' I knowed him', said another, ' and that was afore he comed here. But for that part of it, I never knowed a parson as wasn't a begging for summat or tother'. 'Ah!' says a woman who came forward with some others, also just out of the church: 'And look at wages a comin' down, look at them rich wagerbonds as the parsons hunt and dine and drink with! So help me God we bes more fitter to be taken into the union and starved, than pay for parsons to go abroad'. ' Why don't they', said another, ' send them parsons as be chantering every day in Salisbury Cathedral to nobody but the bare stones, and be so rich as to have so much land all over, why don't they go?' ' *They* don't go ', said the old man who spoke first, ' because they be rich; they wants the money to send away the poor uns; I knows what they want; I been knowing them too long not to know that.'

' But my good friends ', said I, ' you surely don't go to church always and come out of it with such bitter dislike to the parsons as you have expressed now. If you do, why go at all?' ' Why go at all?' said the woman, ' we be like to go, and we wouldn't lose everything, work and all; we be like to go. . . .'

. . . And they could get a few privileges in regard to fuel and ground for potatoes (to be paid for), *if they went to church*. Hence they were hypocrites, ay, and dangerous ones. . . .'

After describing the poverty and ignorance of the agricultural labourers, the correspondent of the *Morning Chonicle* concludes his article with these words:

'. . . Now I assert fearlessly that the condition of these people, their poverty, their hatred of the churches, their outward compliance with, but inward bitterness towards, its dignitaries, is the rule throughout rural England; and that anything to the contrary is the exception. . . .'

In England the life of rural parishes is affected by the presence of a great army of agricultural labourers, but in Wales the situation is quite different, owing to the existence of a class of small tenant farmers. The contrast between property-owning capitalists and wage-earning farm labourers in the English countryside reproduces a situation which we have already examined in the towns. Similarly the condition of the Welsh peasantry reproduces the uninterrupted decline of the urban lower middle classes. The characteristic feature of Welsh agriculture is the existence of small tenant farmers. They sell their products in the same markets as the big English tenant farmers.

---

[1] Engels interpolates: ' The sermon had been on behalf of a mission to the heathen '.

But the small Welsh farmers are not in a position to produce so efficiently or to sell so cheaply as their English rivals. It must also be remembered that in many parts of Wales the nature of the soil forces the farmer to concentrate upon stock rearing, which is less profitable than arable farming. The Welsh farmers hold firmly to their national heritage and this makes them more conservative than English farmers. Competition with English farmers—coupled with rising rents—has had such a depressing effect upon agriculture in Wales that the farmers can barely make ends meet. Yet they do not appreciate the fundamental cause of their misery. Consequently they try to improve their position by agitating in favour of all sorts of minor reforms such as the abolition of high tolls on the turnpike roads. It is true that these tolls restrict traffic and prevent the expansion of agriculture, but they are a fixed charge which everyone who leases a farm knows about and therefore takes into account when agreeing to the rent. Such charges are in fact ultimately paid by the landlord. The new Poor Law, too, has been bitterly attacked in Wales. Even the small tenant farmers fear that one day they may end up in the workhouse. In February 1843 the unrest of the Welsh peasantry came to a head in the famous Rebecca riots.[1] Bands of armed men—who had blackened their faces and donned women's clothes—attacked toll-gates. To the sound of gunfire and loud cheers they pulled down the cottages of toll-keepers. They wrote threatening letters in the name of the imaginary ' Rebecca '. On one occasion they even stormed the workhouse at Carmarthen. In due course the police were reinforced and the troops were called out. But the insurgents showed great cunning in deceiving the champions of law and order. They burned down toll-gates while the troops—whose advance was heralded by bugle cries which echoed in the surrounding hills—marched in the opposite direction. When the number of troops in the district was so great that organized resistance was no longer possible, individual insurgents committed acts of individual violence—including incendiarism and even attempted murder. As always these greater crimes marked the end of the movement. Many of the insurgents were discontented while others were afraid. Law and order was automatically restored and the whole affair ended with the dispatch of a commission to Wales to investigate the causes and the events of the rising. The poverty of the peasantry continues and it will become worse rather than better in view of the existing social circumstances. One day distress in Wales will lead to more serious consequences than the farce of the Rebecca riots.

[1 For these riots see David Williams, *The Rebecca Riots* (University of Wales Press, 1955)].

Having discussed the agrarian economies of England (with its large estates) and Wales (with its small farms) and their social effects we turn now to Ireland, where we have to examine a country of tiny smallholdings. The vast majority of the Irish lease very small plots of land. They live in single-roomed cabins built of mud and rent a patch of ground on which they grow potatoes. They have a very low standard of living because their holdings are so small. The fierce competition for land between these smallholders has driven rents up to an incredible extent. Rents are twice, three times and even four times greater than in England.[1] Every farm labourer in Ireland wants to rent his own little plot and although there has been a great sub-division of farms there is still vigorous competition for every small-holding that a landlord wishes to rent. Ireland has 75,000 *more* agri-cultural labourers than England in spite of the fact that Great Britain has 34,254,000[2] acres of cultivated land compared with Ireland's 14,603,000[3] and that the [supposed] value of the annual agricultural produce of Great Britain is £150,000,000 whereas that of Ireland is only £36,000,000.[4] These statistics reveal the existence of an extremely unsatisfactory situation which greatly aggravates the competition for every scrap of Irish soil. The natural result is that rents are so high that the standard of life of the man who leases a small plot of land is little better than that of the wage-earning agricultural labourer. That is why the Irish people are sunk in such abject poverty, from which they cannot hope to escape so long as the present state of affairs

[1 For the most recent study of Irish agrarian conditions at the time Engels was writing see E. R. R. Green on 'Agriculture' in *The Great Famine: Studies in Irish History*, 1845–1852 (ed. R. Dudley Edwards and T. Desmond Williams, 1956), pp. 89–128.]

[2 In the original German edition Engels gave the figure as 32 millions.]

[3 In the original German edition Engels gave the figure as 14 millions.]

4 *Report of the Poor Law Commissioners for Ireland*, Parliamentary Session of 1837 [This is a reference to the *Third* (Final) *Report* of the Commissioners appointed in 1833 ' to inquire into the condition of the poorer classes in Ireland, and into the various institutions at present established by law for their relief. . . .' This report was published in 1836 (*Parliamentary Papers*, Vol. 34 of 1836). The figures quoted by Engels appear on pages 3 and 5 of the Report itself and on page 12 of Table III of Appendix (H), Part I, to the *Report*. The figure for the area of cultivated land in Great Britain is based on Cowling's estimate of 1827, and the figure for the area in Ireland, on Richard Griffith's estimate. The figure for the supposed annual value of the agricultural produce of Great Britain is an estimate made by the Commis-sioners on the basis of the property tax returns. The estimate of a similar kind for Ireland is the one made by Griffith. In the Marx-Engels-Lenin Institute reprint of Engels's book Adoratskij listed Sir George Nicholls's *Poor Laws—Ireland*: *Three Reports to Her Majesty's Principal Secretary of State for the Home Department* (London, 1838) as a source used by Engels. It appears that Adoratskij confused Nicholls's three reports (dated November 5th, 1836, November 3rd, 1837, and May 5th, 1838) with the three earlier reports of 1835–36 from the Commissioners appointed in 1833.]

continues. [It has been seen that] the people live in miserable mud huts which are hardly fit for animals. During the winter they have to go short of food. The report which we have cited states that for thirty weeks in the year the consumption of potatoes in Ireland gives the people about half the nourishment that they would obtain from a really adequate diet. And for the other twenty-two weeks they must manage as best they can. In the spring a time comes when potato supplies are exhausted or when the remaining potatoes are no longer edible. Then the women and children go round the district begging— the women carrying their teapots with them. After the potatoes are planted the men take jobs as farm labourers either in Ireland itself or in England and they do not return home again until harvest time. That is how nine-tenths of the inhabitants of the Irish countryside live. They are as poor as church mice; they go about in rags; their educational attainments are negligible. In short the Irish can only be regarded as a half-civilized people. According to the report to which we have referred there are in Ireland—with its population of eight and a half millions[1]—no less than 585,000 heads of families who are totally destitute. According to sources quoted by Sheriff Alison there are 2,300,000[2] people in Ireland who can survive only if they receive public or private relief. In other words, 27 per cent of the Irish population are paupers.[3]

We have shown that this poverty is caused by the existing social circumstances—above all by competition, which in Ireland takes the form of the continual subdivision of holdings. Great efforts have been made to explain Irish poverty by drawing attention to other factors in the situation. Some argue that the real cause of trouble is the existence of middlemen between the landowner and the cultivator. The owners of the huge estates lease their land in large farms which in turn are divided and sublet in smaller holdings. In the end there may be as many as ten ' landlords ' between the man who tills the soil and the owner of the land. It has been argued that distress is due to the scandalous law which makes it possible for a landlord to eject a cultivator who has paid his rent because the tenant immediately responsible for paying the rent has failed to do so. But this law merely determines the *way in which* poverty manifests itself in Ireland. What

[1 According to the Census of 1841 the civil population of Ireland was 8,175,124: G. R. Porter, *The Progress of the Nation* (1851 edn.), p. 9.]
[2 The actual figure was 2,385,000. This estimate was given in the *Third Report* (1836, p. 5) of the Commissioners for enquiring into the conditions of the poorer classes in Ireland.]
3 Sir Archibald Alison, *The Principles of Population* (2 vols., 1840), Vol. 2 [p. 218].
[See Sir G. Nicholls, *A History of the Irish Poor Law* (1856), pp. 133-4.]

would happen if the smallholder were actually the owner of his plot of land? Even if they no longer had to pay rent most of them would still not be able to wring a livelihood from their little farms. Any improvement in their situation would soon be lost again owing to the continuing and rapid increase in the population. Those smallholders who were in a better position would find that their children—who now die at an early age owing to the poverty of their parents—would grow up [and this would lead to an increase in population]. Others argue that Ireland's poverty is due to the utterly shameless manner in which the English exploit the country. The English are indeed responsible for the fact that poverty strikes the Irish a little sooner than it would otherwise do. But they cannot be held responsible for the poverty itself. Again, it has been argued that poverty and distress are due to the fact that a Protestant Established Church has been forced upon a Catholic people. But what this Church takes from the Irish amounts to less than six shillings a head [a year]. In any case tithes really come out of the pockets of the landlords, although until 1838 they were actually paid by the tenants. The Commutation Act of that year provided that tithes should be paid by the landlords. But this has made no difference to the tenants since the landlords have raised rents in order to pay the tithes. Hundreds of other reasons have been suggested to account for Irish poverty and they are all wrong. The truth is that poverty and distress are the inevitable consequences of the existing state of society. When we look for other causes we are really examining factors in the situation which determine the way in which poverty strikes the Irish. But we are not dealing with the basic cause of poverty. The actual manner in which poverty strikes the Irish may be explained by the history, traditions and national characteristics of the people. The Irish have a strong affinity with the Latin races such as the French and the Italians. The resemblance to the Italians is particularly strong. We have already quoted a passage from Carlyle which illustrates the less admirable side of the Irish character. Now let us hear what an Irishman has to say about his fellow-countrymen—and he is more likely to understand the Irish than Carlyle, whose sympathies are all with the Teutonic races. It is stated in a pamphlet, written in 1807, that the Irish are ' restless yet indolent, shrewd and indiscreet, impetuous, impatient and improvident, instinctively brave, thoughtlessly generous; quick to resent and forgive offences, to form and renounce friendships, they will forgive injury rather than insult; their country's good they seldom, their own, they carelessly pursue, but the honour of both they eagerly vindicate;

oppression they have long borne, insolence never. With genius they are profusely gifted; with judgment sparingly; . . . '[1]

In Ireland passions and sentiment rule supreme and reason takes a back seat. The sensuous and excitable nature of the Irish prevents them from undertaking tasks which require sober judgment and tenacity of purpose. Obviously such a people are not able to engage in industry as it is carried on to-day. So they must stick to farming—and farming of a very primitive kind at that. In Ireland the land has been divided into tiny plots from time immemorial, whereas in France and in the Rhineland the same result was achieved by carving up great estates.[2] In the present state of agriculture in Ireland a radical improvement of soil would cost so enormous a sum that this would not be a practical solution to the problem. Alison estimates that £120,000,000 would be needed to raise the productivity of Irish land to the admittedly low English level. The English immigration might well have had the effect of raising Ireland's low level of civilisation. In fact the English immigrants have been content to exploit the Irish in a brutal fashion. Ireland has no cause to be grateful to the English immigrants. On the other hand the Irish immigrants in England have added an explosive force to English society which will have significant consequences in due course.

The Irish people have resisted oppression in two ways—by acts of violence and by agitation for the repeal of the Union. Crime is endemic in the rural districts and not a day passes without the perpetration of some serious breach of the law. Nor do the Irish hesitate to kill their oppressors—the agents and other faithful henchmen of the landlords, the Protestant intruders, and the substantial tenants whose farms have been established by evicting hundreds of Irish peasants from their tiny potato patches. These sworn enemies of the Irish people are to be found mainly in the South and West of Ireland [and it is here that crimes of violence are most common].

From what we have written it is obvious that the ignorant Irish inevitably regard the English as their immediate enemies. They consider that the first step towards improving their condition must be to secure national independence. But it is equally clear that the

---

[1] Pamphlet entitled: *The State of Ireland* (London, first edn. 1807, second edn. 1821). [This pamphlet, the correct title of which is *A Sketch of the State of Ireland Past and Present*, was written by John Wilson Croker. The quotation appears on page 27 of the 2nd edition published in London in 1808.]

[2] In the German edition of 1892 Engels added in a footnote: ' Mistake. Smallholdings were common in the middle ages and existed before the French Revolution. What was altered after 1789 was the nature of the *tenure*. The *ownership* of the land was transferred—directly or indirectly—from the feudal lord to the peasant.']

repeal of the Union would not itself automatically put an end to poverty and distress in Ireland. Once the Union has been repealed the Irish will realise that the causes of poverty—which they now think lie outside their own shores—must in fact be sought at home. It is, however, doubtful whether it will really be necessary to secure the repeal of the Union before the Irish realise the true reasons for their misery. Up to the present [it must be admitted that] neither the Chartists nor the Socialists have had much success in Ireland. Since the agitation for the repeal of the Union in 1843 and the trial of Daniel O'Connell have brought the sufferings of the Irish people to the notice of my readers in Germany, it will hardly be necessary for me to say anything more on this subject.

We have now examined all the various working-class groups [—the factory workers, the miners, the farm labourers—] in the British Isles. Everywhere we have found poverty, distress and dreadful living conditions. We have seen how the working classes have become more and more discontented. We have seen how this discontent has grown and has been canalised into organised resistance. We have seen how the workers have openly expressed their discontent and have openly resisted the oppression of the middle classes—sometimes peaceably, sometimes violently. We have analysed the fundamental factors which influence the fate of the working classes. We have considered the basic principles which guide their hopes and their fears. And we see that there is no hope for any improvement in their condition. From time to time we have been able to observe the attitude of the middle classes towards the workers and we have seen that the bourgeoisie is utterly selfish and acts only in its own private interests. We do not wish, however, to pass a hasty judgment on the middle classes and so we propose to examine their conduct in more detail.

CHAPTER XII

ATTITUDE OF THE BOURGEOISIE

When I speak of the 'bourgeoisie' in this chapter I am referring not only to the middle classes proper but also to the so-called aristocracy. This is because the privileges enjoyed by the aristocracy affect their relations with the middle classes rather than with the workers. Since all other privileges sink into insignificance when coupled with the privilege of property, the workers regard both bourgeoisie and aristocracy together as a single property-owning class. The only difference between the middle classes (in the narrower sense) and the aristocracy is this: the former come into direct contact with the factory workers, some of the miners and (if they are farmers) with the agricultural labourers. But the latter have relations only with certain miners and with the farm workers [but not with the factory operatives].

I have never seen so demoralised a social class as the English middle classes. They are so degraded by selfishness and moral depravity as to be quite incapable of salvation. And here I refer to the bourgeoisie proper (in the narrower sense of the term)—and in particular to the 'Liberal' section of the English middle classes which supports the repeal of the Corn Laws. The middle classes have a truly extraordinary conception of society. They really believe that all human beings (themselves excluded) and indeed all living things and inanimate objects have a real existence only if they make money or help to make it. Their sole happiness is derived from gaining a quick profit. They feel pain only if they suffer a financial loss.[1] Every single human quality with which they are endowed is grossly debased by selfish greed and love of gain. Admittedly the English middle classes make good husbands and family men. They have also all sorts of so-called 'private virtues'. In the ordinary daily affairs of life they seem to be as respectable and as decent as the members of any other middle class. One finds them better than Germans to deal with in business. The English do not condescend to that petty haggling which characterises the German trader with his pathetically limited horizon. But what is the use of all that? When all comes to all what really matters to the

---

[1] In *Past and Present* (London, 1843) Carlyle has given a wonderful description of the English middle classes, in which he paints a vivid picture of their revolting greed for money. I may refer my readers to my translation of part of this book in the *Deutsch-Französische Jahrbücher*. [This article by Engels is printed in *Gesamtausgabe*, Part I, Vol. 2, pp. 405-431].

Englishman is his own interest and above all his desire to make money.

One day I walked with one of these middle-class gentlemen into Manchester. I spoke to him about the disgraceful unhealthy slums and drew his attention to the disgusting condition of that part of the town in which the factory workers lived. I declared that I had never seen so badly built a town in my life. He listened patiently and at the corner of the street at which we parted company he remarked: 'And yet there is a great deal of money made here.[1] Good morning, Sir '.

So long as they are making money it is a matter of complete indifference to the English middle classes if their workers eat or starve. They regard hard cash as a universal measuring rod. Anything that yields no financial gain is dismissed as ' stupid ', ' impractical ', or ' idealistic '. That is why these petty Jewish chafferers are such devoted students of economics—the science of making money. Every one of them is an economist. There is no human tie between manufacturers and workers—only an economic link. The manufacturers are ' capital ' and the operatives are ' labour '. The middle classes are utterly dumb-founded if the workers refuse to accept this abstract relationship of ' capital ' and ' labour ' and declare that they are not ' labour ' at all, but human beings who possess other attributes besides the ability to work. The bourgeoisie are quite unable to grasp the point of view of workers who argue that they should not have to offer their ' labour ' for sale in the same way that goods are brought and sold at a market. It lies quite outside the comprehension of the middle classes that there should be any relationship between masters and men other than the purely economic link. The bourgeoisie see in the workers only ' hands '[2] and they call them ' hands ' to their faces. As Carlyle says, the middle classes can conceive of no relationship between human beings other than the cash nexus. Even the relationship between man and wife, in this class of society, is a purely financial one in ninety-nine marriages out of a hundred.

The middle classes in England have become the slaves of the money they worship. Even the English language is permeated by the one idea that dominates the waking hours of the bourgeoisie. People are ' valued ' in terms of hard cash. They say of a man: ' He is worth £10,000 ',[3] and by that they mean that he possesses that sum. Anyone who has money is ' respectable '. He belongs to ' the better sort of people '. He is said to be ' influential ', which means that what he

[1 'And yet there is a great deal of money made here ' is in English in the first German edition of 1845.]

[2 The word ' hands ' is in English in the first German edition of 1845].

[3 ' He is worth £10,000 ' is in English in the first German edition of 1845.]

says carried weight in the circles in which he moves.[1] The spirit of
petty bargaining permeates the whole language. Everything is
expressed in commercial terms or in the categories of the science of
economics. The English judge every aspect of life in terms of ' supply
and demand '.[2] The English middle classes believe in absolutely
unbridled freedom of competition, consequently the principle of
' laissez faire ' is allowed to dominate government and administration,
medicine, education and even religion—for the authority of the Established Church is rapidly declining. The bourgeoisie believe that
free competition should be absolutely unchecked. The State should
have no power whatsoever to interfere with this holy principle. The
bourgeois ideal is a society in which there is no ' State ' at all to
exercise any authority—a state of anarchy comparable with that in
friend Stirner's ' society ',[3] where everybody can exploit everybody
else to their heart's content. But the English middle classes cannot do
without the State just as they cannot do without the workers. They
need the State to keep the workers in order. Nevertheless the bourgeoisie do everything to prevent the State from interfering in any way
with their own affairs.

It must not be supposed that the ' educated ' Englishman frankly
acknowledges his love of money. On the contrary he tries to hide his
selfish greed in the most hypocritical manner. Englishmen are shocked
if anyone suggests that they neglect their duty towards the poor. Have
they not subscribed to the erection of more institutions for the relief
of poverty than are to be found anywhere else in the world? Yes,
indeed—welfare institutions! The vampire middle classes first suck
the wretched workers dry so that afterwards they can, with consum-
mate hypocrisy, throw a few miserable crumbs of charity at their
feet. And then they have the effrontery to appear before the world as
paragons of charity. It never occurs to these pharisees that they are
only returning a hundredth part of that which they have previously
taken away from the broken-down workers whom they have ruthlessly
exploited. Charity—when he who gives is more degraded than he
who receives. Charity—when the recipient is trodden even deeper
into the mud than he was before. Charity—when those who dispense
alms insist that those who receive them must first be cast out of

---

[1 The words ' respectable ', ' the better sort of people ', and ' influential ' are
in English in the first German edition of 1845.]

[2 ' Supply and demand ' is in English in the first German edition of 1845.]

[3 This is a reference to a book by Max Stirner (pen-name for Johann Kaspar
Schmidt) entitled *Der Einzige und sein Eigenthum* (Leipzig, 1845). The words ' in
friend Stirner's " society " ', were omitted in Florence Kelley Wischnewetzky's
English translation of 1887].

society as pariahs and must be deprived of their last shred of self-respect by being *forced to beg*! Only then will the middle classes be graciously pleased to give something in charity—and in doing so the beggar is stamped for ever as one who has lost all claims to be regarded as a human being. There is no need to take my word for it. Just hear what the English middle classes have to say for themselves. It is hardly a year ago since I saw in the *Manchester Guardian* the following letter which the editor printed (without comment) as if the views expressed were the most natural in the world:

Sir,

For sometime past numerous beggars are to be seen on the streets of our town. They attempt—often in a truly brazen and offensive manner—to arouse the pity of the public by their ragged clothes, their wretched appearance, their disgusting wounds and sores, and by showing the stumps of amputated limbs. I should have thought that those of us who not only pay our poor rates but also subscribe generously to charitable appeals have done enough to claim the right to be shielded from such disgusting and revolting sights. Why do we pay such high rates to support the borough police if they cannot even give us adequate protection so that we can leave our home and walk on the Queen's Highway in peace? I hope that the publication of this letter in your paper, which has a large circulation, will lead to the suppression of this nuisance.

I remain

Your obedient servant

A Lady.[1]

There you have it! The charity of the English middle classes springs merely from self-interest. The bourgeoisie give nothing away.

[1 A search has been made for the original version of this letter in the files of the *Manchester Guardian*. No letter corresponding exactly to the one printed by Engels has been found but the following from 'A Female Sufferer', expressing somewhat similar sentiments, appeared in the issue for December 20th, 1843:

STREET BEGGARS

To the Editor of the *Manchester Guardian*

Sir,

Will you allow me, through the medium of your valuable journal, to call the attention of the authorities to the numbers of beggars, who, on market days especially, station themselves in various parts of the town, exhibiting burnt or maimed limbs, and forcibly obtruding themselves on the attention of passers-by, to the great annoyance of all who see them, particularly the ladies, some of whom have received injuries the most deplorable. Had I known any better method of bringing this before the notice of the proper authorities I should have adopted it.

Yours

A Female Sufferer.

Broughton, Dec. 16th, 1843.

The similarity between parts of the two letters is very striking.]

The middle classes make a *bargain* with the poor and say: ' If I pay so much to charity *I am purchasing the right* not to be troubled any more. You must promise to stay in your dark dens and not disturb my delicate nervous system by displaying your misery in public. You may despair but—by subscribing £20 to a hospital—I have purchased the right to insist that you should despair in private '. How infamous is the charity of the English bourgeoisie. The correspondent of the *Manchester Guardian* did well to sign herself 'A Lady '. Happily she did not have the nerve to call herself 'A Woman '. But if that letter is typical of English ' ladies ' what can one expect from English ' gentlemen '?

It may be argued that this letter is an isolated case. Not at all. If the letter had not aptly represented the attitude of the vast majority of the English bourgeoisie the editor would not have printed it and having published it he would have received letters of protest from the public. But I have looked in vain in subsequent issues of the *Manchester Guardian* for any protests. How effective are the charitable efforts of the bourgeoisie? Canon Parkinson states that the poor are helped much more by the workers than by the middle classes. When a decent worker, who knows from personal experience what it is to go hungry, cheerfully shares his crust with one who is starving—that sort of help is something quite different from the charity that the well-fed bourgeoisie disdainfully throw to the poor.

There is no limit to the hypocritical ' humanity ' of the middle classes. But their humanity is always subordinated to their own interests. This applies to their politics and to their economics. For five years they have moved heaven and earth to pursuade the public that they favour the repeal of the Corn Laws because this will benefit the working classes. The long and the short of the matter is that the Corn Laws keep the price of bread higher in England than elsewhere. Consequently the employers have to pay higher wages. This in turn means that the factory owners find that their costs are raised and that it is difficult for them to compete with industries in foreign countries where both the price of bread and the level of wages are lower than in England. If the English Corn Laws were repealed then the price of the loaf would fall and employers would be able to reduce wages to the level of other civilized European countries. All this will be quite clear to those who appreciate the principles—which we have discussed above—concerning the regulation of wages. [If the Corn Laws were repealed and both bread prices and wages fell] the manufacturers would be in a better position than before to compete with their foreign rivals. There would be an increased demand for English goods—

followed by an increased demand for labour in England. This new demand for labour would, it is true, lead to a slight advance in wages. But how long would that last? The ' surplus population of England ' —and especially that of Ireland—would soon supply English industry with all the workers it needed, even if the number of factories were doubled. In a few years the trifling immediate advantages gained by the workers from the repeal of the Corn Laws would be lost again. A new commercial crisis would be upon us and then the workers would be back again where they were at the beginning. [In fact they would be in a worse position than before because] meanwhile the [temporary] trade boom would have led to an acceleration in the rate of increase in the population. The workers understand all this perfectly well. They have said so openly and frankly a hundred times. But the whole race of factory owners can only see the *temporary immediate* advantages that they hope to secure from the repeal of the Corn Laws. The manufacturers are so incredibly stupid that they cannot understand that they cannot secure *permanent or lasting* advantages from the repeal of the Corn Laws because eventually the competition between manufacturers themselves is obviously bound to bring profits back to their former level. Nevertheless the manufacturers persistently scream at the top of their voices that they advocate the repeal of the Corn Laws simply and solely to benefit the workers. They claim that it is only for the sake of the starving masses that the wealthy members of the liberal party pour hundreds and thousands of pounds into the coffers of the Anti-Corn Law League. Yet everyone knows that the manufacturers are in fact throwing a sprat to catch a mackerel. They expect to get ten or a hundred times as much money back within a few years of the abolition of the Corn Laws. The workers, however, are not allowing themselves to be deceived by the middle classes—especially after what happened at the time of the workers' rising of 1842. The proletariat insist that anyone who claims to be a friend of the workers should give proof of his sincerity by subscribing to the Charter. The workers declare that they need no assistance from other classes in society. They demand the Charter so that they can secure the *power to help themselves*. The workers rightly regard as their foes all—be they declared enemies or false friends—who refuse to accept the Charter.

It may be added that the supporters of the Anti-Corn Law League have told barefaced lies and have employed gross deceptions to win over the workers to their cause. They have actually said that money wages must vary in inverse ratio to the price of corn—that low corn prices are accompanied by high wages and *vice versa*. This proposition —supported by the most ridiculous arguments imaginable—is indeed the most truly ridiculous assertion ever made by any economist. If the workers failed to swallow this fairy tale the manufacturer would promise them immeasurable prosperity from the increased demand for labour that they anticipate will follow from the repeal of the Corn Laws. They have actually had the effrontery to parade two models of loaves of bread through the streets. The big loaf bore the legend 'American 8d. loaf. Wages 4s. a day '. The much smaller loaf bore the words: ' English 8d. loaf. Wages 2s. a day '. But the English workers are not taken in by propaganda of this sort. They know their employers too well for that.

In order to appreciate fully the disgraceful hypocrisy of these fine promises it is only necessary to see how the bourgeoisie actually treat the workers in practice. We have already shown how the middle classes exploit the proletariat in every conceivable fashion. Hitherto, however, we have been concerned with the way in which individual members of the middle classes oppress particular workers for their own benefit. Let us now turn our attention to the way in which the workers are treated by the bourgeoisie when they act as a united class and use the power of the State for their own ends. It is obvious that the whole legal system has been devised to protect those who own property from those who do not. The laws are needed only because people exist who have no property. This aspect of the laws is admitted with brutal frankness in only a few cases. The laws against vagrancy and being without visible means of support openly brand the proletariat as an illegal group in society. Nevertheless at the root of all laws lies the idea that the proletariat is an enemy which must be defeated. This can be seen from the way in which the law is administered by the judges. This is particularly true of the Justices of the Peace—themselves members of the middle class—and it is with these that the proletariat for the most part comes into contact. The Justices of the Peace have no hesitation in regarding the administration of the law as a means of keeping the working classes down. Let a prosperous member of the middle classes be summoned—or rather, politely ' invited to appear '—before a magistrate. The court naturally expresses regret that he should have been troubled to appear at all. The magistrate does everything in his power to smooth the path of the accused. And if the charge against the rich man is conclusively proved then the magistrate, with profuse apologies, merely imposes a trifling fine. The rich man flings the money contemptuously on the table and takes himself off. But if some poor devil of a worker appears before the magistrate it is quite a different story. He has nearly always had to spend the previous night—with other prisoners—in the lock-up.

The magistrate shouts at him and assumes from the first that he is guilty. His defence is contemptuously brushed aside with the remark: ' We have heard that sort of excuse before '. Then he is fined and since he has not got enough money to pay the fine he has to go to prison for a month (or even longer) and suffer on the treadmill. If nothing specific can be proved against the poor devil he can still be sent to the treadmill on the grounds that he is ' a rogue and a vagabond '[1]— the two nearly always go together. The prejudice of the Justices of the Peace—particularly in rural areas—against the working classes beggars description. Public opinion accepts this state of affairs and it is only the really scandalous cases of judicial prejudice that arouse any comment in the newspapers. Generally the facts are reported without comment. And this is what one might expect. These ' Dogberries '[2] in fact interpret the law as it was always intended that it should be interpreted. And the Justices of the Peace are, of course, themselves members of the bourgeoisie and really believe that the interests of their own class are the true corner-stone of law and order. The police follow the lead given by the magistrates. A policeman will always treat a member of the middle classes with every courtesy whatever he may do and will stretch the law in his favour as far as he possibly can. But a worker who falls into the hands of the police is immediately treated in a nasty and brutal fashion. The fact that a worker is poor is sufficient for him to be suspected of every crime in the calendar. The worker loses all the legal protection to which he should be entitled against the arbitrary conduct of the police. The protection which the law usually gives is denied to the worker. The police do not hesitate to enter his house, to arrest him and even to knock him about. Only when a trade union, such as the miners' union, secures the services of a man of the standing of W. P. Roberts are such abuses of the law brought to light. Then the public get to know how often the worker has to put up with all the drawbacks of the law without benefitting from any of the advantages which it affords.

The capitalists in Parliament are still trying—against the more enlightened views of those not wholly sunk in degrading selfishness —to keep the workers down as much as possible. One after another of the public commons are taken away from the workers and are used as building sites. The new houses may raise working-class living standards but they do the proletariat untold harm. A common was a place

[1 The words ' a rogue and a vagabond ' are in English in the first German edition of 1845.]

[2 ' Dogberries ' is in English in the German edition of 1845.]

on which poor people could keep a donkey, a pig or a few geese. There the young people could play and amuse themselves. But all this is being stopped. The workers lose a source of income when a common is taken away and the young people, having lost a playground, drift into the public houses. Every session of parliament sees the passing of several Acts for the enclosure of commons.

In the parliamentary session of 1844 the government decided to force the railway companies—those great transport monopolists—to run trains at fares which the workers could afford. A Bill was brought forward which laid it down that on every line one [stopping] train a day should be provided. The third-class fare on these trains was to be one penny a mile. Thereupon that reverend Father in God, the Bishop of London, proposed that no such trains should be run on a Sunday, which is obviously the only day in the week on which a worker with a job to do is free to travel. If the Bishop's proposal had been adopted the rich could have continued to go by train on Sundays while the poor would have been prevented from doing so. This suggestion however, was so shamelessly and so blatantly biased that it had to be dropped.[1]

I have not enough space to list all the disguised attacks on the workers that are made even in a single session of parliament. But I will give just one more example from the same session as before (1844). A certain Mr. [P. W. S.] Miles—quite an obscure Member of Parliament—brought forward a Bill to regulate the relations of masters and men which seemed to be harmless enough. The government assumed responsibility for the Bill and it passed the Committee stage. Meanwhile a great strike broke out in the coalfields of the north of England and W. P. Roberts made his triumphal progress through the country at the head of the strikers whose innocence he had proved in cases which had come before the courts. When Mr. Miles's Bill emerged from the Committee stage it was found that a highly objectionable clause had been inserted. This would have given every employer new rights over his workers. The clauses covered every kind of contract of service from written agreements to quite informal bargains sealed by shaking hands. It was proposed that if an employee broke his contract by refusing to carry out any task which he had agreed to perform or if he were guilty of ' misbehaviour ' of any sort he could be hailed before a Justice of the Peace, who received the power to give him up to two

[1 See article on ' The Railway Bill—More Oppression for the Poor ' in *Weekly Dispatch*, no. 2232, Aug. 4th, 1844, p. 369, col. 4. It was the Bishop of Lichfield who spoke in the House of Lords—in the absence of the Bishop of London—in support of omitting Sundays, Good Friday and Christmas Day from the provision of the Railways Bill.]

months hard labour simply on evidence, given on oath, by the employer himself or by his agents—that is to say by the very people who were making the complaint. The workers, who were already engaged in a powerful agitation in favour of the Ten Hours Bill (which was also before Parliament at this time), were enraged beyond measure at Mr. Miles's Bill [as amended in Committee]. Hundreds of meetings of protest were held. Hundreds of petitions, signed by workers, were sent to Thomas [Slingsby] Duncombe, who represented working-class interests in the House of Commons at this time. Except for Mr. [W. B.] Ferrand (a supporter of the 'Young England' movement), Duncombe was the only Member of Parliament who strenuously opposed Mr. Miles's Bill. But when the other Radicals realised that the people were emphatically against the Bill they crept, one after another, out of their holes and gave Duncombe their support. The 'liberal' middle classes, too, lacked the courage to speak up in favour of the Bill once they realised how strongly it was opposed by the workers. In the end nobody was prepared to flout public opinion by saying a good word for the Bill, which soon came to an inglorious end.[1]

It is, however, Malthus's theory of population—and the new poor law to which it gave rise—which represent the most flagrant warlike aggression of the middle classes against the workers. We have already mentioned Malthus's theory more than once. Let us summarise Malthus's main conclusion once more. He argues that because the world is always over-populated it is inevitable that hunger, distress, poverty and immorality will always be with us. He says that an over-populated world is humanity's eternal destiny from which there is no escape. Consequently men must be divided into different classes. Some of these classes will be more or less wealthy, educated and moral and others will be more or less poor, miserable, ignorant and immoral. From these facts Malthus comes to the conclusion that private charity and public provision for the poor are really useless since they merely serve to keep alive—and even to promote the growth of—the surplus population. And the competition for jobs between the surplus workers and those in employment tends to depress the level of wages. Malthus also argues that it is equally ineffectual to put paupers to work in poor-houses. Only a fixed quantity of goods can be consumed and therefore every time a pauper is set to work another worker loses his employment. In this way private industry is injured

[1 See *Northern Star*, no. 338, May 4th, 1844, p. 4, col. 6, p. 5, col. 1—article headed 'The Damnable Bill Crushed! Government Defeated! Triumph for Labour!']

by competition from 'workhouse industry'. According to Malthus the problem to be solved is not the finding of employment for paupers but the reduction of the number of paupers by one means or another. Malthus calmly dismisses as nonsense the traditional view that every human being has an inalienable right to food, clothing and shelter. He uses the words of a poet to describe a poor man who applies in vain for a share of 'nature's mighty feast'. But 'there is no vacant cover for him'. 'He forgot to ask society before he was born whether there was any room for him or not'.[1]

It is not surprising that this harsh doctrine should have been firmly held by the English middle classes.[2] By accepting this convenient though specious theory as gospel truth the bourgeoisie can cheerfully stand on one side and ignore the whole problem of poverty. Moreover there is much to be said for Malthus's view that the existing economic system and the present structure of society are to be regarded as sacrosant and unchangeable. It is obviously easy to solve the problem of pauperism if no attempt is made to turn the 'surplus population' into *useful* members of society and if all that has to be done is to persuade the paupers to die of starvation without making a fuss and to refrain from bringing too many pauper children into the world. This assumes, of course, that the 'surplus population' accepts the fact that it *is* superfluous and makes no objection to dying of

[1 Engels does not quote Malthus correctly. The notorious passage—frequently criticised by the workers during the troubles of 1842— runs as follows:

A man who is born into a world already possessed, if he cannot get subsistence from his parents on whom he has a just demand, and if the society do not want his labour, has no claim of *right* to the smallest portion of food, and, in fact, has no business to be where he is. At nature's mighty feast there is no vacant cover for him. She tells him to be gone, and will quickly execute her own orders, if he do not work upon the compassion of some of her guests. If these guests get up and make room for him, other intruders immediately appear demanding the same favour. The report of a provision for all that come, fills the hall with numerous claimants. The order and harmony of the feast is disturbed, the plenty that before reigned is changed into scarcity; and the happiness of the guests is destroyed by the spectacle of misery and dependence in every part of the hall, and by the clamorous importunity of those, who are justly enraged at not finding the provision which they had been taught to expect. The guests learn too late their error, in counteracting those strict orders to all intruders, issued by the great mistress of the feast, who, wishing that all her guests should have plenty, and knowing that she could not provide for unlimited numbers, humanely refused to admit fresh comers when her table was already full.

The passage appeared in the *second edition* (1803) of *An Essay on the Principle of Population*, p. 531. It was omitted from the edition of 1807 and from subsequent editions, though the substance of the argument remained. The passage is quoted by J. M. Keynes, *Essays in Biography* (1933). p. 126, and by G. Kitson Clark, 'Hunger and Politics in 1842' in *The Journal of Modern History*, Vol. 25, no. 4, December 1953, p. 357 (note 5).]

[2 Engels wrote 'the genuine middle classes'—i.e. the middle classes in the narrower sense as defined above, p. 311.]

hunger. So far, however, in spite of their most strenuous efforts, the humane middle classes have not been able to make the workers understand this simple theory and it hardly looks as if they are likely to be more successful in the future. The workers, on the contrary, take the view that their labour is essential and that it is the wealthy capitalists, who neither toil nor spin, who should really be regarded as ' superfluous '.

The wealthy, however, are still in power and so the workers must either willingly agree to being treated as ' superfluous ' or they must submit to having laws passed which are based upon the assumption that they are ' superfluous '. And that is what has happened with the passing of the new Poor Law Amendment Act of 1834. The former Poor Law was based upon an Act passed in 1601 (the 43rd of Elizabeth). The authors of this Act naïvely assumed that it was the duty of each parish to support its own poor. Relief was granted to the unemployed. Poor people, as was only reasonable, assumed that the parish was bound to save them from starving for as long as they were unable to provide for themselves. They demanded a weekly dole—not as charity—but as a right. Eventually this proved too much for the middle classes. As soon as they gained power as the result of the passing of the Reform Bill [of 1832]—and this was just when pauperism in the rural districts reached unprecedented proportions—the middle classes inaugurated a reform of the poor law in accordance with their own point of view. A commission was appointed to enquire into the working of the poor law and many abuses were brought to light. It was found that the whole class of agricultural labourers was utterly demoralised. The farm workers were partly or wholly dependent upon poor relief since they were able to supplement their low wages by applying to the poor law authorities. It was found that poverty as such had a claim upon the public purse; that the able bodied unemployed were being assisted; that those who were employed but were receiving low wages were having their incomes supplemented from the rates; and that it was a function of the poor law authorities to make men contribute towards the support of their illegitimate children. The Poor Law Commissioners reached the conclusion that this system was ruining the country and had become

'a check to industry, a reward for improvident marriages, a stimulant to population, and a blind to its effects on wages . . . a national institution for discountenancing the industrious and honest, and for protecting the idle, the improvident and the vicious . . . the destroyer of filial, parental and conjugal affection, a system for preventing the accumulation of capital, for destroying that which exists, and for reducing the ratepayer to pauperism ... [and] a premium for illegitimate children, exhibited in the allowance for illegitimate as compared with that for legitimate.'[1]

This description of the working of the old poor law is, by and large, true enough since the relief [given under the ' Speenhamland System ' certainly] encouraged idleness and promoted the increase of the ' superfluous ' population. Under present social conditions a poor man is obviously forced to be an egoist and if he has the choice between work and unemployment—with the same income—he naturally prefers to live in idleness. All that this proves is that the existing state of society is no good. It does not prove that poverty is an offence meriting severe punishment as a warning to other potential paupers. But that was the view taken by the Poor Law Commissioners who accepted Malthus's views without question.

But these wise Malthusians were so convinced that their theory was right that they lost no time in trying to force the poor into the Procrustean bed of their preconceived doctrines. To do this they treated the poor with incredible savagery. With Malthus and other supporters of free competition, these people are fully convinced that the best thing to do is carry the laissez-faire doctrine to its logical conclusion and leave everybody entirely to his own devices. They would have liked to have abolished the poor laws altogether. Having neither the courage nor the power to do so, they proposed to have as Malthusian a poor law as possible. This is an even more barbaric policy than laissez-faire, for it is an active policy whereas laissez-faire is merely a passive attitude. We have seen that Malthus declared that poverty—strictly speaking inability to earn enough food—made people ' superfluous ' and was really a crime that society should punish by death from starvation. The Poor Law Commissioners were not, in fact, prepared to adopt quite so barbaric a policy as that. Even Poor Law Commissioners drew back in horror from plainly condemning a pauper to death by starvation. So what the Poor Law Commissioners said to the poor was this: ' You have the right to exist— but *just* to exist and no more. You have certainly no right to breed —still less to live in a civilized way like normal human beings. You are like a plague. Even if we do not take steps to get rid of you as we would stamp out any other plague, we shall at any rate make you appreciate the fact that you *are* a plague. We shall at least prevent this plague of poverty from spreading for we shall make it

---

[1] *Extracts from the Information received by His Majesty's Commissioners, as to the Administration and Operation of the Poor-Laws* (London, 1833), [p. xvi. This is not a quotation from the text of the report but from the subject-index, under ' POOR-LAWS, as at present administered '. See below, Appendix V].

impossible for you to breed any more " superfluous " paupers and we shall stop you from contaminating others who might become idle or unemployed through your evil example. We shall let you live —but only as an awful example to others who might be tempted to become " superfluous ".'

They produced the new Poor Law which was passed by Parliament in 1834 and is still in force. It forbade all outdoor relief in money or food. The only relief offered to the poor was admission to the new workhouses which were promptly erected all over the country. These establishments—people call them 'Poor Law Bastilles'[1]—are conducted in such a manner as to frighten away everyone who can possibly survive without accepting this form of public relief. So as to be quite certain that the poor will make every conceivable effort to support themselves and will apply for public charity only in the absolutely last extremity the workhouse has been turned into as truly repulsive an abode as the perverted ingenuity of the Malthusians can devise. The food is worse than that enjoyed by the poorest labourer in employment. In return the pauper is forced to work harder than he would in a normal job. If this policy were not adopted the paupers would obviously prefer life in the workhouse to their miserable existence outside. The workhouse paupers seldom get meat—and fresh meat is very infrequent indeed. Their diet generally consists of potatoes, very bad bread, gruel and little or no beer. Since even prison food is better than this it is by no means uncommon for work-house inmates to commit an offence in the hope of being sent to gaol. The pauper would only exchange one prison for another. The workhouse, after all, is conducted like a prison. The pauper who fails to do the work allocated to him has to go without food. The pauper who wants to go outside must ask the workhouse master for per-mission. Leave is granted or withheld according to the conduct of the pauper and the whim of the workhouse master. Paupers are not allowed to smoke or to receive presents from relatives and friends. They have to wear special workhouse clothes and they are com-pletely subjected to the arbitrary authority of the workhouse master. To prevent pauper labour from competing with private industry the workhouse inmates are set comparatively useless tasks. The men are engaged on stone-breaking and have to do ' as much as a strong man can accomplish with effort in a day '. Women, children and old folk pick oakum—I forget for what useless purpose. Pauper families are separated in the workhouse so as to stop the ' superfluous ' population from breeding and to save the children from the ' demoral-

[1 ' Poor Law Bastilles ' is in English in the German edition of 1845.]

ising' influence of their parents. Fathers, mothers and children are housed in different wings of the workhouse and are allowed to see each other only at fixed, rare intervals, and then only if—in the opinion of the workhouse officials—their conduct has been exemplary. In order that the foul disease of pauperism may be safely restrained within the four walls of the workhouse and never infect anybody outside, the inmates are allowed to receive visitors only in a special room and only by permission of the workhouse master. Indeed, every contact between the paupers and the outside world is strictly controlled by the officials.

Yet there are official regulations to the effect that the food in the workhouse should be wholesome and that the paupers should be treated in a humane manner. But the evil spirit of the Poor Law of 1834 is far too strong for these precepts to be obeyed. The Poor Law Commissioners—and indeed all the middle classes—merely deceive themselves if they think that they can strictly apply the principles of the Poor Law of 1834 without having to face the disagreeable practical consequences that follow from the adoption of that policy. On paper the new poor law makes certain provisions for the humane treatment of paupers in workhouses. But these provisions are entirely at variance with the true spirit of the Poor Law of 1834. That law was firmly based on the idea that since paupers were criminals it followed that workhouses must be prisons. It followed that the inmates of workhouses were people beyond the pale of the law—even beyond the pale of humanity. Workhouse paupers were regarded as objects of horror and disgust. No pious instructions to the contrary from the Poor Law Commissioners can avail against the spirit of the law itself. Workhouse paupers have discovered that in practice it is the *spirit* of the law—and not the *letter* of the law—that counts.

A few examples may be given. In the summer of 1843 a five-year-old boy, who was an inmate of the Greenwich Union workhouse [at Deptford] was punished by being locked up in the mortuary for three nights and he had to sleep on some coffin-lids.[1] At Herne [Common] workhouse a little girl was treated in the same way because she wet her bed.[2] This particular punishment appears to be very popular in the workhouses. The Herne [Common] workhouse,

[1] *Northern Star*, no. 295, July 8th, p. 5, col. 4—'Brutality at a Workhouse'. The small boy was about four years old.]

[2] *Northern Star*, no. 334, April 6th, 1844, p. 6, cols. 2–3—'Inhuman Conduct of the Master of a Union Workhouse'. The Union in question was the Blean Union in Kent. The Poor Law Commissioners held two enquiries after the editor of the *Weekly Dispatch* had raised the matter with Edwin Chadwick. See *Weekly Dispatch*, no. 2214, March 31st, 1844, p. 156, cols. 2–3. This article appears in an abridged form in the *Northern Star*.]

situated in one of the most beautiful parts of Kent, is constructed in an unusual way, because every single window faces an inner court so that the inmates can never enjoy the sight of the outside world. A writer in the *Illuminated Magazine*, who gives this information, closes his description of workhouse conditions with the words: 'If God punish man for crime as man punishes man for poverty, woe to the sons of Adam '.[1]

A man named George Robson died in Leicester in November 1843. Two days previously he had been discharged from the workhouse at Coventry. He had an injured arm which had been grossly neglected. In spite of this injury he had been sent to work the pump with his other arm. He received only the normal workhouse diet and, owing to the neglect of his injury, he became so ill that he could not digest the coarse food. The weaker he became the more he complained. And the louder he complained the more brutally was he treated. When his wife, who was also an inmate of the workhouse, brought him a little beer the matron shouted at her and made her drink it up herself on the spot. Robson grew worse but still received no better treatment. At last, at his own request, he was discharged from the workhouse. As he was leaving the workhouse an official used the most disgraceful language. And two days afterwards he died at Leicester. At the inquest a doctor stated that death was due partly to the injured shoulder, which had been neglected, and partly to the entirely unsuitable food which had been given. When he left Coventry workhouse he had been given letters which contained money which was due to him. These letters had been in the possession of the workhouse master, who—in accordance with the rules of the establishment—had opened them.[2]

Birmingham workhouse was conducted in so scandalous a fashion that eventually—in December 1843—an assistant poor law commissioner was sent to make enquiries. He discovered that four [young] tramps[3]—we have already explained the meaning of this word —were locked in a ' black hole ' under some stairs where they were left for between eight and ten days. It was in the depth of winter[4] and yet the tramps had no clothes. They were kept short of food and

[1 *The Illuminated Magazine*, ed. Douglas Jerrold, Vol. 3, May–Oct., 1844, p. 118. But Jerrold in his article, ' The Two Windows ', pp. 117–8, made it clear that although the original workhouse was built without external windows, two such windows had been put in later by the Guardians.]

[2 *Northern Star*, no. 315, Nov. 25th, 1843, p. 7, cols. 3–6 and no. 316, Dec. 2nd, 1843 (leading article).]

[3 Engels used the word ' trampers '.]

[4 The young men were confined in the ' black hole ' from about Sept. 26th to Oct. 3rd.]

frequently were not given anything to eat before mid-day. A small boy had been confined in all the punishment rooms of the work-house.[1] First he was put into a small, damp and dark lumber room. Next he was twice confined in the ' black hole ' under the stairs. On the second occasion he was kept there for three days and three nights. [Afterwards he was sent to a second ' black hole '.] Then he was put into a dirty, stinking, revolting place which was worse than a store room [' the tramp room '.] He had to sleep on bare boards. The assistant commissioner found two other ragged boys in the place. They had been there for four days[2] and were huddled in corners as it was very cold. Seven tramps were often to be found in the ' black hole ' while as many as twenty were crammed into the casual ward. Female paupers, too, were incarcerated in the ' black hole ' as a punishment for refusing to go to church. On one occasion a woman was locked up in the tramp room for four days—heaven knows in what company—although she was ill and taking medicine. Another female pauper was sent to the lunatic ward, as a punishment, although she was perfectly sane.[3]

A similar enquiry was made in January 1844 at the workhouse at Bacton in Suffolk. Here it was found that a young woman of weak intellect had been appointed to nurse sick paupers and [that another nurse] committed all sorts of blunders. To save herself the trouble of keeping awake at night she used to tie to their beds those paupers who were restless or likely to get up. One invalid was found dead strapped down to his bed.[4]

At St. Pancras workhouse in London, where the paupers make cheap shirts,[5] an epileptic inmate suffocated to death in bed and no one came to his aid. In the same workhouse as many as four—even six—pauper children had to sleep in the same bed.[6]

[1 The boy had been sent into the workhouse as a punishment by the relieving officer, at the request of this mother. The assistant poor law commissioner holding the enquiry (J. Weale) condemned the Guardians for agreeing to his admission and stated: ' You, as Guardians, have nothing to do with punishing the children of the poor. It is an act of great illegality and cruelty '.]

[2 One had been there for four days, the other nearly a fortnight.]

[3 *Northern Star*, no. 317, Dec. 9th, 1843, p. 6, cols. 4–6; no. 318, Dec. 16th, 1843, p. 6, cols. 1–3; no. 319, Dec. 23rd, 1843, p. 6, cols. 1–3.]

[4 *Northern Star*, no. 326, Feb. 10th, 1844, p. 6, cols. 1–2. The nurse who tied a patient to his bed was Mary Dunn. The *Northern Star* report does not state that she was mad, but merely lazy and neglectful. Her ' idiotic assistant ' was Ann Davis, aged 18.]

[5 For the making of shirts at 2d. each in St. Pancras workhouse see *The Times*, Dec. 26th, 1843, p. 7, col. 3.]

[6 *Northern Star*, no. 328, Feb. 24th, 1844, p. 7, cols. 2–3. The inmate was a 6-year-old child suffering from a skin eruption and extensive enlargement of the heart. There was no evidence of suffocation, but the children usually slept five or six in a bed.]

In Shoreditch workhouse in London, a man was put into the same bed as a sick pauper and the bed was full of vermin. A young woman —who was in the sixth month of pregnancy and accompanied by a child under two years of age—was kept in the receiving ward of Bethnal Green workhouse (London) from February 28th until March 19th, 1844[1] without being formally admitted to the institution. She had no bed and did not have access to a lavatory. Her husband was admitted to the workhouse and when he asked [a magistrate] that his wife might be allowed to leave the receiving ward he was punished for this piece of insolence by being locked up for twenty-four hours on a diet of bread and water.[2]

In September 1844 a man lay dying in the workhouse at Slough near Windsor. His wife travelled to Slough and hurried to the workhouse. It was midnight, so she was not admitted. It was only on the next morning that she was allowed to see her husband—and then only for half an hour in the presence of a nurse. The same thing happened on subsequent visits which were all strictly limited to thirty minutes.[3]

At the Middleton workhouse in Lancashire, a dozen—sometimes even eighteen—paupers of both sexes had to sleep in a single room. The position of this workhouse is anomalous. It does not come under the new Poor Law Act of 1834 but is administered under an older Act (Gilbert's Act).[4] The workhouse master had installed a brewhouse which he ran as a private concern for his own profit.

On July 31st, 1844, an old man of seventy-two, an inmate of Stockport workhouse, was hauled up before the magistrate because he had refused to break stones. He said that owing to his age and infirmities—he had a stiff knee—he could not perform a task of this kind. He offered to do any other sort of job which was within his

[1 Engels wrote ' March 20th ', which is incorrect.]
[2 *Northern Star*, no. 333, March 30th, 1844, p. 6, col. 3.]
[3 *Northern Star*, no. 359, Sept. 28th, 1844, p. 6, cols. 1–2.]
[4 Gilbert's Act of 1782 (22 Geo. III, cap. 83) enabled a majority of not less than two-thirds of the substantial ratepayers by number and value in any parish or group of parishes to set up a Board of Guardians. This Board took over from the church-wardens and overseers the power to grant relief. In these ' Gilbert ' unions the workhouses were reserved for the impotent poor and pauper children. Able-bodied paupers were hired out near their place of residence. In 1834 there were about 67 Gilbert Unions, but owing to the omission of any provision for them in the Poor Law Amendment Act of that year they proved to be a great embarrassment to the Poor Law Commissioners. Gilbert's Act was not finally repealed until the early 1870s by 35 and 36 Vict. c. 116: T. Mackay, *A History of the English Poor Law*, Vol. 3 (1899), pp. 86–7; P. F. Aschrott, *The English Poor Law System Past and Present* (1888), p. 84. For the resistance to the introduction of the new Poor Law into Middleton, see the *Manchester and Salford Advertiser*, Nov. 2, 1844, p. 3, col. 5.]

capacity. The magistrate sentenced him to fourteen days' hard labour at the treadmill.

At Basford in Nottinghamshire, an assistant poor law commissioner, who visited the workhouse in February 1844, found that the sheets had not been changed for [from ten to] thirteen weeks. Shirts had not been washed for four weeks, while socks were worn continuously from two to ten months. There were forty-five boys in the workhouse. Only three of them were wearing stockings. All their shirts were in rags. The beds were full of vermin. The tins out of which the inmates ate were ' washed ' in urine buckets.[1] In the West London Union workhouse one of the porters suffered from syphilis, with which he infected [three or] four girls. But he was not dismissed.[2] Another porter took a deaf and dumb girl to his room for four days and slept with her. He, too, was not dismissed.

In death as in life the poor in England are treated in an utterly shameless manner. Their corpses have no better fate than the carcases of animals. The pauper burial ground at St. Bride's in London is a piece of open marshland which has been used since Charles II's day and there are heaps of bones all over the place. Every Wednesday the remains of dead paupers are thrown into a hole which is fourteen feet deep. A clergyman gabbles through the burial service and then the grave is filled with loose soil. On the following Wednesday the ground is opened again and this goes on until it is completely full. The whole neighbourhood is infected by the dreadful stench from this burial ground.

In Manchester there is a pauper burial ground in the Old Town on the other side of the Irk. This, too, is a desolate piece of waste ground. Two years ago a new railway line was built which ran through the burial ground. Had it been a churchyard in which ' respectable ' people were interred the middle classes and the clergy would have protested loudly against the desecration of the burial ground. But since it was only a pauper burial ground—the last resting place of ' superfluous ' paupers—they did not show the slightest concern. No one bothered to give a decent burial on the other side of the churchyard to the half-decayed corpses which were dug up to let the railway go through. The navvies dug holes where they pleased and great stakes were knocked into fresh graves. Since the men were working in marshy land, water containing putrefying matter from these graves was forced up to the surface and the whole district suffered from the

[1 *Northern Star*, no. 328, Feb. 24th, 1844, p. 7, col. 2.]
[2 *Northern Star*, no. 334, April 6th, 1844, p. 7, col. 3—' Horrible Profligacy in the West London Union Workhouse '.]

nauseating and dangerous gases which filled the air. I cannot give the more revolting details about the consequences of this callous and disgusting act.

Can anyone be surprised that the poor refuse to accept public relief which is available only under the most degrading conditions? No wonder that they would die of starvation rather than let the door of the poor-law bastilles close behind them! I have before me accounts of five cases in which people literally starved to death. A few days before they died the poor law authorities refused to grant them any relief outside the workhouse and they preferred to bear their sufferings as stoically as they could rather than go into a workhouse which was a hell on earth. Up to a point, therefore, the Poor Law Commissioners have successfully accomplished what they set out to do. But at the same time the workhouses have led to a marked increase in the enmity between the workers and the capitalists—who are nearly all staunch supporters of the new poor law. No other act passed by the capitalists has so incensed the workers as this. From Newcastle to Dover the working classes are to a man wild with fury at the way in which the poor law is administered. Even the most stupid members of the labouring classes can now have no doubts as to how the bourgeoisie fulfils its duties towards them. Never before have the middle classes made it so plain, without any shadow of doubt, that they regard the workers simply as a class to be exploited, and then to be thrown on the scrapheap to die of hunger when the capitalists have no more use for them. And so the new Poor Law has played an important part in furthering working class movements, particularly Chartism. The effects of the new Poor Law have been felt most acutely in the agricultural counties and this has made it easier for the working class movement to develop in the rural districts.

It may be added that Ireland, too, has had a similar poor law since 1838 and that the 80,000 Irish paupers are treated in the same way as the English poor. The new Poor Law is as hated in Ireland [as it is in England] and if it ever had to deal with really large numbers of paupers it would be hated still more. But what does the bad treatment of 80,000 members of the Irish proletariat matter in a country where the working classes number 3,500,000! Scotland has no poor laws at all—although there are local exceptions.

In view of the description that I have given of the new Poor Law and the way in which it is administered I hope that no one will feel that my condemnation of the English middle classes has been in any way too strong. The true intentions of the capitalists are vividly revealed in the working of the new poor law, for here the bourgeoisie is acting as a class and what it does cannot be hidden. The new Poor Law shows up the middle classes and throws into true perspective the other ways in which this class injures the proletariat. Support for the new Poor Law was not confined to a mere section of the bourgeoisie. The whole middle class is behind it. This can be proved, for example, by examining debates which took place in Parliament in 1844. The Liberal party had been responsible for passing the new Poor Law. The Conservative party, led by Sir Robert Peel, defended the law and made only a few trifling changes in it when the Poor Law Amendment Act of 1844 was passed. The original Act [of 1834] was passed with the aid of a Liberal majority. [Ten years later] a majority of Conservatives reaffirmed the Act. And on both occasions the noble lords in the upper houses gave their assent. In this way the exclusion of the proletariat from the State and from society has been made public. The middle classes have made it perfectly clear that they do not regard the workers as human beings and that they have no intention of treating them in a humane manner. We can confidently leave it to the British workers to regain their rights as human beings.[1]

[1] In order to avoid all misunderstandings—and the criticisms that arise from misunderstandings—I should like to make it quite clear that I am speaking of the bourgeoisie as a *class*. All the examples [of the bad treatment of the workers] that I have given are intended to illustrate how this *class* thinks and how it behaves. I have not had time to differentiate between the different sections of the bourgeoisie or the various middle-class political parties. This subdivision of the middle classes is only of historical and theoretical significance. For the same reason I can refer only in passing to the few members of the middle classes who are honourable exceptions [to the general rule]. Let me mention the left-wing Radicals (who are virtually Chartists)—such as Hindley of Ashton and Fielden of Todmorden (two Lancashire manufacturers and Members of Parliament) and the humane Tories who have recently organised themselves into the ' Young England ' movement. A group of Tory members of Parliament—Disraeli, Borthwick, Ferrand, Lord John Manners etc.—support the ' Young England ' movement. Lord Ashley is closely associated with this group. The supporters of ' Young England ' want to revive the ' Merry England ' of the past with all its colourful romantic feudalism. Their object is obviously unattainable—indeed it is a ridiculous policy which is a satire on the normal process of historical development—but there is something to be said for these young Tories. They have courage and they have good intentions. They oppose the present disgusting state of affairs and they oppose existing prejudices. And that is something to be thankful for. The Germanophile Englishman (*sic*) Thomas Carlyle stands alone. He was formerly a Tory, but now he goes much further than the ' Young England ' group. Of all the critics he probes most deeply into the social anarchy of the English bourgeoisie. He demands proper organisation of labour. I hope that Carlyle, who has found the right road, will follow it to the end. I join with many other Germans in wishing him well. [These last two sentences were left out of the English translation of 1887. In the German edition of 1892 Engels added—' But the [French] revolution of February [1848] turned Carlyle into a complete reactionary. His righteous anger against the [middle-class] philistines turned into a sour-grapes, philistine-like peevishness at the wave of history which had left him stranded '.]

CONCLUSION

I have now described the condition of the workers in England from my own observations during a stay of twenty-one months in the country and from official and other authentic reports. I have often enough declared in these pages that the condition of the English proletariat is an unendurable one and that it cannot continue. I am by no means the only person who has reached this conclusion. Gaskell stated in 1833 that he doubted whether the outcome could be a peaceable one. He thought that it would be difficult to avoid a revolution. A few years later (1838) Carlyle declared that in view of the rise of the Chartist movement and the revolutionary agitation among the workers he was surprised that for eight long years they should have sat peaceably at the feast of the Barmecide[1] and dined off the empty promises of the Liberal bourgeoisie. In 1844 Carlyle pressed for the immediate ' organisation of labour ', ' if Europe, at any rate if England, is to continue habitable much longer '.[2] And *The Times*— ' Europe's leading newspaper '—said plainly enough in June 1844: ' " War to the mansion, peace to the cottage "—is a watchword of terror which may yet ring through the land. Let the wealthy beware.'[3]

Let us take one last look at the future prospects of the English bourgeoisie. The worst that could happen—from the point of view of this class—would be that foreign (particularly American) industry will be able to compete successfully on equal terms with English

[1 T. Carlyle, *Chartism* (1839), p. 92. *Chartism* was written in 1839, and not in 1838.]
[2 T. Carlyle, *Past and Present* (1843), p. 262 (Everyman edn., 1912)—see also p. 188. The same passage was quoted at greater length in Engels's review of *Past and Present* in the *Deutsch-Französische Jahrbücher* (1844), pp. 171–2 (facsimile reprint, 1925). Louis Blanc's *Organisation du Travail* had appeared in 1839.]
[3 This quotation is not from *The Times*, but from the *Northern Star* (June 15th, 1844, p. 7, col. 5—' Horrible Condition of the Agricultural Labourers') commenting on a case reported in *The Times* (June 7th, 1844, p. 6, col. 4—' Effect of the New Poor Law upon Wages '). Two men, Turner and Helps, had been brought before the Lewes (Sussex) magistrates and charged with ' wilfully neglecting to work ' because they had refused jobs at 6s. a week and had thereby become chargeable to the poor law. After some hesitation the magistrates dismissed the case and the men were discharged. *The Times* had a long and highly critical leader on the fumblings of the magistrates and the working of the new Poor Law in the same issue (p. 4, cols. 5–6), but its language was more restrained than that of the *Northern Star*, which prefaced the report with the words: ' The following case exhibits a frightful picture of the awful misery and degradation to which our hardworking peasantry is reduced ', and ended with the words quoted by Engels, who evidently did not take the trouble to check back to *The Times*.]

industry, even although it is to be expected that the Corn Laws will be repealed within a few years.[1] German industry is now making great efforts while American industry is moving forward in a most impressive manner. The United States has immense reserves of wealth, unlimited coal and iron-ore, great resources of water-power, fine navigable rivers, and (above all) an energetic and active people, compared with whom the English are phlegmatic sleepy-heads. In less than ten years the United States has developed a great [cotton] industry which is already competing successfully with English rivals in the coarse branch of the industry (which is particularly important to England). The Americans have supplanted the English in markets of North America and South America. They are also competing with the English in China. The same story can be told of other branches of manufacture. If ever a country had the natural advantages needed to seize the monopoly of supplying manufactured products [to the rest of the world] it is the United States. Such a development would deal a fatal blow to English industry. This is bound to happen within the next twenty years if existing social conditions are not altered. By that time the majority of the working classes will have realised that they are permanently ' superfluous ' and that their only choice lies between starving to death and rising in revolt.

Do the English middle classes realise the gravity of their position? Not at all! J. R. McCulloch, their favourite economist, reassures them from the seclusion of his study. He declares that it is quite unthinkable that so young a country as the United States, which is not yet fully populated, should engage in industry on a large scale. According to McCulloch the United States cannot hope to compete successfully with an old-established manufacturing country such as Britain. It would be madness for the Americans to try to do such a thing. If they did they would only lose their money. McCulloch advises the Americans to stick to farming. Only when all their vast territories are under cultivation will the time have come for the Americans to turn successfully to industry. So says the wise economist and the whole of the English bourgeoisie piously echoes his words. Meanwhile the Americans take one market after another from the English and one foolhardy American speculator recently had the nerve to send a consignment of American manufactured goods to England itself—and, what's more, he sold them for re-export!

Supposing however, that England managed to keep her industrial

[1 See T. Carlyle, *Past and Present* (1843), p. 175 (Everyman edn., 1912): ' The Corn-Laws will go, and even soon go: would we were all as sure of the millennium as they are of going! ']

monopoly. Suppose that the number of her factories continued to increase. What would happen? Commercial crises would continue [to afflict the economy] and they would become ever more serious and ever more disastrous as industry expanded and the number of workers continued to grow. The working classes—augmented by the continual ruin of the lower middle classes and by the ever-increasing concentration of capital in fewer and fewer hands—would expand in geometrical proportion, until the whole nation, except for a few millionaires, would be composed of workers. If that happened it would not be long before the proletariat realised how easy it would be for them to seize power—and then the revolution would come.

In fact neither of these possible developments will in fact occur. The fate of the middle classes will be sealed sooner than we have suggested. Commercial crises of ever-increasing severity (the most powerful stimulus to independent action on the part of the workers), coupled with the effects of foreign competition and the progressive ruin of the middle classes, will bring matters to a head before long. I do not think that the workers will put up with another commercial crisis. The next one—it is due in 1846 or 1847—will probably lead to the repeal of the Corn Laws and the acceptance of the People's Charter. It remains to be seen how far the acceptance of the Charter will encourage the movement towards revolution. After the crisis of 1846 or 1847 the next crisis should (on the analogy of previous crises) occur in 1852 or 1853. It may be delayed by the repeal of the Corn Laws or it may be hastened by foreign competition or other circumstances. But before that crisis arrives the English workers will surely have reached the limits of their endurance. They will no longer be prepared to allow themselves to be exploited by the capitalists only to be thrown on the scrap heap when their services are no longer needed. If the English middle classes have not come to their senses by that time—and there is no reason to anticipate any change of heart in that quarter—then a revolution is to be expected. And it will be more violent than any previous revolution. The English working classes, driven to desperation, will follow the advice of the Reverend Mr. Stephens and will turn to incendiarism. Popular fury will reach an intensity far greater than that which animated the French workers in 1793. The war of the poor against the rich will be the most bloodthirsty the world has ever seen. Even if some of the middle classes espouse the cause of the workers—even if the middle classes as a whole mended their ways—the catastrophe could not be avoided. A change of heart on the part of the bourgeoisie would only lead to suggestions for a flabby compromise. The left wing of the bourgeoisie would join the workers to found a new Gironde party. And such a party would collapse in face of a rising of the workers. A social class cannot rid itself of its inborn prejudices—particularly a class like the English bourgeoisie which is stable, self-possessed and utterly selfish.

These are all conclusions that can be drawn with absolute certainty. They are based upon facts which cannot be disputed—facts of historical development and facts of human nature. It is particularly easy to forecast future events in England because in that country every aspect of social development is so plain and clear-cut. The revolution *must* come. It is now too late for a peaceful outcome of the affair [—the antagonism between the workers and the bourgeoisie—] to be possible. But [if a peaceful solution were possible] it would be due to changes in the proletariat rather than to changes in the bourgeoisie. As the workers absorb more and more Socialist and Communist elements so the revolution will be less bloody, less violent and less vengeful.

In principle Communism stands over and above the clash between the bourgeoisie and the proletariat. Communism is interested in this clash at the present day only because of its historical significance. Communism does not regard this clash as justified in the future. Indeed Communism proposes to remove this rivalry between two social classes. Communism recognises that so long as this rivalry lasts it is inevitable that the workers should be the avowed and bitter enemy of the middle classes. The fury of the proletariat against their oppressors is the most important stimulus to promote a working-class movement *in its early stages*. But Communism rises above the enmity of classes, for it is a movement that embraces all humanity and not merely the working classes. Of course no Communist proposes to avenge himself against any particular individuals who are members of the bourgeoisie. And they quite realise that—in existing social circumstances—it is at the moment inevitable that individual members of the middle classes should behave as they do. English Socialism (i.e. Communism) undoubtedly accepts the doctrine that the individual bourgeois is not, as an individual, responsible for the acts of the middle classes as a whole. The more the English workers accept Socialist doctrines the more superfluous will be their righteous anger against the middle classes. But if that anger is maintained at its present intensity it will have terrible consequences. Should the proletariat become more Socialist in character its opposition to the middle classes will be less unbridled and less savage. Were it possible to turn all the English workers into Communists before the outbreak of the revolution then the revolution itself would be a peaceable one. But that is not possible. It is too late. I think that it is inevitable that *open* war will break out between the rich and the poor in England. But it may be expected that by the time the rising comes the English working classes will understand basic social problems sufficiently clearly for the more brutal elements of the revolution to be eventually overcome—with the help of the appearance of the Communist Party. In this way the tragedy of a new 9th of Thermidor may be avoided. The experience of the French has not been neglected and already most of the Chartist leaders are Communists. And the more enlightened section of the middle class—admittedly pathetically small at the moment and capable of expansion only by the adhesion of young people—may find it easier to join the Communists than the exclusively working-class Chartists because, after all, Communism stands outside the conflicts of proletariat and bourgeoisie.

If we have not advanced enough proof to justify the conclusions that we have drawn we hope to have another opportunity of showing that these conclusions follow inevitably from an examination of the history of England. But I stick to what I have already said. The war of poor against rich in England—which is already being waged by individuals and also by all the workers by indirect means—will [before long] be openly waged by the whole of the proletariat. It is too late for the parties concerned to reach a peaceful solution. The gulf between the two classes is becoming wider and wider. The workers are becoming more and more imbued with the spirit of resistance. The feelings of the proletariat against their oppressors are becoming more and more bitter. The workers are moving from minor guerilla skirmishes to demonstrations and armed conflicts of a more serious nature. Soon it will only be necessary to dislodge a stone and the whole avalanche will be set in motion. When the cry echoes throughout the country: ' War to the mansion, peace to the cottage ', then it will be too late for the wealthy to save their skins.

APPENDICES

Appendix I. The Postscript of 1846: An English Strike.

Appendix II. Preface to American Edition of 1887.

Appendix III. Preface to English Edition of 1892.

Appendix IV. List of sources quoted by Engels.

Appendix V. Examples of Engels's methods of quoting.

APPENDIX I

THE POSTSCRIPT OF 1846: AN ENGLISH STRIKE[1]

In my book on the *Condition of the Working Class in England* it was not always possible for me to give chapter and verse for every one of my facts. So that the book should not be too long and too dull I restricted my references to official documents, impartial authors and publications issued in the interest of political parties whose views I opposed. By doing this I hoped that no one would question certain descriptive passages which were not based upon personal observation. It seems that I was mistaken. It is difficult in these days to convince people by arguments even if they are based on excellent authorities. Modern readers—tired of being told to believe something simply because it has been believed by previous generations—are of a highly sceptical frame of mind. They can be convinced only by striking *facts* which can be proved up to the hilt. Facts are above all else absolutely essential when we are dealing with affairs of major importance, when facts are accumulated so that principles may be established and when we are concerned not with small separate sections of society but with the relations of vast social groups. I have already explained why I

[1 This postscript was written between April and July 1845 when Engels was in Brussels. It was printed in two numbers of the Bielefeld periodical *Das West-fälische Dampfboot*, January 1846, pp. 17–21 and February, 1846, pp. 61–7. It was reprinted in *Gesamtausgabe*, Part I, Vol. 4 (ed. V. Adoratskij) (Berlin, 1932), pp. 393–405. It appears to be based almost entirely on articles in the *Northern Star*.]

could not give all the facts in my book. I hope to remedy this defect from time to time and to supplement what I have said in the book from further sources now available to me. At the same time I am anxious to prove that the description of the condition of the English workers [which I gave in 1844–5] is still true to-day [1846] and so I shall refer only to events which have taken place in England since I left that country last year. I shall deal only with material that has come to hand since my book was published.

Readers of my book will remember that I was mainly concerned with describing the rivalry of the bourgeoisie and the proletariat. I took the view that a clash between the two classes was inevitable. I was anxious to prove conclusively that the working classes were completely in the right and that there could be no shadow of doubt as to the justice of their cause. I was determined that the fine phrases of the middle classes should be exposed and pilloried as they deserved to be. From the first page of my book to the last I was compiling a dossier from which to condemn the English bourgeoisie. I will now lay before you a few additional proofs of their villainy. Incidentally I have vented my wrath often enough upon the English middle classes. I have no intention of doing so again and, if at all possible, I will keep my temper on this occasion.

The first worthy citizen and respected family man with whom we have to deal is an old acquaintance. There are actually two of them —Messrs. Pauling and Henfrey. Their workers had been on strike in 1843. Heaven knows how many previous occasions this firm had been faced with labour troubles. In 1843 the men asked for higher wages because their hours had been increased and no arguments of their employers could deflect them from their purpose. When their demands were rejected they went on strike. Pauling and Henfrey are building contractors who employ large numbers of kiln-firers, joiners, carpenters and so forth. When their men went on strike they engaged fresh labour. This led to disturbances [between strikers and blacklegs] which culminated in a pitched battle with blunderbusses and bludgeons in the brickyard. As a result half-a-dozen workers were sentenced to be transported to Van Diemen's Land. I have already given an account of this affair in my book.[1]

But Pauling and Henfrey are never happy unless they have trouble with their workers at least once a year. Labour troubles began again in October 1844.[2] This time it was the carpenters who were the

[1 See above, p. 256.]
[2 The following paragraphs are based upon the *Northern Star*, no. 362, Oct. 19, 1844, p. 1, col. 6.]

object of the philanthropic attention of their employers. It is a tradition among the carpenters [and joiners] of Manchester and district not to 'strike a light' between Candlemas and November 17th. At the height of summer, when there are many hours of daylight, the carpenters work from 6 a.m. to 6 p.m. As the days become shorter they work from daybreak to sunset. Then from November 17th onwards they work by candle light so as to complete a 12-hour working day. Pauling and Henfrey, who had long disliked this 'barbaric' custom [of working less than 12 hours a day at certain times of the year] decided to overcome the difficulty by introducing gas-lighting. One evening—before 6 p.m.—when it was too dark to see by daylight, the carpenters put their tools away and prepared to put on their coats. The foreman lit the gas and told the men that they must work until 6 p.m. The carpenters employed by Pauling and Henfrey objected to this and they called a meeting of all members of their craft. Mr. [George] Pauling was amazed at what had happened and asked his men if they had any complaints. Some of the men said that the meeting had not been called by the carpenters employed by Messrs. Pauling and Henfrey. It had been called by the committee of the carpenters' union. Mr. Pauling replied that he did not care a damn for the trade union. He suggested that if the carpenters would work a full 12-hour day —if necessary by gaslight—he would give them three hours off on Saturday afternoon. His 'generosity' even went further, for he suggested that the men should be able to earn something extra by being allowed to work for an extra quarter of an hour every day. But he proposed that if other firms adopted the system of working by gaslight the hours worked by Messrs. Pauling and Henfrey's men should be increased by half an hour.

The men examined these proposals. They calculated that Pauling and Henfrey would gain a whole hour's work during the days of shorter daylight in the winter. They reckoned that altogether, in this season of the year, they would work for another 92 hours or 9¼ days. And for this extra work they would receive no additional wages. Taking into account the number of men employed by Pauling and Henfrey, this would mean that the firm would save £400 in wages during the winter months. In the circumstances the men held their meeting and made it clear to their colleagues [in other establishments] that if Pauling and Henfrey carried out their plan other building contractors in the district were likely to follow suit. If this happened the carpenters of Manchester and district would be robbed of about £4,000 a year in wages. So it was decided that on the following Monday all the carpenters employed by Pauling and Henfrey should give three months' notice to terminate their employment. If, in the meantime, Pauling and Henfrey refused to give up their proposals the men would leave the service of the firm when the notice expired. The carpenters' union promised to give financial aid if the carpenters working for Pauling and Henfrey went on strike.

Pauling and Henfrey's carpenters handed in their notices on Monday, October 14th [1844].[1] The firm replied that the men could leave work at once and this they did. On the same evening a meeting was held of representatives of workers in all the building trades and it was decided to give financial support to the carpenters who had gone on strike at Messrs Pauling and Henfrey's works. On the next Wednesday and Thursday all the carpenters in the district came out on strike in sympathy with Pauling and Henfrey's men. So a general carpenters' strike in the Manchester area was now in progress.[2]

The building contractors were left high and dry, for not a single carpenter in the district would work for them. They sought workers all over the place—and even went as far afield as Scotland for blackleg labour. In a few days thirteen carpenters from Staffordshire came to Manchester. The strikers got in touch with these men and explained to them what the strike was about. Several of the Staffordshire men thereupon decided not to work in Manchester. Pauling and Henfrey now summoned the leading strikers before Daniel Maude, Esq., the local magistrate. Before we explain what happened next it may be as well to say a few words about Daniel Maude, Esq.

Daniel Maude, Esq., is the stipendiary magistrate for Manchester. Normally in England the magistrates are [unpaid Justices of the Peace]—rich landlords or members of the middle classes, including clergymen—who are appointed by the Lord Chancellor. But these Dogberries are quite ignorant of the law. They commit the most egregious blunders and so bring the middle classes into disrepute. If a clever lawyer defends a worker skilfully the J.P.s very frequently get themselves into such a muddle that they either condemn the accused improperly—and then their judgment is upset on appeal—or they even dismiss the case and let the worker go. Moreover the wealthy industrialists of the factory districts feel that they cannot spare the time to attend court every day. So they prefer to have a paid substitute. In such towns, therefore, paid magistrates (who are qualified barristers) are appointed at the request of the borough author-

---

[1 Engels wrote ' Oct. 17th ' in error. See *Northern Star*, no. 362, Oct. 19th, 1844, p. 1, col. 6—' Great Meeting of the Carpenters of Manchester and Salford '.]

[2 *Northern Star*, no. 363, Oct. 26th, 1844, p. 5, col. 4—' Manchester—The Strike of Messrs. Pauling and Co.'s Carpenters and Joiners '.]

ities. These stipendiary magistrates faithfully serve the interests of the middle classes. They know all the tortuous byways of the English law—and if necessary they are quite prepared to stretch a point in favour of their patrons. Their behaviour is illustrated by the following example.

One of the 'Liberal' magistrates appointed in a wholesale fashion by the Whig ministry was Daniel Maude, Esq. Let us look at two of his heroic deeds—inside and outside the walls of his Borough Court at Manchester. In 1842 the factory owners of South Lancashire succeeded in goading the workers into open rebellion. The trouble broke out in August of that year in Stalybridge and Ashton. On August 9th, some ten thousand workers marched on Manchester from these towns with the Chartist leader, Richard Pilling, at their head. Their purpose was 'to meet their masters on the Exchange . . . and to see how the Manchester market was '.[1]

At the outskirts of the town the workers were met by Daniel Maude, Esq. He was accompanied by the whole worthy police force of Manchester, to say nothing of a troop of cavalry and a company of riflemen. But this apparent attempt to persuade the workers to go home was a deception. In fact it was in the interests of the factory owners and Liberals that the insurrection should spread. They wished to foment working-class discontent so as to frighten the government into repealing the Corn Laws. Daniel Maude, Esq., was in full agreement with his worthy colleagues as to the merits of this policy. So he began by treating with the demonstrators. On the understanding that they 'kept the peace' and followed a prescribed route, the workers were allowed to enter Manchester. Mr. Maude knew very well that the demonstrators would not fulfil the agreed conditions and he did not want them to do so. Had he acted with proper vigour he could have nipped in the bud this workers' rising incited by the factory owners themselves. But if he had done that he would have played into the hands of the Prime Minister, Sir Robert Peel, and he would not have acted in the interests of his friends the great manufacturers who were demanding the repeal of the Corn Laws. So Mr. Maude ordered the troops to retire and he allowed the demonstrators to enter Manchester. This led the factories in Manchester to close. But as soon as the rising changed its character, as soon as the workers showed no

[1 The resolution put to the meeting at Ashton-under-Lyne on the morning of Tuesday, August 9th, 1842 by Richard Pilling ran as follows:
    That the workpeople would have the wages of 1840, and go to Manchester to meet their masters on the Exchange, as their masters would not meet them, and see how the Manchester market was: *Quarterly Review*, Vol. 71, no. 141, Dec. 1842, p. 294—article VII on the Anti-Corn Law agitation.]

interest in the ' hellish Corn Laws ' but came out openly against the Liberal middle class—then Daniel Maude, Esq., promptly resumed his judicial duties, ordered the workers to be arrested by the dozen and sent them to cool their heels in gaol for a ' breach of the peace '. In this way Mr. Maude first made sure that a breach of the peace would take place and then punished the workers when the breach of the peace occurred.

Here is another characteristic extract from the life-story of this Manchester Solomon. After a number of public meetings of the Anti-Corn Law League had been broken up by hostile demonstrators, the League decided to hold private meetings. Admission to these meetings was by ticket only. Nevertheless it was announced to the world that the resolutions and petitions approved at such gatherings had been passed by *public* [and not by *private*] meetings.[1] The League pretended that decisions taken at these private meetings genuinely represented the ' public opinion ' of Manchester. In order to expose once and for all this impudent deception on the part of the 'Liberal' factory owners three or four Chartists—including my good friend James Leach—got tickets and attended one of these private meetings organized by the Anti-Corn Law League in Manchester. When Mr. Cobden got up to make his speech James Leach asked the chairman if this were a public meeting. Instead of answering the question the chairman promptly called in the police and had Leach arrested! A second Chartist—then a third and then a fourth—asked the same question and were treated in the same way. All were seized by the police (who stood at the door in large numbers) and were packed off to the Town Hall. On the following morning they appeared before Daniel Maude, Esq., who was already perfectly well aware of what had happened. Leach and his friends were charged with having caused a disturbance at a meeting and gave their own account of the affair. Then they had to listen to a pompous lecture from Daniel Maude, Esq. The magistrate said that he knew all about them. They were political troublemakers. They were continuously making disturbances at all sorts of public meetings and they were a nuisance to law-abiding citizens. This must stop. Daniel Maude, Esq., knew very well that he could not punish them and so he let them off on payment of costs.

This Daniel Maude, Esq.—whose bourgeois virtues we have just sketched—was the man before whom the recalcitrant employees of Messrs Pauling and Henfrey were haled. But they had taken the precaution to bring a lawyer with them. The first case to be heard

[1 For Chartist interruptions at an Anti-Corn Law meeting in 1839, see Archibald Prentice, *A History of the Anti-Corn-Law League* (2 vols., 1853), Vol. 1, pp. 116-8.]

was that of one of the Staffordshire carpenters [Ambrose Woodall], who had refused to play the part of a blackleg and to take the place of regular workers who had gone on strike in defence of their interests. Messrs. Pauling and Henfrey laid before the magistrate a written agreement which the Staffordshire worker had signed.[1] For the defence it was submitted that this contract was *ultra vires*, as it had been signed on a Sunday. Daniel Maude, Esq., in a long-winded oration, admitted that ' business transactions ' made on the Sabbath did not have the force of law—but added that he could not believe that Messrs. Pauling and Henfrey regarded the document before him as a ' business transaction '! So without asking him whether *he* regarded the contract as a ' business transaction ' or not, the magistrate told the poor devil that he must either carry out the terms of his agreement with Pauling and Henfrey or enjoy the pleasures of the treadmill for three months. Oh, what a Solomon does Manchester possess![2]

This matter having been settled, the next case was heard. This time Messrs. Pauling and Henfrey prosecuted a man named [John] Salmon, one of their regular workmen, who had gone on strike. He was accused of having persuaded the newly-arrived workmen to join the strikers. A witness—one of the new workers—said that Salmon had held him by the arm and had spoken to him. Daniel Maude, Esq., asked the witness if the accused had either threatened or struck him? ' No,' said the witness. Daniel Maude, Esq.—having just done his duty to the middle classes in the first case—was showing his ' impartiality '. He said that in the case before him no evidence had been submitted to incriminate the accused. Salmon was within his rights in walking on the public highway and in speaking to people there, so long as he used no threats and was not guilty of any act of violence. So Salmon was found ' not guilty '. But Messrs. Pauling and Henfrey,

---

[1] This contract contained the following provisions:—The worker agreed to stay with Pauling and Henfrey for six months and to be satisfied with the wages paid to him. Pauling and Henfrey however were under no obligation to find him work for six months. The firm could dismiss him at any time by giving one week's notice. Pauling and Henfrey agreed to pay him travelling expenses from Staffordshire to Manchester, but this was to be regarded as a loan to be repaid by a deduction of two shillings per week from his wages! What do you think of that for a contract?

[2] *Manchester Guardian*, Nov. 2nd, 1844, p. 4, col. 5 (' Messrs Pauling and Co. and their workmen '):

Mr. Maude said, the mere question was, whether it was in the course of business. He was inclined to think that a contract entered into on Sunday, in the ordinary way of business, was void. It had been held that a contract for the sale [of] a horse, by a horse dealer, was void if made on a Sunday, because it was made in pursuance of his ordinary calling. He thought the contract was not made in this instance by Messrs Pauling and Co. in the ordinary course of business, and therefore was not void.

Woodall promised to start work on the following day, Friday, November 1st.]

in return for paying the costs of this case, had at least had the satis-faction of making the impudent Salmon spend the previous night in the lock-up—and that was something.

And Salmon had little cause for rejoicing. Having been discharged on Thursday, October 31st, he was back in the dock on Tuesday, November 5th [1844] and once more faced Daniel Maude, Esq. This time he was accused of assaulting Mr. Pauling and Mr. Henfrey in the street. On the very Thursday [October 31st] that Salmon had been freed on the previous charge a number of Scottish workers had been enticed to Manchester. They had in fact been brought to the town by Messrs. Pauling and Henfrey on false pretences. They had been told that the strike was over and that the firm needed additional workers to complete the large contracts which they had on hand. On the following day—a Friday—a number of Scottish joiners, who had been working in Manchester for some time, spoke to the newly-arrived Scots to explain to them why the carpenters employed by Pauling and Henfrey had gone on strike. A large number of workers—some 400 or so—collected outside the public house where the Scots were lodg-ing. The Scots were treated by the firm as if they were prisoners and a foreman stood like a sentry at the door. After a time Mr. Pauling and Mr. Henfrey turned up in person to conduct their new carpenters to the workshop. When the Scots came out of the public house, those who were standing outside tried to persuade them not to act as black-legs and so disgrace their own countrymen. They were told that it was not right for them to work in contravention of the rules made by the Manchester union of carpenters. Two of the Scots hung back and Mr. Pauling went to them and tried to persuade them to hurry. The crowd was quiet and merely tried to delay the Scots from going to work. The workers told the Scots not to get mixed up with other people's disputes and urged them to go back home. By this time Mr. Henfrey had lost patience. He recognised some of his regular work-men in the crowd. Salmon was one of their number. Mr. Henfrey seized one of his arms while Mr. Pauling seized the other. Both yelled for the police at the top of their voices. A police superintendent ran up. He asked what charge Mr. Henfrey and Mr. Pauling were making against Salmon. Mr. Henfrey and Mr. Pauling were greatly embarrassed. All that they could say was: ' We know this man '. The superintendent said that if Salmon was known to Mr. Henfrey and Mr. Pauling he could go for the time being. Messrs. Pauling and Henfrey felt that it was necessary to bring some sort of charge against Salmon. They thought the matter over for several days and then, acting on the advice of their lawyer, they brought the charge to

which we have referred. [They accused Salmon of assault]. When the
evidence against Salmon had been heard, who should get up to defend
him but W. P. Roberts—'the Miners' Attorney General' and the
terror of all the magistrates. Roberts asked if it was necessary for him
to call his witnesses since nothing had so far been proved against his
client. David Maude, Esq., said that he wanted to hear the defence
witnesses. These witnesses testified that Salmon had behaved peaceably until Mr. Henfrey had seized him by the arm. When he had heard
all the evidence Daniel Maude, Esq., said that he would give his
decision on the following Saturday. The presence of Mr. 'Attorney
General' Roberts had obviously had the effect of making Mr. Maude
hesitate to make up his mind without considerable reflection.[1]

When Saturday [November 9th], came Messrs. Pauling and
Henfrey were ready with new charges. This time it was a criminal
charge of conspiracy and intimidation and was made against three
regular workers—Salmon, [John] Scott and [John] Mellor.[2] Pauling
and Henfrey wanted to deal a death-blow at the carpenters' union.
Since they had every reason to fear the dreaded Mr. Roberts they put
their case in the hands of Mr. Monk, who was one of the best-known
London barristers. Mr. Monk's first witness was one of the newly-
engaged Scottish workmen named Gibson—a man who had already
testified against Salmon on the previous Tuesday. He said that on
Friday, November 1st, he and other Scottish carpenters had left the
inn and had been surrounded by a milling crowd of workers who had
pushed them to and fro. The three accused were in this crowd. Mr.
Roberts cross-examined this witness. He confronted Gibson with
another worker. He suggested that Gibson had spoken to this workman on the previous Tuesday and had admitted that when giving
evidence against Salmon he had not realised that he was speaking on
oath. Indeed he did not know why he was in court and what he was
supposed to say. Gibson replied that he had been with two men on
the previous evening but it had been dark so that he could not swear
that the worker who had just left the witness box was one of them.

[1 *Northern Star*, no. 365, Nov. 9th, 1844, p. 8, cols. 4–5, article entitled ' Henfrey
v. Salmon—Assault '; *Manchester Guardian*, Nov. 6th, 1844, p. 4, col. 5: ' The
Turn-out at Messrs Pauling and Co.'s.' There are certain discrepancies between
the accounts given in these two newspapers. According to the *Manchester Guardian*,
' Mr. Henfrey was violently seized and twisted about by a man named John Salmon,
with such force, that, had he not been a stout and active man, he would have been
brought to the ground '. The *Northern Star*, however, stated: ' Mr. Henfrey,
being annoyed at the presence of so many men, and seeing some of his old hands
amongst them, seized Mr. Salmon; Mr. Pauling seized him also; and then they
immediately called out for the police to take Salmon into custody '.]

[2 Mellor's name is given as ' Milling ' in the *Manchester Guardian*, Nov. 13th,
1844, p. 5, col. 2.]

But he agreed that he might well have used some of the alleged expressions because the form of oath was different in English and Scottish courts. He could not remember exactly what he had said.

Mr. Monk got up and said that Mr. Roberts had no right to ask such questions. Mr. Roberts replied that in a case of this sort he had every right to make such allegations. He had the right to ask what he liked. He could ask a witness where he was born and he could ask where he had been and what he had eaten on every day afterwards. Daniel Maude, Esq., admitted that Mr. Roberts was within his rights in asking such questions. But he ventured to give Mr. Roberts a little fatherly advice and he hoped that Mr. Roberts would keep as closely to the point at issue as possible.

Mr. Roberts now questioned Gibson further. Gibson agreed that he had not started to work for Pauling and Henfrey until November 2nd—that is to say on the day *after* the events which were the subject of the charge against the three accused. Mr. Henfrey himself was the next witness. He confirmed the account of the affair given by Gibson. Mr. Roberts asked him if he were not seeking an undue advantage over his competitors. Mr. Monk objected to this question. 'Very well', said Roberts, 'I will put it a little plainer'.

He then asked Mr. Henfrey: 'Are you not aware that there are certain rules by which the working hours are regulated of the carpenters and joiners in Manchester?'

Mr. Henfrey: 'These rules are nothing to do with me. I claim the right of making my own rules'.

Mr. Roberts: 'Quite so. On your oath, Mr. Henfrey, are you not requiring the men in your employment to work more hours than other masters in the same trade?'

Mr. Henfrey: 'Yes'.

Mr. Roberts: 'How many hours?'

Mr. Henfrey could not tell, but he would make the calculation, and pulled out his tablets for the purpose.

Daniel Maude, Esq.: 'You need not make the calculations. You can tell us what you think it will be.'

Mr. Henfrey: 'Why, about one hour in the morning and one in the evening for six weeks before the time that the trade generally light up, and the same for six weeks after they cease from lighting'.

Daniel Maude Esq.: 'That will be 72 hours before lighting and 72 after, which makes 144 hours from each man during 12 weeks'.

Mr. Henfrey: 'Yes.'

This reply was received with the most marked indignation by members of the public present in court. Mr. Monk looked wrathfully at Mr. Henfrey—and Mr. Henfrey looked abashed at Mr. Monk. Mr. Pauling tugged at Mr. Henfrey's coat-tails. But it was too late. Daniel Maude, Esq., saw clearly enough that this time his rôle must be that of the impartial judge. Mr. Henfrey's admission had been openly made and Mr. Maude had heard it. The evidence of two further unimportant witnesses was heard and then Mr. Monk said that the case for the prosecution was concluded.

Daniel Maude, Esq., said that the prosecution had failed to show that the defendants were guilty of any criminal offence. The prosecution had not proved that the workers from Scotland, who were alleged to have been threatened, had been employed by Pauling and Henfrey [on or] before November 1st. The contract and the engagement were shown to start on *November 2nd*, but the information [against Salmon, Scott and Mellor] related to events which were alleged to have taken place on November 1st—that is to say at a time when the workers from Scotland were not yet employed by Pauling and Henfrey. [On November 1st] the defendants were in their rights in endeavouring by every legal means to dissuade the Scots from entering the service of Pauling and Henfrey.

Mr. Monk said that in his opinion the Scots had been employed by Pauling and Henfrey from the time that they had embarked on the steamship to leave Scotland. Daniel Maude, Esq., remarked that reference had been made to such a contract of employment, but it had not been put before the court. Mr. Monk replied that the document was in Scotland. He asked that the case should be adjourned so that this contract could be submitted to the court for inspection. Mr. Roberts protested that this was the first time that he had heard a prosecuting counsel suggest that, although the magistrate had been satisfied that no offence had been proved, the case should be adjourned for more evidence to be produced. Mr. Roberts argued that the case should proceed. Daniel Maude, Esq., said that he would not adjourn for further evidence and he would not proceed with the case since no supporting evidence had been put forward by the prosecution. He dismissed the case and discharged the defendants.[1]

Meanwhile the strikers had not been idle. Week after week they assembled either at the carpenters' meeting place or at the Socialist Hall. They appealed to the trade unions for support and they did not appeal in vain. They never relaxed their efforts to let the whole world know how Messrs. Pauling and Henfrey had behaved. They sent

[1 *Northern Star*, no. 366, Nov. 16th, 1844, p. 5, cols. 4–5, article entitled 'Another of Labour's Victories'; see also *Manchester Guardian*, Nov. 13th, 1844, p. 5, col. 2.]

delegates north, east, south and west to every town in which the firm
tried to recruit blackleg labour. Everywhere the delegates told the
workers why Pauling and Henfrey were trying to get carpenters to
come to Manchester. They made every effort to stop new workers
from entering into the firm's employment. Only a few weeks after the
outbreak of the strike seven delegates of the carpenters' union were
stumping the country. At street corners in all the big cities the delegates put up placards which warned unemployed carpenters not to
accept offers of work from Pauling and Henfrey. By November 9th,
some of these delegates were back in Manchester and they gave an
account of their activities. One of them—named Johnson—had been
to Scotland. He stated that one of Pauling and Henfrey's agents had
recruited thirty workers in Edinburgh, but as soon as he explained to
them the truth of what was happening in the building trade in Manchester the Scottish workers declared that they would rather starve
than go to England. A second delegate reported that he had been in
Liverpool and had watched the arrival of the steamships [from
Glasgow.] But not a single recruit for Pauling and Henfrey had
arrived and he had nothing to do. A third delegate said that he had
been in Cheshire. He too had nothing to do, for wherever he went he
found that the operatives had been reading the *Northern Star*, which
is the journal of the working classes. Working men were so well
informed concerning the carpenters' strike at Pauling and Henfrey's
works that none of them had the slightest inclination to seek employment there. Indeed in Macclesfield the local carpenters had already
sent a contribution to the strike fund and they declared that if necessary
they would increase their help by a levy of one shilling per man. The
delegate was able to persuade other carpenters' unions in Cheshire to
promise to contribute to the strike fund.[1]

In order to give Messrs. Pauling and Henfrey another opportunity
of coming to an understanding with their men all the building operatives assembled at the Carpenters' Hall on Monday, November 18th
[1844]. A deputation was appointed to take an address to Messrs.
Pauling and Henfrey. A procession was formed with flags and banners
and the building operatives made their way to the works of the firm.
It was headed by the deputation. Then came the strikers' committee.
Next came the carpenters, the brickmakers, the day labourers, the
bricklayers, the sawyers, the glaziers, the plasterers, the painters, a
band, the stonemasons, the cabinet makers. They cheered loudly

[1 This paragraph is based on the article entitled ' The Carpenters' and Joiners'
Strike ' in the *Northern Star*, no. 365, Nov. 9th, 1844, p. 8, col. 1, and on an account
of a public meeting of the carpenters and joiners of Manchester held on Nov. 9th,
printed in the *Northern Star*, no. 366, Nov. 16th, 1844, p. 5, col. 5.]

when they passed the hotel at which 'Attorney General' Roberts was staying.

On arriving at Pauling and Henfrey's works the deputation fell out, while the remainder of the procession moved on to Stevenson Square where a public meeting was to be held. The deputation was received by the police, who took their names and addresses before allowing them to go inside. When they were admitted to the office they saw the partners, Mr. Sharps and Mr. Pauling, who declared that they were not prepared to receive an address from a mob which had been brought together to intimidate the firm. The members of the deputation denied that there had been any intimidation. The procession had not even stopped outside the works. It had moved on [to Stevenson Square]. While this procession of five thousand workers was marching away the deputation was at last ushered into a room where they found the head of the police force, an officer and [two or] three newspaper reporters. Mr. Sharps, a partner in the firm of Pauling and Henfrey, took it upon himself to preside over the meeting. He began by advising the members of the deputation to take care what they said since everything would be taken down and might, in certain circumstances, be used against them as evidence in the courts.

The members of the deputation were then asked to state their complaints. They replied that the carpenters were fighting to maintain the rules by which members of their craft had long worked in Manchester. The deputation asked if the carpenters who had recently come from Staffordshire and Scotland were working according to these rules. ' No ', was the answer, ' we have made a particular agreement with those men '. The deputation asked if former regular employees of the firm would be re-engaged on the established rules of the district. ' We will not treat with any deputation; if any of our own men . . . will come and ask for work we will tell them what rules they must work by '. Mr. Sharps added that none of the firms which bore his name had ever opposed the interests of the working classes and that his firms had paid as good wages as any firm in the town. Members of the deputation replied that if—as they had heard—Mr. Sharps was associated with Messrs Pauling, Henfrey and Co., they would like to make it clear that this firm had done much in opposition to the best interests of the working men [in Manchester].

A brickmaker—a member of the deputation—was asked whether members of his craft had any complaints to make. ' Nothing at present,' he replied, ' we have had enough.'[1] ' Oh! You have had enough, have you? ', said Mr. Pauling with a [hellish] grin. And then

[¹ He was referring to the shooting affray of May, 1843. See *supra*, p. 256.]

he seized the opportunity to give the deputation a long lecture about trade unions, strikes and so forth. He also drew attention to the misery which the workers were bringing on to their own heads. Members of the deputation retorted that they had no intention of being deprived of their rights one after another, and they were not going to accept the demand now made that they should work for nothing for 144 hours a year. Mr. Sharps remarked that, as against this, the deputation should consider how much had been lost by the workers who had given up a day's pay to take part in the procession, and how much the strikers had lost in wages. One member of the deputation [Bellhouse] observed: ' That is our business, and we don't think that we shall ask for anything out of your pocket towards it.'

The deputation then withdrew and reported on the interview to the workers who had assembled in the Carpenters' Hall. It was reported that the procession had been attended not only by the carpenters, who were on strike, but also by all the building operatives in the district employed by Pauling and Henfrey, who had hitherto stayed at work. It was also stated that several Scots who had just arrived to take up jobs with Pauling and Henfrey had downed tools that very morning. A painter [McGhee] said that Pauling and Henfrey had offered to members of his craft the same unacceptable terms which had already been rejected by the carpenters. The painters were determined to offer every resistance to such an imposition. The meeting resolved that matters must now be brought to a head. In the hope of shortening the struggle it was decided that all building operatives employed by Pauling and Henfrey should now go on strike.[1] This decision was put into effect. The painters stopped work on the following Saturday and the glaziers downed tools on the following Monday. Within a few days Pauling and Henfrey, who had secured a contract to build a new theatre, found that they had got only two bricklayers and four day labourers on the site instead of two hundred men.[2] Many of the newly-recruited workers also joined the strike.

Pauling, Henfrey and Co. foamed at the mouth. When yet another three of the new recruits stopped work they were haled before Daniel Maude, Esq., on Friday, November 22nd. The firm seemed quite undeterred by their previous discomfiture [in the borough court]. The first workman to appear was a man named Read, who was charged with breach of contract. An agreement which he had signed in Derby

[1 *Northern Star*, no. 367, Nov. 23rd, 1844, p. 6, cols. 3–4, ' Manchester—Great Aggregate Meeting of the Building Trades '.]
[2 *Northern Star*, no. 368, Nov. 30th, 1844, p. 1, col. 4—' Extension of the Strike '. The ' new theatre ' was the Theatre Royal, Peter Street, Manchester, opened in 1845.]

was produced in court. Read was defended by Mr. [W. P.] Roberts, who at once declared that there was not the slightest connection between the agreement and the information laid. They were two quite different things. Daniel Maude, Esq., at once saw the point—and he saw it because the dreaded Roberts had made it all too clear—but Mr. Maude found it an exhausting business to make the matter equally clear to counsel for the prosecution, [W. S. Rutter]. Eventually the prosecution asked for permission to amend the information and after a time counsel came back with an amended information which was even worse than the first. When counsel saw that he would not get anywhere with the new charge he asked that the case should be postponed yet again and Daniel Maude, Esq., agreed to give him a whole week to think things over, that is, until Friday, November 29th.[1] Whether counsel for the prosecution ever came back to court, I have not been able to discover, because the issue of the newspaper which must contain this information is missing from my file.[2] Meanwhile W. P. Roberts took the offensive and laid charges against one of Pauling and Henfrey's foremen and also against several of the recently recruited workers, because they had broken into a striker's house and assaulted his wife. He also brought two other charges against men who had assaulted strikers. Daniel Maude, Esq., to his great regret, had to find the charges proved, but he let them off as lightly as possible and merely bound them over to be of good behaviour in the future[3].

At the end of December [1844] Messrs. Pauling, Henfrey and Co., at long last succeeded in securing a verdict against two of their enemies, both of whom were charged with assaulting one of the workers employed by the firm. But this time the court was not so lenient. No hesitation was shown in sending the two men to jail for a month, and they were also bound over to keep the peace.[4]

[1 See *Northern Star*, no. 368, Nov. 30th, 1844, p. 1, cols. 4 and 5: 'More of Labour's Triumphs at Manchester and Wigan'.]

[2 *Northern Star*, no. 369, Dec. 7th, 1844, p. 5, cols. 3–4—'Another Victory for Labour. Manchester, Friday, Nov. 29th'. Roberts won the case by objecting that only a part of the agreement of October 19th between Pauling and Co. and the journeymen joiners was given in the information laid against the accused men. The portion omitted consisted of the 'annexed rules' according to which the joiners were to work. Maude therefore dismissed the cases against the five men, whereupon Roberts told them that they were all discharged. The *Northern Star* added: 'This announcement was received with one simultaneous burst of applause.']

[3 *Manchester Guardian*, Nov. 27th, 1844, p. 6, col. 5.]

[4 On December 24th, 1844, John O'Neile was brought before the Manchester Borough Court, charged with assaulting Michael Burton, an employee of Messrs Pauling and Henfrey. Mr. Maude stated that it was a case of assault only and not one of intimidation. O'Neile was bound over to keep the peace and had to provide two sureties of £10 each: *Manchester Guardian*, Dec. 28th, 1844, p. 5, col. 3. On January 1st, 1845 Thomas Robson, John Crabtree and Thomas Oman were charged

From now on there are few references to the strike [in the press], but on January 18th, [1845] it was still in full swing.[1] I have found no later references to the strike than this, but it probably followed the same course as so many other strikes have done. In time, no doubt, Pauling, Henfrey and Co. will have got together an adequate body of workers. The majority will be new recruits from distant parts of the country, and they will be supplemented by a few strikers who have given up the struggle. The great mass of the strikers will have found employment elsewhere, after being on strike for varying periods. The strikers can console themselves for all the misery they have endured with the reflection that they stood fast and that they kept up the level of their fellow-workers' wages. As for the matters in dispute, Messrs. Pauling, Henfrey and Co. will have found that it is not easy for them to get their own way and that they, too, have suffered losses on account of the strike. But after this bitter struggle it will be a long time before other employers [in the Manchester area] will dare to break the traditional rules of the carpenter's craft.

APPENDIX II

PREFACE TO THE AMERICAN EDITION OF 1887

Ten months have elapsed since, at the translator's wish, I wrote the Appendix[2] to this book; and during these ten months, a revolution has been accomplished in American society such as, in any other country, would have taken at least ten years. In February 1885,

at Ashton-under-Lyne petty sessions with conspiring to intimidate workmen employed by Messrs Pauling and Henfrey in building a new barracks nearby. The prisoners were liberated on bail, pending the hearing of the charge at the following South Lancashire Assizes: *Manchester Guardian*, Jan. 4th, 1845, p. 6, col. 5.]

[1 *Northern Star*, no. 375, Jan. 18th, 1845, p. 1, col. 5—'Aggregate meeting of the Manchester Building Trades.' According to this article a meeting was held on January 11th, 1845 to discuss 'certain proposals made by Messrs Pauling and Henfrey and Co., as the terms on which the Carpenters' and Joiners' strike could be terminated'. The debate was 'somewhat stormy' and a final discussion was deferred to a meeting called for January 14th. No subsequent reports of the strike have been traced. According to the *Manchester Guardian* the strike had ended on December 23rd:

We understand that the strike of the joiners in the employ of Messrs Pauling and Henfrey has terminated, the men having gone to their work yesterday morning, on the condition that their masters would henceforth adhere to the same rules as the other builders in the town (Dec. 24th, 1844, p. 4, col. 5).]

[2 The appendix to the American edition of 1887 was used by Engels as the basis of his preface to the English edition of 1892.]

American public opinion was almost unanimous on this one point; that there was no working class, in the European sense of the word, in America; that consequently no class struggle between workmen and capitalists, such as tore European society to pieces, was possible in the American Republic; and that, therefore, Socialism was a thing of foreign importation which could never take root on American soil. And yet, at that moment, the coming class struggle was casting its gigantic shadow before it in the strikes of the Pennsylvania coal-miners, and of many other trades, and especially in the preparations, all over the country, for the great Eight Hours' movement which was to come off, and did come off, in the May following. That I then duly appreciated these symptoms, that I anticipated a working-class movement on a national scale, my 'Appendix' shows; but no one could then foresee that in such a short time the movement would burst out with such irresistible force, would spread with the rapidity of a prairie-fire, would shake American society to its very foundations.

The fact is there, stubborn and indisputable. To what an extent it had struck with terror the American ruling classes, was revealed to me, in an amusing way, by American journalists who did me the honour of calling on me last summer; the ' new departure ' had put them into a state of helpless fright and perplexity. But at that time the movement was only just on the start; there was but a series of confused and apparently disconnected upheavals of that class which, by the suppression of negro slavery and the rapid development of manufactures, had become the lowest stratum of American society. Before the year closed, these bewildering social convulsions began to take a definite direction. The spontaneous, instinctive movements of these vast masses of working people, over a vast extent of country, the simultaneous outburst of their common discontent with a miserable social condition, the same everywhere and due to the same causes, made them conscious of the fact, that they formed a new and distinct class of American society; a class of—practically speaking—more or less hereditary wage-workers, proletarians. And with true American instinct this consciousness led them at once to take the next step towards their deliverance: the formation of a political working-men's party, with a platform of its own, and with the conquest of the Capitol and the White House for its goal. In May the struggle for the Eight Hours' working-day, the troubles in Chicago, Milwaukee, etc., the attempts of the ruling class to crush the nascent uprising of Labour by brute force and brutal class-justice; in November the new Labour Party organized in all great centres, and the New York, Chicago and Milwaukee elections. May and November have hitherto reminded the

American bourgeoisie only of the payment of coupons of U.S. bonds; henceforth May and November will remind them, too, of the dates on which the American working class presented *their* coupons for payment.

In European countries, it took the working class years and years before they fully realized the fact that they formed a distinct and, under the existing social conditions, a permanent class of modern society; and it took years again until this class consciousness led them to form themselves into a distinct political party, independent of, and opposed to, all the old political parties formed by the various sections of the ruling classes. On the more favoured soil of America, where no mediaeval ruins bar the way, where history begins with the elements of modern bourgeois society as evolved in the seventeenth century, the working class passed through these two stages of its development within ten months.

Still, all this is but a beginning. That the labouring masses should feel their community of grievances and of interests, their solidarity as a class in opposition to all other classes; that in order to give expression and effect to this feeling, they should set in motion the political machinery provided for that purpose in every free country—that is the first step only. The next step is to find the common remedy for these common grievances, and to embody it in the platform of the new Labour Party. And this—the most important and the most difficult step in the movement—has yet to be taken in America.

A new party must have a distinct positive platform; a platform which may vary in details as circumstances vary and as the party itself develops, but still one upon which the party, for the time being, is agreed. So long as such a platform has not been worked out, or exists but in a rudimentary form, so long the new party, too, will have but a rudimentary existence; it may exist locally but not yet nationally; it will be a party potentially but not actually.

That platform, whatever may be its first initial shape, must develop in a direction which may be determined beforehand. The causes that brought into existence the abyss between the working class and the capitalist class are the same in America as in Europe; the means of filling up that abyss are equally the same everywhere. Consequently, the platform of the American proletariat will in the long run coincide, as to the ultimate end to be attained, with the one which, after sixty years of dissensions and discussions, has become the adopted platform of the great mass of the European militant proletariat. It will proclaim, as the ultimate end, the conquest of political supremacy by the working class, in order to effect the direct appropriation of all means of production—land, railways, mines, machinery, etc.—by society at large, to be worked in common by all for the account and benefit of all.

But if the new American party, like all political parties everywhere, by the very fact of its formation aspires to the conquest of political power, it is as yet far from agreed upon what to do with that power when once attained. In New York and the other great cities of the East, the organization of the working class has proceeded upon the lines of Trades' Societies, forming in each city a powerful Central Labour Union. In New York the Central Labour Union, last November, chose for its standard-bearer Henry George, and consequently its temporary electoral platform has been largely imbued with his principles. In the great cities of the North-West the electoral battle was fought upon a rather indefinite labour platform, and the influence of Henry George's theories was scarcely, if at all, visible. And while in these great centres of population and of industry the new class movement came to a political head, we find all over the country two widespread labour organizations: the 'Knights of Labour' and the 'Socialist Labour Party', of which only the latter has a platform in harmony with the modern European standpoint as summarized above.

Of the three more or less definite forms under which the American labour movement thus presents itself, the first, the Henry George movement in New York, is for the moment of a chiefly local significance. No doubt New York is by far the most important city of the States; but New York is not Paris and the United States are not France. And it seems to me that the Henry George platform, in its present shape, is too narrow to form the basis for anything but a local movement, or at best for a short-lived phase of the general movement. To Henry George, the expropriation of the mass of the people from the land is the great and universal cause of the splitting up of the people into Rich and Poor. Now this is not quite correct historically. In Asiatic and classical antiquity, the predominant form of class oppression was slavery, that is to say, not so much the expropriation of the masses from the land as the appropriation of their persons. When, in the decline of the Roman Republic, the free Italian peasants were expropriated from their farms, they formed a class of 'poor whites' similar to that of the Southern Slave States before 1861; and between slaves and poor whites, two classes equally unfit for self-emancipation, the old world went to pieces. In the middle ages, it was not the expropriation of the people *from*, but on the contrary, their appropriation to the land which became the source of feudal oppression. The peasant retained his land, but was attached to it as a serf or villein, and made liable to tribute to the lord in labour and in produce. It was only at the dawn of modern times, towards the end of the fifteenth century, that the expropriation of the peasantry on a large scale laid the foundation for the modern class of wage-workers who possess nothing but their labour-power and can live only by the selling of that labour-power to others. But if the expropriation from the land brought this class into existence, it was the development of capitalist production, of modern industry and agriculture on a large scale, which perpetuated it, increased it, and shaped it into a distinct class with distinct interests and a distinct historical mission. All this has been fully expounded by Marx (*Capital*, Part VIII: 'The So-Called Primitive Accumulation'). According to Marx, the cause of the present antagonism of the classes and of the social degradation of the working class is their expropriation from *all* means of production, in which the land is of course included.

If Henry George declares land-monopolization to be the sole cause of poverty and misery, he naturally finds the remedy in the resumption of the land by society at large. Now, the Socialists of the school of Marx, too, demand the resumption, by society, of the land, and not only of the land but all other means of production likewise. But even if we leave these out of the question, there is another difference. What is to be done with the land? Modern Socialists, as represented by Marx, demand that it should be held and worked in common and for common account, and the same with all other means of social production, mines, railways, factories, etc.; Henry George would confine himself to letting it out to individuals as at present, merely regulating its distribution and applying the rents for public, instead of, as at present, for private purposes. What the Socialists demand, implies a total revolution of the whole system of social production; what Henry George demands, leaves the present mode of social production untouched, and has, in fact, been anticipated by the extreme section of Ricardian bourgeois economists who, too, demanded the confiscation of the rent of land by the State.

It would of course be unfair to suppose that Henry George has said his last word once for all. But I am bound to take his theory as I find it.

The second great section of the American movement is formed by the Knights of Labour.[1]   And that seems to be the section most typical of the present state of the movement, as it is undoubtedly by far the strongest. An immense association spread over an immense

[1 For the Knights of Labour, see J. R. Commons and others, *History of Labour in the United States* (New York, 1926) Vol. 2 and N. J. Ware, *The Labour Movement in the United States* (New York, 1929).]

extent of country in innumerable 'assemblies' representing all shades of individual and local opinion within the working class; the whole of them sheltered under a platform of corresponding indistinctness and held together much less by their impracticable constitution than by the instinctive feeling that the very fact of their clubbing together for their common aspiration makes them a great power in the country; a truly American paradox clothing the most modern tendencies in the most mediaeval mummeries, and hiding the most democratic and even rebellious spirit behind an apparent, but really powerless despotism— such is the picture the Knights of Labour offer to a European observer. But if we are not arrested by mere outside whimsicalities, we cannot help seeing in this vast agglomeration an immense amount of potential energy evolving slowly but surely into actual force. The Knights of Labour are the first national organization created by the American working class as a whole; whatever be their origin and history, whatever their shortcomings and little absurdities, whatever their platform and their constitution, here they are, the work of practically the whole class of American wage-workers, the only national bond that holds them together, that makes their strength felt to themselves not less than to their enemies, and that fills them with the proud hope of future victories. For it would not be exact to say that the Knights of Labour are liable to development. They are constantly in full process of development and revolution; a heaving, fermenting mass of plastic material seeking the shape and form appropriate to its inherent nature. That form will be attained as surely as historical evolution has, like natural evolution, its own immanent laws. Whether the Knights of Labour will then retain their present name or not, makes no difference, but to an outsider it appears evident that here is the raw material out of which the future of the American working-class movement, and along with it, the future of American society at large, has to be shaped.

The third section consists of the Socialist Labour Party. This section is a party but in name, for nowhere in America has it, up to now, been able actually to take its stand as a political party. It is, moreover, to a certain extent foreign to America, having until lately been made up almost exclusively by German immigrants, using their own language and, for the most part, little conversant with the common language of the country. But if it came from a foreign stock, it came, at the same time, armed with the experience earned during long years of class struggle in Europe, and with an insight into the general conditions of working-class emancipation, far superior to that hitherto gained by American working-men. This is a fortunate circumstance for the American proletarians who thus are enabled to appropriate, and to take advantage of, the intellectual and moral fruits of the forty years' struggle of their European classmates, and thus to hasten on the time of their own victory. For, as I said before, there cannot be any doubt that the ultimate platform of the American working class must and will be essentially the same as that now adopted by the whole militant working class of Europe, the same as that of the German-American Socialist Labour Party. In so far this party is called upon to play a very important part in the movement. But in order to do so they will have to doff every remnant of their foreign garb. They will have to become out and out American. They cannot expect the Americans to come to them; they, the minority and the immigrants, must go to the Americans, who are the vast majority and the natives. And to do that, they must above all things learn English.

The process of fusing together these various elements of the vast moving mass—elements not really discordant, but indeed mutually isolated by their various starting-points—will take some time and will not come off without a deal of friction, such as is visible at different points even now. The Knights of Labour, for instance, are here and there, in the Eastern cities, locally at war with the organized Trades Unions. But then this same friction exists within the Knights of Labour themselves, where there is anything but peace and harmony. These are not symptoms of decay, for capitalists to crow over. They are merely signs that the innumerable hosts of workers, for the first time set in motion in a common direction, have as yet found out neither the adequate expression for their common interests, nor the form of organization best adapted to the struggle, nor the discipline required to ensure victory. They are as yet the first levies *en masse* of the great revolutionary war, raised and equipped locally and independently, all converging to form one common army, but as yet without regular organization and common plan of campaign. The converging columns cross each other here and there: confusion, angry disputes, even threats of conflict arise. But the community of ultimate purpose in the end overcomes all minor troubles; ere long the straggling and squabbling battalions will be formed in a long line of battle array, presenting to the enemy a well-ordered front, ominously silent under their glittering arms, supported by bold skirmishers in front and by unshakeable reserves in the rear.

To bring about this result, the unification of the various independent bodies into one national Labour Army, with no matter how inadequate a provisional platform, provided it be a truly working-class platform—that is the next great step to be accomplished in America.

To effect this, and to make that platform worthy of the cause, the Socialist Labour Party can contribute a great deal, if they will only act in the same way as the European Socialists have acted at the time when they were but a small minority of the working class. That line of action was first laid down in the ' Communist Manifesto ' of 1847 in the following words:

The Communists—that was the name we took at the time and which even now we are far from repudiating—the Communists do not form a separate party opposed to other working-class parties.

They have no interests separate and apart from the interests of the whole working class.

They do not set up any sectarian principles of their own, by which to shape and model the proletarian movement.

The Communists are distinguished from the other working-class parties by this only: 1. In the national struggles of the proletarians of the different countries they point out, and bring to the front, the common interests of the whole proletariat, interests independent of all nationality; 2. In the various stages of development which the struggle of the working class against the capitalist class has to pass through, they always and everywhere represent the interests of the movement as a whole.

The Communists, therefore, are on the one hand, practically the most advanced and resolute section of the working-class parties of all countries, that section which ever pushes forward all others; on the other hand, theoretically, they have, over the great mass of the proletarians, the advantage of clearly understanding the line of march, the conditions, and the ultimate general results of the proletarian movement.

Thus they fight for the attainment of the immediate ends, for the enforcement of the momentary interests of the working class; but in the movement of the present, they represent and take care of the future of the movement.

That is the line of action which the great founder of modern Socialism, Karl Marx, and with him, I and the Socialists of all nations who worked along with us, have followed for more than forty years, with the result that it has led to victory everywhere, and that at this moment the mass of European Socialists, in Germany and in France, in Belgium, Holland and Switzerland, in Denmark and Sweden as well as in Spain and Portugal, are fighting as one common army under one and the same flag.

FREDERICK ENGELS.

London, January 26th, 1887.

APPENDIX III

PREFACE TO THE ENGLISH EDITION OF 1892

The book, an English translation of which is here republished, was first issued in Germany in 1845. The author, at that time, was young, twenty-four years of age, and his production bears the stamp of his youth with its good and its faulty features, of neither of which he feels ashamed. It was translated into English, in 1885, by an American lady, Mrs. F. Kelley Wischnewetzky, and published in the following year in New York. The American edition being as good as exhausted, and having never been extensively circulated on this side of the Atlantic, the present English copyright edition is brought out with the full consent of all parties interested.

For the American edition, a new Preface and an Appendix were written in English by the author. The first had little to do with the book itself; it discussed the American Working-Class Movement of the day, and is, therefore, here omitted as irrelevant; the second—the original preface—is largely made use of in the present introductory remarks.

The state of things described in this book belongs to-day, in many respects, to the past, as far as England is concerned. Though not expressly stated in our recognised treatises, it is still a law of modern Political Economy that the larger the scale on which capitalistic production is carried on, the less can it support the petty devices of swindling and pilfering which characterise its early stages. The petti-fogging business tricks of the Polish Jew, the representative in Europe of commerce in its lowest stage, those tricks that serve him so well in his own country, and are generally practised there, he finds to be out of date and out of place when he comes to Hamburg or Berlin; and, again, the commission agent who hails from Berlin or Hamburg, Jew or Christian, after frequenting the Manchester Exchange for a few months, finds out that in order to buy cotton yarn or cloth cheap, he, too, had better drop those slightly more refined but still miserable wiles and subterfuges which are considered the acme of cleverness in his native country. The fact is, those tricks do not pay any longer in a large market, where time is money, and where a certain standard of commercial morality is unavoidably developed, purely as a means of saving time and trouble. And it is the same with the relation between the manufacturer and his ' hands '.

The revival of trade, after the crisis of 1847, was the dawn of a new industrial epoch. The repeal of the Corn Laws and the financial reforms subsequent thereon gave to English industry and commerce all the elbow-room they had asked for. The discovery of the Californian and Australian gold-fields followed in rapid succession. The colonial markets developed at an increasing rate their capacity for absorbing English manufactured goods. In India millions of hand-weavers were finally crushed out by the Lancashire power-loom. China was more and more being opened up. Above all, the United States—then, commercially speaking, a mere colonial market, but by far the biggest of them all—underwent an economic development astounding even for that rapidly progressive country. And, finally, the new means of communication introduced at the close of the preceding period—railways and ocean steamers—were now worked out on an international scale; they realised actually what had hitherto existed only potentially, a world-market. This world-market, at first, was composed of a number of chiefly or entirely agricultural countries grouped around one manufacturing centre—England—which consumed the greater part of their surplus raw produce, and supplied them in return with the greater part of their requirements in manu-factured articles. No wonder England's industrial progress was colossal and unparalleled, and such that the status of 1844 now appears to us as comparatively primitive and insignificant. And in proportion as this increase took place, in the same proportion did manufacturing industry become apparently moralised. The competition of manu-facturer against manufacturer by means of petty thefts upon the work-people did no longer pay. Trade had outgrown such low means of making money; they were not worth while practising for the manu-facturing millionaire, and served merely to keep alive the competition of smaller traders, thankful to pick up a penny wherever they could. Thus the truck system was suppressed, the Ten Hours Bill was enacted, and a number of other secondary reforms introduced—much against the spirit of Free Trade and unbridled competition, but quite as much in favour of the giant-capitalist in his competition with his less favoured brother. Moreover, the larger the concern, and with it the number of hands, the greater the loss and inconvenience caused by every conflict between master and men; and thus a new spirit came over the masters, especially the large ones, which taught them to avoid unnecessary squabbles, to acquiesce in the existence and power of Trades' Unions, and finally even to discover in strikes—at opportune times—a powerful means to serve their own ends. The largest manufacturers, formerly the leaders of the war against the working-class, were now the foremost to preach peace and harmony.

And for a very good reason. The fact is that all these concessions to justice and philanthropy were nothing else but means to accelerate the concentration of capital in the hands of the few, for whom the niggardly extra extortions of former years had lost all importance and had become actual nuisances; and to crush all the quicker and all the safer their smaller competitors, who could not make both ends meet without such perquisities. Thus the development of production on the basis of the capitalistic system has of itself sufficed—at least in the leading industries, for in the more unimportant branches this is far from being the case—to do away with all those minor grievances which aggravated the workman's fate during its earlier stages. And thus it renders more and more evident the great central fact that the cause of the miserable condition of the working-class is to be sought, not in these minor grievances, but *in the capitalistic system itself.* The wage-worker sells to the capitalist his labour-force for a certain daily sum. After a few hours' work he has reproduced the value of that sum; but the substance of his contract is, that he has to work another series of hours to complete his working-day; and the value he produces during these additional hours of surplus labour is surplus value, which costs the capitalist nothing, but yet goes into his pocket. That is the basis of the system which tends more and more to split up civilised society into a few Rothschilds and Vanderbilts, the owners of all the means of production and subsistence, on the one hand, and an immense number of wage-workers, the owners of nothing but their labour-force, on the other. And that this result is caused not by this or that secondary grievance, but by the system itself—this fact has been brought out in bold relief by the development of capitalism in England since 1847.

Again, the repeated visitations of cholera, typhus, smallpox, and other epidemics have shown the British bourgeois the urgent necessity of sanitation in his towns and cities, if he wishes to save himself and family from falling victims to such diseases. Accordingly, the most crying abuses described in this book have either disappeared or have been made less conspicuous. Drainage has been introduced or improved, wide avenues have been opened out athwart many of the worst ' slums ' I had to describe. ' Little Ireland ' has disappeared, and the ' Seven Dials ' are next on the list for sweeping away. But what of that? Whole districts which in 1844 I could describe as almost idyllic have now, with the growth of the towns, fallen into the same state of dilapidation, discomfort, and misery. Only the pigs and the heaps of refuse are no longer tolerated. The bourgeoisie have made further progress in the art of hiding the distress of the working-class. But that, in regard to their dwellings, no substantial improvement has taken place is amply proved by the Report of the Royal Commission ' on the Housing of the Poor ', 1885. And this is the case, too, in other respects. Police regulations have been plentiful as blackberries; but they can only hedge in the distress of the workers, they cannot remove it.

But while England has thus outgrown the juvenile state of capitalist exploitation described by me, other countries have only just attained it. France, Germany, and especially America, are the formidable competitors, who, at this moment—as foreseen by me in 1844—are more and more breaking up England's industrial monopoly. Their manufactures are young as compared with those of England, but increasing at a far more rapid rate than the latter; and, curious enough, they have at this moment arrived at about the same phase of development as English manufacture in 1844. With regard to America, the parallel is indeed most striking. True, the external surroundings in which the working class is placed in America are very different, but the same economical laws are at work, and the results, if not identical in every respect, must still be of the same order. Hence we find in America the same struggles for a shorter working-day, for a legal limitation of the working-time, especially of women and children in factories; we find the truck-system in full blossom, and the cottage-system, in rural districts, made use of by the ' bosses ' as a means of domination over the workers. When I received, in 1886, the American papers with accounts of the great strike of 12,000 Pennsylvanian coal-miners in the Connellsville district, I seemed but to read my own description of the North of England colliers' strike of 1844. The same cheating of the workpeople by false measure; the same truck-system; the same attempt to break the miners' resistance by the capitalists' last, but crushing, resource—the eviction of the men out of their dwellings, the cottages owned by the companies.

I have not attempted, in this translation, to bring the book up to date, or to point out in detail all the changes that have taken place since 1844. And for two reasons: Firstly, to do this properly, the size of the book must be about doubled; and, secondly, the first volume of *Das Kapital*, by Karl Marx, an English translation of which is before the public, contains a very ample description of the state of the British working-class, as it was about 1865, that is to say, at the time when British industrial prosperity reached its culminating point. I should, then, have been obliged again to go over the ground already covered by Marx's celebrated work.

It will be hardly necessary to point out that the general theoretical standpoint of this book—philosophical, economical, political—does not exactly coincide with my standpoint of to-day. Modern international Socialism, since fully developed as a science, chiefly and almost exclusively through the efforts of Marx, did not as yet exist in 1844. My book represents one of the phases of its embryonic development; and as the human embryo, in its early stages, still reproduces the gill-arches of our fish-ancestors, so this book exhibits everywhere the traces of the descent of modern Socialism from one of its ancestors, German philosophy. Thus great stress is laid on the dictum that Communism is not a mere party doctrine of the working class, but a theory compassing the emancipation of society at large, including the capitalist class, from its present narrow conditions. This is true enough in the abstract, but absolutely useless, and sometimes worse, in practice. So long as the wealthy classes not only do not feel the want of any emancipation, but strenuously oppose the self-emancipation of the working class, so long the social revolution will have to be prepared and fought out by the working class alone. The French bourgeois of 1789, too, declared the emancipation of the bourgeoisie to be the emancipation of the whole human race; but the nobility and clergy would not see it; the proposition—though for the time being, with respect to feudalism, an abstract historical truth—soon became a mere sentimentalism, and disappeared from view altogether in the fire of the revolutionary struggle. And to-day, the very people who, from the 'impartiality' of their superior standpoint, preach to the workers a Socialism soaring high above their class interests and class struggles, and tending to reconcile in a higher humanity the interests of both the contending classes—these people are either neophytes, who have still to learn a great deal, or they are the worst enemies of the workers—wolves in sheep's clothing.

The recurring period of the great industrial crisis is stated in the text as five years. This was the period apparently indicated by the course of events from 1825 to 1842. But the industrial history from 1842 to 1868 has shown that the real period is one of ten years; that the intermediate revulsions were secondary, and tended more and more to disappear. Since 1868 the state of things has changed again, of which more anon.

I have taken care not to strike out of the text the many prophecies, amongst others that of an imminent social revolution in England, which my youthful ardour induced me to venture upon. The wonder is, not that a good many of them proved wrong, but that so many of them have proved right, and that the critical state of English trade, to be brought on by Continental and especially American competition, which I then foresaw—though in too short a period—has now actually come to pass. In this respect I can, and am bound to, bring the book up to date, by placing here an article which I published in the London *Commonwealth* of March 1st, 1885, under the heading: 'England in 1845 and in 1885'. It gives at the same time a short outline of the history of the English working class during these forty years, and is as follows:

'Forty years ago England stood face to face with a crisis, solvable to all appearances by force only. The immense and rapid development of manufactures had outstripped the extension of foreign markets and the increase of demand. Every ten years the march of industry was violently interrupted by a general commercial crash, followed, after a long period of chronic depression, by a few short years of prosperity, and always ending in feverish over-production and consequent renewed collapse. The capitalist class clamoured for Free Trade in corn, and threatened to enforce it by sending the starving population of the towns back to the country districts whence they came, to invade them, as John Bright said, not as paupers begging for bread, but as an army quartered upon the enemy. The working masses of the towns demanded their share of political power—the People's Charter; they were supported by the majority of the small trading class, and the only difference between the two was whether the Charter should be carried by physical or by moral force. Then came the commercial crash of 1847 and the Irish famine, and with both the prospect of revolution.

'The French Revolution of 1848 saved the English middle class. The Socialistic pronunciamentos of the victorious French workmen frightened the small middle class of England and disorganised the narrower, but more matter-of-fact movement of the English working class. At the very moment when Chartism was bound to assert itself in its full strength, it collapsed internally before even it collapsed externally on the 10th of April, 1848. The action of the working class was thrust into the background. The capitalist class triumphed along the whole line.

'The Reform Bill of 1831 had been the victory of the whole capitalist class over the landed aristocracy. The repeal of the Corn Laws was the victory of the manufacturing capitalist not only over the landed aristocracy, but over those sections of capitalists, too, whose interests were more or less bound up with the landed interest —bankers, stock-jobbers, fund-holders, etc. Free Trade meant the re-adjustment of the whole home and foreign, commercial and financial policy of England in accordance with the interests of the manufacturing capitalists—the class which now represented the nation. And they set about this task with a will. Every obstacle to industrial production was mercilessly removed. The tariff and the whole system of taxation were revolutionised. Everything was made subordinate to one end, but that end of the utmost importance to the manufacturing capitalist: the cheapening of all raw produce, and especially of the means of living of the working class; the reduction of the cost of raw material, and the keeping down—if not as yet the *bringing down*—of wages. England was to become the 'workshop of the world'; all other countries were to become for England what Ireland already was— markets for her manufactured goods, supplying her in return with raw materials and food. England the great manufacturing centre of an agricultural world, with an ever-increasing number of corn and cotton-growing Irelands revolving around her, the industrial sun. What a glorious prospect!

'The manufacturing capitalists set about the realisation of this their great object with that strong commonsense and that contempt for traditional principles which has ever distinguished them from their more narrow-minded compeers on the Continent. Chartism was dying out. The revival of commercial prosperity, natural after the revulsion of 1847 had spent itself, was put down altogether to the credit of Free Trade. Both these circumstances had turned the English working class, politically, into the tail of the 'great Liberal Party', the party led by the manufacturers. This advantage, once gained, had to be perpetuated. And the manufacturing capitalists, from the Chartist opposition, not to Free Trade, but to the transformation of Free Trade into the one vital national question, had learnt, and were learning more and more, that the middle class can never obtain full social and political power over the nation except by the help of the working class. Thus a gradual change came over the relations between both classes. The Factory Acts, once the bugbear of all manufacturers, were not only willingly submitted to, but their expansion into acts regulating almost all trades was tolerated. Trades' Unions, hitherto considered inventions of the devil himself, were now petted and patron- ised as perfectly legitimate institutions, and as useful means of spreading sound economical (*sic*) doctrines amongst the workers. Even strikes, than which nothing had been more nefarious up to 1848, were now gradually found out to be occasionally very useful, especially when provoked by the masters themselves, at their own time. Of the legal enactments, placing the workman at a lower level or at a dis- advantage with regard to the master, at least the most revolting were repealed. And, practically, that horrid 'People's Charter' actually became the political programme of the very manufacturers who had opposed it to the last. " The Abolition of the Property Qualification " and " Vote by Ballot " are now the law of the land. The Reform Acts of 1867 and 1884 make a near approach to " universal suffrage ", at least such as it now exists in Germany; the Redistribution Bill now before Parliament creates " equal electoral districts "—on the whole not more unequal than those of Germany; " payment of members ", and shorter, if not actually " annual Parliaments ", are visibly looming in the distance—and yet there are people who say that Chartism is dead.

' The Revolution of 1848, not less than many of its predecessors, has had strange bedfellows and successors. The very people who put it down have become, as Karl Marx used to say, its testamentary executors. Louis Napoleon had to create an independent and united Italy, Bismarck had to revolutionise Germany and to restore Hungarian independence, and the English manufacturers had to enact the People's Charter.

' For England, the effects of this domination of the manufacturing capitalists were at first startling. Trade revived and extended to a degree unheard of even in this cradle of modern industry; the previous astounding creations of steam and machinery dwindled into nothing compared with the immense mass of productions of the twenty years from 1850 to 1870, with the overwhelming figures of exports and imports, of wealth accumulated in the hands of capitalists and of human working power concentrated in the large towns. The progress was indeed interrupted, as before, by a crisis every ten years, in 1857 as well as in 1866; but these revulsions were now considered as natural, inevitable events, which must be fatalistically submitted to, and which always set themselves right in the end.

'And the condition of the working class during this period? There was temporary improvement even for the great mass. But this improvement always was reduced to the old level by the influx of the great body of the unemployed reserve, by the constant super-seding of hands by new machinery, by the immigration of the agri-cultural population, now, too, more and more superseded by machines.

'A permanent improvement can be recognised for two " pro-tected " sections only of the working class. Firstly, the factory hands. The fixing by Act of Parliament of their working-day within relatively rational limits has restored their physical constitution and endowed them with a moral superiority, enhanced by their local concentration. They are undoubtedly better off than before 1848. The best proof is that, out of ten strikes they make, nine are provoked by the manu-

facturers in their own interests, as the only means of securing a
reduced production. You can never get the masters to agree to work
" short time ", let manufactured goods be ever so unsaleable; but get
the work-people to strike, and the masters shut their factories to a man.

' Secondly, the great Trades' Unions. They are the organisations
of those trades in which the labour of *grown-up men* predominates, or is
alone applicable. Here the competition neither of women and children
nor of machinery has so far weakened their organised strength. The
engineers, the carpenters and joiners, the bricklayers, are each of them
a power, to that extent that, as in the case of the bricklayers and bricklayers' labourers, they can even successfully resist the introduction of
machinery. That their condition has remarkably improved since
1848 there can be no doubt, and the best proof of this is in the fact
that for more than fifteen years not only have their employers been
with them, but they with their employers, upon exceedingly good
terms. They form an aristocracy among the working class; they have
succeeded in enforcing for themselves a relatively comfortable position,
and they accept it as final. They are the model working-men of Messrs.
Leone Levi & Giffen, and they are very nice people indeed nowadays
to deal with, for any sensible capitalist in particular and for the whole
capitalist class in general.

' But as to the great mass of working-people, the state of misery
and insecurity in which they live now is as low as ever, if not lower.
The East End of London is an ever-spreading pool of stagnant misery
and desolation, of starvation when out of work, and degradation,
physical and moral, when in work. And so in all other large towns—
abstraction made of the privileged minority of the workers; and so in
the smaller towns and in the agricultural districts. The law which
reduces the *value* of labour-power to the value of the necessary means
of subsistence, and the other law which reduces its *average price*, as a
rule, to the minimum of those means of subsistence, these laws act
upon them with the irresistible force of an automatic engine which
crushes them between its wheels.

' This, then, was the position created by the Free Trade policy of
1847, and by twenty years of the rule of the manufacturing capitalists.
But then a change came. The crash of 1866 was, indeed, followed by a
slight and short revival about 1873; but that did not last. We did not,
indeed, pass through the full crisis at the time it was due, in 1877 or 1878;
but we have had, ever since 1876, a chronic state of stagnation in all
dominant branches of industry. Neither will the full crash come; nor
will the period of longed-for prosperity to which we used to be
entitled before and after it. A dull depression, a chronic glut of all

markets for all trades, that is what we have been living in for nearly ten years. How is this?

'The Free Trade theory was based upon one assumption: that England was to be the one great manufacturing centre of an agricultural world. And the actual fact is that this assumption has turned out to be a pure delusion. The conditions of modern industry, steam-power and machinery, can be established wherever there is fuel, especially coals. And other countries besides England—France, Belgium, Germany, America, even Russia—have coals. And the people over there did not see the advantage of being turned into Irish pauper farmers merely for the greater wealth and glory of English capitalists. They set resolutely about manufacturing, not only for themselves, but for the rest of the world; and the consequence is that the manufacturing monopoly enjoyed by England for nearly a century is irretrievably broken up.

'But the manufacturing monopoly of England is the pivot of the present social system of England. Even while that monopoly lasted, the markets could not keep pace with the increasing productivity of English manufacturers; the decennial crises were the consequence. And new markets are getting scarcer every day, so much so that even the Negroes of the Congo are now to be forced into the civilisation attendant upon Manchester calicos, Staffordshire pottery, and Birmingham hardware. How will it be when Continental, and especially American, goods flow in in ever-increasing quantities—when the predominating share, still held by British manufacturers, will become reduced from year to year? Answer, Free Trade, thou universal panacea.

'I am not the first to point this out. Already in 1883, at the Southport meeting of the British Association, Mr. Inglis Palgrave, the President of the Economic section, stated plainly that " the days of great trade profits in England were over, and there was a pause in the progress of several great branches of industrial labour. *The country might almost be said to be entering the non-progressive state* ".

'But what is to be the consequence? Capitalist production *cannot* stop. It must go on increasing and expanding, or it must die. Even now the mere reduction of England's lion's share in the supply of the world's markets means stagnation, distress, excess of capital here, excess of unemployed workpeople there. What will it be when the increase of yearly production is brought to a complete stop?

'Here is the vulnerable place, the heel of Achilles, for capitalistic production. Its very basis is the necessity of constant expansion, and this constant expansion now becomes impossible. It ends in a deadlock. Every year England is brought nearer face to face with the question: either the country must go to pieces, or capitalist production must. Which is it to be?

'And the working class? If even under the unparalleled commercial and industrial expansion, from 1848 to 1868, they have had to undergo such misery; if even then the great bulk of them experienced at best but a temporary improvement of their condition, while only a small, privileged, " protected " minority was permanently benefited, what will it be when this dazzling period is brought finally to a close; when the present dreary stagnation shall not only become intensified, but this, its intensified condition, shall become the permanent and normal state of English trade?

' The truth is this: during the period of England's industrial monopoly the English working class have, to a certain extent, shared in the benefits of the monopoly. These benefits were very unequally parcelled out amongst them; the privileged minority pocketed most, but even the great mass had, at least, a temporary share now and then. And that is the reason why, since the dying-out of Owenism, there has been no Socialism in England. With the breakdown of that monopoly, the English working class will lose that privileged position; it will find itself generally—the privileged and leading minority not excepted—on a level with its fellow-workers abroad. And that is the reason why there will be Socialism again in England.'

To this statement of the case, as that case appeared to me in 1885, I have but little to add. Needless to say that to-day there is indeed ' Socialism again in England ', and plenty of it—Socialism of all shades: Socialism conscious and unconscious and of the middle class, for, verily, that abomination of abominations, Socialism, has not only become respectable, but has actually donned evening dress and lounges lazily on drawing-room *causeuses*. That shows the incurable fickleness of that terrible despot of ' society ', middle-class public opinion, and once more justifies the contempt in which we Socialists of a past generation always held that public opinion. At the same time we have no reason to grumble at the symptom itself.

What I consider far more important than this momentary fashion among bourgeois circles of affecting a mild dilution of Socialism, and even more than the actual progress Socialism has made in England generally, that is the revival of the East End of London. That immense haunt of misery is no longer the stagnant pool it was six years ago. It has shaken off its torpid despair, has returned to life, and had become the home of what is called the ' New Unionism ', that is to say, of the organisation of the great mass of ' unskilled ' workers. This organisation may to a great extent adopt the form of the old Unions of ' skilled ' workers but it is essentially different in character. The old Unions preserve the traditions of the time when they were founded, and look upon the wages system as a once-for-all established, final fact, which they at best can modify in the interest of their members. The new Unions were founded at a time when the faith in the eternity of the wages system was severely shaken; their founders and promoters were Socialists either consciously or by feeling; the masses, whose adhesion gave them strength, were rough, neglected, looked down upon by the working-class aristocracy; but they had this immense advantage, that *their minds were virgin soil*, entirely free from the inherited ' respectable ' bourgeois prejudices which hampered the brains of the better situated ' old ' Unionists. And thus we see now these new Unions taking the lead of the working-class movement generally, and more and more taking in tow the rich and proud ' old ' Unions.

Undoubtedly, the East Enders have committed colossal blunders; so have their predecessors, and so do the doctrinaire Socialists who pooh-pooh them. A large class, like a great nation, never learns better or quicker than by undergoing the consequences of its own mistakes. And for all the faults committed in past, present and future, the revival of the East End of London remains one of the greatest and most fruitful facts of this *fin de siècle*, and glad and proud I am to have lived to see it.

F. ENGELS.

January 11*th*, 1892.

APPENDIX IV

LIST OF SOURCES QUOTED BY ENGELS[1]

1. *Books and Pamphlets*

ALISON, SIR ARCHIBALD
The Principles of Population . . ., (2 vols., Edinburgh, 1840). [Alison was High Sheriff of Lanarkshire and Engels generally refers to him as ' Sheriff Alison '.]

ALISON, WILLIAM PULTENEY
Observations on the Management of the Poor in Scotland and its Effects on the Health of Great Towns (Edinburgh, 1840).

BAINES, EDWARD, jun.
History of the Cotton Manufacture in Great Britain (London, 1835).

CARLYLE, THOMAS
Chartism (London, 1839), *Past and Present* (London, 1843).

CROKER, J. W.
A Sketch of the State of Ireland, Past and Present (2nd London edn., 1808): published anonymously.

DISRAELI, BENJAMIN
Sybil (London, 1845).

FAUCHER, LÉON
Etudes sur l'Angleterre (2 vols., Paris, 1845). Engels used articles in the *Revue des Deux Mondes* which formed the basis of Faucher's book.

GASKELL, PETER
The Manufacturing Population of England . . . (London, 1833).

KAY, J. P. (later KAY-SHUTTLEWORTH)
The Moral and Physical Condition of the Working Classes employed in the Cotton Manufacture in Manchester (1st edn., 1832; 2nd edn., 1832). Engels used the second edition.

LEACH, JAMES
Stubborn Facts from the Factories by a Manchester Operative, published . . . by W. Rashleigh, M.P. (London, 1844): this appeared anonymously.

McCULLOCH, J. R.
A Statistical Account of the British Empire . . . (London, 1837).

MALTHUS, T. R.
An Essay on the Principle of Population (London, 2nd edn., 1803).

OASTLER, RICHARD
The Fleet Papers (4 vols., London, 1841–4).

---

[1] This list includes books, pamphlets, journals, newspapers and official reports to which Engels refers in his text or footnotes.

PARKINSON, R
On the present Condition of the Labouring Poor in Manchester (London and Manchester, 3rd edn., 1841).

PORTER, G. R.
The Progress of the Nation . . . (3 vols., London, 1836–43).

SENIOR, NASSAU WILLIAM.
Letters on the Factory Act . . . (London, 1837).

SMITH, ADAM
An Inquiry into the Nature and Causes of the Wealth of Nations (ed. by J. R. McCulloch, 4 vols., 1828).

STIRNER, MAX
Der Einzige und sein Eigenthum (Leipzig, 1845). 'Stirner' was the pen-name of Johann Kaspar Schmidt.

STRAUSS, D. F.
Life of Jesus (German edn., 1835–36; official English translation, 3 vols., 1846).

SYMONS, J. C.
Arts and Artisans at Home and Abroad (Edinburgh and London, 1839).

URE, ANDREW
The Cotton Manufacture of Great Britain (2 vols., London, 1836).
The Philosophy of Manufactures (2nd edn., London, 1835).

VAUGHAN, ROBERT
The Age of Great Cities (London, 1842).

WADE, JOHN
History of the Middle and Working Classes (London, 3rd edn., 1835).

WAKEFIELD, EDWARD GIBBON
Swing Unmasked; or the Causes of Rural Incendiarism (London, 1831).

2. *Newspapers and Journals*

† *Artizan*
* *Durham Chronicle.*
* *Edinburgh Medical and Surgical Journal*, Vol. 14, (1818).
* *Halifax Guardian.*
Illuminated Magazine.
Journal of the Statistical Society of London, Vols. 2 (1839), 3 (1840) and 7 (1844).
* *Leeds Mercury.*
Liverpool Mercury.
Manchester Guardian.
* *Miner's Advocate* (Newcastle-upon-Tyne).
* *Mining Journal.*
Morning Chronicle.

* Engels referred to these periodicals only once in his book.
† One article in *The Artizan* mentioned on several occasions.

Northern Star (Leeds).
North of England Medical and Surgical Journal.
* *The Sun.*
The Times.
Weekly Dispatch.

3. *Parliamentary Papers*

1831–2   Report of Select Committee on Factory Children's Labour (cited by Engels as ' Sadler's Report).

1833   Factories Inquiry Commission: Report of the Central Board of His Majesty's Commissioners appointed to collect Information in the Manufacturing Districts as to the employment of Children in Factories—First Report June 1833, Second Report July 1833.

1833   *Extracts from the Information received by His Majesty's Commissioners, as to the Administration and Operation of the Poor-Laws* (1833).

1836   Third Report of the Commissioners appointed ' to inquire into the condition of the poorer classes in Ireland, and into the various institutions at present established for their relief '.

1842   Report to Her Majesty's Principal Secretary of State for the Home Department from the Poor Law Commissioners on an Inquiry into the Sanitary Condition of the Labouring Population of Great Britain (by Edwin Chadwick).

1842–3   Report of Commission of Inquiry into the Employment of Children and Young Persons in Mines and Collieries and in the Trades and Manufactures in which numbers of them work together. . . First Report 1842, Second Report 1843.[1] Appendices to both Reports, each in two parts, were published in 1842.

1843   Reports of Special Assistant Poor Law Commissioners on the Employment of Women and Children in Agriculture.

1844   Report of the Commissioners for Inquiring into the state of Large Towns . . . First Report (2 volumes), 1844.

1844   Reports of the Inspectors of Factories . . . for the Half Year ending December 31, 1843 (1844).

[1 There is an official abridgement of these reports entitled *The Physical and Moral Condition of the Children and Young Persons employed in Mines and Factories* (published for Her Majesty's Stationery Office by J. W. Parker, London, 1843) to which Adoratskij frequently refers in footnotes to the Marx-Engels-Lenin Institute edition of Engels's book. Engels, however, almost certainly used the full reports and not the abridged version.]

APPENDIX V

EXAMPLES OF ENGELS'S METHODS OF QUOTING

Two examples may be given to illustrate the way in which Engels's quotations sometimes represent only very garbled and abridged versions of the originals.

1. THE OLD POOR LAW

Extracts from the Information received by His Majesty's Commissioners as to the Administration and Operation of the Poor-Laws (1833), p. xvi.

CONTENTS

POOR-LAWS, as at present administered.

Opinion in Cambridgeshire seems to be in favour of a thorough change of system, 127.

A check to industry, a reward for improvident marriages, a stimulant to population, and a blind to its effects on wages. See scale to able-bodied 2, 65, 78, 82, 127, 132, 143, 189—in Durham 177, 179.

Have become a national institution for discountenancing the industrious and honest, and for protecting the idle, the improvident, and the vicious 2, 14, 27, 40, 63, 74, 76, 79, 108, 116, 119, 120, 121, 149, 161, 162, 165, 188, 218, 241, 247.

The destroyer of filial, parental and conjugal affection, 84, 85, 117, 119, 161, 162, 166—in Durham 175, 188.

Have become a system for preventing the accumulation of capital, for destroying that which exists, and for reducing the ratepayer to pauperism 15, 27, 93, 163, 188.

A premium for illegitimate children, exhibited in the allowance for illegitimate as compared with that for legitimate 392, 393, 394, 395, 396, 397.

ENGELS'S VERSION

. . . it was found that this system was—

'A check upon industry, a reward for improvident marriage, a stimulus to increased population, and a means of counterbalancing the effect of an increased population upon wages; a national provision for discouraging the honest and industrious, and protecting the lazy, vicious, and improvident; calculated to destroy the bonds of family life, hinder systematically the accumulation of capital, scatter that which is already accumulated, and ruin the taxpayers. Moreover, in the provision of aliment, it sets a premium upon illegitimate children'.
(Words of the Report of the Poor Law Commissioners.)

The Condition of the Working Class in England in 1844, English translation by Mrs. Wischnewetzky (edn. of 1892, p. 286).

2. DEFORMITIES AMONG FACTORY WORKERS

Extract from Dr. Loudon's report (Factories Enquiry Commission.   Second Report, C.3, p. 24).

'Although no cases presented themselves of deformed pelvis, varicose veins, ulcers in the young people under 25 years of age, and some others of the diseases which have been described, yet their ailments are such as every medical man must expect to be the probable consequences of young people working, in some instances, nearly forty consecutive hours twice a week, and, besides, labouring from twelve to fourteen hours on those days of the week when night-work was not expected; and they are recorded by men of the highest professional and moral character.'

ENGELS'S VERSION

'Although ', says Dr. Loudon in his report, ' no example of malformation of the pelvis and of some other affections came under my notice, these things are nevertheless so common, that every physician must regard them as probable consequences of such working hours, and as vouched for besides by men of the highest medical credibility.'

The Condition of the Working Class in England in 1844, English translation by Mrs. Wischnewetzky (edn. of 1892, p. 161).

INDEX

This index covers Engels's text of 1845, his Postscript of 1846, and a few of his more important footnotes. It does not cover the majority of the footnotes, Engels's various prefaces or the Editors' Introduction. Topics which occur very frequently in the text are omitted e.g. bourgeoisie, child labour, factory system, female labour, housing, Lancashire, machinery, middle classes, prices, proletariat, slums.

Aaron, 127
Absentees, 202, 203
Accidents, 123, 186–8
Acts of Parliament:
  Beer Act (1830), 142
  Combination Laws (repealed 1824), 243
  Commutation (Tithes) Act, 308
  Factory Acts of 1819, 1825 and 1831, 191, 195
  Factory Act of 1833 (Althorp's Act), 150, 169, 191, 194, 196, 220
  Factory Act of 1844, 25, 197–9
  Health and Morals of Apprentices Act (1802), 168, 191
  Metropolitan Buildings Act (1844), 123
  Mines Act (1842), 284
  Poor Law of 1601, 322
  Poor Law of 1782 (Gilbert's Act), 328
  Poor Law of 1834, 196, 297, 322, 324, 325
  Poor Law of 1844, 331
  Railways Act (1844), 319
  Reform Act (1832), 24, 243, 259, 260, 322
  Truck Act (1831), 204–7
Adam, 128
Adulteration, 81–5
Agriculture, 21, 27, 296–310
Ainsworth and Crompton (of Bolton), 250
Aire, River, 47
Alison (brothers):
  Sir Archibald (Sheriff of Lanarkshire), 113, 130, 135–7, 142, 147, 307
  Dr. William Pulteney, 41, 113, 114
Allendale (Northumberland), 276
Allen's Court (Manchester), 58
Alston, Rev. G., 35
Alston Moor, 276, 277
America, 23, 251, 333
American competition, 332, 333
Anaemia, 229
Ancoats (Manchester), 68, 70, 73, 75, 84, 113

Ancoats Street (Manchester), 68
Anti-Corn Law League, 101, 137, 262–4, 302, 316, 342
Apprentices. See Acts of Parliament (Health and Morals of Apprentices)
Ardwick (Manchester), 54, 55, 71
Ardwick Green (Manchester), 56
Arkwright, Sir Richard, 14, 243
Army recruits, 226
Ashley, Lord (Shaftesbury), 143, 159, 161, 165, 180, 284
Ashton:
  Thomas (senior, of Hyde), 210
  Thomas (junior), 249
Ashton-under-Lyne, 16, 51, 52, 53, 84, 148, 207, 263
Ashworth (brothers), Edmund and Henry (of Turton by Bolton), 180, 210, 254
Asthma, 276, 280
Atheism, 129, 141, 284, 303–4
Athens, 41
Auction system (export trade), 95
Australia, 38
Average wage, 91, 92

Back-to-back houses, 44
Bacon, 85
Bacton (Suffolk), 327
Baines, Edward (the younger), 150
Bankruptcies, 97
Bank Top (Macclesfield), 173
Bardsley, Dr. S. A., 140
Barham, Dr. C. F., 275
Barmecides, 332
Barnsley (Yorks.), 49
Barrack Street (Dublin), 40
Barrows, 98
Barry, Sir David, 172, 173, 174, 175, 183, 184, 185
Barton aqueduct, 22
Basford (Notts.), 329
'Bastilles'. See Workhouses
Bayley, William (and brothers), 263
Bayswater (London), 38

Beaumont, Thomas (surgeon), 172, 177
Bedford, 218, 301
Beer shops, 142, 232
Begging, 85, 98, 100, 156, 314
Belfast, 18
Bellhouse, 350
Belper, 289
Bentham, Jeremy, 273
Bentley and White (of Bury), 250
Bermondsey Street (London), 36
Bethnal Green (London), 35, 328
Bilston (Staffs.), 44, 227, 288
Birley, Hugh Hornby (of Manchester), 257, 264
Birmingham, 20, 23, 31, 44, 45, 52, 102, 126, 224, 225, 226, 227, 258, 261, 266, 273, 326
Bishop, Theresa, 37
Blackburn, 12
Black Country, 226-9
Blacklegs, 246, 247, 251, 256
Blackstone Edge, 47, 50
Bleaching, 16, 220
Blindness, 238
Boards of Guardians, 239, 325-9
Board of Health (Manchester), 76, 77
Bobbin-lacemaking, 218
Bobbin-net, 16
Bobbins, 158
Bohemia, riots in (1844), 243
Bolton, 16, 23, 51, 75, 85, 180, 210, 250
Boom, commercial, 98
Borthwick, Peter, 331
Bourgeoisie, 311-31
Bowers (of Holmfirth), 205
Braces, 99
Bradford, 17, 18, 49, 172, 176, 261
Brandy, 112, 114
Bread, 8
Brighton, 23
Bridge Street (Manchester), 73
Bridgewater Canal, 22
Bridgewater, Duke of, 22
Brindley, James, 22
Bristol, 23, 29, 104, 287
Brocklehurst, John (of Macclesfield), 222
Brougham, Lord, 205
Broughton, 54, 55
Brown Street (London), 37
Buckinghamshire, 218, 300
Builders, 28, 69, 338-52
Buonaparte, 127
Burial grounds, 329, 330
Burns, Major J. A., 218
Burns. See Accidents
Burslem, 233
Bury, 51, 148, 250

Bussey, Peter (Chartist), 261
Butchers, 81
Butter, 82
Byron, Lord, 273

Caledonian Canal, 23
Calder, River, 47
Calico printing, 16, 17, 219-20
Calton (Glasgow), 45
Cambridge, 23
Cambridgeshire, 23, 300, 301
Canals, 22, 23, 28
Capitalists, 28, 91, 236, 252, 334
Carding, 14
Carlyle, Thomas, 104-5, 107, 132, 308, 312, 332
Carmarthen, 305
Carpenters Hall (Manchester), 348
Carter, Mr. (Surrey coroner), 36
Cartwright, Rev. Edmund, 14
Cellar dwellings, 43, 44, 51, 73, 76, 104, 157
Central Asylum, 39
Cemeteries. See Burial grounds
Chadwick, Edwin, 42
Champneys, Rev. William Weldon, 99
Chapel Street (Salford), 74, 143
Charity, 39, 85, 100, 102, 140, 315
Charles Street (London), 34, 35
Charlotte Street (Macclesfield), 173
Chartism, 79, 151, 152, 211, 255, 258, 259, 260, 262, 263, 264, 265, 267, 268, 269, 270, 271, 273, 287, 292, 303, 330, 332, 334, 341
Cheese, 85
Cheetham Hill (Manchester), 54, 55
Chemistry, 17
Cheshire, 19, 119, 219, 301, 348
Chicory, 82
China, 333
Chinaware, 234
Chlorine, 220
Cholera, 73, 76-7
Chorlton-on-Medlock (Manchester), 54, 55, 71, 84, 119, 120
Church, Established, 303, 304, 308, 313
Church Street (Dublin), 40
Cleland, James, LL.D., 16
Clocks in factories, 203
Cloth, 83, 157
Clothing, 78, 115
Clyde, River, 23
Coalmining, 19, 21, 277-93
Coalheavers, 92
Coalfields, 21
Coalminers, 27
Cobden, Richard, 342

Cobridge (Staffs.), 233
Cocoa, 82
Coffee, 82, 85
Colchester, 23
Combinations. *See* Trade Unions
Commercial Crises. *See* Trade Cycle
Commission:
Children's Employment, 125, 126,
   129, 213, 217, 220, 225, 226, 228,
   229, 233, 234, 235, 236, 238, 274,
   275, 277, 283, 284, 291
Factories Enquiry, 165, 166, 167, 168,
   170, 171, 173, 175, 181, 182, 184,
   187, 188, 189, 190, 192, 193, 194,
   195, 203, 214, 254
Religious Instruction, 41
Sadler's Committee, 192
Common land, 318-9
Common lodging-houses, 77
Commons, House of, 25, 258
Communism, 269, 335, 336
Competition, 88-103, 246, 248
Complete Suffrage Association, 266
Compulsory Education (proposed), 124
Congleton (Ches.), 19
Consumption, 111, 184, 231, 234, 235,
   238, 275, 276
Continent, 26
Copper, 21, 274
Cork (Ireland), 22, 113
Corn Laws, 25, 128, 262, 263, 266, 267,
   302, 303, 311, 315, 316, 334, 341
Cornwall, 274, 275, 276, 284
Cottages, 52, 67, 69, 110, 157, 206, 207,
   211, 290, 299
Cotton Industry, 14, 15, 16, 17, 50, 150,
   160
Court:
Borough (Manchester), 340-51
Guild (Glasgow), 47
Leet (Manchester), 80
Queen's Bench, 288
Courts (housing), 43, 44, 49, 53, 57, 65,
   71, 75
Coventry, 326
Cowan, Dr. Robert, 119, 120
Cowell, John W., 166, 167, 172, 179, 184
Craft work, *see* Domestic workshop
Credit, 83, 97
Crime, 98, 145-9, 227, 232, 242, 243,
   269, 309
Crompton, Samuel, 14
Crises, commercial. *See* Trade Cycle
Crisis of, 1842, 101, 102, 340-2
Crockery, 83
Croker, J. W., 308-9
Cross Lane (Salford), 75
Cross Street (Leeds), 47

Darlaston (Staffs.), 227
Davy, Sir Humphry, 22
Davy lamp, 283
Deansgate (Manchester), 51, 55, 73
Death Rate, 119, 123, 159, 276
Deeply Vale printworks (Bury), 219
Deformities, 173, 174, 181, 217, 228,
   279, 280
Deptford, 325
Derby, 16, 23, 44, 213, 215, 219, 289,
   301, 350
Derbyshire, 219
Devon, 300
Diderot, Dénis, 272
Diet (working-class), 80, 81, 85, 86, 218,
   299
Dissenters. *See* Nonconformists
Disraeli, Benjamin, 139, 331
Division of Labour, 24, 50
Divorce, 269
Dockers, 92, 99
Doffers, 158
Domestic workshops, 24, 224-5, 236
Double-decking, 152
Douglas (of Pendleton), 173
Dorset, 18, 300
Draw-boys, 176
Dressmakers, 237, 238
Drink, 105, 115, 116, 141, 142, 143, 284
Drinkwater, J. E., 172
Drury Lane, 34, 35
Dublin, 34, 35, 40, 41, 45, 113, 137
Ducie Bridge (Manchester), 58, 60, 61
Dudley, 44, 227
Dukinfield, 186, 253
Duncombe, Thomas Slingsby, 25, 292,
   320
Dundee, 18, 174
Dunfermline, 174
Durham, 21, 275, 280, 282, 287, 288,
   289, 291, 292
Dyeing, 16, 17, 220

Earthenware, 21, 234
Eastern Asylum (London), 39
East Lothian, 281
Eccles, 257
Edinburgh, 23, 41-3, 77, 113, 119, 348
Education, *See* Schools
Engineering, 28, 232
Epilepsy, 234, 235
Essex, 301
Established Church. *See* Church
Etruria, 233
Exeter, 23
Expectation of Life, 122, 276-7, 281, 282

Explosions in mines, 282, 283, 292
Export trade, 95
Eye complaints, 213, 216, 217, 235, 238

Factory inspectors, 158, 194-5
Factory rules, 201
Family relationships, 145, 160-6
Faraday, Michael, 292
Farm labourers, 13, 296-310
Farmers, 13-4, 296-310
Farming, 14, 21, 296-310
Faucher, Léon, 224
Fennel Street (Manchester), 57
Ferrand, W. B., 320, 331
Feudalism, 207-8, 331
Fever, 112, 113
Fielden, John, 331
Fines (in factories), 201-4, 223, 287
Fire lighters, 99
Firwood (Lans.), 14
Flannel, 83
Flax, 14, 18, 160, 174, 184-5
Food (of workers). *See* Diet
Frames, 158
Framework knitting, 213, 216
France, 22, 23, 24, 147, 260
Fraudulent practices, 81-5
Free Trade, 266
French Revolution, 26, 336
Frost, John, 261
Fustian:
    cutters, 220, 221
    jackets, 79

Galway, Ann, 36
Game Laws, 300
Gas lighting, 20
Gaskell, Peter, 9-12, 78, 117, 142, 147-8, 332
Geese, 81
Genoa, 74
George Street (Macclesfield), 173
German competition, 333
German merchants in Manchester, 265
Germany, 22, 23, 85, 214, 260, 333
Gibson (building worker), 345, 346
Gin, 142
Ginger beer, 99
Girard, Philippe de, 18
Glasgow, 16, 23, 41, 45, 46, 47, 104, 113, 119, 136, 142, 143, 174, 181, 250, 251, 287, 348
Glass workers, 235
Gloucester, 23
Godfrey's Cordial, 118
Godwin, William, 273

Golden Hill (Staffs.), 233
Graham, George (Registrar General), 119
Graham, Sir James (Home Secretary), 196, 197, 198
Graham (artisan), 261
Grainger, R. D., 126, 214, 217, 218, 227
Gravel Lane (Salford), 74
Great Ancoats Street (Manchester), 68, 70
Great George Street (Macclesfield), 173
Greenacres Moor (Oldham), 186
Greengate (Salford), 74
Greenwich (London), 325
Greg (brothers):
    Robert Hyde, 179, 210
    Samuel, 179
    William Rathbone, 179
Grinders, 230
Grosvenor Square (London), 37

Habeas Corpus, 288
Halifax, 17, 18, 23, 49
Hamilton, Duke of, 285
Hanley (Staffs.), 233
Hanover Square (London), 35
Hargreaves, James, 12
Harpur, 180
Haslam, Messrs. (of Belper), 289
Haswell colliery (Co. Durham), 282, 292
Hawking, 98
Hawkins, Dr. Francis Bisset, 160, 165, 166, 167, 172, 178, 179, 181, 182, 193, 200
Health of workers, 109, 110
Heathcote, John, 16
Helvétius, Claude-Adrien, 272
Henfrey. *See* Pauling and Henfrey
Hennen, John (surgeon), 42
Herne (Kent), 325
Hertfordshire, 301
Hey, William (surgeon), 171, 172, 173
Heywood (Lancs.), 51
Higher Broughton, 54
Highlands (Scotland), 22
High Street:
    Edinburgh, 42
    Glasgow, 45
Highworth, 303
Hindley, Charles (of Ashton), 331
Hinckley (Leics.), 214, 215
Hobhouse, Sir John Cam, 191, 195
Holbach, Baron (or D'Holbach), 272
Holland, 147
Holland, P. H. (surgeon), 120, 121
Holmfirth (Yorks), 205
Home Office, 146
Hood, Thomas, 239
Hope Street (Salford), 75

Horne, R. H., 127, 229
Horner, Leonard (Factory Inspector), 158, 195
Horse dung, collection of, 98, 99
Hosiery, 16, 214, 215
House of Industry (Dublin), 40
Howard Street (Sheffield), 249
Huddersfield, 17, 18, 36, 49, 50
Hudson, River, 23
Hull, 23, 29
Hulme (Manchester), 54, 55, 71, 73, 84
Huntsman, Benjamin, 20
Hyde, 210, 249, 253, 263

Ibbetson (of Sheffield), 249, 250
Illnesses of workers. *See* particular diseases, e.g. scrofula
Import duties, 19
Incendiarism, 232, 250, 300–1
Industrial democracy, 224–5
Industrial Revolution, 9–26, 88, 95, 242
Industrialisation, results of, 108–49
Infirmary (Manchester), 186, 187
Inspectors of Factories, 194
Ireland, 18, 22, 23, 24, 25, 64, 85, 89, 113, 114, 274, 306–20
Ireland, Little (Manchester), 71, 72, 75, 113
Irish immigrants, 27, 34, 41, 71, 73, 77, 79, 89, 90, 103, 104–7, 139, 141, 157, 309
Irish Sea, 47
Irish Town (Manchester), 65, 75
Irk, River, 54, 56, 58, 60, 61, 62, 63, 65, 71, 329
Iron Industry, 20, 21
Ironstone, 277
Irwell, River, 22, 50, 53, 54, 71, 74
Islington (Salford), 75
Italy, 125

Jacobinism, 266
Jenny, 12, 13, 15, 151
Jerry shops, 142
Jersey Street (Manchester), 202
Johns, Dr. William, 161
Johnson (building worker), 348
July Revolution (France), 300
Justices of the Peace, 289, 290, 317, 318, 319, 340

Kay, Dr. J. P. (Kay-Shuttleworth), 58, 73, 74, 75, 76, 77, 105
Kennedy, John (McConnel and Kennedy) (of Manchester), 148, 201

Kent, 300, 325
Kerry, 22
Kersal Moor (Manchester), 53, 260
King Street (London), 34
Kirkgate (Leeds), 47
Kitchen (of Sheffield), 250
Knight, Dr. Arnold (of Sheffield), 230, 231
Knitters, 213
Knobsticks. *See* Blacklegs

Labourers, 107
Labour movement. *See* Chartism: Trade Unions
Lace industry, 16, 215, 216, 217, 218, 237
Lanark, 174, 180
Lanarkshire, 16, 147
Lancashire. *See* Manchester and other Lancashire towns
Lancaster, 23
Lane Delph (Staffs.), 233
Lane End (Staffs.), 233
Lawlessness. *See* Crime
Lead, 21, 274
Leach, James (Chartist), 151, 152, 202, 203, 204, 219, 221, 223, 224, 342
Lee, Dr. John (Edinburgh minister), 41
Leeds, 17, 18, 23, 31, 47, 49, 60, 61, 102, 162, 171, 172, 173, 177
Leicester, 16, 23, 44, 102, 167, 213, 214, 215, 279, 281, 326
Leigh, 148, 223
Liberals, 197, 266
Lichfield, Bishop of, 319
Limerick, 113
Lincoln, 301
Lindley, John, 16
Linen, 18, 174, 184–5
Little Ireland (Manchester), 71, 72, 73, 75, 113
Liverpool, 16, 23, 29, 43, 44, 60, 74, 104, 113, 119, 121, 122, 160, 348
Loaders, 281
Lockjaw, 185
Lodging houses, 77, 277
London, 23, 29, 30–9, 77, 85, 98, 99, 104, 109, 111, 112, 123, 127, 144, 146, 148, 237, 238, 290, 325, 327, 328
London, Bishop of, 319
London Bridge, 30
London Fever Hospital, 112, 224
London Road (Manchester), 56
Londonderry, Marquis of, 291
Long Acre (London), 34
Long Millgate (Manchester), 57, 58, 62
Longport (Staffs.), 233

Lords, House of, 259
Loudon, Dr. Charles, 171, 177, 178, 181
Lovett, William (Chartist), 259
Lower Broughton, 54
Lyell, Professor Charles, 292
Lyons, 9

MacAdam, J. L., 22
Macclesfield, 19, 173, 348
McCulloch, J. R., 15, 333
McDurt, Thomas, 183
McGhee, 350
Machine-breaking, 156, 243
Machinery, 24, 150, 154, 232, 233
Mackintosh, Robert, 174, 181, 185, 193
McPherson, Mrs., 251
McQuarry (blackleg), 251
Mainwaring's Pills, 117
Makellar, Dr., 281
Malthus, Rev. T. R., 92, 93, 155, 320, 321, 323
Manchester, 16, 19, 23, 29, 31, 47, 50, 52, 53, 55, 55–57, 83, 102, 104, 105, 111, 113, 117, 119, 120, 121, 122, 123, 140, 142, 143, 144, 148, 151, 156, 160, 161, 162, 165, 167, 178, 179, 180, 181, 183, 184, 185, 186, 197, 201, 210, 211, 233, 255, 256, 257, 258, 264, 265, 273, 312, 329, 338–52
Manchester Infirmary, 117
Manners, Lord John, 331
March Lane (Leeds), 47
Market Street (Manchester), 56
Marlborough Street police court (London), 38
Marylebone (London), 39
Master and Servant Bill (1844), 25, 319
Matches, 99, 156
Mathew, Father Theobald, 144
Maude, Daniel (stipendiary magistrate), 340–51
Mead, Edward P., 208
Meat, 85, 102, 228
Mechanics Institutes, 271
Medlock, River, 53, 54, 56, 71, 73
Mellor, John, 345, 347
Mendicity Association (Dublin), 40, 41
Menenius Agrippa, 253
Menstruation, 184
'Merry England', 29
Mersey, River, 22, 50, 52
Metal trades, 224–235
Middlesex, 146–147
Middleton (Lancs.), 51, 328
Middleton (Teesdale), 276
Mile End cotton factory (Glasgow), 251
Miles, P. W. S., M.P., 319, 320

Milk, 85
Mill Lane, (Macclesfield), 173
Miller, Capt. (of Glasgow), 46
Miller's Street (Manchester), 66
Milliners, 237
Milling, John. See Mellor
Minimum Wage, 90, 91
Miners, 274–93
Miners' Association, 285
Miners' Union, 287, 288, 289, 290, 291, 292, 293
Mitchell, Dr. James, 275, 277
Money, 312
Monk, Mr. (barrister), 345, 346, 347
Mons Sacer (Kersal Moor), 54, 260
Moorside (Leeds), 162
Morrison's Pills, 117
Mortality, 112–4, 120–3, 160, 169, 275–6
Moses, 127
Mottram Moor (Hyde), 263
Mule. See Jenny

Nailmakers, 20, 232
Naples, 40
Napoleon. See Buonaparte
Narcotics, 114, 118, 161
National Charter Convention, 266
Needlewomen, 238–40
Nelson, Lord, 127
Netherlands, 147
Nettle beer, 99
Newcastle-upon-Tyne, 23, 287, 289
New Lanark, 191
Newspapers:
   Durham Chronicle, 21
   Examiner (London), 266
   Halifax Guardian, 207
   Leeds Mercury, 205
   Liverpool Mercury, 82
   Manchester Guardian, 81, 82, 84, 85, 119, 148, 160, 186, 283, 285, 314, 315
   Morning Chronicle (London), 214, 303–304
   Northern Star (Leeds and London), 205, 254, 301, 302, 332, 348
   Sun (London), 207
   Times (London), 38, 148, 299, 332
   Weekly Chronicle (London), 266
   Weekly Dispatch (London), 78, 123, 266
Newton-le-Willows (Lancs.), 23, 29
New Town:
   Edinburgh, 41
   Manchester, 64–8, 71
Nightwork, 170–1, 191, 194, 216, 218
Nonconformists, 196

Norfolk, 301
Northampton, 218
North Riding, 177
North Sea, 47
Northumberland, 21, 280, 287, 288, 289, 292, 293
Nottingham, 16, 44, 174, 213, 215, 218, 227

Oakbank factory (Glasgow), 251
Oastler, Richard, 162, 196, 197, 261
O'Connell, Daniel, 310
O'Connor, Feargus, 79
Old Church:
  Edinburgh, 41
  Manchester, 55, 57, 74
Oldfield (Road) (Salford), 75
Oldham, 16, 20, 51, 53, 148, 186, 207
Oldham Road (Manchester), 68, 70
Old Town:
  Edinburgh, 41, 42, 119
  Manchester, 56, 63, 64, 65, 73, 74, 75, 113, 329
Opium, 114
Oranges, 99, 156
Ores, mineral, 274
Owen, Robert, 191, 269
Overlookers, 158
Oxford, 218, 300
Oxford Road (Manchester), 71
Oxford Street (London), 34

Padgin (of Sheffield), 249
Paine, Thomas, 20
Paisley, 19
Paris, 19, 42
Park Green (Macclesfield), 173
Parker Street (London), 34
Parkinson, Richard (Canon of Manchester), 140, 315
Parliament, 25
Parliament Passage (Manchester), 74
Parliament Street (Manchester), 74
Parr's Life Pills, 117
Patent medicines, 117, 118
Patteson, Sir John (Judge at Court of Queen's Bench), 288
Pauling and Henfrey (Manchester), 256-7, 338-52
Pauperism. See Poor Law
Pawnshops, 143
Peasants, 131, 298
Peel:
  Sir Robert (the elder), 168, 191
  Sir Robert (prime minister), 198, 262, 292, 331, 341

People's Charter. See Chartism
Pencaitland (East Lothian), 281
Pendleton (Lancs.) 54, 55
Pentrich colliery (Belper), 289
Pepper, 82
Percival, Dr. Thomas (of Manchester), 168
Periodicals:
  Artizan (London), 44, 47, 111, 122
  Deutsch-Französische Jahrbücher (Paris, 1844), 28
  Edinburgh Medical and Surgical Journal, 41
  Fleet Papers (London), 162-3, 196
  Illuminated Magazine (London), 326
  Journal of the Statistical Society (London), 48
  Miners' Advocate (Newcastle-on-Tyne), 287
  Mining Journal (London), 283
  North of England Medical and Surgical Journal (Manchester), 183
  Punch, 240
  Westfälisches Dampfboot (Bielefeld), 337
Peter Street (Manchester), 73
Philanthropy. See Charity
Phoenix Mill (Manchester), 202
Piccadilly (Manchester), 56
Pickford Street (Macclesfield), 173
Piece rates (Wages), 154-5
Piecers, 158
Pig iron, 21
Pigs, 63, 81, 106
Pilling, Richard, 341
Pills, 117
Pin-making, 232
Playhouse Yard (London), 39
Plug Plot riots (1842), 255-8, 263-5, 341-2
Poachers, 22, 300
Point-net, 16
Pool of unemployed, 97, 98
Pool's Place (London), 37
Poor Law, 25, 102, 267, 297, 322-31
Poor Law Commissioners, 100, 322-31
Population, 16, 18, 20, 28 (see also surplus population)
Porridge, 85, 157
Port wine, 82
Porter, G. R., 15
Porters, 92, 107
Portman Square (London), 34
Portugal, 82
Potatoes, 85, 86, 89, 105, 157
Potteries, 21, 102, 128, 233, 235
Pounder, Robert, 162-3
Power, A., 176, 214
Power looms, 50, 153, 157, 158
Prescot (Lancs.), 119, 288

Preston (Lancs.), 14, 20, 51, 265
Princess Street (Manchester), 73
Privies, 73, 76
Profits, 91, 95
Proletariat, 150–240
Prostitution, 34, 38, 45, 46, 74, 136, 143, 144, 167, 203, 218, 232, 284
Proudhon, Pierre-Joseph, 272
Public houses, 116
Puddling. *See* Iron Industry

Quack remedies, 117, 118
Quaker Court (London), 37
Quakers, 126, 266
Quarry Bank (Ches.), 210
Quay Street (Manchester), 73

Radicals, 25, 95, 225, 258, 262, 266, 267, 275, 320
Radnor, Earl, 303
Railways, 23, 28, 47, 319
Rashleigh, William, 151
Read (building worker), 350, 351
Reading rooms, 211, 271
Rebecca riots, 305
Refuge of Houseless Poor, 39
Regent Road (Salford), 75
Registrar General of Births, Deaths and Marriages, 119
Religion, 284
Refrewshire, 16
Revolution, threat of, 334–6
Ribble, River, 50
Rice, 82
Richmond Road (Leeds), 47
Rickets, 115
Riots:
  Plug Plot (1842), 101–2, 340–2
  Rebecca (Wales) (1843), 305
River transport, 22–3
Roads, 22, 28
Roberton, John (surgeon), 183
Roberts, Richard (engineer), 253
Roberts, W. P. (miners' attorney general), 287, 288, 289, 290, 291, 292, 293, 294, 318, 319, 345, 346, 347, 351
Robson, George, 326
Rochdale, 16, 20, 51, 84, 148, 207
Rutter, W. S. (barrister), 351

Sacred Month, 263
Saddleworth, 186
Sadler, Michael Thomas, 192, 193
St. Bride's (London), 329
St. George (London parish), 35

St. George's Channel, 104
St. George's Road (Manchester), 65
St. Giles (London), 33–4, 45, 135
St. James (London), 38
St. Helens (Lancs.), 22, 162
St. John (London parish), 35
St. Michael's Church (Manchester), 62
St. Paul, 127, 128
St. Pancras (London), 239, 327
St. Peter, 128
St. Philip's Church (London), 35
Salford, 54, 55, 74, 75, 119, 143, 148, 160, 197
Salford Hundred, 74
Salisbury Cathedral, 304
Salmon, John, 343, 344, 347
Salt, 156
Salt market (Glasgow), 45
Samson, 127
Sankey Brook Canal (Lancs.), 22
Saunders, J. R. (factory inspector), 195
Savings (of workers), 96
Saxony, 214
Scarborough, 177
Scarlet fever, 111
Schmidt, J. K. *See* Stirner
Schools, 124–9, 195, 211, 226, 228, 231, 235, 279
Scotland, 17, 23, 41–3, 45–7, 100, 113, 114, 119, 147, 170, 174, 184, 191, 219, 232, 244, 274, 278, 281, 285, 289, 340, 347, 349
Scotland Bridge (Manchester), 62
Scott, John, 345, 347
Scottish joiners, 344
Screw making, 20
Scriven, Samuel, 235
Scrofula, 115, 214, 217
Seaham Harbour (Co. Durham), 291
Sealing wax, 99
Seamstresses, 237
Seats in factories, 174
Sedgeley (Staffordshire), 227–8
Self-actors, 151
Senior, Nassau William, 75
Sewing girls, 237
Sexual behaviour, 144, 167
Shaftesbury, Lord. *See* Ashley
Shales Moor (Sheffield), 249
Sharp, Francis (surgeon), 171, 172, 177
Sharp, William (junior), 177
Sharp, Roberts and Co. (Manchester), 253
Sharps (associate of Pauling and Henfrey), 349
Sheep-rearing, 20
Sheffield, 20, 23, 44, 128, 224, 229, 231, 232, 249, 250, 261

Shelley, Percy Bysshe, 273
Shepherd, Jack, 127
Shipping, 23, 30
Shirtmakers, 238, 239
Shoe-laces, 99, 156
Shoreditch (London), 328
Short time, 96, 219
Shudehill (Manchester), 57, 62
Silk, 18, 19, 222, 223
Slavery, 93, 131, 200
Slough, 328
Smallholdings, 267, 307
Smellie, James (surgeon), 181
Smith, Adam, 93
Smith, John (blackleg), 251
Smith, Dr. Thomas Southwood, 112, 281
Smuggling, 22
Soap, 82
Socialism, 225, 267–73, 303, 335
Socialist Hall (Manchester), 347
Soho Grinding Wheel Works (Sheffield), 250
Solomon, 127
Somerset, 19
Somerville, Alexander ('One who has whistled at the Plough'), 303–4
Southampton, 23
Southwark Bridge (London), 20
Spain, 125
Speculation, 96
Speenhamland, 323
Spirits, 82, 85, 106, 111, 112, 142
Spitalfields (London), 37, 224
Staffordshire, 21, 224, 227, 281, 288, 340, 343, 349
Starvation, 32–3, 36, 85–6, 89–90, 96, 108, 321
Stalybridge (Ches.), 16, 51, 53, 263
Stanhill (Lancs.), 12
Stanhope (Weardale), 276
Stealing, 98
Steam engine, 14, 175
'Steam King' (verses), 209, 210
Steamships, 23, 30
Stephens, Rev. J. R., 260, 267, 334
Stevenson Square (Manchester), 349
Stirner, Max (nom de plume), 31
Stocking-frames, 16, 213–5
Stocking-knitters, 16, 213–5
Stockings, 83
Stockport (Ches.), 51, 52, 101, 152, 180, 197, 264, 328
Stoke-on-Trent, 233
Stomach disorders, 114, 115, 280
Strand (London), 34
Strauss, David Friedrich, 272
Street sweepers, 156

Street traders, 98–9, 156
Strikes, 254
    Kennedy's mill (Manchester), 201
    Pauling and Henfrey (Manchester), 256–7, 338–52
    Miners, 288–92
String, 99
Stuart, James, 174, 185, 188
Sturge, Joseph, 266
Suffolk, 301, 327
Suicides, 130, 148, 239
Sugar, 82, 85
Sunday work, 215
Sunday Schools, 125, 126
Sunday trains, 319
Surplus population, 93, 94, 95, 96, 98, 99, 100, 156, 300, 321, 333
Survey, 36, 300
Sussex, 301
Swedish tables of mortality, 276, 277
'Swing' riots, 301
Symons, J. C., 45, 46, 128, 130, 155, 232, 243, 279

Tame, River, 52, 53
Tancred, Thomas, 235
Taylor, P. A. (Chartist), 261
Tea, 82, 85
Teachers, 124
Temperance societies, 143, 144
Ten Hours Bill (1844), 159, 192, 193, 197, 198, 199, 261, 266
Thames, River, 20, 30
Theft, 98
Thornhill, Thomas, 196
Throstle, 14, 15, 151, 158
Thugs (of Glasgow), 250, 251
Timber, 20
Tin, 21, 274
Tithes, 308
Titley, Tatham and Walker (of Leeds), 203
Tobacco, 82, 83
Todd Street (Manchester), 56, 57
Tolls, road, 305
Tommy shops, 204, 206, 211
Tories, 95, 135, 189, 196, 198, 243, 262, 263, 302
Townley Street (Macclesfield), 173
Towns, industrial, 30–87
Trade Cycle, 95, 97, 98, 102, 131, 247, 334
Trade Unions, 89, 246, 249
    Builders, 338–5
    Carpenters, 338–5
    Miners, 287, 288, 289, 290, 291, 292
    Weavers, 244

Trafalgar Square, 34
Tramping system, 245
Transport. *See* Canals, Roads, etc.
Treacle, 118
Trongate (Glasgow), 45
Truck System, 204–7, 211, 215, 285, 289
Tuberculosis. *See* Consumption
Tufnell, Edward Carlton, 166, 172, 173, 181
Tunstall (Staffs.), 233
Turnpike Roads, 22
Turpin, Dick, 127
Turton (near Bolton), 210
Typhus, 111, 113, 114, 117, 137

Unemployment. 85–7, 94, 95, 97, 165, 225, 244
Union, proposed repeal of, 309, 310
United Kingdom, 23, 24, 25, 40, 56, 95, 146, 159, 282
United States, 23, 251, 333
Universal suffrage, 259, 260, 266
Upper Ogle Street (London), 39
Ure, Dr. Andrew, 137, 150, 189, 190, 191, 194, 211, 252, 253

Vagrancy laws, 207
Van Diemen's Land, 338
Vaughan, Robert, 134
Vegetables, 86, 99
Victoria, Queen, 38
Vitriol throwing, 249

Wade, Dr. John, 120
Wages, 24, 28, 29, 80, 87, 89, 90, 91, 93, 94, 96, 102, 107, 152, 248, 255, 267, 278, 286
Wakefield (Yorks.), 289
Wakefield, Edward Gibbon, 297, 298, 299
Wales, rising in (1839), 256, 261, 304, 305
Walsall (Staffs.), 227
Wapping (London), 39
Warrington, 29, 148, 232
Warwickshire, 279, 281
Waste land, 22
Watercots (Macclesfield), 173
Waterford (Ireland), 113
Watt, James, 14

Weavers, 12, 88, 107, 158, 216, 221, 222, 223, 224
Wedgwood, Josiah, 21
Wednesbury (Staffs.), 227
Wednesfield (Staffs.), 227
Wellington, Duke of, 127
Wesley, John, 128
West Derby (Liverpool), 119
West London Union Workhouse, 329
West Riding. *See* Yorkshire
Westminster, 35
Wheat, 22
Whigs, 95, 191, 331
Whitechapel, 35
Whitecross Street (London), 39
White Lion Court (London), 36
Wigan, 23, 51, 81, 148, 232, 285
Wightman, Sir William (Judge), 288
Willenhall (Staffs.), 127, 227, 228, 229
Williams, Sir John (Judge), 288
Wine, 112
Wiltshire, 16
Winders, 216
Windsor, 328
Withy Grove (Manchester), 57, 62
Wolverhampton, 44, 127, 224, 227
Wood (factory at Bradford), 177
Wood:
    Francis, 251
    James, 251
Woodhall, Ambrose, 343
Woodhouse (Leeds), 162
Wool, raw, 14, 17, 274
Woollen Cloth, 17
Woollen Industry, 17, 160
Woollen Yarn, 17
Woolwich (London), 30
Workhouses, 61, 324–31
Working-class movements, 241–73
Working Men's Association, 259
Worship St. police court (London), 36
Wright (factory manager), 173
Wynds (in Scotland), 42, 43, 45, 46

Yarn, 151, 180
Yearly bond (contract) in mining, 286
Yeoman farmers, 9–13
York, 23
Yorkshire, 17, 18, 47, 67, 119, 162, 177, 224, 225, 261, 280
Young England, 320, 331

Zinc, 274